Social Research

SECOND EDITION

Social Research

SECOND EDITION

Sotirios Sarantakos
Charles Sturt University, Australia

This edition first published 1998 by
MACMILLAN PRESS LTD
Houndmills, Basingstoke, Hampshire RG21 6XS
and London
Companies and representatives throughout the world

ISBN 0–333–73868–3 paperback

A catalogue record for this book is available from the British
Library.

10   9   8   7   6   5   4   3
07 06 05 04 03 02 01 00 99

Printed in Hong Kong

Contents

Preface

This is an introductory text on social research and is designed for students undertaking basic-level undergraduate courses in social sciences and related disciplines. Its main aim is to introduce methods and techniques of social research and their methodological frameworks in their diverse and pluralistic nature, and to demonstrate their purpose, relevance and effectiveness.

This book has many distinctive features. First and foremost, it offers a full coverage of the area of social research. Whereas most texts operate in one methodological domain or focus on one specific method or technique, this text integrates all popular methodologies and methods, and presents a relatively complete and pluralistic model of social research, in both theory and practice. In this sense, the text is concise and comprehensive, and offers a large amount of information in a relatively small space.

The text also introduces the most popular statistical techniques employed by social researchers and discusses the use of computers in social research. It also covers a wide area of study, ranging from the traditional research models of positivism and neopositivism to more recent developments in the area, such as grounded theory and feminist research, issues that are rarely presented in other standard texts of social research. Finally, the text presents social research as a dynamic process leading from the beginning to the end, and from questions to answers, showing clearly how researchers progress from one stage to the next, how decisions are made, how options are chosen, and how conclusions are drawn. This is an advantage over the many texts that concentrate on introducing methods and techniques of social research, placing less emphasis on their framework and their processual nature.

This text offers undergraduate students almost everything they need to know about social research: what it is, what it does, how it is used, when it is used and for what purpose, what methods it employs, how good they are, and a multiplicity of issues enabling a clear and critical understanding of modern social research. Obviously, preoccupation with comprehensiveness leaves little space for in-depth analysis and discussion of the elements of social research. Nevertheless, the choice of extent of coverage over intensity of discussion is preferable, because knowledge and understanding of the total context of social research is more important for the undergraduate than intensive analysis of a few specific methods or processes. Such an intensive analysis may be accomplished through further reading, or more specific course work.

As a basic-level text, the book is oriented towards practice and substance, leaving more critical and theoretical issues for the initiated and advanced student. In essence, it offers a solid basis for further developments, and prepares undergraduates for a more detailed study of advanced, specialised and theoretically demanding aspects of research, which might be undertaken, as stated above, in other courses, or for which information may be sought in more specialised literature.

Due to its comprehensive nature and the diversity of issues presented in it, the text lends itself to a variety of uses and diverse services. It can be used in courses with diverse structure, and as a guide to diverse research projects. The variety of issues covered allows students and teachers to concentrate on issues that suit the nature and purpose of their course. As a result, this text might prove to be useful to students of sociology, social work, psychology, nursing, education, administration, politics, and social sciences in general, and can be employed at lower as well as higher undergraduate levels.

The book is divided into four parts. In the first part the historical, theoretical and methodological foundations of social research are introduced. The research process is presented in a series of steps, in the form of a research model. Here, an attempt is made to show how to plan a research project, and to familiarise the reader with the kind of decisions that need to be made regarding the methods and techniques, their relevance and their advantages and disadvantages. In the second part, the process of data collection is outlined in nine chapters. The theoretical formulation of the topic, the most common methods of data collection and the process of data gathering are discussed briefly in this part.

The third part deals with the analysis and interpretation of the data. The bias here is quantitative, but qualitative analysis is not neglected. The mode employed in quantitative analysis is pragmatic and functional; it is important to know how analysis is done and when and how statistical methods are used, leaving mathematics and advanced statistics to the experts. The basic methods of analysis are introduced here but only the most popular statistical techniques are discussed briefly in this part.

The process of writing a report and the rules and standards employed for this purpose are presented in the last part of the book. A glossary of some common terms as well as an index and the bibliography follow this part.

Ideally, this text is written for the beginner who wishes to develop an understanding of social research and who intends to carry out an elementary investigation. Nevertheless, the advanced student may find the book a good model for ordering, categorising and integrating knowledge of research methodology in the social sciences.

The second edition

This second edition has followed several reprints of the original book and extensive communication and discussions with those who had most to do with the book: students and particularly colleagues who reviewed the book and/or used it as a text in their courses. They pointed to needs, options for expansion and opportunities for adjustment. The suggestions were constructive and resulted in a reorganisation of content, and in minor additions and deletions, which made the text more suitable and more relevant to a variety of student groups. Still, the author's goals remain true to the principles entailed in the previous edition.

More specifically, apart from revising, updating and reorganising, the major changes introduced in the text are as follows: (a) the chapter on surveys was split into two, one on questionnaires and one on interviewing; (b) the order of three chapters was changed; (c) sections on action research and evaluation research were added; (d) the section on ordinal tests of significance was reduced; and (e) computer-aided statistical analysis was added. The SPSS package (Windows Version 6.1.3) is employed. SPSS is one of the most popular programs in the USA, Europe and Australia, and its accessibility and user friendliness (especially in the windows version) makes it the preferred option for many students. Still, manual analysis of data is as fully explained in the text as before.

The inclusion of a discussion of a computer statistical package is one of the major improvements of the text. Computer-aided research design and data analysis has become an integral part of modern research, and the demand for computer skills in social research and for speed and accuracy in analysis is becoming increasingly evident at the level of tertiary institutions as well as to the employers of social researchers. In this sense, *Social Research* is the first text that integrates fully computer-aided analysis with a comprehensive discussion of quantitative and qualitative research methods.

In a nutshell, the second edition retains the strengths of the original book, presents an enriched version of the first edition, includes 19 chapters (one more than the previous edition), contains sections on action research and evaluation research and incorporates computer-aided analysis by using SPSS, and this without changing the size of the text substantially. Students and teachers who found the text useful in the past will find it now even more attractive. It is hoped that in its new form the text will be more effective, more accessible and more useful to students, and suitable to more courses than the old edition.

S. Sarantakos
October 1997

Acknowledgements

The author and the publishers are grateful for permission to reproduce the following copyright material:

- Educational and Psychological Measurement, Inc, Table 6.2
- Harper Educational Publishers, Table 6.1
- Institute of Mathematical Statistics, Table 17.2
- *The Bookseller*, 10 July 1992, Figure 15.10

While every care has been taken to trace and acknowledge copyright, the publishers tender their apologies for any accidental infringement where copyright has proved untraceable. They would be pleased to come to a suitable arrangement with the rightful owner in each case.

PART I Introduction

1

Introduction

The aim of this book is to present, in a clear, concise and practical manner, the methods and techniques of social research. These methods and techniques have been developed, modified and practised throughout the history of the social sciences, and constitute the methodological heritage of modern researchers: each method is the result of continual efforts of many researchers and social scientists, and contains elements contributed by academics from all parts of the world.

With this element of history that permeates not only the single methods and techniques but also the whole body of methodology of the social sciences we will begin the discussion of this chapter. Following this, we will explore the types of social research and methodologies practised in the social sciences, the way they contribute to the development of theory, and finally the aims, applications, motives and principles of social research.

1 Social research: a historical overview

Beginnings
Social research is by no means an invention of the modern social scientist. Although the form used by many social scientists today might be less than 150 years old, and in some special forms even younger, as a tool of gaining knowledge and of gathering information about people and their social life, social research has been used extensively for more than 2000 years. In some cases, it was employed in much the same way and in about the same methodological context as many social researchers use it today.

Greek philosophers such as *Socrates* investigated the structure of society and the causes of social problems more than 2000 years ago, and produced very impressive accounts of social life and of society. They carried out research at different levels, collected information on various social phenomena and interpreted their findings in a political and philosophical context (see, for example, Menzel 1936; Stergios 1991).

More particularly, signs of empirical science were shown even before Socrates. *Thales* (640–550 BC) is an example of a researcher who employed an empirical–rational framework to understand the world of his time: instead of using the traditional explanation based on religious principles, beliefs and superstitions, he applied observation of natural events and offered what could be termed an 'empirical–scientific' approach to the world. On the other hand, *Anaximander* (611–547 BC) with his theory of evolution, *Empedocles* (*c.* 450 BC) and *Xenophanes* (*c.* 600 BC) are other examples of empirically thinking philosophers of the distant past. *Hippocrates* (*c.* 450 BC) was even more involved in empirical research than his contemporaries; his experiments in health and illness opened up general knowledge and weaned public opinion away from superstitions and powers of demons and bad spirits and established guidelines and findings based on observation and empirical science.

The interest in controlled research including observation and experimentation increased with time, and by 400 BC it had partly displaced the theological religious explanations of the past. Empiricism emerged as the antipode of old-style mysticism, augmented by the works of great philosophers such as *Aristotle* (384–322 BC), who saw empirical events as manifestations of fundamental principles of an ordered universe. It was *Socrates* (and of course *Plato*) who turned the course of research back to speculation and mysticism.

The work of Greek philosophers was pioneering. At times descriptive and comparative and at other times critical and normative, this type of research was received very positively by contemporary intellectuals and politicians. Many of the works of these writers are read today, and the methods they used are still employed by modern researchers.

This methodological approach introduced by the Greek philosophers influenced researchers throughout Europe and became more profound, particularly during the sixteenth and seventeenth centuries, the time of *scientific revolution*, when many researchers displayed a strong interest in understanding nature. Examples are *Descartes*, who offered the mathematical foundations for this endeavour; *Bacon*, who developed experimental models and used experimental data to develop theories; and *Newton*, who related experiments to mathematics.

Experimentation was gradually believed to be the way that would allow social researchers to unlock the mysteries of nature, and to gather 'truths' about society; it ultimately became accepted into the system of science.

During the seventeenth and eighteenth centuries, in the context of the so-called *political arithmetic*, serious research was undertaken by social philosophers to discover regularities in social and economic phenomena. Nevertheless, it was the nineteenth century that brought research into its real place, namely to people, by studying real problems such as poverty and the plight of the working classes; and it established research as a form of intellectual enterprise containing most of the elements of modern-day social research.

Following this path, *Le Play* investigated in France the conditions of European workers in a systematic way, using 'family monographs', a method still employed today in some form. *Boots*, on the other hand, studied workers by using surveys and participant observation. Similar techniques were employed in Norway and Denmark. Increasing social problems in agriculture and agrarian populations, caused by a progressively higher industrialisation, motivated social researchers to intensify their efforts in order to provide more convincing explanations of and solutions to these problems.

Positivism

Although the methodological attempts to understand people, society and social problems were reported in many countries, social research as it is known today originated in France, introduced by a distinct social philosopher, *August Comte*, whose name is inseparably connected with sociology. Comte believed that the approach employed in the past, and also by his contemporaries, to study society was by no means uniform, and the methodology used was torn between rationalism and empiricism; and the arguments were based either on reason or empirical observation. Nevertheless, the emphasis on metaphysics, speculation and theological thinking was particularly dominant; and this was, according to Comte, insufficient and inadequate to study social life. In 1848 Comte simply denounced in his *Positive Philosophy* the methodology of his time and proposed the introduction of a *positive method*, which was to dominate the field of social research for more than a century.

In Comte's view, researchers employed metaphysical principles and theological beliefs to explain social problems, attempting to relate ailments and social structures to supernatural phenomena. He believed social investigators should not seek explanations of social problems in theological principles or metaphysical theories, but rather in society itself and in the structure of social relations. He argued, for instance, that it is not God who makes people poor or rich but the social forces that dominate society. Therefore, the new methods must be 'scientific' and it was essential to study society and people as we see them rather than as they are interpreted by philosophers and theologians. *Scientific methods* were, according to Comte, the most appropriate tools of social research. His aversion to metaphysics, and speculation in general, was more than obvious.

Comte's theory, known as *positivism*, had a profound impact on the thinking of many social scientists of the time, leading to the introduction and development of sociology as a new science of society; positivism became the backbone of social sciences in Europe and in other countries, revolutionising the methodological thinking of the time. The new methodology shifted its domain from philosophy to science and from speculation to the gathering of empirical data, and became a *positivistic methodology*, which was to study *positive phenomena*, that is, phenomena that can be perceived through the senses, and to employ *scientific methods*, namely methods similar to those employed by physical scientists.

The social and intellectual atmosphere created by positivism influenced thinking and research in other academic areas such as psychology, which for some time is reported to have been dominated to a certain extent by theological principles. Positivism helped to strengthen the efforts to look at the psyche from a different perspective and explain problems through 'scientific' methods and principles. Psychology gained new support and strengthened its foundations as a discipline and as a way of looking at the world. The new positivistic trend made this discipline more popular among academics as well as in the context of educational institutions. Wilhelm Wundt (1832–1920), for instance, established in 1879 in Leipzig the first psychological laboratory, with experiments becoming the central method of psychological research; experimentation (next to psychoanalysis) dominated the psychological thinking and research of that time.

Positivism flourished also in the USA, where, especially in the twentieth century, it gained many supporters. Social research became institutionalised, with many research centres being established and many universities gradually becoming research institutions. The establishment of research centres inside and outside universities formalised this trend further, and studies of social issues, such as integration of migrants into the USA, earned a high status and prestige and their reports are still being read today. The 1930s produced very respectable works. The social psychologists of Columbia University, with their quantitative studies, followed the trend of the time. Market research and opinion research became more popular and more sophisticated and led to the development of Gallup studies, which are still currently used. England followed this trend (with some hesitation) later, and Australia adopted the British tradition, in all aspects of epistemology, research and methodology.

As a result, until the 1960s social sciences in general and sociology in particular were largely positivistic in theory as well as in methodology, with the typical sociological research including mainly survey methods and experiments, and being directed towards quantification and the use of statistics and computers.

The challenge

Comte's attempt to resolve the conflict between the *logicians* and the *empiricists* was greeted with some considerable resistance and opposition. Such an opposition came, in the first instance, from within positivism. Branches of positivism emerged, with *logical positivism* (also called logical empiricism) being one of the most influential. A group of academics of the early twentieth century (Rudolf Carnap (1891–1970), Hans Reichenbach (1891–1953), Bernard Russel (1872–1970) and Ludwig Witkenstein (1889–1951)) joined forces to prove that science is both logical and interested in observable facts. It was argued in this context that logic and empirical evidence together provide the avenue for experiencing social reality. This is done through operationalism and verification. Theoretical terms have their corresponding empirical reflections, which can be subjected to scientific examination. Karl Popper (1902–94) was one of the last and most influential logical positivists.

Positivism was challenged further by a number of schools of thought, this time from outside the positivist domain. Examples of such schools of thought are *symbolic interactionism, phenomenology, philosophical hermeneutics* and *ethnomethodology*; all questioned most theoretical points of positivism, especially its methodology and its perception of social reality (this point will be discussed later in more detail).

Symbolic interactionism criticised positivism from the very beginning, and was strongly supported by a group of US and European sociologists and social psychologists. Its influence gradually became stronger and gained recognition among wider audiences of social scientists in Europe and the USA. Its theoretical orientation and its objection to positivism made this school of thought a legitimate and also well-respected alternative. In addition, symbolic interactionism offered the basis for other theoretical developments, which were equally critical of the theoretical and methodological direction of positivism. In this way, the criticism against positivistic theory became wider, and undermined its 'hegemony' in the social sciences.

On a more practical and methodological level, the work of critics of positivism, as well as reports communicating findings gained through non-positivistic methods, began to appear and to be read by many academics and students, not only in the USA but also in Europe. Blumer's theoretical contribution in this context was pioneering. But reports of actual research contributed further to make this type of research more acceptable. Becker's 'Outsiders' (1960) and Whyte's 'Street-corner society' (1943) are two good examples. In the 1970s, the ethnomethodologists continued this trend even further.

Criticism of and attack on positivism came also from other directions. Members of the *Frankfurt School*, for instance, introduced a critical debate that culminated in the late 1960s in the so-called conflict of positivism. Beyond this, *Marxists* exercised an equally sharp critique of positivism, while the *interpretive school* of thought and the *action-research* group of sociologists continued their efforts with equal strength and commitment.

Equally significant and effective indeed was the *feminist critique* of positivism. Unlike other critics, feminists concentrated on basic philosophical and methodological premises of positivism. Most of all, feminists argued that positivism has a gendered character, is based on a male paradigm that derives knowledge in an androcentric way (Brieschke, 1992; Harding, 1990), and places women in a position of inferiority and hence oppression and exploitation. In addition, feminist research critically addressed issues resulting from this methodological perception of the world, such as objectivity, the relationship between researcher and researched, its methodolatry or physics envy and so on, which they considered inadequate, inappropriate and oppressive ways of data generation and analysis.

Many researchers began to express more openly their dissatisfaction with the positivist thinking and methodology. Many criticised, for instance, positivism's perception of reality, the goals it pursued, the methods it employed, the moral prescriptions it made, and also its perception that the world was 'mathematically drafted' and, therefore, mathematics was a guarantee of precision. Critics from all sides proposed a new methodology that focused on subjective elements and a constructed world, on critical thinking, on interpretive attributes and on political issues that rejected the notion of taking the world for granted. This has motivated some writers to talk about the emergence of a new stage of research, the *post-empiricist* period, marked by the notion that the scientific method is not the only source of knowledge, truth and validity.

In summary, the early attacks by symbolic interactionism, followed by the works of the members of the Frankfurt School, were augmented later by the establishment of women's studies, phenomenology and ethnomethodology and the introduction of semiotics, post-structural linguistic theory, existentialism, etc. in the context of sociology as well as by the introduction of other methods, so far not accepted in the domain of this discipline. As a result, the number of alternative methodologies increased, and positivistic methodology lost, more or less, its privileged position in the social sciences, giving way to 'the post-positivist' era (see Lather, 1992). Sociological methodology is no longer a uniform body of theory and research based on positivism only, as it was in the past, but a body of diverse methodologies with diverse theoretical backgrounds and diverse methods and techniques, all of which appear to be equally acceptable, equally valid and equally legitimate.

2   Types of social research

The diverse perception of methodology discussed above has been expressed in many ways in practice. Several research models have been introduced and practised by many social researchers, some being unique. The diverse practices and uses of social research are shown in the following descriptive list:

*   *Quantitative research*   This refers to the type of research that is based on the methodological principles of positivism and neopositivism, and adheres to the standards of strict research design developed before the research begins. It employs quantitative measurement and the use of statistical analysis.
*   *Basic research*   This research is usually employed for the purpose of gaining knowledge that will advance our understanding of the social world. It may also help in rejecting or supporting existing theories about the social world.
*   *Applied research*   This type of research is directly related to social and policy issues and aims at solving specific problems and establishing policy programs that will help to improve social life in general, and specific conditions in particular. Types of applied research are *social impact studies, action research, evaluation research* and *cost–benefit analysis.*
*   *Longitudinal research*   Longitudinal research involves the study of a sample on more than one occasion. Versions of this type of research are *panel studies* and *trend studies.*
*   *Qualitative research*   This type of research refers to a number of methodological approaches, based on diverse theoretical principles (e.g. phenomenology, hermeneutics and social interactionism), employing methods of data collection and analysis that are non-quantitative, and aiming towards exploration of social relations, and describes reality as experienced by the respondents.

    Barton and Lazarsfeld (1979), for instance, see in qualitative research: (1) exploration, which helps to analyse research objects, identify indicators and establish classifications and typologies; (2) discovery of relationships between variables, enabling comparisons and conclusions to be made about the significance of certain factors for the relationship; (3) establishing integrated constructs; and (4) testing of hypotheses.
*   *Descriptive research*   This form of research is quite common, in most cases as a preliminary study or an exploratory study, but also as an independent investigation; it aims to describe social systems, relations or social events, providing background information about the issue in question as well as stimulating explanations.
*   *Classification research*   The aim of this research is to categorise research units into groups, to demonstrate differences, explain relationships and clarify social events or relationships. Putting youth into categories on the basis of their political preference, ranking groups according to their attitudes to immigration and classifying people on the basis of their views on multinational operations in Australia or according to their body form are a few examples of classification research.

- *Comparative research* In this type of research, the researcher is interested in identifying similarities and/or differences between units at all levels, for example at a historical or cultural level. The differences between British and Australian families, between forms of exploitation of women in the nineteenth and twentieth centuries and classes in the USA and Australia are a few examples.
- *Exploratory research* This research is usually undertaken when there is not enough information available about the research subject. In certain cases it is undertaken in order to provide a basis for further research, for example to define certain concepts, to formulate hypotheses or to operationalise variables; in other cases it is undertaken to gain information on the issue *per se*. The use of library research, case studies or expert consultation as sources of data is commonly employed in this form of research. Qualitative studies are more likely to use this type of research as a study *per se* than quantitative research.

  Exploration is a process that, according to some writers, is useful for developing an accurate picture of the research object, is a central element of qualitative research and can offer assistance not only in formulating hypotheses and theories but also in modifying and testing hypotheses and theories.
- *Explanatory research* Here, research aims at explaining social relations or events, advancing knowledge about the structure, process and nature of social events, linking factors and elements of issues into general statements and building, testing or revising a theory.
- *Causal research* This is considered the most 'respected' type of research in the social sciences and is employed to explain the causes of social phenomena and their consequences. The research aims at establishing a relationship between variables so that the one is the cause of the other; and so that when the one variable occurs the other will also occur.
- *Theory-testing research* Its aim is to test the validity of a theory. Theory-testing research may employ other types of research to achieve its purpose.
- *Theory-building research* For many social scientists, the purpose of research is to establish and formulate theories. It is expected to provide the data and the evidence that support a theory. For instance, research with criminals led to the development of the theory of differential association; and research with married couples led to the theory of complementary needs.
- *Action research* Action research is 'the application of fact finding to practical problem solving in a social situation with a view to improving the quality of action within it, involving the collaboration and co-operation of researchers, practitioners and laymen' (Burns, 1990: 252). This type of research is characterised by a number of criteria. Burns (1990), for instance, notes that action is *situational* (it diagnoses a problem and attempts to solve it), *collaborative* (since it requires the efforts of researchers and practitioners), *participatory* (in that researchers take part in the implementation of the findings) and *self-evaluative* (for it involves a constant evaluation of its process and modifications to adjust research and practice).

  Action research criticises the theoretical and methodological basis of conventional social research, both by its challenges and by its claims. As Winter (1987: 2) put it, 'it challenges a scientific method of inquiry based on the authority of the "outside" observer and the "independent" experimenter, and it claims to reconstruct both practical expertise and theoretical insight on the different basis of its own inquiry procedures'.

* *Participatory action research (PAR)*   This is a form of research characterised by the strong involvement and degree of participation of members of organisations or communities in the research process (Whyte, 1991). In PAR, some members of the units under study are expected and indeed encouraged to participate actively with the researcher throughout the study. This participation begins with the initial identification of the research topic and design and continues up to the publication of the findings.

These types of social research are not mutually exclusive. Researchers usually employ more than one type of research in a project. It is, for instance, possible that descriptive research is used in an investigation together with classification research, theory-building research and comparative research. The investigator has to decide about the types and combinations of research forms that, in his or her opinion, best serve the goals of the study. Nevertheless, the two well-established major domains of social research are quantitative and qualitative research; these types of research will be discussed at length in the next chapter.

3   Research and theory

a   Theory construction in quantitative research

Theory and research are very closely interrelated, especially in two ways: on the one hand, theory guides research by providing guidelines and basic assumptions; on the other hand, research provides the way of establishing, formulating, strengthening and revising a theory. It is the second form of this relationship that we shall explore in this section.

As stated above, constructing a theory is a goal of many methodologists. In this sense, many researchers try to produce findings that will support a theory. Nevertheless, the notion of theory construction, which seems to dominate the mind of many methodologists and researchers, and at least for some appears to be the ultimate goal of research, has often been criticised. It is argued, for instance, that theory construction is neither the aim of all methodologists nor the purpose of all types of research. In theoretical terms it is a characteristic of some researchers and types of research; but for many investigators, theory construction is a less significant element of their research activities. In the context of positivism, for instance, theory construction is not a ubiquitous methodological task. A number of positivists prefer to direct their research interests towards description and classification rather than towards theory construction, while others prefer to talk about *paradigms* rather than about *theories*. However, since theory construction *per se* is a task of a number of social researchers, a few words on this issue are in order.

The process of theory construction is complex and diverse. What is a theory, which process of theory construction is the best and even whether theory can be constructed (or should in the first place be constructed) are issues over which theorists have been arguing for decades without reaching agreement. We will see below how social scientists (e.g. Bergmann, B., 1991; Johnson, 1989; Stergios, 1991; Turner, 1982) approached the issue of theory construction in the past.

Many methodologists would agree that *a theory is a set of systematically tested and logically interrelated propositions that have been developed through research and that explain social phenomena*. This understanding is partly based on the neopositivistic belief that social sciences and physical sciences share many basic theoretical and methodological principles, that one should avoid subjectivity and speculation, and that one should avoid discursive argumentation based on metaphysical speculation and theoretical appeals to subjective plausibility, so that the basic elements of theory construction are presented clearly and objectively. Further, one should be in a position to distinguish between social philosophy and abstract speculation; and fact-related and supported theory is of paramount importance for this school of thought. No vague or sloppy approach to social reality is allowed (Bergmann, B., 1991; Johnson, 1989; Stergios, 1991; Turner, 1982).

Theory construction is based on a systematic approach employing clear, explicit and formal procedures in all aspects of the research process: in defining concepts, variables and classificatory systems; in developing propositions, in making these statements and in operationalising and measuring concepts and variables. The intention of this process of methodological thinking is to arrive at a set of logically interrelated propositions that describe, interpret, explain and/or predict social phenomena, so that they can be assessed and reassessed and ultimately lead to the development, acceptance, rejection or modification of a theory.

In more detailed presentation, this process of theory construction as described by social theorists (e.g. Johnson, 1989; Stergios, 1991; Turner, 1982) contains the elements of concepts, classification systems and theoretical propositions discussed below.

Concepts and variables

The first step towards theory construction is developing concepts; concepts are the elementary blocks of a theory. They are words that label, name, classify or define objects, experiences, events, phenomena or relationships. Concepts enable us to construct our experience and structure our perception of reality.

Concepts can be either *observables* or *constructs*. Observable concepts refer to items that can be perceived by the senses; constructs refer to items that are not objects to our senses but can be inferred from observables. To what extent concepts are observables or constructs is difficult to define. For some theorists even observables have a portion of constructs in them; and all constructs are developed through experience. Besides, many concepts are a combination of several observables and constructs. The *student role*, for instance, contains observables such as 'man' or 'woman', 'white', 'tall' and so on, as well as constructs such as 'intelligent', 'liberated', 'politically engaged', etc.

Classification systems

The next step in theory construction is analysing, testing and understanding concepts and, most of all, classifying them into systems or categories. This helps to organise our knowledge of reality and leads to understanding its structure and composition. The models of classification depend mainly on the criteria employed; such criteria are determined by the purpose of classification and can be gender, educational status, class, occupation or political orientation.

Propositions

The next step of theory construction is the development of *propositions*, that is, general statements regarding relationships between concepts. Such propositions answer the question *why* as against concepts and classification systems which answer the question *what*. Propositions have a limited explanatory power but still provide answers to certain important questions.

Propositions can be original, that is, they may not be derived from other propositions (*postulates*); or they may be derived from other propositions (*theorems*); or they may be generally accepted statements, repeated and accepted as true propositions (*laws*) (see Johnson, 1989; Stergios, 1991).

Theories

Theories are a set of logically interrelated propositions, presented in a systematic way, which describe and explain social phenomena. They are logically constructed statements that summarise and organise knowledge in a particular area, and are open to testing, reformulation, modification and revision. How these propositions are to be arranged in order to offer a valid description and explanation of reality, and ultimately to constitute a theory, varies; while some writers (e.g. Turner, 1982) see statements as being arranged in *axiomatic formats, causal process formats* and *typological* or *classification formats*, others (Johnson, 1989) perceive two models of theory construction, namely the *hypothetico-deductive* model and the *pattern* model, which we shall refer to briefly below.

Hypothetico-deductive model

According to this model, the basic logical form of theory should be deductive or hierarchical. This means that propositions must be arranged in a hierarchical order from the most general to the more specific hypotheses, so that the lower level propositions are derived from the higher level propositions. In this sense the model presents a typical form of a standard categorical syllogism.

Pattern model

Here, reality is presented at two levels, the theoretical and the empirical. The theoretical pattern contains elements and relationships that mirror relationships in an empirical world. The empirical model represents phenomena that are seen and interpreted as a specific instance of the theoretical elements of the first model. In this case, theory is an intellectual model of the empirical model. Constructing a theory, then, means establishing the concepts and the patterns of relationships between these concepts; testing a theory implies a comparison between the concepts and their relationships as stated in the theory, on the one hand, and the empirical facts included in the empirical model, on the other. What is important here is that no predictions are made.

Also, no hypotheses are formulated which need to be tested. A theory is regarded as 'fruitful' if 'the interpretation it leads to is meaningful, or adds new insights in understanding some aspects of the empirical world' (Johnson, 1989).

These models are by no means contradictory. Pattern theory can well progress to a deductive theory.

Causal relationships

For many writers, establishing a causal explanation is a step towards developing theories. For this reason, causality is a central concept in this context. Nevertheless, the establishment of a causal relationship between two variables is a very difficult task and even when it is established, it is not a guarantee of certain, scientific knowledge. In any case, for a relationship to be defined as causal a number of conditions should be met, of which the following are most important (see Bergmann, B., 1991; Minichiello *et al.*, 1990: 40–1; Williamson, Karp and Dalphin, 1977; Turner 1982):

- *A relationship* between two variables or events, measured in terms of magnitude and consistency of the association, must be established, for example that feminism is associated with improved working conditions of women.
- The one variable or event must *explain* the other consistently (not just once) so that whenever the former occurs, the latter follows. The variable that explains another is the *cause* while the variable that is explained is the *effect*; for example, feminism (the cause) *caused* the improvement in the working conditions of women (the effect).
- *Time order* is very important; this means that the causal variable appears before the change occurs in the dependent variable, that is, that the cause precedes the effect, for example the improvements in working conditions of women occurred after feminism was established.
- Cause and effect must be *contiguous*, that is, close together in both time and space.
- The relationship between the variables must not be *spurious*.
- There must be a *rationale*, which explains and/or justifies the causal relationship between the variables in question, for instance that feminism did help to improve the working conditions of women through raising the consciousness of women and also establishing favourable conditions in the community which were conducive to female employment.

Nevertheless, the researcher should be aware of a number of problems that might interfere with establishing a relationship, and might cause potential errors and problems. The following are the most important (see Berger *et al.*, 1989; Lamnek, 1988; Vlahos, 1984):

- *Mismatch* When association between variables is being established for the purpose of ascertaining a causal relationship between them, the generalisation of the evidence must be restricted to the level of the variables studied, and should not be expanded to other levels. When, for instance, evidence stems from a study of individuals, generalisations are not allowed to include groups, and vice versa.

- *Spuriousness*   Association between two variables does not necessarily mean a causal relationship. The relationship may be spurious (false). It may be that the relationship is determined through a third unidentified variable, without which association does not exist. The real cause in such relationships may be the third variable.
- *Teleology*   Often, specific relationships are explained in terms of general, abstract and vague conditions that are to take place in the future.
- *Tautology*   Tautology does not offer any valid explanation of relationships between variables.

b   Theory construction in qualitative research

Theory construction in quantitative research has been criticised by several theorists in many and diverse ways (as we shall see later). Qualitative researchers, and theorists in particular, expressed serious doubts about the way theory is defined, constructed and used in quantitative research, and the way knowledge is gained and organised. In contrast, qualitative researchers present an image of theory and its relationship to research that is fundamentally different, impressive and most of all popular.

An example of a specific and systematic approach to theory construction in qualitative research is offered by *grounded theory*, a theory that will be discussed later in this volume. At this stage, a few relevant elements will be presented only to show how, according to some writers, theory building in qualitative research can be done, and is being done very successfully, by many researchers.

Summarising the views of the founders of that theory (Glaser and Strauss, 1979; Strauss, 1991), qualitative research is set to produce theories that are *grounded* in empirical data from which they are generated (thus 'grounded theory'), and are the result of social research that goes through a number of steps, as presented below.

Step 1
The researcher first enters the field without preconceptions, strict designs, categories, hypotheses or knowledge about the research object, without firm concepts, and without relevant theoretical definitions. The researcher resembles a newborn person (Glaser and Strauss, 1967; Strauss, 1987, 1991) who is not socialised in the world in which he or she is born; research for the mature researcher is a process of resocialisation.

Step 2
The researcher studies single cases or groups and records the findings, making observations about certain aspects of the research object.

Step 3
The study is then expanded to more cases and groups through the process of *theoretical sampling*, which is different from statistical sampling and is guided by the already gathered knowledge and experience and the emerging theory.

Step 4
Next is *comparison* between groups and other elements, which allows the researcher to test and validate the collected facts, to develop categories and their dimensions, correct already made statements and concepts, identify changes, refine data and categories, *integrate* data, categories and hypotheses, make some empirical generalisations, identify similarities and differences between categories, integrate similar categories and formulate hypotheses.

Step 5
Such hypotheses are integrated into more general statements related to a central object, and establish what is called a *substantive theory*. This theory is the first major step towards establishing a grounded theory.

Step 6
Throughout the process of research, data collected are simultaneously analysed; collection and analysis take place concurrently.

Step 7
When such theories are constructed, the researchers subject their findings to a *comparative analysis* and attempt to *generalise* their statements. The result of this process is what is labelled a *formal theory*. Such a theory emerges out of many substantive theories but is pitched at a higher degree of generality and abstractness, and has no time or space limits. Nevertheless, they are not 'grand' theories but middle-range theories.

Despite the fact that there are not many specific examples verifying and validating the development of a grounded theory, the creators of that school of thought seem to 'feel certain of [their] general position and the ways that formal theory should be generated' (Glaser and Strauss, 1967: 80).

Nevertheless, writers have pointed to a number of problems of grounded theory. Lamnek (1988), for instance, makes the following points:

- The notion of entering the research scene without preconceptions is sociologically very questionable.
- The notion of personal involvement in the research raises the point of subjectivity and the level of validity of the findings.
- The extent to which new information is expected to be added must become clearer. We shall see later that Glaser and Strauss refer to the concept of *saturation*.
- There is not enough explanation given about how hypotheses are expected to be verified.
- The process of data collection needs to become clearer. There is no information about what should be included in the study, that is, what is useful, suitable, theoretically relevant, etc.
- Validity of data needs to be defined in some way, namely when data are considered as offering empirical validation of the relationships contained in the theory.
- The method of theory building (especially of formal theory) is not adequately precise.

- Grounded theory is not an alternative to quantitative theory, since it is presented by its creators (Glaser and Strauss, 1967: 17) as a model suitable to both qualitative and quantitative theory.

In a more general sense, theory construction in qualitative research has been criticised by social scientists and methodologists in a number of ways. The main argument in this context is related to the nature of this type of research and to its theoretical approach. Qualitative research involves a small number of cases, often chosen by means of non-probability sampling procedures, and for that reason cannot claim representativeness. Consequently, qualitative research, it is argued, cannot produce findings that are valid enough to support the development of a theory. The most that qualitative research is assumed to be able to produce is hypotheses that can be tested by quantitative researchers who, on the basis of this, can relate them to theory.

For a number of writers, however, such a perception of theory construction is incorrect. In the first place, it is argued, qualitative research is being judged in terms of quantitative standards. Besides, theory may be defined in a way that is different from that of the neopositivists, thereby allowing qualitative researchers an avenue into theory construction. In this sense, there are theorists who argue that exploration can lead not only to formulating hypotheses and theories, but also to modifying and testing hypotheses and theories.

It is further believed that comparisons allow the development of some type and degree of explanation, and the establishment of *trend theories*. Real examples can then verify whether the phenomenon in question or trends in general really exist.

c   Theory construction in comparison

The process of theory building in the context of the two types of research is obviously different (see Table 1.1). Not only the theoretical framework that guides this process but also the research process itself vary in the two fields. The main differences between the two types of research will be discussed in the next chapter; with regard to theory building, the major differences can be summarised as follows (see Flick *et al.*, 1991; Lamnek, 1988; Vlahos, 1984):

- *Logic of theory*   In qualitative research the logic of theory building is inductive, in quantitative research it is deductive.
- *Direction of theory building*   Qualitative theory building begins from reality, quantitative theory does not.
- *Process of theory building*   The course of theory building in qualitative research moves from data generation to verification, with both processes taking place concurrently; in quantitative research verification takes place when theory building is completed.
- *Concepts*   Concepts in qualitative theory are developed during the research process, that is, researchers enter the field without any notion of concepts; the concepts are either *orienting* (McCall, 1979) or *sensitising* (Denzin, 1970) or are just flexible concepts (Witzel, 1982). In quantitative theory building, concepts are already available and firmly defined before operation begins.

- *Generalisations* Quantitative theories normally warrant generalisations; qualitative theories allow *analytic generalisation*, or *exemplar generalisation* (Firestone, 1993), that is, the sample units can act as typical representatives of a class or group of phenomena.

Table 1.1 Theory building in quantitative and qualitative research

Differences	Quantitative research	Qualitative research
Logic of theory	Deductive	Inductive
Direction of theory building	Begins from theory	Begins from reality
Verification	Takes place after theory building is completed	Data generation, analysis and theory verification take place concurrently
Concepts	Firmly defined before research begins	Begins with orienting, sensitising or flexible concepts
Generalisations	Inductive, sample-to-population generalisations	Analytic or exemplar generalisations

4   Aims of social research

The driving force behind any type of social research is its philosophical framework. This dictates not only the general perception of reality and social relations but also the type of methods and techniques available to researchers and the motives and aims of social research. The aims of social research vary significantly, depending on the theoretical orientation of the framework that guides the research; Fay (1987: 23), for instance, referring to critical research, argues that its aims are to 'simultaneously explain the social world, critique it, and empower its audience to overthrow it'. These aims may not be accepted by all researchers, particularly those who support different paradigms. In general, writers usually refer to the following aims:

1 to *explore* social reality for its own sake or in order to make further research possible;
   to *explain* social life by providing reliable, valid and well-documented information;
   to *evaluate* the status of social issues and their effects on society;
   to make *predictions*;
   to *develop* and/or *test theories*.
2 to *understand* human behaviour and action.
3 to offer a basis for a *critique* of social reality;
   to *emancipate* people;
   to *suggest possible solutions* to social problems;
   to *empower* and *liberate* people.

It is obvious that the aims of social research presented above are neither exhaustive nor mutually exclusive. Research projects may be undertaken for a number of reasons and may serve many and diverse aims. These aims depend primarily on the paradigm that guides the project. As stated above, positivist research strives to achieve the aims listed under 1 above, that is, to *explore, explain, evaluate, predict* and *develop/test* theories; while interpretive research is more interested in *understanding* people (point 2 above). Critical research aims at *criticising* social reality, *emancipating* people, *empowering* them to change social reality by suggesting possible solutions and thus liberating them from oppressive and exploitative social structures (point 3 above). Still, the boundaries between these three perspectives seem to be rather flexible. There are qualitative researchers, for instance (e.g. Miles and Huberman, 1994), who include prediction and causal analysis in the aims of qualitative analysis.

In a more general sense, the information and knowledge gathered when pursuing the above aims are further used to achieve other more specific goals of social research, mainly of a practical nature. Researchers and those having an interest in social research may aim at one or more of the following applications (Becker, 1989; Vlahos, 1984):

- *General goals*   Understanding for its own sake.
- *Theoretical goals*   Verification, falsification, modification or discovery of a theory.
- *Pragmatic goals*   Solution of social problems.
- *Political goals*   Development of social policy, evaluation of programs and practices, and social criticism; social change and reconstruction; empowerment and liberation.

These goals are not mutually exclusive. Their selection depends largely on the philosophical orientation of the researcher, and his or her understanding of the role of social sciences in the community. 'Conservative' sociologists, for instance, might see the goals of their research in describing and categorising social reality. Critical sociologists, on the other hand, might see the application of their research to be social criticism, social change and social reconstruction, that is, empowering people to overthrow oppressive and exploitative social structures.

5   Motives of social research

In most cases, the aims of social research coincide with the motives, but in some cases the motives are quite often unknown to the respondents or even to the researchers themselves, as, for example, in the case of contracted research. As a result, motives can be intrinsic, that is, related to personal interests of the researcher in the study object; or they can be extrinsic, that is, related to the interests of those contracting the research.

Some of the motives that are not included in the list of the aims discussed above, which have quite often been identified in research studies and quoted in the literature (Mahr, 1995: 84), are:

- *educational*: to educate and inform the public;
- *'magical'*: to offer credibility to views held by researchers and/or their sponsors;
- *personal*: to promote the academic status of the researcher;
- *institutional*: to enhance the research quantum of the institution for which the researcher works;
- *political*: to provide support to political plans and programs;
- *tactical*: to delay decision or action for as long as the investigation is under way.

Often, the initiation of a research project and the type of its outcomes depend on the social and political context in which research is undertaken. In socialist countries, for instance, the goal of social research, its principles and strategies are to a very significant degree dictated by the political system. Although, for a social researcher of the former German Democratic Republic, research was reported to relate to the structural, processual, organisational and developmental aspects of the society, its guiding principle was the *theory of historic and dialectic materialism, and the principles of Marxist–Leninist sociology* (Berger *et al.*, 1989: 68).

In the case of contracted research, the motives often given by the sponsors or researchers are not always clear. There are instances in which the sponsors of a project (or even researchers) have reasons to hide their real motives, and to mislead the public and certain interest groups. The trained researcher and the critical reader should be able to identify the real motives of research and to act on it accordingly.

6   Principles of social research

Modern social research is generally expected to comply with certain standards and principles. Investigators use them as guidelines for their operations, irrespective of their theoretical or methodological orientation. The following seven are the most significant principles of quantitative methodology. Nevertheless, as we shall see later, while quantitative researchers adhere to all the principles listed below, qualitative researchers adhere to only a few:

- Precision in measurement
- Replication
- Validity
- Reliability
- Objectivity
- Ethics
- Representativeness

The first four principles are discussed in Chapter 4, and will be referred to directly or indirectly and implicitly or explicitly in other parts of the book. Objectivity and issues of ethics and representativeness in social research are discussed below.

7   Objectivity in social research

a   Objectivity in quantitative research

Objectivity is considered by many quantitative researchers to be one of the most significant elements of sociological enterprise, and has been practised by many social scientists throughout the history of social science. Objectivity is regarded by many as a virtue that every social researcher should try to achieve, although it is realised that reaching a high degree of objectivity is not easy or even possible.

Objectivity is generally employed to minimise personal prejudice and bias, and to guarantee that social reality will be presented as it is, rather than as it is interpreted or imagined by the investigator. But the issue has divided social scientists, one group supporting objectivity and the other being against it. The former believe in *value neutrality,* while the latter do not, and subscribe to what we know as *normativism.*

Value neutrality
The inherent presupposition of the first school of thought is that the researcher ought to be limited in his or her own biases. Social scientists are thought to be 'technicians' or consultants and not reformers. They should be neutral observers and analysts and not philosophers or moralists. The researcher's personal views and value judgements should be kept out of research.

More particularly, the main principles of objectivity (or value neutrality) are these:

- Sociology (and the social sciences in general) is value free, that is, its goal is to study *what is* and not *what ought to be.* For this reason, the structure of theory and research should adhere to the inherent principle of value neutrality, and try to achieve the highest possible degree of objectivity.
- Social scientists should be value free, that is, they should rule out value judgements, and should exclude subjective views, personal bias and personal convictions when working as academics.
- Value judgements should be reserved for politicians, who are more familiar with the whole social process of social life, and not for social scientists.

Normativism
The opposite view constitutes the theoretical position of normativism. This position entails a number of principles, the most important of which are listed below (see, for example, Abercrombie *et al.*, 1988; Fay, 1980; Mills, 1959; Wadsworth, 1984):

- Objectivity or value neutrality is unattainable, unnecessary and undesirable. For some theorists, objectivity is used as an excuse for an uncritical acceptance of the established status quo. One cannot consider intrinsic evaluation, feelings, beliefs and standards as insignificant or not influential.
- Social scientists ought to have a standpoint on social issues, and they must produce value judgements if they wish to solve social problems.

- Our general orientation is based on and is constructed with values; these values direct our thinking and action and cannot be isolated or ignored.
- Disclosing the inevitable bias or personal beliefs is less dangerous than pretending to be value free.
- Social sciences are normative. Apart from studying what is, they should be concerned with what ought to be.

From a feminist perspective it is argued (see, for example, Keller, 1985; Reinharz, 1992) that objectivity has adverse effects on women, and abandoning objectivity is expected to free thinking from inappropriate constraints and 'unconscious' mythologies through disengaging thinking from notions of what is generally considered to be objective, given that such constructs are determined by patriarchal perceptions about life and social relations.

The middle view
A third view on this issue seems to stand between 'pure' value neutrality and normativism. Here it is argued that although complete value neutrality may be unattainable, some degree of value neutrality is possible and some aspects of objectivity should be preserved and defended (see, for example, Fee, 1986). At least in some stages of social research, for example during the collection of data and the planning of the research, this might be possible and even desirable. In this sense, objectivity requires independence of data and results from the person of the investigator.

In a more general context, objectivity is a diverse and complex concept. It may refer to the relationship between research methodology and society, but it may also concern the relationship between the researcher and the researched. And while in the former, objectivity and detachment may be impossible and undesirable, in the latter it may be a virtue to adhere to. What would be the value of research findings, it is argued, if planning, collection, analysis and interpretation of findings are the result of personal preference and bias?

b   Objectivity in qualitative research

Qualitative researchers reject fundamentally the notion of objectivity. As we shall see later, the notion of establishing intersubjective reliability (so that if a research study is carried out by two or more researchers the same results are achieved) is neither desirable nor possible. This attitude is based on methodological and theoretical grounds.

In the first place, objectivity is associated with and results from standardisation — a methodological tool that is incompatible with the main principles of qualitative research (Vlahos, 1984).

In addition, objectivity requires that the researcher remains distant from and neutral to the research object, the respondents, the methods and techniques of data collection and analysis, and to the findings — requirements that are against the fundamental principle of qualitative research, which encourages intersubjectivity, closeness between the elements of the research and involvement of the researcher in the whole research process (Becker, 1989; Stergios, 1991).

For the qualitative researcher, social reality does not exist objectively but is created in interaction and through interpretation, of which the researcher is an integral part. The researcher experiences reality through interaction and interpretation. Our world is something we make, not something we discover (Rorty, 1989). In this sense, objectivity is impossible in qualitative research.

For some qualitative researchers, objectivity seems to take on a different meaning in qualitative research. Here, objectivity is 'emergent', that is, it evolves out of the subjectivity of the parties of interaction. Qualitative research uses an intersubjective concept of objectivity in as far as one wants to break away from the subjectivity through generalisation.

For other qualitative researchers, what is important is validity, and if validity is assured — as it is believed to be — research should be reliable as well as objective. Finally, it is argued (Bogumil and Immerfall, 1985: 71) that instead of attempting to neutralise the relationship between researcher and researched by means of artificial techniques, which is unachievable anyway, one should look for 'transparency', that is, stating openly the course and elements of the research process, and let others judge its quality.

From a different perspective, qualitative researchers accept objectivity but see it as being identical to solidarity (see Rorty, 1985: 10; Smith, 1992: 101). Here, objectivity is expressed in the form of agreement among colleagues and researchers. Subjectivity, on the other hand, means disagreement or concern expressed by colleagues. In simple terms this means that a piece of research is objective if colleagues agree with the results and praise the researcher. In this sense, there are no objective standards of evaluation; there is 'no permanent, overarching justification for knowledge claims, and there are no permanent criteria for distinguishing knowledge from belief or opinion' (Smith, 1992: 102).

Still, the debate about objectivity, validity and reliability in qualitative research is not over yet. On the contrary, the number of qualitative researchers looking favourably at objectivity and numerical treatment of data is on the increase. The words might change but the essence seems to remain solid. Guba and Lincoln (1989), for instance, confirm that any qualitative study of rigour is expected to contain what they call truth value, applicability, consistency and neutrality. The latter is another word for objectivity and is expected to provide 'confirmability'. Neutrality or objectivity are central elements of qualitative research, although the extent of that objectivity is different from that of quantitative researchers.

8   Ethics in social research

a   Introduction

Social research is a dynamic process, which involves researchers and respondents, and which is based on mutual trust and cooperation, as well as on promises and well-accepted conventions and expectations. On the basis of this, researchers enter the research field with relatively few limits and many options for action. This freedom of action has always been thought to offer the best opportunities for answering the research question or solving the problem under investigation.

Nevertheless, research practice has shown that this freedom can have adverse effects on the participants, causing serious problems to the subjects and the community in general. Often uncontrolled freedom violates directly and/or indirectly the rights of those involved in the research process — a violation that is often justified by the researchers on the grounds that research findings might offer benefits to the public that greatly outweigh the problems and hardship suffered by a relatively small number of respondents. For example, forwarding confidential information to the police, thereby violating promises and hurting the respondents concerned, may be justified by the fact that such information helps authorities to prevent crime or to restore justice; or testing certain drugs on people without their knowledge, although this may affect their health adversely, may be justified by the fact that it may help to produce medicine that could improve public health and save lives.

But is such action permissible? The answer to this question is by no means uniform; while the majority of social researchers are in favour of upholding promises and avoiding at all costs violation of the rights of the respondents and the community in any way, others still believe that 'after all the end justifies the means'. Consequently, there may be researchers who still misuse the power and privileges of their position, and carry out research that hurts respondents and the community in many ways.

As stated earlier, research bodies as well as contractors and consumers of research are aware of the possibility that such malpractices can happen and have raised their objections and made concrete suggestions about how malpractices can be avoided or prevented. Nevertheless, such suggestions were answered by the claim that 'ethics' should be the controlling factor, with research being guided by unwritten standards and principles, which were left to the researcher to accept or reject.

With the passing of time, and with research becoming not only more frequent but also more intrusive, pluralistic (i.e. including several researchers in the same project) and highly computerised, and with the findings becoming increasingly more open to abuse than before, the need for some regulation of the research process beyond self-regulatory mechanisms of the researcher became a necessity.

In the USA and in other countries, universities and other professional bodies began to formulate guidelines delineating the limits of freedom in research and defining the rights of the respondents and the community. The American Association for Public Opinion Research (AAPOR), for instance, published in May 1977 a code of ethics and included it in its by-laws, offering a good guide as to what is and what is not allowable in research practice. Obviously, this was not the first attempt to 'control' the researcher and to provide clarity in the area of social investigation. It was not the last either. Other organisations have followed this trend, producing a sound basis for carrying out research with people, and also with animals.

In Australia, ethics was taken for granted, and the attitude towards having or not having control over the process and consequences of social research was similar to that of other countries. But still, the final decision was always left up to the individual researcher to uphold ethics, interpreting it the way she or he considered most fitting. Nevertheless, the need to establish a written code of ethics was recognised in this country as it was in other countries, and attempts to introduce such codes produced very encouraging results. The Australian Psychological Society (APS) is one example; in its *Code of Professional Conduct* it defined, in 1986, some 'General Guidelines for Psychological Research with Human Participants'.

In 1990, the Australian Vice-Chancellors Committee (AVCC) produced (in consultation with universities, unions, associations and other groups) a document entitled *Guidelines for Responsible Practices in Research and Dealing with Problems of Research Misconduct*, which was forwarded to Australian universities with the advice that tertiary institutions develop a code of ethics of their own to guide research carried out by their members and to establish an environment that will ensure responsible research practice. Most universities have already established such codes and others are in the process of doing so.

But what are the areas of concern that served as the basis for taking such actions? Most codes of ethics produced by Australian and overseas organisations deal with many and often diverse issues. The most common areas, however, are: (1) professional standards and ethical conduct, (2) the researcher–respondent relationship, (3) the researcher–researcher relationship, and (4) the treatment of animals in research. In the following we shall list some details related to these broad areas, as presented in the documents listed above (i.e. those produced by the APS, AAPOR and AVCC) as well as in relevant literature (e.g. Bailey, 1982, 1988; Sproull, 1988; Vlahos, 1984). The issues related to research practice that have been incorporated in the codes of ethics and that seem to concern social scientists are presented in the lists that follow.

b   Professional practice and ethical standards

The following issues relate to ethical standards in professional practice:

- *Accuracy in data gathering and data processing*   With regard to collection and processing of data, ethical codes contain a clause suggesting that researchers are expected to plan, collect and process data by employing high professional standards, a systematic and objective procedure and well accepted ethical standards.
- *Relevant research methodology*   Further, methods and techniques should be chosen as required by the research objective and not for other reasons.
- *Appropriate interpretation of the data*   The researcher is expected to interpret the data in full according to general methodological standards.
- *Accurate reporting*   Researchers are expected to include in a report the research findings accurately expressed and in an unbiased manner and also to explain the methods employed in the collection and analysis of the data. Research problems, errors or distortions known to the researcher should be stated in the report.
- *Fabrication of data is misconduct*   Researchers should not publish findings on data they did not collect.

- *Falsification of data is misconduct* Researchers should abstain from falsifying data, or even changing words.

Ethical considerations in research

---

1 It is a basic assumption of institutions conducting research that their staff members are committed to high standards of professional conduct. Research workers have a duty to ensure that their work enhances the good name of the institution and the profession to which they belong.

2 Research workers should only participate in work which conforms to accepted ethical standards and which they are competent to perform. When in doubt they should seek assistance with their research from their colleagues and peers. Debate on, and criticism of, research work are essential parts of the research process.

3 Institutions and research workers have a responsibility to ensure the safety of all those associated with the research. It is also essential that the design of projects takes account of any relevant ethical guidelines.

4 If data of a confidential nature are obtained, for example from individual patient records or certain questionnaires, confidentiality must be observed and research workers must not use such information to their own personal advantage or that of a third party. In general, however, research results and methods should be open to scrutiny by colleagues within the institution and, through appropriate publication, by the profession at large.

5 Secrecy may be necessary for a limited period in the case of contracted research.

Source: Australian Vice-Chancellors Committee, *Guidelines for Responsible Practices in Research and Dealing with Problems of Research Misconduct,* 1990.

c The researcher–respondent relationship

- *Proper identification* Codes of ethics suggest that the researcher should identify herself or himself to the respondent and avoid giving false impressions of the researcher or the project sponsor.
- *Clear outset* Researchers should inform the respondent of the type of questions, the degree of question sensitivity or stress and the possible (true) consequences that the questioning and the research in general might have on the respondent.
- *Welfare of the respondent* The researcher should always be concerned with the welfare of the respondent, including mental and physical health and safety, and take all possible precautions to avoid incidental injury. The researcher should also avoid questions or issues that may cause embarrassment, guilt, discomfort, hazards or risks to the respondent (Bailey, 1982, 1988; Sproull, 1988; Vlahos, 1984). Where such conditions might occur, the researcher should inform the respondent accordingly at the outset of the study.
- *Free and informed consent* Respondents should participate in the research freely and not be pressured to do so or deceived in any way. They should

also be fully informed about the nature and goals of the study before they are asked to take part in the project (see below).

*   *Right to privacy*   Researchers should respect respondents' privacy when entering their private sphere and when asking questions, and should allow respondents to leave unanswered questions for which they do not wish to provide the information required.
*   *The right to anonymity*   Data collected by the researcher should be anonymous, that is, not related to names or other forms of identification.
*   *The right to confidentiality*   Information offered by the respondent should be used by the researcher only, and only for the purpose of the study; it should not be made available to other people for any reason or purpose.

d   The researcher–researcher relationship

*   *Misleading ascription of authorship*   Researchers should not list authors in their report without their permission, should not attribute work to persons who have not contributed and should attribute adequately work completed by students, trainees or associates.
*   *Misuse of authority or role*   Authority given by a researcher to a colleague should not be misused, and when criticising works or research studies of others this should be guided by 'honesty, sincerity, justice, and responsibility rather than by polemic, personal bias or collective interests'.
*   *Plagiarism*   Researchers should abstain from using other people's work without appropriate acknowledgement.

Informed consent

1   Research procedures must be described accurately and its goals presented in easily understandable terms.
2   The possibility of risks, injury or discomfort must be explained.
3   Eventual benefits from the research for the subjects and science in general must be stated.
4   Alternative procedures that might be advantageous must be revealed.
5   Subjects must be given the opportunity to ask questions about methods and procedures pertaining to the research.
6   Subjects must be given to understand that they can leave the project at any time without prejudice.
7   The availability of care and compensation in case of an eventual physical injury must be explained.

Source: Department of Health Education and Welfare (1975), 'Protection of human subjects — technical amendments', *Federal Register*, **40**, pp. 1854–8.

e   The researcher–animal relationship

*   *Maintenance*   Animals should be maintained under acceptable conditions and should not be deprived of basic needs for food, water, sleep and companionship.

- *Reasons for research* There should be good reasons for subjecting animals to research.
- *Stress and suffering* Animals should not be put under stress or pain, or be injured in any way.

The points referred to above are some of the issues contained in guidelines or codes of ethics produced by universities and other sources (e.g. Bailey, 1982, 1988; Sproull, 1988; Vlahos, 1984) in their publications listed above. Other organisations (e.g. the American Psychological Association or the National Health and Medical Research Council) have produced similar codes and stressed more or less similar issues to those listed above. This demonstrates an increased concern with and commitment to sound standards of research and the rights of the respondents, the community and the institutions sponsoring research.

Although these guidelines are contained in codes of 'ethics' their violation may result in punitive action on the part of the academic community as well as by other interested parties and they are gradually becoming institutionalised by many groups in Australia. In the AVCC document cited above, the committee clarified the nature of, as well as procedures regarding, *misconduct* resulting from doing research. Stressing that misconduct does not include 'honest errors or honest differences' during interpretation or judgement of data, it outlined a number of elements that can constitute misconduct, most of which have already been presented above.

Nevertheless, prevention of problems is better than establishing sanctions and devising punitive structures. In this context, the AVCC recommended ways of protecting ethical standards and principles. It was suggested among other things by the AVCC that data must be securely retained for future reference and evidence; that multiple authorship should be clarified, recorded and evidenced, including principal author; that publications of multiple papers from the same data is improper; and that potential conflicts of interests should be disclosed. Finally, the AVCC referred to the relationship between research supervisors and students and the concern with animal and human experimentation as well as with the handling of hazardous material.

This discussion shows that the issue of how research is carried out, which was originally left up to the good faith and subjective judgement of the researchers and was primarily guided by 'codes of ethics' partly in a written and partly in an unwritten form, has now become — in most cases at least — a part of the legal structure of rights and regulations of this country. In this sense, research is no longer 'guided' by codes of ethics in the old style, but is controlled by strict rules and standards that are as binding and effective as any other legal regulation.

9   Representativeness

a   Quantitative research

One of the most important qualities of quantitative research is the requirement that the sample employed reflects the attributes of the target population, the findings it produces relate to the whole population, and the conclusions drawn through the study are pertinent to the whole population. This attribute of social research is referred to as *representativeness*.

To achieve representativeness is one of the aims of quantitative research; several methods have been devised for this purpose. Most of these methods deal with probability sampling as well as with determining the right sample size and composition of the sample in general. In addition, statistical techniques have been developed to assist in this process. Standard errors, for instance, are calculated, and techniques used that can assist in achieving a sample size that will allow the study to claim representativeness.

Researchers try to achieve representativeness in their studies, not only for its own sake but also because such studies allow generalisations that their findings can be thought to be applicable to the whole population being sampled. The higher the representativeness, the higher the generalisability of the findings and therefore the higher the quality of the study.

b   Qualitative research

In qualitative research, representativeness and generalisability are approached differently. While some qualitative researchers reject the notion of representativeness as employed by quantitative researchers, others find it a useful and indispensible element of qualitative research and make an effort to assure that principles of representativeness are adhered to.

For many qualitative researchers, although representativeness is generally considered irrelevant and unimportant, generalisability is valued highly, although in a manner different from that of the quantitative researchers. For this reason, sampling in qualitative research is not based on probability theory, and the size of the samples is usually too small to reflect the attributes of the population in question. Instead, the choice of subjects is guided by the principles of *theoretical sampling* and is geared towards essential, typical and theoretically important units.

Although qualitative researchers consider generalisations to be important, they relate them to the typical cases they study, not to random theory and principles. Generalisation becomes obvious out of the intersubjective clarification of validity. The essential argument here is that generalisation is based on the typical case studied, which is thought to be representative of a species; what qualitative research claims is that such findings can be interpreted beyond the cases studied and are examples of an 'exemplar generalisation', or 'analytic generalisation' (see Mueller, 1979: 13; Wahl *et al.*, 1982: 206).

This is one view of representativeness in qualitative research, but, as stated above, not the only one. There are qualitative researchers who consider representativeness as an indispensable element of qualitative research and take serious precautions to make sure that their conclusions are representative. Miles and Huberman (1994), for instance, stress the importance of representativeness and point to possible pitfalls qualitative researchers should be aware of. Such pitfalls are 'sampling nonrepresentative informants, eg by overrelying on accessible or elite respondents'; 'generalising from unrepresentative events or activities' and 'drawing inferences from nonrepresentative processes' (p. 264). They advise that weak non-representative cases should be expanded, and suggest the following ways (p. 265):

1 Increase the number of cases.
2 Look purposely for contrasting cases.
3 Sort the cases systematically . . . and fill out weakly sampled case types.
4 Sample randomly within the total universe of people and phenomena under study.

The last suggestion brings qualitative research the closest one can get to quantitative research and is a controversial suggestion indeed.

10 The politics of social research

Social research provides reliable and verifiable knowledge about the social world. This knowledge can be used in many areas of social relations and can help to improve social conditions in modern societies. However, the applicability of research findings is restricted, and depends on many factors, some related to social conditions and others to academic issues. The quality, usefulness and applicability of research findings are believed (Becker, 1989; Vlahos, 1984) to depend on the following factors, but all are related to political factors of some kind.

The questions that are important here are not about how research is done but rather about issues such as why it is done the way it is done, who gains the most out of the research, how the findings are used by those in power, how choice of research topic and research procedures is arranged, the extent to which sponsors influence research, and how research funds are distributed among researchers. The underlying theme here is that politics means power, and research and the findings it produces is associated with both politics and power; and those who have the opportunity to control research outcomes do so if and when they have the power to do so. The government, the industry and the researchers are involved to some extent in the power game and influence the research process significantly. This in itself is of considerable significance for research and the researcher, but is also compounded by factors associated with the research culture, which in certain cases and under certain circumstances makes research a difficult task.

In the first instance, it is not unusual for different academics to study the same problems and obtain different results, or make quite often contradictory recommendations. This obviously creates confusion among the policy makers and the community in general and restricts the credibility and applicability of such findings. This confusion is quite often exploited by interest groups and politicians who might have a vested interest in certain areas of the research study and use inconsistency of findings as a reason not to take action.

Added to this factor is the fact that social scientists have a reputation for attacking each other on academic and ideological issues. Quantitative and qualitative researchers, for instance, consider each other as unable to provide reliable information about the social world. As a consequence, traditional consumers of social research services often lose faith in social research and mistrust social scientists and their findings.

Further, social research is an expensive enterprise, requiring an immense amount of time, expertise and personnel, all of which make high economic demands. It therefore depends on the availability of adequate funds, the lack of which often makes the study of important issues impossible. In a different context, economic considerations determine the chance of findings being publicised and implemented. It has quite often been shown that findings are evaluated in terms of their economic significance for certain interest groups, and that they are considered and implemented only if they favour the economic interests of these groups.

Research and political interests
Research is as much subject to political factors and conditions as any other venture in social life. Everyone is exposed to research, and research findings affect the lives of people, from choice of products in supermarkets to choice of political parties at election times: market research and polls are a part of the decision-making process of the ordinary Australian. Hence, research is power that allows those who have access to it to control others; and the options for using that power are many.

1 Contract research often implies, implicitly or explicitly, the expectation that results support the interests of the sponsor. Providing the funds for the research often gives the impression that researchers are hired hands and therefore must produce the findings sponsors prefer. This is so in some areas more than in others, but there is a possibility that the research process may be influenced. This affects the quality of the research as well as the credibility of the findings. How valid is research on the effects of smoking on cancer if it is conducted by researchers of tobacco companies? And how credible are the findings of a study carried out by a factory saying that the waste products dumped in the nearby lake pose no threat to the environment? Not all sponsored research is affected by the views of the sponsor, but as stated above the possibility of influencing research outcomes cannot be excluded.

2 Even if the sponsors do not directly influence the process and outcomes of the research, they do have the opportunity of using results produced through the research as they wish; findings that do not support their views or question the soundness of their plans and programs can be put away for ever, without reaching the public, particularly when contractual arrangements prohibit researchers from publishing their findings without the permission of the sponsor.

3 Equally powerful is political ideology and the power of the status quo. Those in power can control research funding as well as publication of findings. Interest groups of many kinds infiltrate the right committees and editorial boards of journals and publishing houses and channel funds and publications according to their personal beliefs and ideologies. Project findings that attack common beliefs or vested interests are not published. At the time of writing, research grants on same-sex families or husband

abuse were literally impossible to obtain, and publication of such findings is indeed limited.

4 Political interests also control access to research topics and research materials. Access to prisons, military academies, nuclear plants, schools, etc. is controlled by the government, and is allowed only if the government is satisfied that such research will not violate its interests. Similarly, data and materials already collected can only become available to researchers if the government allows it.

5 Finally, governments and funding bodies set priorities on what issues they wish to be studied, promoting only what they consider as important, and suppressing research in areas which they do not wish to see explored. For instance, for many government-funding bodies, wife abuse is top priority, while husband abuse is low-priority research. Who determines the priority level of each research type? And how is differential treatment of victims of domestic assault justified? Priorities are often biased, and certain minority groups (e.g. homosexual couples, ethnic families) are neglected and certainly disadvantaged. The government appoints assessors of research grant applications to select the proposals that deserve support. But who are the assessors and who determines the parameters of choice?

11 Summary

We have seen that social research has a long history. Since antiquity, it has been used in many different ways to explore social reality, and taken many and varied forms. It has been used and is still being used for a number of diverse goals and motives, and in many methodological contexts.

The most dominant type of research has been the positivistic research, as devised by A. Comte around the middle of the nineteenth century. Positivism has been challenged by other forms of research, but still remains the central element of modern investigation in the social sciences.

Research appears in a variety of forms, each of which has a particular purpose and use. Theory construction is one of them; this is true for qualitative and quantitative research.

Research is conducted to achieve certain aims; these aims vary with the type of research, ranging from description to understanding and to empowering people.

Research follows certain principles. Precision, validity, reliability, replicability, representativeness, objectivity and ethical standards are the most important.

In this diverse form, social research will be studied in the chapters that follow. We shall see how social research is initiated, developed, guided and used to produce answers to questions of social significance.

Key concepts

Action research
Causal research
Explanatory research
Logical positivism
Objectivity
Participatory research
Positivistic methodology
Quantitative research
Value neutrality

Causal explanations
Ethics
Exploratory research
Normativism
Positive phenomena
Positivism
Qualitative research
Theories

2

Varieties of social research

1 Introduction

One of the characteristics of social research introduced in the previous chapter is that it is complex, diverse and pluralistic. The way research is conducted, its goals and its basic assumptions vary from case to case. More specifically, there are at least two major ways of doing research, and actual investigations fall into one of them. These are quantitative and qualitative research. This diversity in social research will be addressed in this chapter.

More specifically, in the discussion that follows we shall discuss first the theoretical foundations of social research that have been developed throughout the history of the social sciences, followed by a presentation of the dominant and representative types of methodologies; we shall conclude this discussion with some general thoughts on recent developments in social research.

2 Paradigms, methodologies and methods

a Definitions

The emergence of paradigms and the extensive employment of diverse research methods by diverse investigators in many and diverse aspects of social life have created a relative confusion among students of methodology, many of whom use paradigms, methodologies and methods incorrectly. It is often not clear whether a writer refers to a paradigm or to a methodology or, even worse, whether a question is about methods or methodologies. This becomes even more crucial when one considers whether a research model is to be accepted as a 'methodology' or not — an issue that is rather topical, as we shall see later.

In our discussion, a distinction is made between the concepts in question based on logical and methodological principles. In simple terms, a *paradigm* is a set of propositions that explain how the world is perceived; it contains a world view, a way of breaking down the complexity of the real world, telling researchers and social scientists in general 'what is important, what is legitimate, what is reasonable' (Patton, 1990: 37). A *methodology* is a model, which entails theoretical principles as well as a framework that provides guidelines about how research is done in the context of a particular paradigm (see, for example, Cook and Fonow, 1990: 72; Harding, 1987: 2; Lather, 1992: 87). In simple terms, a methodology *translates* the principles of a paradigm into a research language, and shows how the world can be explained, handled, approached or studied. *Methods* refer to the tools or instruments employed by researchers to gather empirical evidence or to analyse data.

b   Paradigms

Discussion of the nature, types, purposes and legitimacy of paradigms in the social sciences is an issue beyond the scope of this treatise. Here, our intention is briefly to explain the types of paradigms or perspectives that are instrumental in thinking and operating in the context of the social sciences, as well as in devising methodologies and methods and in doing social research.

A paradigm is a set of beliefs, values and techniques which is shared by members of a scientific community, and which acts as a guide or map, dictating the kinds of problems scientists should address and the types of explanations that are acceptable to them (Kuhn, 1970: 175). However, as in other domains of sociological enterprise there is no complete agreement about the usage of the term 'paradigm'. Although for most sociologists paradigm has the meaning stated above, that is, the world view or the general perspective, this view is used very widely in some contexts but very narrowly in others. As a consequence, for some social scientists there are as many paradigms as there are groups of like-thinking social scientists, while others use this concept only with regard to the major theoretical directions in the social sciences.

For the first group, phenomenology, symbolic interactionism, existentialism, Marxism, feminism, postmodernism, ethnography, hermeneutics, sociolinguistics, etc. are paradigms; for the second group, the paradigms are two, namely the positivist and postpositivist paradigms (see, for example, Lather, 1992), the latter including 'the great ferment over what is seen as appropriate within the boundaries of the human sciences' (Lather, 1992: 89), or, in more general terms, everything that is not positivist. Although such a distinction might make sense to some, it is rather too general and does not allow expression of the diversity of schools of thought grouped under postpositivism.

In a similar fashion, most social scientists opted in the past for a dyadic model, this time including the *positivist* and the *interpretive* (or naturalist) paradigm — a model that was fully accepted in social sciences and that has offered a valid guide for theory and research during the past 20 years. This model was later expanded to include *critical theory* as a third paradigm, and in this triadic form it seems to have been accepted by most social scientists in Australia and overseas. (In a more recent debate (see Lather, 1991), a fourth paradigm is proposed (postmodern) but has not yet been fully accepted or established in the area of the social sciences.)

For the purpose of this text, the second option is accepted. For this reason, in the following, reference will be made to the three major paradigms — the positivistic, the interpretive and the critical — which will also be employed as the context in which methods and methodologies are usually discussed and employed. A description of these paradigms is given in Table 2.1.

Table 2.1   Main paradigms in the social sciences

Positivistic	Interpretive	Critical
Positivism	Symbolic interactionism	Critical sociology
Neopositivism	Phenomenology	Conflict school of thought
Methodological	Ethnomethodology	Marxism
positivism	Hermeneutics	Feminism
Logical positivism	Psychoanalysis	
	Ethnology	
	Ethnography	
	Sociolinguistics	

It must be noted that although there is a clear distinction between the positivist paradigm on the one hand and the other paradigms on the other, the distinction between the critical and the interpretive, although significant, is rather weaker. As we shall see later, particularly with regard to the methodological issues, although the positivist and the non-positivist paradigms may be considered incompatible, the critical and the interpretive paradigms are not.

c   Methodologies

The relative confusion about paradigms referred to above is present also in the context of methodology. This is evident with regard to perception as well as types of methodologies. The view of what constitutes a methodology and under what circumstances a research model becomes a methodology as well as the number of methodologies that deserve a place in the context of social research is a contentious issue.

In the first place, methodology is defined in at least two ways. In one form, methodology is identical to a research model employed by a researcher in a particular project, including basic knowledge related to the subject and research methods in question and the framework employed in a particular context (see Lather, 1992: 87). In this sense, every investigation has a distinct methodology, and every researcher employs his or her methodology, which might vary from study to study. By this definition, it would seem that there are as many methodologies as there are projects, since most projects are unique in nature and approach. I tend to perceive this as a *research model* rather than a methodology.

Another definition relates the nature of methodology to a theoretical and more abstract context, and perceives it in conjunction with distinctive, unidimensional and mutually exclusive theoretical principles. Here, a methodology offers the research principles which are related closely to a distinct paradigm translated clearly and accurately, down to guidelines on acceptable research practices. Methodology is determined not by the research model but rather by principles of research entailed in a paradigm. The methodologies that result from this definition are the quantitative methodology and the qualitative methodology.

Between these two extremes, several versions of 'methodology' have been proposed explicitly or implicitly by social scientists, some being close to what we termed research models, and others being closer to 'methodologies'. And while some researchers, and social scientists in general, argue that every branch of a theory or theoretical direction has several methodologies, and thus talk, for example, about 'feminist methodologies', 'Marxist methodologies', 'existential methodologies' and so on, others ask the logical question about whether talking about methodologies is in fact reasonable, sensible or practical, since setting up methodological paradigms might homogenise views, create an obstacle to open debate, encourage dogmatism or be counterproductive (Hammersley, 1992a). In this book, the methodologies considered are those related to the basic perspectives presented above.

d   Methods

Methods are the tools of data generation and analysis. Practically, methods are the tools of the trade for social scientists and are chosen on the basis of criteria related to or even dictated by the major elements of the methodology in which they are embedded, such as perception of reality, definition of science, perception of human beings, purpose of research, type of research units and so on.

'Methods' are obviously different from methodologies. Literally, 'methodology' means the science of methods (method + *logy*, the latter being a Greek word which can liberally be translated to mean 'the science of', in the same way it is used in geology, psychology, sociology, etc.) and contains the standards and principles employed to guide the choice, structure, process and use of methods, as directed by the underlying paradigm.

In a sense, methods are a-theoretical and a-methodological (meaning independent from methodology). Interviews, for instance, like observation, experiments, content analysis and so on, can be used in any methodology type, and serve any chosen research purpose. The same methods can be used in the context of different methodologies, and the same methodology can employ different methods.

Nevertheless, although methods in general are a-methodological, their content, structure and process are dictated by the underlying methodology. Although interviews, for instance, can be used in a qualitative and in a quantitative methodology, the former employs an unstructured, open or in-depth interview, while the latter normally employs standardised interviews. In a similar vein, participant observation is used in qualitative studies while structured observation is employed in quantitative studies.

Methods have never been and should never be used as criteria for determining the type of methodology without considering factors relating to its purpose, structure, process, type of analysis and other similar factors.

3   Theoretical perspectives

a   Dominant perspectives

The theoretical perspectives that have influenced the structure, process and direction of social research are many and diverse. However, three perspectives, or paradigms as they are usually referred to, are most dominant and provide a theoretical basis for the methodologies employed in the social sciences. These are positivism, interpretive social science and critical theory. In the following we shall first describe these paradigms and then compare a number of relevant theoretical and methodological principles as understood and presented by modern researchers and writers (see Bergmann, B., 1991; Johnson, 1989; Neuman, 1991; Stergios, 1991).

The positivist perspective
Positivism is the oldest theory in the social sciences. As a school of thought and as the basis of research, positivism dominated the scene for the largest part of the history of social sciences; as a philosophical perspective it is a school of thought that for some social scientists means it 'currently holds intellectual sway within the domain of social research though, these days, this hold is weakening, sometimes significantly' (e.g. Hughes, 1990), particularly after new theories were developed or old ones were adopted in social sciences from the area of philosophy or psychology. Nevertheless, while as a theory positivism seems to be neglected, as a basis of methodology it is still influential. The majority of social scientists still employ a positivistic methodology in a pure positivistic theoretical context, or in the context of another theory. As Schrag (1992: 6) put it, 'despite the attacks levelled against it, the positivist paradigm is hard to avoid'.

Positivism is linked with the work of A. Comte (1798–1857) and E. Durkheim (1858–1917), and was expanded later by other theorists either of the same school but a different branch (e.g. logical positivism, methodological positivism or neopositivism) or from another school of thought (e.g. functionalism and exchange theory).

The interpretive perspective
Interpretive social science relates to the works of Giovanni Batista Vico (1668–1744), Dilthey (1833–1911) and most of all of Weber (1864–1920), and his emphasis on *verstehen*, that is, the empathetic understanding of human behaviour. Equally significant is the contribution of symbolic interactionism, phenomenology, ethnomethodology and hermeneutics. On these foundations, several schools of thought have been developed, and a special methodology has been established, which we shall discuss later.

The critical perspective
Critical social science was developed out of the work of Karl Marx (1818–83) and the critical theorists and feminists, and although it was originally developed in the second half of the nineteenth century, it became fully accepted in the social sciences and especially in sociology after the Second World War. The

theoretical backbone of the critical perspective is a combination of conflict theory, critical sociology and Marxism and feminism.

In the following discussion we shall address a number of fundamental theoretical elements, and examine the way in which they are perceived and evaluated in relation to the three perspectives listed above.

b   Perception of reality

Reality is perceived in terms of the three perspectives in different ways.

Positivism

Positivism defines reality as everything that can be perceived through the senses; reality is 'out there', independent of human consciousness, is objective, rests on order, is governed by strict, natural and unchangeable laws, and can be realised through experience. All members of society define reality in the same way, because they all share the same meanings.

The interpretive perspective

By contrast, interpretive theorists believe that reality is not 'out there' but in the minds of people; reality is internally experienced, is socially constructed through interaction and interpreted through the actors, and is based on the definition people attach to it. Reality is not objective but subjective, reality is what people see it to be (see Hughes, 1990: 89–114).

The critical perspective

Critical theorists see reality in a different manner. Reality is created not by nature but by the people; this does not mean the acting self but the powerful people who manipulate, condition and brainwash others to perceive things and to interpret them the way they want them to: reality is constructed by the powerful to serve their needs. Beyond this, reality is not in a state of order but of conflict, tension and contradiction, resulting in a constantly changing world. Critical theorists also distinguish between appearance and reality; what 'appears to be' is not reality, for it often does not reflect the conflicts, tensions and contradictions that are eminent in society, and appearance is based on illusion and distortion.

While positivists give reality an objective structure and interpretive scientists give it a subjective nature, critical theorists stand somewhere in between and believe that although subjective meanings are relevant and important, objective relations cannot be denied. The interest of the critical theorists is to uncover these myths and illusions, to expose real structures and present reality as it is.

The feminists who adhere to the theoretical perspective of Marxism–Leninism, socialism, critical theory, etc. see reality as presented above. Radical feminists see reality as being based on conflicts and tensions caused by gender divisions and patriarchal attitudes. Reality is seen as being dominated by male views and interests, which work against the interests of women, and is perceived in objective as well as subjective terms.

c   Perception of human beings

Positivism
For positivists, human beings are rational individuals who are governed by social laws; their behaviour is learned through observation and governed by external causes that produce the same results (the same causes produce the same consequences). There is no free will. The world is, however, not deterministic; causes produce effects under certain conditions, and predictions can be limited by the occurrence of such conditions.

The interpretive perspective
In interpretive social science human beings occupy a central position; reality and the social world is created by the actors through assigning meaning systems to events. For most theorists of this school of thought there are no general laws of a restrictive nature. Despite this, subjective meanings, patterns and regularities of behaviour emerge as a result of social conventions, established through interaction. Interpretive social science has the task of searching for the systems of meaning that actors use to make sense of their world.

The critical perspective
Critical theory proposes that humans have a great potential for creativity and adjustment. They are, however, restricted and oppressed by social factors and conditions and exploited by their fellow men, who convince them that their fate is correct and acceptable. Beliefs in such illusions create a false consciousness and prevent people from fully realising their potential.

Feminists are concerned with human beings but primarily with women and their position in contemporary societies. Women are seen in a dynamic context, with options and opportunities which, however, are being misused and appropriated by men. Men are seen as oppressing and exploiting women in all social contexts (family, community, work, etc.) as well as in their personal world. Long-standing propaganda and conditioning have resulted in the development of a negative or false consciousness among women that helped to perpetuate inequalities and injustices for centuries.

d   The nature of science

The nature of science is perceived differently by the three groups.

Positivism
For positivists: (1) Science is based on strict rules and procedures, fundamentally different from speculation and common sense; it is unsuitable for studying social reality because it is biased, unsystematic and logically inconsistent. (2) Science is deductive, proceeding from general/abstract to specific/concrete. (3) Science is nomothetic, namely, it is based on universal causal laws which are used to explain concrete social events and relationships. (4) Science relies on knowledge derived from the senses; other sources of knowledge are unreliable. (5) Science separates facts from values; it is a value-free science.

The interpretive perspective

Interpretive social scientists perceive the nature of science in a rather different way. They propose that: (1) The basis for explaining social life and social events and for understanding people is not 'science' in the positivist sense but common sense, for it contains the meanings people use to make sense of their life. (2) The approach employed is inductive, proceeding from the specific to the general and from the concrete to the abstract. (3) Science is not nomothetic but ideographic; it presents reality symbolically in a descriptive form. (4) Knowledge is not derived through the senses only; understanding meanings and interpretations is more important. (5) Science is not value free; value neutrality is neither necessary nor possible.

The critical perspective

Critical theorists perceive science from a standpoint that is between positivism and interpretive social science; between determinism and humanism or voluntarism. They propose that actors are confronted by socioeconomic conditions that shape their life; they are, however, also capable of assigning meanings to their world and act on it to change it. Critical theorists see people as creators of their destiny, for example through fighting illusion and the structures that support and promote it, and it is not value free. On the contrary, they assume that critical science employs values and works with values. Critical social science is an 'engaged' science, meaning that it assumes involvement and activism on the part of the researcher and theoretician. Researchers don't only study reality; they act on it.

Applied in the area of feminism, critical social science sees women as being exposed to inequality, injustice, oppression and exploitation stemming from patriarchy, but they are also capable and motivated to fight against the cause of the problem and change their fate. Feminist science sees people as the creators of their destiny, encourages engagement and action for the purpose of changing the conditions of people's lives, and is normative, not value free.

e   The purpose of social research

Positivism

Positivism perceives social research in an instrumental way; research is a tool for studying social events and learning about them and their interconnections so that general causal laws can be discovered, explained and documented. Knowledge of events and social laws allows society to control events and to *predict* their occurrence.

The interpretive perspective

In interpretive science social research has no direct instrumental value. Research helps to *interpret* and *understand* the actors' reasons for social action, the way they construct their lives and the meanings they attach to them as well as to comprehend the social context of social action. What is important here is not observable social actions but rather the subjective meaning of such actions.

The critical perspective

The purpose of social research for the critical theorists (Marxists and feminists alike) is determined by the critical and activist nature of the theory, which is research oriented. It enables the social scientist to get below the surface, to expose real relations, to disclose myths and illusions, to show people how the world should be, how to achieve social goals and, in general, how to change the world. In Fay's words a critical social science 'explains social order so that it becomes the catalyst that leads to the transformation of the social order' (Fay, 1987: 27), or explains social reality, criticises it and empowers people to overthrow it (Fay, 1987: 23), or, in milder form, helps to understand and change social reality (Lather, 1992: 87).

In summary, critical science sees in social research the goals of removing false beliefs and ideas about society and social reality, perceives humans as creative and compassionate human beings and is critical of the power systems and inequality structures that dominate and oppress people in societies.

The main characteristics of the three theoretical perspectives that are dominant in the social sciences are summarised in Table 2.2.

4 Perspectives and methodologies

Although in theory the three perspectives discussed above are clearly distinguished from each other, in reality the situation is more complex and, for the novice, rather confusing. Positivism, for instance, is not a solid and monolithic approach but a system with diverse theory, principles and views on theory and method. There are also 'branches' of positivism, which deviate to a certain extent from the portrait presented above. Logical positivism, neopositivism and methodological positivism are a few examples.

Equally diverse is the interpretive perspective. As we shall see later, the theoretical background of this perspective is pluralistic, and its theoretical principles are varied. Here, we do not talk about 'branches' but rather about distinct theories such as phenomenology, hermeneutics and symbolic interactionism.

An even stronger diversity is evident in the critical perspective and in feminism. Marxism, for instance, has now become so diverse that it is more accurate to talk about 'Marxists' rather than 'Marxism'. In a similar fashion, feminism draws from a number of theoretical perspectives and is as diverse as, if not more diverse than, Marxism. Biological feminism, Marxist feminism, liberal feminism, socialist feminism and radical feminism are a few examples. The branch that is more relevant to methodology is radical feminism, primarily because it presents a model of researching women and their place in the world that is different and distinct from the other perspectives (also from Marxism).

Despite this internal diversity, the perspectives share many common principles and demonstrate many basic similarities, the most important of which were displayed below. These basic principles reflect the theoretical and

Table 2.2   Theoretical perspectives in the social sciences

Criterion	Positivism	Interpretivism	Critical perspective
Reality is . . .	• objective, 'out there', to be 'found' • perceived through the senses • perceived uniformly by all • governed by universal laws • based on integration	• subjective, in people's minds • created, not found interpreted differently by people	• both out there and in people's minds • complex: appearance is not reality • created by people not by nature • in tension/full of contra-dictions • based on oppression and exploitation
Human beings are . . .	• rational individuals • obeying external laws • without free will	• creators of their world • making sense of their world • not restricted by external laws • creating systems of meanings	• creators of their destiny • oppressed, alienated, exploited, restricted • brainwashed, misled, conditioned • hindered from realising their potential
Science is . . .	• based on strict rules & procedures • deductive • relying on sense impressions • value free	• based on common sense • inductive • relying on interpretations • not value free	• conditions shape life but can be changed • emancipating, empowering • relying on sense impressions & values • not value free
Purpose of research:	• to explain social life • to predict course of events • to discover the laws of social life	• to interpret social life • to understand social life • to discover people's meanings	• to explain, interpret and elucidate • to disclose myths and illusions • to emancipate, and empower

methodological basis of the perspectives and determine to a large extent the way in which research should be conducted. If the world is structured in a certain way, if social research has a certain purpose and if people are perceived in a certain context and display certain criteria, then methods have to be perceived in the context of a certain framework and should also fit into the theoretical and methodological model of the perspective in question.

This commonality in principles, perceptions and methods is shared not only among the branches of the same perspective but also among a number of perspectives. This is obvious with regard to the perspectives of Marxists and feminists: they not only have similar perceptions of science and humans, they also share many perceptions of the world and of the purpose of science. As a consequence, their methodologies are diverse but also similar — diverse in some aspects but similar in others.

As a result of similarities and differences in the nature and principles of the various perspectives, two major methodologies, *quantitative* methodology and *qualitative* methodology, have emerged in the social sciences, each of which contains certain theoretical and methodological principles we shall discuss later. A third methodology, *critical* methodology, entailing Marxist and feminist research, has been practised among social scientists for some time, but has not been fully accepted in the social sciences as a distinct, clear and independent methodology of the level of the other two.

In the discussion that follows we shall explain the nature and structure of the two major methodologies and then explore the structure and status of the emerging critical methodology.

The methodologies will be presented in their 'pure' form, as ideal types and as the extreme ends of a methodological continuum. It goes without saying that, in practice, modified versions or even combinations of elements of both methodologies are employed.

5   Quantitative methodology

a   Theoretical background

Quantitative methodology is based on the positivist or neopositivist philosophy, already explained above. For more than a century, its structure, process and theoretical background offered the basis for the development and practice of *the* standards for the methods of the social sciences. These standards (already introduced earlier) constitute the theoretical principles of quantitative research, and can be summarised as follows:

- Reality is objective, simple and positive and consists of sense impressions; there is one reality in nature, one truth.
- Human beings are determined by their social world in the same manner that the naturalistic world is governed by fixed laws; they are subject to

fixed patterns that are empirically observable (the thesis of nomological thinking). The task of the sociologist is to discover the scientific laws that explain human behaviour.

- Facts should be kept apart from values; social scientists should not make value judgements (the thesis of value neutrality).
- Natural and social sciences share common logical and methodological foundations. Social scientists ought to employ the methods of the physical sciences.
- Metaphysics, philosophical reasoning and speculations are a mere sophistry or illusion; they cannot offer reliable and verifiable data, they do not have empirical relevance, and do not employ a clear procedure that would allow replication and retesting.
- Explanation is restricted purely to positive phenomena and is derived exclusively from experience. In terms of construction of knowledge, social scientists are committed to explicit, exact and formal procedures in defining concepts, establishing propositions and operationalising and measuring concepts and variables so that the validity of new propositions can be reassessed by other researchers and the results accepted, rejected or modified.
- The logical form of a theory is deductive.

As can be seen from these statements, neopositivism is set to establish a 'clear' and 'objective' orientation, a vigorous, disciplined and systematic procedure, and a reality-bound methodology, which allows scientists to arrive at a theory that will be free from vague and sloppy approaches, speculative thoughts about reality, and a theory that should be distinguished from a social philosophy, abstract speculation and everyday assumptions (Stergios, 1991; Vlahos, 1984).

The ideological bases of this school of thought are, apart from Comte's positivism, 'quantitativism' (placing emphasis on measurement and quantification), 'behaviourism' (stressing the exclusive interest in the study of observable behaviour), and 'positive epistemology' derived from the philosophy of James and Dewey (Timasheff and Theodorson, 1976: 196–7). This philosophical orientation has been supplemented by modern and highly sophisticated statistical techniques and computer models, and is considered to be the school of thought with the strongest influence on social research in the modern world. The vast majority of research articles published in leading journals employ a positivistic methodology, including advanced statistical models and the use of computer-aided data analysis.

b   Critique of quantitative methodology

Despite the prevalence of studies based on positivistic data collection and analysis, positivism as a theory is rather neglected. Most theory texts have already dropped positivism from their list of contents; and the number of critics of positivism in general and of quantitative methodology in particular has increased. And so has the number of theoretical and methodological elements they criticise.

This critique has been expressed systematically in the works of philosophers and social critics from the schools of philosophical hermeneutics (e.g. Gadamer 1960); of Husserl's phenomenology (Husserl, 1950) and Schuetz (1969); of symbolic interactionism, ethnomethodology (Cicourel, 1970); by Marxists and feminists and the followers of the qualitative methodology. Such criticisms reflected a basic dissatisfaction with a number of elements of quantitative research, some being related to theoretical principles and others to methodological practices. Girtler levelled a critique against positivism mainly from a qualitative stance (Girtler, 1984). In the following we shall present Girtler's critique together with some additional criticisms (Brieschke, 1992; Collins, 1992; Hughes, 1990; Konegen and Sondergeld, 1985; Lamnek, 1988):

- Social phenomena exist not 'out there' but in the minds of people and their interpretations.
- Reality cannot be defined objectively but subjectively: reality is interpreted social action. Objectivity can only lead to a technocratic and bureaucratic dehumanisation (Brieschke, 1992: 174).
- The overemphasis positivists place on quantitative measurement is wrong and unjustifiable, for it cannot capture the real meaning of social behaviour. Quantification often results in 'meanings' that are closer to the beliefs of the researchers than to those of the respondents.
- The use of hypotheses is problematic for many reasons but especially because it determines the course of the study at the outset, and restricts the options of questions and responses, forcing upon the respondents opinions or intentions which they might otherwise have not expressed.
- Quantitative research restricts experience in two ways: first by directing research to what is perceived by the senses; and second by employing only standardised tools, based on quantifiable data, to test hypotheses.
- Quantitative research fails to distinguish between appearance and essence of social events; it neglects the essence of life, studies 'appearance' and assumes that appearance is reality.
- This methodology employs a theoretical perspective and a form of research that supports the status quo and existing power structures.
- In quantitative research, methods are considered to be the most important element of the research process: they are more important than the research object; research is carried out by using already established methods; methods determine what is allowed to be studied; methods determine what is experience. As a result, research is limited to what can be approached through the existing methods; what is not approachable through quantitative methods is insignificant, is not worth studying, is not considered. Instead of trying to adjust methods to reality, reality is adjusted to methods. Quantity is more important than quality.
- Quantitative research perceives reality as a sum of measured or measurable attributes; and its primary purpose is to quantify and measure social events, a characteristic often referred to as quantaphrenia! The whole research process is geared towards quantifying and measuring: measurement is taken for granted, and introduces a peculiar and biased perception of the world.

- Quantitative research attempts to neutralise the researchers or to reduce or eliminate as much as possible their influence on the researched, to the extent that they become 'disembodied abstractions' and depersonalised (Collins, 1992: 183). This is accomplished through bracketing out personal experiences and views of the researcher as well as through refinement and standardisation of methods and techniques. Critics argue in this context that such a process of neutralisation is neither possible nor beneficial.

  In another context, it is further argued that the neopositivist methodology employs a 'technocratic' perspective, which sees the researcher as an expert who aims at discovering and documenting law-like generalisations. The researcher appears in the context of the society as a technician who serves technocratic needs. The logic the researcher employs is a *reconstructed logic* in the sense that it is reconstructed into logically constructed rules, terms and principles.

- Quantitative research takes natural sciences as a model (often referred to as *methodolatry* or *physics envy*). However, such an attempt is feasible neither in their theoretical perception of reality nor in their methodological approach (Konegen and Sondergeld, 1985). First, natural sciences operate in isolation, that is, to dissect the research object into elements and analyse them in parts; social sciences do not. Second the natural sciences try to quantify the experience and to reproduce the findings through repetition of the research; this should not be the guide for social sciences. Finally, natural sciences assume a nomological regularity behind the natural process, which does not exist in society.

  The methods of natural sciences are not suitable for social research. People are not just natural elements but social persons, acting individuals with their own wishes, perceptions and interests; neither is there such regularity in social action as in natural phenomena. Therefore, it is argued, the methodological rule should be understanding (*verstehen*) rather than measuring.

- Because quantitative research works on the principles of natural sciences (i.e. objectivity, neutrality), research objects are seen as scientific objects and are treated as such. Respondents are therefore treated as *objects* and as informants or producers of data. But social sciences are not natural sciences, and respondents are not objects but partners and 'experts' whose views are sought.

- Quantitative researchers endeavour to achieve objectivity in their research, which they consider to be one of the most important properties of social research, and employ several methods to achieve it, such as standardisation. Qualitative researchers criticise this in three ways: (1) Objectivity is not possible. Standardisation and distance from the research object does not guarantee objectivity because the perceptions and meanings of the researcher penetrate the research process in many ways. A state of objectivity is therefore just an illusion. (2) Standardisation results in converting the social world under study into an artificial world which has nothing in common with the real world. (3) Objectivity is not necessary. The personal involvement of the researcher is required in order to help to take the position of the respondent and see human life as seen by people themselves.

- The research procedure employed by the quantitative researchers pre-supposes the presence of a research design, including hypotheses, before the research begins. Consequently, this design determines what is relevant and how it will be studied, and what is meaningful and required, even before the study starts. This restricts the options of the research process, blocks initiative and the motivation of the researcher, limits the effectiveness of research, and produces artificial data, which do not reflect reality as a whole.
- Quantitative researchers believe that in order to maintain objectivity they have to be distant from the researched and eliminate any form of subjectivity that could bias the findings. This distance is obvious in the way research is done, the instruments they use and the manner in which data analysis is conducted. Respondents are turned into 'units' or 'objects' and are treated as such. As a result, researchers are removed from the research process, lose contact with the researched and become alienated from the world they are supposed to study.
- The methods employed by quantitative researchers seem to separate the research object from its context. Data collection, for instance, is usually taken out of the context of the research object. In most cases, controlling variables is a virtue. Factors such as the Hawthorne-effect or reactivity-effect must then be avoided at all costs. Excluding natural processes, isolating the study object from its environment and implanting it in an artificial context is considered ideal. Such procedures are criticised strongly by qualitative researchers who argue that research must be done as it unfolds in real life situations, and that the researcher should not change the structure and process of social life.

    Positivism employs unidirectional research practices, which present the researcher as a separate, objective and autonomous expert, who acts on the respondent. This has many diverse consequences, for example the aim of hiding the identity of the researcher, legitimating a sense of unconnectedness, encouraging exclusion of women from the construction of knowledge, and creating a political structure of domination, exploitation and oppression (Brieschke, 1992: 173–4).
- Positivism has a gendered character based on the inherent trend to separate the world into fundamental dichotomies (culture versus nature, subject versus object, etc.), one of which is the masculine versus feminine division. This separation is strengthened by the fact that men are presented as the experts, the 'knowing' subjects, while women are seen as the objects, the 'known' objects, which are also taken to be inferior. This results in a form of construction of knowledge that ignores women and works against their personal interests.

6   Qualitative methodology

Qualitative methodology is associated with many diverse methods employed in the social sciences. For some, qualitative methodology is everything that is not quantitative. It is also perceived by some as a supplement to quantitative research and by others as its opposite or alternative.

Qualitative research as an alternative to traditional, established, conventional or quantitative research has been developed through a cooperative effort involving a number of factors, which we shall discuss in this section. As a result the structure of this methodology is diverse and to a certain extent not as distinct or as explicit as that of its adversary. Information about this new methodology is thought to be not as clear, as advanced or as integrated as that of quantitative methodology. This makes a discussion of this research form rather cumbersome. (For a very good discussion of qualitative methodology see Flick *et al.* (1991), Lamnek (1988 and Crabtree and Miller (1992). Many of the points presented in this section have been taken from these works.)

In the discussion that follows we shall introduce a number of fundamental aspects of qualitative methodology, including its main criteria, theoretical basis, central principles and foundations. Because information related to this type of methodology is not as systematised or as readily available as for quantitative research, the need to offer more detail is obvious and justifiable.

a   General criteria

In principle, qualitative methodology demonstrates the following characteristic elements (Berger *et al.*, 1989; Crabtree and Miller, 1992; Lamnek, 1988; Patton, 1990; Vlahos, 1984):

- It assumes that the social world is always a human creation not a discovery (Smith, 1992: 101, 1990); consequently interpretive science tries to capture reality as it is, namely as seen and experienced by the respondents.
- It tries to capture reality in interaction.
- It studies a small number of respondents.
- It employs no random sampling techniques.
- It attempts to present the information gathered verbally in a detailed and complete form, not in numbers or formulae (no statistical analysis).
- It uses no quantitative measures or variables.
- It tries to approach reality without preconceived ideas and prestructured models and patterns.
- It perceives the researcher and the researched as two equally important elements of the same situation. Respondents are not reduced to variables, units or hypotheses, but are seen as parts of the whole. Reducing people to numerical symbols and statistical figures results in loss of a perception of the subjective nature of human behaviour.
- It aims to study reality from the inside not from the outside.
- Its purpose is to interpret meaningful human actions and interpretations that people give of themselves or others.
- It attempts to capture the meaning and regularities of social action.
- It aims to understand people, not to measure them.
- It employs research procedures that produce descriptive data, presenting in the respondents' own words their views and experiences.

- It leads to an interpretive inquiry which ultimately is a moral inquiry (Smith, 1992).

The main elements of this approach have been criticised by many social scientists, particularly for their almost exclusive micro-sociological interest, their assumed degree of 'fluidity' of social structures and high degree of subjectivity and relativism ('anything goes'), their indeterministic perception of the world, and several other methodological and theoretical issues. Despite these criticisms, this school of thought grew in popularity among young sociologists and social scientists after the Second World War and especially in the 1980s.

Features of qualitative research

Qualitative inquiry means:

1 Naturalistic inquiry, which studies real-world situations as they unfold.
2 Inductive analysis in which the evaluator is immersed in the details and specifics of data to discover important categories.
3 Holistic inquiry, in that the whole phenomenon under study is understood as a complex system that is more than the sum of its parts.
4 Qualitative data, detailed, thick description.
5 Personal contact and insight, with the researcher getting close to the people, situation and phenomenon under study.
6 Dynamic systems, with attention to process and change.
7 Unique case orientation, assuming each case is special and unique.
8 Context sensitivity, placing findings in a social, historical and temporal context.
9 Empathetic neutrality, with the researcher passionately seeking understanding of the world, rather than either ephemeral objectivity or a subjectivity that undermines credibility.
10 Design flexibility, with the evaluator open to adopting inquiry as understanding deepens.

Source: M. Patton (1990), *Qualitative Evaluation and Research Methods,* Newsbury Park, CA: Sage, pp. 40–1.

b Theoretical foundations of qualitative methodology

Qualitative research is diverse not only in form but also in its theoretical framework, which provides the guidelines for the actual research process. In its entirety, qualitative methodology relates to a vast number of theoretical bases, which make it rich, pluralistic and diverse. Jacob (1987, 1988) identified six 'domains' of qualitative methodology, which are listed below. For the social scientist, most important are the foundations that contribute most to social research and are most frequently applied by social scientists, namely phenomenology, hermeneutics and symbolic interactionism.

The six domains of qualitative research

- *The human ecology domain*, which is interested in the behaviour patterns demonstrated by people in their everyday life; it employs observation techniques.
- *The ecological psychology domain*, which investigates the relationships between people and their environment in order to identify ways of shaping their life; it employs mainly observation techniques.
- *The holistic ethnography domain* concentrating on culture and the effects it has on people; it employs participant observation.
- *The cognitive anthropology domain*, which studies people's perspectives as organised in schemata and categories of meanings and inter-related to each other; it employs in-depth interviewing.
- *The ethnography* or *communication domain* relating to linguistics and interested in verbal and non-verbal interaction.
- *The symbolic interactionism domain* which is interested in how people make sense of their world and assign meanings in interaction with others

Source: E. Jacob (1988), 'Classifying qualitative research: a focus on tradition', *Educational Researcher*, 17, pp. 16–24.

Phenomenology

Husserl's phenomenology criticises positivist thinking and especially the underlying assumption that people, through their senses, can capture the world around them. It is also critical of the idea that positivist research can create knowledge about the world, and that the human mind is an empty vessel, passively delivered to its environment. Instead, it suggests that people are active creators of their world and have a consciousness that communicates to them everyday experiences and knowledge (Husserl, 1950).

Although against the notion of the objectively experienced world, phenomenology does not reject outright its existence; rather, it argues that although there is an objective world, it is experienced only through consciousness — in a sense, the objective world becomes real through consciousness in about the same way that consciousness becomes real by referring to an object or experience: one is conscious of something.

Husserl sees the world as a highly ordered system (Freeman, 1980) created by people who actively participate in producing and maintaining that order. People, however, are not aware of the fact that they create this ordered world. Instead, they take order as a natural phenomenon and hence do not question it. This is what Husserl calls the *natural attitude* (Husserl, 1950; Ritzer, 1983). This natural attitude is, for Husserl, an obstacle, a distortion and a bias, which for the phenomenologist need to be overcome if one wishes to come to the essence of the subjects and understand them.

Husserl (1950) regards this 'essence' as the consciousness, the 'transcendental ego', which resides not in people's heads but in their relationships with others (a notion termed *intentionality*). The most important function of Husserl's phenomenology is to penetrate and look beyond the various layers constructed by actors in the real world so that the essential structure of their consciousness and its basic properties become clear (Ritzer, 1983). This is done by disconnecting or setting aside (Husserl uses the term *bracketing*) the natural attitude (Freeman, 1980) and the 'incidental experiences of life which tend to dominate consciousness' to arrive at the 'transcendental ego'. This way, science for Husserl is a philosophy that is vigorous, systematic and critical (Ritzer, 1983).

This brief description of some minute elements of phenomenology demonstrates very clearly how much qualitative methodology owes to it. The perception of the world as being created by people, the notion of natural attitude or natural standpoint, the process of getting down to the essence of people, the perception of reality through the minds (consciousness) of the respondents and the process of bracketing are a few examples.

Hermeneutics

Hermeneutics is a special technique based on text interpretation. In its original (Greek) meaning it denotes the art of translating and constitutes an approach to texts and fixed expressions of human life with the purpose of understanding and interpreting them as well as their creators. The central point of this approach is *verstehen*, that is, understanding, and its original sociological meaning comes from the work of Max Weber. It was Weber and those who followed his theory who gradually extended the idea of understanding texts to understanding people and social life in general. Such verstehen can be a 'psychological verstehen' (especially with regard to empathetic understanding); 'meaning-verstehen' (*sinn-verstehen*), directed towards the actual meaning; 'elementary verstehen' and 'higher verstehen'.

In the context of hermeneutics, understanding becomes a very complex process, leading researchers and theorists to various levels of human life, and it takes various forms (see Danner, 1979), an explanation of which is beyond the scope of this book. Nevertheless, its emphasis on understanding people as well as on interpreting objects and actions and the emphasis on meanings are elements that have proved to be very useful for interpretive social science and for qualitative methodology.

Symbolic interactionism

Most qualitative researchers opt for theoretical frameworks, which draw predominantly on symbolic interactionism. The basic assumptions, elements and directives of this framework are many and diverse. Some of these principles have already been presented explicitly or implicitly (in previous discussions) where the theoretical perspectives were discussed (see Section 3 in this chapter). Some of the points that are relevant primarily to qualitative research can be summarised as follows:

- Social life is formed, maintained and changed by the basic meaning attached to it by interacting people, who interact on the basis of meanings they assign to their world; social life and objects become significant when they are assigned meanings.
- Social life is expressed through symbols. Language is the most important symbolic system.
- The purpose of social research is to study the structure, functions and meaning of symbolic systems.

- The most appropriate method of social research is the *naturalistic* method, which incorporates two major procedures, *exploration* and *inspection* (Blumer, 1969; Vlahos, 1984; Wallace and Wolf, 1986). Exploration studies new areas, looks for details, and offers a clear understanding of the research question. Any method is useful here. Inspection, on the other hand, is an analytical method and contains a more intensive and more concentrated testing. (Blumer called this type of approach *sympathetic introspection* — Blumer, 1969.)
- Data and interpretations depend on context and process and must be steadily verified and, when necessary, corrected.
- Meanings are established in and through social interaction. They are learned through interaction and not determined otherwise.
- Meanings are employed, managed and changed through interaction.

Principles of symbolic interactionism

---

1 Human beings, unlike lower animals, are endowed with the capacity for thought.
2 The capacity for thought is shaped by social interaction.
3 In social interaction people learn the meanings and the symbols that allow them to exercise their distinctively human capacity for thought.
4 Meanings and symbols allow people to carry on distinctively human action and interaction.
5 People are able to modify or alter the meanings and symbols they use in action and interaction on the basis of their interpretation of the situation.
6 People can make these modifications and alterations because, in part, of their ability to interact with themselves, which allows them to examine possible courses of action, assess their relative advantages and disadvantages, and then choose one.
7 The intertwined patterns of action and interaction make up groups and societies.

Source: G. Ritzer (1983), *Sociological Theory,* New York: Knopf, pp. 306–7.

The relevance of this theoretical paradigm for qualitative methodology is more than obvious. Most of the principles of this methodology come from symbolic interactionism.

c   Central principles of qualitative methodology

The main principles of qualitative research are based on and centre around a number of fundamental concepts, such as communication, verstehen, subject and everyday life. These principles are somewhat diverse, since the philosophical background of qualitative methodology is diverse. Lamnek (1988: 21–9) summarises the basic principles of this methodology in the following six points:

1 *Openness*   Qualitative research is not predetermined or prestructured by hypotheses and procedures that might limit its focus, scope or operation.

Its perception and approach are open in all aspects, namely with regard to its research subjects, the research situation or the research method to be employed. Hypotheses in this research process are not a condition but the aim of the research. The aims of qualitative research are open and also geared towards general exploration.

2 *Research as communication* Qualitative research is embedded in a process of communication between researcher and respondent. There is no intention to establish independence of the researcher from the respondent or the data; researcher and respondents are working together for a common goal, and the respondents are 'subjects' who define, explain, interpret and construct reality, and as such they are as important as, if not more important than, the researcher.

3 *The process-nature of the research and the object* Reality, according to this form of research, is created and explained in interaction. In this process, reality is constructed, managed, explained and presented. The purpose of social research is, therefore, to identify the process of reality construction, and the construction of patterns of meanings and actions. Statements collected through this research are therefore parts of this process of creation, reproduction and explanation of social reality.

4 *Reflexivity of object and analysis* In qualitative research every symbol or meaning is considered to be a reflection of the context in which they were developed. A symbol is an *index* of an embracing regulated context ('indexicality'). The meaning of an object of expression is understood through a reference to its symbolic or social context. This requires a flexible method that is ready to react to change and to adjust its instruments according to changing circumstances and contexts.

5 *Explication* Qualitative research is set to explain clearly and accurately how respondents will be approached. The steps of the research process, as well as the rules of its operations, are expected to be made known as far as possible.

6 *Flexibility* Qualitative methods are flexible in many ways, for example with regard to the choice of research instruments and research procedures. Research is not rigidly set but rather flexible, and can change during its execution. In qualitative research, a design is more likely to include guidelines than strict rules.

d   Research foundations of qualitative methodology

Qualitative research is based on certain foundations or is marked by certain criteria that differ from those of quantitative research. These criteria as summarised by Lamnek (1988) (see also Flick *et al.*, 1991; Miles and Huberman, 1994; Smith, 1992) suggest that qualitative research has these characteristics:

• It is *interpretative*, that is, social interaction is a process of interpretation; social reality is constructed through interpretation of the actors; social relations are the result of a process of interaction based on interpretation, and theory building is a process of interpretation.

- It is *naturalistic*, that is, it perceives reality as a natural setting; it uses naturalistic methods, such as fieldwork, field study and generally methods that are familiar to the people living in these settings. Such methods are considered to be mostly descriptive in nature, describing people and events in natural settings.
- It is *communicative*, that is, it is understood and operates in the context of the process of communication, of which it is a part.
- It is *reflective*, that is, it should reflect critically the aspects of reality that are considered to be a theoretical and practical problem of sociology and social research.
- It is *qualitative*, that is, it uses no traditional quantitative procedures, but methods known to be suitable for the research object.

A research study based on interpretive research assumes an identity of its own based on internal quality, perhaps supported through collegial solidarity. Judging the value of an interpretive inquiry consequently is different from assessing the quality of a quantitative study. The rules applied are loose and definitely not quantitative. Smith (1992: 102) suggests the following three points should be considered when judging an interpretive inquiry:

1 The standard of evaluation should be *values* not rules. Any criterion considered by the judge as appropriate is relevant.
2 It is useful to construct a list of traits to describe the expectations judges have of an inquiry; such attributes might be 'consistency and scope of interpretation', 'length of time spent in the field', and 'evidence that the interpreter entertained alternative possible interpretations' (Smith, 1992: 103). Such a list will change from case to case and will depend on many factors related to the nature of the study, the researcher and the research object.
3 The judgement is based on practical and moral issues.

This view makes some interesting points; it is, however, not shared by many qualitative researchers who tend to employ more specific and objective standards of evaluation which go beyond practical and moral issues.

e   Strengths and weaknesses of qualitative research

Qualitative research has both strengths and weaknesses. Both relate to its nature as an approach concerned with studying people as persons and being interested in their everyday life experiences and interpretations. Of the summaries presented by many writers (e.g. Miles and Huberman, 1994; Stergios, 1991; Vlahos, 1984), the one given below is most comprehensive.

Obviously many of the 'weaknesses' of this type of research are related to its very nature and reflect the positivistic prejudice of assessment. We should understand that qualitative research is a unique type of academic activity and should be assessed in its own context.

Strengths and weaknesses of qualitative research

Strengths:	*	Researching people in natural settings.
	*	Stressing interpretations and meanings.
	*	Achieving a deeper understanding of the respondent's world.
	*	Humanising research process by raising the role of the researched.
	*	Allowing higher flexibility.
	*	Presenting a more realistic view of the world.
Weaknesses:	*	Problems of reliability caused by extreme subjectivity.
	*	Risk of collecting meaningless and useless information.
	*	It is very time-consuming.
	*	Problems of representativeness and generalisability of findings.
	*	Problems of objectivity and detachment.
	*	Problems of ethics (entering the personal sphere of subjects).

Source: B.A Chadwick, H.M. Bahr and S.L. Albrecht (1984), *Social Science Research Methods,* Englewood Cliffs, NJ: Prentice-Hall, pp. 214–15.

7 Similarities and differences in qualitative and quantitative methodology

The division between qualitative and quantitative methods is perceived by methodologists in a diverse fashion. For a few writers, qualitative methodology is an easy way of doing research, a soft option — 'anything goes', as some put it — and quantitative methodology is very complex and very demanding. But while some consider these two methodologies as contradictory and fundamentally different, others see them as the extreme positions of the same continuum: two ideal types that are employed only in exceptional circumstances. In concrete cases, researchers employ a methodology that, although predominantly quantitative or qualitative, in essence contains some aspects of the other methods. The perceived differences are summarised in Table 2.3 (see Lincoln and Guba, 1985: 35; Stergios, 1991; Vlahos, 1984).

Table 2.3 shows that the two methodologies have developed quite distinct research techniques and modes of operation. Quantitativists employ highly structured techniques of data collection that allow quantification, hypotheses, measurement and operationalisation, as well as the use of quantitative methods of data analysis including statistics and computers. Qualitative researchers on the other hand use less structured techniques of data collection and analysis. Participant observation is the most common method; other methods, however, are also employed. Their emphasis is on discovery and exploration rather than on hypothesis testing.

Table 2.3 Perceived differences between quantitative and qualitative methodology

Feature	Quantitative methodology	Qualitative methodology
Nature of reality	Objective; simple; single; tangible sense impressions	Subjective; problematic; holistic; a social construct
Causes and effects	Nomological thinking; cause–effect linkages	Non-deterministic; mutual shaping; no cause–effect linkages
The role of values	Value neutral; value-free inquiry	Normativism; value-bound inquiry
Natural and social sciences	Deductive; model of natural sciences; nomothetic; based on strict rules	Inductive; rejection of the natural sciences model; ideographic; no strict rules: interpretations
Methods	Quantitative, mathe-matical; extensive use of statistics	Qualitative, with less emphasis on statistics; verbal and qualitative analysis
Researcher's role	Rather passive; is the 'knower'; is separate from subject — the known: dualism	Active; 'knower' and 'known' are interactive and inseparable
Generalisations	Inductive generalisations; nomothetic statements	Analytical or conceptual generalisations; time-and-context specific

The researcher in quantitative research is thought to assume a rather 'passive' role during data collection. In qualitative research the investigator is taken to be actively involved in the process of data collection and analysis and to be more aware of the flow of the process than the quantitative researcher.

Quantitative researchers, finally, are thought to be interested in inductive generalisations of the research findings. Qualitative researchers on the other hand seem to be interested in exploration and in making analytical or conceptual generalisations only. A more detailed contrast of the two types of research is presented in Table 2.4.

Some writers (e.g. Kleining, 1991) argue that both methodologies have the same origin — the everyday methods of the past; quantitative methods are simplifications of the qualitative methods, and can only be meaningfully employed when qualitative methods have shown that a simplification of identified relations is possible.

Nevertheless, qualitative methodology remains fundamentally different from quantitative, not only in theory but also with regard to the way it extracts information and analyses it. It employs a nonpositivist perspective, a 'logic in practice' rather than a reconstructed logic, and a non-linear path (Neuman, 1994), as we shall see later.

Table 2.4 Comparison between the essential features of qualitative and quantitative research

Quantitative research	Qualitative research
• Its purpose is to explain social life	• Its purpose is to understand social life
• Is nomothetic — interested in establishing law-like statements, causes, consequences, etc.	• Is idiographic — describes reality as it is
• Aims at theory testing	• Aims at theory building
• Employs an objective approach	• Employs a subjective approach
• Is etiological — interested in *why* things happen	• Is interpretative — interested in *how*
• Is ahistorical — interested in explanations over space and time	• Is historical — interested in real cases
• Is a closed approach — is strictly planned	• Is open and flexible in all aspects
• Research process is pre-determined	• Research process is influenced by the respondent
• Researcher is distant from respondent	• Researcher is close to the respondent
• Uses a static and rigid approach	• Uses a dynamic approach
• Employs an inflexible process	• Employs a flexible process
• Is particularistic, studies elements, variables	• Is holistic — studies whole units
• Employs random sampling	• Employs theoretical sampling
• Places priority on studying differences	• Places priority on studying similarities
• Employs a reductive data analysis	• Employs an explicative data analysis
• Employs high levels of measurement	• Employs low levels of measurement
• Employs a deductive approach	• Employs an inductive approach

8   Quantitative and qualitative methods

a   Quantitative methods

The methods of data collection employed by quantitative researchers are many, diverse, simple and straightforward; and deserve no comment at this stage. Long history of application has made them a household item not only for the researcher but also for the uninitiated person. The most common methods are *surveys, documentary methods, observation, sociometry* and *experiments*. In many instances, quantitative researchers employ qualitative methods in their studies, adjusted to meet the criteria of quantitative research, or in their real nature. In other cases such methods are used in addition to quantitative methods, as a preparation step to a quantitative study, or to refine conclusions reached by means of qualitative research.

b   Qualitative methods

The methods employed by qualitative researchers vary in type, structure and quality. While some of the qualitative methods are in principle the same as those of the quantitative methodology, others are totally different and are employed only in the area of qualitative methodology. Many methods are more complicated and involved than quantitative methods.

In general, writers (e.g. Berger *et al.*, 1989; Lamnek, 1988) refer to three major types of qualitative methods; each of these methods is embedded in a rich theoretical tradition structure and methodology. Such methodologies can be subject directed, object directed, or development orientated, as shown below.

Subject-directed methodologies
These methodologies place emphasis on the significance of the subject in the process of collection, analysis and interpretation of the data and the social research in general. The following three methodologies are well accepted in the area of sociology:

1   *Hermeneutics*, which stresses the process of text *interpretation* as a central element of its approach. Used in many contexts it is directed towards interpreting speech and text and, more generally, interpretation of the world. It stresses the significance of the interpreting subject and its ability to understand the world.
2   *Phenomenology*, stemming from philosophy and Husserl's work; this methodology aims at understanding everyday life by means of unravelling taken-for-granted assumptions.
3   *Ethnomethodology*, which studies structures of the world that are taken for granted with the intent of making sense of them by clarifying them.

Object-directed methodologies
Emphasis in these methodologies is placed on the object, that is, the researched; they are explorative and directed towards reconnaissance rather than interpretation. They still entail a portion of criticism. There are three main object-directed methodologies, namely psychoanalysis, ethnology and symbolic interactionism.

1 *Psychoanalysis* is based on Freud's theory of personality and the work of his followers; it is more influential in psychology than in sociology, although as a theory it has attracted the interest of some sociologists and social anthropologists.
2 *Ethnology* (also known as social anthropology or cultural anthropology) is the study of entire cultures. It entails *living* in, and becoming part of the culture one intends to study, for extended periods of time, *conversing* and *communicating* with the members of the group being studied, and *gathering* information while being a part of that group.
3 *Symbolic interactionism* of the Chicago School was developed in 1892 at Chicago University in the USA; it influenced the sociological thinking of the country up to the 1930s. It employs a qualitative methodology based on observation, questioning and document analysis. The main aim of this research is exploration. This is also the type of qualitative methodology that is most commonly used by sociologists (in a direct and/or indirect way).

Development-oriented methodologies
Emphasis in this group of methodologies is placed on change and development of individuals, groups and societies rather than on individuals as subjects or objects. Of these methods, *dialectic* social research seems to be common among sociologists. This research rests on the principles of the laws of motion of society and the mind; and on theory and practice of society. The work of many members of the Frankfurt School belongs in this group of methodologies.

9   The right methodology

Diversity in social methodology, as presented in the two types discussed above, has often been perceived as differences in quality. The conflict about which methodology is the best choice for a researcher is as old as the methodologies themselves. And the answers to this question cover all possible options.

Quantitative researchers stress the shortcomings of qualitative research and argue that quantitative methods are better than qualitative methods. In a similar fashion, qualitative researchers present their methods as the most appropriate form of research, for similar reasons. And the conflict continues.

Marshall and Rossman (1989: 6) have listed suitable applications for qualitative research. This list identifies the nature of qualitative research and indicates that it is mainly descriptive or exploratory, and places emphasis on context, setting and the subject's frame of reference. Nevertheless, this does not necessarily mean that one type of research is better than the other; on the contrary, it means that both types of research are important, although suitable for different types of inquiry.

Research on which qualitative inquiry can concentrate

- Research that cannot be done experimentally for practical or ethical reasons.
- Research that delves in depth into complexities and processes.
- Research for which relevant variables have yet to be identified.
- Research that seeks to explore where and why policy, folk wisdom and practice do not work.
- Research on unknown societies or innovative systems.
- Research on informal and unstructured linkages and processes in organisations.
- Research on real as opposed to stated organisational goals.

Source: C. Marshall and G.B. Rossman (1989), *Designing Qualitative Research,* London: Sage, p. 46.

To follow the line of thought of a number of writers (e.g. Berger *et al.*, 1989) advocating a Marxist–Leninist perspective, the two types of research are equally legitimate. The following arguments have been presented:

- Every social unit is a dialectic unit with quantitative and qualitative aspects; therefore, both methods are acceptable.
- Both are correct approaches to the essence of social reality. Quantification progresses to qualitative data; and qualitative data become 'hardened' into quantitative data.
- Quantitative and qualitative analyses must have a theoretical basis.
- Criteria that can be measured must be measured; they must be determined quantitatively.
- The trend in Marxist–Leninist sociology is to split complex social issues into criteria that can be determined quantitatively and to develop in that way theoretical conditions for qualified understanding.
- A summary of mere quantitative data alone gives no scientific perception. Marxist–Leninist sociology is against empiricism, which produces statistical data without being able to say what the data mean and how they fit into the social context.

The answer to the question which methodology is the best is that there is no 'better' or 'right' methodology. Both methodologies are good and right depending on the circumstances. Quantitative and qualitative methodologies are the tools of the trade of social scientists and both are useful and have a purpose. The one complements the other, and both together offer a stereoscopic picture of the world. Quantitative researchers use qualitative elements in their work, and qualitative research is not free of quantitative elements of study, such as numbers, statistics and quantitative data in general. Quantitative elements are thought to complement and supplement qualitative work, a notion supported by many qualitative researchers, critical theorists and feminists (Sprague and Zimmerman (1989: 82). Hence, both ways are legitimate and useful, although they are used for different purposes and to answer different questions.

10   Emerging methodologies

Quantitative methodology dominated the research scene throughout the early and middle history of social sciences. Qualitative methodology was accepted, although reluctantly, in the ranks of social methodology much later. Only recently did texts on social research include discussion of qualitative research (e.g. Neuman, 1991), with most texts either ignoring qualitative methodology or including it as research 'methods' rather than as a research 'methodology'.

Obviously, the expansion of the methodological scope of social sciences legitimated qualitative research and widened immensely the enterprise of the social sciences. Simultaneously it defined more clearly its domain as well as the various types of research undertaken by social scientists. Practically, research models which did not fit into the frameworks of these methodologies (e.g. Marxist research or feminist research) were considered either as lying outside the area of social science (e.g. as being philosophical, speculative, ethnological, anthropological, etc.) or as a version of the existing methodologies. Views supported by many Marxist and feminist researchers, suggesting for instance that the world should be seen as a totality, or the trend to reject the employment of a strict methodological procedure, arguing for instance that Marxist or feminist research cannot be set in steps or be controlled by prescribed methodological rules, or, finally, that research should be seen as a process in which there are no researchers and researched but researchers only (classifying the respondents as researchers) presented an image of this type of research that could easily be considered to be outside the area of social sciences. On the other hand, the fact that these research models employed, in most cases at least, standard methods of social science tempted social scientists to believe that this social research was either quantitative or qualitative.

This is the attitude currently held among social scientists in Australia and in many other countries; they tend to support the view that social research is carried out in the context of a quantitative or a qualitative methodology, and are sceptical about accepting critical research — and more so Marxist or feminist research — as a separate methodology. Some writers are more vocal and more serious about it than others, but the current methodological repertoire of the social sciences seems to contain only the two established methodologies. The closest many social scientists would come to accepting critical research as a new methodology is to see it as an *emerging methodology*, leaving its real position in the social sciences to be established in the future.

11   The basis for a methodological distinction

Why is critical research not accepted as a new methodology? When can a research model become a methodology? What makes methodologies inherently different from each other is possession of *distinct* research principles, which make one research methodology *significantly different* from the other methodologies. But, does critical research possess these principles? Below, we shall explore some points related to this question.

Perception of reality

In the first place reality is perceived by critical theory in a way that is different from the perceptions of the other two paradigms. While for positivists it is a set of sense impressions, which can best be ascertained through quantitative methods, for interpretivists it is a set of subjective meanings, which call for qualitative methods; for critical researchers reality is complex, diverse and multifaceted. It entails appearances, it reflects 'real facts' that are hidden behind appearances, it contains personal perceptions and actions that are expressions of a correct or a false consciousness; it is seen as the result of historical processes and reflects the powerless position of people acting in well-orchestrated and institutionally reinforced systems of power that researchers are supposed to actively address.

In this sense, a researcher who is to operate in the context of a critical paradigm is expected to devise a research model that will address aspects of interpersonal relationships, systems and situations that are unique to this researcher. The model may address people, families or power relationships, the same issues that positivists or interpretivists address; however, the aspects of these issues, their nature, their conceptualisation and their origin and relation to other issues or social units will be different from those addressed by positivists and interpretivists. If critical theorists were to employ a positivist methodology (which they openly criticise and reject anyway) or an interpretive methodology they would not be able to capture the aspects of reality they are interested in.

Critical theorists are not primarily interested in what people do or the subjective meanings they assign to aspects of their world. In the first place interpretive researchers do not normally address the same issues that critical researchers address. Even if they do, while interpretive researchers would be interested in what types of meanings they give to certain events, critical researchers would be interested in why they interpret issues the way they do, how such meanings are created, who facilitates such interpretations, who benefits out of such interpretations, how do such interpretations affect labourers and social organisation, how such mechanisms of cultural determination or social arrangements can be broken down and so on. This means that the whole theoretical and practical organisation of critical research is tuned to a different environment and to a different level than that of the positivist and interpretive research. This is a fundamental issue and a very legitimate reason for establishing a critical methodology.

Nevertheless, for many social scientists, critical theory does not seem to refer to a third dimension of reality, a new or a different perception of the world. Irrespective of the way in which it views reality (e.g. in a critical manner) it still sees it in objective and/or subjective terms, and for that reason there is no justification for a new methodology.

How humans are perceived

A similar trend can be identified in the way the various paradigms view human beings. While positivists see them as guided or controlled by social rules and general laws (which are best accessible to quantitative methods), and interpretivists as free acting people who create their own social world, critical theorists perceive them as being both enslaved in cultural and social constraints as well as in their own perceptions of self, and as being subjected to the powers ultimately determining interpretations: subjective meanings about their world which interest the interpretivists very much are controlled by power structures that allow no freedom of interpretation. Interpretations are given on the basis of standards, conditions, practices and conventions all supplied and controlled by subtle powers outside the individual. Even researchers are victims of this intellectual and cultural determination because they are biased through socialisation and conditioning to see things the way they are supposed to see them. And while positivists and interpretivists ignore these elements, critical researchers consider them as fundamental to their research. Thus, *what* is to be studied, *how* it will be captured, and *in what* contexts and ways it will be analysed are issues that among critical researchers are defined in a unique and distinct way.

Nevertheless, as in the previous section, although the significance of the critical perspective is not denied, there is currently no justification for a new methodology, because the critical paradigm does not present any research-related elements that are not included in the already existing methodologies. The additional concerns of the critical paradigm relate to theoretical/ideological but not methodological issues.

The nature of science

The nature of science presents a case in which the difference between the paradigms and therefore between their methodologies is more than obvious. Science among positivists is controlled, deductive, nomothetic, positivistic and value free, and among interpretivists it is inductive, ideographic, normative and based on common sense; among critical researchers it is part of both but most of all it is engaged, emancipating and empowering. This, in conjunction with the other elements considered above, supports the point that a critical paradigm is justified.

Again, from a different perspective, the perception of science held by critical theorists can hardly justify a new methodology. The fact that critical science is engaged, emancipating and empowering makes it different from the others, but this difference refers to theory and not necessarily to methodology. For many social scientists, critical science is a step further than the positivist and interpretive science, but not different enough to justify a new methodology.

Purpose and procedures

The factors considered above generate a kind of research model that varies from one paradigm to another. While for positivists, research is there to explain and predict, and for interpretivists to interpret and understand people, for critical researchers it has the purpose of emancipating, empowering and liberating, that is, to get below the surface, to expose real relations, to disclose myths and illusions, to remove false beliefs and ideas and to show how the world should be, how to achieve goals and how to change the world. These aims, it is argued, cannot be achieved in the context of the traditional paradigms because methodologies do not provide the options, principles and means to achieve that purpose.

Nevertheless, for reasons similar to those presented above, critical theory does not have a basis for establishing a new methodology. It is argued that the purpose of the research alone does not create significant differences in its processes of research design, data collection and analysis. The principles and procedures employed by critical theorists are thought to be the same as those used by positivists and interpretivists.

Obviously, there is a difference of opinion regarding whether the elements of the critical paradigm can justify a critical methodology. As far as we are concerned, there is no sufficient agreement among social scientists and researchers to warrant the inclusion of a 'critical methodology' as a separate entity in this text. It is hoped that debates on this issue (see, for example, Geldsthorpe, 1992; Hammersley, 1992a; Ramazanoglu, 1992) will clarify this issue further, and help to define the status of research models employed in social sciences.

12   Feminist research

a   Introduction

The extent, quality and diversity of feminist research during the past 20 years and its immense impact on society in general and on the position and role of women are more than obvious. Based on Marxist principles or views related to patriarchal elements of social analysis, feminist research has made tremendous achievements in the area of social theory and research

The emphasis on the significance of capitalist relations of production for the analysis of oppression of women in modern societies, as well as on the ways in which ownership of private property leads to ideological subordination of women (socialist feminism), has helped to establish a new basis for the analysis of women and their roles in modern societies. New solutions to social problems arose, such as integrating women into social production as a way of emancipation (Sayers *et al.*, 1987). On the other hand, a new perspective is introduced into the area of social analysis, namely the 'gender' perspective, as a separate approach or in combination with class analysis, seeing capitalism as conspiring with patriarchy to achieve more profits through 'patriarchal ordering'.

As a result of this new ideology and approach countless studies have been conducted, producing a body of research and knowledge that cannot be ignored. Feminist research established a framework that demonstrates criteria of separate identity, and deserves special consideration.

b   The nature of feminist research

The question about what constitutes feminist research has been answered by feminists in many and diverse ways. According to one view (Reinharz, 1992: 6), feminist research includes methods used (1) in research projects by people who identify themselves as feminists or as part of the women's movement; (2) in research published in journals that publish only feminist research or in books that identify themselves as such; and (3) in research that has received awards from organisations that give awards to people who do feminist research. Be that as it may, Nielsen (1990: 6), quoting Reinharz (1983), describes feminist research as being 'contextual, inclusive, experiential, involved, socially relevant, multidimethodological, complete but not necessarily replicable, open to the environment and inclusive of emotions and events as experienced'. Reinharz (1992), on the other hand, argues that feminist research involves an ongoing criticism of non-feminist scholarship, is guided by feminist theory, may be transdisciplinary, aims to create social change, strives to represent human diversity, includes the researcher as a person, frequently attempts to develop special relationships with the people studied and, finally, frequently defines a special relationship with the reader.

Feminist research has concentrated on a number of issues and has employed types of research methods ranging from positivistic to interpretive and critical research, and has been based on a number of principles that reflect its nature and purpose. In general, feminist research is thought by many writers (see, for example, Lather, 1991, Reinharz, 1992) to have the following characteristics:

- It puts gender in the centre of social inquiry; making women visible and representing women's perspectives are a major part of feminist critical research (Harvey, 1990: 154).
- It places emphasis on women's experiences, which are considered a significant indicator of reality (Harding, 1987) and offer more validity than does method; in a wider context feminist research seems to involve the development of women's history, for example by recasting history to take account of women's roles and by reconstructing it in terms of women's rather than men's concerns; or by writing the history of women's realms (Harvey, 1990: 154).
- It discloses distortions related to such experiences.
- It sees gender as the nucleus of women's perceptions and lives, shaping of consciousness, skills, institutions and distribution of power and privilege.
- It is preoccupied with social construction of 'knowing and being known'.
- It is politically value laden and critical, and as such it is not methodic, but clearly dialectical. This implies that it is an imaginative and creative process which engages oppressive social structures (Harvey, 1990: 102–3).
- It is not solely *about* women but primarily *for* women, taking up an emancipationist stance; it entails an anti-positivistic orientation.
- It is supposed to use multiple methodologies and paradigms.

At the beginning of feminist research the emphasis was mainly on positivistic methods, using conventional methods as used by positivists or by eliminating inherent sexist bias in method and approach. This is what Harding (1987) refers to as *feminist empiricism*. Nevertheless, this changed very quickly towards the use of different and less androcentric methods; still while some feminists were urging researchers to develop distinct feminist methods that would correspond to women's intuitive rationality and also to feminist political commitments (Stanley and Wise, 1983), others (Reinharz, 1983) were suggesting that feminist methods should be derived from qualitative methodology. Harding

(1987: 2) finally was recommending the use of listening to respondents, observation and documentary methods, for example by studying historical records.

The significance of the position of males in culture and society with reference to the construction of knowledge was stressed by many feminists and began to influence the position of women in and attitudes towards society and the males. The struggle that followed strengthened this situation and created a *standpoint* from which women could view social life and the world and eliminate traditional distorted views. This created a position referred to by Harding (1987) as the *feminist standpoint theories of knowledge*, which characterised the developmental step in feminist research at that time. Following this, and the resulting multiplicity of standpoints (diverse experience leads to diverse standpoints), it was argued that reliable knowledge was gained through the struggle against oppression rather than through the traditional impression of a peaceful and loving coexistence of the sexes.

From this stage, some authors (Harding, 1987; Simons, 1989) reported that research had progressed to *feminist postmodernism*, which took a critical stance towards what traditional theory and research considered as right, proper and useful, namely universal theory, reason, enlightenment, etc. (for more information on postmodernism see Nicholson, 1990). Brieschke (1992: 174) defines post-modernist feminist research as follows:

> Postmodernist research in the social arena at its most evolved has been multi-dimensional, that is, reciprocal and mutual, moving back and forth from self to other(s), concerned with the social structures that enable the self and other(s) to communicate symbolically and intersubjectively. It values and is based upon a sense of connectedness that recognises the interdependent construction of both self and other through different ways of knowing. Philosophically, postmodernist paradigms view rationality itself as a social symbolic construction.

Methods employed by feminists are many and varied; however, the association between gender and qualitative research is obvious (Pilcher and Coffey, 1996). Still, methods may come from quantitative or qualitative frameworks, for example structured questioning, in-depth interviews, participant observation and document analysis, but also from ethnographic and ethnological studies, deconstruction (historical or structuralist deconstruction) and semiological analysis. Nevertheless, innovative applications of research strategies as well as new feminist methods have recently been suggested by feminist researchers. Cook and Fonow (1990), for instance, writing about innovative applications, referred among other things to visual techniques, triangulation, linguistic techniques, textual analysis, refined quantitative analysis and collaborative strategies.

Reinharz (1992) reported some originality in feminist research in methods as well as in procedure. Studying groups never studied before, using original sampling techniques, reporting in a manner that involves a variety of people never considered before, inventing new words and concepts and attributing authorship to groups or collectives are some examples of procedures used in this form of research. Nevertheless, inventing new methods is equally popular and interesting. The following methods have been reported (Reinharz, 1992) to be new additions:

- *Consciousness-raising method*   This is a group discussion technique involving groups; however, there is no leader or imposed theme of discussion; the discussion is guided by the group facilitator.
- *Group diaries*   Diaries are kept by members of a group anonymously. Emphasis is placed on the group and can involve group interview or memory work whereby stories are written by the group, read to the members, with discussion and analysis following later.
- *Dramatic role play*   Views, opinions and feelings are expressed in the form of a drama. The discussion issue is introduced by the researcher; then members of the group discuss the main issues and identify general trends or themes. Members of the group improvise, reflecting their feelings in their expressions; this is expected to generate further discussion.
- *Genealogy and network tracing*   This involves inquiring into a woman's history, tracing her relationships, friendships and origin.
- *Non authoritative and neutral research*   Information is collected and presented to the respondent to make sense of it. Emphasis is placed on the respondent and on subjectivity.
- *Conversation, dialogue*   A conversation involving a number of people discussing a topical issue, some impersonating historical figures, without division into questioners and answerers, is used in this method.
- *Using intuition or writing associatively*   This uses a way of 'blending dreams, reading and thought' (Reinharz, 1992: 232), in which the writer appears in a deep non-chronological, non-topical intuitive process and which requires passivity alternating with integration (Reinharz, 1992: 231).
- *Identification instead of keeping distance*   The researcher is expected to identify herself with the subjects, display this identification with the reader and encourage the reader to identify with the writer.
- *Studying unplanned personal experience*   Personal experience, for example illness, operation, etc. (alone or in addition to additional data), is used as the basis of the study.
- *Structured conceptualisation*   This involves recording, analysing and synthesising information related to certain issues, ideas, etc. in order to demonstrate how feminists define and understand concepts.
- *Photography or talking picture technique*   This technique involves a collection of pictures taken at certain intervals to be used in an interview kit; subjects choose pictures to be included in the interview kit and orders them in the album according to certain categories. Pictures are used in conjunction with questionnaires. They can also be analysed and interpreted according to the information they contain, such as sitting order/position, gestures, posture and so on.
- *Speaking freely* into a tape recorder or answering long, essay-type questionnaires. This technique involves a set of questions sent to the respondent with the instruction to record the answers on tape.

Nevertheless, what really matters in feminist research is not the method but the way and the context in which the results of the research are used to answer substantive questions about the nature of oppressive social structures. Unlike traditional methods, critical methods are directed towards breaking down taken-for-granted concepts and rebuilding them into new entities. 'In so doing they lay bare the essential concepts of the research and use this as the basis for revealing what is really going on' (Harvey, 1990: 101, 102, 152).

Central to feminist (and in general to critical) research is the dialectic method the essence of which lies in a process of constantly moving between concepts and data as well as between society and concrete phenomena, past and present issues, appearance and essence. In this process, after the initial concept has been chosen, the researcher looks for connections and reflections regarding surface appearances and real situations, forming opinions about the issue in question and thus new concepts, relating them to method and approach, re-examining the new concepts, correcting elements, getting deeper below the surface, and refocusing on the concept in the historical process. This process is continued until the analysis produces a coherent model (Harvey, 1990).

The process entailed in the dialectic method is based on a constant motion of deconstruction followed by reconstruction, which leads to new deconstruction and reconstruction, and so on. A comprehensive description of this process is given by Harvey (1990: 31–2) as illustrated in the following quotation:

> The dialectical deconstructive–reconstructive process can be construed as a process of focusing on the structural totality or historical moment and critically reflecting on its essential nature. The totality is initially taken as an existent whole. The structure presents itself as natural, as the result of historical progress, that is, it is ideologically constituted. The critical analysis of the historically specific structure must therefore go beyond the surface appearances and lay bare the essential nature of the relationships that are embedded in the structure. This critique ostensibly begins by fixing on the fundamental unit of the structural relationships and decomposing it. The fundamental unit must be broken down until its essential nature is revealed, the structure is then reconstituted in terms of the essentialized construct. The reconstructive process reveals the transparency of ideology. The whole is grounded in historically specific material reality.

This brief reference to feminist research demonstrates that it employs a comprehensive approach and a set of methods, the majority of which are shared with positivists and interpretivists, although their use is different. It also uses methods that are unique to this type of research only (e.g. the dialectic method).

c   Feminist research and conventional research

Feminist research is different from, incompatible with (Miller and Treitel, 1991: 7) and also critical of (Nielsen, 1990: 7) conventional research in the social sciences, which it describes as the 'male paradigm'. This research is thought to present a distorted view of the world (Westkott, 1990), which is perceived in the conventional way as being dominated by male ideology and to suffer from problems related to reliability, validity and representativeness (related to non-response, incomplete sampling frames, hired-hand effect, etc.). It also creates a view of research that is biased towards objectivity, detachment and hierarchy (Oakley, 1981), using unidirectional instruments executed dispassionately, and assigning researchers the role of an objective and detached observer, and devaluing, manipulating and exploiting the respondents. It is argued that investigations should be geared not towards standardised ideals of statistical principles but rather towards self-defined objectives.

Feminist researchers are equally critical of the use of interviewing practice, which many (e.g. Oakley, 1981: 41) find morally indefensible. Interview practice that employs unidirectional methods and is based on a hierarchical relationship between the researcher and the researched is thought to undermine the feminist reassessment of the interrelationship of women with one another (Harvey, 1990: 117). In-depth interviews are a better option than standardised interviews for many other reasons, but also because they encourage subjectivity and intensive dialogue between equals, which are intrinsic features of feminist analysis of gender experience.

Feminist research is also critical of the sexist orientation of social research and of social sciences in general. Social sciences are not only based on the writings of their founding *fathers*, but are also dominated by male stereotypes and attitudes created through socialisation and professional training of social scientists, the majority of whom are males. Many feminists (e.g. Eichler *et al.*, 1985; Eichler, 1988; Reinharz, 1983) have pointed to the many ways in which sexist practices exist and affect social life. Eichler (1988), for instance, lists these seven problems of sexism:

1 *Androcentricity* This refers to the fact that the world is perceived and presented from the view of the male. In this context, women are presented as passive objects rather than as acting persons. This can lead to two extreme phenomena, namely *gynopia*, where women are totally invisible, and *misogyny*, characterised by hatred of women.
2 *Overgeneralisation/overspecificity* This situation occurs when statements are made about both sexes, whereas the study might have referred to one sex only, for example where researchers generalise about single parenthood from studies of single mothers, or where reference is made to police officers when they in fact mean 'policemen'.
3 *Gender insensitivity* This occurs when gender as a factor is totally ignored, for example in studies of the effects recession has on people, gender is not considered, or when a study of parents' influence on the socialisation of female children does not differentiate between fathers and mothers.
4 *Double standards* Here, different standards or instruments are used to measure issues related to males and females.
5 *Sex appropriateness* This is a problem derived from the application of double standards and relates to attitudes and expectations that assign behaviour patterns, traits, attributes or roles considered appropriate to a particular gender.
6 *Familism* This is a particular case of gender insensitivity and refers to the common practice of referring to families while in fact the issue in question concerns men, women or members of the family; or when, referring to families it is assumed that all family members are affected by a particular issue or problem uniformly.
7 *Sexual dichotomism* This is another example of double standards and refers to practices that tend to consider genders as distinctly separate without considering the interrelationships and interdependence that exist between them.

d   Is there a feminist methodology?

The question about whether feminism has developed distinct methodological principles that could justify the establishment of a distinct methodology next to the qualitative, quantitative or critical paradigms is by no means new. Claims for a separate place in the ranks of paradigms and methodologies were made long ago, and are still being made. The responses to these claims are diverse, with some arguing in favour and others against such a recognition.

Arguments in favour of a feminist methodology
Those in favour of a feminist methodology argue, among other things, that (1) feminism has developed a characteristic approach that is valid and also different from the approaches of the other methodologies. This approach rejects the male paradigm and the associated methodology and deserves a place in social methodology as a separate and distinct entity. (2) A feminist methodology places emphasis on women and their position in society and contrasts it with the emphasis on males, which is portrayed in the other methodologies. (3) It explains the world in a unique way (e.g. based on patriarchy), which is important for the type of methods used and the way the results are analysed and interpreted. (4) It sees women as the chief researchers, because it is believed that only women can truly understand women and their unique position. This is what is generally termed (Stanley and Wise, 1983) *feminist standpoint epistemology*. Finally, (5) a feminist methodology is the sum of feminist methods (e.g. Reinharz, 1992: 240) and deserves to be recognised as such.

Arguments against a feminist methodology
There are many arguments against a feminist paradigm, such as: (1) Feminists do not have a perspective of their own; rather, they use theoretical and methodological principles of other paradigms, such as Marxism, naturalism, critical theory, psychoanalysis, etc. Without their own and distinct principles it is not possible to claim a separate methodology. (2) Feminists are very diverse (Marxist feminists, liberal feminists, socialist feminists, psychoanalytic feminists, structural feminists, etc.) and do not present 'a coherent and cogent alternative to non-feminist research' (Hammersley, 1992a: 202). (3) Many of the ideas on which feminist methodologists draw can also be found in the non-feminist literature or are unconvincing (Hammersley, 1992a: 202). (4) Unique attention to gender is not justified; even post-structural feminists (Alcoff, 1988: 407) argue that such a practice should be reconsidered and replaced by an emphasis on a plurality of differences. (5) Its objection to positivistic methodological practices such as the value of method versus experience, its objectivity, its emancipation as a goal of research or a criterion of validity, and the relationship between researcher and researched (hierarchy), which many theorists use as a justification for a feminist methodology, are all questionable (Hammersley, 1992a). (For a response to these criticisms, see Geldsthorpe, 1992; Ramazanoglu, 1992). The fact that positivism is considered 'inappropriate' does not justify a feminist methodology as its alternative. Qualitative methodology may be the answer, since its principles seem to be similar to those proposed by feminist critics.

A different and more realistic position is taken by Cook and Fonow (1990), who see feminist methodology as being in the process of development. They argue that there is no agreement among feminists about the right methodology, and go on to say that there is in fact no 'correct' feminist methodology in the field of sociology; they conclude that 'at least within the field of sociology, feminist methodology is in the process of *becoming* and is not yet a fully articulated stance' (Cook and Fonow, 1990: 71). Nevertheless, they seem to have a concrete impression of what a feminist methodology is, and describe its main criteria as follows:

- *Female prism* Feminist methodology is marked by a gender bias, viewing women as the focus of inquiry and seeing reality through a 'female prism'; it rejects the notion that equates 'masculine' to 'universal', recognising the central place men have held in sociological research and lifting the 'androcentric blinders' allowing a better vision of reality, and locates the researchers as a gendered being in the web of social relations.
- *Consciousness raising* In feminist methodology, consciousness raising is central not only as a specific methodological tool but also as a general orientation. Cook and Fonow (1990) argue that women are in the best position to carry out research because, due to their particular position as members of an oppressed group and as scholars, they possess a 'double vision' and are therefore better equipped to identify, understand and interpret women's experiences (p. 74). The research process becomes a process of 'concientization', and through this a research object becomes a research subject and learns to perceive contradictions and to work against oppression.
- *The subject–object dichotomy* Feminist methodology rejects the artificial separation of the researcher and the researched as well as the implied notion that such a separation produces more valid results, demonstrates how the research process encourages and reinforces subjugation of women, and challenges the norm of objectivity that it entails and the beliefs that objectivity can be achieved through quantification and statistics (p. 72). Instead, it advocates a dialectic relationship between subject and object of research, a form of participatory research and a 'conscious partiality', that is, the 'researcher's understanding of the connectedness to the experiences of the research subject through partial identification' (p. 76).
- *Feminist ethics* Feminist research points to new areas in which ethics is being violated. Such violations create or perpetuate forms of oppression of and discrimination against women, for example when using sexist language that perpetuates female subjugation, when using unfair practices related to publication of feminist works, intervening in the respondents' lives and withholding information from women subjects (p. 78).
- *Empowerment and transformation* The purpose of feminist research is to empower women to transform oppressive and exploitative conditions, to provide visions for the future and to attend to policy complications of research.

These points indicate that there is a good reason for raising the status of women in the research arena and assigning them the position they deserve. However, the argument that Cook and Fonow (1990) present is neither strong nor convincing that there is a place for a feminist methodology. The points listed above speak more for a qualitative, flexible and involving research procedure rather than for a feminist methodology.

The question of whether a feminist methodology exists has not been answered fully yet; the debate is still alive (see, for example, Geldsthorpe, 1992; Hammersley, 1992a; Ramazanoglu, 1992) and promising. Without denying the value, extent and significance of feminist research, at this stage it is reasonable to say that it is more appropriate to talk of feminist research than feminist methodology.

13   Summary

The discussion in this chapter has shown that social research is based on a variety of methodologies and methods. Of the models employed by social researchers the qualitative and quantitative frameworks and methods are the most commonly used, sometimes in their own context, and at other times in the context of critical, Marxist or feminist frameworks. Employing a quantitative or a qualitative methodology or framework and choosing quantitative or qualitative methods and techniques seem to be choices all researchers make in some way and at some stage during their investigations.

The description and evaluation of these two forms of research activity of social scientists presented in this chapter may be perceived as extremist in the sense that they refer to extreme forms or ideal types of methodologies — models that might not be employed fully by investigators in real-life situations. Researchers are more likely to employ a model that borrows elements from both the qualitative and the quantitative framework, provided of course that the combined elements are compatible.

In this sense, this text offers 'pure' methodologies, which researchers approximate in some form and to some degree. These models can well be placed at the two extreme ends of a continuum, offering in the space between them a variety of permutations and a high degree of freedom for individual choice, innovation and creativity set in a conservative, critical, Marxist or feminist framework. Researchers are then creators of individual research models, which they ultimately employ in their project(s); such models may contain elements of one or both methodological frameworks, bringing them close to or away from the ideal models of quantitative or qualitative research.

Quantification, for instance, normally reserved exclusively for positivistic methodology and also rejected by many qualitative researchers, may be negotiated in the context of the individual research model and be presented and employed at a high level, a low level, at a nominal, ordinal or interval level, or not considered at all. The same holds for methods and techniques of collection and analysis of data. Researchers usually employ research models that are often not strictly reflections of the ideal models of social research.

Key concepts

Androcentricity	Critical perspective
Explication	Flexibility
Feminist methods	Gender insensitivity
Gynopia	Hermeneutics
Interpretive paradigm	Method
Methodology	Misogyny
Openness	Paradigms
Phenomenology	Reflexivity
Sexual dichotomism	Symbolic interactionism

3

Measurement and scaling

1 Introduction

The first step in our research model is the theoretical preparation or formulation of the research topic — a step which is as complex as it is diverse and pluralistic. This step will establish the foundations for the remaining part of the study and is therefore very important, and deserves special consideration. However, before we commence our discussion of this step, we need first to consider another more general and equally fundamental element of the research process and one of the principles of social research, namely measurement. You would remember that in the the first chapter we stated that research is expected to be systematic, accurate and precise. Measurement is a central element of social research and also fundamental for the procedures which will be introduced in the next chapter, where the preparation step of the research is considered.

In this chapter, we shall first introduce the concept, nature and types of measurement and a number of issues associated with it. We shall look at measurement as an element of social research, and explore some of its qualities, such as validity and reliability. Following this we shall turn our attention to scaling.

2 Nature of measurement

Social research, irrespective of type and nature, entails a degree of measurement. In some cases measurement is exact, quantitative and complicated. In other cases it is qualitative, involving simple operations and aiming at classification or labelling of variables. Measurement is pluralistic and can be accomplished in a number of ways.

Measurement involves categorising and/or assigning values to the variables in question, and can be diverse in nature and level of operation. Generally, measurement is quantitative or qualitative. *Quantitative measurement* concentrates on numerical values and attributes. Qualitative measurement refers to labels, names and qualities.

Qualitative measurement describes attributes by using common concepts or symbols or introducing new ones; a common procedure involves description of categories and classifications. The classification of Australian families for instance into Anglo-Saxon and ethnic families is a qualitative measurement. In the view of some writers, qualitative measurement does not qualify as 'measurement' since it does not demonstrate the main criteria of measurement, such as precision, reliability and validity; rather, it is thought to be a process of labelling, classification and description. Nevertheless, as we shall see soon, this view is not correct.

3   Variables

Definitions
Measurement relates to variables. A variable is a concept that can take two or more values; for example, sex (male, female), marital status (single, married, divorced, widowed, deserted), age and education are variables. Variables can be 'dependent' or 'independent'. An *independent variable* causes changes in another; a *dependent variable* is a variable that is affected or explained by another variable. For instance, in a research study of 'family status and scholastic achievement', the independent variable can be family status, and the dependent variable scholastic achievement.

Discrete and continuous variables
Variables can also be discrete or continuous. Discrete and continuous variables differ from each other in terms of *scale continuity;* the former are not continuous but use whole units only, while the latter are continuous and can be fractioned indefinitely. In *discrete variables* (also called *binomial variables*), measurement uses whole units or numbers, with no possible values between adjacent units. For instance, family size can be 3, 4, 5 and so on, not 2.5, 3.8, or 5.4. Family size is a discrete variable. However, weight is a *continuous variable*; it can use smaller increments of units, for example it can be 73.2, 78.1 or 85.6 kg. Discrete variables are counted, not measured; continuous variables are measured, not counted. Examples of discrete variables are ethnicity, race, sex, marital status, cause of death or blood type. Examples of continuous variables are height, distance, time, age, temperature or IQ scores.

More definitions
Some writers also differentiate between quantitative and qualitative variables. *Qualitative variables* use nominal scale measurement; racial origin, ethnic origin, religious affiliation or sex are qualitative variables. *Quantitative variables* use either ordinal or metric scales.

4   Levels of measurement

Measurement can be performed at four levels, which vary in many ways, but especially with regard to the degree to which they match the characteristics of the real-number system. The four levels of measurement and four corresponding scales are: the nominal, the ordinal, the interval and the ratio level. Nominal-level measurement has the lowest and ratio-level measurement the highest match with the real-number system.

a   Nominal-level measurement

This is the simplest, the lowest and the most primitive type of 'measurement'. At this level, measurement involves classification of events into categories that must be distinct, unidimensional, mutually exclusive and exhaustive; and the resulting scales are 'naming' scales. Such a measure indicates that there is a difference between the categories considered.

Such differences refer to nature but not to magnitude. Thus, dormitory no. 10 is not twice as large as dormitory no. 5. In a similar fashion, numbers assigned to categories have no mathematical meaning, are used only for identification and cannot be added, subtracted, multiplied, divided or otherwise manipulated mathematically. Classifying the respondents in categories such as male–female, black–white, young–old, single, married, cohabiting, separated, divorced, remarried or widowed, or Catholic, Protestant, Anglican, Orthodox is based on nominal measurement. Classifying respondents according to their place of birth, religious affiliation, political affiliation, car type and place of residence are additional examples. Further examples of nominal measurement are: nationality, type of shoes, skin colour, type of music and brands of drinks.

Characteristic of the nominal-level measurement is that:

- it involves nominal categories and is essentially a qualitative and a non-mathematical measurement; it actually names and classifies data into categories;
- it does not have a zero point;
- it cannot be ordered in a continuum of low–high;
- it produces nominal or categorical data;
- it assumes no equal units of measurement;
- it assumes the principle of equivalence: all units of a particular group are taken to be the same. All Greeks, Aborigines, jogging shoes, IBM computers, personal vehicles, etc. are the same.

It must be noted that only statistical measures designed for nominal data must be used.

b   Ordinal-level measurement

Measurement at the ordinal level involves not only categorising elements into groups but also ordering of data and ranking of variables in a continuum ranging according to magnitude, that is, from the lowest to the highest point (transitive relationship). Here, numbers offer more information since they not only indicate differences between categories but they also rank them; however, they do not allow mathematical operations such as addition or subtraction. Characteristic of this level of measurement is that:

- it refers to ranks based on a clear order of magnitude of low and high signifying that some elements have more value than others;
- the numbers have actual mathematical meaning as well as having identification properties;
- it is essentially a quantitative measurement;
- it shows a relative order of magnitude.

With regard to the last point, order of magnitude allows categories to be ranked (who is first, second, last) but does not indicate the amount of difference between the groups (how much above or below a certain category neighbouring categories are). So the difference between the first and second may be different from that between the sixth and seventh category. The intervals between the categories are not necessarily equal.

Examples of such forms of continuum employed in ordinal measurement are: *status* — low, middle, high; *size* — smallest, small, big, biggest; *quality* — poor, good, very good, excellent; *class* — low, middle, high; *achievement at school* — poor, moderate, high; *income* — low, middle, high. Ranking occupations is another example.

Only nominal and ordinal statistical measures are permissible for ordinal data.

c Interval-level measurement

This level of measurement, as well as demonstrating the properties of ordinal level measurement, provides information about the distance between the values, and contains equal intervals, ordering subjects into one of them. This method allows the researcher to judge differences between respondents and to obtain more detailed information about the research topic.

Characteristic of this level of measurement is that it includes equal units, and that it is essentially a quantitative measurement. In addition to allowing differentiation and classification and also incorporating orderings, it specifies the numerical distance between the categories. In other words, interval measurement allows the researcher to determine whether two values are the same or different (as in nominal measurement), whether the one is greater or smaller than the other (as in ordinal measurement) and the degree of difference between them. Nevertheless, it does not have a true zero point, and if a zero is used it is set arbitrarily, is done so for convenience and does not mean absence of the variable.

For example, if the IQ of two students is 105 and 125 respectively, in nominal terms this means that they have a different IQ; in ordinal terms that the first student has a lower IQ than the second; and in interval terms, that the IQ of the second student is 20 points higher than that of the first student, but not, say, one-fifth smarter than the other student.

In mathematical terms, at this level numbers assigned to categories are used to count and rank, but can also be added to and subtracted from each other. This indicates that interval-level measurement is superior to the other two. However, given that there is no true zero, they cannot be multiplied or divided. Statistical measures for nominal, rank and interval data can be used.

Examples of this type of measurement are degrees of temperature, calendar time (day, week, month), attitude scales and IQ scores.

d   Ratio-level measurement

Measurement at this level includes all the attributes the other three forms offer, plus the option of an absolute true zero (0) as its lowest value, which in essence indicates absence of the variable in question. This allows the researcher to make statements about proportions and ratios, that is, to relate one value to another. For instance, a comparison of speed of response of two students to a stimulus, say, 10 seconds and 20 seconds, allows the researcher to conclude that the first is twice as fast as the second.

In the social sciences this level of measurement is employed mainly when measuring demographic variables; however, it is considered inappropriate for measuring attitudes and opinions. This is because indicating a 0 option in an attitude scale means no attitude, or no opinion; given the nature of the research question, this is incorrect since even stating that the respondent has no opinion is in itself an opinion.

In terms of mathematics, numbers arrived at through ratio ordering indicate counting as well as ranking, and can also be added, subtracted, multiplied or divided. As far as statistical tests are concerned, measures appropriate for all levels can be used.

Examples of this type of measurement are those given for the interval level above, with the addition of a 0 point in the continuum. Other examples could, for instance, come from the following areas: number of family members, weight, length, distance, number of books that subjects own, reaction time and number of products produced per hour.

e   Measuring variables

Variables are not by nature measured at one specific level only. Whether a variable will be measured one way or another depends very much on how it is conceptualised and on the type of indicators used during measurement. The same variable can be measured in a variety of ways. Age, for instance, can be measured nominally, if it is defined in broad and discrete categories, such as infancy, adolescence, adulthood, middle age and old age; or as young and old. It can be measured also at the ordinal level, when respondents are ranked according to age from the oldest to the youngest. Age can also be measured at the interval level, given that units are equal and we can determine how many units of difference there is between age levels. Interval-level measurement tells us here not only whose age is higher (as in ordinal-level measurement) but also how much higher it is. Age can, finally, be measured at the ratio level, since it has an absolute (non-arbitrary) zero. One cannot be younger than 0; and a 20-year-old person is twice as old as a 10-year-old person.

Table 3.1   Levels of measurement: a summary

Criteria	Nominal	Ordinal	Interval	Ratio
Properties of measurement	Naming	Naming and ranking	Naming, ranking and equal intervals	Naming, ranking, equal intervals and zero point
Nature of measurement	Categorical	Ranking	Scoring	Scoring
Mathematical functions	None	None	Addition and subtraction	All four functions
Relevant statistical tests	Lambda test χ^2 test; CI%	Spearman's ρ Mann–Whitney U test Sign test	Pearson's r t-test ANOVA	Pearson's r t-test ANOVA
Nature of under-lying construct	Discrete	Discrete or continuous	Continuous	Continuous
Examples	Marital status, gender, race, birth place, residence, ethnicity	Income status, achievement, social class, size	Temperature, calendar time, IQ scores, attitude scales	Length, Weight, Distance, No. of children, Age
Typical answers to questions	Male, female single, married, divorced, widowed	Very high, high, moderate, low, very low	Scores Likert scales Degrees	Years Kilograms Kilometres

Despite this degree of freedom researchers enjoy when measuring variables, there is a rule of thumb which states that *variables are measured at the highest level possible.* Overall, discrete variables are measured at the nominal or ordinal level, and continuous variables at the interval or ratio level.

Arbitrary and true zeros
The use of true zero as the distinguishing characteristic of ratio scales has caused some confusion. This is due to the fact that students find it difficult to distinguish true zeros from arbitrary zeros. Zeros are not always *true.* True zeros are meaningful, arbitrary zeros are not. For instance, when we measure temperature, a zero degree reading does not mean no temperature at all! And measuring attitudes, a zero does not mean no attitude at all (having no opinion on an issue is an opinion!). These zeros are not *true zeros,* they are arbitrary zeros. However, when measuring income, number of cars or number of children, a zero indicates no presence of these criteria: it means no children, no income, no cars, etc. These are true zeros; and only measurement based on using these true zeros is conducted at the ratio level.

f   Summarising

All levels of measurement are effective and useful in their own context and the purpose for which they have been developed. However, nominal-level measures are the least precise, followed by ordinal-level measures, and then interval-level measures, with ratio-level measures offering the highest degree of precision. Measuring at the interval and ratio level has many advantages, but not all variables can be measured at these levels (Wang and Mahoney, 1991).

Measurement is a very important and also relatively complicated process, but it is associated with many problems and errors. It is limited by the nature of our social world and the variables in question, the perceptions of researchers and their personal bias. Its value depends on the accuracy of the instruments used and the model of operationalisation employed.

5   Validity

a   Validity in quantitative research

As stated in the first chapter, attainment of validity is one of the basic principles of social research. Validity means the ability to produce findings that are in agreement with theoretical or conceptual values; in other words to produce accurate results and to measure what is supposed to be measured. If an instrument employed to measure the extent of cheating in examinations revealed that 32 per cent of the students regularly cheat, the measure used has validity if the proportion of students who cheat is actually 32 per cent. A valid measure produces true results that reflect the true situation and conditions of the environment it is supposed to study.

There are two ways of checking the validity of an instrument: empirical validation and theoretical validation. In the former, the validity of a measure is checked against empirical evidence. In the latter, the validity of an instrument is ascertained through theoretical or conceptual constructs. In both cases, validity is claimed if the findings produced through the measure in question are supported by empirical evidence or by theoretical principles.

Empirical validation
Empirical validation tests *pragmatic* or *criterion validity*. If an instrument has, for instance, produced results indicating that students involved in student union activities do better in their exams, and if this is supported by available data, the instrument in question has pragmatic validity. Again, validity here is assumed if the findings are supported by already existing empirical evidence. In this case the validity is *concurrent validity*.

Quite often, the validity of a measure is checked by the degree to which predictions made by the results of this measure are supported by findings that appear later. Validity is then claimed if new data support the predictions of the measure in question. For example, if a study found that an eventual introduction of advanced statistics into the social sciences degree would result in a significant drop-out of older students, and if this prediction in the meantime was found to be correct, the measure has validity. This is known as *predictive validity*.

Theoretical validation

Theoretical or conceptual validation is employed when empirical confirmation of validity is difficult or not possible. A measure is taken to have theoretical validity if its findings comply with the theoretical principles of the discipline, that is, if they do not contradict already established rules of the discipline. There are several types of theoretical validity.

Face validity

An instrument has face validity if it *seems* to measure what it is expected to measure. 'On the face of it' it appears to have validity. For example, a question-naire aimed at studying sex discrimination has face validity if its questions refer to discrimination due to sex. The standards of judgement here are not based on empirical evidence, as it was in the case of the other type of validation, but on general theoretical standards and principles, and on the subjective judgement of the researcher.

Content validity

A measure is supposed to have content validity if it covers all possible aspects of the research topic. If a measure of alienation, for instance, does not include normlessness or powerlessness (two elements generally considered to be important aspects of alienation) the researcher cannot claim content validity for this instrument.

Construct validity

A measure can claim construct validity if its theoretical construct is valid. For this reason, validation concentrates on the validity of the theoretical construct. For example, if discrimination of female students is the research topic, we proceed as follows: an instrument is constructed to study this topic. Then two student groups known to differ in their views on basic issues related to the research question are identified. Next, the instrument whose validity is to be checked is administered to both groups and the results recorded separately for each group. If the findings obtained from each group differ, the instrument is thought to have construct validity.

Here is another example. To test the validity of a questionnaire developed to measure the attitudes of female students to the student union of their institution, a questionnaire is constructed and then administered to both male and female students, two groups already known to have different attitudes to the research issue. The results of each group are checked with regard to whether they differ from each other. If the results show differences in the attitudes of male and female respondents to the student union, the instrument is considered to have construct validity.

Other forms of validity

There are two other forms of validity: *internal validity* and *external validity*. The former relates to the instrument's significance for the study situation; the latter is associated with the generalisability of the findings gathered by means of the instrument in question.

b   Validity in qualitative research

Validity is a methodological element not only of quantitative but also of qualitative research (Miles and Huberman, 1994; Lancy, 1993). Qualitative researchers aim to achieve validity, which they consider to be a strength of their research, since it frees data from interference and contamination, control or variable manipulation (LeCompte and Goetz, 1982); this is facilitated in a number of ways, particularly through their orientation towards, and the study of, the empirical world (Blumer, 1979a: 49), through construction of appropriate methods of data collection and analysis (Volmerg, 1983: 124) or through specific measures such as communicative, cumulative, ecological or argumentative validity (see Koeckeis-Stangl, 1980). Still, while some qualitative researchers speak of validity, others use different names to refer to validity. Miles and Huberman (1994), for instance, speak of 'credibility', 'trustworthiness' and 'authenticity' instead.

To guarantee validity in their work, qualitative researchers apply a number of measures. These measures vary from case to case, with some researchers proposing one set of measures and others suggesting another. Some of these types of validation, referred to by a number of writers (see Becker, 1989; Drew *et al.*, 1996; Lamnek, 1988; Terhardt, 1981: 789), are presented below.

Cumulative validation
A study can be validated if its findings are supported by other studies. The researcher can compare the various findings and make a judgement about the validity of the studies.

Communicative validation
The validity of the findings can also be ensured through additional questioning of the respondents; the researcher is then expected to re-enter the field and collect additional data.

Argumentative validation
This form of validity is established through presentation of the findings in such a way that conclusions can be followed and tested.

Ecological validation
A study is thought to be valid if carried out in the natural environment of the subjects, using suitable methods and taking into consideration the life and conditions of the researched.

Other 'tactics'
In a different manner, Miles and Huberman (1994, 1984a) suggest 'tactics' for testing or confirming findings, which, although not direct forms of validity, have a similar function. Some are similar to those presented above

(e.g. cumulative or communicative validation); others are close to the form of validation employed by quantitative researchers. The tactics these writers propose are as follows:

- *Checking for representativeness* The findings are confirmed by manipulating the sample, for example by increasing the sample size or adding contrasting cases, and observing whether the findings are changed in any way.
- *Checking for researcher effects* This includes avoiding or preventing effects of the researcher on the site and of the site on the researcher. Avoiding elite bias, showing the notes to another researcher to check, staying on the site for as long as possible, using unobtrusive methods and explaining the purpose of the study clearly are some of the ways that can help to reduce researcher effects.
- *Triangulation* Here, the quality of findings is tested through triangulating not only with methods but also with other researchers.
- *Weighing of evidence* Testing the quality of the findings can be accomplished also through weighing the evidence that supports them, for example by using better informants, collecting data under better circumstances and through validating the data.
- *Checking the meaning of outliers and extreme cases* Studying extreme cases and unusual events provides information that can be very useful in identifying the strength of the findings and therefore the quality of the conclusions.
- *Following up surprises* The idea behind this point is that a surprise entails something that is outside the researcher's experiences and expectations. Such surprises can be indicative of trends the researcher had not anticipated and need to be pursued further.
- *Looking for negative evidence* This operates in a manner similar to the previous tactic.
- *Making if–then tests* The association between two factors that follows the if–then patter is a useful tool for exploring relationships in the field and for formulating hypotheses. Miles and Huberman (1994: 271) describes if–then tests as the 'workhorse of qualitative data analysis'.
- *Ruling out spurious relations* This is a very useful concept and it will certainly benefit evaluation of the data. However, spuriousness has to be identified and this is not a very simple task; this procedure may than replace one problem with another.
- *Replicating a finding* This is supposed to offer additional information, which is expected to be similar to or different from that obtained originally. Replication is expected to strengthen or weaken the original finding.
- *Checking out rival explanations* Such explanations might throw light on different impressions and allow a more accurate evaluation of the original findings.
- *Getting feedback from informants* The quality of findings or conclusions can be checked through informants, who may be respondents or a panel of judges. It is hoped that their opinions will allow judgements about the quality of the original findings. If they are disputed by the respondents or judges their quality is obviously questionable.

- *Making contrasts or comparisons* Using the method of differences, findings can be contrasted or compared with other findings. This can help to identify strengths and uncover weaknesses in the data.

In addition to these criteria, Miles and Huberman (1994: 277–80) give serious attention to issues of validity and reliability in qualitative research and argue that qualitative research does consider these attributes to be very important. In particular they stress the following five criteria:

1 *Objectivity/confirmability* Research is expected to comply with rules of neutrality and freedom from bias. This means external reliability and replicability of the findings.
2 *Reliability/dependability/auditability* Here the research is expected to be consistent and relatively stable across time and methods.
3 *Internal validity/credibility/authenticity* These criteria indicate that validity in qualitative research is as important as in quantitative research, although in a different manner.
4 *External validity/transferability/fittingness* The issues contained in this item relate to transferability and generalisability of findings. There are many types of generalisability (Firestone, 1993; Maxwell, 1992), a number of which apply fully to qualitative research. Miles and Huberman (1994: 279) note that here 'the researcher needs to know whether the conclusions of a study have any larger import'.
5 *Utilisation/application/action orientation* This item relates to 'pragmatic validity' and has the purpose of exploring the question of whether the findings have an impact on the researcher, the research and the community in general. Here the theme of the question is about relevance, effects, evaluation and emancipation.

To demonstrate the diversity of opinion as well as the pluralist nature of qualitative research it is worth referring to a few more models of controlling rigour in qualitative research. Lincoln and Guba's attempt to cope with the traditional demand for every research output to meet standards and principles of evaluation is one of them. Lincoln and Guba (1985) propose four alternatives to validity, reliability, generalisability and objectivity, namely credibility, transferability, dependability and confirmability.

In their view: (1) In qualitative research, investigators do not need to demonstrate validity but rather methodological excellence, that is, doing research in a professional, accurate and systematic manner. (2) Instead of generalisability, transferability is suggested. This means that the researcher should state how research was undertaken and explain methods, instruments and parameters, leaving it up to those who are interested in the findings to decide whether they can be generalised or not, and also to use triangulation. (3) On the notion of consistency and reliability, Lincoln and Guba suggest that, in a constantly changing world, dependability is the closest one gets to reliability. (4) Instead of aiming for objectivity, confirmability is proposed. Confirming data shifts evaluation from the researcher, who was the centre of objectivity, to the data themselves.

Likewise, Drew and associates (1996: 169–71) propose that there are several ways of protecting validity in qualitative studies. *Duration and intensity* of data gathering is one of them. This involves a wide coverage and prevention of being misled by unrepresentative events (outlier data). Another factor is *rich description;* this entails collection of rich and supportive data from a variety of sources and detailed, accurate and vivid description and aims to produce a valid description and a complete and valid analysis. Drew and associates note also that qualitative research should safeguard against threats to validity. Such threats are (1) history and maturation; (2) setting, participant or context mortality; (3) observer/researcher effects on events and behaviour; and (4) spurious conclusions.

Value of validation of qualitative research
The above forms of validation, especially cumulative, communicative, argumentative and ecological validation, are thought to be effective and to allow qualitative researchers to achieve not only validity but also, at least in the opinion of some writers, a higher degree of validity than quantitative researchers achieve. Lamnek (1988: 154–9) argues that qualitative studies achieve higher validity for the following reasons:

- In qualitative research the data are closer to the research field than in quantitative research.
- The collection of information is not determined by research screens and directives.
- The data are closer to reality than in quantitative research.
- In qualitative research, the opinions and views of the researched are considered.
- The methods are more open and flexible than in quantitative research.
- In qualitative studies, there is a communicative basis that is not available in quantitative research.
- A successive expansion of data is possible

6   Reliability

a   Reliability in quantitative research

Reliability refers to the ability of an instrument to produce consistent results; reliability is equivalent to *consistency*. Thus, a method is reliable if it produces the same results whenever it is repeated, even by other researchers. Reliability is also characterised by precision and objectivity. Without precision and objectivity reliability cannot be achieved. Social scientists are interested in achieving *internal reliability* and *external reliability*. Internal reliability means consistency of results within the site, and that data are plausible within that site. External reliability refers to consistency and replicability of data across the sites.

At least three types of reliability are considered by social scientists:

1 *Stability reliability*, relating to reliability across time. Here the question is whether a measure produces reliable findings if it is employed several times.
2 *Representative reliability*, which relates to reliability across groups of subjects. The question here is whether the measure will be reliable if employed in groups other than the original group of subjects.
3 *Equivalence reliability*, which relates to reliability across indicators and to multiple indicators in operationalisation procedures. Will the measure in question produce consistent results across indicators?

There are several methods for testing reliability of an instrument. The most common methods are the following:

• *Test–retest method*   The same subjects are tested and retested with the same instrument. If the same results are obtained the instrument is reliable.
• *Split-half method*   According to this method, responses to the items of an instrument are divided into two groups (e.g. odd/even questions) and the scores correlated. The type and degree of correlation indicate the degree of reliability of the measurement.
• *Inter-item test and item–scale test*   In this case, inter-item correlations or item–scale correlations indicate the degree of reliability of the instrument.
• *Alternate-form reliability*   Here, reliability is tested by administering two similar instruments in one session, and is assessed by the degree of correlation between the scores of the two groups.

b   Reliability in qualitative research

Although qualitative researchers try to achieve high reliability in their studies, they do not accept methods that quantitative researchers employ to reach high reliability. They reject, for instance, the use of methods to control the environment, achieve high standardisation or control the researcher–researched relationship which are practised by quantitative researchers. They believe that quantitative researchers check reliability by creating artificial situations, for example by means of techniques based on measuring, and this is considered unacceptable. As well, the process of testing reliability is thought to alienate the researcher from research and the research environment, and to be counterproductive.

So qualitative researchers employ other, in their view, more effective forms of reliability, for example by increasing the variability of perspectives in research or by setting up a list of possible errors or distortions which researchers should endeavour to avoid (McCall, 1979). Overall, qualitative researchers strive for rigour but their standards vary from those employed by quantitative researchers. Instead of attempting to achieve validity they strive for 'credibility' and 'applicability'; and instead of talking about reliability they speak of 'audit-ability'; objectivity is replaced by 'confirmability' (Guba and Lincoln, 1989).

Other investigators suggest alternative ways of guaranteeing quality of research without resorting to reliability. Bogumil and Immerfall (1985: 71), for instance, recommend that instead of talking about reliability, control of variables or subjectivity in social research, one should rather consider looking at options such as the following: *coherence*, that is, the extent to which methods meet the goals; *openness*, the degree to which otherwise suitable methods are allowed to be used; *discourse*, that is, the extent to which researchers are allowed to discuss the researched data and interpret them together and evaluate the consequences of such findings.

In a similar manner, Drew and associates (1996: 169) agree that qualitative researchers should strive for rigour, and suggest that the following sets of steps should be followed if reliability in qualitative research is to be achieved. With regard to internal reliability they propose the following five steps:

1. Use low inference descriptors.
2. Use multiple researchers whenever possible.
3. Create a careful audit trail (record of data that can be followed by another scholar back from conclusions to the raw data).
4. Use mechanical recording devices where possible (and with permission).
5. Use participant researchers or informants to check the accuracy or congruence of perceptions.

With regard to external reliability, the same authors propose the following five steps:

1. Clearly specify the researchers' status or position so that readers know exactly what point of view drove the data collection.
2. Clearly state who informants are (or what role they play in the natural context) and how and why they were selected or chosen (while maintaining confidentiality).
3. Carefully delineate the context or setting boundaries and characteristics so that the reader can make judgments about similar circumstances or settings.
4. Define the analytic constructs that guide the study (describe specific conceptual frameworks used in design and deductive analysis).
5. Specify the data collection and analysis procedures meticulously.

Regardless of the significance of these approaches to reliability, it is generally believed that qualitative research does not provide as high a reliability as does quantitative research. Nevertheless, as stated above, the definition of reliability and the type of measurement of the degree of reliability must be considered when the quality of reliability in the two research contexts is evaluated.

7 Validity and reliability

Students quite often confuse validity with reliability. An example might help to distinguish them. If a male student weighs himself on a scale 20 times and every time he receives a reading of 65 kg (which is also his true weight), the scale is both reliable and valid. If all recorded readings are 40 kg, the measure is reliable but not valid. But if he obtains different readings each time he weighs himself (40 kg, 45 kg, 63 kg, etc.) the scale is neither valid nor reliable.

Validity and reliability of a measure are interrelated. If an instrument is valid it is expected to be reliable too. However, if it is reliable, it is not necessarily valid.

Although validity and reliability can easily be tested, the results must be treated with caution. Reliability can be affected by factors associated with the researcher, the respondents and the conditions of the study. Variations in the tests might reflect these factors rather than the quality of the instrument.

8   Indexes

Indexes are an integral part of surveys and questionnaires. They are commonly used in social sciences in many contexts and for varied purposes. They are used to describe and measure accurately global concepts by considering a number of specific and representative aspects of the concept. They represent a summary figure and a composite measure in which each item measures one element of the concept and provides information on this element or part of the concept.

An index is a measure containing a combination of items, the values of which are summed up to provide a numerical score. An example is 'The quality of life index' for the city of Albury. Such an index may include the following items: employment opportunities, recreation opportunities, weather, pollution level, medical services, educational opportunities, child care, safety, crime rate and racial problems. These items will be transformed into questions/statements and the index presented for evaluation. Each question will be scored and their total will present a single measure.

The items of an index can be given the same or different values. The latter option is preferred when, for instance, some index items are thought to be more important than others. In the example given above, employment rate, safety and crime rate may be considered as more important for the quality of life in a country town than the weather or child care. If this is the case, these items will be given a higher value (and therefore a higher score) while other items will obtain a lower value. Depending on the actual weight allocated to each item, two types of index can be distinguished: *the weighted index*, where items have different weights, and *the unweighted index* in which items have the same weight.

Indexes are useful measures and can be employed in every aspect of life, such as economy, politics, education, social life, teaching and religious observance. The main aim of this measure is to include all significant elements of the issue in question so that the items present a representative picture of the issue. A researcher may use such a measure to evaluate the quality of an educational institution by considering the educational level of the staff, their research and publications, the quality of library resources, the staff to student ratio, the number of female staff in the institution and their level of employment, promotion opportunities, and so on. A teacher might develop an index to use as the basis of a test that is supposed to cover, for instance, theory, statistics and methods, or simply different parts of a subject; and a social worker might develop a criminality index to look into aspects of life in a community.

9   Scaling

Scales are techniques employed by social scientists in the area of attitude measurement. They consist of a number of statements or questions and a set of response categories, related to a score. They place respondents in a continuum between very low (or negative), over a neutral, to a very high (or positive) position. Each item is chosen so that persons with different points of view on this item react to it in a different way. In this sense they are a part of surveys and questionnaires and are considered during the process of questionnaire construction.

Scaling involves a high degree of operationalisation and allows researchers to measure complex issues. Furthermore, it enables researchers to summate values of several variables into one score and this with a relatively high degree of reliability. In general, it offers respondents a choice of picking their answers out of given sets of alternatives, which, as we shall see, are established in a very careful but also a cumbersome way.

There are nominal, ordinal and interval/ratio scales. Of these, nominal scales are not very common. Most popular are the Likert scales, the Thurstone scales and the Guttman scales, which do not use nominal measurement.

Scales vary not only in their level of measurement but also in their aims and their method of construction. Some are constructed by means of a very complicated process, while others are built in a relatively simple manner. In all cases, however, there are some basic points that experts such as Edwards (1957) and Likert (1932) some time ago said should be considered during scale construction — points that are still respected and practised in social research today by many investigators. The following are some examples:

- Language must be simple, clear and direct.
- Items must be brief (up to 20 words) and contain one issue only.
- Complex sentences must be avoided.
- Items referring to past events and factual items must be avoided.
- Ambiguous and irrelevant items must be avoided.
- Items that may be accepted or rejected by all respondents must be avoided.
- Words such as all, always, no one, never, only, exactly, almost should be avoided.
- Use of professional jargon and double negations should be avoided.
- Response categories must be mutually exclusive, exhaustive and uni-dimensional (i.e. measuring one single construct).

a   Reasons for using scales

Scales are used for a number of reasons. Apart from general methodological motives, the following reasons are most common (see Vlahos, 1984):

- *High coverage*   Scales help to cover all significant aspects of the concept.

- *High precision and reliability*   Scales allow a high degree of precision and reliability.
- *High comparability*   The use of scales permits comparisons between sets of data.
- *Simplicity*   Scales help to simplify collection and analysis of the data.

Scales are a most useful tool of social research and also one that is very difficult to construct. Construction and statistical testing are very involving and time-consuming tasks and therefore not easily accessible to the ordinary researcher. However, researchers developed and tested in the past a very large number of scales which have been adequately tested and are available to other researchers to use. In this sense, scale construction is less common than scale use. Scale construction may be a step to consider after having completed your current course of study. In the meantime using already available scales may be the way to go when addressing issues for which scales are available.

b   The Thurstone scale

Description
This scale was developed in the USA in the 1920s; it consists of a list of items constructed with the aid of experts who are very closely related to the construction of the scale. It is employed mainly in the area of attitude measurement, and is developed through a cumbersome and demanding process, as explained below.

Construction
The construction of the scale is as follows:

Step 1
The researcher selects a number of relevant statements containing a set of response categories ('agree', 'disagree') allowing respondents to express their attitudes to the issue in question freely.

Step 2
These statements are given to a number of judges, who are asked to order them on a continuum from 1 to 11, according to the way they judge the statements. If in the opinion of the judge the statement describes the most favourable attitudes to the study object, it is given the score 1; if it describes slightly less favourable attitudes, it is given the score 2 and so on. In this way, statements are allocated a *scale value*.

Step 3
The statements are scrutinised in terms of the values they received from the judges. Statements that were ordered by the judges uniformly are retained and given an average scale value (the closest to the average); those that received a diverse value are discarded.

Step 4
The remaining statements are processed further by the researcher, and their number reduced. The resulting scale is constructed so that statements are distributed evenly between 1 and 11 and each statement is identified through its scale value.

Evaluation
Although Thurstone scales are still used, they are criticised, among other things, for their demanding and time-consuming manner of construction, and the emphasis they place on the views of the judges. They are a valuable tool of methodology, and are employed as the sole technique or together with other methods of attitude measurement.

c   The Likert scale

Description
Developed by Likert in 1932, this scale operates in a way similar to that of the Thurstone scale. It consists of a set of items of equal value and a set of response categories constructed around a continuum of agreement/disagreement to which subjects are asked to respond. It is very popular among social scientists, is relatively easy to construct and is believed to be more reliable than the Thurstone scale.

Construction
Likert scales are constructed in the following way:

Step 1
A number of items related to an issue are collected. In general, 80 to 120 items are thought to be sufficient, but four times as many items as needed are generally considered.

Step 2
Five-answer response categories are assigned to each item, ranging from 'strongly agree' through 'agree', 'undecided' and 'disagree' to 'strongly disagree', including numerical values, for example from 1 to 5 respectively

Step 3
Statements are administered to respondents in a pilot study, and total scores are computed and further processed to determine, for instance, *uni-dimensionality*, that is, measuring one and the same concept (usually through factor analysis), and *internal consistency* (e.g. correlation with the total score is calculated).

Step 4
Items with a substantial correlation are retained; items with low correlation are discarded. The constructed scale is then administered to all respondents.

Example	'There is a lot of sexism going on in this community'			
Strongly agree	*Agree*	*Undecided*	*Disagree*	*Strongly disagree*
1	2	3	4	5

Evaluation

Likert scales are very popular among social scientists and have been so for more than half a century. The reason for this is that they: (1) have a high degree of validity even if the scale contains only a few items; (2) provide single scores from a set of items; (3) have a very high reliability (between 0.85 and 0.94); (4) allow ranking of the respondents; and (5) are relatively easy to construct. Nevertheless, researchers point to some drawbacks of this method. For example, total scores referring to many and diverse items say little about a person's response to the various aspects of the research object; also, it is difficult to achieve equal items in the scale (Kimmon, 1990).

d   The Bogardus social distance scale

Description

This scale was developed in the USA and was employed to measure 'social distance' between the respondents and persons of other nationalities or races; it is still used to determine how close a respondent is willing to place himself or herself to persons of other races or nationalities.

The scale consists of a number of statements that indicate the degree of distance between the respondent and the groups under study. More particularly, the respondents are asked to state their reactions to a set of statements varying in intensity of closeness to a population group. As a concrete example, respondents could be asked to state which of the following seven statements (which actually make up the scale) reflect accurately and honestly their true feelings towards Aborigines, and whether they would accept an Aborigine as a:

- close relative by marriage
- personal friend
- neighbour
- colleague at work
- speaking acquaintance only
- visitor to their country
- person to be kept out of their country

Interpretation

The results obtained through this procedure are evaluated as shown below:

- Compute the mean values for each group.
- Rank each group according to the value of the mean.
- The higher the value, the greater the social distance, that is, the lower the willingness to assume contacts with that group; and the stronger the negative prejudice and attitude to that group.

Application

This scale, although originally developed to measure distance among ethnic groups, can be equally successfully employed in other areas, for example in market research and studies of race relations. One could, for instance, develop a range of questions related to a certain item (car, television set, record player, etc.) that could best describe a person's intention and willingness to buy this item. For example, questions ranging from 'I would most certainly buy this product' to 'I will never buy such a thing in my life' can be used to measure the degree of a person's readiness to purchase the item.

Evaluation

This scale has been used very extensively by social scientists. The three most common advantages of the scale are the following (see Kimmon, 1990):

1 A very high split-half reliability (r is equal to or greater than 0.90).
2 A high content validity of the scale items.
3 A satisfactory overall validity and reliability.

Although there are some problems associated with the construction of the steps of the scale and their order, the scale is considered to be a very useful tool of social research.

e The Guttman scale

Description

This is another scale that measures social distance, or rather 'proximity'. It consists of a number of statements placed in a hierarchical order ranging from low to high in such a way that if respondents reject one statement they will also reject all other statements above it; and if they accept one statement they will accept all other statements below it.

Respondents are normally asked to state whether they agree or disagree with each of the statements. The results obtained are expected to show the degree of proximity or distance of the subjects from the research object (e.g. migrants, blacks, homosexuals, etc.). More particularly, it will show how far the respondents will allow certain people to come close to them.

Construction

Construction of such a scale is complicated and time consuming. In a simplified form it can be constructed in the following way:

Step 1
A number of statements thought to be cumulative, that is, they fall in a hierarchical order ranging from low to high, are formulated in such a way that if respondents reject one statement they will also reject all other statements above it; and if they accept one statement they will accept all other statements below it.

Step 2
These statements are presented to a number of subjects (say, 10), who are asked to state whether they agree or disagree with each statement.

Step 3
A table with the numbers of the statements on the top, and the side, is constructed; the agreements of the subjects with each statement are entered (note that disagreements are not recorded).

Step 4
The statements are then ordered so that the one accepted by one subject only is placed first, the statement accepted by two subjects second, the statement accepted by three subjects comes third and so on.

Step 5
The reproducibility value, which is 1 minus the fraction consisting of the number of errors (numerator) and the number of responses (denominator), is computed. If the score is 0.90 or better the scale is satisfactory.

Evaluation
This scale has been employed very extensively in the past and is still considered to be a valid and useful way of measuring social proximity. But, it is considered to be more cumbersome than the Bogardus social distance scale, which is used more frequently.

f   The semantic differential scale

Description
This technique was developed by Osgood, Suci and Tannenbaum in 1957 and has been used by social scientists to measure the impression concepts make on people and the meaning they invoke. Concepts are measured independently as well as in comparison with other concepts, and can be related to a variety of contexts, issues or objects, in this way allowing the researcher to draw relevant conclusions about the respondents.

The semantic differential scale consists of a number of opposite concepts, which may range from 7 to over 70. Examples of such opposites are given below. The data sheet containing the sets of opposites is administered to the respondents with instructions to place an individual (e.g. a teacher) or a group of individuals (e.g. Asian migrants) in a specific position between the extremes of a continuum.

Example   Some opposites

Good	6	5	4	3	2	1	0	Bad
Democratic	6	5	4	3	2	1	0	Authoritarian
Sociable	6	5	4	3	2	1	0	Unsociable
Strong	6	5	4	3	2	1	0	Weak
Flexible	6	5	4	3	2	1	0	Rigid
Cooperative	6	5	4	3	2	1	0	Uncooperative
High	6	5	4	3	2	1	0	Low
Hard	6	5	4	3	2	1	0	Soft
Conformist	6	5	4	3	2	1	0	Non-conformist
Fair	6	5	4	3	2	1	0	Unfair
Difficult	6	5	4	3	2	1	0	Easy
Active	6	5	4	3	2	1	0	Passive
Sharp	6	5	4	3	2	1	0	Dull
Independent	6	5	4	3	2	1	0	Dependent
Irritable	6	5	4	3	2	1	0	Calm
Hot	6	5	4	3	2	1	0	Cold
Harmonious	6	5	4	3	2	1	0	Unharmonious

The numerals indicate the degree of agreement or disagreement of the subjects regarding the concepts under evaluation. In the examples, 6 stands for *very* good, strong, high, etc., 5 for *moderately* good, strong, etc., 4 for *fairly* good, strong, etc., 3 for *undecided,* 2 for *fairly* bad, unsociable, weak, low, etc., 1 for *moderately* bad, unsociable, weak, etc. and 0 for *very* bad, unsociable, weak, low, etc.

The subject's judgement is based on three distinct characteristics, namely evaluation of the *individual,* judgement of the *potency* or *power* of the individual, and judgement of the *activity of the individual. General evaluation* is judged by opposites such as good–bad, sociable–unsociable, high–low and harmonious–unharmonious. *Potency* is judged by means of opposites such as hard–soft, large–small, difficult–easy and unyielding–lenient. *Activity* is judged by opposites such as hot–cold, active–passive, sharp–dull and irritable–calm. Of these three dimensions the first (evaluation) seems to be the most important.

Respondents are advised to evaluate the study person or group, by indicating the number that corresponds to their feelings on the specific item. If the respondents think that the person in question is moderately good they are advised to circle '5' at the 'good and bad' item, if they feel that this person is fairly unsociable they should circle '2' in the second line, and so forth. Each circle represents a score which can be high or low depending on the subject's judgement of the concept or the individual, for example the teacher. When the evaluation is completed, a total score for the impression of the concept or the person in question is computed by adding up all individual scores. A high score represents a high impression and a low score indicates a low impression of the concept or the person.

This scale can be employed successively in a number of different groups, such as Asian migrants, Italian migrants and British migrants, allowing comparisons to be made between these groups.

Interpretation

The results of this procedure can be interpreted and presented in many ways. The method of adding up the individual scores mentioned above is one. Drawing profiles, computation of correlation coefficients and of the semantic distances are other ways.

Evaluation

The semantic differential method offers precise information about the attitudes of people toward others. It allows evaluation of concepts, comparisons and measurement of different types on the same measure, and is relatively easy to construct. It has, however, to be treated with caution. For instance, a long list of points to choose from might cause confusion and also inaccurate results. The use of equal intervals or ordinal data is another issue. Definitions of the concepts and their meanings might vary from one respondent to another, causing problems and distortions.

10   Summary

The concept and practice of measurement are two important and also controversial issues. However, the controversy in this case is not about whether to employ measurement in social research or not but rather about how and in what way measurement should be employed. The practice of measurement is well accepted in social research, regardless of type and nature. Some studies may use nominal measurement, others may use ordinal and others interval/ratio measurement.

All types of measurement are employed. The notion that one type of research is better than the other is incorrect. Qualitative researchers may opt for nominal measurement, but this does not make other types of measurement less effective. Quantitative researchers often use all types of measures simultaneously. In one and the same research instrument one may find some variables being measured at the nominal level and others at the ordinal or interval/ratio level. The latter provides different types of information than the former; but it nevertheless produces equally useful information.

The level of measurement is useful for itself, but more so for further research and analysis. The level of measurement determines the type of measures that are to be employed in the analysis. As we shall see in Chapters 16 to 19, there is a close relationship between level of measurement, type of variable and statistical tests. For this reason, having a clear understanding of the levels of measurement is important for doing research, and for assuring high levels of accuracy.

Measurement together with objectivity and ethics on the one hand and with validity and reliability on the other constitute major principles of social research. The latter are central to any type of research, regardless of its nature and ideological affiliation. Adherence to reliability and validity is a fundamental requirement which researchers have to consider seriously when doing research. Reliability and validity are indicators of consistency, truthfulness and accuracy, and such concepts are structural ingredients of any type of research.

Measurement, validity and reliability, together with scaling, which was discussed in the last part of this chapter, are very useful research tools. They help establish the parameters for producing well-founded and respectable findings. In the following chapters we shall see how these parameters fit in the context of data collection and analysis.

Key concepts

Measurement	Cumulative validation
Dependent variable	Triangulation
Ordinal level	Equivalence reliability
Validity	Split-half method
Theoretical validation	Indexes
Concurrent validity	Thurstone scale
Content validity	Guttman scale
External validity	Independent variable
Communicative validation	Qualitative measurement
Argumentative validation	Ratio level
Test–retest method	Empirical validation
Unweighted indexes	Criterion validity
Scaling	Face validity
Bogardus social distance scale	Internal validity
Research model	Ecological validation
Variable	Stability reliability
Nominal level	Representative reliability
Interval level	Alternate-form reliability
Reliability	Weighted indexes
Pragmatic validity	Likert scale
Conceptual validation	Semantic differential
Construct validity	Conceptual frameworks

4

The research process

1 Introduction

This is where the actual research process begins. The question that comes up first is, 'What do we do next?' or better, 'What is the first step towards doing research?' and then, 'What follows right after that?'. This chapter will show how actual research is initiated and planned, and what type of decisions are to be made in order for the research to achieve its purpose. In addition, the nature, types and levels of measurement and the concepts of validity and reliability will be considered.

The first step towards doing research is to develop a model that will present a summary of the main elements of the research, namely what will be studied, how, when and where it will take place; then, how it will be executed and, finally, how the data will be analysed and published. Such a model can be very prescriptive or rather loose and flexible, depending on the type of methodology employed and the type of research to be undertaken.

Quantitative researchers tend to be more prescriptive than qualitative investigators, who prefer to operate with as few prescriptions as possible. Some writers, for instance, propose a research model of 25 steps, while others suggest models with significantly fewer steps, even with vague and flexible guidelines. Nevertheless, a form of model is employed by all researchers. We shall soon see why.

2 Quantitative research: the research model

a Basic assumptions

The general assumptions regarding the use of a research model rest on the belief that:

- research can be perceived as evolving in a sequence of steps which are closely interrelated, and in which the success of the one depends on the successful completion of the preceding step;

- the steps must be executed in the given order — this is imperative, particularly for models with a few steps;
- planning and execution of the research is more successful if a research model is employed.

To the qualitative researcher, the second point might cause some concern, but the other two points are difficult to dismiss.

b   Content of the research model

The form of the research model employed in practical situations varies according to the nature and purpose of the project and the type of method used. Thus, exploratory studies employ a model that differs from that of surveys, experiments and causal studies. Despite this, there are several common points to be considered, and decisions must be made in all types of design

Research decisions

Which topic? Which methodology?
The first decision the researcher must make in the context of a research model is about the research topic to be studied and then the methodology that will be used in the investigation. In addition, the researcher will have to prepare the research topic in some way (e.g. operationalise it) for further analysis. As we shall see later, in certain cases some of these points might not be employed or may be executed in a different way.

Sampling procedure?
The next step is equally ubiquitous and important, and relates to the decision about the sampling procedure. The researcher must decide where the study will be carried out, how many respondents will be included in it, who these respondents will be, how they will be chosen, and what proportion of the population will be considered. While quantitative researchers must finalise this issue before they proceed to the next step, qualitative researchers will, in most cases, begin choosing the subjects at this stage but will continue the selection throughout the research.

How to collect data?
The issue to be considered next is the selection of the method of data collection. The investigator will decide how the necessary information will be collected, and will evaluate the available methods, consider their advantages and limitations as well as their suitability for the study and make the final choice.

Method of analysis?
The fourth important decision to be made during this step is related to the method of analysis to be employed in the study. This issue is very important since it will influence the other aspects of research planning. For instance, if

the study is to employ quantitative statistical methods and the analysis is to be undertaken electronically, arrangements must be made to prepare the study accordingly, for example by appointing appropriate personnel and by making arrangements for the use of computers and for preparing relevant methods of data collection.

How is the research to be administered?
The fifth issue concerns the administration of the research, and more particularly the type and number of *assistants* required, the type of *supervision* of the research to be employed, the *arrangements* needed for the execution of the major steps of the research process, for example approaching respondents, training personnel, preparing forms, questionnaires, forms of recording data, permits, etc. and other relevant issues.

Other decisions
The planning of the research is further expected to include factors that will control *bias* and *errors* and will allow transition from one step of research to another without problems, and be *free from distortions or unnecessary delays*. Apart from this, the researcher will have to consider factors related to *timing* and *costing* of the project, as well as other restrictions associated with the nature of the research topic, the type of respondents or the limits set by the employer.

c   Purpose of the research model

Irrespective of their nature and length, research models contain a research design and provide very useful guidelines to researchers, both in terms of the use of resources and of personnel and administration and the validity and reliability of the study. Some methodologists (e.g. Berger *et al.*, 1989) suggest that the use of research models:

- offers a guide that directs the research action, helping to reduce time and costs to a minimum;
- helps to introduce a systematic approach to the research operation, thereby guaranteeing that all aspects of the study will be addressed and that they will be executed in the right sequence;
- encourages the introduction of an effective organisation and coordination of the project;
- helps in the planning of the research and use of the resources effectively, avoiding errors and bias and preventing distortion;
- enables researchers to direct and control the research operation most effectively, especially when research assistants are employed.

The degree to which a design will prescribe the operation of the project will depend on the methodology used. As stated earlier, qualitative researchers employ more open and guiding models than do quantitative researchers; the latter employ more accurate, detailed and prescriptive designs.

Although a research model can provide many advantages, there are critics who argue that such models can also restrict the research, by not allowing freedom and flexibility, and by excluding from the investigation other issues and approaches that might not have been realised at the initiation of the study. Despite this, models are an indispensable aspect of the research process. The question often asked in this context is not whether a model will or will not be used, but rather, whether it will be written down, or, more often, how prescriptive it will be.

d Structure of the research model

We have already seen what research models are expected to include. But how detailed are these models expected to be? How many points should they contain? How prescriptive are they supposed to be? And in what order should the steps be executed? The answers to these questions vary from case to case. Most frequently, however, researchers seem to agree that too many points hamper the flexibility that every researcher wants to enjoy; and too few points leave many questions unanswered, and allow too much freedom to research assistants, which can be misused.

In the following discussion, we introduce a research model consisting of five steps, each of which relates to one major part of any research project (see Table 4.1). Studying any research topic begins with the first step, and then proceeds to the other steps until the last step is reached; this step is expected to answer the research question.

Although some researchers might be flexible about how the steps of a research model are executed, in the majority of cases it is believed that a model can only be effective if employed in its original sequence. One cannot, for instance, begin collecting data unless the research question has been chosen and adequately defined and formulated, and unless the research has been adequately designed and the necessary arrangements made.

Despite this, as we shall see later, some points of the basic steps of the research model can be interchanged with others, where conditions permit or dictate it. An attempt will be made briefly to describe these steps, in order to gain a better understanding of the whole model.

e Steps of the research model

In a general manner, the items expected to be included in a research model were presented earlier in this section. What we intend to present here is a more detailed discussion of the content of the various steps of the research model and to give relevant examples.

Step 1: Preparation
This step contains two major decisions, namely the selection of the research topic and the choice of research methodology. This means that before any research takes place the researcher must know what is to be studied, and then what type of methodology will be employed.

Table 4.1   The research model

Step	Elements
Preparation	Selection of research topic Selection of research methodology Formal definition of the topic Exploration Operationalisation Formulation of hypotheses
Research design	Selection of sampling procedures Selection of methods of data collection Selection of methods of data analysis Arrangement of administrative procedures
Data collection	Data collection
Data processing	Grouping and presentation of data Analysis and interpretation of data
Reporting	Publication of the findings

The research topic
Any type of social research starts with selection of the research question. Sometimes ideas about the research topic have been expressed and formulated before the actual selection of the question; and the question can even be adjusted and changed to a certain extent after the selection. Nevertheless, there is a time in the course of the research process when the actual question is formally chosen or adopted by the investigator or the research body. For instance:

Topic: Traditional families and family size

Type of methodology
Following this, the researcher must decide about the type of methodology that will direct the study. The choice is usually between quantitative and qualitative research. Which methodology will be chosen is not important but a choice must be made before further decisions are made. For instance:

Methodology: Quantitative methodology

The researcher decides to use a quantitative study, either because this methodology is more suitable for the intended study or because the researcher has already established a methodological conviction that motivates him or her to carry out predominantly, or even exclusively, quantitative research. This decision will of course restrict, to a certain extent, the choice of methods available to the researcher, as we shall see later.

Formal definition of the topic
Here, the researcher will explain clearly and accurately the concepts, for example what one would define as 'families'. The actual content and ideological bias of the definitions are not important. Still, these concepts must be defined before one progresses to the next step. For instance:

> *Definitions:*   **Family:** For the purpose of this study, a family is a group of people related by blood or marriage.
> **Family size:** The number of children per family.

Exploration
An exploration is required in order to collect information about the research topic, review relevant literature and so on which will ultimately constitute the framework of the study, and help refine definitions, provide the necessary elements for operationalisation and formulate hypotheses. Examples of exploration are:

> *Exploration:*   (1) Literature review; (b) Expert surveys; (c) Case studies

Operationalisation
This element of research has the purpose of translating abstract concepts into measurable indicators. It entails a rather complex procedure but is very useful nevertheless. Most quantitative researchers use operational definitions of some kind. An example of how a quantitative researcher will address the research question is given below:

> *Operationalisation:*   **Traditional families** are operationalised as families in which the husband is the only provider and makes the most important decisions.
> **Family size** relates to number of children living in or out of home and not other relatives.

Formulation of hypotheses
Formulating hypotheses is a routine step of research for many researchers, particularly those who employ statistical tools of analysis. A hypothesis is an assumption about the possible outcome of the study and provides a guideline for the research process. A possible hypothesis is shown below.

> *Hypothesis:*   The family size of traditional families is larger than the national average.

Overall, some researchers might 'treat' the question in detail, using very sophisticated techniques (e.g. operationalisation, exploration, formulation of hypotheses). Others might isolate it in intellectual terms, but without losing touch with the real world, and study it in its real environment. In either case, the research question is introduced to the arena of research, and is also linked with possible methods of data collection.

Step 2: Research design

This step is the most significant element of the research process. Here, all of the research will be designed, options considered, decisions made and details of the research laid down for execution. Most decisions about how the research will be executed and how respondents will be approached, as well as when, where and how the research will be completed, are made during this step. Depending on the methodological orientation of the researcher, certain methods of data collection will be chosen, and sampling procedures will be selected; the day to day operations associated with the research will be decided in this step. No research can be undertaken without some portion of planning.

For this reason, this step occupies a central position in the research model and has attracted the interest of many researchers who developed specific designs to meet the special needs of certain methods. In general, during the step involving research design the following points will be considered.

Sampling procedures
Here, the researcher is expected to decide whether the whole population will be studied or only a sample will be considered. If the latter is chosen, decisions will be made about the type, size and representativeness of the sample. For instance:

> *Sampling:*   The sample should consist of 300 traditional families. The method used involves a two-phase sampling procedure.

Data collection
In addition, during this step the method(s) of data collection will be chosen, which will be used in the study. The choice here is between the methods that are available in the context of the research methodology chosen. The characteristics of these methods and, most of all, their suitability and availability of personnel and resources will be considered during this stage. For instance:

> *Method of data collection:*   Standardised interviewing.

Administrative procedures
Here, the researcher is expected to consider issues such as type of material needed during the study, the funds required and how they will be distributed to cover the needs of the study, the assistants who might be needed for the execution of the investigation, the training of the personnel, and eventual permits needed for the execution of the study and so on. For instance:

Administrative procedures:	It may be decided to include female research assistants, employ and train interviewers in due time and opt for a large number of assistants so that the study is completed in a minimum amount of time.

Data analysis

The form of analysis and interpretation of the data are decided next. The use of statistics, for instance, will require not only additional personnel, but also relevant adjustments of the methods and techniques of the study and eventual use of computers. Relevant arrangements must be made.

Data analysis:	It may be decided that statistical analysis should be considered, using computers; the services of a statistician must be secured, and accessibility to relevant computers arranged.

Reporting the results

At this stage, some thoughts must be made about whether the results will be publicised in the form of a report, a paper, a journal article or a book. To facilitate this, publishers, editors of journals and state departments interested in this issue will be contacted.

Reporting:	It may be decided that a report will be prepared to be sent to the relevant authorities, and that further publications in journals will be undertaken.

The list of activities included in step 2 indicates the significance of the step for the whole project. Everything that needs to be done in the study has, in fact, to be decided upon at this stage of the project.

Step 3: Data collection

The objective of this step is to collect the data. For many researchers, collection of data is the most important part of any research, because it is the way to secure information about the research question, which is of course the main aim of social research in general. The choice is wide and will be affected by factors related not only to personal preferences of the researcher but also to methodological affiliation and ideological convictions. Nevertheless, a choice must be made and the researcher will collect the necessary information either alone or with the assistance of other research personnel. This stage will provide the raw material to study the issue in question.

Data collection:	During this step interviewers are sent to respondents to collect the information

Step 4: Data processing
In this step the collected information is analysed and interpreted in the manner specified earlier during the planning stage of the study. Raw data are processed in a way that allows the researcher to examine the question and to make statements about the question as a social issue. The analysed data are put in context and given meaning and social relevance and also studied to provide answers to the research question. The details of this operation will vary significantly according to the type of methodology employed. In quantitative studies, analysis employs statistical techniques and is undertaken after the previous steps of the research process have been completed. In qualitative studies, the analysis usually contains no measurement or statistics and takes place during the stage of data collection.

> *Data processing:*   Data are grouped and subjected to statistical analysis by using computers in order to uncover trends and patterns of behaviour of women in their families.

Step 5: Reporting
The interpretations, conclusions and recommendations made in the previous step of the research process are finally published in some form, for example as a conference paper, an article in a journal, a report or a book. Reporting is the last part of the intellectual activity involved in the research process.

> *Reporting:*   A report to be sent to relevant authorities will be prepared. However, given that the issue in our example concerns people of all walks of life, the findings will be published in a variety of ways, ranging from popular media to journal articles and conference papers.

3   Research design in qualitative research

a   Introduction

It has quite often been argued that qualitative researchers do not employ a design and therefore have no need for a research model. The principles of openness and flexibility discussed in the previous chapter, for instance, are thought to offer the researcher freedom of choice and make designs an unnecessary restriction.

This view is not correct. Qualitative researchers are equally expected to develop a design and to specify in some way how, where, when and under what conditions they will collect and analyse their data. The content of the research process and the form in which it will be executed may be more open and perhaps vague, but making some firm decisions about the research process is unavoidable. For instance, the methodology to be employed, the object to be studied, the place and time of research, the specific methods of collection and analysis of the data and the nature of the research units must all be defined.

As Miles and Huberman (1994: 16, 17) have shown, 'contrary to what you might have heard, qualitative research designs do exist. Some are more deliberate than others. At the proposal stage and in the early planning and start-up stages, many design decisions are being made — some explicitly and precisely, some implicitly, some unknowingly, and still others by default . . . any researcher, no matter how unstructured or inductive, comes to fieldwork with some orienting ideas, foci and tools' such as focusing on families and not on schools or churches, and inside these families investigating, for example, perceptions of power relationships, abortion or adultery 'through the eyes of an architect'.

The characteristics of qualitative and quantitative methodologies are summarised and compared in Table 4.2.

Table 4.2 Comparison between the two methodologies: research models

Procedure	Quantitative methodology	Qualitative methodology
Preparation	*Definition*: precise, accurate and specific *Hypotheses*: formulated before the study Employs *operationalisation*	*Definition*: general, and loosely structured *Hypotheses*: formulated through/after the study Employs sensitising concepts
Design	*Design*: well planned and prescriptive *Sampling*: well planned before data collection; is representative *Measurement/scales*: employs all types	*Design*: well planned but not prescriptive *Sampling*: well planned but during data collection; is not representative *Measurement/scales*: mostly nominal
Data collection	Uses quantitative methods; employs assistants	Uses qualitative methods; usually single handed
Data processing	Mostly quantitative and statistical analysis; inductive generalisations	Mainly qualitative; often collection and analysis occur simultaneously; analytical generalisations
Reporting	Highly integrated findings	Mostly not integrated findings

Miles and Huberman speak of *focusing and bounding* as a way of preparing a study and getting ready for data collection. They admit that conventional qualitative research implies a 'loosely structured, emergent, inductively grounded approach' in which research models emerge from the field while the research is being done, that questions are clarified and settings and respondents chosen during the course of the study, and research instruments emerge and become refined while research is in progress, but they also state that such a perception of qualitative research is good for 'exploring exotic cultures, understudied phenomena or very complex social realities' (Miles and Huberman, 1994) and will be totally useless if the researcher already has sufficient knowledge about the research subject.

The view of these authors is that a case can be made for tight, prestructured qualitative designs *and* for loose emergent ones, arguing that much qualitative research now lies between these two extremes (p. 17). In most cases the investigator knows enough about the setting but not enough about the research question; at least not enough to support a conclusion or a theory. The investigator usually knows, before the fieldwork begins, what questions require an answer, what settings to investigate, which actors to approach, which processes to consider, what types of events to register and what instruments to employ. Miles and Huberman state (p. 28) that 'at the outset, then, we usually have at least a rudimentary conceptual framework, a set of general research questions, some notions about sampling, and some initial data gathering devices'. Whether this conceptual framework will be prescriptive or not and to what extent depends on many factors, ranging from personal preferences of the investigator, state of knowledge of the research subject, type of subject, nature of setting, availability of time and money, to type of methods used.

b   Conceptual frameworks

The question here, then, is not about whether qualitative investigators use a research design, but rather about the type of the design and the degree of restriction it implies. Miles and Huberman speak of *conceptual frameworks* instead of designs or models, which in our view mean the same thing. Using their descriptions, conceptual frameworks have certain properties that resemble those of quantitative research designs.

In Miles and Huberman's view 'a conceptual framework explains, either graphically or in narrative form, the main things to be studied — the key factors, constructs or variables — and the presumed relationships among them. Frameworks can be rudimentary or elaborate, theory-driven or commonsensical, descriptive or casual' (1994: 18). Frameworks are not blinders or strait-jackets; they emerge from experience, they are revised and corrected through research, and refocused to serve the needs of the study. In this sense they guide research and coordinate research activities in a multi-researcher and multi-site context.

The structure of a conceptual framework varies, according to these writers, from case to case but in general it seems to contain the following elements: (1) it explains the main dimensions of the study (e.g. key factors, variables); (2) it describes the presumed relationship between factors and variables; (3) it specifies who and what is to be studied as well as events, settings, processes, theoretical constructs (e.g. organisational rules) considered in the study; (4) it also specifies outcomes of the study; (5) it guides the researcher through the research process, at the same time being receptive to change, by focusing and refocusing data collection and analysis; (6) it coordinates research activities by the members of a research team.

We used in this discussion Miles and Huberman's work because it takes a firm and specific view on data collection and analysis in qualitative research but also because their work is well known among many social scientists and researchers in this region. They undoubtedly present a view that is dominant among qualitative researchers and deserves some thought and recognition. Their views also provide guidelines for research design in qualitative research. Most qualitative researchers will agree with most propositions they made in this context.

Marshall and Rossman (1989), for instance, take the existence of a research design in qualitative research for granted and state that it contains among other things details concerning how the researcher will deal with the following issues:

- Site and sample selection
- Researcher's role management, including entry, reciprocity and ethics
- Research strategies
- Data collection techniques
- Managing and recording data
- Data analysis strategies
- Management plan, time line and feasibility analysis

Qualitative researchers do employ research designs, plan their studies carefully and guide their activities towards their goals in an integrated and systematic manner. The content and complexity of their designs might vary but their presence cannot be denied.

4   Examples of other research designs

The majority of research models and designs employ the steps of the research process as presented above. They include a model which will guide the study throughout its process. Details may change but the basic steps of the research process remain the same. However, there are certain studies which are thought to deviate from the model presented above. Changes in the content of the steps of the research process are interpreted to mean that a different research model is being used. As we shall see below, the difference between these studies and the research model presented above lie not in the model but rather in the design of the model. And even in that context, the differences are not significant enough to speak of a different research model.

Two examples of research models in which the design varies partly from the research model presented in this chapter are *evaluation research* and *action research*; these types of research will be introduced briefly below. The basic deviations from our research model relate to the way respondents are involved in the study (action research) and the arrangements of data collection and analysis (evaluation research).

a   Evaluation research

Evaluation research is a type of research which is usually conducted by practitioners, social workers, psychologists and economists. It is a form of applied research, which by nature aims to search for solutions to problems, assess the significance of existing policies and practices, and evaluate the need for new approaches, plans and programs. In this sense, evaluation research is expected to be systematic and precise in its operations, and this requires a clear plan, program or design.

In the area of psychology, psychotherapy and social work, evaluation research can look at clinical programs and interventions concerning individuals with mental illnesses or interpersonal difficulties (family conflicts and violence) (Ellis, 1994).

The purpose of evaluation research varies with many factors. The goals of evaluation research are (Ellis, 1994; Bauer, 1994):

1 To discover gaps in services and to investigate the alternatives employed to meet the unmet needs.
2 To predict whether a planned program will be successful.
3 To assess the quality and effectiveness of a program, and the impact it has on the community.
4 To establish whether the program is cost effective, and whether benefits outweigh the costs.
5 To identify the need for and ways of improving the effectiveness of an existing program.

This list of goals indicates that there are many types of evaluation research. The most common are *feasibility studies* or *needs analysis, process analysis* and *impact analysis.* Some writers (e.g. Judd *et al.*, 1991: 329) prefer the names formative and summative evaluation research, with the former referring to process research (What is the program all about? How does the program work?), and the latter being another name for outcome research (Does the program work? What are its effects?).

The steps of evaluation research
As stated above, in evaluation research the steps of the research process are the same as those described above for any research project. Details regarding the content of the various steps of the model may vary; however, the basic structure of the model remains the same, as we shall see next.

Step 1: Preparation
Evaluation research begins with the basic elements included in the preparation step of the research model presented above. The first task to be accomplished is to define the research topic. There are two major topics investigated in this type of research. These are *program* and/or *community.* For instance, program evaluation research studies programs; feasibility studies or needs analysis studies investigate communities with a view to identifying gaps in services, evaluating their offerings and looking for ways of improving them, including need identification and need assessment.

The next items in the list of tasks of the preparation step of the research model are *definition* and *operationalisation,* which are part and parcel of evaluation research. The extent to which definition and operationalisation will go depends among other things on the type of evaluation. Programs are often conceived as formally defined by the government, and operationalisation will be geared towards the aspect of the program to be evaluated. Some might study the *process* and others the *outcomes* of the program.

Finally, hypotheses can be formulated as much in evaluation research as in any other type of research.

Step 2: Design
As in other research types, during this step evaluation research will consider two major questions, namely those regarding sampling procedures and methods of data collection and analysis.

1 *Sampling* The study will address respondents who will be in a position to provide useful information about the program or needs in question. These will be: (a) persons who have knowledge of the program and its effects on the community, (b) the persons responsible for its development and/or introduction, (c) those working with the program or who are responsible for the services it provides, (d) stakeholders, (e) experts, (f) government authorities, and (g) community groups. The *methods of sampling* which will be employed in evaluation research to identify the respondents will be taken from those available to other researchers.
2 *Methods* The methods of data collection vary significantly from one type of research to another. Overall, the main methods used in evaluation research are those employed by other researchers and in most cases are observation (observing clients, agency employees, practices and intervention strategies), case studies, documentary analysis (service records, files, agency records, log books, statistics, etc.), community surveys, interviews with employees and clients, social indicators and experimental research (Ellis, 1994). Service evaluation techniques and cost–benefit analysis are also used.

Step 3: Data collection
The actual collection of data varies slightly from the way it is conducted by other researchers in that it uses additional practices and procedures and relies more on respondent participation than other studies. Such practices are the use of:

1 *steering committees* consisting of members from sponsors, management of agency, staff and clientele which are established for the duration of the study and offer advice on many important issues;
2 *focus groups* which are small groups called for a one-off meeting and consultation/discussion of problems; and
3 *Delphi groups,* which act in a similar manner to steering committees.

It must be noted that the difference here is not that evaluation research employs methods which other studies do not use, but rather that it uses these methods to a greater extent and it gives them more weight than other types of research.

Step 4: Data processing
This step depends entirely on the type of methodology, methods and techniques chosen by the researcher. In most cases, analysis is qualitative but community surveys, surveys of clients, etc. often are analysed by means of quantitative methods or a combination of both. This is common when attitude surveys or experimental designs are used, which lend themselves to advanced statistical analysis. Following this, the findings will be interpreted to show whether the evaluation is positive or negative, that is, whether the program succeeded in achieving the intended outcomes or not.

Step 5: Reporting

As in any other research type, the findings of the study will be communicated through all possible channels. The final report will clearly show the trends identified in the research, the conclusions and eventual recommendations, for example whether the program should be continued in its present form, continued in a modified form, or be discontinued. In many cases, evaluation research takes place in the context of *action research,* which by nature not only involves the participants but also takes steps towards changing conditions, influencing government and the community in their decision regarding the issue in question, and working towards implementing the recommendations contained in the report. Policy recommendations, advocacy and action often are corollaries of the research outcomes of evaluation research.

It is obvious from this presentation that the methods used to conduct evaluation research are not different from those employed by other researchers. Noting this, Judd and associates (1991: 329) state: 'Outcome evaluations use experimental, quasi-experimental and survey research designs. Process evaluations use techniques more like participant observation . . . Outcome research usually uses statistical analysis of quantitative data. Process research is usually qualitative research and uses histories rather than statistics to make a point'. We shall see later that all these methods and designs are employed by other researchers and fall within the boundaries of the standard research model presented above.

b   Action research: research in action

Introduction

As stated in the previous chapters, for some investigators political interests and research should be kept apart. Researchers are not politicians. Their task is to create knowledge and explain social phenomena, not to reorganise society. Certainly, new knowledge can lead to social reconstruction; however, this should be the outcome of political action, not of research action.

This is one view. Another view is that research can take dimensions which can involve political action, involvement of respondents in the process of research and through this in political action as a part of the research process. This converts research practice to political action, or better to action research. In this sense, political interests are associated not only with politicians and interests groups but also with the researcher. Researchers become the source of direct and/or indirect influence on the investigation through the decisions they make, the methods they choose and the extent to which they accept the demands of their sponsors.

But politics goes even deeper than that. There are cases where the researchers identify themselves fully with political ideologies and programs, and take positive (or negative) action in an attempt to put their views and opinions into practice (Schensul and Schensul, 1992). Research becomes for them a political instrument and a tool for social change and reconstruction; in this sense it is often used to promote personal convictions and political interests. *Action research* is the best example of this and represents a research type that has been employed by researchers since the 1920s (Whyte, 1991) in almost all areas of social research, for example in critical ethnography (Thomas, 1993).

The question that concerns us at this stage is to do with the research model it employs. Is action research a different type of research? Does it employ a different research model or a model that is similar to that introduced above? Is action research conducted as any other type of research or in a significantly different way? The view we shall present in the discussion that follows is that action research employs the same type of research model other research types employ with some modifications regarding the role of the respondent and the manner in which data collection is conducted. To a large extent, action research employs the same research model evaluation research does.

What is action research?

We understand action research to be 'the application of fact finding to practical problem solving in a social situation with a view to improving the quality of action within it, involving the collaboration and co-operation of researchers, practitioners and laymen' (Burns, 1990: 252; Oja and Smulyan, 1989). This type of research is characterised by a number of criteria. Burns (1990), for instance, notes that action is *situational* (it diagnoses a problem and attempts to solve it), *collaborative* (since it requires the efforts of researchers and practitioners), *participatory* (in that researchers take part in the implementation of the findings) and *self-evaluative* (it involves a constant evaluation of its process and modifications to adjust research and practice).

Briefly, action research criticises the theoretical and methodological basis of conventional social research, both by its challenges and by its claims. As Winter (1987: 2) put it, 'it challenges a scientific method of inquiry based on the authority of the "outside" observer and the "independent" experimenter, and it claims to reconstruct both practical expertise and theoretical insight on the different basis of its own inquiry procedures'.

The research model

The model employed by action researchers follows the same steps other types of research follow. It will begin with the arrangements entailed in the preparation step, and proceed to the steps of research design, data collection and analysis and finally the step of publication of the findings. Below is an example of this.

Step 1: Preparation

In the first instance the researcher will begin with the choice and *definition of the topic*. Like every other researcher, the action researcher will identify an issue that needs investigation and define it to make it clear and specific. Here the researcher identifies the discrepancies and injustices and names the problem (Wadsworth, 1991: 5). The difference between this researcher and other researchers may be that the former is more likely to opt for a topic that is controversial, relates to problems, neglect and oppression and so on. However, this is not an element of the research model but rather of the type of theoretical perspective chosen; this means that action research is more likely to be guided by critical, Marxist or feminist principles than positivist principles and standards. Still, these parameters are already a part of the model introduced above.

An example of this may be a study of oppression of homosexuals in Sydney's Western Suburbs. Here the researcher will have to clarify what types of homosexuals are referred to (gays, lesbians, single, committed, with/without children, etc.), the types of oppression that need to be investigated and the specific suburbs that will be considered in the study.

Operationalisation of the topic will be as much a part of action research as it is in any other research type. If issues are to be explored that need refinement and processing before they are taken to the respondents, operationalisation is an element the researcher cannot do without. In the example introduced above, oppression will definitely have to be clarified and specified and most of all prepared for measurement, that is, if measurement is a part of the study. If this is not the case, oppression will be addressed as in any other qualitative study. The same is to be said about hypotheses.

Step 2: Research design
1 *Sampling*   The sampling procedures employed by action researchers are the same as those employed by other researchers. They may be probability or non-probability samples, and they may include a few or many respondents.
2 *Methods*   In a similar fashion, the methods employed by action researchers are the same as those employed by other investigators.

Step 3: Data collection
For the most part, data collection in action research is the same as that in other types of research. This is true with regard to the technical aspects of getting to the respondents and collecting the required information. However, there are some differences here. Action research supports a higher degree of respondent participation in the research. Some members of the units under study are expected and indeed encouraged to participate actively with the researcher throughout the study. This participation may begin with the initial identification of the research topic and design and may continue up to the publication of the findings (Whyte, 1991). Homosexual groups will be consulted and researched but also guided about how to become active in their own environment and with regard to approaching the authorities with the view of changing the conditions in which they live.

Step 4: Data analysis
Analysis and interpretation of the findings are conducted within the parameters of the underlying research methodology. As in any other type of research, action researchers will use appropriate methods to identify trends and to justify conclusions pertinent to the research question.

Step 5: Reporting
As in previous steps, so here reporting will basically follow the path of other types of research. Nevertheless, the nature of the research implies a more proactive perception of the findings, with the researcher and the researched making a concerted effort to give the findings the attention they deserve. While other researchers will be content to see their findings published in a professional journal or report of some kind, action researchers will make the effort to bring

the findings to the attention of the authorities and make sure that they are implemented. This may even require additional pressure put upon the relevant authorities to do so.

The essence of action research

We consciously left out of the model presented here the factor of *theoretical perspective*. The reason for this is that the perspective permeates the whole process of research and offers guidance and direction; and this guidance and direction are the determinants of action research and of any research in general. This means that if one takes away the theoretical and methodological bias, the technical aspects of action research are not very different from those of other types of research. Consequently, the factor that makes the difference here is politics, as entailed in the theoretical framework of action research

The elements that characterise action research are the personal involvement of the researcher, the emancipatory nature of the research, the active involvement of the researched, and its opposition to certain established policies and practices. This will set action research within the parameters of the critical perspective explained in Chapter 2 of this volume. The researcher here takes the side of the respondents, helps them understand their real situation (discrimination, disadvantage, etc.), explains to them the reasons for this, and shows them ways of change and 'liberation'. The researcher together with the respondents work towards change. Research becomes the vehicle of change and reconstruction. For instance, the respondents are shown how social order is shaped, how they came to be what they are in the community and their personal life, who benefits from it and what can be done to improve their life.

In certain cases, the background motives are related to deep-seated beliefs, convictions and theories which demand a radical reconstruction of the social order; Marxism is an example of this. In other cases, the motivating theory is less radical but equally influential. Feminism, for instance, influenced research activity that implied a strong element of participation, action and emancipation. Finally, action research is undertaken by researchers who wish to change conditions which, although not as fundamental as the previous two, are still socially significant.

In all cases, action research is based on the researchers' political convictions, initiates action-loaded investigation of social conditions, involves people, mobilises their forces, guides them to set goals, produces findings and follows them through until they are implemented The researcher carries the work through, and makes sure that the research findings are given the attention they deserve. In this sense, the researcher is not just an investigator but a collaborator and a facilitator: the political nature, the participatory character, the emancipatory elements and the direct, committing and personal involvement of the researcher are at the front of the research activity. Ultimately, action research helps to empower participants and to develop the skills and knowledge required to effect change in their own environment (McNiff, 1992).

Political interests, priorities, values and ideologies affect the nature, type and extent of research and the nature and application of its findings. In a similar fashion, research affects social and political life. It is this that motivates politicians and policy makers to be cautious about what type of research to support and what types of findings to make public. It is this interrelationship that social researchers must be aware of, and hence they must make their decisions according to ethical standards and principles.

5 Summary

We have seen that starting a research study involves careful development of a systematic model which will define or guide all significant elements of the study. All steps of the model are interactive in the sense that they influence each other so that the model is a perfectly functioning dynamic system.

In an oversimplified form, the model includes the stages of preparation, design, action and reporting. In the first step, the research topic is chosen, specifically formulated and embedded in a methodological framework; in the second step, the already chosen topic is related to the anticipated execution (data collection, analysis, etc.) and certain plans are made about how the required information is to be gathered; the action stage includes data collection, analysis and interpretation; and in the last step the findings are communicated in some way to the interested parties.

Although each research model has individuality, in principle it will vary very little from that described above. The context of the model is always the same; only the content will vary. For instance, it is essential for success that the topic is chosen, the design carefully planned and the plan carefully executed. Whether the topic is alienation of the aged or the empty-nest syndrome, and whether the sampling procedure is stratified sampling or theoretical sampling, has no significance for the quality or necessity of the model. It is important that the steps of the model are followed as designed by the researcher (strictly or loosely) and that the right decisions are made and executed as specified in the design.

Research becomes, therefore, a well-planned, and systematically organised system of investigation, related to a certain topic and methodology, aiming at collecting valuable information and analysing it in the context of a certain framework. The process of data collection is goal oriented, well thought out and often predictable (even if the predictions are of a general nature or expressed in a set of options). If the model is developed with care, and if it is executed precisely as planned, it is very unlikely to fail.

Research models are equally useful for the quantitative and the qualitative researcher, although in different ways. In both cases the model guides the researchers through the process of study and helps them to complete the project with economy of procedure and accuracy of operation, as well as avoiding errors, bias and distortions. While in the one context the model might *direct* the operations, in the other it might just *remind* the researcher of the decisions made and the steps that have to be undertaken in order to complete the study. In either case, a model is a tool that helps to administer the research most effectively and facilitates order in the course of the study.

Research models may vary to some extent in their content but are ubiquitous. Evaluation research and action research, which are often thought to be 'different', employ a research model which does not deviate significantly from the model presented in this chapter. The difference here is about involving respondents more in the research process than do other types of research, giving the research model a political character, strengthening the degree of commitment to the study and putting pressure upon the government to implement the findings. In all cases, however, the research model, its steps and the way research moves from the first to the last step remain relatively the same. The steps of the research model presented in this chapter and the political–ideological boundaries are wide enough to allow for adjustments required to fit the criteria of the various theoretical perspectives.

Key concepts

Research model	Processing
Research steps	Reporting
Research preparation	Focusing
Bounding	Design
Conceptual frameworks	Execution

PART II Data collection

5

Initiating social research

1 Introduction

In our discussion so far we introduced some theoretical and practical issues to familiarise the reader with the framework of social research, the varieties of thought in this area, the problems and issues related to it, the methods researchers use to measure reality and, finally, the manner in which research is carried out. It was shown there that social research is a diverse and pluralistic enterprise and that research is best carried out in the form of a more or less systematic process, which can be presented in the form of a model.

In the last part of that discussion we saw that the research process begins with the selection of the research question, followed by the selection of the methodology. The steps that follow have the purpose of securing the respondents and the data, and lead to establishing the material required to address the research question.

In this chapter we shall concentrate on that part of the research process related to the foundations of a project, namely the process of initiating the study. This process includes three elements, namely the selection of the research topic, the selection of the research methodology and the theoretical and methodological preparation of the research topic. In the following, we address these three issues in turn.

2 Selection of the research question

One of the first steps the investigator has to take is to choose the research question; this is a methodological necessity: no research can be undertaken unless the research question is chosen and accurately and clearly defined — it deserves serious consideration.

Choosing and formulating a research question is not the prerogative of quantitative research only. In qualitative studies, formulating research questions is a central element of research and while in some cases it may precede construction of the conceptual framework of the study, in other cases it may follow it. In all cases, it makes the theoretical assumptions in the framework more explicit, and most of all it indicates what the researcher wants to know *most* and *first*; formulating questions represents the facets of an empirical domain that the researcher most wants to explore (Miles and Huberman, 1994).

Mayntz *et al.* (1978) (see also Selltiz *et al.*, 1976; Puris, 1995) note that there are at least three major questions associated with the selection of the research topic that deserve some attention and which the researcher must be aware of, namely (1) what can be studied in a research project, (2) who decides about the selection of the research topic, and (3) what are the factors that influence the decision to study a certain research question. Let us briefly look at these three points in turn.

a   The nature of the research question: what can be studied?

Practically, social scientists can investigate any social issue. The research topic can be related to individuals, groups, ideas, ideologies, attitudes and opinions, structures and processes, methods and practices, and causes and effects of social events. Units of study can be taken from any level, that is, from the individual to individual level, individual to group level, or group to group level. A research project might operate on one or more levels.

The only restrictions relate to issues of researchability, feasibility, relevance and ethics. *Relevance* relates to whether the study of the research topic is relevant to the purpose of the study, for example to solve problems and show avenues for appropriate action. *Researchability* refers to whether the research topic is approachable methodologically. Topics that do not lend themselves to methodological scrutiny, such as whether there is a God or whether there is life after death, are not suitable and cannot be studied empirically. While research can approach the perceptions people have of God or life after death, a direct empirical study of the existence of these issues is not possible. *Feasibility* relates to whether the researcher has the means and resources to complete the study. *Ethics,* finally, refers to whether the proposed study is ethically justifiable and follows ethical standards and principles in its design, execution and application of the findings.

Any topic that is relevant, researchable, feasible and based on ethics can be studied. Nevertheless, it must be borne in mind that of these four factors only the second and third are directly relevant to the question *What can be studied?* Obviously topics that are not relevant or are not based on ethical standards can be studied. There are two levels of rules regarding what researchers should study: one relates to what researchers *can* study, and the other refers to what researchers *should* study. Both sets of rules are important, although the former seems to generally receive more attention than the latter.

b   The right to make the choice: who chooses the research question?

The researcher
Generally it is taken for granted that the right to choose the research topic rests with the investigator, who generally investigates issues that lie in the

area of his or her personal expertise and interests. These interests might be related to external factors, such as salary, prestige, promotions, advancement of knowledge or improvement of social conditions (extrinsic motivation); or to internal factors, such as the research issue *per se* (intrinsic motivation).

The social reality

This view is not shared by some critical theorists who believe that research has a social function, which must be carried out irrespective of the personal preferences and interests of the investigator. It is argued here that the researcher is a part of community life and is guided by the needs of that community. For these critics, the choice is governed by social conditions and the needs of society, and the researcher has a responsibility to research issues dictated by social reality.

In practical terms, researchers are expected to select a research topic that is socially significant and requires serious attention, even if they are not personally interested in it. To make such a choice possible and rational, it has been suggested that a team of experts compile a list of issues in order of priority, to be investigated in that order (Mayntz *et al.*, 1978).

The sponsor

Practical circumstances and working conditions also play an important role in selection of the topic. Many researchers work for employers, who, in turn, determine the research topic. Contract research does not allow freedom of choice in this area; in certain cases the researcher is employed for the purpose of investigating a topic that has already been chosen.

c Selection in a social context

A number of factors usually affect the choice of a certain research question by the researcher or his or her employer. These factors may be of a practical or theoretical nature; others may be guided by personal views and interests. Some of the factors affecting the selection of a research topic are the following (Bailey, 1982; Becker, 1989; Puris, 1995):

- *Financial restrictions* Limited funds might favour the selection of a topic that does not require expensive procedures to study. The availability of 'social premiums' are thought by many researchers (Singleton *et al.*, 1988: 68) to have a significant influence upon the decision regarding the topic to be studied.
- *Time* Time restrictions may force the researcher to opt for research topics that can be studied in a short period of time, avoiding topics that may require years of preparation and work.
- *Availability of assistants and experts* If assistants are available the researcher can choose a complicated issue to study; otherwise the selection may be restricted to easily studied approachable issues.
- *Methodology* Each methodology is appropriate for studying certain issues. If the sponsor or the researcher supports a theoretical paradigm which is associated with a definite methodology, the selection of the research topic will be biased by this.

- *Politics and personality*   These factors motivate some researchers to choose only topics that are in accordance with their beliefs and standards and to avoid those topics or aspects of topics that are against their ideology and values. Personal preferences and academic specialties of the researchers partly influence the choice of the research topic. A religious academic is more likely to research religious issues than an atheist; a Marxist is more likely to research the contradictions of the capitalist system than a non-Marxist; and a feminist is more likely to study the role of women in modern families than a non-feminist. On the political side, research topics that are not favoured by those providing the funds, by interest groups or publishers are avoided by social investigators.
- *The need for data*   Researchers are normally compelled to study areas which need first-hand information, and do not carry out research in areas that are well researched and in which knowledge is well advanced.

d   Basic questions

After the research topic has been chosen, the investigator usually explores further methodological issues related to the researchability of the topic and related factors. The extent of such an exploration depends on factors related to the nature of the topic; nevertheless, some questions are thought by writers (e.g. Koenig, 1978; Mayntz *et al.*, 1978; Puris, 1995) to be important in this context. Examples of such questions are given below:

- *Is the topic researchable?*   Whether or not a topic is researchable is a question that has been answered differently by the various schools of thought. For some theorists any question is researchable; others are more cautious about making such statements. Moreover, while some issues might not be researchable through quantitative methods they might be researchable through qualitative methods. Further, while a topic might not be approachable through direct observation it might be researchable through indirect questioning. In any case, the researcher is expected to explore this issue carefully before embarking on a research project.
- *What is the research unit?*   Before entering the next section of the research, the researcher should know exactly what the research unit of the study will be. 'Research units' are quite often defined very differently; thus the researcher should make it clear from the outset that the research will deal with a certain unit, in a certain context, and having certain specific characteristics. It is important to stress that this is the unit the investigator will refer to when conclusions, statements or generalisations are made at the end of the research.
- *What is the level of research?*   Defining the research unit helps to establish the level of the research. It should be made clear at this stage what level the research objective is related to, namely whether it is (1) first-level research, that is, the relation between individuals, (2) second-level research, that is, the relation between individuals and groups, or (3) third-level research, that is, the relations between groups. An investigation may be carried out on more than one level. It is the task of the researcher to define these levels adequately during the first step of the research process.

- *Objectivity*   For some writers the issue of objectivity might be considered irrelevant. Nevertheless, the position of the researcher regarding objectivity should be made clear at the outset. If measures to preserve objectivity have been taken, these should be stated. If objectivity was considered to be irrelevant this should be made known, in order to allow the reader of the research report to judge the research effectively and to evaluate the 'usefulness' of the findings and their generalisability.
- *Code of ethics*   Ethical issues should be considered at all stages of the research process, and measures taken to guarantee that the respondents will not be affected in any way by the research or the publication of the findings.

3   Selection of the research methodology

a   Introduction

The extent to which identification and definition of concepts and variables will go depends on many factors, but the underlying methodological frame-work is the most important. For this reason, it is imperative that at this stage the researcher defines and outlines clearly the type of methodology that will guide the research project. In some cases just stating that the investigation will be based on a quantitative or qualitative framework might suffice. In other cases more information may be required.

As stated earlier (Chapter 2), many investigators devise their methodological framework by combining elements of both major methodologies and establish an approach that cannot be explained by simply referring to a methodology. In such cases more information is required to inform the reader or critic of the underlying assumptions, standards, rules and principles that guide the research and the expectations associated with the study.

In most cases, the definition of the methodological framework will begin with a reference to the methodology closest to the investigation (e.g. qualitative or quantitative); beyond this, researchers often explain more details of their approach by demonstrating their bias — explicitly or implicitly — towards a critical, Marxist, feminist or positivist framework.

It is important to note that bias regarding the methodological framework or its purpose is an inherent element of any study; nevertheless, it should not be hidden but expressed openly so that the research does not suffer from hidden subjective motives of the investigator, and the readers are not misled in any way. Explaining the basis of the project offers a better understanding of the research, and allows a clear, just and valid interpretation and assessment of the findings.

Whether the methodological framework will be quantitative or qualitative, whether the orientation of the framework will be critical, empowering or descriptive, and whether the definition of the framework will be general or specific and detailed depends on many factors, some related to the research object and others to the theoretical perspective that dominates the thinking and operation of the researcher. We already know that any decision is acceptable and legitimate, if it is justified in terms of methodological standards; and in this sense there is no right or wrong methodological framework.

Finally, it must be stressed that the choice of the methodological framework must be made very early in the research process, because that choice affects the direction, structure and process of the whole project. It is usually made after the choice of the research object, but in many cases it is chosen even before that, when, for instance, researchers employ only one major methodology. It must be kept in mind that the research process is not divided into distinct steps and stages separate from and unrelated to the other parts of the study. The research process is to be perceived as a dynamic process, each part of which affects the others in some way and to some extent.

b   Quality criteria

It has already been discussed earlier in the book that social research can be carried out in the context of a quantitative or qualitative study and that the employment of either type of research is equally legitimate. Here the question is no longer about whether one methodology is better than the other; nor is it about their merits or deficiencies. Rather it is about which methodology is most suitable for the project.

In many cases no option is available since researchers usually work within the context of one methodology only, and employ only the methods of their preferred choice. Nevertheless, for others this choice is an issue, to decide upon. In either case, a systematic research project will contain a statement defining the type of methodology employed and in most cases a justification for such a choice.

Normally, the choice of a suitable methodology is directed by theoretical and methodological principles. The nature of such principles has been studied by sociologists and methodologists, who have taken a position on this issue and have produced a set of criteria that generally guide that choice. Berger *et al.* (1989: 152), for instance, propose that the choice of a methodology is influenced by:

- the appropriateness of the method for the theoretical goals;
- the adequacy of the method for the research object;
- the realisation of methodological rules which determine its structure, possibilities and limitations; and
- the examination of the prerequisites and conditions which must be considered for the performance of mathematical–statistical tests.

Similar suggestions were made also by Drew and associates (1996: 162) who suggest that qualitative methods are employed when researchers seek to understand how people make sense of their environment and the factors and conditions which shape their lives (Drew *et al.*, 1996; Bogdan and Bilkin, 1992). The important point here is that the choice of methodology is not left up to the personal preference of the researcher or methodological convenience, but rather is based on factors related to the nature of the research topic, the structure and composition of the population, the type of information sought, the perception of reality and the availability of resources: the choice has to be made on theoretical and methodological principles.

In a wider context, and with regard to the choice of qualitative versus quantitative research, Flick and colleagues (1991) suggest that a choice in favour of the former is made under the following conditions:

- When the standard of knowledge in the area of the research subject is inadequate and provides no sound basis for a quantitative study, for example for defining the research question, familiarising oneself with the research environment, operationalising the variables, etc. The qualitative research takes here the form of an exploratory study.
- When there is a need to study reality from the inside rather than from the outside, that is, to understand it from the point of view of the subject.
- When the study object is too complicated and complex and a quantitative method is of little use. It is argued here that quantitative methods are simplifications of the qualitative methods, and can only be meaningfully employed when qualitative methods show that a simplification of identified relations is possible (Kleining, 1991). Consequently, an exploratory qualitative study can provide clues about the research environment and the issue in question, and can on the one hand make quantitative research possible, and on the other guide it towards more realistic goals.
- When there is a need to capture reality as it is, that is, in interaction.
- When the researcher intends to present the information gathered not in numbers or formulae but, rather, verbally, in a detailed and complete form.
- When the researcher wishes to approach reality without preconceived ideas and prestructured models and patterns.
- When the investigator perceives researcher and researched as elements of the same situation and the research process as a whole unit.
- When the researcher wishes to capture the *meaning* and the regularities of social action

It must be stressed that for many investigators qualitative research is neither a stepping stone to nor a servant of quantitative research. The reasons stated above show clearly that a qualitative study is in many cases undertaken for the same reason a quantitative study is carried out.

4   Formulation of the research question

So far we have explored the choice of methodology and choice of the research topic. The next step is to see how the research topic is to be 'prepared' in order to be approached methodologically. In some cases this 'preparation' or formulation might be very simple or even not necessary at all. This is the case, for instance, in qualitative research, where definitions are usually achieved during the research and not stated before it starts.

In quantitative research, the formulation of the research topic can be very complex indeed, and involves, as we shall see later, very complicated methods and very sophisticated procedures. During the process of formulating the research topic, additional information is gathered to clarify the object of study and to organise the research project. In particular, this step aims: to refine the research question, to make it more specific and to prepare it for investigation; to develop a framework for the research project; and to link the research question with research methods and procedures.

More specifically, while formulating the research topic the following points are being considered:

• Definition of the topic and associated variables
• Exploration
• Operationalisation
• Formulation of hypotheses

Quantitative researchers usually consider all the above five points to be important, although to a different degree. Qualitative researchers are somewhat interested in the first three points; apart from this, they seem to approach these points in a more unstructured and general manner than do quantitative researchers. Miles and Huberman (1994), for instance, state that research questions can be general or particular, descriptive or explanatory. They can be formulated at the outset or later on, and can be refined or reformulated in the course of the fieldwork, a practice not encouraged in quantitative research. In the next sections of this chapter, these five points are examined further.

5   Definition of the topic

After the research question is chosen the researcher will proceed with defining the topic and its related variables. The definition employed depends on a number of factors, of which the type of methodology is important. Quantitative researchers usually define the topic accurately and specifically; qualitative researchers prefer to define it loosely and in general terms. Nevertheless, both will define their topic clearly enough in order to make their study object clear, explicit and distinguishable from other objects.

For example, if the research question is about the *influence the family has on delinquency*, quantitative researchers are expected to explain what they mean by both 'family' and 'delinquency', and define these concepts accurately. In doing so, the researcher will not necessarily develop a new definition for each concept, since there are many and well-accepted definitions for both concepts. However, since there are many types of families and of delinquency, the researchers will specify the kind of families they intend to investigate. Will, for instance, one-parent families, *de facto* families, reconstituted families, extended families, migrant families, city families or country families be included in the study?

It is also necessary in this context that researchers state their perception of the family. For instance, they might define the family as a group consisting of a man, a woman and a number of children living together under the same roof. It is possible that the family is defined as a man and a woman who are legally married and who live together with their children. Although other types of definitions are possible, the investigator cannot deviate significantly from the generally accepted definitions of the concepts being considered.

When defining the topic, researchers may reduce the topic significantly. They might, for instance, reduce the family into 'families in which at least one partner was born outside Australia', 'families with children under five years of age', 'white Australian families', or 'families with teenage children'. Quite frequently, researchers begin their definition with the statement 'for the purpose of this study we define family as . . .' and describe in this way the type of units they intend to deal with in their study.

In a similar fashion, the researcher will define 'delinquency' and 'influence'. These definitions are expected to be specific enough to enable the researcher and the respondent to differentiate between the issues in question and other matters that are excluded from the study; furthermore, the researcher will have to employ the defined terms uniformly throughout the study. If, for instance, the family is defined as a group consisting of a man and a woman legally married to each other and who live with their children, who live in Griffith, New South Wales, this definition has to be employed throughout the whole study and when conclusions are made. These families might be quite different from other Australian families (e.g. due to the high proportion of Italian migrants), and should not be taken as representative or typical for all Australian families. The reader should be frequently reminded that the concept 'families' in this study refers to Griffith families, and not to all Australian families in general.

As stated earlier, especially with regard to quantitative studies, defining the topic makes it concrete and specific and more understandable and in doing so the study is 'prepared' for an effective methodological operation to follow. The topic in the previous example 'Family and delinquency' might read, after the definition: 'Children of working-class families and delinquency rate (property crimes)'. At this stage in the research process, both concepts (family, delinquency) are clearly defined, and have become concrete and specific.

The process of defining the research question is predominant in quantitative research. In qualitative investigations, definitions are loosely structured, and it is expected that during the study more information will be collected that will help to refine concepts and define them more clearly in a more concrete and specific manner. The more information gathered and the more respondents included in the study, the clearer the definitions become. It must be kept in mind that qualitative researchers are interested in people's interpretations of objects and events, and this includes definitions.

6   Exploration

a   Introduction

Some exploratory work is undertaken in any study, irrespective of its methodological framework or its purpose. In some cases this work is elementary, and serves as a guide for the formulation of hypotheses and/or for the operationalisation of the concepts. In other cases, exploration is a major part of the research study. The latter is, for instance, the case in certain forms of qualitative research.

Most frequently, exploratory studies are carried out when there is not sufficient information about the topic and, thus, the formulation of hypotheses and the operationalisation of the question are difficult or even impossible. More specifically exploration is undertaken for the following reasons (see, for example, Becker, 1989; Selltiz *et al.*, 1976; Puris, 1995):

- *Feasibility* In the first place, exploration will show whether a study on the issue in question is warranted, worthwhile and feasible. If this is not the case, the main study will be abandoned.
- *Familiarisation* Exploration will familiarise the researcher with the social context of the issue in question, with details about relationships, values, standards and factors related to the research topic, its theoretical framework, and with methods.
- *New ideas* An exploratory study may help to generate ideas, views and opinions on the research object, which will help in the construction of an effective research design.
- *Formulation of hypotheses* In this context, exploration may show whether variables can be related to each other, in what way and to what degree.
- *Operationalisation* Here, exploration can help to operationalise concepts, by explaining their structure and by identifying indicators.

It must be noted that exploration in qualitative research often constitutes — as we shall see later in detail — a full and independent study, rather than a prelude to quantitative research.

b   Types of exploratory studies

Exploratory studies can take many forms, depending on the nature of the main study, the purpose of the research, the study object, the state of knowledge in the area of investigation and more specifically on the purpose of exploration. As a prelude to a quantitative study, Selltiz *et al.* (1976), when talking about exploration, refer to the following forms:

- review of available literature;
- expert surveys; or
- analysis of case studies.

Most projects employ more than one type of exploratory study, with literature research being predominant. This constitutes also the first step of exploration, when more types of exploration are employed. Library research or literature review will determine whether additional exploration is required and, if so, what type of exploration will be necessary.

Literature review

This involves a secondary analysis of available information already published in some form. It can be a study of the research object alone, with the aim of collecting information about its structure, process and relationships, increasing the familiarity of the researcher with the research object and establishing the credibility of the project.

In addition, it can consider previous research, attempting to link it with the study currently planned. It may also be geared towards a historical or comparative analysis of the issue in question so that the current study can be placed in a historical context. Finally, it may review a theory or the methods and techniques most suitable for the study, simply by looking at the ways other researchers have approached the topic, and by evaluating their suitability and effectiveness.

The methods employed when undertaking literature reviews are diverse and are known as *documentary methods*. These methods will be discussed later in this volume.

Expert surveys

Expert surveys involve interviews with experts who have substantial knowledge and experience in the research area, although their findings might not have been published yet. This unpublished information is quite often very relevant to the research object, and can only be obtained through such interviews. How surveys are conducted will be discussed later in the book.

Case studies

Selltiz *et al.* (1976), when writing about this third type of exploratory studies, referred to 'insight stimulating examples' and were cautious about distinguishing between this type of exploration and case studies in general. Nevertheless, case studies can be helpful as an avenue of exploration.

When information collected through literature review and expert surveys is insufficient, or when qualitative research is employed, researchers collect first-hand information through case-study research. Single cases relevant to the issue are selected and studied, in order to collect information for the main study.

It must be noted that case studies as a concept can be a research model as well as a method of data collection. The former is more appropriate for qualitative studies; the latter is mostly used as a prelude to quantitative research in the context of exploration. Both types of case-study research will be discussed later.

7   Operationalisation

a   Operationalisation in quantitative research

For the quantitative researcher, operationalisation is a very useful and also indispensable tool. It is employed in most studies in some way, and to some degree it helps to establish an accurate definition of the variables to be considered in the study. Try, for instance, to investigate with some degree of objectivity and accuracy love, patriotism, morale, oppression, ambition, pride, motivation, esteem, joy, anxiety, temperament and learning ability without employing some form of operationalisation. Even concepts such as social class are difficult to operationalise, given that they incorporate elements such as wealth, education and occupational status (Ellis, 1993).

Definition

The notion of operationalisation is based on the principles of *operationalism* developed in the nineteenth century, which suggests that a concept is identical with its measurement; for example, intelligence is identical with the IQ measurement. Operationalisation is thus the process of converting concepts into their empirical measurements, or of quantifying variables for the purpose of measuring their occurrence, strength and frequency. It is employed when concepts are vague, unclear or abstract, thus involving a process of translating abstract concepts into synonymous empirical referents; it contains three major elements:

1 *Selection of indicators*, which reflect the presence or absence of the element the researcher has set out to measure.
2 *Quantification of the indicators*, that is, identification of the continuum of values the indicators can assume, and *assignment of scores* that represent the degree of presence or absence of the concept or variable.
3 *Quantification of the variable*, that is, identification of the continuum of values the variables can assume, and assignment of scores, as above — here, for the main variable.

Rules of operationalisation

The basic rules of operationalisation are associated with the selection and quantification of the empirical referents, and are as follows:

• The *rule of empirical relevance*, which suggests that indicators should adequately reflect the concept they set out to measure. Empirical referents should measure one concept, the whole concept and only this concept. Indicators should be synonymous with the concept.
• The *rule of correspondence,* which proposes that indicators correspond fully to the concept.
• The *rule of empirical adequacy*, which states that indicators should have the capacity to measure all aspects of the concept adequately.
• The *rule of quantification*, which suggests that uniform quantification procedures should be employed when indicators and the variables are quantified.

Example A: Assume we are to study *class* in a small country town. The intention of the study is to find out how the community is divided into classes, and how the various classes compare to each other, by employing quantitative methods. The question arises about how to measure class so that a relatively accurate estimation of the classes in the town is achieved.

There are many ways of operationalising class. One such way, and also the most common, is described below:

1 *Selection of the indicators*   The following indicators reflect the basic characteristics of class: income, education and occupation. Here measurement will concentrate on identifying the respondent's income (personal income or family income), level of education and occupation.

2 *Quantification of the indicators*   Each indicator will be ranked from low, through moderate, to high, and numerical values will be given to each point, ranging from 0 to 9, for example. The pattern of quantification will be held uniform for all indicators. We shall see later that each indicator will be translated into a number of questions and each question will provide the required information for the quantification expressed in general or average scores. If a respondent obtained, for instance, for the indicators of class the scores 6, 4 and 3, this person would have obtained a general class score of 4.3.

3 *Quantification of the variable*   The procedure employed in the previous step will also be employed when quantifying the variable (class). Its continuum will be ranked from low to high (0 to 9); the values 0–3 may indicate low class score, 3.1–6 middle class and 6.1–9 upper class. In our example, the average class score of 4.3 will be taken to indicate middle class.

Operationalisation makes it possible to compute a score for each indicator (e.g. income, education and occupation) and for class as a whole. This allows the researcher to differentiate between the various types of class and to obtain an overall impression of class in the country town.

In most cases, the transition from the variable to the indicators is simple and direct. Class is one such example. Educational achievement and sociability are additional examples. In the former the indicators will be scores achieved in the central areas of study; in a primary school environment, this may be the scores in, say, English, maths and social studies. In the latter, indicators may include number of friends, number of visits received from friends, club membership, etc. There are, however, cases in which the transition from variables to indicators is more complex than that. The variable may include many areas which deserve special consideration, and which require special attention, definition and analysis. In such cases, these areas must be taken into account before indicators are chosen. These areas are usually referred to as *dimensions* and *contexts*. Dimensions refer to aspects of the variable; contexts refer to the areas in which the variable is measured.

An example of variables with dimensions is *alienation.* Studies from the USA, for instance, divide alienation into five dimensions, namely powerlessness, meaninglessness, normlessness, social isolation and self-estrangement. Each of these dimensions will be studied carefully and a number of indicators will be chosen from each of them. Powerlessness, for instance, may be measured in terms of indicators such as control, decision making and so on. With regard to contexts, alienation can be measured in at least five contexts, namely polity, economy, education, religion and family. Since the five dimensions of alienation can be measured in each of the five contexts, 25 combinations can be identified in this study, such as political powerlessness, economic normlessness or religious self-estrangement.

Another example of a complex variable that requires a more elaborate treatment is religiosity. Researchers have, for instance, identified the following dimensions, namely religious beliefs, religious practice, religious emotions, religious understanding and religious effects. The contexts in which religiosity can be employed are similar to those mentioned above for alienation, but it can be expanded to include contexts such as mass media and peer groups.

Choosing indicators
The most difficult part of operationalisation is the selection of the indicators. This is due to the nature of the concepts and indicators. It is quite often difficult to define concepts clearly and to translate them into empirical referents which are synonymous with and cover all aspects of the concept.

Indicators are selected in many ways. In some cases they are chosen by means of *theoretical principles*, in other cases through *speculation*. In both cases it is assumed that a relationship between concepts and their empirical equivalents exists. *Experience* is another source of indicators. *Analysis* of real definitions is still another. However, the most secure way of choosing indicators is to use *exploratory studies*, especially case-study analysis based on primary experience with respondents. For instance, if one wanted to study religiosity, and wished to select the relevant indicators, a qualitative study of a small part of the population, looking at what is generally considered in that community to be 'religious', and what makes a person 'religious', 'non-religious' or 'anti-religious', should reveal valid information and be an invaluable guide to selection.

b   Operationalisation in qualitative research

Qualitative researchers do not employ operationalisation. Instead, when there is a need for creating such concepts *sensitising concepts* are used. The general view of operationalisation is that it is an inadequate research instrument; many researchers point to a number of deficiencies. Most critics of operationalisation (see, for example, Lamnek, 1988) refer to the following problems:

- *Inadequacy* Operationalisation is often based on common sense, and therefore it does not link concepts with reality but rather concepts with other concepts, leaving reality untouched; it is considered an inadequate way of approaching reality.

- *Incompleteness*   Operationalisation does not and actually cannot cover all aspects of the concept in question just by using existing knowledge. If there were sufficient knowledge about the concept there would have been no need for research. As a result, operationalisation can only cover some aspects of the concept.
- *Subjectivity*   The structure of operational definitions often depends on the personal understanding of the researcher. For this reason the same concept can be operationalised in many different ways by the various researchers. Such forms of operationalisation may be of little use.
- *Concept and scores*   Quite often, concepts are taken to be equivalent to the scores of tests arrived at through operationalisation (e.g. IQ scores and intelligence), an assumption that is not always true.
- *Timing*   Operationalisation is completed before the research has started. For this reason, instead of explaining and enriching the concepts in question, it reduces the options of the research and limits its scope. Concepts are not explored through the 'researched' but through the researcher, before the study is completed. One proceeds from theoretical concepts to empirical data, not from empirical data to theoretical concepts. Operationalisation is conducted too early in the research process.
- *Validity*   Due to these problems the validity and reliability of the whole study is questionable.

c   Value of operationalisation

Although for many qualitative researchers the best operationalisation is *no operationalisation at all*, for quantitative researchers operationalisation remains as significant as ever. In general, and in the context of what was said above, operationalisation is an indispensable tool of quantitative research, but its methodological significance should not be overestimated. One should remember that operationalisation is valuable only if used properly, aiming at establishing ideal structures and offering operational definitions that approximate the concepts included in the study. The results obtained through operationalisation should finally be interpreted in the context of the indicators used.

8   Formulation of hypotheses

a   Introduction

After variables are operationalised the researcher will proceed to formulate one or more hypotheses. The purpose of formulating hypotheses is to offer a clear framework and a guide when collecting, analysing and interpreting the data. In many cases hypotheses serve as a testing tool of the relationships between variables. In this sense, a hypothesis contains a possible solution to the research problem, and as such is expected to be verified or falsified (accepted or rejected) by the evidence gathered by the study.

Quantitative and qualitative researchers employ hypotheses in a different form and for a different purpose. While the former see hypotheses as a step towards research, the latter perceive hypotheses as emerging out of the research. In the following section we shall refer to hypotheses as employed by quantitative researchers. The place and purpose of hypotheses in qualitative research will be explained later on in this book.

A hypothesis is *an assumption about the status of events or about relations between variables*. It is a *tentative explanation* of the research problem, a possible outcome of the research, or an *educated guess* about the research outcome. And while some methodologists suggest that any logically justifiable assumption can be formulated into a hypothesis, others add that such an assumption should be scientifically justifiable, and created on the basis of sufficient theoretical or empirical evidence.

b   Criteria of hypothesis construction

Hypotheses can be in any form except in the form of a question. Nevertheless, they have to meet a number of standards, listed below. While some method-ologists are convinced that all these criteria should be met, others require that only a few of these conditions are necessary. In general, hypotheses are required (see, for example, Bailey, 1982; Becker, 1989; Selltiz *et al.*, 1976) to demonstrate the following characteristics:

* to be empirically testable, that is, they can be empirically proven right or wrong;
* to be clear, specific and precise;
* to contain statements that are not contradictory;
* to describe variables or establish a relationship between variables;
* to describe one issue only.

Hypotheses can be formulated in a

* *descriptive* or *relational* form; in the former they describe events, in the latter they establish relations between variables;
* *directional, non-directional* or *null form*, depending on whether or not they make a concrete suggestion about the research question.

c   Generating hypotheses

Hypotheses are generally translations of research questions and can be generated in many ways. They can be developed, for instance, through existing theories; they can be based on social policy, research findings of other studies, evidence, commonly held beliefs, intuition and the findings from exploratory studies especially designed for this purpose (Selltiz *et al.*, 1976).

Table 5.1   An example of a State doctrine regarding hypotheses

A scientifically justified hypothesis or a system of hypotheses must meet the following criteria:

- They must correspond to the world view of the principles of historic and dialectic materialism.
- They must be formulated on the basis of the approved theoretical position of the Marxist–Leninism sociology.
- They must consider the experiences won so far by the relevant branch of sociology.
- They must accurately reflect the approved relevant sociological facts which are known to them.
- They should not be in contradiction with approved relevant statements of other scientific disciplines.

The ideology of the researchers and their personal preferences, interests and convictions quite often dominate the structure as well as the direction of the hypothesis. While State rules and political doctrines are not important in Australia, they are of paramount importance in some countries. Table 5.1 contains an extract from a methodology text published in 1989 in the German Democratic Republic (now a part of Germany) (Berger *et al.*, 1989: 68). It must be noted that this methodology text was approved by a relevant committee of professors in sociology, who acted as referees for the validity and accuracy of the text. The significance of the above statement and its representativeness for the sociological and methodological practice in this country is shown in the opening statement of the editors in the preface of the book (p. ix), which in a free translation reads as follows:

> This handbook presents the experiences of social research which have been systematically employed for more than a quarter of a century in the German Democratic Republic.

d   Nature of hypotheses

Hypotheses cannot be described as true or false; they can only be relevant or irrelevant to the research topic. If we were to study, for instance, the effects of education on religiosity, a relevant hypothesis would be that 'high education is associated with low religiosity'; equally possible would be the following hypotheses: 'education is adversely related to religiosity'; 'education is positively correlated with religiosity'; and 'there is no relationship between education and religiosity'.

e   Types of hypotheses

There are many forms and types of hypotheses, mainly depending on their structure, goals and nature. A few examples of types of hypotheses are described briefly below.

Working hypotheses
This type of hypothesis is understood and used by researchers in various ways. In general, researchers see a working hypothesis as a preliminary assumption about the research topic, particularly when there is not sufficient information available to establish a hypothesis, and as a step towards formulating the final research hypothesis. Working hypotheses are used to design the final research plan, to place the research problem in its right context, and to reduce the research topic to an acceptable size.

Statistical hypotheses
A statement or set of statements developed by means of statistical models related to a probable distribution of certain criteria of the population, characterised by the use of parameters and/or statistics, is referred to as a statistical hypothesis. Statistical hypotheses are used as a part of the process of verification, lend themselves to statistical testing, and are expressed in the context of a null hypothesis and an alternative hypothesis. Statistical testing should prove whether a statistical hypothesis is accepted or rejected.

Research hypotheses
This is a general concept to describe the hypothesis used in a study, without reference to its particular attributes.

Null hypotheses (H_o)
This is one of a set of two hypotheses (the other is the alternative hypothesis) formulated by the researcher to be used in the context of hypothesis testing. A null hypothesis might state, for example, that all differences identified between samples are by chance and caused by the sampling procedures; or that all samples stem from the same population and that their means are equal.

Alternative hypotheses
This is one of the set of two hypotheses referred to above (the other is the null hypothesis), which states the opposite of the null hypothesis. In statistical tests of null hypotheses, acceptance of H_o means rejection of the alternative hypothesis; and rejection of H_o means similarly acceptance of the alternative hypothesis.

Scientific hypotheses
These refer to hypotheses containing statements based on or derived from sufficient theoretical and empirical data.

f   Formulating hypotheses

In the form of a model, the process of formulating a hypothesis may start with developing working hypotheses, which are then gradually upgraded to research hypotheses and finally translated into statistical hypotheses (null hypotheses and alternative hypotheses). The collection of relevant data will then allow statistical testing and show whether the research hypothesis is accepted or rejected. In qualitative research, data collection and analysis is expected to provide data that will lead to formulating hypotheses and strengthening their theoretical and conceptual basis.

g   Functions of hypotheses

In summary, in the context of a quantitative study, hypotheses are expected to fulfil at least one out of three major functions:

1 to guide the social research, by offering directions to its structure and operation;
2 to offer a temporary answer to the research question;
3 to facilitate statistical analysis of variables in the context of hypothesis testing.

h   Critique of hypotheses

Although not mandatory, hypotheses are being used very widely in the context of quantitative methodology. It is argued that any study needs a hypothesis; even descriptive studies can benefit from the formulation of a hypothesis.

This position has been criticised by other researchers who argue that hypotheses make no positive contribution to the research process. On the contrary, they may bias the researchers in their operation (e.g. data collection, data analysis and interpretation); they may restrict their scope and limit their approach, and may, finally, predetermine the outcome of the research study.

Qualitative researchers, apart from stressing the criticisms mentioned above, argue that although hypotheses *per se* are important tools of social research, they must not precede the research but rather result from an investigation.

Despite these criticisms, many investigators employ hypotheses in their research, implicitly or explicitly. It is generally believed that hypotheses offer a guide only, and tend constantly to remind the researchers of their topic, their aim and their limits, and help in this way to rationalise the research process by concentrating on the important aspects of the research topic by avoiding peripheral and less significant issues.

9   Summary

The step that deals with the initiation of the research project contains elements which assist the researcher to make the research topic clear and specific, and to convert it to a form that will allow detailed measurement. This is more so for quantitative studies, but the basic elements of this process are found also in qualitative research. The points which are covered during this step of research are as follows:

1 Choosing the appropriate methodology; this will be either quantitative or qualitative.
2 Choosing the research question, that is, the topic that will be investigated.
3 Defining the variables.
4 Conducting exploratory research.
5 Operationalising the variables.
6 Formulating hypotheses.

This step of the research process is very significant. The success and value of the research outcomes will depend very much on the accuracy and effectiveness of the tasks which are completed during this step.

Key concepts

Exploration	Statistical hypotheses
Case studies	Alternative hypotheses
Empirical relevance	Expert surveys
Working hypotheses	Indicators
Null hypotheses	Hypotheses
Literature review	Research hypotheses
Operationalisation	Scientific hypotheses
Empirical adequacy	

6

Sampling procedures

1 Introduction

One of the most significant issues investigators have to consider when designing a project concerns the type and number of the respondents who will be included in the study. A number of very important questions have to be answered, such as: Will the whole population or a sample be studied? If sampling is preferred, which sampling procedure is most suitable? How large should the sample be? Is there a sampling frame required? If yes, is one available? How representative should the sample be? How will possible problems, errors, distortions be prevented? What kind of administrative arrangements are required for the frictionless completion of these sampling procedures? Are the required time, funds and staffing available and, if so, how can they be rationally employed? How is non-response going to be dealt with in the study? Are there any issues of ethics and objectivity to be considered at this stage, and how will such requirements be met?

The answers to these questions are diverse. One might opt for a *complete coverage* of the population (*saturation survey*), whereby all units of the *target population* (i.e. the units for which the information is required) will be studied. In this case the target population is also the *survey population* (i.e. the units actually studied).

In general terms, sampling enables the researcher to study a relatively small number of units in place of the target population, and to obtain data that are representative of the whole target population. In most cases, however, researchers opt for an incomplete coverage, and study only a small proportion of the population, a *sample*. *Sampling* is, thus, the process of choosing the units of the target population which are to be included in the study.

a Reasons for sampling

Opting for a sample survey is guided by a number of factors. The following are most common (Becker, 1989; Selltiz *et al.*, 1976):

- In many cases a complete coverage of the population is not possible.
- Complete coverage may not offer substantial advantage over a sample survey. On the contrary, it is argued that sampling provides a better option

since it addresses the survey population in a short period of time and produces comparable and equally valid results.

- Studies based on samples require less time and produce quick answers.
- Sampling is less demanding in terms of labour requirements, since it requires a small portion of the target population.
- It is also thought to be more economical, since it contains fewer people and it requires less printed material, fewer general costs (travelling, accommodation, etc.) and of course fewer experts.
- Samples are thought to offer more detailed information and a high degree of accuracy because they deal with relatively small numbers of units.

b   Problems of sampling

Despite these positive qualities, sampling is associated with problems. Two of the most common objections to sampling are that:

1 sampling procedures require more administration, planning and programming than saturation surveys;
2 sample studies may not be as valid as saturation surveys.

Despite these problems, sampling offers many advantages, which make it a standard procedure of social research.

c   Principles of sampling

Samples are expected to be representative. For that reason, samples are expected to be chosen by means of sound methodological principles. With regard to quantitative research, the following are the most important (see Selltiz *et al.*, 1960, 1976):

- Sample units must be chosen in a systematic and objective manner.
- Sample units must be easily identifiable and clearly defined.
- Sample units must be independent of each other, uniform and of the same size, and should appear only once in the population.
- Sample units are not interchangeable; the same units should be used throughout the study.
- Once selected, units cannot be discarded.
- The selection process should be based on sound criteria and should avoid errors, bias and distortions.
- Researchers should adhere to the principles of research (discussed in the introductory part of the book).

2   Types of sampling

There are basically two types of sampling, random or probability sampling and non-probability sampling.

Probability (random) sampling
This employs strict probability rules in the selection process: every unit of the population has an equal, calculable and non-zero probability of being selected for the sample. It allows computation of accuracy of selection and offers a high degree of representativeness; however, the method is expensive, time consuming and relatively complicated since it requires a large sample size, and the units selected are usually widely scattered.

Non-probability sampling
This method is less strict and makes no claim for representativeness. It is generally left up to the researcher or the interviewer to decide which sample units should be chosen, and is employed in exploratory research, observational research and qualitative research.

3   Probability sampling

The majority of social researchers employ probability sampling for several reasons, but especially due to its high reliability, degree of representativeness and high generalisability of the results. Probability sampling is employed in many forms. Simple and systematic random sampling are two types of probability sampling widely employed by social researchers either as the only sampling procedure or as part of other types of probability sampling. These two types and the forms they appear in will be presented below.

a   Simple random sampling

This type of sampling gives all units of the target population an equal chance of being selected. The sample units are selected by means of a number of methods of which the following are the most common.

The lottery method
Choosing respondents by the lottery method follows a procedure that can be described in the following steps:

Step 1
Identify or construct a *sampling frame*, that is, a list of the units of the target population. Such frames are, for instance, the electoral role, student records, rating records, etc. and include names and addresses of sample units in alphabetical order and numbered accordingly.

Step 2
Substitute names listed in the sampling frame for numbered marbles (or discs) so that each marble corresponds to a name from the sampling frame. All marbles are placed in an urn.

Step 3
Mix well and remove one marble from the urn. The number of this marble is registered and the corresponding name in the sampling frame is ascertained. This is the first respondent. The marble is returned to the urn or is left out (both methods are legitimate). This process is continued until the required number of respondents is reached. If an already drawn number is selected for a second or third time it is ignored.

Example A: Assume that we are interested in the attitudes of university students to feminism, for which a sample of 500 students is required. Using the lottery method the sample is chosen as follows:

1 From the university administration, a list of the names of all students (this is the sampling frame) arranged in alphabetical order, numbered and containing the addresses of the students is obtained.
2 An urn with as many numbered marbles as the number of students on the list, for example 6000 marbles numbered from 1 to 6000 for 6000 students, is obtained.
3 The marbles are mixed and the first marble drawn. If the number on that marble is 679, the name on the list that corresponds to that number is identified and recorded, together with the address and telephone number (if required). This process of drawing and recording names is continued until the number of recorded names has reached 500, that is, the required sample size.
4 The 500 names drawn constitute the sample which will be studied in this survey.

The random numbers method
This method is similar to the lottery method, except that the urn and marbles are replaced by tables of random numbers, which are available in separate publications or in the appendix of texts on statistics.

Example B: A small table of random numbers

9212	7120	5909	8020	2904	1949	3612	1450
3740	0200	7686	1842	2704	0964	6901	9455
9686	1832	5865	3240	9695	1418	5218	9572
8024	7323	1312	7240	0103	7208	0192	7911
1780	9028	7233	1358	2466	8896	7509	1452
1410	0860	0371	2392	8227	3417	2625	8204
2385	8166	6914	0475	1253	9421	6835	2116
4245	1735	5180	1466	8932	1309	1972	2816
2621	0735	4709	2177	0067	0536	1785	1728
1535	6150	1712	0177	1621	1838	2032	9329

Choosing the sample by using the random numbers method involves the following:

Step 1
A sample frame is identified or constructed as in the lottery method.

Step 2
Appropriate tables of random numbers are selected.

Step 3
Numbers are picked from the tables randomly and registered; the names in the sample frame corresponding to these numbers constitute the sample.

> *Example C*: We use the same example as shown in the lottery method, but we prefer to select the sample by means of random numbers; we proceed as follows:
>
> 1 A list of all students' names (from the sampling frame) is obtained, numbered and ordered accordingly.
> 2 A list of random numbers that contains all numbers included in the sampling frame is used. If, for instance, there are 6000 students on the list, the list should contain numbers up to 6000. Such lists are readily available in various forms, sizes and number combinations.
> 3 Pointing randomly with a finger or pencil at the list of random numbers, the number that is under the finger or the pencil point is recorded.
> 4 The name on the student list that is next to that number is identified. This is the first respondent. This process is continued until the required number of students is achieved.

The computer method
This is similar to the methods described above. It only differs in the second step, whereby the urn or table of random numbers is replaced by a computer; instead of seeking numbers through the urn or the list of numbers we instruct the computer to give us a set of numbers, for example 500 numbers ranging between 1 and, say, 6000. Obviously this method is more convenient and less time consuming than the previous methods. This makes the computer method the preferred option particularly when dealing with large numbers. The selection of the respondents through this method is as follows:

Step 1
A sampling frame is identified or constructed.

Step 2
The computer is instructed to print randomly x numbers (as many as the sample units), to be selected randomly between the numbers 0 and n (n being the number of units in the target population and sampling frame).

Step 3
Identify the names which correspond to the numbers chosen by the computer. These are the subjects of the study. (See Example D at the top of page 144.)

Other methods
A number of additional techniques have been devised to identify respondents. In most cases, these methods employ the techniques described above. The difference lies in the criterion used to select the respondents from a sampling frame. The following techniques are common.

Example D: The sample of the 'students and feminism' study is to be selected by the computer method; we proceed as follows:

1 The appropriate sampling frame (which might contain 7000 students) is obtained.
2 The computer is instructed to randomly select 500 numbers from 1 to 7000.
3 The respondents are identified as in the previous examples.
4 These respondents constitute the sample for the study.

Birthday

When the birthday is used as a criterion of selection, all those subjects born on a certain date are chosen. The identification of the respondents will follow one of the methods mentioned above. Here the use of computers makes the selection very easy. Needless to say, the choice of the birth date (e.g. July, 5 May) must adhere to the rules of random sampling.

First letter

Here, the choice of the subjects is decided on the basis of the first letter of the first name, or last name, or a combination of both. For example, the sample may include all respondents whose surname begins with P and their first name with L. The identification of the respondents is accomplished as above, in the context of a sampling frame and according to the rules of probability.

PIN number

In this method respondents are chosen on the basis of the personal identification number (PIN), which must, of course, be available in the sampling frame. The researcher might decide, for instance, to include in the study all those whose number begins with or ends in 3, or whose first number is 5 and third number 9, and so on. The personal identification numbers must be listed in an objective manner; the choice of numbers may be done by means of one of the methods presented above.

b Systematic sampling

Systematic sampling and simple random sampling differ in that in the latter the selections are independent of each other; in systematic sampling the selection of sample units is dependent on the selection of a previous one (Moser and Kalton, 1971: 83).

The population units are specially prepared and the sample selected in a *systematic* way by means of various techniques, of which the sampling fraction method is very common.

When the *sampling fraction method* (symbolised by k) is employed, samples are drawn from a sampling frame on the basis of the sampling fraction that is equal to N/n, where N is the number of units in the target population and n the number of units of the sample. For instance, if the target population is 4800 and the intended sample size 600, the sampling fraction is 8 (i.e. 4800/600 = 8).

To select a sample by using the sampling fraction method, the following steps are followed:

Step 1
Identify or construct a sampling frame.

Step 2
Compute the sampling fraction k (as above, $k = N/n$).

Step 3
Randomly select a number between 0 and k. (In the above example, since $k = 8$, the random number would be between 0 and 8.)

Step 4
Identify all numbers between 0 and N that result from adding k to the random number. The process is repeated until N is reached. For example, if the random number is 6 and k is 8, the numbers are 6, 14 (6 + 8), 22 (14 + 8), 30 (22 + 8), etc.

Step 5
Locate the names on the sampling frame that correspond to the numbers drawn above.

Step 6
These names correspond to the respondents who constitute the sample.

c   Stratified random sampling

This is a special form of simple or systematic random sampling, in which the population is divided into a number of strata and a sample is drawn from each stratum. These subsamples make up the final sample of the study.

The division of the population into strata is based on one or more criteria, for example sex, age, economic status and so on. The sample size can be *proportionate* or *disproportionate* to the units of the target population. For instance, the target population (consisting of equal numbers of males and females) may be divided into two strata, for example males and females. Then, if a proportionate stratified sample is drawn, 5 per cent from each group may be taken. If the researcher decides for a disproportionate sample, 5 per cent of males and 10 per cent of females may be taken.

A stratified sample is employed when there is a need to represent all groups of the target population in the sample, and when the researcher has a special interest in certain strata. In this sense, the method is very economical, offers accurate results and a high degree of representativeness, and is very useful.

A stratified sample is drawn in the following way:

Step 1
First the target population is divided into a number of strata according to the number of the significant groups in the population.

Step 2
The sampling frames for each of these groups are identified; if not available, relevant sampling frames must be developed.

Step 3
Employing one of the methods discussed above, a sample is drawn from each group. This can be proportionate or disproportionate to the number of units in the population.

Step 4
The individual samples are merged into one; this constitutes the sample for the study.

Example E: We were asked to study the attitudes of our community to the government's foreign aid policy. In order to include in the study all ethnic groups, stratified sampling was chosen. To obtain the names of the respondents, we proceed as follows:

1 Sampling frames are identified or prepared for each ethnic group living in the community.
2 A decision on whether proportionate or non-proportionate stratified sampling should be employed is made.
3 The number of subjects to be chosen from each ethnic group is determined. This can be 60 per cent for Australians, 20 per cent for Italians, 15 per cent for Greeks and 5 per cent for Germans.
4 One of the methods discussed above (e.g. the lottery method, random numbers, sampling fraction) is used to choose the subsamples (i.e. separate samples from each ethnic group).
5 The subsamples are merged into one sample.

---

d   Cluster sampling

Cluster sampling is a popular sampling method and is employed primarily:

• when no sampling frame is available for all units of the target population;
• when economic considerations are significant; and
• when cluster criteria are significant for the study.

Characteristic of this sampling method is that first groups of elements (clusters) are selected (schools, classes, etc.) and then individual elements are selected from these clusters. To choose the clusters and the respondents from the clusters one of the methods discussed above can be employed.

Caution: Cluster sampling is biased by the fact that the respondents come from a specialised population group (dictated by the choice of clusters) and may not, for that reason, represent the whole spectrum of the population.

Example F: We are interested in the attitudes of NSW secondary school teachers to last year's national wage policy, and we wish to study these attitudes by means of a survey. The sampling procedure is cluster sampling in order to allow school teachers from as many parts of Australia as possible to be included in the study. To compile the sample we proceed as follows:

1 A list of all NSW secondary schools is constructed (sampling frame), or such a list is obtained from the Department of Education if available (and if accessible).
2 The number of schools required for the study is determined by employing appropriate standards.
3 Schools are chosen from the sampling frame by means of one of the sampling methods introduced above (the lottery method, sampling fraction, etc.).
4 The number of teachers required for the study is determined and then divided by the number of schools to determine the number of teachers to be chosen from each school (proportionate or disproportionate numbers to be considered).
5 The sampling frame is ascertained for each school, and the required number of respondents chosen using one of the methods introduced above.
6 The sum of all teachers chosen this way constitutes the sample.

e   Multi-stage sampling

In this method, a sequence of samples is drawn from samples already selected but only the last sample of subjects is studied. In all other aspects the multi-stage sampling is similar to the simple or systematic sampling.

The main advantage of this sampling procedure is that it allows the establishment of a sample that is directly related to the research object. With every additional drawing, the sample becomes more specific and more relevant to the research question, and the results are expected to become equally relevant and more representative.

The process of choosing a sample through the multi-stage sampling method proceeds as follows (see Moser and Kalton, 1971):

Step 1
A sampling frame for the target population is identified.

Step 2
A large probability sample is chosen; the units of this sample are usually referred to as *primary selection units*. A sample from the primary selection units is then chosen.

Step 3
After the criteria of the respondents have been identified, another sample is drawn from within the previous sample. The procedure is repeated until the targeted sample size is reached.

Step 4
The last drawing constitutes the sample of the study.

Example G: We are to study the attitudes of Australians of Asian origin to sex education of primary school children, by using multi-stage sampling. To obtain the sample we proceed as follows:

1 A list of Asian immigrants is obtained from any possible source (such as Department of Immigration, Asian Club or electoral roll).
2 From this list a large number of respondents (say, 2000) are chosen.
3 The respondents are screened with regard to certain socially significant criteria; a sampling frame is then developed according to these criteria, and 600 respondents are chosen.
4 These respondents are further screened for relevant criteria, and a new sampling frame is developed on the basis of these criteria.
5 These respondents are further screened (not studied) to identify additional relevant criteria, and a sampling frame is developed on the basis of these criteria.
6 From this sampling frame, say, 25 per cent (150), or any other proportion, of suitable respondents are chosen. These respondents constitute the final research sample.

f   Area sampling

Area sampling is multi-stage sampling applied in geographical areas. In this case, the sample of the study is the final-stage sample drawn in a series of samples taken from geographical areas where each stage refers progressively to smaller and more concrete areas, for example state, region, city, suburb, street, household. In addition, this method is a form of cluster sampling related to areas as clusters.

This procedure takes into consideration the fact that respondents are widely spread geographically and attempts to rectify this problem by considering areas as the clusters of selection. Such a method guarantees that an equal representation of respondents from as many geographical areas as possible will appear in the study.

Example H: We are interested in the views of country Australians on hospital-bed shortages, and the sample is to be area sampling. In this typical case, area sampling starts as follows:

1 A sampling frame of country towns is established; by means of the sampling methods discussed above a number of towns (say, 25 per cent of the towns on the list) are drawn.
2 The chosen towns are divided into suburbs, and, say, four suburbs from each town are chosen randomly.
3 The streets in each chosen suburb are identified and five streets from each suburb of the chosen towns are chosen.
4 The households on each of the chosen streets are now identified. This constitutes a sampling frame of thousands of households.
5 From this sample the required number of households are randomly chosen, using one of the sampling methods introduced above.
6 The sample will include the heads of all households chosen in the last drawing.

g   Multi-phase sampling

The process of unit selection in a multi-phase sampling procedure is the same as in multi-stage sampling. First, the primary selection units are chosen. Then a sample is drawn from these units and so on. However, in a multi-phase sampling procedure each sample is adequately studied before another sample is drawn from it. Consequently, while in multi-stage sampling only the final sample is studied, in multi-phase sampling all samples are researched. This offers an advantage over other methods, because the information gathered at each phase helps the researcher to choose a more relevant and more representative sample.

Example I: We are interested in the division of labour among homosexual couples in Sydney. The sampling procedure is to be multi-phase sampling. To compile the sample we proceed as follows:

1   A sampling frame of homosexual persons living in Sydney is constructed, and 5000 units are randomly chosen.
2   These respondents are studied with regard to their relationships and presence of young children.
3   Of these respondents, 1000 having a permanent partner and at least one child living in the same household were chosen randomly.
4   After studying these couples, 150 lesbian and 150 gay couples are chosen. This stratified sample will be the final sample used to study the division of labour among homosexual couples.

---

h   Panel studies

Longitudinal research is characterised by the fact that it employs a sampling procedure in which the respondents of the original sample are studied on more than one occasion. In general, the sample contains the same respondents who are interviewed every year for a period of five years, for instance, or before and after the occurrence of certain significant events. This form of longitudinal research is known as *panel studies*.

Longitudinal studies appear also in another form, known as *trend studies*. In this form, the research is repeated several times as above, using the same methods and instruments, but different samples are studied at each stage of the project.

Longitudinal research is employed when the investigator is interested in changes or just continuity over time, or in recognition and examination of patterns of behaviour (Minichiello *et al.*, 1990: 202). In this sense, the method has many advantages over other forms of sampling, particularly with regard to facilitating comparisons over time as well as precision and economy in procedure. It is, however, affected by a number of problems that must be kept in mind. Writers (see, for example, Bailey, 1982; Stergios, 1991) suggest that the following problems must be kept in mind when using panel studies; they are related to:

- convincing respondents to take part in the study;
- motivating respondents to fill in relevant questions accurately, especially those of a personal and sensitive nature;
- maintaining the same structure and same criteria at each stage;
- avoiding or minimising drop-outs;
- mortality, migration and change of residence;
- preparation of data;
- panel conditioning, whereby respondents become gradually interested in the research study, learn more about it and can, in this way, cause distortions in the research findings.

Nevertheless, this is a very useful method, and is widely used by social scientists all over the world in the context of industry, household studies, service industries and sociological and psychological studies.

Example J: In an effort to understand better the changes that occur in attitudes towards living in old people's homes, we decided to study a number of Australians at various periods of time. The sampling panel study was constructed as follows:

1 A sample of 250 55 year olds was chosen and studied with regard to whether they thought old people should be encouraged to live in old people's homes.
2 Five years later, the same old people were studied again on the same issues.
3 Another five years later the same respondents were studied when they were 65 years old and aged themselves, and their responses were compared point by point with those obtained previously. This allowed the researcher to ascertain whether attitudes towards aged care changes with increasing age, and with changed circumstances.

i Spatial sampling

This is a method of sampling people temporarily congregated in a space. A typical example of how this method operates would be as follows: A number of interviewers approach the crowd (e.g. in a mass demonstration in the city square) and choose their respondents randomly and in a systematic way, for example by walking three steps into the crowd and interviewing the person on their right. This process is then repeated until the interviewers have walked through the crowd. The people interviewed in this way constitute the sample of the study.

Example K: In a sit-in at the University of NSW students occupied the main administration building and refused to leave. The Department of Sociology quickly decided to study the reasons for participating in this sit-in and the type of students joining such a demonstration. The sampling procedure was as follows:

1 Ten interviewers were lined up in the front of the room where students were gathered.
2 As instructed, interviewers addressed the person who happened to be in front of them, and asked the study questions.
3 Then, each moved five steps forward and approached the person who was now in front of the interviewer.
4 They proceeded in the same way until they reached the back of the classroom.
5 The students interviewed constituted the sample for the study.

4   Non-probability sampling

Non-probability sampling procedures do not employ the rules of probability theory, do not claim representativeness, and are usually used for exploration and qualitative analysis. Some of these techniques can, with some adequate 'treatment', be converted into probability methods. The accidental sampling, the purposive sampling, the quota sampling and the snowball sampling are examples of non-probability sampling techniques; they are presented below.

a   Accidental sampling

This type of sampling is employed in qualitative research and in other studies where representativeness is not an issue. It is also known as 'convenience sampling', 'chunk sampling', 'grab sampling' and 'haphazard sampling'. When this sampling technique is employed, all units for study that the researcher accidently comes in contact with during a certain period of time are considered. The investigator might stand at a street corner, in front of a shopping centre or at a university entrance and interview a certain number of persons passing by between, say, 11.00 and 12.00 o'clock on certain days of the week.

Such samples are easy to construct and evaluate. Nevertheless, they are not representative of the whole population. However, in studies where this sampling procedure is employed, representativeness is not significant.

Example L: The local chamber of commerce in a small country town wanted to study the reasons for people shopping in the four large supermarkets. The sampling procedure was accidental sampling. They proceeded as follows:

1 Two interviewers were positioned at the door of each supermarket with the instruction to address 100 women passing by with relatively full shopping trolleys, asking them the relevant questions.
2 The completed forms were to be returned to the researcher on the same day for evaluation.

b Purposive sampling

In this sampling technique (also known as judgemental sampling) the researchers purposely choose subjects who, in their opinion, are thought to be relevant to the research topic. In this case, the judgement of the investigator is more important than obtaining a probability sample.

The process of sampling in this case will involve identification of the informants and arranging times for meeting them.

> *Example M*: A researcher is interested in studying the problems of migrant groups in a particular community. In order to study these problems it is decided to interview key informants, for example the local priests, club secretaries and functionaries of ethnic welfare groups. In the view of the investigator, these persons offer more valid and useful information than would interviewing the migrants.

c Quota sampling

Quota sampling is a version of stratified sampling with the difference being that instead of dividing the population into strata and randomly choosing a number of respondents, it works on 'quotas' set by the researcher. It is a non-random stratified sampling procedure.

In simple terms, the researcher sets a 'quota' of respondents to be chosen from specific population groups, by defining the basis of choice (gender, marital status, ethnicity, education, etc.) and by determining its size (e.g. 60 parents of toddlers; 35 policewomen; 66 teachers and so on). The choice of the actual respondents is usually left up to the interviewer.

The way quotas are determined varies, depending on a number of factors related to the nature and type of research. For instance, the researcher might advise the interviewer to survey 50 female students who will attend the next Monday methodology class and 50 male students who walked out of the student union immediately after 5 pm on the last Friday of June; or 100 fathers who attend the local Baby Health Clinic immediately after 9.00 am on the next Monday. The choice is left to the interviewer or left up to chance (as in the last sample).

Another way of determining the quotas is based on more strict procedures. One such method is by choosing respondents according to their proportion in the entire population. For instance, if the study is about attitudes of ethnic and non-ethnic Australians to youth homelessness, and the respondents are to be chosen by means of quota sampling, the investigator, after considering the composition of the population, may decide that of the 400 respondents required for the study 104 should be ethnic and 296 non-ethnic Australians.

In another form, quota sampling considers all significant dimensions of the population and ensures that each dimension will be represented in the sample. This is usually referred to as *dimensional sampling* and is used particularly when the sample is small. In such cases, this procedure guarantees that at least one case from each dimension of the population will be included in the sample.

Quota sampling is quite common in the social sciences because it is less costly than other techniques, does not require sampling frames, is relatively effective, and can be completed in a very short period of time. It is, however, limited, especially with respect to representativeness, control of sampling and fieldwork requirements. Problems of abuse and bias caused by the interviewer, who may turn to the first available, convenient and least resistant person, are hard to avoid. However, quota sampling is normally not meant to be a random procedure, and should not be expected to provide random data.

Example N: The Australian Health Commission is interested in identifying the state of health of workers employed in mining industries around the country. Instead of going through the process of compiling sampling frames in each industry, and then choosing the respondents, the researcher decides to use quota sampling. The researcher proceeds as follows:

1 Interviewers are sent to each major mining industry.
2 The interviewers are told to study 10 workers aged below 20; 10 workers aged between 21 and 30; 10 aged between 31 and 40; 10 aged between 41 and 50; 10 aged between 51 and 60; and 10 aged over 60.
3 The interviewers are told to interview the same proportions of workers employed in these industries for more and for less than two years.

d Snowball sampling

In this type of sampling researchers begin the research with the few respondents who are available to them. They subsequently ask these respondents to recommend any other persons who meet the criteria of the research and who might be willing to participate in the project. If and when such respondents are recommended, the investigator approaches them, collects the information required and asks them to recommend other persons who might fit the research design and be willing to be studied. This process is continued until the topic is *saturated*, that is, until no more substantial information is achieved through additional respondents, or until no more respondents are discovered.

Example O: This method was employed during a study of *de facto* relationships in Australia, Germany and Greece. The sampling design was as follows:

1 A number of cohabiting couples identified through a family study carried out previously were interviewed.
2 These respondents were asked to recommend other cohabiting couples.
3 After these new couples were interviewed, inquiries for further cohabiting couples were made, and additional respondents were secured.
4 This process was continued until the topic was *saturated*.

This method is employed when the lack of sampling frames makes it impossible for the researcher to achieve a probability sample, when the target population is unknown, or when it is difficult to approach the respondents in any other way.

5 Sampling procedures in qualitative research

It has quite often been argued that qualitative researchers do not use sampling procedures. This is not correct. It is more accurate to say that they employ sampling procedures that correspond to the philosophy of this type of research, and that are less structured, less quantitative and less strict than the techniques quantitative researchers employ.

Normally, qualitative studies employ a form of non-probability sampling, such as accidental or purposive sampling (Kuzel, 1992), as well as snowball sampling and theoretical sampling. Qualitative sampling is biased by the nature of the underlying qualitative framework, which is perceived as an investigative process, not very different from detective work, where 'one makes gradual sense of a social phenomenon, and does it in large part by contrasting, comparing, replicating, cataloguing and classifying the objects of one's study' (Miles and Huberman, 1994). Sampling here comes after factors and conditions become clear and directive, and making decisions about sampling before the study has begun is neither proper nor useful.

Nevertheless, qualitative research has no strict agreed-on rules of sampling employed by all researchers. Sampling procedures employed by qualitative researchers are those mentioned above (accidental, purposive, snowball sampling and so on) or a version or combination of quantitative sampling procedures. In all cases, sampling is closely associated with theory. It is therefore either theory-driven 'up-front' (Miles and Huberman, 1994: 27), where subjects are chosen before data collection, guided by theory or, progressively, during data collection. The latter is known as *theoretical sampling* and is connected with grounded theory.

For some researchers theoretical sampling is a new concept. This form of sampling has been very well established in the context of grounded theory, and is characterised by the fact that the collection of data is controlled by the emerging theory (Burgess, 1984; Strauss, 1991), in that the researcher has constantly to look for new units and data, and justify the theoretical purpose for which each additional group is included in the study.

The researcher who employs theoretical sampling will continue adding new units to the sample until the study has reached a saturation point, that is, until no new data are produced through inclusion and analysis of new units.

Irrespective of the type of sampling chosen, several sampling parameters have to be considered before a qualitative study can begin. Although qualitative sampling is a function of the research process itself and is decided on while the research is in progress, depending on the outcome of the study, researchers do have to decide at the outset at least about a number of issues, such as the informants or respondents who will be studied, the setting where research will take place, the events and processes to be considered in the investigation, and the time when research will be conducted. In any case, sampling procedures in qualitative research are inevitably related to a number of issues and choices.

Qualitative researchers have to make a choice at some stage about the *kind of people* (actors) who will be included in their study, particularly since the number of subjects in these studies is very small. If they intend, for instance, to study the quality of life of single fathers in Broken Hill, they have to decide whom they will include in their study, at least whom to begin with. Given that the number of lone fathers can be larger than the intended sample, a choice is inevitable.

Equally inevitable is the choice of *time*. Qualitative researchers will have to decide whether to contact their respondents on working days, on weekends, during the school holidays, in summer or winter, in the afternoons, in the evenings or any other time. Choosing the 'right' time is important and has significant effects on the results.

Apart from this, the qualitative researcher will make a choice about the *kind of event* or *processes* to be studied, namely whether it will be a routine event, a special event, an unexpected event or all types of events. In any case, making a choice is inevitable.

Finally, a choice regarding the *setting* in which the research will be conducted (the home, the club, the work place, a friend's house, etc.) has to be made.

The sampling procedures employed by qualitative researchers demonstrate a number of characteristics; many writers (e.g. Berger *et al.*, 1989; Lamnek, 1988; Miles and Huberman, 1994) note that qualitative sampling is directed:

- not towards large numbers of respondents but rather towards *typical* cases;
- not towards fixed samples but towards a sample that is flexible in size and type or subjects;
- not towards statistical or random sampling but towards purposive sampling;
- not towards 'mechanical' sampling but towards *theoretical sampling*;
- towards fewer global settings than quantitative sampling;
- not towards choosing a sample before the study has started, but (often) while the study is in progress;
- not towards a strictly defined size but a sample whose number will be adjusted while the study is in operation;
- not towards representativeness but rather towards *suitability*.

As stated earlier, the range of qualitative research has significantly widened in scope and purpose during the past 10 years, allowing researchers more choice than before. It is interesting, then, to see Miles and Huberman note that qualitative sampling 'puts flesh on the bones of general constructs and their relationships' (1994: 27), or that 'just thinking in sampling-frame terms is healthy methodological medicine' (1984a: 41).

Table 6.1 Quantitative and qualitative sampling: a brief summary

Quantitative sampling	Qualitative sampling
Is relatively large	Is relatively small
In most cases it employs statistics	In most cases it employs no statistics
Is often based on probability theory	Is often based on saturation
Allows no researcher bias in selection	Allows researcher influence in selection
Its size is statistically determined	Its size is not statistically determined
Occurs before data collection	Occurs during data collection
Involves complex procedures	Involves simple procedures
Its parameters are fixed	Its parameters are flexible
Involves high costs	Involves very low costs
It is time consuming	It is not time consuming
It is representative	It is not representative
It is laborious	It is easy
It treats respondents as units	It treats respondents as persons
Facilitates inductive generalisations	Facilitates analytical generalisations

6 Non-response

The various types of sampling enable the researcher to identify the respondents who will be included in the study. In most cases the sampling procedures will result in a list of names and addresses to be used at a later stage in order to approach the respondents. In other cases sampling will bring the researcher or the interviewer face to face with the respondent.

Despite efforts made by the research personnel to contact the respondents selected through the sampling methods, several subjects will not be able to be contacted or suitable. Research experience shows that some respondents will not be at home at the arranged time; others will be unsuitable due to inability to communicate; while others will have moved away, and others will simply refuse to cooperate. A certain number of respondents will remain unavailable even after intensive efforts on the part of the researcher. How will the investigator compensate for this loss of subjects? Can they be ignored? Can equivalent or similar subjects be taken from the same area as a substitute for the unavailable subjects?

There are various answers to these questions. Some theorists suggest that the best way of meeting this problem is prevention. This means that the researcher should test the response rate of his or her study by means of pilot studies, estimate the expected drop-out rate and take a sample that is larger than the required sample, that is, large enough to compensate for the expected non-response rate. This method, however, causes obvious problems which cannot be justified methodologically.

Some researchers prefer to ignore the non-respondents and to proceed with the rest of the sample. The underlying justification for this is that the missing units are thought to be similar to those who responded, and the study is not affected by the lost units. This seems to be a popular way of responding to the problem, especially if the response rate is relatively high and if the necessary steps for reducing the non-response have been followed, but again this is not without problems.

The suggestion to ignore the non-respondents has been criticised by many methodologists who believe that such a device has negative effects on the results. Missing respondents are often different from those who responded, and for this reason the study consciously excludes a significant part of the target population. Their view is that non-respondents should not be left out. Some suggest that they have to be substituted, in a manner similar to quota sampling, whereby the researcher advises the interviewer to select extra respondents who are similar in certain characteristics to the non-respondents. Others suggest that the substitute respondents should be similar to those who responded after the second or subsequent reminder. In any case, for these researchers substitution seems to be imperative once all possible methods of approaching the original respondents have been fruitless.

Non-response is a research problem, but it can be solved with some degree of success if the research has been planned accurately and systematically.

7   Sample size

The question about the right sample size in quantitative research is one that concerns not only the beginner but also any social investigator. In simple terms it refers to basic questions such as: How large or small must the sample be for it to be representative? Is 10 per cent of the population sufficient? Are 300, 900 or 2000 respondents required?

Obviously the answers to these questions vary with many factors. In the first place the notion of representativeness might be questioned; do you need a representative sample? Can you even achieve representativeness? Apart from this, the views of the researchers vary, with some arguing that the ideal sample size can be estimated in general qualitative terms while others see statistical procedures as the proper method.

a   Non-statistical estimations

For a number of investigators sample size is related to the nature of the population as well as the type of analysis employed in the project. For many researchers, a minimum of 100 subjects is required to allow statistical inferences; but this is not always correct. Many statistical measures are designed for samples smaller than 30. Similarly the nature of methodology is important. In qualitative studies, theoretical sampling does not resort to numerical boundaries to determine the size of sample; instead, subject selection will cease after saturation has been reached. Similarly, when purposive sampling or accidental sampling procedures are used, it is left up to the researcher to decide when a number of respondents is considered sufficient, since actual numbers are not of primary importance for the study. In these cases, the sample size is evaluated in the context of the study, on the basis of criteria and theoretical principles not known to the researcher at the beginning of the investigation, or, even if they are, not dependent on the number of subjects considered. In such cases, representativeness relates to quality rather than quantity, and generalisations are associated with quality rather than with quantity.

Nevertheless, there are cases in which investigators are interested in quantitative aspects of their study and wish to select a sample that will be representative of the target population. In such cases, standards applied to estimate the 'correct' sample size are derived from statistical operations and procedures as we shall soon see. However, in many cases estimates are based on different criteria and on factors associated with the type of population, the type of methodology employed, the availability of time and resources, the aim of the research, the type of instruments used, the accuracy required and the capacity of the research team.

More particularly, the following considerations are made:

- If the population is homogeneous with respect to the study object, a small sample may suffice; if it is found (e.g. through an exploratory study) to be heterogeneous, a larger sample may be required.
- If a high degree of accuracy is required, a large sample must be drawn.
- If the approach is qualitative the sample will be relatively small. The intensity of research employed in qualitative research, the type of questions it explores, the purpose it pursues and the methods and techniques it employs make the choice for small samples inevitable. Quantitative studies require larger samples.
- In quantitative studies, if the resources are sufficient and if adequate personnel are available, a large sample can be considered. Finally, if time is not a problem and if the research units are not widely spread, the sample can be large.

It must be stressed that large samples do not always guarantee a higher degree of precision, validity or, in general, success in a research study. The quality of the results depends on several factors and the sample size is only one of them. Nevertheless, if probability sampling procedures are employed, the sample size is expected to be large in order that claims of representativeness can be made.

b   Statistical estimations

Many quantitative researchers employ statistical methods in order to define the 'right' size of the sample. This is based on the assumption that if certain data are available, the sample size can be statistically computed so that sampling errors can be reduced to a minimum or to an acceptable or expected level. There are several methods employed by statisticians and social researchers, some of which are quite complicated and also beyond the limits of this treatise.

In general, the logic of many statistical methods relates sampling error to the standard error (S.E.): if the standard error is reduced, the sampling error is reduced also. The standard error depends on the size of the sample: with increasing sample size the standard error is decreased. Thus an acceptable standard error can be achieved by changing the sample size. This method tries to manipulate the size of a sample by increasing or reducing it, until it corresponds to a standard error that is considered acceptable. This is then the ideal sample size.

The standard error varies inversely with the square root of the sample. If, for instance, we intend to halve the standard error, we have to quadruple the sample size. Thus, if we wish to determine the sample size that will reduce sampling errors, we start with a sample size taken at random, compute the standard error and increase the sample size until the relevant standard error is at an acceptable level. This manipulation works well with small samples, where increases in sample size result in increases in accuracy (i.e. decreases in sampling error), but it does not work equally well with large samples. Above a certain point, the increase in sample size required to achieve a significant decrease in the error is so large and therefore so costly that it makes such an increase unacceptable.

In the main, the method employed depends on whether the estimation is directed towards means or proportions. In the former, investigators are interested in ascertaining trends and average scores in the area of study. For example, how large should my sample be to study the average amount of money spent by female students on alcohol per year? In the latter, researchers endeavour to estimate the proportion of people acting in a certain way. For instance, what is the proportion of female students who support affirmative action in Australia? There are statistical techniques available to help to estimate the relevant sample size in both cases.

For proportions

There are several ways of estimating sample size when proportions are investigated, some being more complicated than others. Using a simple technique, employing the following formula, seems to be popular (see Foddy, 1988: 105):

$$\text{Sample size} = \frac{pqZ^2}{E^2}$$

To estimate the sample size we need the value of p, which is a population estimate; q, which is derived by subtracting p from 100; Z, which is the value corresponding to the confidence level chosen for the study; and E, which denotes the maximum deviation from true proportions that can be tolerated in the study. The value of p is estimated on the basis of assumed parameter values, on existing knowledge or results of pilot studies; the value of Z and E are chosen freely by the investigator.

Z refers to the level of confidence, namely that our estimates are correct in 95 per cent of cases or even 99 per cent of cases, and that the risk of the estimates being incorrect are 5 per cent and 1 per cent respectively. If we are content with a 95 per cent probability, the value of Z is 1.96; but if we wish to raise this probability to 99 per cent, the value of Z is 2.57. Of course, there are more than these two options, but social researchers usually choose one of these two values.

If, for instance, we were interested in studying the proportion of female students who object to investigating police practices related to Aborigines in custody and the estimated proportion of such students was 15 per cent ($p = 15$), the value of q would automatically be 85 per cent ($q = 85$). If we opted for a

95 per cent confidence level ($Z = 1.96$) and the researcher allowed a deviation from the true population percentages that is not higher than 5 per cent ($E = 5$), the appropriate sample size is estimated as follows:

$$\text{Sample size} = \frac{15 \times 85 \times 1.96^2}{5^2} = \frac{1275 \times 3.8416}{25} = \frac{4898.04}{25} = 195.92$$

Obviously, the sample size depends on the values of factors p, q, Z and E. In general terms, the larger the product of p, q and Z, the larger the required sample; and the larger E becomes, the smaller the required sample. For example, when E is 5, the required sample size is 196 respondents; but if E is halved from 5 per cent to 2.5 per cent, the required number of respondents is increased four times, that is, from 196 to 784. This is shown below:

$$\text{Sample size} = \frac{15 \times 85 \times 1.96^2}{2.5^2} = \frac{1275 \times 3.8416}{6.25} = \frac{4898.04}{6.25} = 783.68$$

In a similar fashion, if p is 15, the required sample size is — as shown above — 196. If p is 50, and if all other factors remain the same, the required sample size is increased to 384, as shown below:

$$\text{Sample size} = \frac{50 \times 50 \times 1.96^2}{5^2} = \frac{2500 \times 3.8416}{25} = \frac{9604}{25} = 384.16$$

For means

A similar procedure is employed to estimate the sample size when the research question is related to averages, for example when it aims to estimate the average amount of time spent by males drinking, by students reading, by nurses talking to patients, or by politicians speaking in parliament sessions. Here again, if E and Z are available, and if the standard deviation of the population (σ) can be estimated, the sample size can be computed. The formula employed for that purpose is:

$$\text{Sample size} = \left(\frac{\sigma \times Z}{E}\right)^2$$

Example P: We are interested in investigating the study patterns of university students, and in particular the amount of time spent per month in reading. What is a reasonable sample size required for this study? We want Z to be set at 1.96, and if we accept an estimate that cannot be more or less than five hours from the true population mean (i.e. $E = 5$), then, employing the formula given above, we can estimate the sample size. But we still need the value of the standard deviation for the population, namely σ. This can either be estimated on the basis of existing information, or computed through data obtained by means of a pilot study. As soon as the value of σ is secured, the sample size can be estimated. With $\sigma = 50$, $Z = 1.96$ and $E = 5$, the sample size is as follows:

$$\text{Sample size} = \left(\frac{50 \times 1.96}{5}\right)^2 = \left(\frac{98}{5}\right)^2 = 19.6^2 = 384.16$$

Changes in the factors of the equation affect the sample size in the same direction as shown above for estimating the sample size for proportions, for example the larger σ is, the larger the required sample size, and vice versa. Thus, if σ is doubled (from 50 to 100), the required sample is quadrupled (from 384 to 1537), as shown below:

$$\text{Sample size} = \left(\frac{100 \times 1.96}{5}\right)^2 = \left(\frac{196}{5}\right)^2 = 39.2^2 = 1536.65$$

c Determining sample size through tables

There is an easier way of estimating the 'right' sample size, without needing to use formulae and computations. This is done by means of tables. The researcher who wishes to know how large the sample should be needs only to look at the table and, considering the necessary factors, such as *p, q*, level of confidence and so on, ascertain the figure that corresponds to the required sample size.

Such tables are many and diverse and are constructed as shown above, that is, by means of the relevant formulae, this time for every possible combination of *p, q, E* and *Z* values. The more factors considered and the more detailed the values of these factors, the more detailed and accurate the table and, unfortunately, the more cumbersome the identification of the sample size figure. In tables with many factors and factor values, for instance, one has to decide on the right factors and values, search for the right column and row and determine the required figure. When fewer factors are used the tables are easier to use but offer limited information. Such tables offer, for instance, advice about a certain *p/q* combination, one confidence level (95 per cent or 99 per cent) and one option for degree of accuracy.

Parten, for instance, published in 1950 two tables, one for the 0.05 confidence level and one for the 0.01 confidence level. The tables offer sample size estimates for dichotomous population percentages (*p* and *q*) for two levels of confidence and for error limits ranging from 0.25 to 10. They provide useful information and save time and energy when deciding about the required sample size (see Table 6.2).

Krejcie and Morgan (1970) offered an even easier table for estimating sample size. The only information needed to estimate sample size is the size of population. Consequently, their table gives figures for populations ranging from 10 to 1 000 000 people and the corresponding figures for the required sample size. This table computes the sample size by means of another formula, which takes into consideration chi-square for 1 degree of freedom, the population size, the population proportion, which is set at 0.50, and the degree of accuracy, which is set at 0.05, by using a formula developed by the research division of the National Education Association (USA), published in 1960. For those interested in the statistical expression of the definition of sample size, the formula is (see Krejcie and Morgan, 1970):

$$s = \frac{\chi^2 NP(1 - P)}{d^2(N - 1)} + \chi^2 P(1 - P)$$

Table 6.2 Estimating sample size for dichotomous percentages

Percentage and level of confidence

Limits of errors (+/−...%)	1 – 99		5 – 95		10 – 90		20 – 80		30 – 70		40 – 60		50 – 50	
	0.05	0.01	0.05	0.01	0.05	0.01	0.05	0.01	0.05	0.01	0.05	0.01	0.05	0.01
0.25	6 085	15 510	29 195	50 425	55 317	95 543	98 341	169 853	129 073	222 933	147 512	254 780	153 658	265 396
0.50	1 521	2 627	7 299	12 606	13 829	23 886	24 585	42 463	32 268	55 733	36 878	63 695	38 415	66 349
0.75	676	1 168	3 244	5 603	6 146	10 616	10 927	18 873	14 341	24 770	16 390	28 309	17 073	29 488
1.00	380	657	1 825	3 152	3 457	5 971	6 146	10 616	8 067	13 933	9 220	15 924	9 604	16 587
2.00			456	788	864	1 493	1 537	2 654	2 017	3 483	2 305	3 981	2 401	4 147
3.00			203	350	384	663	688	1 180	896	1 548	1 024	1 769	1 067	1 843
4.00			114	197	216	373	384	664	504	871	576	995	600	1 037
5.00			73	126	138	239	246	425	323	557	369	637	384	663
6.00					96	166	171	295	224	387	256	442	267	461
7.00					71	122	125	217	165	284	188	325	196	339
8.00					54	93	96	166	126	218	144	249	150	259
9.00					43	74	76	131	100	172	114	197	119	205
10.00					35	60	61	106	81	139	92	159	96	166

Source: M. Parten (1950), Survey Polls and Samples, New York: Harper and Row, pp. 314–15.

where *s* is the required sample size, χ^2 is the table value of chi-square for 1 degree of freedom (3.841), *N* is the population size, *P* is the population proportion, and *d* is the degree of accuracy.

Estimating the required sample size by using this table is just reading numbers! (See Table 6.3.) For example, to specify the required sample size you need to know the size of the target population. For a population of 260 people the suggested sample size is 155; for a population of 1600 the sample size is 310, and for a population of 20 000 the sample size is 377.

A word of caution: The statistical procedures presented above provide a handy tool for estimating the sample size required in each case when a study is to be carried out and when the sample is to be representative. Although these procedures are statistically sound, it should always be kept in mind that they relate to estimations based on assumptions and conditions, on which the estimates depend. As shown above, the sample size depends on the values of *p*, *Z* and *E*, chi-square and so on — values that are often difficult to estimate. How can we be sure, for instance, that *p* is 10, 25 or 48, or that σ is 50, particularly when our knowledge of the population is restricted? Guessing the value of the standard deviation of a population for which we intend to estimate the unknown mean is again a daring estimation. These issues must always be kept in mind when the representativeness and even validity of estimations of sample sizes are considered.

Table 6.3 Table for determining sample size from a given population

N*	S†	N	S	N	S	N	S	N	S
10	10	100	80	280	162	800	260	2 800	338
15	14	110	86	290	165	850	265	3 000	341
20	19	120	92	300	169	900	269	3 500	346
25	24	130	97	320	175	950	274	4 000	351
30	28	140	103	340	181	1000	278	4 500	354
35	32	150	108	360	186	1100	285	5 000	357
40	36	160	113	380	191	1200	291	6 000	361
45	40	170	118	400	196	1300	297	7 000	364
50	44	180	123	420	201	1400	302	8 000	367
55	48	190	127	440	205	1500	306	9 000	368
60	52	200	132	460	210	1600	310	10 000	370
65	56	210	136	480	214	1700	313	15 000	375
70	59	220	140	500	217	1800	317	20 000	377
75	63	230	144	550	226	1900	320	30 000	379
80	66	240	148	600	234	2000	322	40 000	380
85	70	250	152	650	242	2200	327	50 000	381
90	73	260	155	700	248	2400	331	75 000	382
95	76	270	159	750	254	2600	335	1 000 000	384

*N is the population size
†S is sample size

Source: R. V. Krejcie and D. W. Morgan (1970), 'Determining sample size for research activities', *Educational and Psychological Measurement*, 30, pp. 607–10.

8   Summary

Sampling is one of the most fundamental elements of research, and one that has attracted the interest of many social researchers and critics alike. In this chapter we described and explained the main elements of sampling and noted that:

1   sampling is the method of choosing the respondents of a study and one which is widely used in social research;
2   there are two major types of sampling, probability and non-probability sampling; the former is used mainly by quantitative researchers and the latter by qualitative researchers;
3   some form of sampling is employed by quantitative and qualitative researchers, although to a different extent and in a different form;
4   non-response is a serious issue and researchers make a concerted effort to reduce its occurrence;
5   investigators have developed several methods to determine the appropriate sample size, most employing statistical operations.

Having outlined the nature, types and relevance of sampling, we will now proceed to the next step of the research model, namely to the methods of data collection. In the next chapter we shall begin this discussion by exploring experiments and focus groups.

Key concepts

Saturation survey	Complete coverage
Random sampling	Lottery method
Birthday methods	Systematic sampling
Cluster sampling	Area sampling
Spatial sampling	Non-probability sampling
Snowball sampling	Longitudinal studies
Target population	Sample
Sampling frame	Random numbers
First-letter method	Dimensional sampling
Sampling fraction method	Multi-stage sampling
Multi-phase sampling	Accidental sampling
Purposive sampling	Non-response
Survey population	Sampling procedures
Simple random sampling	Computer method
Number method	Stratified random sampling
Primary selection units	Panel studies
Trend study	Quota sampling
Sample size	Saturation

7

Methods of data collection: experiments and focus groups

1 Introduction

The successful completion of a sampling procedure connects the research with the respondents and specifies the kind and number of respondents who will be involved. The investigator knows at this stage not only *what* will be studied, but also *who* to approach to collect the required information. The information will be available, provided that the right 'connection' between the researcher and the respondents is made. This connection is made through the *methods of data collection.*

The next step in the research process is therefore to choose methods that will enable the researcher to collect relevant information. The researcher has to study the available methods and their relevance to the research topic, to weigh the advantages and limitations of these methods, to consider the available resources and personnel and the nature of the research and the research topic, and finally to select the method that appears to be the most suitable and most adequate for the research project.

The decision regarding the method(s) of data collection will be influenced by many factors but the research methodology that provides the framework for the study is one of the most important. If the qualitative framework has been chosen, it is very likely that the researcher will choose unobtrusive methods of data collection, while the choice of a quantitative framework will involve methods requiring direct participation of the respondents in the study, for example the use of surveys.

In the following pages we shall explore some questions that are relevant to the type and choice of method. In the chapters that follow, we shall introduce the methods and techniques of data collection employed by social scientists. The most relevant questions in this context are first of all about the nature and type of the diverse methods of social research and about the choice researchers have to make between the various methods available to them: What are the methods of social research available to social investigators? Which methods should be employed in a particular situation?

We begin our discussion with a more general question, that is, whether qualitative or quantitative methods should be used — a question introduced, although in a different context, in Chapter 2. Here, in addition to discussing the nature of the two types of methods of data collection, we shall explore the criteria that influence the researchers' choice for one or the other type.

2   Methods in quantitative and qualitative research

In principle, qualitative methods have the same purpose as quantitative methods, namely to collect the data that will provide the basis for further thinking and operation. Nevertheless, their structures are rather different, predominantly because they are based on a theoretical basis and are geared towards a methodology which are fundamentally different.

In some cases, qualitative and quantitative researchers employ different methods. Nevertheless, in most cases, the methods employed in both research contexts are similar. Both may employ, for instance, content analysis, interviewing or observation. However, in these cases their structure and theoretical orientation are different.

It must be stressed that in principle it is not the primary nature of the method that determines its affiliation with one type of research or the other, but rather its theoretical framework and its design. One method may be designed to operate in quantitative research in one project but in qualitative research in another. For example, interviewing can be designed as a quantitative method (e.g. in the form of standardised interviewing) or as a qualitative method (e.g. narrative interviewing or intensive interviewing). Similarly, content analysis can be designed as a quantitative method or as a qualitative method.

This design assigns to methods certain attributes that change their structure and approach, places them in a theoretical framework with definite principles, standards and goals, and equips them with methodological attributes to suit the research environment in question. A number of relevant criteria stressed by writers of diverse backgrounds (e.g. Berger *et al.*, 1989; Flick *et al.*, 1991; Lamnek, 1988; Miles and Huberman, 1994) addressed in such designs are given below.

Closeness of the researcher
Methods in qualitative research are designed to bring the researcher closer to social reality and social interaction than are quantitative methods. They expect the researcher to become a part of the research environment and experience interaction as it is experienced by the respondents.

Openness of the methods
Methods in qualitative research are open in the sense that they can be changed and adjusted while they are employed and while data are being collected. This is not the case with quantitative research, where methods are standardised and fixed, leaving no options for correction and adjustment.

Flexibility of design

In qualitative research, the research design is as *flexible* as the methods, allowing for modification in order to adjust it to the data. In quantitative research the design is developed at the beginning of the project and deviations of any kind are not permitted. Such deviations are thought to cause problems and are to be avoided.

Communicative method

This refers to the nature of the research object that is about to be studied. Whether, in other words, methods are set to capture reality in *communication and interaction* (qualitative methods) rather than in an objectively defined fashion (quantitative methods).

Naturalistic methods

The important point here is about whether or not methods are designed to study interaction in the world of everyday life, as it unfolds and as it is interpreted by the respondents. In qualitative research, reality is seen as emerging from the interaction and communication of the members of the society in its natural setting.

Collection and analysis

In a number of qualitative studies, data collection is closely associated with, and takes place simultaneously with, data analysis, the one leading to and enhancing the other. In these studies, the initial steps of data analysis take place during data collection. In quantitative research, data analysis takes place only when the process of data collection has been completed.

Instrumentation

A question relevant to qualitative research is when instruments should be chosen. Whereas in quantitative research instruments are chosen before the study begins, in qualitative research instruments can also be chosen during the study. Some researchers believe that choosing methods prior to research is inappropriate and ineffective, while others argue that under certain circumstances choosing the instruments prior to the study is advisable. Miles and Huberman (1994: 35–6) argue that there are factors which speak for little instrumentation prior to the study and other factors which speak for a lot of instrumentation prior to the study; they refer also to cases in which instrumentation prior to a study is allowed under certain conditions. These factors are shown below.

Instrumentation prior to the study

Arguments for:	Prior instrumentation . . .
Little instrumentation:	. . . may blind the researcher to the site; cause important phenomena to be over-looked or misinterpreted. . . . is context-stripped; lusts for universality, uniformity and compatibility. . . . is inappropriate for single-case studies. . . . is a misnomer for fieldwork where everything unfolds during the study.

A lot of instrumentation:	. . . is appropriate if sufficient information is available about the research topic. . . . helps to avoid collection of too much superfluous information. . . . allows comparability. . . . guarantees dependable and meaningful findings and avoids collection of invalid and unreliable data.
'It depends':	Instrumentation prior to the study depends on: . . . the type of study: it can be employed in confirmation studies but not for exploratory studies, where instrumentation is loosely defined. . . . the type of site: advisable for multiple-site studies but not for single-site studies, where instruments are loosely defined. . . . the type of unit of analysis: advisable for large, multi-site units; in single-site, small research units, instrumentation is loosely defined.

Source: Miles and Huberman (1984a: 42–3; 1994: 35–6).

3   Triangulation

In general, a research design will describe the number and nature of the methods to be employed in the research project. Normally, the research will employ one basic methodology and one basic method, taken from one method-ological context, the qualitative or the quantitative. Nevertheless, it is becoming increasingly popular for a combination of methods to be employed. Quite often, researchers combine different methods of data collection, for example surveys and experiments, experiments and observation or observation and documentary methods when studying the same social issue. Such a combination of methods is called *triangulation*, a concept that has been discussed very intensively in the area of social research, and which is equally employed by quantitative and qualitative researchers.

Triangulation can be of two types (see Denzin, 1989): *inter-method tri-angulation*, which includes two or more methods of different methodological origin and nature; and *intra-method triangulation*, which employs two or more techniques of the same method. It is not unusual for researchers to employ mixed-method designs to investigate different aspects of the same phenomenon (Crawford and Christensen, 1995).

Triangulation is employed for a number of reasons. Using two methods, for instance, is thought (see, for example, Blaikie, 1988; Burgess, 1984) to allow the researcher:

- to obtain a variety of information on the same issue;
- to use the strengths of each method to overcome the deficiencies of the other;
- to achieve a higher degree of validity and reliability; and
- to overcome the deficiencies of single-method studies.

From a feminist stance, triangulation is thought to 'express the commitment to thoroughness, the desire to be open-ended and to take risks' as well as to 'increase the likelihood of obtaining scientific credibility and research utility' (Reinharz, 1992: 197).

Although the use of triangulation is generally thought to produce more valid and reliable results than the use of single methods, there are researchers who disagree. They argue that generalisations of this kind are unfounded and point to the fact that expanding the spectrum of methods employed to collect the data does not necessarily guarantee better results; it is suggested that one should also test the validity and reliability of all methods separately.

Problems and conditions of triangulation have been discussed by many writers (e.g. Blaikie, 1988; Lamnek 1988: 240; Silverman, 1985: 105–6). In addition to problems emerging from the theoretical justification of triangulation and the positivistic impression it seems to entail, there is no evidence to suggest that studies based on triangulation necessarily produce more valid results. Even if all diverse methods support each other's findings, all findings might be invalid. In simple terms, the findings of a study based on several methods are not necessarily 'better' than the findings of a single-method study. What happens if multiple methods employed in the same study produce different findings? Which method is valid? Beyond this, if methods from different methodological contexts are employed, to what extent can their results be compared?

Lamnek (1988) warns further that the use of triangulation might be associated with serious methodological problems. He argues, for instance, that:

- triangulation and single-method procedures can be equally useless if they are based on wrong conditions and wrong research foundations;
- triangulation can be used as a way of legitimising personal views and interests;
- triangulation is difficult to replicate;
- triangulation *per se* is not more valuable than a single-method procedure, which can be more suitable, useful and meaningful to answer certain questions;
- triangulation therefore is not suitable for every issue.

It is generally suggested that the number of methods that are most appropriate in each research design must be evaluated in the context of the project in question. Although expanding the spectrum of methods is desirable (Koeckeis-Stangl, 1980) one must be very careful about the value that can be given to such expansions or combinations.

4 Summary

The discussion above has demonstrated that data collection is a complex and diverse procedure, which can vary from case to case and from one methodology to another. In addition, we have seen that more than one method can be used simultaneously, coming from the same methodology or from different methodologies. This can offer a stereoscopic analysis of the issue in question and help test the validity and reliability of the methods used. Certainly, triangulation has its critics, but it is nevertheless very common.

A number of the methods which are used in social research will be discussed in the next chapters. Some of these methods are used by qualitative researchers and others by quantitative researchers or by both. Such methods are experiments, document analysis, indirect methods, observation and, last but not least, surveys, including questionnaires and interviews. These are the main channels that will provide us with the data we need to answer our research question. We begin our discussion with two traditional methods of data collection: experiments and focus groups.

A   Experiments

1 Introduction

Experiments have always been used in everyday life. Since the dawn of humanity people experimented in many ways to ascertain the best ways of coping with everyday problems and to improve the quality of their life in general. The cook experimented with various ways and ingredients to improve the quality of food, the husband or wife with various communication methods to improve the quality of marriage, the child with a number of techniques to win the attention of the mother, the teacher with various teaching methods to convey mathematical principles to mentally handicapped children more effectively, the young man with various techniques to win the heart of the girl he loves, and the businessman with a variety of methods to win the largest part of the market.

This everyday method was adopted and improved by physical scientists and it became the standard method of discovery of knowledge. From the physical sciences experiments moved to psychology, where they are still used today. They were introduced by Wilhelm Wundt (1832–1920), a German psychologist, and William James (1842–1910), an American philosopher and psychologist, and are used as much as they are used in the physical sciences. The step from psychology to sociology and other social sciences was a small one. Although experimentation is more common in psychology than in other social sciences, it is currently used by researchers of a diverse affiliation and background, and is used in a variety of forms and ways.

In this section, we shall explore experiments as a method of data collection and in particular their nature, structure, types and the process as they are employed in the social sciences. We begin with the nature of experiments.

2   The nature of experiments

Experiments are used to ascertain the presence, type and degree of a *causal* relationship between two variables. As a rule, experiments involve some degree of *manipulation* of the surroundings and an assessment of the effects of this manipulation on behaviour, attitudes, relations and so on. The aim of this procedure is ultimately to establish a causal relationship between variables.

Manipulation of the environment takes place in a very systematic form, and is based on *controlling for*, *ruling out* or *closing off* all factors except those included in the 'manipulation'. (This process is usually referred to as *closure*.) The logic behind this technique is that if a certain type of behaviour changes after the introduction of a variable, the change has been caused by this variable.

In the most elementary form an experiment consists of the following processes:

- Establishing and controlling the experimental conditions.
- Measuring the dependent variable.
- Introducing the independent variable.
- Testing the dependent variable.
- Assessing the presence and extent of change in the dependent variable.

3   Steps in experimental research

Experiments are carried out in a manner that, in principle, is no different from that employed in other areas of research. The steps of the research model presented in the introductory chapters of this book apply also in the area of experimentation. Some differences between this general model and that employed in the process of experimenting do exist in relation to the content of some steps, but only with respect to details. The stages can be described as follows:

Step 1: Selection of the topic
Experiments begin with the selection of the topic to be researched. Any topic that can be put under experimental conditions lends itself to experimentation.

Step 2: Formulation of the topic
The selection of the research topic is followed by the methodological formulation of the question. As in the general research model, concepts must be defined, variables must be chosen and operationalised, and categories established. Selection of the independent variable, that is, the causal or test variable,

and selection of the dependent variable, that is, the variable supposed to be changed or affected, are made. Finally, hypotheses are formulated.

Step 3: Research design
Experiments are designed in a number of ways, resulting in several types of experiments, which we shall discuss later in this chapter. Basically, experimental designs include decisions related to the selection of the subjects and arrangement of the experimental conditions that will guide the execution of the experiments.

Step 4: Collection of the data
Collection of the data in experimentation differs from that discussed so far. It includes a number of steps that ultimately consist of subjecting the respondents to certain conditions and ascertaining the effects that resulted from that procedure (see below).

Step 5: Analysis and interpretation
The methods of analysis employed in experiments are quantitative and concentrate on experimental conditions, on assessing the difference between pre-test and post-test results, and on statistical techniques (e.g. establishing correlation, covariation, causal relationships or independence).

In the following sections we shall look more closely at some aspects of experimental designs, examine some important elements of experimentation in more detail and compare them with those of other methods.

4   Experimental sampling

a   Characteristics of the sample

Selection of the subjects in an experimental design is usually undertaken by means of probability sampling procedures discussed earlier in this book. The experimental sample demonstrates the following characteristics:

- It includes two subsamples, namely the *experimental group* and the *control group*. The experimental group is the group that will be exposed to the independent variable; the control group is the group not subjected to the independent variable.
- The two groups must be checked for any systematic differences.
- The subjects in the experimental and control groups must be the same or similar.
- The selection of the subjects should be free from sampling bias.

These criteria indicate that sampling in experimental designs has to meet at least two conditions, namely (1) that it produces a representative sample free from bias and distortion; and (2) that it establishes two similar subsamples.

A pool of subjects or a sampling frame from which the two groups will be established is required and is usually gained in several ways. As a rule, the nature and objective of the study will indicate the area from which the subjects will be obtained. The selection will also comply with the principles of sampling introduced earlier in this book.

b   Methods of selection

There are at least three methods of sample selection in experiments (Becker, 1989; Mahr, 1995).

Randomisation
When this method of sampling is employed, subjects are selected randomly from a sampling frame and then placed in the experimental and the control group in turn. Any random sampling method can be used to assign subjects to the experimental groups, but simple random sampling is used more often than other methods. The method of randomisation is employed when the experimenter is convinced that this method will result in similar groups and that it will not affect the results of the study.

Subject matching
From a pool of eligible subjects (sampling frame), pairs of matched subjects, that is, persons with the same or similar (relevant) characteristics, are chosen. One subject is placed in the experimental group and one in the control group. This process is continued until sufficient subjects are obtained.

Group matching
In this method, pairs of matched groups, that is, groups with the same or similar characteristics (e.g. average age, education, status, achievement and performance) are chosen at the same time, with one group being placed in the experimental group and the other in the control group. The selection continues until the expected number of groups is reached. Group matching is generally employed when groups are the unit of analysis and when they are available for sampling.

Matching is a more effective sampling method than randomisation for many reasons but primarily because it assures a higher degree of similarity than other methods. Randomisation can assure that the sample is representative and that there is no experimenter influence on the choice of subjects but cannot assure equivalence and similarity of the treatment groups to the degree matching does.

It is finally worth noting that matching can be done either before data collection (*a priori matching*), or after data collection (*ex post facto matching*). The examples given above relate to *a priori* matching. Here the subjects are chosen before treatment. *Ex post facto* matching employs a multi-phase sampling procedure whereby matching is facilitated during the second or third stage of sampling, that is, when more knowledge about the nature of the subjects is gained.

c   Strengths and weaknesses

All three methods, although widely used, have their strengths and limitations. The subject-matching method is affected by the inherent difficulty in matching subjects; when similarity is the principle of selection, it is not easy to define consistently what is and what is not similar. Group matching is equally affected by this problem; in addition, the use of averages (where employed) results in individual differences not being considered. Randomisation is more objective and freer from bias than the other two methods, and is useful, especially if subject matching is not possible. But it still replaces individual judgement with 'objective' selection, and quite often it is not possible to argue that such a method guarantees the establishment of similar groups, especially when the samples are relatively small.

5   Arrangement of experimental conditions

In order to be able to make definite statements about the causal relationship between the independent and the dependent variables, the experimenter should ensure that factors other than the independent variable do not affect the dependent variable. All possible factors that could have an influence on the progress of the experiment should be controlled. Where control of these factors is not possible, the experimenter should be in a position to assess the influence of such factors and to consider their effect when interpreting the findings.

Arrangements usually undertaken refer to group composition, the process of selection, structure of the setting in which the experiment is to be performed, time of the test, nature of the stimulus (independent variable) and its meaning for the subjects, time between pre-test and post-test, opportunity for manipulation or conditioning during the time between pre-test and post-test, strict supervision, instructions given during the experiment and similar factors and conditions that might have a differential impact on the subjects.

6   The process of data collection

Data collection begins with the establishment of first contact with the subjects and continues with manipulation and measurement of the variables. The three basic steps of data collection in experiments are as follows:

Step 1: Pre-test
During this step, the subjects will be tested. This test is called pre-test because it takes place before the subjects are subjected to the experimental treatment. The pre-test includes measurement of the dependent variable, usually of both the experimental group and the control group. This measurement is taken as a basis for assessing eventual changes of the dependent variable during the experiment.

Step 2: The test
During this step the subjects are exposed to the independent variable. More specifically, the experimental group is exposed to a stimulus or treatment (independent variable); this may entail taking part in a discussion, reading a book, taking a certain medicine, consuming an amount of alcohol, watching a film, attending a lecture or visiting a club. The nature and duration of the stimulus varies with the nature of the experiment and the independent variable. In some cases it might take only a few minutes; in other cases it might take significantly longer.

Step 3: Post-test
After the experimental treatment has been completed, the subjects are tested again. This test is referred to as post-test because it takes place after the experimental treatment. During this test the dependent variable is measured again in order to ascertain its present status. Following this, the results of the pre-test and post-test are compared and any variations in the results are recorded.

Example A: Let us assume that we are interested in testing the hypothesis that media has a strong influence on the attitudes of students towards Aborigines. We decided to use experiments as our method. The steps to follow are shown bellow:

1 The experimental and control groups are chosen by using one of the methods described above.
2 The experimental conditions are established.
3 Both groups are pre-tested to measure the attitudes of the subjects towards Aborigines, by using attitude scales and by computing attitude scores for each subject.
4 The members of the experimental group are shown a film dealing with Aborigines and their life and which includes a speech from the Prime Minister and an interview with an activist. The members of the control group were not allowed to watch this film.
5 Both groups were post-tested by remeasuring their attitudes to Aborigines by using attitude scales and computing the attitude scores for each subject.
6 The results of the pre-tests and the post-tests are compared to ascertain whether there were any significant differences. Relevant conclusions are drawn.

---

7   Analysis and interpretation of experimental data

The analysis and interpretation will concentrate on data collected through the pre-test and post-test. These data will be analysed, compared and the differences computed, most likely by using statistical methods; an attempt will be made to establish a causal relationship between the variables in question. For instance, if the results of the pre-test and post-test of the control group show no difference, but the post-test results of the experimental group are significantly different from the pre-test results, and given that other factors were controlled, the conclusion may be that the independent variable was the cause of the change.

8   Types of experimental designs

Psychologists and social scientists use several types of experimental designs to establish relationships between variables. The differences between these designs lie mainly in the number of experimental and control groups employed in each experiment, in the use of pre-tests (i.e. in the experimental group only or in both groups), and in the way in which the independent variable is treated. The aim of the experimenters who introduced the various types of designs is to eliminate or at least control the effect of any factors that could affect the process and/or the results of the study. There are several other and more complicated experimental designs that are beyond the scope of this treatise, but the following are some of the most commonly used designs.

Before–after design
This design employs only one group, the experimental group, which is treated as demonstrated above (pre-test, stimulus, post-test). The differences between the pre-test and post-test scores indicate the possible effects of the independent variable on the dependent variable.

Classical experimental design
Here, two groups are employed, the experimental group and the control group. Although both groups are adequately prepared for the experiment, for example with regard to experimental conditions, the control group is not exposed to the independent variable. This is the most common form of experimentation.

After-only experiment
This is identical to the classic experimental design, except that neither the experimental group nor the control group are pre-tested.

Solomon two-control-group design
This design employs one experimental group and two control groups. In principle, one control group and the experimental group are treated as in the classic experimental design. The second control group is not pre-tested, but is exposed to the independent variable and post-tested.

Randomised group design
Here, the design includes two experimental groups and one control group. Randomised group design is similar to the classic design, except that it includes two experimental groups.

Solomon four-group design
This design employs two experimental groups and two control groups. One experimental group and one control group are treated as in the classic experimental design. The second experimental group and the second control group are not pre-tested but are exposed to the independent variable and are also post-tested.

There are many other experimental designs (e.g. factorial design) which are extensively used in the area of psychology. In sociology and other social sciences such complex designs have little use. Social scientists are more likely to use field experiments or quasi-field experiments rather than laboratory experiments or multi-group and multi-design experiments.

9   Types of experiments

Regardless of the design they employ, experiments appear in various forms. Some of these forms are used predominantly by psychologists, others by sociologists and other social scientists. The following three types are the most common forms of experiments in the social sciences.

Laboratory experiments
This is the traditional form of experimentation which is usually referred to by writers when they talk about experiments without qualification. Their major characteristic is that they are conducted in a laboratory, where all external factors can be controlled.

Field experiments
These experiments are performed not in a laboratory but in natural situations, such as in city blocks, in bars, meeting places of migrants, villages, churches and classrooms.

Demonstration experiments
Demonstration experiments are field experiments or laboratory experiments but with one group (experimental group) only. Although they help to 'demonstrate', highlight or illustrate trends in or aspects of human behaviour, they are not true experiments because: (1) they do not contain a control group, and therefore no comparisons can be made; (2) they do not select subjects randomly; and (3) there is no clear timing for the experimental treatment, since it can continue for as long as the subjects remain in the treatment (Williamson *et al.*, 1977). Milgram's study is a perfect example of this type of experiment.

10   Field experiments

Field experiments are experiments like those described above; they differ from other experiments in that they are conducted in natural situations, that is, in the field. The basic elements of experimentation are maintained; this relates to the use of control and experimental groups, the assignment of subjects to groups randomly, the control over conditions and timing of treatment, the procedure regarding pre-testing, post-testing and so on. Due to their nature, field experiments have gradually become more popular among social scientists, particularly during the past 25 years.

An example of field research is a study which was conducted in Germany (replicating a US study) and which was carried out to test reactions of people to violations of their private space. How do people react if others invade their private space? In this study, violation of private space was conceptualised in terms of someone sitting next to the subject and at a distance that was closer than 6 inches. In this study, students sitting alone on benches were approached by another person, who was working for the researcher, and who sat very close to them. The researcher who observed the process from a distance recorded the reaction. The researcher also recorded the reaction of the students to the same person sitting more than 6 inches from them. The question was, are subjects more likely to leave the bench if the 'intruder' sits closer than 6 inches to them than if this person sits further away? The answer to this question allowed the researcher to make conclusions about the boundaries of private space among students.

Field experiments are more suitable for social research, not only due to their closeness to social reality but also because they promise higher generalisability of the findings. However, they do demonstrate some basic problems which must be kept in mind (see Williamson *et al.*, 1977):

- The choice of similar groups or subjects in natural environments is rather difficult and sometimes impossible. For this reason it is difficult to determine the cause of any change in the behaviour of the subjects, since its origin cannot be determined. This problem might force researchers to apply field experiments only to such areas in which similar units are available. This of course reduces its applicability markedly.
- In a similar fashion, it is difficult to choose natural environments that are comparable. The problem here is as serious as in the previous case. This reduces the applicability and usefulness of this method even further.
- Even if similar environments are available, it is illogical to assume that they will affect the research units in a similar way, particularly if the similarity of these units is questionable.
- Field experiments are very involved, time-consuming and costly methods.

These problems indicate that field experiments require strict control of units and environmental conditions before validity and reliability claims can be made. The question is how far one can go in controlling the process of experimentation and still retain the naturalness of the setting. There are many valid ways of guaranteeing that balance, but the problem arises when the field experiment becomes an experiment in a 'natural laboratory', which in some cases might not differ very much from a real laboratory experiment. The researcher should be conscious of this.

As stated above, field experiments in their true form require a complete adherence to the principles of experimentation. When such elements or conditions are met, the experiments are referred to as *true field experiments*. Nevertheless, depending on the design, often subjects are assigned to groups not through randomisation but through identification of individuals or groups in natural settings. This selection otherwise complies with the general principles of experimentation: units, for instance, must be comparable, and environments must be similar.

When the condition of assigning subjects to groups is not accomplished randomly, we are dealing with what researchers (e.g. Wiliamson *et al.*, 1977) have termed *quasi-field experiments*. Quasi-field experiments are common in the social sciences, but do not produce the evidence true field experiments offer.

11   Validity of experiments

Validity of experiments is considered in two forms: internal and external validity. In *internal validity* the probability is tested that factors associated with the *process* of experimentation (instead of or in addition to the independent variable itself) are responsible for the changes in the dependent variable. *External validity* refers to the extent to which the experiment allows generalisations of the findings to be made. Writers (Berger *et al.*, 1989; Sproull, 1988; Suls and Rosnow, 1988) stress the following risk areas of experimentation:

- *Maturation*   The change in the dependent variable may not be caused by the independent variable but rather by maturation of the subjects. The views of the subjects may change over time and/or subjects may by the time they come to the post-test be tired, hungry or influenced by others.
- *Conditioning*   Pre-testing might sensitise subjects and predispose them to develop an interest in the experiment and respond atypically to experi-mentation.
- *The history effect*   Historical events might take place during the time between the pre-test and post-test, and might affect the responses to the latter.
- *Changes in samples*   These are changes due to mortality, spatial mobility and general unavailability of subjects and/or experimenters.
- *Instrumentation*   There is a possibility that changes in the dependent variable are due to changes in the nature of the tests during pre-testing and post-testing rather than due to the effects of the independent variable (measurement decay).
- *Interaction*   Changes in the dependent variable might be caused by a combination of several factors, including or not including the independent variable.
- *Sampling*   Changes in the dependent variable might be caused by sampling problems.
- *The Hawthorne effect*   Changes might be caused by the fact that subjects know that they are being studied (also referred to as the reactivity effect).
- *Modelling*   The dependent variable might change because the experimenter expects the subjects to behave in a certain way and the subjects wish to please the experimenter.

- *Ecology*   Changes in the dependent variable might have been caused by the 'ecology', or the experimental setting and measurement.

These problems can affect experiments in many ways; for this reason experimenters are expected to take precautions to avoid such problems as much as possible. This can be achieved by organising the experiments very carefully and by employing well-trained experimenters as well as by controlling the experimental setting, using extreme caution. Other problems can be controlled by introducing more than one experimental and control group and by manipulating them accordingly. In any case, these problems should be considered when the data are analysed and results interpreted.

Despite their popularity, experiments have their critics. Many qualitative researchers as well as feminists are critical of experiments. The latter stress structural and ideological deficiencies of experiments, for example that they express a male agentic style, not a feminine communal mode, that they demonstrate a sexist bias, that they mistreat animals, that they attempt to generalise from animals or specific groups to the whole population and that they do not capture the subjects' true feelings (Reinharz, 1992).

Focus groups

1   Introduction

You may think that focus groups have little to do with experiments, and in this sense they should not be discussed together in the same chapter. You may in fact be right. Many psychologists will agree with you, because they would not consider focus groups and experiments as belonging to the same family group of research methods. However, these two methods have some fundamental similarities. The most important similarity is that in both methods, respondents are brought together in an 'artificial' environment created for that purpose, and are examined according to some methodological criteria. Of course, experiments can take place in natural environments, but so do focus groups. Another similarity is that focus groups can be subjected to 'treatment' in a controlled environment, converting them to a kind of quasi-experimental method. Consequently, knowledge of experiments, their nature, strengths and weaknesses can help us to use focus groups more constructively.

Focus groups are employed extensively among many social researchers (Stewart and Shamdasani, 1990); the range of social scientists using focus groups is steadily increasing (Morgan, 1996). They are used as a preliminary study leading to quantitative research (McQuarrie, 1996), as a self-contained and principal method of research, as a supplementary source, or as a part of a multi-method study (Morgan, 1997). In any case, focus groups involve persons specially selected owing to their particular interest, expertise or position in the community in an attempt to collect information on a number of issues, as well as to brainstorm a variety of solutions, and ultimately facilitate group discussion as a tool of data collection and possibly policy construction. This method is therefore often referred to as 'group discussion', particularly among European researchers.

Focus groups are used as a form of (quantitative and qualitative) data collection that employs discussion in a non-standardised form and observation as its sources. This discussion includes more than one person at a time. This method was introduced by Kurt Lewin in 1936 in the USA, in the context of small-group experiments, and later in other areas of research, including market research and opinion research, in the USA and other countries. In the 1950s, group discussion was employed systematically and on a large scale by the Frankfurt Institute of Social Research to study opinions and attitudes. With the revival of symbolic interactionism and the spread of qualitative methods the interest of sociologists and social psychologists in group discussion was intensified but has lately decreased.

Originally, this method concentrated on group processes, but later it was used to study the content of the discussion. Although it is conducted in a group environment, its main aim is not to analyse the group; it is primarily a way of gaining information in a short period of time about the breadth or variation of opinions, and of establishing a mechanism of opinion formation. In this section we shall refer to a number of issues related to group discussion, as accepted, practised and presented by modern researchers (especially Berger *et al.*, 1989: 339–44; Dreher and Dreher, 1991: 186–8; Flick *et al.*, 1991).

The basic assumption that underlies this method is that a group environment will, through mutual stimulation, encourage discussion related to topical issues; increase the motivation to address social and especially critical issues; enable the discussion leader to lead the discussion towards focal points and topical issues through encouragement or discouragement or manipulation of the environment; and allow significant points of view to be presented in a real, emotional and summated form as spontaneous expressions (in other words, reducing the opportunity for a controlled presentation of personal views).

This is expected to occur when (1) addressing, describing or explaining an issue introduced by the leader or a member of the group; (2) comparing different points of view, evaluating views and discussion outcomes, and judging relevant arguments; or (3) making decisions or drawing conclusions presenting alternative points of view, trying to achieve or suggesting a possible consensus.

2   The purposes of focus groups

In the context of social research, focus groups and group discussion can serve several purposes. The following are thought by many researchers (e.g. Dreher and Dreher, 1991; Mariner, 1986) to be the most significant:

- As a pre-research method it can help to prepare the main study by providing sufficient information about the study object, about operationalisation by defining indicators and about preventing possible errors.

- As a post-research method it can explain trends and variances, reasons and causes, through the views of the respondents.
- As a main study it offers information about group processes, spontaneous feelings, reasons and explanations of attitudes and behaviour as adequately as any other method.
- In one form it can bring about changes in the group and its members as a result of the direction and intensity of the discussion.
- In another form, group discussion allows access to valuable information about group processes, attitude changes and manipulation, attitudes and opinions of group members, the group or the public, the effectiveness of certain methods and so on.

In Australia, focus groups are used extensively in the field of social work and social welfare and to a lesser extent in other areas.

3   The discussion process

Different writers see the conduct of group discussion in different ways. While some (e.g. Mucchielli, 1973) suggest that there are three major steps in group discussion (i.e. warm-up, confrontation and relaxation), others refer to six or even more steps. Lamnek (1988), for instance, lists the following steps: being strange, orientation, adjustment, intimacy, conformity and fading out of the discussion.

In more general terms, group discussion as a method of data collection unfolds in a way that is parallel to that of our model of social research. Nevertheless, there are some special points that mark this particular model (see especially Berger *et al.*, 1989: 339–44; Dreher and Dreher, 1991: 186–8; Flick *et al.*, 1991).

a   Choice of respondents

Choice of respondents is accomplished through a random procedure, systematic or cluster sampling, or other ways that can be justified by the object of study, nature of the respondents or the underlying methodology. Questions of interest here may be related to the structure of the group, that is, whether it should consist of similar or different people, age and gender of the respondent and so on.

The *size of the group* must be large enough to provide a basis for a reasonable discussion but not too large to become uncontrollable. In the view of some writers, the group size should be between 5 and 12 but no larger than 20. A size of around 10 seems to be ideal.

The *group composition* has been described by writers in diverse ways, depending of course on methodological factors. While most researchers agree that the members of the group must be talkative, knowledgeable of and interested in the research topic, views regarding their homogeneity and the cohesiveness of the group are divided. Some writers believe that the group must be homogeneous with reference to the research issue; others see more value in diversity of opinion. This will depend very much on the nature of the research question and the purpose of the study.

b   Introduction of a goal-directed discussion

After a group is selected for investigation, a *goal-directed discussion* is introduced by the group leader. This is accomplished through the introduction of a 'discussion-generating question' supplied by the researcher. The group leader will intervene as required, directing the discussion to the research goals and keeping its course interesting and balanced, that is, equally distributed among all members of the group. The way in which discussion will be introduced, organised and controlled is summarised in an *interview guide* which is given to group leaders.

Discussions are led on the basis of *strict instructions*, particularly when there are many leaders and/or when the research is extended over a longer period of time. The discussion-generating question must be the same among all group leaders and presented to them in a similar fashion. How the discussion will be arranged, what is to be discussed and how, as well as the limits of the debate, must be clearly outlined from the outset. Whether this degree of standardisation will be continued throughout the study is a decision for the researcher to make. In general, while the introduction is standardised, the discussion itself is not.

In physical terms, the *environment* in which the discussion will take place should be conducive to encouraging debate. Noisy places with excessive traffic and overly warm rooms with restricted air circulation should be avoided. In addition, rooms must be arranged so that all respondents can see each other and communicate with all participants freely.

c   Controlling the discussion

The discussion will be *controlled by the leader* as required by the situation. Discussions that are slow to start will be helped to gain momentum through additional questions, probes and other appropriate means; non-talkers will be encouraged to participate and those who dominate the discussion will be controlled. Motivation, encouragement, stimulation and control will bring about a balanced environment that is conducive to group discussion. In a qualitative context, such controls might be unacceptable; other ways of intervention may have to be used. Perhaps taking a reserved and non-directive position in the group or opting for controlling the form of discussion but being permissive with regard to the content of the discussion might be preferable.

d   Recording the data

The *type of information* to be collected depends on the research question and the purpose of the study. While in some cases it might be descriptive and exploratory, in other cases it might be theory testing. In a similar fashion, while in some cases it might be of a quantitative nature, in others it might not be. If the data are collected in a qualitative context, interpretation in a reductive or explicative form will be most appropriate. In other cases, a hermeneutic method might be chosen.

4   The leader

The leader — often referred to as the *facilitator* — occupies a central position in the context of group discussion. The extent to which this method achieves its purpose depends to a large extent on the quality of the group facilitator. Consequently, leaders are expected to have the following qualities:

- Theoretical and methodological knowledge of the research topic and general intellectual capacity.
- Experience with group work as well as the ability to control the discussion effectively by encouraging involvement, controlling dominating participants and keeping the discussion moving in the right direction.
- Leadership qualities.
- The ability to develop a warm atmosphere among the members of the group.

Ideally, the leader should be a facilitator. Guiding rather than controlling the discussion should be the rule. The research design should also include arrangements which will help to avoid or reduce bias generated by the leader.

5   Recording

There are many ways of recording data produced in group discussions. *Electronic recording* is common, but demonstrates several shortcomings, for example it can cause some distortions (members might feel intimidated or not wish to talk when their statements are recorded), especially when used at the beginning of the discussion, since it might distract the respondents and lead to selective participation in discussion. Electronically recorded data also require additional time for analysis and evaluation and this is a very time-consuming exercise.

Writing down the discussions *manually* is the good old way of recording such data, but this is still not without problems. Intensive discussions might be too big a task for the researcher; employing an assistant might be the solution, but such assistants need to have extensive experience with recording. Perhaps having two leaders, with both of them taking notes in turn or one recording the data and the other leading the discussion, may be the ideal solution.

Another issue is the *content of the recording*. When several recorders are employed, and if a comparison between the various groups is intended, some standardisation of the data is unavoidable. A summary evaluation for the question being discussed is presented at the end of each debate, of the type such as 1 = all in favour; 2 = most in favour; 3 = undecided; 4 = most against; 5 = all against might make comparisons much easier. This will, however, be difficult to reconcile with the intention of the method if the framework is qualitative.

6   Evaluation

Evaluation will take place in the context of the aim of the research. However, identifying trends as well as diversity in the group, views that dominate and their justification and outcomes of comparisons between the various groups might be one way of evaluating the results of group discussions.

As stated above, statistical analysis and evaluation is quite common when group discussion is conducted in a quantitative context. Developing variables related to each other in some form in the context of a hypothesis and operationalised adequately will allow statistical measures to be employed. If the context of the study is qualitative, the collection and analysis of the data can occur simultaneously, and interpretation of the data, establishing of categories, comparative analysis and formulation of hypotheses might be the way of analysis. When the discussion is recorded and transcripts are available, the analysis has a wider scope. Content analysis and perhaps objective hermeneutics are also possible.

7   Problems of group discussion

Group environments do encourage people to express views and to evaluate situations, especially when 'encouraged' or 'manipulated' by the leaders. Nevertheless, this advantage may cause several problems, such as those listed below (see Berger *et al.*, 1989: 339–44; Flick *et al.*, 1991; Dreher and Dreher, 1991: 186–8; Mahr, 1995; Puris, 1995):

- Group conditions might force people to hide their real opinions, especially if their views can have effects on their personal life or professional career.
- There are problems with recording the data.
- Domination of the discussion by some persons might affect the direction and outcome of the discussion.
- Some members may not participate in the discussion.
- A trend of the group to please the leader might occur, for many reasons (e.g. to 'get it over with', or to please the leader when he or she holds a decisive position in the respondents' personal, political or professional life).
- Success of the method relies very much on the qualities of the leader and the composition of the group.
- There may be difficulties with keeping discussion on track.

- The group might have reasons to attempt to offer to the leader a con-
solidated front and mislead him or her.
- The findings are not representative.

In the social sciences, focus groups as a research design are currently not
employed as much as other methods; where they are employed, it is used as
a form of exploration rather than as an independent and autonomous study
(Mahr, 1995: 112).

8 Summary

In this chapter we discussed briefly the context in which methods are
employed. We saw that methods are chosen and constructed according to the
methodology in which the research is to be developed. While some methods
are employed primarily in the context of qualitative or quantitative research,
others are employed in both methodological contexts. In such cases the
methods will be adjusted to meet the principles and standards of these
methodologies.

It was also demonstrated in this chapter that projects often include more
than one method to address the same question; we called this arrangement
triangulation. The methods can come from one methodological framework or
from both frameworks. Triangulation intends to offer a stereoscopic view of
the issue in question and improve the quality of the findings. Whether this is
the case or not is another issue. We saw that there are writers who express
doubts about the efficacy of this arrangement.

The second issue discussed in this chapter was experiments. This method
is well advanced, complex and demanding, and is employed almost exclusively
by psychologists, although sociologists are beginning to use it more than before.
Conducting a simple experiment may be an easy task, but guaranteeing
experimental conditions and establishing causality are very demanding tasks.
Those who intend to use experiments in their work or just want to know more
about experiments might have to consult specialist literature.

The last issue considered in this chapter was focus groups, or group
discussion, as it is known in central Europe. It is a very useful method which
is very common among those working in the field of social work and social
welfare and among community psychologists. As a method group discussion
is very effective and provides useful information predominantly of a qualitative nature. As such it has become increasingly more attractive than before
to sociologists and those interested in community work, participatory research
and action research.

The next step of our discussion will take us to a similar area, namely to
field research. This includes research that brings the researcher as close to
respondents as one can get. Methods which can facilitate this are case studies,
ethnographic research and grounded theory. These methods will be discussed
in the next chapter.

Key concepts

Triangulation	Experiments
Field experiments	Ruling out
Conditioning	Group matching
Hawthorne effect	Post-test
Before–after experimental design	Laboratory experiment
Group discussion	Maturation
Controlling for	Instrumentation
Subject matching	Ecology
Pre-test	After-only design
Randomised group design	Closure
Demonstration experiments	Closing off
History effect	Randomisation
Modelling	Classic experimental design

8

Field research and grounded theory

The methods grouped together in this chapter are new additions to the arsenal of some social researchers. Although they have been used for some time by social anthropologists, social workers and other social scientists, the extent to which they were used and the intensity of use was relatively low. Apart from this, sociologists in particular did not embrace these methods as much as other researchers did, showing a marked preference for the hard-line traditional methods of social research, and especially for survey research.

With the development of ethnomethodology and the gradual acceptance of symbolic interactionism, hermeneutics, phenomenology and feminism in the area of sociology, coupled with the relative displacement of neopositivism from the centre of attention and hegemony in the social sciences, the interest in these methods during the last 25 years grew markedly.

These methods are often referred to as naturalistic research by some or low-constraint methods by others. In the following discussion we shall explore some basic aspects of these methods, including case studies and ethnographic research. The last section of the chapter will focus on grounded theory. Case-study research is not always pure field research, since it is not always conducted in a natural setting; researchers doing case-study research do impose some constraints on the environment; nevertheless case studies are closer to nature than other methods of social research. The same is to be said about ethnographic research, although this can be developed in a clear naturalistic form. Grounded theory, finally, is just an example of qualitative research which can be employed in field research or in other contexts. We begin first with a general overview of field research.

A Field research

Field research is a form of social inquiry into real-life situations. Field research takes place in the 'field', that is, in a natural setting, a setting that is not established for the purpose of conducting research. Equally important for field studies is the fact that respondents do not always know they are being observed.

Field research has the purpose of exploring real-life situations, studying behaviour patterns and the reasons behind social interaction. It investigates, for instance, how people behave in natural situations in which interventions have been introduced in one way or another, particularly when they do not know that they are being investigated, and when they act without instructions from the researchers. In general, (qualitative) field researchers begin with some general notions or tentative hypotheses, formulate questions, accumulate data that may support or eliminate guesses maintained so far. Where supported, guesses become formal hypotheses and the research begins to centre around them, eventually leading to tentative conclusions and to propositions.

The nature of this form of research has motivated a number of researchers to believe that field research is a kind of soft-option research with relatively low status and a lack of rigour, producing biased and sloppy results. The results were thought to lack the sound basis required for making 'scientific' generalisations, and were considered to be too costly and excessively time consuming, resulting in excessive and unsystematic information which was of little use, except as a basis for further research (exploratory study).

Nevertheless, in its context, field research is now considered to be as demanding and useful as any other method of social research. Field research is not just methods of data collection but is also a research model which employs a number of techniques of data collection and analysis. Field research is not characterised only by the *place* of the study, although the element 'field' is central in its research design. The most important element of this type of research and its central design is the underlying theory, which integrates the field and the selected methods into a meaningful tool of social investigation.

1   Types of field research

Field studies vary in a number of ways. According to the purpose they serve, they can be exploratory, descriptive or hypothesis-testing forms of research.

Exploratory studies
As exploratory studies, they are usually developed in a qualitative context, and aim at gaining general information for the purpose of defining the research topic, operationalising or explaining variables or aspects of the topic, or generating hypotheses. Field studies can equally be developed and executed in a quantitative context, and produce quantitative findings.

Descriptive studies
This type of field research is as common as the previous one and is often designed in a qualitative context. As a rule, qualitative studies produce descriptions of the research topic, and in a number of cases without the use of quantitative measurement or statistics. However, as in exploratory research, quantification of the approach and the findings is equally possible.

Hypothesis-testing studies
This form of field research is geared towards hypothesis testing, which can be a qualitative as well as a quantitative approach. Testing of hypotheses is undertaken in a descriptive and logical fashion in qualitative studies but in a statistical–quantitative manner in quantitative studies.

Other categories
Field studies can also be categorised according to the methods and techniques they employ to pursue their goals. In this sense they can be *non-experimental studies* or *experimental studies*. The former are studies of natural happenings in the context of an environment chosen for that purpose; they do not refer to events induced by the investigators. Examples of non-experimental studies are studies of natural disasters, blackouts caused by unforeseen events, floods and strikes.

Experimental studies, on the other hand, include investigations that refer to events artificially induced by the investigator, for example a study of the reaction of customers who witness the theft of clothes, or reaction of pedestrians to an assault on a young Vietnamese by Australians (both being 'arranged' by the researcher). Other examples are artificially introduced programs, such as minimum income schemes, where a number of families are involved; the investigator is interested in the way the research units react to these programs and the effects they have on the quality of their life.

From a different perspective, field research appears in a variety of forms. Examples of such types are *case-study research, ethnographic research* and research based on *grounded theory*. The former is geared towards an intensive analysis of single cases (or a few cases) in their own right, often with little relationship with each other or with the social context. Ethnographic research is a form of research that places groups or units of analysis in the context of the whole culture, studying them in a holistic context. Grounded theory research falls between the two. Overall, the nature of these studies (borrowing elements from different sources and applying in most cases different principles, and following different goals) makes them distinct examples of field research which warrant special consideration.

2   Field design

The design of field studies varies with a number of factors but primarily with the type of study. When the design is developed in the context of a quantitative framework, it is expected to be relatively rigid and deterministic. This form of design has already been discussed elsewhere in the book and requires no further consideration. Where, however, the study is developed in a qualitative context the design is quite different. Here, its structure will conform to the principles of qualitative research discussed earlier. The basic steps of the qualitative field research design are given below. As far as the analysis of the findings of such a study is concerned, this will be discussed later on in this treatise.

Stages in qualitative design

Stage 1: Preparation
During this stage the investigator chooses both the research object and the unit of analysis. The object of study may, for instance, be students demonstrating against the state government, and the unit of analysis female first-year nurses or a subgroup of union activists and so on.

Stage 2: Entering the field
This stage includes very basic but also complex and demanding activities. This is what many researchers refer to as 'going native', and is mainly orientated towards establishing the research environment and building up contacts. The completion of the stage quite often depends on a number of factors, most of which are out of the control of the researcher. Identification of key persons, manipulating accessibility, choosing methods of contact and settling into the group are examples of activities the researcher must undertake to make the study possible. Such activities are time consuming and require personal qualities and availability of resources (social, economic, political, etc.), which in many cases are rather scarce. These activities become even more demanding and difficult when the event under study is a temporary one and requires immediate attention, for example a disaster situation, a demonstration or a strike.

Stage 3: Exploration
Much of what will be done in this stage depends very much on the type of study as well as the intentions of the researcher. Exploration here might just mean identification and description of issues related to the research subject; in other cases, this might also include analysis of some kind, as well as evaluation of the findings. Analysis and evaluation will, as a rule, be conducted in a qualitative fashion; it may, however, include some quantitative procedures and computations. In terms of the research model introduced earlier in this volume, exploration includes both data collection and analysis.

B Case studies

1 Introduction

Case-study research involves studying individual cases, often in their natural environment, and for a long period of time (Kromrey, 1986: 320) and employs a number of methods of data collection and analysis. A typical definition defines a case study as 'an empirical inquiry that investigates a contemporary phenomenon within its real-life context when the boundaries between phenomenon and context are not clearly evident; and in which multiple sources of evidence are used' (Yin, 1991: 23). Although case studies are usually referred to as a method of data collection and are also discussed together with other methods, for many researchers they are a research model or design that deals with all aspects of research (Hartfield, 1982: 160; Witzel, 1982: 78).

Writers such as those mentioned above (and especially Hartfield, 1982; Yin, 1991) suggest that case-study analysis is a type of research that is different from other forms of investigation, and demonstrates the following distinguishing characteristics:

- It studies whole units in their totality and not aspects or variables of these units.
- It employs several methods primarily to avoid or prevent errors and distortions.
- It often studies a single unit: one unit is one study.
- It perceives the respondent as an expert not just as a source of data.
- It studies a typical case (Hartfield, 1982).

For a long period of time, case studies have been considered an inferior method of inquiry, being of little use and of minimal significance, since they allowed very little quantification and no generalisations. However, the interest in this method has recently increased, particularly with theoretical developments in the area of the social sciences and improvement in the structure and methodology of case studies.

Today, case studies are considered to be valid forms of inquiry in the context of descriptive as well as evaluative and causal studies, particularly when the research context is too complex for survey studies or experimental strategies, and when the researcher is interested in the structure, process and outcomes of a single unit.

2 Case studies in quantitative and qualitative research

Case studies are employed indiscriminately in both quantitative and qualitative research, although to a different extent and for different reasons. Case studies are employed to a lesser extent in quantitative research than in qualitative research, are less popular and also assigned less value. Case studies are also employed for the purpose of exploration, and for the following reasons (see Bauer, 1994: 38–45; Berger *et al.*, 1989: 334; Lamnek, 1988):

- to gain more information about the structure, process and complexity of the research object when relevant information is not available or sufficient;
- to facilitate conceptualisation;
- to assist with formulating hypotheses;
- to guide the process of operationalisation of the variables;
- to illustrate, explain, offer more detail or expand quantitative findings;
- to test the feasibility of the quantitative study.

This shows that case studies in quantitative research are employed (1) as a prelude to the 'real' research; (2) as a form of pre-test; or (3) as a post-research explanation of the 'main' study. In all cases it is obvious that case studies are not used as an autonomous research project but as a supplement to other studies.

In qualitative research, case studies do not serve as a stepping stone to quantitative studies but as a research enterprise of their own, aimed at developing hypotheses or even theories. They are not second-rank research or a supplement to quantitative studies, but a research model that is as significant and worth pursuing as quantitative research.

As a scientific inquiry, case-study research has the aim of studying in an open and flexible manner social action in its natural setting as it takes place in the form of interaction or communication and as interpreted by the respondents. This type of case-study research in the qualitative field illustrates its main criteria, which were already introduced earlier in our discussion. Among these criteria are openness, communicativity, naturalism and interpretativity.

3   Research design

The design normally contains, among other things, the logical sequence in which the study is to be carried out, as well as the elements of the study, its methods of data collection and analysis and all administrative procedures that need to be considered for the study to be carried out without problems or delays. In case-study research the design of the research is contained in the *case-study protocol*, which is described below.

4   The case-study protocol

The protocol contains, among other things, the main steps of the research process, offering details about the decisions that need to be made and the techniques that must be employed in the context of the study. According to Yin (1991: 70) the most relevant points contained in the protocol are the following:

- *An overview of the case-study project*, that is, what it is all about, the case(s) to be investigated, special characteristics of the research unit(s), the aim of the study, expected outcomes and so on.
- *Field procedures*, that is, choosing the case(s) to be studied, the ways of gaining access to the research unit(s) including key organisations and informers, the resources required in the field for the completion of the study, communication patterns while in the field, an outline of data collection activities to be considered at the various stages of the study, and in general planning for unexpected events that might affect the study.

- *Case-study questions*, mainly acting as reminders of the issues that need to be addressed in the study.
- A *guide for preparing the report*, that is, the elements it must contain, its style, format and the audience it might address.

This description shows that the case-study protocol does not differ significantly from the research model introduced earlier in this volume and employed by social researchers working in a quantitative or qualitative context.

5   Aspects of the research design

The fact that the case-study protocol is similar to the research model employed by social researchers indicates that many aspects of the research design of case-study research are similar to those of mainstream social research. This is shown in the discussion of the following points contained in the case-study protocol (see Becker, 1989; Yin, 1991).

a   Sampling

Case studies can investigate a large variety of research objects, ranging from behaviour and interrelations, to persons and groups, to organisations and whole cultures (Reinecker, 1987; Witzel, 1982; Yin, 1991). The choice of cases is determined by one of the sampling methods discussed earlier in this book. In case-study investigations the following options are available: single-case designs and multiple-case designs, both of which may include a holistic or an embedded approach. In quantitative studies, the choice is based on their suitability for the main study.

In qualitative research, when more than one case is studied research begins with one case chosen by the researcher according to its suitability for the research; the first case is normally chosen as a typical case, that is, a typical example of a category of cases. Additional cases are chosen by means of snowball sampling, or other methods such as *theoretical sampling*, which we introduced earlier in another context and which will be discussed later in this section. In this case, expansion of cases follows the principles of the emerging theory, and can include similar or different cases.

b   Planning data collection

The instructions contained in the design regarding data collection relate to procedures as well as to methods. The usual procedure is to study the case completely and then write down the information obtained before entering another unit. Each case is handled separately.

Data collection takes place in the natural environment of the research unit; the methods employed in case studies are many and diverse. The most common methods involve the use of: open interviews, narrative interviews, observation, documents (e.g. biographical methods, life-story methods), archival data, cohort analysis and some indirect methods, for example analysis of physical artifacts. The choice of method will depend on methodological factors, most important of which is the type of research.

c   Planning data analysis

Although the analysis of data in case studies follows its own rules and procedures, it is to a certain extent similar to that employed in the qualitative methods and will be discussed in the appropriate place. However, *pattern-matching*, *explanation building* and *time-series analysis* are the most dominant methods of analysis (Yin, 1991). Analysing embedded units, making repeated observations and case survey are also employed, although to a lesser extent.

In more detail, a qualitative analysis will involve first the assigning of meanings to data and devising concepts that will be analysed, refined and put in categories, followed by a comparative analysis. The analysis will take different dimensions depending on whether the study includes single or multiple cases, but categorisation, development of typologies and formulation of hypotheses will be the steps to follow in the context of such an analysis. It should be remembered here that in many cases analysis takes place concurrently with collection of data.

d   Interpretation and reporting

Finally, some guidelines will be included in the design regarding the way in which the collected data will be integrated into a logical argument or conclusion, and how they will be reported.

C Ethnographic research

1 Introduction

Literally, ethnography is the science of 'ethnos', that is, nations, people or cultures. The specific definition of this discipline as well as its name vary significantly among social scientists in the various parts of the world. While some retain name and definition as stated, others use the names social anthropology, cultural anthropology or ethnology instead. And while some use these concepts interchangeably, others consider them as separate disciplines.

In general, ethnography and ethnology were considered to be the areas of interest of anthropologists who were generalists and interested in relationships between people and the physical, sociopolitical, personal, cultural and historical aspects of their life, and they were kept out of the area of social sciences.

Ethnographic studies were thought to be the prerogative of anthropologists, mainly because these workers were dealing with primitive cultures. Nevertheless, with recent developments in the social sciences, and especially with the advent of feminism and women's studies, ethnographic research, particularly critical ethnography, has become rather popular (see, for example, Anderson, 1989; Hammersley, 1991, 1992b; Hammersley and Atkinson, 1983). In this section, some of the aspects of ethnographic research will be outlined.

2   Theoretical foundations of ethnographic research

Ethnographic research derives its structure and principles from anthropology. These elements determine the perspective and direct theory and research in a way that is different from other, already established research models. The main elements of anthropology are those given below.

Culture
Ethnography and social anthropology are centred around the concept of culture: anthropologists and ethnographers study culture as an entity in itself; they study the ways it is established, changed or destroyed, and the ways in which culture is transmitted from generation to generation. Culture is perceived as a system shared by groups of people, who learn its main elements or configurations through interaction and living in its context. Social anthropology is interested in the structure and process of culture and tries to understand the patterns of behaviour, values, norms and standards as experienced and practised by people (Peoples and Bailey, 1988).

Holism
The approach employed by ethnographers and anthropologists is holistic in that it perceives human action in the context of the whole system, for which it is an expression. Social action is a part of the whole and derives a meaning through the place and purpose it has in the context of the system. Individual actions are, therefore, manifestations of cultural standards and principles of the large sociocultural system and can be better understood if they are seen in the context of the whole system. Many feminists, for instance, have employed critical ethnography to explain invisibility, oppression and exploitation of women in modern societies, or views and practices related to the role of women in the family and society.

In-depth studies
Anthropologists and ethnographers are primarily interested not in 'surface counting' or survey data relating to a small number of people but in in-depth studies. They therefore do not rely on information obtained through a question–answer style of questioning lasting for a small period of time, but rather on information gained by living in the groups they investigate, and experiencing culture the way their subjects do.

Chronology

Traditionally, anthropologists were interested in primitive cultures, leaving modern societies and cultures to sociologists and other social scientists. With time, this notion changed, resulting in various branches of anthropology, some being interested primarily in primitive cultures and others in modern cultures. Despite this division, ethnography as a method is still employed by anthropologists irrespective of their chronological orientation. Sociologists and social scientists in general use ethnography as a method to study modern societies.

3 Methodology in ethnographic research

Ethnographic research uses a number of methods, most of which are employed by other researchers in the context of different paradigms and methodologies. In this sense, ethnographic research is not different from positivist or interpretive research. Nevertheless, the methodological approach is different and the way in which the methods are employed in actual situations is different indeed.

Structure

The methods employed in ethnographic research are of two kinds, namely descriptive or critical. The first type is usually referred to as ethnographic and the latter as ethnological. Ethnographic research describes trends in the area of study, establishes typologies and categories and is sociographic in nature. Ethnological research uses ethnographic material collected for that purpose or available through ethnographic research to make further conclusions regarding causes and effects, particularly with regard to macro-social elements. Common in social sciences (especially in Marxist and feminist research) is *critical ethnographic research*. This relates mainly to ethnological research that critically analyses the relationships between social practices and overarching macro-cultural principles. While ethnographic research is descriptive, ethnological and ethnographic critical research are theoretical, causal, critical, emancipatory and empowering. In the following, when we talk about ethnographic research we shall refer to all types — ethnographic, ethnological and critical ethnographic research.

Purpose

The purpose of this research depends on the paradigm that underlies the project. If the research employs a positivistic paradigm, the purpose of the ethnographic research may be to describe, explain and categorise social events, whereas if it is an interpretive paradigm it may aim at understanding the dynamics of a sociocultural system as well as of how people interpret their world. In critical studies, ethnographic research aims to emancipate, empower and liberate people. It is important to remember here that while ethnographic research in anthropology is carried out for the purpose of primarily understanding cultures in the social sciences it has the purpose of understanding people in their social environment and of explaining the social justification of their role and position in that culture.

Methods

As stated earlier, the methods and techniques employed in ethnographic research are the same as those employed in positivist and interpretive research. The most common methods are:

- *ethnographic fieldwork*, which entails data collection through standard methods such as participant observation and interviewing, conducted while the researcher is living with the people he or she studies; and
- *ethnohistoric research*, that is, methods of data collection that rely on the study of documents, such as personal accounts, life histories, diaries, personal letters and reports related to the group in question (Peoples and Bailey, 1988).

4   Criteria of ethnographic research

In the area of anthropology, ethnographic research is executed in a way that demonstrates a number of criteria. Many of these criteria are no different from those encountered in case-study or field research. Nevertheless, their context, purpose and meaning are different from those employed in field research or other research models. Zaharlik (1992: 119–21; Zaharlik and Green, 1991) lists the following characteristics of ethnographic research:

- *Social relationships*   Ethnographic research assumes that researchers establish a long-term and diffuse relationship with the respondent, that is, extending over a long period of time and in a variety of contexts.
- *The researcher as learner*   The researcher assumes a role that is inferior to that of the researched. The researcher knows very little and wants to learn from the respondent, who knows more about the research issue. Learning goes beyond the specific research topic and includes patterns of communication (including language), habits and cultural imperatives of the environment under investigation.
- *First-hand information*   The essential information gathered by the ethnographer is gained through direct contact with the respondents (first-hand information). This is important in the understanding of complex issues, ideal structures and deviations.
- *Long-term observation*   Ethnographic research requires long-term contact with the respondents, that is, long enough to allow experience with regular routines and patterns of life as well as with reactions of people who find themselves in different situations and circumstances. In many cases this might require years of contact with the group in question.
- *Participant observation*   A part of ethnographic research is living in the community under investigation and participating in its life as much as the members of the group. Participant observation in which participation is stronger than just observation is the rule.

- *The ethnographer as a research instrument*   Practically, the ethnographer does not use an instrument in the sense that positivistic researchers do; she or he is the instrument. The whole personality of the researcher is involved in the research.
- *Naturalistic observation*   This means that research captures social life as it unfolds and also in natural situations, not in artificial settings.
- *Eclectic approach*   Eclectic means here the use of different data collection techniques and of cross-checking to enhance 'scope, density and clarity of constructs' gained through one way or another.
- *Interactive–reactive approach*   Ethnographic research employs a dynamic form of data collection and analysis that is based on flexibility, reactivity and self-correction. Initial questions that generate response and information act as an instrument of regulation and result in correction and redirection of the initial design and methods. New knowledge and information are used not only for understanding and explaining the research object but also for adjusting the approach, design and methods so that the research topic can be studied most effectively.
- *Holistic approach*   Ethnographic research is holistic in that it attempts to understand social structures and processes of elements of the system in terms of reference to the whole sociocultural system, and in that it assigns meanings to parts of the system by 'connecting' them to the whole. Parts are evaluated in the context of the whole system.
- *Humanistic perspective*   Ethnographic research is geared towards more humanistic concerns and values that explain the essence of the culture in which people live and the experiences gained through living in that culture.
- *Cross-cultural frame of reference*   A final characteristic of ethnographic research is that it is comparative. In this sense it uses previously collected information to understand other cultures and environments and to direct the study towards more effective and realistic goals.

In the area of feminism, ethnography becomes a powerful methodological tool, particularly because it relies on interpretation and on the researcher's immersion in social settings, calls for intersubjective understanding between researchers and respondents, and aims at: (1) documenting the lives and activities of women, (2) understanding the experience of women from their own point of view, and (3) conceptualising women's behaviour as an expression of social contexts (Reinharz, 1992: 51).

5   Evaluation of ethnographic research

Ethnographic research has in the past been used almost exclusively in the area of anthropology and only exceptionally outside this context. Nevertheless, during the past 20 years, and particularly during the 1980s, this form of research has been applied systematically in areas other than its traditional domain. Marxist and feminist research are the two most common areas of applications but it has equally been applied in other contexts such as educational research. Particularly when social conditions, attitudes, roles and interpersonal relationships are explored in conjunction with fundamental cultural prescriptions, this type of research is more than effective and useful.

Feminist research, for instance, through ethnographic research, has challenged the ways in which gender is culturally defined and how perceptions of gender roles are manifestations of general cultural imperatives such as patriarchy. Relating common beliefs held by women to cultural imperatives, asking how such beliefs are developed, supported and maintained, who encourages the perpetuation of such practices, who benefits from such beliefs and practices and how they affect women are issues that have been examined and can be addressed through ethnographic research. The characteristic element in this research is not primarily living with people as it is in anthropology, but familiarity with the subject, closeness to the respondents, quality and type of relationship between researcher and the researched, which must be at least equalitarian and referenced to the large sociocultural system as the explaining source. This last point is very important and makes this approach different from the other research models.

D Grounded theory research

1   Introduction

This theory was developed by Glaser and Strauss (1967) and has become popular among many social scientists. It is 'grounded' because it is related to, emerges out of, is created through and grounded on empirical data. The centre of its interest is not on collecting volumes of data but organising the variety of thoughts and experiences the researcher gathers during the analysis of data.

Grounded theory is associated with a type of qualitative or interpretive research that is representative of many other qualitative methods.

Central criteria of grounded theory
Bruno Hildebrand states in the introduction to Strauss's book *Grundlagen qualitativer Sozialforschung* (1991) that the most important criteria of grounded theory are the four described below.

An autonomous unit
In grounded theory the case under investigation is an autonomous research unit. This means that a case is considered to be not an amorphous piece of reality but an autonomous unit with its own structure, boundaries and history, and should be studied as a case and reconstructed as a case, not as an element of something else. Studying cases, then, under the rules of grounded theory involves this particular perception as well as a process of interaction between researcher and the research unit.

In addition it involves the notion that research is directed by the interests of the researcher. In one sense, grounded theory guides research under the notion that 'something appears *as* something *to* someone'. The expression 'to someone' demonstrates the emphasis placed on the researcher as an element of the research process; the rest of the statement 'something appears as something' shows the nature of the perception of reality and a process involving researcher as well as research object alike.

Interpretation of reality
Scientific interpretation of reality resembles that of an artist. This element suggests that social scientists who employ grounded theory as their guide approach and interpret reality the same way as artists do. Like artists, social scientists approach reality in an unprejudiced manner (like newborn babies), and they also form and shape reality. So they both create reality in an unbiased manner.

Everyday thinking
There is continuity from everyday thinking to scientific thinking. Being grounded to data means that grounded theory is close to everyday behaviour and action. Everyday knowledge is an unrenounceable resource, which this theory makes a central element of its structure and approach. Primary experience is very significant for the development of grounded theory.

Development of concepts
Openness of social scientific formation of concepts is the feature here. This element suggests that the development of concepts and categories is made in a form that does not demand continuous validity, that is, concepts and categories change as soon as knowledge of them and their environment changes and as soon as new ideas emerge and new explanations dominate. The development of concepts is a process not a structure; it is constantly changing.

Theories are consequently developed and then further refined and tested, in a continuous and unending process. In qualitative research this means:

- *induction* (development of temporary/conditional hypotheses);
- *deduction* (derivation of implications of hypotheses); and
- *verification* (testing of the validity of these hypotheses).

The whole research process is based on this work pattern.

2   Main steps of the research process

In general terms, the major steps in qualitative research based on grounded theory are similar to those of other qualitative models; for instance, (1) thinking about the research issues, searching for material, asking generative questions, etc.; (2) entering the field; (3) making observations, interviewing; (4) taking notes (analysing the data). The central points of such research are data collection, coding and writing of memos.

3 Main procedures and elements of the research process

The main procedures of the qualitative research based on grounded theory are as follows (Strauss, 1991: 51; Glaser, 1992):

- The concept-indicator model
- Data collection
- Coding
- Key categories
- Theoretical sampling
- Comparisons
- Saturation of the theory
- Integration of the theory
- Theoretical memos
- Sorting of theoretical memos

These steps are closely interrelated, and while in some cases they may be followed in the order given above, they may also be employed simultaneously. Whether they will be introduced in one way/order or another depends on many factors, such as the type of data, the personality, interests and experience of the researcher, the respondents and finally the nature of the theory being developed.

In a practical and methodological fashion, according to the founders of the theory, the procedures stated above serve to establish a grounded theory in a manner that can be described in the following steps:

1 Identifying indicators in the research topic.
2 Studying indicators and comparing them with each other.
3 Coding indicators; looking for answers and formulating hypotheses.
4 Categorising similar indicators as a *class*.
5 Naming the class and perceiving it as a *coded category*, which reflects the indicators' similarities, and the smallest common denominator. This is the conceptual code, the *concept*.
6 Comparing indicators with concepts and with other indicators; this helps to refine them and relate them optimally to the data.
7 Working through more attributes of the categories, refining them and getting additional information until the codes are tested and *saturated*, that is, until no more new information is gained. The more similar the indicators regarding the concept in question, the higher the degree of saturation of the attributes of the concept.
8 Developing and saturating more categories through the process of *constant comparisons*.
9 Including in the theory concepts and their attributes developed in that way.
10 Further testing, contrasting and comparing of theories and perhaps refining and changing them.

4   Details of the main procedures

Most of the procedures used in the research based on grounded theory are self-explanatory and not very different from those employed in other types of research. Nevertheless, the content and context in which the processes take place vary, giving these procedures a separate identity. The following descriptive details of the main procedures are by no means exhaustive. More details on this methodology will be presented later when discussing the various aspects of social research.

Developing the concept-indicator model
This procedure is very important because it covers the largest part of the research process, and introduces most other procedures. The identification of indicators and the establishment of concepts seems to be at the heart of this research model.

Empirical indicators are concrete data, such as behaviour patterns and social events, which are observed or described in documents or interview texts. Such data are indicators for a concept, which the researcher develops, initially temporarily and then with more confidence. Such concepts occupy a central position in the context of grounded theory.

Data collection
This means searching for sources, establishing access to such sources and, finally, studying and collecting information. This also involves among other things coding, asking new questions, writing theoretical memos, collecting new data, coding again and so on, continuing the process until saturation is achieved.

Coding
The concept here is different from the concept employed in computer-aided data processing. It refers to asking questions about categories and their relationships. A code resulting from this process is, for instance, a category, a relationship and so on. Coding, consequently, helps to discover categories and subcategories, which are then named and further processed as stated above.

Coding appears in one of three types: open coding, axial coding and selective coding. *Open coding* serves to initiate coding, is rather 'open' and general, and allows further refinement and reinterpretations. Only significant data are considered for coding. Codes are then verified and saturated. *Axial coding* concentrates on issues related to the *axis* of a category and involves more intensive analysis. *Selective coding*, finally, concentrates on coding key categories.

Coding is performed in an accurate and responsible way and is expected to adhere to the following basic rules (Strauss, 1991: 122–3):

- One should not paraphrase sentences but discover and name genuine categories.
- One should set categories as directed by the coding paradigm (i.e. in reference to conditions, strategies, consequences, etc.).
- One should set categories in relationship with subcategories, one by one.

- One should always relate to data and refer adequately to them.
- One should underline, which makes sorting easier.
- Categories and subcategories must be interrelated.
- Unrelated categories must either become related or eliminated.

Key categories

When discovering and naming categories the following points should be considered: (1) condition, (2) interaction between actors, (3) strategies and techniques, and (4) consequences. But discovering categories has the purpose of allowing the researcher to identify the key categories that are central to the context of grounded theory, which lead to theoretical sampling and data collection and which offer the nucleus around which a theory may be developed. Key categories explain the largest part of variance in behaviour and help to integrate, tighten and saturate a theory.

For this reason, the researcher is expected to look for a key category, that is, for a category that possesses the explaining power. Beyond this, a key category must meet the following criteria (Strauss, 1991: 67–8); it:

- must be neutral;
- must appear frequently in the data;
- should allow an easy reference to other categories; and
- should possess clear implications for the formal theory.

In a study, Ravagniani (1991) employed grounded theory to examine the meaning of care among staff of an institution for people with severe developmental disabilities. Ravagniani identified six interrelated categories of care, namely 'real work', 'routinisation', 'expertise', 'the partial parent', 'developmental care' and 'intimate care'. The categories were unified with a core category, which was termed 'circumstantial relationship'.

Theoretical sampling

This is a form of sampling that is guided by the principles of the theory that is to be developed. This process directs the researcher on an analytical basis to the additional data, which are to be collected next in order to explore aspects of the theory that have now become important, and to where such data can be found, for example which groups should be approached and what theoretical view to adopt. This shows that theoretical sampling is directly related to data collection, which obviously is controlled by the theory being developed (Strauss, 1991: 70).

Comparisons

This is a very central tool of analysis in this form of qualitative research. It takes place at all levels, such as between indicators, indicators and concepts, and continues at higher levels until saturation is achieved.

Saturation and integration of the theory

The concept of saturation seems to be a very useful tool in controlling the extent to which a process of analysis must go. It means that analysis, comparisons, etc. will continue until all available information has been obtained. This is demonstrated by the extent to which new information can achieve a change in the existing data. When such a change is not available, saturation is considered to have been reached, and the process is completed.

Theoretical memos

Memos are written at all stages of research. In the early stages they may relate to instructions, while in later stages they may refer to more serious and factual issues, for example coding, ideas, key categories, gaps in analysis and so on. Memos vary with the phase of the research and with the research style, experience of the researcher and the research dynamics, that is, one researcher or a team, etc.

Memo writing is expected to follow certain rules, of which these are the most important (Strauss, 1991):

- Data and memos should be kept separate.
- Memo writing must be done as soon as the need arises, without delay.
- Memo writing should not be forced, but should be written as the need for it arises
- Memos can be modified at wish.
- Keeping a list of codes helps when writing memos.
- Keeping similar issues in the same memo, and one issue per memo, is advisable.
- Memos should be marked 'saturated' when the category becomes saturated.
- Techniques of memo writing should be flexible.

Memos can take a variety of forms, depending on their content and purpose, for example orientation memos, inspiration memos, memos about categories or discoveries, comparison memos, expansion memos, summary memos and so on (Strauss, 1991: 174).

Sorting of theoretical memos

This is a part of the process of identifying, categorising and analysing information contained in the memos. The degree to which this procedure will be demanding depends on several factors, particularly the number of memos, the size of memos, their structure, the writing style of the researcher and the organisation of the memos.

E Summary

In this chapter we explored three distinct research methods which are gradually becoming very popular. One of the reasons for this is the increased acceptance of qualitative research as a legitimate form of research, which provides the methodological framework for these research methods. In addition, the emergence and establishment of feminist research contributed further to the popularity of the methods presented in this chapter. Many feminists use case studies and ethnographic research, and demonstrate a marked preference for grounded theory rather than the traditional positivist research.

Nevertheless, overall case studies are not high in the preference order of social researchers. Poor representativeness and poor replicability are two of the reasons for many researchers deciding against case studies. However, for the purpose they are used case studies are accepted as a legitimate form of investigation and are often used in qualitative research.

Ethnographic research is used less frequently by social researchers than other methods. Still, its capacity to address relationships between cultural phenomena and social practices seems to make it a very useful tool of descriptive but also critical research. The ways in which cultural conventions and imperatives affect life chances of individuals can clearly be demonstrated by this type of research, and in this sense it is very useful. This has been shown for instance in the areas of feminism and women's studies.

Finally, grounded theory has progressed within the same paths and constraints as case studies and ethnographic research. Whether grounded theory has been accepted for its innate qualities or as a preferred alternative to 'inflexible' and 'biased' research methods and methodologies is difficult to say. In any case, grounded theory has a lot to offer, and has been accepted by a significant number of researchers, if not as the only research method, at least as one of them. The number of researchers using grounded theory types of research is growing.

Key concepts

Field research	Saturation
Hypothesis-testing studies	Descriptive studies
Fieldwork	Field design
Ethnographic fieldwork	Ethnographic research
Grounded theory	Holistic approach
Concept-indicator model	Selective coding
Theoretical sampling	Axial coding
Exploratory studies	Theoretical memos
Experimental studies	Open coding
Case study	Coding
Eclectic approach	

9

Observation

1 Introduction

Observation is one of the oldest methods of data collection. Until it was introduced to sociology it was largely employed by social anthropologists and ethnologists, with sociologists and other social scientists opting in larger numbers for survey and other techniques. Nevertheless, with time observation gradually became popular outside anthropology and ethnology and particularly in the social sciences. Today, observation is proclaimed to be one of the fundamental techniques of social research.

Literally, observation means a method of data collection that employs vision as its main means of data collection. It is used as the only technique of data collection, or jointly with other techniques, for instance in intensive interviewing, documentary study or case studies. Observation is an indirect method of data collection since in most cases it collects information without the full knowledge of the respondent. Often, even if the respondent knows that he or she is being observed, the actual nature and purpose of observation are not known.

In this chapter we shall explore the nature, types and process of observation and examine its significance for social research.

2 Types of observation

Observation is open to all observable social phenomena. However, there are some limitations. In the first place there are issues that do not lend themselves to an observational analysis, for example personal, sensitive issues or causes and consequences of social phenomena. Also, past or future events cannot be observed. Further, observation is limited by the fact that it can only study observable phenomena.

There are several types of observation, some more popular than others. Although basically similar, they do differ from each other in the degree of the observer's participation in the environment, in the setting in which it occurs, and in the manner in which it is organised. Some examples of observation are given below.

Naive and scientific observation

Naive observation refers to everyday, unstructured observation which people use when they interact with others in social situations. Observation becomes scientific when it is systematically planned and executed, when it is related to a certain goal and when it is subjected to tests and controls.

Participant and non-participant observation

In general, the degree of the observer's involvement in observation varies from no participation at all to full participation. In the first case, observers study their subjects from outside the group without becoming a part of the environment of the observed; in the second case, they actually become members of the group they are supposed to study. The first type of observation is known as *non-participant* observation; the other is *participant* observation.

In participant observation, the observers observe from inside the group, and ideally their identity as a researcher is not known. For instance, researchers who want to observe criminals in action manage to become members of criminal gangs; those who wish to study homosexual behaviour pretend to be homosexuals, and are accepted by the members of the group they intend to study; and investigators who want to study the work conditions of labourers in a factory are employed in a plant for a certain time, working along side the workers. As members of these groups, they can study among other things their structure, process, problems and attitudes from the inside, and as experienced by the members of the groups.

In the case of non-participant observation, the observers are not a part of the environment they study. Their position is clearly defined and different from that of the subjects. In ideal terms the observers are invisible, unnoticed and outside the group they observe. The best example of non-participant observation is laboratory observation, where the subjects interact in a laboratory and the researcher observes them from the outside, for example through an one-way vision glass. Observing children playing in the school playground through a window is another example of non-participant observation. In both cases the observer does not actively participate in the group under study.

Many cases of observation lie somewhere between these two extremes of participant and the non-participant observation. In certain cases investigators are more observers than participants; in others they are more participants than observers — the difference between the various forms of observation is a matter of degree rather than a matter of substance.

Structured and unstructured observation

These two types of observation differ in terms of the degree to which they are structured. *Structured observation* employs a formal and strictly organised procedure, with a set of well-defined observation categories, and is subjected to high levels of control and differentiation. It is organised and planned before the study begins. Unstructured observation is loosely organised and the process of observation is largely left up to the observer to define.

Semi-structured observations lie somewhere between these two techniques, and may be structured, for instance, in their approach but unstructured in their setting. They are relatively common in social research and combine advantages (and limitations) of both the structured and unstructured techniques of observation.

Natural observations and laboratory observations
The main difference between these two techniques lies in the type of setting in which they unfold. In the former, observations take place in natural settings; in the latter they are performed in a laboratory.

Open and hidden observation
This distinction refers to the degree to which the identity of the researcher as an observer as well as the purpose of the study is known to the participants. While in the case of open observation the participants are well informed of the nature of the study and the identity of the researcher, in hidden observation they are not.

Active and passive observation
This type of observation refers to the degree to which the observer is involved in the process and purpose of observation. Active observation presupposes full engagement of the observer in the cause of the study, while passive observation sees the role of the observer as being just a strict recording of data. In this case observation is a job to be done in an objective and neutral fashion.

Direct and indirect observation
Direct observation studies the subject it intends to explain; for example, if the study intends to explain the patterns of conflict in marital dyads, and observation involves married couples, this is a direct observation. Indirect observation does not involve the object of study, either because the subject refuses to take part in the study or a direct observation is not possible (the subject is deceased). Instead, researchers observe the physical traces the phenomena under study have left behind and make conclusions about the subject. The discussion of physical traces in this volume also applies here.

3   The process of observation

a   Steps in observation

Observation takes place in the same form as the general research model introduced earlier in this book. Nevertheless, the content of each step includes elements that are more or less influenced by the nature of observation. The following is a brief summary of the basic steps of research as employed in the area of observation, mainly by quantitative researchers. Qualitative investigators may use the same steps but their content will have to be adjusted to the principles of the underlying theoretical framework.

Step 1: Selection of the topic
This step entails the selection of a theoretical approach and the issue to be studied through observation. This must be an observable social phenomenon at any level.

Step 2: Formulation of the topic
This involves a specific definition of the topic; exploration of its elements and structure; development of observation categories; establishment of the observer–subject relationship; and explanation of what is to be observed, where required.

Step 3: Research design
Here, the researcher will determine the subjects to be observed; select the setting for observation; and make arrangements for entry into the setting for recording the data and printing the documents.

Step 4: Collection of data
This involves familiarisation with the setting and subjects; initial interaction; observation and recording.

Step 5: Analysis of data
At this stage the researcher will undertake data reduction, presentation (e.g. in tables and graphs), cross-tabulation and interpretation.

Step 6: Report writing
This involves the writing of the report to be published in some form.

b   The structure

The structure and process of observation depend on many factors, especially with regard to the underlying methodology. While in some cases observation is employed as participant observation, in other cases it might appear as non-participant observation. In case-study research, for instance, both direct observation and participant observation can be employed; however, in both cases its process is quite clearly explained and outlined in the protocol.

In some cases observation is employed in a structured way, where everything must be followed to the last detail as prescribed; in other cases it is done only while employing other methods, for example while interviewing respondents.

4   Selection and formulation of the topic

Here, apart from choosing the topic to be observed, the researcher will establish the logical and normative structure of the study. This involves an explanation of the purpose of observation. This is required in both participant and non-participant observation, and in qualitative and quantitative research.

Definition of the topic and categories

In quantitative studies and structured observation, the topic is expected to be precisely defined so that the observers are well aware of the specific elements of the object to be observed. In addition, specific *categories* will be developed. This will help the observer categorise the material (i.e. behaviour, relationships, etc.), for example according to the behaviour or intentions of the actor(s), according to the reaction of the observed or according to the nature of the situation. In a class observation, 'teacher centred', 'student centred', 'authoritarian', 'democratic' and 'oppressive' are some examples of categories that might be employed. These categories are developed in consultation with experts and before the observation has begun. Once these categories have been formulated and refined, they are employed in the same form throughout the study. This allows the researcher to categorise the units of analysis, it also allows comparisons to be made. Category construction will, finally, enable investigators to direct their attention to the elements close to the goal of the study, to collect valid and accurate data and, where multiple observers are employed, to produce more accurate, detailed and comparable findings.

In the case of a *qualitative research* and where participant observation is employed, the approach is relatively different. Certainly, the topic has to be chosen; the definitions, however, are not expected to be very specific, and the categories not explicit and deterministic. Here observation means exploration of the area under study. One of the tasks of this exploration is the establishment of categories; when categories have been formulated, it is expected that observation will enable the investigator to refine them, to expand them or to reduce them. The process of observation in this context is flexible and open in its approach.

The approach

The investigator makes a number of important decisions. The most significant are related to: (1) the most appropriate theoretical and methodological framework, that is, whether the study will employ a quantitative or a qualitative methodology, and (2) the type of observation, that is, whether structured or unstructured, participant or non-participant observation will be used.

Degree of participation

Depending on the type of observation chosen, the investigator will determine the type of relationship to be established between the observer and the observed. In structured situations observation does not allow flexibility. In the case of participant observation, the observer can take up a variety of roles: for example, complete participation, where she or he is fully absorbed in the group under study; partial participation, in which the observer is more a participant and less an observer; and partial observation, where the investigator is more an observer and less a participant.

Unit of observation

At this stage the investigator will finally decide about the *unit of observation*. This is not a serious issue in unstructured observation; it is, however, of considerable significance in structured observation. In this case the observer determines the element that will be observed, for example action, speech, attitudes or behaviour, as well as the intensity of these elements. Many researchers have developed very complex and impressive techniques which help to direct observation to certain issues and to record the data in an accurate and convenient manner.

Related to the definition of the unit of analysis is the development of categories to be observed. This issue was introduced above.

5   Research design

a   Selection of the sample

The most important issue of this step is the *selection of the sample* required to study the research topic. As far as structured observation is concerned, selection of the respondents is largely made by means of probability sampling and less by using other sampling procedures. With respect to unstructured or participant observation, the subjects are often chosen by means of purposive sampling or theoretical sampling.

As stated earlier, sampling refers to more than just the selection of the subjects (see Mahr, 1995). Rather it relates to more issues of which the following are the most important.

Time
Observers have to decide at this stage about the *time* when observation will be carried out. This is more significant in the case of participant observation, since certain times might offer different environments and experiences than other times (days, weeks, months, etc.). For this reason, choosing a definite time will have implications for the type, quality and quantity of information gathered. The structured observer does not necessarily need to comply with such requirements, since it is expected that observations will take place under controlled conditions (including time).

Place
Sampling refers also to the *place* in which observation will be conducted. If schools, hospitals or clubs, for instance, are to be observed, one has to determine where in these systems observations will take place, that is, in which room, level or specific location. The choice of place is significant.

Type of event
In addition, the *type of event* to be studied has to be determined. Will the researcher observe everything, some events, routine events, unexpected events or special events? This decision must be made regardless of the methodological orientation of the study.

Subjects
Most importantly, sampling will determine the *persons* to be observed. Even when the selection of the primary units has been completed (schools, clubs,

etc.) the specific persons who will be observed have to be selected. When marriages, for instance, are the research units and after the actual units have been selected, it still has to be determined which specific persons will be observed, namely: both husband and wife; only one spouse; with or without the children? These questions have to be answered adequately by the investigator.

b   The arrangements

As well as the sampling procedures, the investigator decides about the *arrangements* regarding entry into the setting and recording the data. As far as the entry into the setting is concerned, this affects the participant observers and is a very important aspect of observation. It mainly involves gaining permission to enter the environment in question, which is quite often difficult to obtain. While it might be relatively easy to gain permission to observe school children during lunch time, it is quite difficult to gain entry into a gaol, a street gang, a club of homosexuals or certain government committees. Arrangements have to be finalised before the process of observation can begin.

6   The observer

During the research design stage, decisions about whether the investigator or an assistant will carry out the observations must be made. If an observer is to be appointed, issues such as the skills and training required must also be considered.

a   Observer skills

The quality of the observer is often more significant in the context of observation than that of assistants working in the context of other forms of data collection; this is because observation, particularly participant observation, relies very much on the attributes of the researcher for both amount and quality of information. Skills are more in demand here than in experiments or surveys. Particularly with regard to observation employed in the context of case studies, this is more crucial since the observer is often expected to carry out the study single-handedly. Although this is a questionable assumption, it does indicate how significant the observer is for the success of observation.

For this reason observers who possess the qualities required to complete their task successfully must be chosen. These qualities will vary from case to case, particularly with reference to the type of observation chosen. But intelligence and previous experience with observation, exact knowledge of the topic and (where appropriate) of the categories, flexibility and adaptability, ability to get along with others, to follow instructions to the smallest detail, to be unbiased and free from ideological constraints and to be honest and trustworthy are of paramount importance.

b   Observer training

This calls not only for careful selection of the observer but also for effective and well-planned training. In most cases the significance of observation makes it necessary for the investigator to carry it out alone; this occurs more so in participant observation and with regard to qualitative research and case-study research. Where, however, more than one observer is employed, and where the observer is not the investigator, training becomes unavoidable.

When this is the case, training must concentrate on issues that are central to the study, or possible sources of distortion and aspects of the study that require further explanation. Pilot studies will certainly show the way. Nevertheless, concentration on the following points is thought by many writers (e.g. Becker, 1989; Flick *et al.*, 1991; Martin, 1988) to be very useful:

- thorough understanding of the research topic;
- knowledge of the peculiarities of the population;
- understanding of possible problem areas of the study;
- familiarity with the categories (where appropriate) and their effective use;
- introduction to ways of overcoming unexpected problems and conflicts;
- ability to follow instructions accurately and adjust them without causing bias or distortion of the data;
- adaptability and flexibility;
- ability to observe several subjects and categories at the same time.

Even when only one observer will be involved in the study, training is important. What will be observed, when and how are issues with which the observer must be very familiar. The extent of involvement is another issue. Also, how to become a genuine participant observer is a difficult question, and observers only seldom reach that stage (Wolcot, 1992: 20). Training is always helpful.

7   Collection of the data

During this stage the researcher executes all the instructions and employs all the techniques outlined during research design. In practical terms, the observer approaches the subjects and collects the information. This issue will be discussed later on in this book. Only a few general points will be mentioned now.

Initiation
Preparation of and introduction to the appropriate setting and offering adequate instructions are the initial duties of the observer. More particularly, the structured observer *contacts the subjects* and invites them to the laboratory, explaining to them their task in detail, such as offering a couple one hundred dollars and asking them to discuss how they would spend it. How much of the process of observation will be disclosed to them depends on the nature of the study.

If the structured observation takes place in natural settings the approach is similar. The subjects are, under normal circumstances, not informed of the fact that they are being observed, and there will be no arrangements made regarding the setting either. The observer visits the subjects and observes them from outside the group, without being noticed by the respondents. Recording will take place here and in laboratory observation in a manner determined by the investigator.

In the case of *qualitative observation*, for example participant observation, the choice of the respondents and the initiation of the study are rather different. As stated above, no random sampling procedures are used here, and the participant is more than just an informant. The observer is expected to respect the observed, to be understanding and tolerant and also familiar with the life conditions of the observed. The observer–observed relationship is close, based on understanding and mutual trust and also directed towards cooperation for the purpose of answering the research question.

Data collection

In participant observation, *collection of the data* begins after entry to the setting is gained. Notes are taken in the way that best suits the circumstances. When the framework is qualitative, collection and analysis of data take place simultaneously.

Observation focuses on research units over a set period of time. In this sense data collection can relate to various time spans and therefore focuses on different time frames, generating different types of data collection. Below are a few examples.

Continuous observation

In its most common form, observation is *continuous*; this means it records occurrences for the entire duration of the event. For instance, the observer will record the activity level of aged patients in a geriatric ward from 8 am to 10 am for a period of four weeks.

Time-point observation

Data collection can also focus on a specific point (*time-point*); here the observer is interested in what happens at a particular point in time; for example recording the place where aged patients are at 9.00 am sharp. Are they still in bed sleeping, staring at the ceiling, reading, talking to others, walking around, helping others and so on. Time-point observation produces 'snap shot' data, like a picture, separate from context or time frame.

Time-interval observation

Between continuous and time-point observation is *time-interval observation*. Here, data collection is focused on what happens between two set times, say, between 9.00 am and 9.10 am. With regard to our example, the observer has good reasons to collect data during that interval and record everything that is significant.

Event observation

This form of data collection relates to behaviours which occur because other behaviours (events) also occur. The presence of an observation unit is conditional on the occurrence of another event. In our example, activity levels of aged patients in a geriatric ward are recorded after the doctor entered the ward. Here the observer is interested to see whether the patients are more/less active when the doctor is present than when the doctor is absent.

Recording

Recording of data is an issue that must be considered during the planning stage of the research. This includes three issues, namely what will be recorded, when and how. This refers to the methods of recording, the events to be recorded and to coding.

Methods of recording

The method of recording varies from one type of observation to another. In participant observation recording is different from that employed in non-participant observation. It also varies according to the type of events studied, the density of information and the size of the group.

Recording can take place in a manner most suited to the research topic and with which the observer is most familiar. It can, for instance, be constructed in a chronological or a systematic way. The most common methods of recording are (1) writing down information verbatim, in summary or in key words; (2) tape recording conversations; (3) video recording events; (4) taking photographs.

Writing down information is the most common method; it is, however, not always possible, for instance when information to be recorded is dense, when many persons are to be observed, and when the identity of the observer is hidden. Apart from this, taking notes may divert the attention of the observers from the scene to the paper, causing them to miss part of the happenings in the group. If the conditions of observation do not allow taking notes, the observer should write down key words or phrases as a guide, and should complete them after observation; or leave the scene for a moment and while away write down important notes.

Tape and video recording make recording easier and certainly more efficient. The tapes can be listened to or viewed as many times as required, including using more than one observer, and this produces more accurate and more valid recordings. However, there are cases when recording is not possible or respondents object to it, and this limits its use. Apart from this, recording adds to the work of the observer — taking notes is just postponed and often a lot of recorded information is of no use. Taking photographs, finally, is of limited use.

Events

Recording is done in the context of a methodological framework. In quantitative studies observation is conducted on the basis of the observational categories developed by the investigator before the observation process. Such categories relate to items and subjects, indicating the existence of some characteristics, their content, trend and intensity. Observation may focus on the content of discussions, on feelings, facial expressions, aggression, patterns of communication and behaviour and on general issues and items defined through the operationalisation process. In qualitative studies observers may initially record whatever happens around them indiscriminately, that is, regardless of whether it seems at that point to be important or not, and keep accurate and detailed records and complete notes. Description of the setting, persons, discussions, relations and so on is the rule. Often, in qualitative research, while describing, observers will evaluate their observations and make tentative hypotheses or explanations; they will also revise their hypotheses and categories in the light of their data and make new suggestions and explanations continuously.

Time
Most researchers believe that where possible, recording should be done as events unfold, and should be as detailed as possible. Recording after the event is only done by necessity.

Coding
Where observation categories have been developed and the items of observation are clear, specific and known in advance, codes can be used to record the data. Codes serve as symbols, a shorthand recording, where actions and behaviours are replaced by numerals or keywords. Codes make recording easier, particularly when there are many items to be recorded and also many persons to be observed. If categories are distinct and easily identifiable, mechanical devices can be used to record observation data. The *interaction chronograph* developed by Chapple, the *audio-introspectometer* developed by Thelen and the *interaction recorder* developed by Bales and Gerbrauds are a few examples. Tape recorders and video tapes are more recent additions to traditional methods of recording, mainly employed in structured observations.

Number of observers
In most cases observation is completed by one person only. In other cases more than one observer is employed. Multiple observers usually observe their groups alone and produce data which are included in the final analysis. The use of multiple observers speeds up data collection but can also cause problems, especially with regard to inter-observer variability.

8   Analysis of data and reporting

How data will be analysed and the way in which they will be published is an important part of the research process, and will be discussed in another chapter. At this stage it is important to note that in participant observation and where qualitative research is employed, collection and analysis of the data are often interwoven, and take place concurrently.

9   Participant observation

In the previous discussion reference was made to participant observation in general and to specific aspects of its structure and process in particular. In this section we shall summarise some aspects of this discussion and introduce more specific points related to participant observation as a tool of qualitative research. It must be noted here that under certain conditions, participant observation can be developed in the context of a quantitative methodology and be considered as a quantitative method. Here this method will be discussed in a qualitative framework.

As stated earlier, a method is thought to be qualitative if it shows, among other things, at least the following characteristics:

- A commitment to studying everyday life events, which are studied the way they are experienced and understood by the participants.
- A perception of reality as constructed through interaction and communication of the participants.
- Performance of the study in the natural environment of the participants without changing it in any way.
- Perception of reality in an interpretative manner — in this sense, participant observation is set to study social events under all these conditions, bringing data close to reality, the people living in it and the way they construct and experience it.

More particularly, participant observation is characterised by the fact that it observes communication and interaction in an unstructured and natural manner, where the design is developed and modified while observation is carried out, in a face-to-face relationship, and in an open and flexible way. Here observation is directed towards a social situation, which only later and after the study has been initiated is broken down into single elements.

10   Ethical issues

As in other methods of data collection, ethical issues should be considered very carefully. The nature of observation makes ethics a real issue since observers have the opportunity to interfere directly with the personal life of the subjects, and since in many cases observation takes place without the subjects being aware of it. This becomes even more serious when the subjects do not know the identity of the observer, for example when the observer pretends to be a genuine member of the group under study.

For some writers ethics is not an important issue and should not hinder researchers from pursuing their research interests if they think that the investigation is carried out for a good purpose. They believe it is therefore justifiable for them to conceal their identity if the research will eventually benefit society and perhaps the subjects.

Other researchers argue that ignoring ethical issues is not permissible, that observers should disclose their identity when entering the private domain of individuals, that they should disclose their real intentions and the objectives of the research and that they should be honest in their intentions.

11   Advantages and limitations of observation

Advantages

Observation as a method of data collection is generally considered to have the following advantages over other methods (Mahr, 1995):

- It provides information when other methods are not effective.
- It employs a relatively less complicated and less time-consuming procedure of subject selection.
- It can offer data when respondents are unable and/or unwilling to cooperate or to offer information.
- It approaches reality in its natural structure, and studies events as they evolve.
- It offers first-hand information without relying on the reports of others.
- It allows the collection of a wide range of information, even when this information is thought to be, at the time of study, irrelevant. This is particularly true of participant observation.
- It is relatively inexpensive.

Limitations

Observation also has some limitations, of which the ones listed below are the most significant. It must be noted that while some limitations occur in qualitative observation, and others in quantitative observation, they are often addressed indiscriminately by many writers (e.g. Becker, 1989; Mahr, 1995), as they relate to observation as a method.

- It cannot be employed when large groups or extensive events are studied.
- It cannot provide information about past, future or unpredictable events.
- It cannot offer data related to frequency of behaviour.
- It cannot study opinions or attitudes directly.
- It is inadequate when studying certain phenomena, such as sexual behaviour, family violence, etc.
- It is a relatively laborious and time-consuming method.
- It is exposed to the observer's bias, selective perception and selective memory.
- In participant observation the observer is a part of the situation that is being observed.
- It offers no control measures regarding bias, attitudes and opinions of the observer.
- It cannot offer quantitative generalisations on the results.

Despite these limitations, observation is one of the most popular methods of data collection, employed by researchers of both the quantitative and qualitative domains.

12   Problems of observation

Observation is limited in its approach in many ways and is affected by several problems. Some of these problems are caused by the observer, others by the nature and purpose of observation as well as by methodological problems. While a few of these problems have already been discussed, others are presented below as summarised by many writers (see Becker, 1989; Berger *et al.*, 1989).

a   Sources of errors

The observer as a source of errors

Lack of ability
Errors may occur due to lack of ability, interest or willingness, as well as tiredness, boredom or attention problems of the observer.

Observer inconsistency
Inconsistency exists in the performance of each observer as well as among observers. This occurs in two ways: the inability of an observer to perform observations in exactly the same way throughout all observations; and different observers involved in the same study cannot perform observations uniformly.

Non-verbal communication
This may affect the attitude and expectation of the observed and influence their behaviour accordingly.

Observer bias
This refers to an observer's consistent tendency to perceive situations according to personal ideology and bias, producing a distorted reality.

Deviation
The behaviour of the observer and his or her relation with the observed may deviate from the prescribed and expected behaviour.

Deception
Observers might deceive the researcher; this is a problem that is difficult to detect and control, particularly in participant observation.

Lack of knowledge
Some observers may lack knowledge of the categories employed in the research.

Problems in recording and analysing data
Facts may not be recorded truthfully and the analysis might be non-systematic and subjective.

Lack of familiarity with the observed group
The observer may not be familiar enough with the group he or she is to observe.

Observer distortion
The phenomena or settings observed are distorted by the fact that the observer

is added to the structure under study (participant observation), or that the respondents have to operate in an artificial environment (laboratory observation).

The purpose of observation as a source of errors
Problems can be caused when the purpose of the study has not been made clear to the participants.

Tools as a source of errors
Inadequate tools of observation may make recording cumbersome and at times impossible, leaving important information unrecorded.

Categories as a source of errors
When categories are inadequate or inadequately defined the collection of relevant data will be affected enormously.

Expectations as sources of errors
Expectations regarding the amount of responses and the direction of responses as well as frequency and/or consequences of categorisation can produce errors.

b   How to prevent errors

The researcher should make a serious effort to prevent errors and, where they have occurred, to reduce their significance and eliminate their consequences. The researcher should act as follows:

- Take the necessary steps to construct a design that will avoid errors as much as possible, for example by making the study object and goals clear and the categories specific and easy to understand, providing effective tools for recording the data and, where possible, offering an environment that will have the least possible negative effect on the research process as well as on the quality and quantity of the data.
- Choose observers and research assistants who have the ability and interest to work on the project, that is, who possess the personal qualities required for the project, have the capacity to learn and adjust to the research needs as required, and be willing to work under diverse and demanding conditions with people of diverse nature and origin.
- Train observers adequately so that they have full knowledge of all aspects of the project, its goals and problems, and particularly the categories and their accurate and meaningful application.
- Supervise observers so that (1) eventual deviations can be identified and controlled, (2) advice can be given when questions arise, and finally (3) plans and categories can be improved through experience.

Errors occur in all types of research, and observation is not an exception. Errors are a part of any investigation. It is the task of the researcher to make the necessary arrangements to prevent errors and problems, and where errors are suspected, to adjust the analysis and interpretation of data accordingly.

13   Summary

In this chapter we described observation, one of the oldest methods and also a popular and effective method of data collection, employed widely across many areas of social endeavour. In social sciences, observation has been used very intensively by many researchers and is becoming increasingly popular, particularly with the rapid expansion of qualitative research and of feminism.

Observation is employed in a number of forms, ranging from participant to non-participant, from structured to unstructured and from direct to indirect observation. Regardless of its type, observation follows a set of steps, beginning with a general definition of the topic and the setting, and proceeding to entry into the field and gathering the data. As in other methods, the chief investigator, here the observer, has a strong impact on the process of data collection; it is therefore a central element of the whole process and for this reason requires serious attention, for example with regard to the choice and training of the observer.

Data collection in this method is as organised and as systematic as in any other method. The fact that it is often used in a qualitative context does not make research easier. For many researchers, it is even more difficult and more demanding to conduct observation than, say, when using a survey, where questions are read from a questionnaire. Observation requires researchers with particular expertise which many do not possess. This is one of the reasons for observation being affected by many problems. Researchers make a serious effort to avoid or at least reduce these problems and their consequences.

In the next chapter we shall introduce another method of data collection which is equally popular and effective: the mail questionnaire, which is a part of what we know as surveys.

Key concepts

Observation	Semi-structured observation
Participant observation	Open observation
Unstructured observation	Passive observation
Laboratory observation	Scientific observation
Active observation	Structured observation
Indirect observation	Natural observation
Naive observation	Hidden observation
Non-participant observation	Direct observation

10

Surveys: mail questionnaires

Surveys are the most commonly used method of data collection in the social sciences, especially in sociology; so common, that they quite often are taken to be *the* research method of social sciences. This perception is strengthened by the fact that almost everyone has been surveyed sometime, for example has participated in census surveys, has received a mail questionnaire at home or at work, or has filled out a questionnaire when applying for admission to a tertiary institution, for a bank loan or for becoming a member of a club. Everyone is familiar with what surveys are all about. Surveys are not only a common research tool, but also a part of a person's life experience.

In general, surveys are methods of data collection in which information is gathered through oral or written questioning. Oral questioning is known as *interviewing*; written questioning is accomplished through *questionnaires*. These are the types of methods we shall discuss next. In this chapter, we shall explore the central elements of mail questionnaires, such as their nature, structure, content, design and construction, their strengths and weaknesses and the forms in which they are employed. Interviews, the other form of surveys, will be discussed in the next chapter.

1   Introduction

As noted above, the use of questionnaires is very common in the social sciences. In most cases, questionnaires are employed as the only method of data collection. In other cases they are used in addition to other methods. In either case they are administered to the respondents by mail or personally by the researcher. The main characteristic of this method is that data are offered by the respondents, with limited interference on the part of research personnel.

In this chapter we shall explore some fundamental issues of questionnaires. Due to the fact that interviews also employ a form of questionnaire, in the format of an interview guide, and since such guides are quite often as rigid and as standardised as questionnaires, the information presented in this chapter is also pertinent to interviewing. Hence we will study questionnaires in a more general manner, concentrating primarily on questioning rather than strictly on questionnaires. We shall see, for instance, that issues such as questionnaire format, type of questions, content of questions and the response format are as relevant to interviewing as they are to questionnaires.

A number of general and specific questions will be emphasised here, of which the following are a few examples:

- Are questionnaires the appropriate method of data collection?
- What type of questions should be considered?
- How many questions should be included in the questionnaire?
- In standardised questions, what types of responses should be considered?
- How will the language of the questionnaire be chosen?
- What are the aspects of the study that must be covered by the questionnaire?
- What is the specific unit of analysis that must be addressed by the questionnaire?
- What elements will be included in the instructions and cover letter of the questionnaire?
- How long should a questionnaire be to do justice to its purpose?
- How will ethics and objectivity be observed in the questionnaire?

2   Advantages and limitations of questionnaires

Questionnaires, as methods of data collection, have strengths and weaknesses and thus advantages and disadvantages that the researcher must be aware of. Strengths and weaknesses are factors which have a significant impact on a researcher's decision about whether or not to use questionnaires in the study. The advantages and limitations which most researchers and writers consider as significant are listed below.

Advantages
- Questionnaires are less expensive than other methods: in the words of Selltiz *et al.* (1976), 'questionnaires can be sent through the mail; interviewers cannot'.
- They produce quick results.
- Questionnaires can be completed at the respondent's convenience.
- They offer greater assurance of anonymity.
- They offer less opportunity for bias or errors caused by the presence or attitudes of the interviewer.
- Questionnaires are a stable, consistent and uniform measure, without variation.
- They offer a considered and objective view on the issue, since respondents can consult their files and since many subjects prefer to write rather than talk about certain issues.
- The use of questionnaires promises a wider coverage, since researchers can approach respondents more easily than other methods.
- They are not affected by problems of 'no-contacts'.

Limitations
- They do not allow probing, prompting and clarification of questions.
- They do not offer opportunities for motivating the respondent to participate in the survey or to answer the questions.
- The identity of the respondent and the conditions under which the questionnaire was answered are not known. Researchers are not sure whether the right person has answered the questions.
- It is not possible to check whether the question order was followed.
- Questionnaires do not provide an opportunity to collect additional information (e.g. through observation) while they are being completed. There is no researcher present, for instance, to make observations while the questions are being answered.
- Due to lack of supervision, partial response is quite possible.

3 Structure of the questionnaire

Regardless of whether the questionnaire is administered personally or by mail, it has to be constructed according to certain standards and principles. In the first place, it has to include three main elements, each having a certain purpose: the cover letter, the instructions and the main body.

The cover letter
The main aims of the cover letter are to introduce the respondents to the research topic and research team, to neutralise any doubt or mistrust respondents might have about the study, to motivate them to participate in the study and answer the questions, and to assure them of anonymity and confidentiality. More specifically, the minimum number of points the cover letter must address are:

- the main objectives and social significance of the study;
- the research team and its sponsors;
- the reasons why the respondent should complete the questionnaire;
- assurance of anonymity and confidentiality;
- requirements for completion such as maximum time, conditions, etc.;
- issues related to ethics.

The cover letter has been recognised as one of the factors that influence the response rate: the way the questionnaire is presented and introduced and the type of assurances given to the respondents determine to a large extent whether the respondent will complete the questionnaire or not, and whether he or she will answer all the questions. Some writers (e.g. Becker, 1989; Mahr, 1995), for instance, suggest that even the way the cover letter addresses the respondent (for example, Dear Sir; Dear Sir/Madam; Dear Mr Jones; Dear Householder, etc.) and also the colour of the paper used, the form of letter head and the style and format of the letter are very significant. Pilot studies and teams of experts are quite often employed to help prepare an effective cover letter.

Instructions

Instructions about how to fill in the questionnaires are mentioned only briefly in the cover letter (e.g. '. . . it shouldn't take more than 30 minutes of your time' or '. . . you only need to tick the box in front of the questions'). Instructions will be given on the questionnaire and/or on a separate sheet. As well as giving details of how to state their answer or preference (e.g. in pre-coded questions) the instructions usually remind the respondents that they should not try to please the researcher, that there are no right or wrong answers and that all questions should be attempted, and instructs them about what to do with the completed questionnaire, for example that it should be returned to the project director in the self-addressed envelop by a certain date. For obvious reasons the instructions are expected to offer as much information as possible and must be written in a simple language. Inadequate instructions are one of the major sources of non-responses and should be avoided.

The main body

The main body of the questionnaire includes the questions that are to be answered. In order to be effective, this part of the document must be worked out very carefully, for example with regard to content, structure, wording, flow, format and so on, and adhere to the basic rules of questionnaire construction (Foddy, 1993). This is the part of the questionnaire that will enable the researcher to collect the data required for the completion of the study, and will be discussed next.

4   The questionnaire format

Questionnaire construction is a very demanding task which requires not only methodological competence but also extensive experience with research in general and questioning techniques in particular. This expertise provides the researchers with the necessary skills required to cope with the major issues of this process, which relate to how the format of the questionnaire should be moulded, what types of questions should be considered and what they should contain, how long the questionnaire should be, and in general how the questionnaire should be presented so that it is clear, easy to read and attractive to the respondent and, most importantly, so that it achieves its purpose.

Questionnaire format refers to the general model which provides guidelines on how the questions should be placed in the context of the questionnaire; there are several models of questionnaire format. Nevertheless, a common requirement of all models is that the questions have to be listed in a *logical order*, allowing for *transition and flow*, that is, for a smooth passage from one topic to the next, and avoiding distortions and problems.

These criteria have been integrated by researchers into a number of *questionnaire formats*. The following six formats deserve to be mentioned:

1 *Funnel format*   The questioning moves from general to specific, from impersonal to personal, and from non-sensitive to sensitive questions.

2 *Inverted funnel format*   The questioning progresses from specific to general, from personal to impersonal, and from sensitive to non-sensitive.

3 *Diamond format*   A combination of the inverted funnel format and the funnel format, where questions progress from specific to general and back to specific, from personal to impersonal and back to personal and so on.

4 *X-format*   The first part of the questionnaire has a funnel format and the second part an inverted funnel format. The questions here change from general to specific and back to general, from impersonal to personal and again to impersonal and so on.

5 *Box format*   Questions are uniform throughout the questionnaire, with all questions being kept at the same level.

6 *Mixed format*   Here questions appear according to the logic of the project, shifting from general to specific and so on as required. Mixed format may also contain sections, each adopting one of the above formats; for example, the first section may employ the funnel format, the second the box format and the last the inverted funnel format.

The type of questionnaire format is chosen to suit the nature of the survey, the type of respondents, length of questionnaire, nature of administering the questionnaire, and the findings of a pilot study. It is important that the format chosen serves the purpose of the study and is not the personal preference of the researcher. Factors such as those controlling soundness of questions must be taken into account when determining the questionnaire format. It is logical, for instance, to avoid asking contingency questions (e.g. 'How often do you read the bible?') before or without asking the relevant filter or screening question (e.g. 'Do you read the bible?'). Using contingency questions without filter questions being asked first, in order to 'trick' the respondent, is unethical and can affect adversely the researcher– respondent relationship. It is also important that the questions are related to each other logically and are interesting and relevant to the topic; above all, the presentation and structure of the questionnaire should make the respondents feel at ease and worthy, rather than the subject of a strict interrogation.

It should be borne in mind that an adequate format ensures a frictionless completion of the questionnaire, allows the respondent to feel a part of the research process, and helps to avoid fatigue and boredom, which can cause disinterest and lack of cooperation. If the questions are arranged according to the logic of the respondent, if they are adequately linked together and if the respondent does not notice the passing of time and the intellectual effort required to answer the questions, a positive attitude to the study is maintained and the respondent is more likely to complete the questionnaire and return it to the researcher.

5   Size of the questionnaire

The size of the questionnaire depends on factors such as the research objective, the type of respondents, the methods of analysis and availability of resources.

The number of questions ranges from only a few to several hundred. However, the golden rule with respect to questionnaire size is that one should include as many questions as necessary and as few as possible.

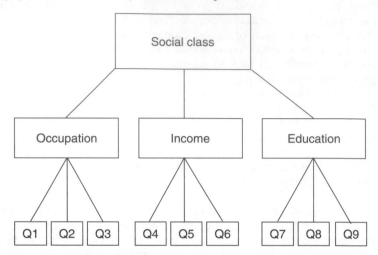

Figure 10.1   Diagrammatic representation of where questions fit in the context of the study and questionnaire

Some more specific guidelines will be introduced in the following sections. At this stage it should be mentioned that the questionnaire, regardless of whether it is offered to the respondent in a written form or in the form of an interview, must contain a translation of the central elements of the research topic: whether a questionnaire will be long or short depends on the number of variables, and the number of indicators considered in the study, as well as the number of questions required to address fully the indicators. If, for instance, the research contained one variable only (e.g. social class), and the indicators of the variable were occupation, income and education, the questionnaire would include as many questions as is required to address the indicators. Figure 10.1 shows diagrammatically where questions fit in the context of the study and the questionnaire. It shows, for instance, that you may include three questions for each indicator; in this case nine questions are sufficient. The questionnaire may include questions about the occupation of the respondent (Q1), the occupation of the respondent's partner (Q2) and the occupation of the respondent's father (Q3). If information about the occupation of the respondent's mother, brother, sister, grandfather, etc. are required, more questions will be included under the indicator 'occupation'. The number of questions related to the indicators 'income' and 'education' will be considered in the same context. The important point here is that there is a straight line between a question, an indicator and a variable. Questions without that link should not be included in the questionnaire unless there is a good reason for it (e.g. they may be secondary or tertiary questions; see below).

The size of the questionnaire also depends on the methodology used and the type of study. For instance, a Gallup poll might include a few question a census survey many more questions and a detailed study of a social issue (e.g. a national family survey) a few hundred questions.

6   Types of questions

Questions contained in a questionnaire vary with respect to a number of criteria, especially those relating to their relevance to the research topic, their approach and structure, content and wording, and with regard to the type of response they require. A brief description of a few of the most common types of questions is given below.

Primary questions
Primary questions elicit information directly related to the research topic. Each question provides information about a specific aspect of the topic, that is, an indicator of a particular variable. In a study of marital power, the question 'Who is the boss in your marriage?' is a primary question.

Secondary questions
Secondary questions are questions which do not relate directly to the research topic. They are of secondary importance in that they provide information on secondary issues such as consistency of opinions or reliability of the instrument used. They do not add new information about the research topic; they guard methodological soundness, integrity of the questionnaire or truthfulness of the respondents.

Tertiary questions
Tertiary questions have neither primary nor methodological significance. They help to establish a framework that allows convenient data collection and sufficient information without exhausting or biasing the respondent. Two examples are padding questions and probes.

Padding questions
These questions are not central to the research but are of interest to the respondent. Acting as a 'breather', they are usually placed before or after sensitive questions.

Probes
These questions are used in interviewing and have the purpose of completing, amplifying or expanding information given by the respondent, stimulating and guiding the discussion and establishing a friendly atmosphere free of bias.

There are several techniques of probing, with interviewers developing and applying them according to need; the two techniques often referred to by writers (e.g. Becker, 1989; Kahn and Cannell, 1957; Moser and Kalton, 1971) are the *summary technique* and *controlled non-directive probing* (see the next chapter).

Direct and indirect questions

Direct or personal questions ask the respondent to offer information about himself or herself. An example of a direct question is: 'Do. you believe in God?'. Indirect questions ask the respondent to offer information about other people, assuming that in this way the respondent will indirectly tell about himself or herself. An example of an indirect question is: 'Do you think that people of your status and age believe in God nowadays?'.

Indirect questioning is mainly used when the respondent is unable or unwilling to offer direct information on the research question; this is the case, for example, when the questions deal with sensitive, embarrassing or threatening issues, or when the topic of research is too difficult for the respondent to answer a direct question. In such cases, indirect questioning makes it easy for the respondent to answer the question. However, indirect questioning raises many serious ethical questions which need to be considered.

Suggestive questions

Suggestive questions presuppose that the respondent holds a particular view on the issue in question that is similar to that of the researcher and contain an implied attempt to tempt the respondent to confirm this view. For example, if we were to test the views of students to examinations, a direct question could have been: 'Do you believe that examinations should be abolished in all sociology subjects?' In a suggestive mode this question could read as follows: 'Don't you also think that examinations should be abolished?'. Suggestive questions *lead* the respondent and *bias* the direction of the findings.

Filter and contingency questions

Filter questions aim at eliciting, for the first time in the study, information related to a general aspect of the research topic, and are usually followed by another more specific question (i.e. a contingency question). An example of such a question is: 'Do you smoke?'.

Contingency questions are geared towards eliciting additional and more specific information on an issue already addressed by a filter question. After an issue has been addressed through a filter question (e.g. 'Do you smoke?'), the contingency question may read as follows: 'How many cigarettes do you smoke each day?'. Asking contingency questions before filter questions are introduced is not a correct practice.

Fixed-alternative and open-ended questions

According to their response format, questions can be divided into two categories: open-ended (free answer) and closed, pre-coded or fixed-alternative questions. In the case of open-ended questions the respondents are free to formulate their answers the way they consider to be the most appropriate, in their own way and in their own words. When the question is pre-coded, the responses are fixed and the respondent is expected to choose the option with which he or she agrees most.

For example the question 'What is your marital status?' followed by an empty writing space is an open-ended question; here it is left up to the respondent to state his or her answer. The question 'Are you currently: (1) Single, (2) Married, (3) Cohabiting, (4) Divorced, (5) Separated,

(6) Widowed?' is a fixed-alternative question. In this case the respondents are expected to indicate their status by placing a tick next to the relevant category or by circling the number that corresponds to their marital status.

Whether to choose pre-coded and open-ended questions or not depends on a number of factors. In a discussion quite a few years ago (which, nevertheless, is still relevant today), Kahn and Cannell (1957) explained these factors as follows: If the researcher is interested in ample information, if the attitudes, ability to communicate and the motivation of the respondents are not known, if they cannot communicate, and if they are not well informed and have not yet structured an opinion, open-ended questions are advisable. If, on the other hand, the researcher is interested in classifying responses or respondents, if the situation of the respondents is known, if they can communicate, and if they are well informed and have formed an opinion, pre-coded questions can be employed.

Open-ended questions have many advantages and several limitations. The advantages are as follows:

- they allow freedom to express feelings and thoughts, especially when complex issues are being studied;
- they offer more details than pre-coded questions, especially qualifications and justifications;
- they offer information in areas that might not have been foreseen by the researcher;
- they allow conclusions about the respondents' way of thinking and logic; and
- they allow the respondent to show creativity, self-expression and initiative.

Despite these strengths, open-ended questions are thought to have certain limitations (Becker, 1989). These are:

- they are not very suitable for sensitive questions;
- they produce large amounts of information which require extensive time and effort to code and/or evaluate;
- they are time consuming and allow no accurate comparisons;
- they can offer useless or irrelevant information;
- they are not suitable if the respondents have problems articulating well; and
- they require additional processing if statistical analysis is intended.

Pre-coded questions have the advantage of being easy to administer, to code and to answer; they allow comparisons and quantification and they help to produce fully completed questionnaires and to avoid irrelevant answers. Their limitations are, for instance, difficulty in covering all possible answers, restriction of freedom, creativity and expressiveness of the respondent, and a high chance of guessing the answers.

The construction of the response categories in pre-coded questions is a relatively difficult task. Alternative answers are primarily constructed so that they are accurate, unidimensional, exhaustive and mutually exclusive (see below). Their final structure should be determined by experts and pilot studies, and they may be formed on a nominal, ordinal, interval or ratio level. The final goal of such a construction should be easy application, reduced stress on the respondent, reduced time required for completion and high precision. It must be kept in mind that too many (more than five) responses may overtax the respondent's ability to differentiate; although more options offer more details they may also offer more options for bias! In general, while well-educated respondents may be in a position to respond effectively to long lists of responses without difficulties or bias, less educated people may not.

Whether or not the response categories should contain neutral options such as 'I don't know', 'no opinion', etc. is a contentious issue (Becker, 1989). While some researchers argue that such an option is required to allow for unexpected answers and to guarantee that the response set is exhaustive, others argue that this encourages the respondent to take the 'soft option' and avoid answering sensitive questions. In methodological terms, the inclusion of a neutral category will depend on the nature of the study and the respondents. If direct answers are required a neutral option has no place in the response set. A compromise position is to employ a filter question to eliminate the need for neutral responses, for instance to ask whether the respondents have an opinion on the government's taxation policy, and then direct questions regarding the nature of the opinion only to those who do have an opinion.

7   Response format

a   Introduction

A characteristic of open-ended and fixed-alternative questions is that the former are easy to construct but difficult to process and the latter difficult to construct but easy to process. Consequently, constructing response sets for fixed-alternative questions is a serious and very demanding task. In this section, we shall look at the options available for responses to pre-coded questions, leaving an examination of the factors affecting the choice of options to be discussed elsewhere. (For an interesting discussion of this issue see Berger *et al.*, 1989.)

It is a strict methodological requirement that response sets to fixed-alternative questions adhere to certain standards and principles of which the most important is that response categories are accurate, exhaustive, mutually exclusive and unidimensional. A brief description of such options is given below.

Accurate sets
Response sets must be accurate; they must address the central point of the question to be relevant and related to the essence of the question. A response set developed to provide responses to the question 'How successful are you with your progress?' containing the response categories 'very satisfied', 'satisfied', 'unsatisfied' and 'very unsatisfied' is not accurate because it relates to *satisfaction* and not to *success*. These two issues may be interrelated but different nonetheless: a business manager may be 'very satisfied' with the progress of his or her branch, but also rate the degree of success of this business as 'moderate'.

Exhaustive sets

Response sets must cover all possible options. If required, the option 'other' is added, to make the response set *exhaustive*. Nevertheless, care must be taken to avoid high proportions of respondents opting for this option. It is desirable and advisable that researchers explore thoroughly the research item before establishing the response categories. Pre-tests, for instance, can determine the type of response categories required for a question, and can assist in reducing the number of respondents opting for 'other' to a minimum.

Mutually exclusive categories

A set of categories is expected to include items that are clearly distinguishable from each other and mutually exclusive. The respondents should only be able to choose *one response,* without confusion and ambiguity. The responses included in the set 'Single', 'Married', 'Living together', 'Divorced', 'Separated', 'Widowed' are — strictly speaking — not mutually exclusive, because it allows a certain group of respondents to choose more than one option. For instance a separated man who is cohabiting can equally tick the third or the fifth option. The same is true for a divorced woman who is cohabiting. This problem can be corrected by making the question specific and more discriminating, for example by asking 'Are you *currently* "Married" . . .' or 'Is your *current* status "Married" . . .' Still, such solutions are not always successful. In the above example, a divorced wife may be obtaining alimony, and therefore considers herself a divorced woman, while cohabiting with another person, establishing that way two *current* statuses.

Unidimensionality

This refers to the requirement that a set of categories should refer to and measure only one construct, in only one dimension. A response category that includes the items 'very reliable', 'reliable', 'unreliable', 'very unreliable' is unidimensional because it measures reliability. The response set 'very reliable', 'reliable', 'unacceptable', 'very unacceptable' is not unidimensional because it relates to two dimensions, namely reliability and acceptability.

b Response sets

The following are possibilities for forming response sets in the context of questionnaires; while some are more common than others, all have been and are currently being employed by social researchers in various studies using questionnaires or interviews.

Numerical responses

This response category includes a continuum, with two opposite adjectives at each end and a range of numbers in between, one of which must be circled or otherwise marked by the respondent.

> *Example A*: The response of the Prime Minister regarding maternal employment was: (Please circle the appropriate number.)
>
> Very satisfactory   5   4   3   2   1   Very unsatisfactory

Verbal scales

In many cases the expected response to a question is formulated in words. The respondent in such cases is expected to tick one of the words in the space provided for that purpose.

> *Example B*: The support provided by the Union was:
>
> Very high   ( )
> High   ( )
> Moderate   ( )
> Low   ( )
> Very low   ( )

Scales of increasing strength

Some researchers opt for response categories that are described simply by an adjective and are followed by a set of numbers ranging from low to high, from which the respondent is expected to choose one. The meaning of the numbers (e.g. 1 standing for very low and 10 for very high) will be explained in the instructions.

> *Example C*: The conditions of Aborigines in this country can be characterised as: (Please circle the appropriate number.)
>
> Acceptable   1   2   3   4   5   6   7   8   9   10
> Discriminating 1   2   3   4   5   6   7   8   9   10
> Just   1   2   3   4   5   6   7   8   9   10

Graphic responses

The use of graphic responses is not new in social research. In its simplest form, a response contains a continuum whose extremes are defined by two opposite adjectives connected by a line. The respondent is expected to mark the line at a point that expresses the strength of his or her view. The researcher will then evaluate the answer according to the position of the mark by means of a standard pattern.

> *Example D*: Last Sunday's elections of the municipal officers were:
>
> Fair .... Unfair

Graphic–numerical responses

A combination of graphic symbols and numerals is being used quite often by social investigators. The direction of choice and evaluation is based on the selected position of the tick, which is not defined in words.

Example E: My wife's reaction to last week's rise in taxes was: (please tick)	
( )	+3
( )	+2
( )	+1
( )	−1
( )	−2
( )	−3

Thermometer scales

In these scales, the responses are set in the form of a thermometer, containing a continuum that is the reading range of a thermometer, the extremes of which are being described by opposite adjectives, for example 'unsatisfactory', 'satisfactory'. The divisions given on the thermometer are used as points of response for the respondent.

Face scales

Another graphic scale employed to record answers to pre-coded questions in a simple manner is the use of faces. Here, usually five to seven faces of equal size and structure are ordered on a line. The faces are identical, except for the shape of the mouth, which at one end is shaped in a U-form giving the impression of happiness, and progressively changes through a neutral position (straight line) to an inverted U at the other end describing unhappiness. There are no explaining adjectives here as it is assumed that the faces offer a clear indication of the implied feeling. The respondents are asked to indicate their feelings to the question by marking the appropriate face.

Ladder scales

In a response set that employs a ladder scale the responses are given on a ladder presenting a continuum of five or more steps, whose extremes are defined by two opposite adjectives (e.g. 'high', 'low' or 'strong', 'weak'). The question could be, for example, 'Whereabouts do you stand on the social ladder?', advising the respondents to place an X on the point of their choice.

Constant-sum scales

These scales ask respondents to score two or more objects or concepts so that they together add up to a given amount (e.g. 100). This relative measure is most suitable to ascertain, for instance, the psychological distance between stimuli. The respondents may be asked to allocate 100 points to the Labor Party or to the Liberal Party, according to their handling of taxation issues. The rating can be 100 to 0 or vice versa; it can be 20 to 80, 60 to 40 and so on. Scores allocated by the respondents can be further computed and evaluated, for instance, by constructing relations of the pattern A/B = 60/40 = 6/4 = 1.5, and vice versa.

Likert scales

Likert scales are widely used, particularly as a means for studying attitudes. The response categories range between two extreme positions divided into five points corresponding to a verbal–numerical scale.

Example F: The reaction of the members of the Teachers' Union of NSW to the salary increase suggested by the government was, in my opinion:

Very positive   5
Positive   4
Neutral   3
Negative   2
Very negative   1

(Please circle the relevant number.)

Ranking scales

Unlike many scales in which respondents are asked to tick one response only, in ranking scales it is required that all responses be answered, for example by ranking them from highest to the lowest. In such cases there are as many ranks as there are items.

Example G: My ranking of the performance of the five political parties from 1 (low) to 5 (high) is as follows:

Democrats   ...( )
Labor Party   ...( )
Independents   ...( )
National Party   ...( )
Liberal Party   ...( )

(Please enter numbers in the spaces provided.)

The structure of the set of responses, its nature and size depends on many factors, but mainly on the nature of the study, the nature of the respondents and the extent to which statistical analysis will be used. For an accurate and effective construction of response categories of this kind, several techniques have been developed and are frequently used by researchers. Those introduced by Likert, Thurstone and Guttman are three examples. Such scales have already been introduced in another chapter. We now turn our attention to another aspect of questionnaire construction, namely the content of the question. The main issues related to the content of questions are described below.

8   Question content

The content of the questions is obviously the most important element of the construction of a questionnaire or an interview guide. While form and order of questions may influence accessibility to information, the content of the questions will lead to the type of information sought in the study. In order that the questionnaire achieves its purpose, the content of questions must be organised according to the following criteria (see Becker, 1989; Mahr, 1995; Puris, 1995):

- *Composition*   The composition of each question is expected to address one item only. Double-barrelled questions are not allowed. For instance, the question 'Are your parents caring and supportive?' addresses more than one issue: first it does not differentiate between father and mother. It is not possible here for the respondent to state the specific feelings of each parent. And, second, it asks about care and support. Such questions should be avoided. If information for all these issues is required, four separate questions should be asked.
- *Relevance*   The content of each question *must be related* to the research topic. Questions not directly related to the topic may be asked only if they can be well justified and if they serve a certain purpose.
- *Symmetry*   The questions should address a specific element of the research topic and be symmetrical: there should not be many questions on one aspect and few on the others unless there are reasons to justify it. Each sector in the questionnaire should be symmetrical to the whole questionnaire.
- *Clarity and simplicity*   The content of the questions must be *clear and simple* in language and in content. Questions that are too general, ambiguous, vague and embarrassing should be avoided. Personal questions should be employed very carefully.
- *Language*   Questions should be formulated in the language of the respondent.
- *Attitude*   Questions should convey a positive attitude towards the respondent and the study, in general, based on friendliness and collegiality.
- *Presuming questions* are not permitted. It is also unethical to ask, for instance, a student, 'When did you stop cheating in the examinations?' without introducing a filter question first regarding cheating.
- *Suggestive questioning* is when the respondent is encouraged to give a certain answer ('Don't you also think . . .'); *prestige bias* occurs when the respondent is motivated to follow some generalised views of important people (e.g. 'Gerontologists believe that progressive age causes alienation and hostility among older males; what is your view on this issue?'). This form of questioning must be avoided.

Some important rules regarding the content of questions will be presented in the next section.

9   Rules of questionnaire construction

It is common practice for questionnaires to be constructed according to set rules and standards. Some rules are more important than others, but overall they are expected to be taken into consideration during the construction of the questionnaires (or interview schedules). Many writers (Berger *et al.*, 1989; Mahr, 1995) refer to the rules listed below.

a   Layout

- Questions must be well presented in the questionnaire, easy to read and easy to follow.
- Questions and response categories must be easy to identify and distinguishable from other questions and response categories. For this reason, sufficient space should be provided between the questions.
- Clear instructions regarding the way of answering the questions must be given, for example 'circle the appropriate number' or 'tick the right box'. Nothing should be taken for granted.
- Sufficient space should be left for the respondent to make relevant remarks if required.

b   Content of the questions

- Every question must be relevant to one or more aspects of the study.
- Ambiguous, non-specific and hypothetical questions are to be avoided.
- Leading, double-barrelled and presuming questions should not be employed.
- Embarrassing, personal or threatening questions should be avoided.
- Vague words and academic jargon should not be used.
- The language of the respondent should be employed. If impossible, a simple language should be used, without jargon, slang or complicated expressions.
- Easy flow and logical progression in the questionnaire should be assured.
- Each question should ask what it is supposed to ask.

c   Questionnaire format

- The questionnaire must have a professional appearance and should give the impression of a document that deserves respect and invokes feelings of responsibility.
- The questionnaire should be presented in a way that encourages the respondent to complete and return it.
- Writing on one side of the page is, for smaller questionnaires, preferable to writing on both sides.

- Print and colour of paper and ink must correspond with the preferences of the respondents.
- The questionnaire should be presented as a complete document with an inviting and reassuring introductory cover letter and a concluding note containing instructions regarding the return of the questionnaire.
- The questionnaire size should be kept to a minimum, and restricted to as many questions as necessary, and as few as possible.
- Sufficient instructions and probes should be provided where necessary.
- Pre-coded questions should offer adequate response categories.
- All questions should be checked for possible bias and ethical adequacy.

It must be noted that the success of the questionnaire in general and the response rate in particular depend to a large extent on the factors stated above — factors that motivate the respondent to read the questionnaire, to complete it and to return it. Sending the questionnaire directly to a 'person', rather than to the 'householder', giving it a professional appearance, arranging for a free return, and timing the arrival of the questionnaire at a convenient time for the respondent may guarantee a high response rate.

The issues presented above relate more to quantitative than to qualitative studies. As we shall see later, qualitative investigations use a less rigid structure and a more flexible approach than do quantitative studies. This discussion is also relevant to qualitative research using an interview guide rather than a questionnaire.

10   Steps in questionnaire construction

Questionnaires are constructed in a very sophisticated and systematic manner. The process of construction goes through a number of interrelated steps, and offers a basis for the research stage to follow. Some steps seem to receive more attention than others, and the following are the most commonly mentioned steps of questionnaire construction (see Becker, 1989; Berger *et al.*, 1989; Puris, 1995):

Step 1: Preparation
The researcher decides what is the most suitable type of questionnaire and determines the way it will be administered. As well, a search for relevant questionnaires that might have already been developed by other investigators is undertaken. If suitable questionnaires are found they can either be adopted for the study or used as guides in the construction of the new questionnaire. If the search is unsuccessful, a new questionnaire is developed.

Step 2: Constructing the first draft
The investigator formulates a number of questions, usually a few more than required, including questions of substance (directly related to aspects of the research topic), questions of method (those testing reliability and wording), and secondary as well as tertiary questions.

Step 3: Self-critique
These questions are tested for, among other things, relevance, symmetry, clarity and simplicity, as well as for whether they comply with the basic rules of questionnaire construction presented above.

Step 4: External scrutiny
The first draft is then given to experts for scrutiny and suggestions. It is anticipated that some questions might be changed or eliminated, while new questions might be suggested.

Step 5: Re-examination and revision
The critique offered by the experts and group leaders will be considered and eventual changes implemented. If the revision is not significant, the investigator proceeds to the next step. If the revision is substantial, the questionnaire is presented again to experts and later re-examined and revised until it is considered satisfactory. The investigator then proceeds to the new step.

Step 6: Pre-test or pilot study
In most cases a pilot study or a pre-test is undertaken to check the suitability of the questionnaire as a whole (pilot study) or of some aspects of it (pre-test). A small sample is selected for this purpose, and the respondents requested to respond to the whole or part of the questionnaire; the results are then analysed and interpreted.

Step 7: Revision
The pre-test and pilot study usually result in some minor or major changes. If the changes are minor, the investigators will proceed to Step 8. But if the changes are major they will return to Step 4.

Step 8: Second pre-test
The revised questionnaire is then subjected to a second test, mainly with regard to the revised questions. The response is considered and adjustments and revisions follow.

Step 9: Formulation of the final draft
In this final step, apart from implementing the suggestions derived from the pre-tests, the investigator concentrates on editorial work, checking for spelling mistakes, legibility, instructions, layout, space for responses, pre-coding, scaling issues and general presentation of the questionnaire. This copy will finally be sent to the printer.

11   Reviewing the questionnaire

The questionnaire review often involves a large number of points, many of which relate to the nature of the particular research topic. However, many writers (Berger *et al.*, 1989; Selltiz *et al.*, 1960: 552–74, 1976; Puris, 1995) stress that the following points should be considered in the review:

- *Size of the questionnaire*   Is the questionnaire too large or too small? In ideal terms it should include as many questions as necessary and as few as possible. Often, large research topics require many questions, small topics fewer questions. The rule here is that every question should have a specific purpose; if not, it has no place in the questionnaire.
- *Relevance of the procedure*   Which point of the topic is the question related to? Is it strictly relevant? Does it ask what it is meant to ask? Questions must be tuned to one specific point in a clear and unambiguous way.
- *Necessity*   Is every question required? Could some questions be omitted? Is there any repetition in the questions? Is more than one question needed for each item? Questions will be retained only if they have a certain purpose and if they are really necessary.
- *Clarity*   Are the questions easy to understand, clear and unambiguous?
- *Tone and content*   Is the tone of the questions acceptable? Are the questions unethical, threatening, insulting, patronising or otherwise biasing? Such questions must be changed or omitted.
- *Set-up of the questionnaire*   Is sufficient space provided for recording answers given to open-ended questions?
- *Pre-coded questions*   Are the response categories to pre-coded questions easy to understand, exhaustive, unidimensional and mutually exclusive? If not, they need to be restructured.
- *Adequacy*   Are all aspects of the topic adequately covered? If not, new questions have to be added.
- *Instructions*   Are sufficient instructions given for filling out the questionnaire and for proper use of probes?
- *Level of pitching*   Is the wording of the questions appropriate for the respondents' linguistic ability, education, interest and intellectual capacity?
- *Cover letter*   Is the cover letter constructed adequately? Does it offer the required information? Are there any points missing? Is it too long or too short? Are the respondents properly addressed in the cover letter?
- *Layout*   Are the layout of the questionnaire, the colour of the paper and the print size adequate and acceptable?
- *Pre-coding*   Is pre-coding (where required) recorded adequately and in accordance with the computer program used?
- *Statistical data*   Are all statistical data of the respondent (age, education, occupation, etc.) required? Are they sufficient? Are they positioned in the right place on the questionnaire?
- *Guides*   Are the guides introduced to direct the respondent through the questions clear and adequate?
- *Principles*   Have the methodological principles regarding the questionnaire construction been adhered to?
- *Legal responsibilities*   Are any questions likely to cause violation of rights of the respondents or third parties?
- *Ethical considerations*   Is the questionnaire ethically sound?
- *Overall impression*   Is the questionnaire easy to read and pleasant to follow overall?

There are, of course, many more points mentioned by writers on this topic that need to be considered when reviewing a questionnaire (or interview schedule). The list presented above offers a guide only, concentrating mainly on issues referred to most frequently by writers. Individual projects will raise additional and more specific issues that will need to be addressed by the investigator.

12   Relevance of the questionnaire

As stated earlier, questions must be relevant to the research topic. Each question will be related to one or more aspects of the topic, and all questions together will cover all elements of the topic. To ensure that questions are relevant to the topic and evenly distributed among the different aspects of the research question, and that parts of the research issue will not be omitted from the questionnaire, researchers usually follow a number of steps. These steps were mentioned earlier in this chapter and were described in Figure 10.1. These steps are summarised below:

- *Step 1*   The variable(s) to be studied is (are) identified.
- *Step 2*   Variables are divided into a number of indicators.
- *Step 3*   Indicators are translated into a number of questions.
- *Step 4*   These questions are put in a questionnaire following the rules and points stated above.

This way, developing questions for a questionnaire is a *process of translating* research topics into variables, variables into indicators and indicators into questions. This process ensures that each question has a certain purpose and elicits information related to a specific aspect of the research object.

Let us see how this works in practice. Assume that we wished to study the 'Effects of religiousness on the scholastic achievement of teenagers'. Following the suggestion contained in Step 1 above we identify the variables, which in this example are 'religiousness' and 'scholastic achievement'. Following Step 2, we translate the variables into a number of indicators; for example, for the first variable belief in God, church attendance, bible reading and participation in religious activities and for the second variable grade in English, grade in mathematics, grade in science and grade in social studies.

These indicators are then translated into questions (Step 3) such as whether they believe in God; whether they attend church; whether they read the bible; whether they participate in religious activities; and what grade they achieved in English, in mathematics, science and social studies. However, while some indicators might be translated into one or two questions, others might require more questions. One might wish to know, for instance, about the frequency of church attendance of the respondents as well as their sibling(s), parent(s) or other relatives at the present time, last year or two years ago. Nevertheless, the important point is that questions translate the meaning of a topic or variable and provide information for a particular aspect of the research topic.

Table 10.1   Chain of translation

Variables	Indicators	Questions
Religiousness	Belief in God	*Do you believe in God?* *Does your father believe in God? . . .*
	Bible reading	*Do you read the Bible? If so, how often? . . .*
	Church attendance	*Do you go to church? If so, how often? . . .*
	Religious activities	*Do you participate in any religious activities? . . .*
	. . . .	. . . .
Scholastic achievement	Grade in maths	*What grade did you receive last term in mathematics?*
	Grade in English	*What grade did you receive last term in English?*
	Grade in science	*What grade did you receive last term in science?*
	Grade in social studies	*What grade did you receive last term in social studies?*

If this chain of translation is followed carefully, all questions will be relevant to the research topic and the researcher will know exactly the purpose of every question in the questionnaire. As a result, every point of the research issue will have one or more corresponding questions, and every question will have one or more corresponding points in the research problem for which they intend to provide information.

13   Questionnaires in the computer age

Due to their structure, questionnaires, especially those with a standardised structure, lend themselves to computer assistance. To a certain extent, the use of computers goes further than just assisting the researcher in data collection. In certain cases the computer takes over questioning, and collection of data occurs between the computer and the respondent without the involvement of the researcher.

This is obvious in the area of interviewing, which will be discussed more extensively in the next chapter. The packages CAPI, CATI, CODSCI and CISUR allow interviews to be run through a computer, where the respondent reads questions on the screen and answers these questions as instructed (by the computer). Interviews are administered like questionnaires; interviews become electronic questionnaires, often without the presence of the interviewer.

Apart from this, there are computer packages that take over the administration and completion of the questionnaires, replacing the traditional research assistant. The program 'Computerised self-administered questionnaire' (CSAQ) is one example. The respondent is given no questionnaires to fill in but is asked instead to sit in front of a computer terminal; the computer displays the questions on the screen, giving the necessary instructions and offering advice on technical aspects of the questionnaire when required. The respondent enters the responses in the computer and the computer then saves the data in its memory and adds the responses to the research data, gradually preparing them for analysis.

Other programs operate in a similar way. The computer has, obviously, extended its function from its traditional role of the assistant in the statistical analysis to data preparation and collection, functions that were accomplished in the past predominantly by research assistants.

14   Summary

In this chapter it was shown that the questionnaire is one of the forms of survey research, and one that uses written questioning as its medium. More specifically we saw that the questionnaire is a popular method of data collection and one that has many advantages over other methods but also a number of weaknesses. The coverage of many respondents in a relatively short time and the low costs as well as the reduced interference on the part of the researcher in the collection of data are the most important advantages; overall, the advantages of the questionnaire outweight its weaknesses.

The questionnaire is an integral part of the process of operationalisation in that it extends the process of translation of variables to dimensions and indicators further; it translates variables to questions, ultimately connecting abstract concepts to specific questions. Questionnaires are the instruments used to bring to the researcher the information that is required for formulating answers to the research question.

Questionnaire construction is not only employed in the area of mail questionnaires, it is also employed by researchers using interviews. Here questions are formulated and response categories constructed and issues relating to the format and length of the questionnaire debated and resolved. The only difference is that in the end they are not sent to the respondent by mail or handed to them in some way; they are instead communicated to the respondent by the researcher reading the questions one by one. Here the communication between the researcher and the respondents is closer and more intense than it is in mail questionnaires. How this is conducted we shall discuss in the next chapter.

Key concepts

Questionnaire format
Tertiary questions
Indirect questions
Numerical response
Constant-sum scale
Questionnaires
Primary questions
Padding questions
Controlled directive probing
Suggestive questions
Contingency questions
Verbal scales
Face scales
Cover letter

Secondary questions
Probes
Direct questions
Fixed-alternative questions
Unidimensionality
Graphic response
Ladder scale
Ranking scales
Summary technique
Filter questions
Thermometer scale
Prompts
Likert scale

11

Surveys: interviewing

1 Introduction

Interviewing is a form of questioning characterised by the fact that it employs verbal questioning as its principal technique of data collection. Together with questionnaires, interviews make up the survey method, which is one of the most popular techniques of social research.

Interviews are a common occurrence in everyday life, but as a tool of social research, or better as a method of data collection, interviewing is different. This is so with regard to its preparation, construction and execution, first because it is prepared and executed in a *systematic* way, second because it is *controlled* by the researcher to avoid bias and distortion, and third due to the fact that it is *related* to a specific research question and a specific purpose.

Interviews are employed as methods of data collection in most research designs, regardless of the underlying methodology. Qualitative studies employ unstandardised forms of interviewing, such as intensive interviewing and focused interviewing, while quantitative studies employ predominantly structured interviews. Feminists, finally, consider (especially semi-structured) interviewing a very useful method, value it for its openness, qualitative nature and interviewee-guided mode, employ it often for social reform purposes, and think it is very useful for feminist research. Reinharz (1992), for instance, argues that interviewing is 'particularly suited to female researchers' and feels that it 'draws on skills in the traditional female role' (p. 20). She goes on to say that this method is very useful when conducted by a woman; for a woman to be understood it may be necessary for her to be interviewed by a woman (p. 23).

In the discussion that follows we shall examine the most central issues of interviewing, starting with the types of interviews.

2 Types of interviews

There are many types of interviews, each of which differs from the others in structure, purpose, role of the interviewer, number of respondents involved in each interview, and form and frequency of administration. In the international literature, these interview types appear under many and different names. Some types of interviews are employed in both quantitative and qualitative methods; others are used in one research type only. Semi-structured interviews, for instance, are employed in qualitative and quantitative research, but structured interviewing is mostly used in quantitative research.

a   Interviews in qualitative and/or quantitative research

Structured versus unstructured interviews

Structured interviews are based on a strict procedure and a highly structured interview guide, which is no different from a questionnaire. A structured interview is in reality a questionnaire read by the interviewer as prescribed by the researcher. This rigid structure determines the operation of this research instrument and allows no freedom to make adjustments to any of its elements, such as content, wording or order of the questions.

The interview is based on a schedule, and strict adherence to the questions and the instructions is paramount. In this type of interviewing (at least in its extreme form) the interviewer is expected to perform like a 'robot', acting in a neutral manner, keeping the same tone of voice, offering the same impression to the respondents, using the same style, appearance, prompts, probes, etc., and showing no initiative, spontaneity or personal interest in the research topic. The purpose of this is to reduce interviewer bias to a minimum and achieve the highest degree of uniformity in procedure. This form of interview is employed in quantitative research.

Unstructured interviews have no strict procedures to follow of the kind described above. In their extreme form they are theoretically inconceivable, for every interview has a structure of some kind, and is structured in some way and to some degree. Nevertheless, the strict control reported above is lacking here. There are no restrictions in the wording of the questions, the order of questions or the interview schedule. The interviewer acts freely in this context, on the basis of certain research points, formulating questions as and when required and employing neutral probing. The structure of these interviews is flexible and the restrictions minimal, being presented in most cases in the form of guides rather than rules. This type of interview is mostly used in qualitative research.

Semi-structured interviews lie somewhere between structured and unstructured interviews. They contain elements of both, and while some are closer to structured interviews, others are closer to unstructured interviews. The degree to which interviews are structured depends on the research topic and purpose, resources, methodological standards and preferences, and the type of information sought, which of course is determined by the research objective. They can be both qualitative or quantitative techniques.

Standardised versus unstandardised interviews

Interviews vary also in terms of the degree to which the answer to each question is standardised. In *standardised interviews* the answers are determined by a set of response categories given for this purpose. Respondents are expected to choose one of the given options as the answer. The number of options usually varies from case to case. An example of an option with two answers is 'Yes', 'No' or 'Male', 'Female'; an example with more response categories is 'British', 'Italian', 'Greek', 'German', 'Asian', 'American', 'Canadian', 'Other', or 'Strongly agree', 'Agree', 'Undecided', 'Disagree', 'Strongly disagree'. Multiple response categories are more common when Likert scales are employed. They belong mainly to quantitative research.

Unstandardised interviews are characterised by the fact that their responses are left open. The respondent is free to formulate responses the way he or she finds most fitting. In these cases we speak of *open questions*. They are employed mainly in qualitative research.

Individual versus group interviews

When individual interviews are employed the researcher interviews one respondent at a time. This is the most common form of interviewing. The interviewer asks direct or indirect questions to one respondent, who in turn answers these questions. In group interviews more than one respondent is involved in the interview situation. They are also addressed by the interviewer simultaneously. In a small-scale group two people (e.g. husband and wife, or mother and daughter) are interviewed concurrently.

On a larger scale, a group of, say, 20 persons might be interviewed. For example, a class of students might be interviewed together. In such cases, the interviewer hands the students response sheets (e.g. with or without the questions, or computer cards), reads the questions one by one and asks the respondents to enter their answers on their sheet or card. In some cases, the interviewing becomes a dialogue between the interviewer(s) and the respondents. For example, the interviewer asks a question, suggests possible answers (yes, no, I don't know, no answer) and asks respondents to indicate their preferences by raising their hands. The number of positive, negative or neutral answers is counted and recorded in a grouped form. (Adequate measures are taken to ensure that external factors will not affect the answers of the respondents.)

A slightly different form of group interviewing is *group discussion* (focus groups), which was discussed in Chapter 7. Individual and group techniques are employed by both types of methodology, although qualitative studies favour individual interviews.

Other-administered versus self-administered interviews

In *other-administered* interviews the interviewer asks the questions and enters the answers on a response sheet or computer card. When prompting is employed, the prompts are read by the interviewer. As a rule, the respondent does not see the interview schedule, the questions or any other relevant material, and does not write answers or any statements.

In *self-administered interviews* the respondent is supplied with a list of questions and relevant instructions and enters the answers in the appropriate place on the interview form, on a response sheet or a card. The majority of group interviews are self-administered interviews.

Computer-administered interviewing entered the social research scene as a new form of interviewing and is gradually becoming very popular. In this form of interviewing, the computer takes the place of the interviewer and the process of interviewing evolves between the computer and the respondent.

Although quantitative researchers employ all three forms of interview, qualitative investigators tend to favour the first.

Unique versus panel interviews

Unique interviews take place only once. The interviewer approaches the respondent, collects the information and concludes the interview at the same time. Interviewing a respondent for the second time occurs if the first interview is incomplete or additional information is sought. In the case of *panel interviews*, the interviewer collects information from the same group of respondents two or more times at regular intervals. In *trend studies* the same questions are asked at regular intervals but different respondents are involved in the various stages of the research. Quantitative researchers employ both forms; qualitative investigators prefer unique studies.

'Hard' versus 'soft' interviews

In their extreme form, *hard interviews* are conducted in a form that resembles police interrogation, where the interviewer requests information, receives it with some doubt and scepticism, questions (mostly indirectly) the validity and completeness of the answers obtained, often warning the respondents not to lie and forcing them to give an answer when they hesitate. This form of interview is more likely to appear in quantitative than qualitative studies.

In *soft interviews*, the interviewer holds a secondary position in the process of data collection, with the respondent being given a leading role in this process. Here the interviewer guides the interviewees through the process of interviewing without putting any pressure on them. This is predominantly a qualitative method.

A third form of interviewing, the *neutral interview*, demonstrates criteria that stand between those of the hard and soft interviews. The interviewer is neutral, factual, encouraging, friendly but also distanced and impersonal.

Personal and non-personal interviews

Personal interviews are conducted in a face-to-face situation, usually with the interviewer presenting the questions and the respondent giving answers. In the non-personal interview there is no face-to-face relationship; interviews are administered through a medium other than the interviewer (e.g. via telephone or computer). Quantitative researchers employ both forms; qualitative investigators use personal interviews.

Oral and written interviews

By definition, all interviews are 'oral'; as such, this division does not seem to be of any significance. In a similar fashion, although the concept 'written interviews' is used among some researchers, it actually is not logical since written inquiries are referred to as questionnaires rather than interviews. The essence of the distinction here is that oral interviews are administered orally, and written interviews in a form that resembles self-administered questionnaires. The latter is the case, for instance, in group interviewing and in computer-aided interviewing. Here, the questions are presented to the respondent in writing, often without oral intervention, and the answers are given again in writing.

Oral interviews are employed by quantitative and qualitative researchers; written interviews are predominantly used by quantitative investigators, although some qualitative interviews may require written responses.

Open interviews

In this form, interviews are mainly unstructured and unstandardised and allow the interviewer a high degree of freedom to manipulate the structure and conditions of the method. Openness refers to the degree to which the interviews are open to change and manipulation by the interviewer. They are 'open' to changes and contain a minimum of control. Open interviews are used by quantitative and qualitative researchers, although they are more common in qualitative studies.

Informative interviews

Although this concept is used in international literature, such a designation is of little significance since all interviews are informative. Those who use this concept usually refer to interviews that are employed to gather information of a rather descriptive nature. This form of interviewing is employed by both groups of researchers.

Telephone interviews

Interviewing using the telephone as the medium of data collection is a popular method, and is also predominantly employed by quantitative researchers.

Computer interviews

This form of interviewing is conducted with the assistance of computers and is gradually becoming very popular, for several reasons. Using computers is supposed to reduce the research costs significantly, provide a neutral interview environment particularly with regard to sensitive questions, anonymity and confidentiality, and to aid significantly the grouping and analysis of the data. It is predominantly a quantitative method.

Analytical interviews

This type of interview is based on certain theoretical principles and serves to analyse concepts, theories, social relationships and events. They are found more frequently among qualitative than quantitative researchers.

Diagnostic interviews

Diagnostic interviews aim to ascertain specific attributes of the respondents, offering a diagnosis of the respondent who is expected to assist in achieving a goal. This form of interviewing is employed in both quantitative and qualitative research.

'Inquiring' interviews

This form of interviewing is more common in Europe, especially in Germany (ermittelndes interview). Although all interviews are to a certain extent 'inquiring', this type of interview seems to be connected with an interviewer–interviewee relationship, in which the latter is seen as an informant who participates equally in the process of data collection along with the interviewer. This form of interview can be employed by both types of researchers but especially by qualitative investigators.

Guided interviews

This is another name for semi-structured interviews, whereby, although the interviewer is provided with an interview guide, there is ample freedom to formulate questions and to determine the order of the questions. This is both a qualitative and a quantitative method.

Structure or dilemma interviews

In these interviews the interview guide and the order of questions are relatively firmly set, but there is freedom to add supplementary questions. In a typical case the interviewer presents the interviewees with a story (or stories) containing a decision problem (dilemma) which they must solve; they must also justify the suggested solutions. During the interview, the responses are recorded by the interviewer or an assistant. This can be done manually and/or electronically. Depending on the goal of the interview, both the solutions as well as the reasons offered by the interviewees are considered and evaluated. This is predominantly a qualitative method.

Ethnographic interviews

Although developed and initially employed by ethnographers and social anthropologists, this form of interviewing is now also common in the social sciences. In its general form it has the purpose of studying cultures and their manifestation on people. It aims to discover cultural meanings as conceptualised by individuals, search for cultural symbols, establish relationships between cultural symbols and in general explain the meaning of the culture for the people.

In one of its common versions, ethnographic interviews are conducted not with ordinary people of the community but rather with *key informants,* that is, people who have knowledge of the issues and situations in which the researcher is interested. Through discussions with such *experts* the researchers gain a valid picture of the structure and processes of the cultures and groups under study. Studying subcultures as manifested in certain groups, such as women, migrants and street gangs, has proven to be very successful. The assumption here is that such people have acquired a culture that is unique and characteristic and has certain cultural and social bases that deserve special consideration. As a descriptive instrument such a study allows researchers to explain and understand the ways of life found in these groups. As a critical instrument, it aims to emancipate and empower respondents to work towards liberation. This is predominantly a qualitative method.

Delphi interviews

This is a version of the ethnographic interview, employing a multi-stage ethnographic approach. The interviewer questions persons who are experts in the area of study. These experts are asked to offer information, pass judgements on the issue in question and make relevant predictions. The interviewer or researcher summarises this information in a logical and sociological context and offers the summary to the experts for comments and discussion. Special attention is given to extreme answers and comments, and justifications of such deviations explained. Eventual comments or identified deviations are discussed and considered again, often with new questions. This process is continued until the differences of opinion among the experts are reduced significantly.

After the discussions are integrated into the initial report, they are offered again to the experts for further comment and discussion. This procedure of interview, discussion and consideration continues until a stable judgement is reached. This form of interview is considered to be similar to or identical with *discursive interviews*. This method is suitable for qualitative and quantitative research, but is employed predominantly by qualitative investigators.

Originally the delphi technique (also known as dephic poll) was used in the 1940s in war situations and was used to predict future events, hence the name the 'delphi' method. It can also use questionnaires instead of interviews as a method of data collection, ensuring the anonymity of the experts.

Clinical interviews
Used more in the area of psychology, social work and social welfare, this form of interview is employed mainly in order to diagnose and interpret a certain illness. It is, however, also employed outside these areas, such as in sociology when, for instance, the effects of certain environments (e.g. family) on personal development, deviant behaviour or moral character of young children are studied. In methodological terms, the clinical interview is often an unstructured and unstandardised interview, and is in essence different simply because of its purpose and application rather than because of its structure or the techniques it employs. This method is suitable for both types of research, although it is employed predominantly by qualitative researchers.

Biographical interviews
A biographical interview is an interview form employed to study the life history of a respondent. It is often carried out in conjunction with document analysis, and can take several forms, some of which are very open while others are relatively strict (semi-structured). In one particular form, biographical interviews employ a very specific procedure known as narrative interview, which will be discussed later in this section. Biographical interviews are more common among qualitative researchers.

Problem-centred interviews
This type of interview is a semi-standardised interview based on a vague and flexible interview guide, allowing the interviewer to direct, control and adjust the process of the interview freely. The main characteristic of this procedure is that it concentrates on *problems*, which are the main concern of the interview. For this purpose it encourages the interviewee to talk freely about problems in general or specific problems in particular. The interviewer leads the discussion to problem areas of particular interest, and encourages critique and discussion of these problems. This is predominantly a qualitative method.

When employed in a qualitative context, the researcher is expected to adhere to the standards and principles of that methodology, particularly with regard to how the problem concept is presented and researched. Here the interviewer enters the field with a vague concept, which gradually becomes modified, tested and then more concrete and specific during the process of the interview.

In most cases, when the qualitative version of the interview is employed, the interviewer does not explain the purpose of the interview or the research 'problem' to the respondent. In some cases the interviewee is given a list of the questions, which are then discussed with the interviewer. In this form, the qualitative interview resembles a quantitative model. The interviewee is encouraged to discuss the issue critically, stress interesting points and reveal gaps in the guide or the research design.

Focused interviews

This form of interview was developed by R.K. Merton in the 1940s in the context of propaganda research and analysis of mass communication. In a sense, it is similar to structure–dilemma interviews except that it is more open, offers more freedom to the interviewer and is directed towards a specific point. In a more general sense it is a semi-structured interview.

It is called a *focused* interview because it focuses on a specific topic, which respondents are asked to discuss, thereby providing their views and opinions on the research question. More particularly, the interviewer introduces a stimulus related to a film, an article or a situation that the interviewees are familiar with and discusses these issues with them. Originally this technique was employed in group situations but it can equally be employed in individual research. The discussion is meant to be free and open, with the interviewer *guiding* rather than leading and restricting the respondent.

The aim of the focused interview depends primarily on the research goals and the specific interests of the researcher and the study. In general, however, this method aims at *maximising* the potential of the study, in at least two ways, namely by allowing the discussion to go beyond the originally planned themes and topics, and by encouraging the respondents to discuss as many issues of the themes as possible.

The use of focused interviews offers the following advantages: (1) a mild interviewer role; (2) relative freedom for the respondent; (3) opportunities for increased information; and (4) more specific information. Nevertheless, these advantages can cause problems. For instance: too much freedom might divert the discussion towards irrelevant points; some respondents might dominate the discussion, making it difficult for other views to be heard; and discussion leaders might bias the discussion by directing it towards their personal preferences and ideologies.

This form of interview is employed in both methodological contexts.

Narrative interview

This interview form was developed by Schuetze (1979) in his studies on communal power structures; it is often used in conjunction with the study of life stories. Contemporary social scientists use it in a variety of areas outside its original field. The question addressed in these interviews varies with the research object. In most cases, as it is used in qualitative research, the study question can be related to the respondent's whole life, to some aspect of his or her life or any other general or specific point.

In any case, this interview form involves less 'interviewing' and more narration, and aims at obtaining a personal account from the respondent about a life situation retrospectively reconstructed through continuous input on the part of the respondent. There is very little conversation, or question–answer interview in this method. Instead, the interview situation is dominated by the story-telling respondent. The interviewer is passive-stimulating, friendly and permissive (non-authoritarian). This is predominantly a qualitative method.

In a typical case, when the researcher has chosen the respondent and established rapport, a story-generating question is put to the respondent, who in turn offers relevant information. After the story is completed, the researcher may ask additional questions and the session is completed in a friendly way. In a more structured way, the procedure can be described in the following five steps: (1) entering the field; (2) initiating the interview; (3) story-telling; (4) additional questioning; and (5) closure.

During the story-telling step, the respondent offers a complete reconstruction (and evaluation) of a certain topic: (1) as it occurred in the past; (2) in the context of conditions and factors as they unfolded at that time; (3) without preparation, that is, as the respondent recalls it; and (4) as experienced by the respondent. This helps to gain an insight into a segment of a person's life, as experienced, understood, explained and justified by that person.

Intensive interviews

These interviews are similar to clinical interviews, in that they aim to advance deeply into the personality structure of the interviewee and to ascertain problems of which the interviewee might not be aware. As a quantitative technique, the intensive interview has been applied in more general situations as an unstructured interview with some degree of freedom in determining the conditions of the interview situation. In this sense intensive interviews are considered long-lasting, discussion-based and interviewer-guided research tools.

Receptive interviews

This type of interview was introduced by Kleining (1988) in Germany. The main characteristic of the receptive interview is that it is a one-way communication (from the respondent to the researcher), that is, a situation in which the interviewer is not the traditional researcher who asks questions but rather an *active listener,* namely a person (1) who empathetically listens to the interviewee, without becoming lethargic-passive, and (2) who actively encourages the interviewee to continue talking without personally making any verbal statements. Instead, miming and gestures are employed.

As a qualitative method, the receptive interview follows the standards of the underlying methodology, and is set to explore issues of interest to the researcher. This way it considers the respondent's everyday-life perception of the world, openness and the fact that the researcher enters the field without preconceptions, or with some ideas that, however, are expected to be changed, modified and expanded. Receptive interviews are very useful tools of social research.

There are two types of receptive interview: the *spontaneous receptive interview*, in which the respondent talks about a certain issue uninvited and unprovoked; and the *provoked receptive interview*, where the interview situation is organised in some way and the interviewer is invited to take part in the study.

Convergent interviews

This form of interview was proposed by researchers (Callan, 1991: 136–46; Dick, 1987) as a tool of data generation for those employing qualitative methods, particularly in the area of family studies. It is based on a procedure that takes interviewing to higher levels of operations and allows complex techniques which promise interesting and valid results.

The convergent interview demonstrates the following characteristics: (1) it involves two interviewers collecting data independently; (2) it employs unstructured techniques of interviewing; (3) it includes family members who are thought to have divergent views; further, (4) interviewers plan the content of the interview and issues to be covered before meeting the respondents; (5) after interviews are completed, the interviewers summarise and compare their findings and prepare a progress report containing points of agreement and disagreement — only shared issues being considered; (6) the cycle is repeated with another pair of respondents, now with more refined questions, until the purpose of the study is achieved.

Elite interviews

This interview type differs from those described above in that it involves *elites*, that is, well-known personalities, prominent and influential people, as respondents. It therefore aims to collect information that is exclusive and unique to these informants. That information is very valuable because of the special position of the respondents. For this reason, elite interviewing is a very useful technique of data collection. Nevertheless, it has several weaknesses. In the first place, it is difficult to access the respondents and arrange an interview; but even when an interview is arranged, it is often difficult to establish rapport and trust between the interviewees and the interviewer. Besides, these respondents are quite knowledgeable and 'demanding', and require high-quality experienced interviewers, who are not always available. Apart from the nature of the respondent, this type of interviewing is similar to all other interview types.

b   Interviews in qualitative research

In qualitative methodology, interviews are basically *semi-standardised and open* and use a standard technique of data collection. In principle they are similar to the interviews employed by quantitative researchers: they contain interviewers and interviewees, who discuss certain questions. Nevertheless, qualitative interviews vary markedly in their theoretical framework, structure, process and orientation from those employed in quantitative methodology.

More particularly, qualitative interviews vary significantly in structure, length, intensity, order and type of questions, and interviewee participation. The important criteria distinguishing qualitative interviews are the following:

- They use open-ended questions only.
- They are predominantly single interviews, questioning one person at a time.
- The question structure is not fixed or rigid, allowing change of question order, even the addition of new questions where necessary.

- They offer interviewers more freedom in presenting the questions, changing wording and order, and adjusting the interview so that it meets the goals of the study.

In a different fashion, Lamnek (1989) identifies the following methodological aspects and technical elements of qualitative interviewing (see also Pannas, 1996):

- *Reflexivity* Qualitative interviewing employs methods and a process of analysis that reflect the nature of the research object rather than the methodological conviction of the researcher.
- *Naturalism* Qualitative interviews are directed towards studying everyday life events.
- *Primacy of the respondent* The respondents are experts who provide valuable information. They are as important as the researcher and not just a source of data.
- *No standardisation* The guiding element of the interview process is the respondent in his everyday life, not the methodological expertise of the researcher. As a result, qualitative interviews are unstandardised interviews.
- *Communicativity* Communicativity is expressed in communication; this system of communication determines the course and structure of the interview.
- *Openness* Qualitative interviews do not use a strictly standardised approach. Rather, they employ a readiness to change, to correct and adjust the course of study as required by the research. Interviewers are expected to engage in an open discussion with the respondent, and to maintain a passive and stimulating, but not dominating, role.
- *Flexibility* The qualitative researcher follows the course that emerges through the interview.
- *Life as process* Qualitative interviews ascertain aspects of personal experience as displayed in everyday life.
- *Grounded theory* Qualitative interviews in most cases aim at developing a data-based theory, a grounded theory.
- *Explication* Findings emerge through the study and are interpreted during the process of interviewing.

These methodological and technical aspects show that qualitative interviews are far from a soft methodological option and an easy form of research. On the contrary, conducting qualitative interviews is a difficult task, which meets certain important and also difficult requirements and demands. It is generally accepted (e.g. Lamnek, 1988: 68; Pannas, 1996: 76–9), for instance, that although they involve a few typical cases, qualitative interviews:

- require the development of trust, collegiality and friendship between inter-viewer and respondent;
- require a high competence on the part of the interviewer;
- require a high ability of the respondent to verbalise views, opinions and ideas;
- are demanding and time consuming.

So interviewers performing qualitative interviews have a very difficult task, and must have certain personal and professional qualities, as we shall see below.

3   The interviewer

a   The interviewer's tasks

Interviewers hold a central place in the research process. They are assigned significant tasks, and failure to fulfil them accurately has serious consequences for the research as a whole. Becker (1989) lists the following tasks:

- *Selecting and/or approaching* the respondents; this is very obvious in the case of quota sampling; however, it is typically used in other types of research that are based on interviewing, whereby the interviewer approaches the respondents and prepares the interview environment.
- *Arranging* the time, date, duration and conditions of the interview. Here the interviewer's contribution is of paramount importance. Personality, manners and capacity to persuade count very highly towards achieving a high response rate.
- *Performing* the interview. Under normal circumstances this involves asking questions and in general following the instructions of the researcher.
- *Controlling* the interview situation. Involved here is work geared towards reducing or eliminating resistance, suspicion, prejudice and negative forces within the interview environment.
- *Avoiding bias* This means, among other things, that the interviewer adheres to the principles of social research and works towards an objective and ethically based data collection.
- *Recording* the answers accurately.
- *Establishing and maintaining positive relations* with the public; this, as well as guaranteeing continuity of research, helps to preserve the reputation of the research bodies and reinforce their position in the community.

b   Interviewer selection

Due to the significance of the interviewer in the research, investigators employ a very systematic process when selecting the interviewer. The criteria usually considered as significant are: (1) honesty, trustworthiness and self-control; (2) intelligence, maturity and friendliness; (3) sociability and social acceptability; (4) carefulness, conscientiousness and ability to concentrate; (5) accuracy and dependability; (6) objectivity and lack of prejudice; (7) adaptability, independence and initiative; (8) verbal ability and ability to listen to others carefully; (9) interest in and familiarity with the research topic; and (10) ability to work with others in a team of experts (see Becker, 1989; Berger *et al.*, 1989).

The qualities which interviewers are expected to have may vary from case to case and will depend on the type of interview employed. Intensive interviewing, for instance, requires more personal qualities, knowledge of the topic, initiative, creativity, long experience and more maturity than other types of interviewing. In general, a decision will have to be made about the qualities the researcher considers important for the particular type of research. In order to make this decision possible, the researcher will interview prospective interviewers, test the applicants, and ask them to perform an interview in front of the research team to prove that they have the required qualities.

c   Interviewer training

After selection, interviewers usually undergo training, the degree and intensity of which depend on the interviewers' skills and experience, as well as on the nature of the research topic. The training is generally thought to include these features (see Martin, 1988; Vlahos, 1984):

• Developing and practising interviewing skills, mainly through observation, practice and criticism. Observation includes using films and videos, actual interviews and videos of the interviewer's own interviewing, which is exposed to general criticism.
• Learning how to present oneself to the respondents, appropriate manners about the lifestyle of the subjects and about presentation and appearance (including clothing, grooming, etc.) and how to enter the interview situation without affecting the environment to be studied.
• Learning essential techniques of persuasion necessary to convince uncooperative respondents to participate in the study.
• Acquiring knowledge and skills related to obtaining relevant information and recording the responses accurately.
• Establishing standards of value neutrality, ethics, anonymity and confidentiality.

Training can last from a few days to a few weeks, depending on the quality of the interviewers and the nature of the research object. The criteria considered during training vary according to the background methodology. They also vary according to the researcher's ideology; for a number of researchers techniques of persuasion as well as objectivity and neutrality might not be the criteria an interviewer needs to acquire in order to accomplish the required tasks.

Supervision
In addition to selecting and training the interviewers thoroughly, the researcher is expected to make sure that interviewing is performed adequately. Often the investigator employs field supervisors, who control the process of interviewing, for example by checking the quality of interviewing, whether the claimed interviews have been performed, the frequency of certain answers (e.g. 'I don't know'), the use of probes, the relative response rate, completeness of the interviews and the general performance of the interviewer.

Interviewer bias

The interviewer is obviously one of the most important elements of interviewing. The interviewer can influence the outcome of the study in positive as well as in negative ways. Interviewer bias can cause problems and distortions which the researcher must isolate and eliminate or at least control. It is therefore important to identify such biases and error-producing factors before they occur. There are many sources of errors and bias, which relate to a number of factors; they can be summarised as follows (see Neuman, 1991; Pannas, 1996: 89–91):

- *Quality of the interviewer* The interviewer can influence the results through lack of administrative and professional abilities, sloppiness, or through contacting the wrong person, omitting or misreading questions, reading them out of order, recording the wrong answers, misunderstanding the respondent and leaving questions unanswered.
- *Misconduct* The interviewer can intentionally alter or omit answers, reword questions, replace respondents and cheat by not contacting the respondent but answering the questions personally.
- *Presentation* The interviewer's own presentation may cause distortion and influence the data. Appearance, tone of voice, attitude to the respondent and the research, reactions to answers or comments made are some examples.
- *Expectations* The expectations interviewers have of the respondent's answers as a result of his or her appearance and living conditions may influence the process and outcome of interviewing.
- *Probing* The research can also be influenced by the interviewer's use of probing, that is, whether probing is done, where and when, and also whether it was carried out as instructed. Improper probing is a definite source of distortion which should be avoided.

Knowledge of the nature and source of errors helps researchers to take measures to eliminate problems or at least to reduce their occurrence. The type and number of measures to be introduced will depend on many factors, but conducting a thorough screening during the selection of the interviewer, effective interviewer training and strict supervision of the interview process are reported to be useful measures.

4 The process of interviewing

Interviewing is conducted in a number of stages, with each stage including certain tasks. The various types of interviewing are conducted in different ways, but some common steps can be identified in all forms of interviewing.

a Seeking the respondents

The interviewer, after having been trained for a certain period of time, is supplied with a list of names and addresses of individuals, whom she or he has to approach and seek cooperation from. Visiting the individuals is preferable to writing or telephoning. When meeting the prospective respondent the interviewer must introduce himself or herself, explain the intention of the visit and the purpose of the research, disclose the sponsor, ensure anonymity and confidentiality, explain details of the research (e.g. how long the interview will take, how the results will be recorded, etc.), and arrange a date for the interview.

Quite often initiating the interview is associated with problems. The person chosen for the study may not be at home, may have moved away or died, be incapable of communicating, or may refuse to cooperate.

When reasons for refusal are given, they are likely to be of the following nature (Becker, 1989; Puris, 1995): not interested in the topic; do not agree with the research objective; no time; not sure about the research objective (due to suspicion or fear); research is against the respondent's professional work or commitment; or the spouse is against it. The interviewer should be prepared to face such refusals and to provide evidence that would help gain the respondent's trust, such as an ID card, reference letters, brief publications of previous studies and additional information about the significance of the research findings.

Often, refusals can be avoided if one knows ahead of time the possible reasons for a refusal to cooperate. The interviewer can then be equipped with the right argument to motivate the respondent to change his or her mind. Equally important is knowing the reasons for the respondent's cooperation. In this case, the interviewer can reinforce factors that would encourage the respondent to take part in the study. Such reasons may be, for instance, altruism, politeness, interest in talking about contemporary issues, emotional relief through talking about one's own problems, feelings of being important, obligation to the sponsor or research agency, boredom and curiosity.

The *place* where the interview is to be performed will be chosen after considering several factors, of which the research objective and topic are two. As well as these factors, the length of the interview, the nature of the questions and the degree of concentration and accuracy of the answers required are also significant. The environment should be stimulating, comfortable and conducive to quiet, private and relaxed talk. If the interview is brief and simple, it can be performed on a street corner or at the front of a supermarket. Long and more demanding interviews are better performed in a more structured environment.

Time is another significant factor. The rule here is, again, that the interview should be conducted at a time most suitable to the respondent, that is, not only when the respondent has time but also when he or she can have an unhurried talk without disturbance. Generally, considerations related to the preferences of the respondent determine this factor.

b   Asking and recording the questions

Asking questions depends of course on the type of interviewing. In the case of standardised interviewing, for instance, the questions should be asked according to the instructions of the researcher, and initiative should never be used unless the researcher has given his or her consent. Nevertheless, the interviewer should show interest in the research topic and the respondent and should avoid bias, leading questions and suggestive questioning. The interview guidelines should be observed accurately.

Recording should take place as given in the instructions. In many cases this means ticking or crossing boxes on the interview schedule and this is not expected to cause any difficulties. However, when interviewers have to take notes there may be some problems, especially when the interviewer has promised anonymity and confidentiality. Some respondents may interpret taking notes as a breach of promise, or get confused. In other cases, taking notes is perceived positively, since some people think that the interviewer who records notes takes their views very seriously.

Some ways to overcome such difficulties include writing down key words only, and completing the notes at the end of the interview; or stealing a few minutes' time during the interview (e.g. by going to the bathroom) and writing down more detailed notes. The most successful way is the use of tape recorders. However, there are problems associated with their use; for instance, the reluctance of some respondents to speak in front of a microphone, and also the fact that listening to tapes after the interview is very time consuming. Video recording is becoming popular and is equally powerful but has the same problems.

c   Field supervision and checks

Data collection is the most significant part of the research, and its administration should not be left entirely up to the interviewer. Especially when more than one interviewer is employed, supervision and checking are indispensable. As stated above, supervisors should make sure that the research progresses as planned. Some interviewers may not be as thorough as they should be, and cheating is not unusual. The researcher or supervisor might have to contact the respondent to determine whether the intended interview has taken place, or otherwise check that the interview has been performed as expected.

Supervision and checks are important in helping to avoid incomplete answers and interviews, refusals to answer certain questions or even to take part in the interview, too much or too little probing and inadequate recording of the data. In this context, the supervisor should control the operation of each interviewer in relation to the work of others, and deviation from the typical performance must be followed up by the supervisor before the data collection is completed. Checks for bias, honesty, politeness, objectivity, ethics and interviewer–respondent relationships should also be made.

d   Completion of the interview

The friendly relationship between the interviewer and the respondent should end with some care, smoothly and in a friendly atmosphere after the questions have been answered and after completion checks have been made. Ending the relationship should be accomplished in a spirit of trust, cooperation and mutual respect, and by letting the respondent feel that the contribution made to the research and to society through the interview was appreciated. In many cases the researcher outlines the way of ending the interview by offering one or more statements that the interviewer has to read or memorise and communicate to the respondent. Most of these statements are standardised and also left up to the interviewers to choose, since they are familiar with the interview situation and the interviewee.

5   Interviewer–respondent relationship

The type of relationship that develops between the interviewer and the respondent depends on such factors as background methodology, research topic, research objective and type of interviewing. However, there are some common features of the relationship that need to be adhered to in all situations. The following discusses some of these.

Background and appearance
Interviewers are more likely to develop a positive and effective relationship with the respondent if they come from a similar background. For this reason, researchers tend to select interviewers who are of the same race, ethnicity, sex and age as the respondents. This not only makes the entry to the respondent's world easier, it also promotes trust, understanding and cooperation, and allows the development of a close and rewarding relationship between the interviewer and the respondent.

Equally important is how interviewers present themselves. Arrogant and intruding persons are not successful. Clothing and grooming are also considered. The interviewer is expected to be dressed neutrally, ideally in a way similar to that of the respondent, and unobtrusively, so that the centre of the interview is the research topic and not the interviewer.

Status of the parties
The interviewers should never patronise the respondents, show disbelief in statements given or evaluate their answers. The interviewer should not appear as the wise judge but rather as the interested researcher who wishes to learn from the respondent. Neither should they appear as if they are rewarding or punishing respondents, or encouraging or discouraging certain types of answers. It is preferable to be neutral, receptive and eager to know the view of the respondent, which for the interviewer is interesting and valuable. The traditional relationship between interviewer and interviewee has been criticised by a number of writers, for example feminists, who see in the researcher a person who asks the questions 'from above', who is the expert and who treats the respondent as the inferior and 'ignorant' party. These writers suggest that the relationship between the two parties must be more egalitarian and more humanised (Reinharz, 1992; Westkott, 1990).

6   Prompting and probing

Prompts and probes are very common in social research and help respondents to offer accurate information and/or refine and complete their answers. They were introduced earlier in this chapter.

A *prompt* is a question that offers a list of possible answers, of which the respondent is expected to select one or more. An example is the question 'Which religious activities have you attended during the past four weeks?'. The interviewer either reads possible activities to the respondent, or shows a list of such activities. This makes answers to certain questions easier and more accurate. Prompts are usually developed after careful pre-tests and pilot studies.

A *probe* is a question which helps to gain more information about an issue addressed in a primary question, exemplifying and extending statements, and stimulating, guiding and assisting the respondent to answer the questions.

In general, probes are employed when a partial, irrelevant or inaccurate response is given, when the respondent has difficulty in answering a question or remains silent. In intensive interviewing, probing helps to encourage the respondent to talk and to direct the discussion towards the objectives of the study without causing bias or distortion. For this reason, probes are neutral statements that do not affect the respondent's direction of thinking. There are at least two types of probe, non-directive probing and the summary technique (see Moser and Kalton, 1971; Selltiz *et al.*, 1976).

Controlled non-directive probing
This technique is used when the respondent gives an incomplete, inadequate or general answer. In this case, the interviewer will ask non-directive and unbiasing questions, in most cases taken from a list provided by the researcher. The content of these probes depends on the type of the respondent's answer. For instance, if the answer is too general, the interviewer may ask 'What do you mean by that?', or 'What would be an example of it?'. If the respondent's answer needs amplification, the interviewer may make simple remarks, for instance 'I see' or just remain silent, expecting that the respondent will provide more information. To encourage the respondent to complete the answer, the interviewer may use probes such as 'That's interesting, tell me more about it' or 'What makes you think that way?'.

Summary technique
This technique is used when the respondent for any reason gives an incomplete or inadequate answer. Probing in this case consists of summarising the respondent's last statement, encouraging and motivating them (without leading them) to offer additional and more detailed information. An example would be 'So, money is one of the reasons . . .', followed by silence. In non-standardised interviewing probes are chosen freely by the interviewer according to the direction of the discussion. In standardised interviewing the use of probes is controlled by the researcher. Where probes are allowed, the researcher specifies when and under what conditions probes will be used, and offers a list of appropriate probes to be used.

7   Intensive interviewing

This is an unstructured and unstandardised interview technique employed by sociologists and psychologists as the only method of research or in addition to other methods. This technique is known also as 'depth' interviewing. It is a very sophisticated technique, requiring extensive knowledge of the research topic, extensive experience with interviewing, and the ability to communicate effectively and to establish and maintain relationships with respondents.

The format of intensive interviewing is unstructured and flexible. There are no specific questions to be asked. The interviewer is expected to develop the questions when they are required and as they best fit into the interview situation. For this reason, the actual formulation and order of the questions might differ from interview to interview. Intensive interviews are usually long and they sometimes extend over two or more sessions.

The value of intensive interviewing relies to a large extent on a number of factors, such as: (1) the relationship established between the interviewer and the respondent — rapport and making the respondent feel important; (2) the degree of commitment of the parties and their interest in the relationship and discussion; (3) economic and other advantages; and (4) the ability of the interviewer to use listening and empathy as significant tools of interaction.

Intensive interviewing is a very valuable technique in social research. It allows social scientists to study relationships in a relaxed unstructured way, where there is less chance of being misunderstood and more opportunity to check inconsistencies and to obtain accurate answers. Questions are presented as part of the discussion rather than as a prestructured questionnaire, and this allows flexibility, continuity of thought, freedom of probing, evaluation of behaviour during the interview, and interest in all aspects of the opinions of the respondent including those not in the areas covered by an interview schedule.

Intensive interviewing is limited in its effectiveness because: it depends on the skills, values, standards and ideology of the interviewer; it does not allow generalisations of the findings; it cannot justify comparisons between cases studied since the elements of the interview may differ from case to case; and it is a very expensive and time-consuming technique. The need for a well-qualified interviewer with extensive experience and personal qualities makes this type of interview a difficult technique and limits its applicability in the social sciences.

8   Telephone interviewing

Particularly since the Second World War, telephone interviewing has become a popular and widespread method of data collection, where and when conditions and the nature of the research topic allow it. It was never intended to replace the main form of interviewing but it is now often used where earlier standard interviewing was employed.

Telephone interviewing demonstrates the same structural characteristics as standard interviewing techniques, except that it is conducted by telephone. Although this difference might not be very significant in many cases, it does have certain effects on some aspects of the research process.

In the first place, telephone interviewing is employed when the interviews are simple and brief, when quick and inexpensive results are sought, when it is not required to approach the respondent face to face and when sampling inaccuracies (e.g. non-subscribers and unlisted numbers) are not considered important.

The subjects are usually chosen through a variety of sampling frames but mainly through the telephone directory, using one of the methods discussed earlier. Random-digit-dialling techniques are also common. The choice is, however, restricted only to those who own a telephone, a rather weak point of telephone interviewing.

Nevertheless, telephone interviewing has attractive advantages over other methods of data collection. The most important advantages commonly reported (e.g. Berger *et al.*, 1989; Mahr, 1995; Martin, 1988) are that it:

- produces quick results;
- allows the study of relatively large samples;
- is relatively economical;
- allows more open communication since the respondent is not confronted with the interviewer;
- reduces bias in that factors such as race, ethnicity, appearance and age do not influence the respondents;
- offers more anonymity than other techniques, particularly when random-digit-dialling techniques are used.

Telephone interviews have many limitations, the most important being:

- telephone interviews are associated with a high refusal rate;
- in telephone interviews the identity of the respondent is not known; it is therefore impossible to determine whether the respondent was the one chosen for the research;
- in telephone interviews it is not possible to control the interview completely;
- telephone interviews are restricted in their coverage by the fact that a part of the target population has no telephone or has unlisted numbers.

Despite these disadvantages, telephone interviewing is a very useful technique of data collection and is very popular.

9   Advantages and limitations of interviewing

Interviewing is so commonly used in the social sciences that it is quite often considered to be *the* method of social research. Its popularity is often justified in terms of several of its qualities, which give it an advantage over other methods of data collection. Feminists, for instance, stress among other things the fact that interviewing allows women to speak in their own words and not in the words of the researcher; it allows the study of non-verbal communication which is used by subordinate people to express themselves, is particularly suited to female researchers, avoids alienation between researcher and respondent and encourages the development of a sense of connectedness (Reinharz, 1990).

Advantages

The advantages of interviewing have been stressed by most writers (see Berger *et al.*, 1989; Mahr, 1995; Roth, 1987). Although they refer primarily to standardised forms of interviewing, they also apply in the area of qualitative interviewing. The advantages are:

- *Flexibility*   Interviews can be adjusted to meet many diverse situations.
- *High response rate*   Interviewing attracts a relatively high response rate.
- *Easy administration*   Interviews do not require respondents to have the ability to read, handle complex documents or long questionnaires.
- *Opportunity to observe non-verbal behaviour*   Such opportunities are obviously not available when questionnaires or indirect methods are used.
- *Less patience and motivation* to complete are needed than are required by questionnaires. Interviews need 'participation', not just 'response'. Participation involves another person with whom the respondent completes the task, so interviewing is often perceived as a cooperative venture rather than a one-sided exercise.
- *Control over the environment*   Here the interviewer has an opportunity to control the conditions under which the questions are answered.
- *Capacity for correcting misunderstandings by respondents*   Such an option is very valuable and not available in other forms of data collection, such as questionnaires.
- *Control over the order of the questions*   Respondents have no opportunity to know what question comes next, or to alter the order of the questions they answer. When the order of the questions is significant, an interview is much more useful than a questionnaire.
- *Opportunity to record spontaneous answers*   The respondent does not have as much time available to answer questions as when questionnaires are employed. When spontaneity is important, interviews offer a real advantage over other methods.
- *Control over the identity of the respondent*   When interviews are employed, the identity of the respondent is known; this is not so when other methods (e.g. questionnaires) are used.
- *Completeness of the interview guaranteed*   The fact that the interviewer presents the questions guarantees that all questions will be attempted.
- *Control over the time, date and place of the interview*   If the information must be collected at a certain time (e.g. after the evening news or on Friday evening, etc.), date or place, interviews offer a guarantee that it will be collected according to the specified conditions. Such a guarantee cannot be given when questionnaires are used.
- *More complex questions* can be used because the presence of the interviewer can assist in answering the questions.

- *Greater permissible length* is more possible in interviewing than when other methods (e.g. questionnaires) are used.

Limitations
Despite its advantages, interviewing is limited by a number of factors; the following are the most important:

- Interviews are more *costly* and *time consuming* than other methods, such as questionnaires.
- Interviews are affected by the factor 'interviewer' and the possible bias associated with it.
- Interviewing is more *inconvenient* than other methods, such as using questionnaires
- It offers *less anonymity* than other methods since the interviewer knows the identity, residence, type of housing, family conditions and other personal details of the respondent.
- It is *less effective* than other methods when sensitive issues are discussed. For example, many people prefer to write about sensitive issues than to talk about them.

Apart from these limitations, interviewing is affected by factors common to other techniques of data collection, for example deliberate misrepresentation of facts, genuine mistakes, unwillingness or inability to offer information and similar problems. In such cases, however, it is easier to detect problems when interviewing than when using other methods.

10   Interviewing in the computer age

The development of computers has affected many aspects of the life of every Australian and consequently the researcher, the interviewer and the interviewee. New developments in this area have led to computer packages that have changed not only the relationship between the researcher and the respondent, the interviewer and the interviewee, but also the process and nature of interviewing.

Interviews can now be held between the interviewee and a computer, and if the researcher is also present, his or her input into the process of interviewing is restricted to giving instructions and to helping the respondent. The following are some examples of computer packages that are relevant to interviewing.

Computer-aided personal interview (CAPI)
This program allows interviews to be carried out through the assistance of computers, whereby to a certain extent the computer takes the place of the interviewer. Questioning and control of the responses is done through the computer.

In this case, the interviewee sits in front of a computer next to the interviewer. The questions appear on the screen; the interviewee reads the questions and enters the responses in the computer through the keyboard, mouse or otherwise. The responses are processed automatically by the computer and prepared for analysis. This program can be used individually or with a group of respondents.

Computer-driven self-completion interview (CODSCI)

This is a fully automated interviewing program in which there is no need for the presence of an interviewer. The interview is carried out in a computer session in which the respondent reads the questions from the computer screen in direct communication with the computer; the computer 'asks' the questions, explains problems and assists in answering the questions. After completion of the interview, the responses are saved automatically in the memory and added to previous interview data.

Computer-aided telephone interview (CATI)

Here the computer is used by the interviewer, who reads the questions to the interviewee over the telephone as they appear on the screen and records the response in the computer. The computer can do more than just present the questions and receive the answers. It can draw the sample, choose the telephone number, dial the respondent through a self-dial system and 'connect' the interviewer with the interviewee.

Computer-integrated survey research (CISUR)

This fully integrated computer program is further advanced than the previous ones in that it contains more functions in a wider area of the research process. This is another example of how computers enter the arena of research over and above the statistical analysis of data, gradually replacing the human factor.

'The data collector'

This is a program that works on the same principles as the above programs, and has similar goals and functions. Although a data collection device, it does have additional features that make it a useful tool for social researchers.

The program allows the development of questionnaires and interview schedules, including a variety of question styles (including Likert scales, semantic differential, cafeteria questions, etc.) and response categories, such as single or multiple choice, fill in the missing words, complete questions and so on, and can handle quantitative and qualitative analysis of the results. The statistical measures available in this program are basic, and include descriptive statistics, frequency distributions, chi-square, analysis of variance, Mann–Whitney test and correlations (r, rho and lagged correlations). The qualitative analysis contains word counts, word/phrase searches and a variety of other forms of searching text.

Overall, it is a useful device for self-administered interviews or for entering and handling questionnaire data of a diverse nature, and in its commercial version it can even be used for telephone interviewing.

11   Problems and errors in interviewing

Every method of data collection can become a source of problems, errors and distortions, and interviewing is certainly not free from such problems. Such errors are very serious and can affect the quality of the data. So the researcher should be particularly aware of the ways in which such problems can occur and must prevent their occurrence as much as possible. It must be noted that the same errors can appear in other forms of data collection, such as observation, fieldwork and so on. The following lists a few examples of such errors, as identified by Berger *et al.* (1989: 228–31).

Recording errors

The errors listed below are caused during the recording of data and are associated with:

* selective hearing or vision;
* misunderstanding of the respondent;
* too-early or too-late registration of the responses;
* incomplete, faulty or illegible responses.

Evaluation errors

These include the:

* *leniency effect*, when extremely negative responses are avoided;
* *severity effect*, when extremely positive responses are avoided;
* *projection effect*, when personal prejudice and stereotypes are projected onto the respondent, affecting perception and evaluation of responses;
* *contact effect*, when loss of objectivity caused by knowing the respondent leads to a mild evaluation of responses;
* *central tendency effect*, when the researcher tends to avoid recording extreme responses;
* *reference-group effect*, when the researcher develops expectations related to the reference group of the respondent and judges the respondent's responses on the basis of these expectations, examples being:
  — the grandpa effect: expecting too little from the respondent;
  — the authority effect: feeling intimidated by the respondent's position of authority;
  — the Santa Claus effect: expecting more or too much from the respondent (e.g. people thought to be more intelligent, sympathetic people treated in a more forthcoming and understanding way, etc.);
  — the identification effect: errors associated with the researcher's tendency to identify himself or herself with the respondent and therefore treating him or her more mildly, and vice versa.

Instruction errors

This type of error includes:

* replacing non-responses with another person's responses;
* withholding information collected;
* introducing changes in operation against the instructions of the researcher, for example changing questions or the order of the questions;
* forgery of parts of the data;
* showing consent or rejection of responses while collecting data.

Interviewing offers many opportunities for errors and problems to distort the process of data collection. However, this is not a characteristic of this method. Any method of data collection is bound to lead to difficulties. It always depends on the way methods are used and on the extent to which precautions are taken to avoid such problems. Certainly interviewing has its share of problems but it is indeed one of the most useful and popular methods.

12   Survey forms in comparison

It has often been asked which survey method — face-to-face interview, telephone interview and mail questionnaire — is the best or most appropriate to be used. This is one of those questions that has no direct and simple answer. The only answer to this question that deserves to be mentioned is that all methods are effective, valid and useful, depending on the type of information needed, nature of the sample and nature of the question.

Table 11.1   A comparison of face-to-face, telephone and mail surveys

Major considerations	Face to face	Types of surveys Telephone	Mail
Access to respondents	Limited only by hearing or speech impairment or disability	As in face to face Plus no access to phone or unlisted numbers	Limited by disability or illiteracy
Response rate	Very high	High	Low
Interviewer bias	High	Moderate	No bias
Control over the respondent's identity	Very high	Low	Very low
Allowed complexity of instrument	Very high	Moderate	Very high
Costs	Very high	Moderate	Low
Inconvenience	High	Moderate	Low

Source: This is a modified version of a table presented in G. Wilhoit and D. Weaver (1980), *Newsroom Guide to Polls and Surveys,* Washington DC: American Newspaper Publishers Association.

Questionnaires are effective when they are used in the right context, with the right people and for the right topic. As shown in the previous chapter, there are many problems and difficulties with questionnaires; and there are many problems and difficulties with face-to-face interviews and telephone interviews. They all also have strengths and these strengths make them suitable tools of data collection for certain topics, certain respondents and certain types of information. Table 11.1 compares the characteristics of these three methods. This information is presented to help the researcher decide which method to choose rather than to show which one is better. All methods are tools of the researcher's trade and are equally useful and effective in their own context.

13　Summary

In this chapter we offered a brief description of the main elements of interviewing, the types and process of interviewing, its advantages and disadvantages, the role of the interviewers and their relationship with the respondent, and outlined the major errors and problems of this method of data collection. This description completes our attempt to demonstrate how surveys are planned and conducted in social research.

Interviewing, and surveys in general, is a practical and effective method of data collection, and one that can be adjusted to serve the needs of both the quantitative and the qualitative researcher as well as critical researchers and feminists. Interviews are used by social scientists in descriptive research as well as in applied research, in action research and participatory research. Their versatility makes them a useful tool of social research, more useful than many other methods; and one that is popular among researchers of all convictions and ideological backgrounds.

There are, however, cases in which interviewing is not possible. The issue in question may belong in the past and as such it may not allow surveys to be conducted. Or it may not be the appropriate research method. In such cases other methods are used. One such set of methods, the indirect methods, is discussed in the next chapter.

Key concepts

Surveys	Open interviews
Soft interviews	Unstructured interviews
Panel interviews	Personal interviews
Intensive interviewing	Unique interviews
Semi-structured interviews	Hard interviews
Computer interviews	Structured interviews
Analytical interviews	Guided interviews
Delphi interviews	Focused interviews
Receptive interviews	Interviewer bias
CAPI	CISUR
Informative interviews	Diagnostic interviews
Dilemma interviews	Clinical interviews
Problem-centred interviews	Convergent interviews
CODSCI	'The data collector'
Telephone interviews	Inquiring interviews
Ethnographic interviews	Biographical interviews
Narrative interviews	Elite interviews
CATI	

12

Indirect methods of data collection

1 Introduction

Interviewing and the use of questionnaires are two methods of data collection that rely very much on the involvement, participation and contribution of the respondents. These methods act directly on the respondents, who in turn provide information about themselves or about other people. The findings of survey-based research are the result of a concerted effort of both researchers and respondents, the latter being fully aware of being studied and thus in a position to influence the results in some way.

There are methods, however, that do not rely on the direct participation of respondents. In these methods data are obtained without the knowledge of the subjects, in an indirect and non-disruptive way. These methods are called *indirect* or *unobtrusive methods* (on this see Kellehear, 1993). In some cases the respondents are not aware of the fact that they are being investigated. In other cases, although they may know that they are involved in a research project, they do not know what is really being studied.

Indirect methods are diverse in nature and can be divided into the following groups:

- Physiological methods
- Non-reactive methods including:
  — analysis of physical traces
  — analysis of documents
- Projective methods
- Concealed methods (observation)

In this chapter we shall briefly introduce some indirect methods that are well known among social scientists, and then focus on those methods that are more relevant to the social sciences and more frequently used by social researchers. (Observation was already discussed in Chapter 9.)

2   Physiological methods

Physiological methods study the physiology of the respondent's body and aim at measuring aspects of its functioning. The results obtained in this process are related to aspects of the research topic, which might be, for example, criminal behaviour, interpersonal relationships in marriage, states of mind and attitudes. In such cases, the respondents are aware of the fact that they are being tested; nevertheless, they do not know what is actually being studied or how these results will contribute to the research questions. In most cases the respondent does not even know that the tests are part of a research project.

Physiological methods are not as common in the social sciences as other methods. In sociology, however, especially with the development and growth of microsociology and sociobiology, these methods have gradually become more popular than before, particularly in the USA and in Europe.

Physiological methods appear in two forms: primary and secondary methods. *Primary physiological methods* measure aspects of the respondent's body, such as electromagnetic signals in the heart or skin, or mechanical signals such as blood pressure and circulation. *Secondary methods* measure information derived from primary methods.

3   Disguised methods

Disguised methods are indirect methods in which the respondent is aware of being investigated but does not know how and in what context the responses will be evaluated. The following are some examples of such techniques:

- Knowledge tests
- Personality questionnaires
- Perception tests
- Memory tests
- Fill-in tests (filling in the missing words)

These methods are used by some social scientists, but they appear to be still significantly more common in psychological research.

4   Study of physical traces

Physical traces are the products of human activity, and indicate certain social trends, habits, behaviour patterns and cultural configurations of a group of people or a community. Here, social investigators, instead of asking people about their habits and preferences, study their 'traces' and make relevant conclusions about the people and their social and cultural life.

The study of physical traces can offer information about the culture and life of past communities, exemplified, for instance, in studies conducted mainly by anthropologists or ethnologists. Studies of traces can provide useful information and are employed as the sole method or in addition to other methods.

There are several areas in which the study of physical traces can be very useful. For example, by observing the floor of a museum, one can draw some conclusions about the popularity of certain exhibits: if the floor in front of an exhibit is heavily worn out or dirty it indicates more traffic and more visitors coming to observe it, and it can support the conclusion that this exhibit is popular, and perhaps more popular than other exhibits. Another example is the study of household garbage, which can offer some strong evidence about the eating habits of residents of certain suburbs — perhaps a more reliable information source than direct statements by the residents.

Social researchers also use physical traces to infer about the habits of certain population groups or social categories. In a recent study, for example, a researcher observed the accumulation of beer bottles exposed in backyards of low-class employed and unemployed people to judge their drinking habits; another managed to study the quality and type of clothes and toys donated by unmarried mothers to charitable institutions in order to make some inferences about the spending habits and consumption patterns of these people.

5 Documentary methods

Documents have always been used as a source of information in social research, either as the only method or in conjunction with other methods. They are employed in the context of many diverse studies, such as quantitative studies, qualitative methods and case-study research. It is most unusual that any research study is carried out without employing some form of documentary method (e.g. a library search).

a Types of documents

In this context, documents are usually referred to as *secondary material*. Their analysis is therefore called *secondary analysis*. They are called 'secondary' because they are not primarily developed for the study in which they are used (Becker, 1989; Stergios, 1991). The most common documents used in this context are:

- *public documents*, namely census statistics, statistical year-books, court archives, prison records, mass media and literature (novels, poetry, etc.);
- *archival records*, such as service records of hospitals, doctors and social workers, and records of organisations;

- *personal documents*, such as life histories, diaries, memoranda, confessions, autobiographies, suicide notes and letters;
- *administrative documents*, such as proposals, memoranda, progress reports, agendas, minutes of meetings, announcements and other internal documents;
- *formal studies and reports* related to the research topic.

With respect to their closeness to the event they describe, one can distinguish between (Becker, 1989; Stergios, 1991):

- *contemporary documents*, namely those compiled at the time the events took place;
- *retrospective documents*, which have been produced after the event took place;
- *primary documents*, that is, sources compiled by eye witnesses of the described events;
- *secondary documents*, being sources derived from primary documents.

b Applications

Documentary research can be employed in every aspect of social life, provided that relevant documents are available. If one, for instance, is interested in the factors that promote traditional family values among Irish-Australians, or the effects of depression on suicide rates in pre-war Germany, a study of relevant documents will provide answers.

c Forms of research

Documentary research can take many forms, of which the following seem to be very popular:

- *Qualitative research*, in which the researcher identifies and interprets information contained in the documents; ascertains aspects of the issue in question and the main ideas, statements and thoughts on the subject; investigates the main theme of the document, who the author is, when the document was written, the reliability of the source, and arrives at relevant conclusions. Methods employed in this context are qualitative and generalisations are limited to analytic generalisations.
- *Quantitative research*, in which data collection is directed to the same issues listed above, but the research design is more strict and specific than in qualitative research, and the methods of data collection and analysis quantitative in nature. Here more emphasis is placed on frequencies than in qualitative research and the conclusions entail inductive generalisations.
- *Descriptive-comparative research*, in which documents are studied to describe the event in question and, using the information available, to facilitate inter- or intra-cultural comparisons as well as comparisons over time. This type of research is usually based on first-level factual information, without manipulating or otherwise analysing the documents.

- *Content analysis*, which implies more complicated and sophisticated analysis. The research focuses on the manifest or latent content of documents, namely it concentrates on text (words, sentences, paragraphs, etc.) in a very detailed and analytical way, or on meanings. Both allow conclusions to be made on issues that are beyond the text and language, in a qualitative or a quantitative framework. This method will be discussed in the following section.

d   The process of documentary research

The study of documents is accomplished in a number of successive steps. Generally, these steps follow the research model introduced earlier in the book. This process can be summarised by describing the following stages.

Stage 1: Identification of relevant documents
The choice of documents depends on availability, accessibility, relevance and the personal interest of the researcher. Sometimes a single source may be chosen. In other cases several documents may be employed. While often the use of documents may constitute a part of a larger study (e.g. in the form of a literature review, or exploration), at other times it might make up the main study.

Stage 2: Data collection
The content of this stage depends on several factors, primarily related to the factors referred to above, as well as on the method of analysis. If description is the purpose of the study and if the methodology is overly qualitative, reading and note taking may be sufficient. When, however, methods such as content analysis are employed, organisation of the data as well as their analysis become more sophisticated and very complex, as we shall see in the next section.

Stage 3: Data analysis
This is a very diverse step. The type of evaluation depends on the nature of the documents, the methodology chosen and the purpose of the study. This diversity becomes even more complex when the plethora of documents is considered. In general, data will be related to the assumptions made before or during the study and assessed with regard to the degree to which these assumptions are valid. Whether the findings can be generalised in statistical or analytical terms depends on the evidence obtained as well as on the type of methodology used.

Stage 4: Interpretation of the findings
Interpretation of the findings will be made in the context of the research topic and will depend on the nature of the study, the purpose of the project and the type of methodology employed. While in some cases inductive generalisations can be made, in other cases analytical generalisations will be produced.

e   Advantages and limitations of documentary methods

Documentary methods demonstrate a number of strengths and weaknesses. They are therefore used only if and when the strengths outweigh the weaknesses.

A brief summary of advantages and limitations of documentary methods is listed below (see Becker, 1989; Berger *et al.*, 1989; Puris, 1995).

Advantages
The following advantages are most commonly mentioned:

- *Retrospectivity* Documentary methods enable researchers to study past events and issues.
- *Quick and easy accessibility* This applies at least to many documents, more so since the introduction of electronic media and the spread of personal computers. The availability of data banks and sophisticated computer programs have made this method an invaluable tool of social research for many researchers. The availability of documents through the Internet strengthens this point.
- *Spontaneity* In most cases, documents are produced by the writers without being requested to do so by researchers. This reduces researcher bias significantly.
- *Low cost* Documentary research is more economical than most other types of research.
- *Sole source* Often, documents are the *only* source of information (e.g. when studying past events).
- *High quality* of information.
- *Possibility of retesting*.
- *Non-reactivity* The method itself and the act of measurement do not affect the results.

Limitations
Despite the advantages, documentary methods demonstrate some *limitations* of which the researcher must be aware. The most common limitations are listed below.

- Documents are *not necessarily representative* of their kind and thus they do not allow generalisations; only a few people, for instance, write autobiographics, and only a few autobiographies survive. However, this limitation applies mainly to personal documents.
- Some of these documents are *not easily accessible* (private letters, diaries, etc.).
- Some documents are *not complete* or up to date.
- The *reliability* of some documents is questionable.
- *Comparisons* between some documents are not always possible.
- They demonstrate *methodological problems*, such as coding problems and state of presentation.
- Documents are *biased*, since they represent the view of their authors.

Despite their limitations, documentary methods are a very useful tool of social research and an indispensable one, particularly when the research is focused on events of the past. In such cases documentary methods are the only way of collecting data on this issue. This is one of the reasons why documentary methods are relatively popular in social sciences.

6   The biographical method

This method is a special version of the documentary method because it uses written documents as the basis of its research. Nevertheless, the biographical method entails elements that allow it to be classified into other research models, such as case-study research, simply because it predominantly deals with single cases. On certain occasions the biographical study seems to be equated with narrative interviews because it shares with them the intention to ascertain individual views of reality as experienced and reported by one individual.

This suggests that the biographical method is not a research model in itself but a branch of another model (Fuchs, 1984). Be that as it may, the biographical method has been used as a source of data for a long time, and has concentrated on the *study of personal and biographical documents*, which intentionally or unintentionally offer information about structure, dynamics and function of the consciousness of the author. Such documents are diaries, memoirs, autobiographies, letters, witness statements and other sources of a personal nature.

As a systematic approach in the social sciences this method was used for the first time by Thomas and Znaniecki (1958) in their famous study of Polish people, and by Shaw (1930, 1966) in his study of juvenile delinquency. Such studies opened up the way for this form of research to become an established methodology of the social sciences.

In the context of qualitative research, biographical methods attempt to present a perception of self and the world from the viewpoint of the author of the biography (Friedrichs, 1987; Lamnek, 1989). This contains two major goals, namely to explore:

1 the author's definition of self and of social action, which demonstrates the way this person perceives and interprets the world in its totality. Nevertheless, the point of analysis is not the individual but rather the biography (Fischer and Kohl, 1987: 26; Voges, 1987);
2 the social regulation of individuality (Lamnek, 1989). This is based on the assumption that the way authors explain their subject reveals information about their life; it also indicates the way in which they perceive reality, the relations between their opinions and their social environment, the influence reality has on their life and actions and, most importantly, the social origin of their individuality. It is proposed here that individual narrations are constructed by society (Hildebrand *et al.*, 1984: 29; Kohli and Robert, 1984), and in that way allow an insight into the process of constructing individuality. Biographical methods, it is argued, allow the identification of determinants of individuality.

How documents are studied through the biographical method is a question that has been answered in a number of ways. This diversity is related to the nature of the method and most of all to its methodological framework and the purpose of the study. The following methods are examples of how biographical research is conducted:

- *The holistic method*, where a document is studied in its entirety with the aim of identifying elements relevant to the research objective. Here emphasis is placed on the overall impression the document makes of the study object. Analysis is based on the overall image of the document.
- *The particularistic method,* which concentrates data collection on one specific aspect of the document or a small number of aspects. This provides detailed information which, if processed systematically, can be used as a basis for further research and analysis.
- *Comparative method,* which is employed when a large number of auto-biographies are studied. Here the documents are studied through holistic or particularistic methods. The aim of the study is to identify similarities and differences between the sets of documents as well as to provide a basis for valid conclusions.
- *Content analysis*, which is employed to analyse the manifest and/or latent content of the biographical documents. The way content analysis is conducted will be discussed later in this section.
- *The quantitative method*, which aims to establish associations between variables and to test hypotheses. In this analysis, emphasis is placed on measuring dependencies and relationships. Obviously, the other methods listed above can equally be quantitative in nature but not to the extent of the quantitative method.
- *Classification method*, in which the analysis of the biographical material concentrates on establishing and classifying categories.

It goes without saying that since the biographical method belongs to the broader category of documentary studies, all methods employed in documentary analysis are suitable also for biographical studies.

7   Content analysis

Content analysis is an everyday means of communication employed by all people who live and communicate in groups. Understanding the meaning of certain statements in radio announcements or the message conveyed in a TV commercial is an everyday occurrence for most Australians.

As a scientific means of data collection and analysis, content analysis employs a systematic approach as well as standards and principles found in all methods of social research. The spectrum of such a method is wider and the purpose of the method is beyond the definition of simple open or hidden media messages.

As a method of social research, content analysis is a documentary method that aims at a qualitative and/or quantitative analysis of the content of texts, pictures, films and other forms of verbal, visual or written communication. Feminists, for instance, have studied children's books, fairy tales, billboards, feminist fiction and non-fiction, children's artwork, fashion, fat-letter post cards, girl scout handbooks, works of fine art, newspaper rhetoric, clinical records, research publications, introductory sociology textbooks and citations (Reinharz, 1992:

147). This analysis may be related to forms of communication, intentions of the communicator, techniques of persuasion, text style, the audience and any aspects of communication, especially those not obvious to ordinary receivers.

As a qualitative technique content analysis may be directed toward more subjective information, such as motives, attitudes or values. As a quantitative method it may be employed when determining the time, frequency or duration of an event (Eckhardt and Ermann, 1977).

In the context of a quantitative study, content analysis investigates the thematic content of communication and aims to make inferences about individual or group values, sentiments, intentions or ideologies as expressed in the content of communication and to assess the effects of communication on the audiences reached (Mahr, 1995).

This discussion indicates that in both contexts, content analysis studies the 'content' of documents, and this can be the manifest content or the latent content.

- The *manifest content* refers to the visible, surface text, the actual parts of the text as manifested in the document, that is, the words, sentences, paragraphs and so on; here analysis relates to the straight and obvious, the visible content of the document, and involves counting frequencies of appearance of the research unit.
- The *latent content* is the underlying meaning conveyed through the document. Here the researcher reads between the lines, and registers the messages, meanings and symbols that are inferred or hidden and which are significant for the object of study. Still, words and sentences are manifestations of implied meanings and in this sense they are used as indicators of the presence and frequency of occurrence of 'meanings'.

Content analysis can concentrate on one type of content or study both types.

a   Steps in content analysis

The general pattern of the research process applied in content analysis is identical to the general model of social research described earlier in this book. The only difference lies in the content of each step, which is obviously expected to be directly related to the nature of the technique as well as to the area of study. The research process of content analysis involves the following steps:

Step 1: Selection of the research topic
The topic can be any issue displayed in the media, for example sexist language, role identification or significance of 'previous experience' as a factor influencing academic appointments in tertiary institutions.

Step 2: Formulation of the research topic
This involves the process of defining, exploring and operationalising the topic and, where necessary, formulating hypotheses. The operationalisation of the topic includes selection of the units and construction of the categories, which will be discussed in the next section.

Step 3: Research design
In this step, the project director determines (a) the nature and size of the sample; (b) the methods of recording and analysing the data (including formulation of categories and construction of code books where required); and (c) methods of checking reliability.

Step 4: Collection of data
Data collection involves primarily counting of frequencies, prominence, direction and intensity of the research units. This process is known as *coding* (see below). More specifically, it is generally accepted (see Becker, 1989; Martin, 1988) that among other things data collection in content analysis will address the following:

- Whether or not the chosen units *appear* in the text, for example whether 'previous experience' is included in the advertisements for academic positions in tertiary institutions.
- The *frequency* of appearance of the units in the text studied. For instance, 'previous experience' as a requirement for an academic position may appear in 85 per cent of the advertisements.
- The *significance or prominence* of the units that appear in the document, for instance whether 'previous experience' is stated before or after qualifications, publications, etc.; its prominence might be defined in terms of the emphasis and space given to this unit in the text.
- The *evaluation* of the unit, that is, whether it is positive, neutral or negative. In our example it may be stated that 'previous experience is an advantage' or that 'previous experience is not essential'.
- The *intensity* of the statement regarding the research unit. In our example, it will be recorded whether 'previous experience' was not stressed at all, was stressed somewhat, strongly or very strongly.

Step 5: Analysis and interpretation of the data
Depending on the orientation of the researcher and the objective of the study, the collected data will be analysed in some way. More particularly, the following specific methods can be employed:

- Computation of frequencies of symbols and indicators.
- Analysis of symbols and indicators collected in the study.
- Analysis of values derived from the analysis of symbols and indicators.
- Analysis of the form, direction and quality of evaluation identified in the study (evaluation analysis).

The results will then be reported in some way and form, depending on the nature of the study and the type of audience.

b   Construction of categories

The collection of data becomes possible through the construction of categories and the process associated with them. A category is a set of criteria which are integrated around a theme or value. For instance, if we were to study documents in order to establish the factors which influenced young people's decisions when choosing their marital partner in the 1970s, two categories could be *emotionality* and *rationality*. The former would include factors such as love, attraction, affection, etc; the latter could include factors such as employment status, assets and economic security, education, etc. The process of constructing categories is explained below (see Becker, 1989; Berger *et al.*, 1989; Roth, 1987).

Selection and definition of categories
Categories are selected in order to make classification of the text possible. Categories must be accurate, unidimensional, exhaustive and mutually exclusive. They must also be clearly defined, so that they can be used as the coding manual when media are being studied. If, for instance, the objective of the study is to describe the status of women as presented in the *Women's Weekly*, the categories might be 'dominant', 'egalitarian' and 'submissive'. What each of these categories exactly means must be explicitly defined.

Selection of the units of analysis and coding
In general, units of analysis can be, for instance, words, symbols, items, sentences, characters and themes, as well as messages, meanings and symbols which indicate the presence of one of the categories. Similarly the context unit, that is, the context in which the unit of analysis will be sought, is chosen. This might be a sentence, a paragraph or a chapter. More specifically, the type of units of analysis depends on the type of content the study aims to analyse, namely a manifest or a latent content.

In either case, following the identification of the research unit the researcher will commence coding, that is, recording the presence, frequency, intensity, etc. of the units in the document. These units can be manifest or latent; hence there are two types of coding, the manifest and the latent coding. Manifest coding deals with parts of the text. Latent coding deals with meanings, as they become evident through more general reading.

Reliability tests
After the categories, units and contexts have been chosen and defined, reliability tests are in order. One way of doing this is to use the expertise of other researchers; for instance, experts are given samples of relevant texts and asked to define the categories, and to select the recording units independently. If there is substantial agreement between the categories identified by the experts and those of the research director (say, about 80 per cent) the reliability test is satisfactory. Otherwise, the researcher must refine and redefine categories and units of analysis.

c   The meaning of data

Content analysis provides data like any other method of data collection. Irrespective of whether the approach is qualitative or quantitative, the data will offer some evidence about the dominant category, for example trends, covariations or causal relationships. If quantitative methods are being employed, the data will be presented in the form of proportions, graphs, tables or diagrams, supported by mathematical tests, such as tests of significance. If qualitative methods are used, the analysis and presentation of the data will be different; however, the evidence of content analysis must be equally convincing. In general, the common methods of analysis and presentation of data that are discussed later in this book will be employed also in content analysis.

d   Coding

In general terms, the type of coding employed in content analysis depends on a number of factors and particularly on the type of content the study is referring to. Coding means the assignment of codes to units identified in the study. Codes can be numbers, words or symbols. If the research relates to manifest content, then manifest coding is employed. Likewise, if the research relates to latent content, the investigator will use latent coding.

- *Manifest coding* implies the identification of presence and frequency of visible, surface text elements such as words, sentences, symbols, etc; in more general terms here the analysis will relate to the manifest units which were chosen for analysis.
- *Latent coding* implies the identification of presence and frequency of semantic units, that is, those related to meanings, as defined in the early stages of the study. Here the researcher will read text from the document and assign to it a label indicating the criteria considered in the study, preparing it for counting and analysis. This form of coding is more complex, complicated and time consuming than manifest coding.

Both types of coding are employed in content analysis either separately or together in the same study. Given that it deals with concrete units that involve no interpretation and personal judgement, manifest coding by nature is more reliable than latent coding.

e   Methods of content analysis

Quantitative analysis
The methods and techniques of analysis employed by quantitative researchers to analyse data collected through content analysis are many and varied. Examples of some common methods of analysis are given below (see Pannas, 1996):

- *Descriptive analysis*   Here analysis means counting the frequency in appearance of certain elements of the research question and comparing it with other elements.
- *Categorical analysis*   Here analysis involves a study of the documents by means of a set of categories, producing nominal as well as ordinal and interval data, which are then processed statistically.

- *Valence and intensity analysis*   In this form of analysis, data are processed by means of multi-step scales based on theoretical criteria. In valence analysis the scales have no discrete criteria but have polar values, such as in favour of or against. Intensity analysis employs scales with multiple steps (Lamnek, 1988).
- *Contingency analysis*   This analysis is basically a semantic communication analysis that is usually employed to make an inference from the text about the personality of the author (Merten, 1983).
- *Contextual analysis*   Here the sequence in which certain concepts appear together in set texts is examined. The systematic appearance of certain concepts together is not considered to be accidental but is taken to express the thinking patterns of the author or to correspond with communicative intentions of the speaker. Such occurrences are thought to signify 'cognitive representations of social reality'.

Qualitative analysis

The type of content analysis employed in qualitative research is fundamentally different from that of quantitative studies. The differences relate to theoretical and methodological standards and principles of qualitative analysis, such as openness, communicativity, naturalism and interpretation. Briefly, qualitative data will be analysed as follows: after the units of analysis have been ascertained (e.g. texts of books, transcripts of interviews, or other forms of verbal or visual communication), the researcher will identify and evaluate the items that appear to be theoretically important and meaningful and relate them to the central question of the study. In some cases, the researcher will study the text semantically and syntactically, employ the rules of logic, relate the meaning of parts of the text to the whole document and the general thinking of the author, and develop relevant hypotheses (Danner, 1979). In other cases, the processes of collection and analysis of data are seen as an attempt to identify criteria in the text that may refer to actions, effects of expressions and principles that will allow statements about the emotional and cognitive background as well as about the behaviour of the communicators. More particularly, Mayring (1983, 1985, 1988) proposes that the analysis here will proceed in one of three ways:

- *Summary*, in which analysis will mean a reduction of the data, as well as integration, generalisation and classification of the data into categories.
- *Explication*, in which analysis will aim at explaining the text or parts of it. This can be done in two ways, namely through using information from the same protocol (narrow context analysis), or using sources outside the protocol (wide context analysis).
- *Structuration*, which involves development of structures by putting the material in some kind of order, for example by means of already defined criteria (Mayring, 1988: 75). Such structuration may be related to formal criteria (formal structuration), content criteria (content structuration), type or dimension criteria (type structuration), or criteria related to dimensions of scales (scaling structuration).
- *Objective hermeneutics*   This is another method of analysis employed in the context of content analysis; it is also a complete research model. It was developed by Oevermann (Oevermann *et al.*, 1983) primarily in the

context of his work with families, socialisation and family therapy. In that context it was used to analyse interview transcripts of family members of patients.

This method is based on the assumption that behind the single forms of action there are *latent structures of meaning*, which direct individual action: such individual actions are expressions of these latent structures of meaning, which ultimately become for the interacting people autonomous forms of reality, which influence them. Objective hermeneutics aims to work out these latent structures of meaning, in which actual 'assignments of meanings' (*Sinnzuweisungen*) are contrasted. The difference between the two allows judgements about the status of individual meaning and action, for example whether there are any developmental problems in the process of socialisation.

Objective hermeneutics explores the objective and subjective inter-pretation (Deutung) of a social situation. This is accomplished in a number of ways (Heinze, 1987: 77; Oevermann *et al.*, 1983: 110). However, the specific technique employed is *feinanalyse* (fine analysis). This includes eight steps, beginning with analysis of written communication, explanation of intentions of the actors and their subjective motives and objective consequences, the function of the interaction, characterisation of linguistic criteria of the interaction, exploration of the interpretation up to the explanation of more general interrelationships.

Historically, a shift is evident in the methods of content analysis from quanti-tative to qualitative analysis. Although both methods are employed, there are more qualitative approaches to content analysis now than before.

f Content analysis in the computer age

The nature of content analysis lends itself easily to computer services. The fact that this method deals to a large extent with words and symbols of some kind makes it easy to employ electronic devices, which assist not only in the area of reading text and identifying occurrence and frequency of units and categories, but also in the actual analysis of the findings.

There are already computer programs available for this purpose, such as 'The general inquirer'; 'Oxford concordance program' and so on, which are employed to identify the occurrence of words and combinations of words and offer rapid and very accurate coding, replacing laborious work previously performed by coders. This assistance is, however, not applicable when thematic coding is used. Here coders are, as always, invaluable.

'The general inquirer', for instance, is used to list and compare various indices. Using programs such as KWIC (Key-word-in-context) and MWOC (Key-word-out-of-context), the computer can identify important concepts in text automatically, compute their frequency, present the findings in graphs, arrange them into systems of categories and compute some basic statistical tests. A comprehensive reference to computer programs employed in content analysis (and social research in general) will be presented in another section of this volume (Chapter 14).

g   Strengths and weaknesses of content analysis

Content analysis is a very effective method of data collection and analysis and is currently used not only as a method in itself but also in the context of other methods. Almost all methods that deal with text and some form of text analysis use some form of content analysis. As a documentary method, content analysis demonstrates all the strengths and weaknesses of the documentary methods presented above. Here reference will be made to only a few points.

Strengths
1   Content analysis is unobtrusive and therefore has no effects on the respondent.
2   Content analysis can be used when access to the research topic or research units is not possible. In some cases the research topic might not be currently accessible and cannot be approached through other methods. Content analysis is the only way of data generation.
3   Content analysis does not require respondents, a factor that is quite often associated with a number of problems.
4   The fact that content analysis involves already completed material and no respondents eliminates researcher bias.
5   Accessibility of the research material is a significant advantage. Texts are readily available for testing and retesting. This is not possible when the human factor is involved in research.
6   Content analysis is a low-cost method compared with other methods, such as surveys.
7   Content analysis entails less bias than other methods, given that text offers information in a neutral form, ready to be researched by the investigator.

Weaknesses
1   Some documents may not be accessible to the researcher; personal letters and diaries, for instance, might be difficult to obtain.
2   Documents often contain information related to a small proportion of people, and are therefore not representative.
3   Content analysis cannot study unrecorded events: it is therefore restricted to what has been documented.
4   Documents often are not complete and the information can therefore be biased and often unreliable.
5   Content analysis is less suitable for making comparisons than other methods.
6   Content analysis is susceptible to coder bias.

8   Projective methods

a   Introduction

Projective methods help to gather information about the personality of the respondents and to bring about an understanding of their behaviour, relationships and problems. The underlying assumption in this method is that stories, associations, drawings and other personal expressions collected through these methods reflect aspects of a person's social orientation, wishes and attitudes, philosophy of life, world outlook, motives, needs, drives, impulses and other traits; and thoughts expressed through projective methods point to this person's views, emotions and needs.

In practical terms, projective methods study individuals by confronting them with a situation or a stimulus and prompting them to react according to the meaning they assign to this stimulus. This response is analysed and interpreted in the context of the research question, and explains how the regularities between reaction and projected traits take place.

b Types of projective methods

There are several types of projective techniques used by social scientists and especially psychologists. The following are the most common.

Word association
In this method, the investigator reads out a set of words in succession and asks respondents to reply with a word which in their opinion is associated with that read by the investigator. The words read by the investigator are chosen carefully to cover the range thought to be important and relevant to the research question. The analysis focuses on the type and direction of the subject's response, and aims to identify patterns of reaction. Such responses are analysed like any other form of data.

Fill-in methods
These methods are more common among social scientists than the word association technique. In this method the researcher offers the structured start of a sentence and asks the respondent to fill in the missing part, as the respondent feels it should be. In a different form the beginning of a story or fairy tale is given, again requesting the respondent to complete it according to the way she or he feels it should go. The content and direction of the filled in parts are analysed to discover attitudes, preferences and also problems, and ultimately help the researcher to form a judgement about the respondent.

Count tests
In this method the respondent is asked by the investigator to count in a set period of time 10 objects of their environment. The speed at which the task is accomplished, as well as the type of objects, are evaluated to indicate the structure and organisation of the respondent's personal world.

Comic-strip tests
In this test the respondent is offered drawings or pictures containing empty 'speech bubbles', depicting people showing aggression, frustration or other feelings. The respondents are asked to guess what each person is saying, and to explain the reasons for feeling that way.

Rorschach test

This method involves 10 pictures of symmetrical ink-blots, formed through the folding of a page with wet ink on it. Pictures 1, 4, 5, 6 and 7 are black and white; pictures 2 and 3 also contain red, while pictures 8 and 10 are multi-coloured. These pictures are shown in succession to the respondent, who is instructed to say what each shape could be. The time taken to give an opinion as well as the context in which the picture is interpreted are recorded.

The answers given by the respondents are interpreted with regard to (1) the way in which the pictures were perceived (the whole picture or parts of it), (2) the size of the parts 'recognised', (3) the type of parts considered (the black parts only or also the white insets), (4) the quality of perception (forms, movements, colours), and (5) the content of perception, for example whether the pictures related to people, animals, parts of both, geographic items, landscapes, plants or non-living objects.

Thematic aperception tests

Here 31 black and white pictures, with no clear indication as to what they mean, are given to respondents in two sessions, with the instruction to tell a story about each picture. It is anticipated that the respondent will create an imaginative character in the story, which will reflect personal traits, identify the respondent with the protagonist and create a story that will allow the researcher to identify drives, emotions, attitudes and eventual conflicts and complexes of the respondent. It is assumed that subjects will communicate, through their responses, hidden or oppressed motives and drives.

The researcher will try to identify the figure with which the respondents identified themselves, and will also study the story with regard to the hero(es), the motives, trends and feelings of the hero(es), the forces of the hero's environment, the outcome of the story with regard to whether the respondent is the hero or the victim, the underlying themes and the interests and sentiments displayed in the story. The experience gained through the story is taken as a working hypothesis for further study.

Game tests

Game tests are employed by clinicians and psychologists in the area of child diagnosis. Children are given items that they are expected to order in the way they see most appropriate. In one case, they are given a box of toys (flexible dolls, animals, trees, flowers, building blocks, etc.) with the instruction to build something. In other tests, they are given items that might be found in a village, such as houses, a church, a castle, a factory, the council chambers building, a bridge, a train station and so on, and asked to use the materials to build a village. The researcher will try to identify the basic philosophy which the respondent uses to create the environment.

In another test the respondent is given 456 wooden or plastic parts in five forms and six colours. The task is to use them to cover a board. In a further test only seven black squares are given to the respondent with similar instructions. The reaction of the respondent and the accompanying behaviours are expected to offer useful information to the experts that will help them to understand the respondent better.

Drawing and colour tests

In a different kind of test, investigators employ drawings instead of pictures or toys to explain some of the background characteristics and behaviour patterns of the respondent. In some cases drawings are incomplete and the respondent is asked to complete them. This is the case, for instance, with the Wartegg–ZeichenTest (WZT), which consists of a print with eight square fields arranged in two rows on A5 paper. In each square are drawings, which the respondent is asked to complete. The investigator records the time required to complete the drawings, the way the drawings are completed, their content and other aspects that seem to be significant. The respondent is finally asked to explain the completed drawings.

In a similar fashion, colours are considered indicative of personality criteria and eventual disturbances. In this way, the choice of colours and colour combinations indicate for the expert ways of self-expression, and constitute methods of understanding thought processes and other aspects of an individual's personality. On the basis of this assumption, the 'Colour-pyramid-test' was developed; it requires the ordering of 24 colours into a 15-field pyramid base, first to make a beautiful combination, and then to put together an 'ugly' set. What is important for the expert is the number of chosen colours, the colours themselves and their arrangement, as well as the meaning of colours and colour combinations and the flexibility of choice.

These tests have been employed extensively by psychologists in clinical settings as well as by social researchers in other areas, such as market research, where the respondents' impressions, ideas, ideologies, preferences, etc. regarding a particular product can be ascertained. Pictures, for instance, containing a certain product can be shown to respondents, who would be asked to respond in a way similar to that contained in the tests described above. The view presented here is that these tests can be easily employed in areas outside psychology and can be very useful to sociologists and other social scientists.

9   Summary

In this chapter we presented a brief description of a sample of indirect methods of collecting data as they are employed in social sciences in general and in psychology in particular. Our focus has been mainly on social sciences, and with regard to this only a few of these methods are being regularly employed by social scientists. Some are the priority of social anthropologists. The study of traces is an example, although many sociologists have begun to give this method more attention than before. In a similar fashion, other methods are employed more by psychologists than by other researchers.

Overall, although these methods are used to a certain extent by social scientists, content analysis is the most common. This method is equally employed by quantitative and qualitative researchers, as well as by critical and conservative social scientists. This is one of the methods which is gaining ground constantly in the area of social research, and is becoming dominant in almost all fields of research.

With the presentation of the indirect methods of data collection we completed the discussion of the methods of data collection employed by investigators in the area of social research. We offered a brief account of the methods of data collection that are available to social researchers. It is now time to demonstrate how researchers go about employing these methods in practice, that is, the steps they take to actually collect the data. The way these methods are employed in social research will be presented in the next chapter.

Key concepts

Physiological methods	Frequency analysis
Projective methods	Structuration
Retrospectivity	Comic-strip test
Constructive method	Game tests
Content analysis	Physical traces
Explication	Disguised methods
Count test	Non-reactivity
Thematic aperception tests	Typological analysis
Non-reactive methods	Valence analysis
Concealed methods	Objective hermeneutics
Spontaneity	Rorschach test
Exemplification method	Wartegg–ZeichenTest

13

Data collection

When the planning stage of a research program is completed the researcher moves to the next step, namely collection of the data. During this stage the plans are executed, the subjects are approached and the information required for the study is gathered. If the previous step was mainly a stage of thinking, planning, judging and decision making, the step of data collection is a stage of action.

The actual content of this step and the researcher's degree of involvement in the project depend on the method of collection and its nature. While in some cases the researcher will be totally involved in data collection (e.g. when a qualitative study based on participant observation is carried out), in other cases the execution of the research plans will be carried out by assistants, for example research assistants, interviewers, fieldworkers or group leaders. In these cases the researcher will sit back waiting for the data to arrive. Some involvement in supervision and checking may be inevitable, but the actual collection of the data will be performed by the assistants. However, before the actual data collection takes place, some other research strategies are employed to make sure that the research design in general and the research tools in particular are appropriate and effective.

In this chapter, the process of data collection will be described, as employed by quantitative and qualitative researchers, beginning with a brief introduction of pre-tests and pilot studies.

1   Pre-tests and pilot studies

As stated above, when the research has been planned, and the instruments chosen and prepared, data collection can begin at any time provided all other arrangements have been made. However, there may be unanswered questions and some doubts about the effectiveness of the instruments or even the whole project and the reaction of the respondents to the study or parts of it, and unknown problems might exist and might have to be solved before the main study can begin. Researchers never begin a study unless they are confident that the chosen methods are suitable, valid, reliable and effective and free from problems or errors, or at least that they have taken all precautions to avoid any problems and/or distortions in the preparatory stages of the research.

One way of checking the effectiveness of the research design and other issues related to data collection is to use pre-tests and pilot studies, both of which have become a part of any survey research and a standard feature of modern research methodology. Each of these miniature preparatory studies serves a similar purpose; they are, however, different, as we shall see next.

a   Pre-tests

There are cases in which the researcher is not sure about the effectiveness or suitability of one small part of the instrument developed for the study, for example one question or a small section of the questionnaire or the interview schedule. The investigator might think, for instance, that the response categories of the question(s) concerned are not adequate, or the wording of one question is ambiguous and the respondent's interpretation of that question could be doubtful. In such cases, pre-tests are employed. *Pre-tests* are small tests of single elements of the research instrument and are predominantly used to check eventual 'mechanical' problems of these instruments.

Assume, for instance, that a study has been designed to investigate the workload of spouses at home and evaluate their involvement in housework as an economic activity. A questionnaire has been developed for this purpose. However, the researcher is not sure about the adequacy of the 15 optional response categories that have been devised for one question, one of them being 'Other, please specify'.

The researcher is concerned that the response set to this question might not be effective; as a result the option 'Other, please specify' may attract a disproportionally large number of responses, a problem the researcher wishes to avoid. In this case, a pre-test containing this question (alone or with a few other questions) administered to a number of respondents will prove to be very useful.

The results of this pre-test will show whether the question is adequate or whether it needs to be adjusted. If the proportion of respondents opting for 'other' is relatively small the question will remain as it is. If, however, the number of the responses falling on 'other' is relatively high, and if there are specific items frequently mentioned in this option, an adjustment of the response set is imperative. It is very likely that the researcher will add these items to the existing response set, thus offering a more exhaustive list of household items and reducing the likelihood for the respondents to opt for the 'other' option.

A similar procedure will be employed if the researcher is doubtful about whether the subjects will in fact answer a sensitive question directly or opt for the neutral category 'Undecided' or 'I don't know'. Certainly, some of these questions/problems would, under normal circumstances, have been answered/solved during the preliminary (exploratory) study. However, there are cases in which exploratory studies have not been undertaken or were not sufficient. There are also questions that arise after exploratory studies have been completed. In such cases a pre-test is employed.

b   Pilot studies

A pilot study is a small-scale replica and a rehearsal of the main study. While pre-tests help to solve isolated mechanical problems of an instrument, pilot studies are concerned with administrative and organisational problems related to the whole study and the respondents.

Pilot studies serve many purposes, but the following are considered by most writers (e.g. Oppenheim, 1992; Moser and Kalton, 1971; Sproull, 1988) to be the most common:

- To estimate the costs and duration of the main study and test the effectiveness of its organisation.
- To test the research methods and research instruments and their suitability.
- To show whether the sampling frame is adequate.
- To estimate the level of response and form of drop-outs.
- To gain information about how diverse or homogeneous the survey population is
- To familiarise researchers with the research environment in which the research is to take place.
- To give researchers and their assistants the opportunity to practise research in real situations and before the main study begins.
- To test the response of the subjects to the method of data collection and through that the adequacy of its structure.

The structure and purpose of pilot studies vary from case to case, depending on the type of research and the structure of the methodology used. In the context of case studies, for instance, pilot studies aim to establish whether respondents are accessible, whether the site is convenient, whether the techniques of data collection generate enough (not enough or too much) information, whether the plan is well adjusted and whether any changes or adjustments are needed

In a nutshell, the purpose of the pilot studies is to discover possible weaknesses, inadequacies, ambiguities and problems in all aspects of the research, so that they can be corrected before actual data collection takes place.

c   Designing pre-tests and pilot studies

The design of pre-tests and pilot studies varies with many factors, such as availability of resources (e.g. money, time, assistants), the nature of the study, type of methodology, nature of the population, size of the sample and degree of necessity for these studies. However, in any case the principles of social research employed in any (main) study are expected to be employed here too.

Sample procedures need to be accurate and valid; the sample required for these studies has to be chosen according to common standards and procedures, in order to produce representative results, that is, in order to allow as many groups of the population as possible to express their views of or concern with, and to attract their reaction to, certain aspects of the project or the whole study. Some researchers include 1 per cent of respondents in this study. Others include more.

In the context of *qualitative studies*, pilot studies are not usually employed. If a researcher, however, decides on a pilot study, the choice of the units is not as accurately defined as in quantitative methods. In *case-study research*, for instance, the units of pilot studies may be chosen according to the personal convenience of the investigator, accessibility of subjects as well as geographic proximity.

d   Nature of pilot studies

As indicated above, the nature of pilot studies depends on the nature of the underlying methodology. In quantitative research, for example survey research, pilot studies need to be very well planned and executed, exactly as the main study is expected to be carried out. When qualitative research is undertaken, pre-tests and pilot studies are generally not employed. If, however, they are included, their nature is, as already stated, rather general and less strict, and the execution broad and less focused. Further, their nature depends very much on the structure, purpose and type of the main study.

e   Evaluation

The results of the pre-tests and pilot studies will be evaluated in the context of the aims described above. The findings will offer straight answers to basic questions asked, and will definitely indicate whether there are any problems that require attention.

If, for instance, the researcher cannot establish the expected rapport with the respondents, if there are difficulties in convincing the majority of the respondents to take part in the study, if the respondents refuse to answer certain questions or give high proportions of 'I don't know' answers, if answers are given but with small notes or qualifications, and if the observed subjects tend unexpectedly to be distracted by the video camera or other environmental factors, then certain adjustments must be made (Becker, 1989).

As this discussion indicates, pre-tests and pilot studies are two very useful research tools, and offer invaluable information that can be used very effectively when preparing the final stage of the research.

2   Data collection in qualitative and quantitative studies

In principle there is no difference in data collection between quantitative and qualitative studies. In both cases data will be collected as designed by the researcher. The chosen methods will be employed and plans will be executed as previously designed and arranged.

Nevertheless, there are basic differences between the two methodologies in this area, stemming from their theoretical uniqueness and methodological preferences, which, as already shown elsewhere, differ from each other significantly.

The first major difference is related to the fact that in many cases of qualitative research the process of data collection is not a distinct part of the research process but an aspect of it that is difficult to delineate from other elements of the process, especially data analysis. The process of qualitative research does not allow the steps of research to be as distinct as in quantitative research. Quantitative and qualitative researchers have different tasks during the process of data collection. While in quantitative research collection means just gathering data, in qualitative research it involves a dynamic process of gathering, thinking, evaluating, analysing, modifying, expanding, gathering further, thinking again and so on. Although the purpose of data collection is the same in both types of research, their content, intensity and nature vary significantly.

In addition, data collection in qualitative research is geared towards natural situations, everyday-life worlds, interaction and interpretation, and for that reason the researcher has to organise this element of investigation to meet these methodological requirements. Beyond this, the qualitative researcher is engaged in the research situation/problem and is more tolerant, flexible, permissive and 'understanding' than the quantitative researcher. Finally, the nature of qualitative research dictates that the researcher employs means and techniques (e.g. language) that are closer to the research situation, so that the everyday life situation is reflected fully and clearly in the findings.

These differences are not accepted by all social investigators. There are quantitative researchers, for instance, who disagree with a number of the assumptions made by qualitative workers presented above. For them, the quantitative researcher is by no means estranged from the research subject and the techniques employed in this context are not 'strange' to the respondent. The quantitative researchers may not be as 'permissive' in their research work as qualitative researchers are and as they define it. What permissiveness is, however, and to what degree one can be permissive and still produce valid results are questions which are difficult to answer.

3   Interviewing

After the pre-tests and pilot studies have been conducted and the findings considered, or after the final plans of the research have been made, the researcher will begin with the actual collection of the data. If interviewing has been chosen as the method of data collection there are several tasks that must be accomplished during this step of the project, the most significant of which are described below.

a   Tasks to be accomplished

Advertising for interviewers and supervisors
If the study is small the researcher might decide to carry out the interviews personally. This is more likely if the study requires an intensive or in-depth

interview. If additional personnel are required appropriate advertisements will be placed in professional journals and newspapers. The number of interviewers and supervisors depends on many factors, such as the sample size, the length and complexity of the interview, the degree of dispersion of the respondents, the study objective, the time by which the data need to be collected and the resources available for the study.

In some cases the researchers make all arrangements for interviewing during the stage of research design, leaving only the actual gathering of information to the stage of data collection. In other cases many arrangements are made at the beginning of the data collection step. As far as the research process is concerned, it is not important when arrangements are made; they may be considered at the end of the research design or at the start of data collection.

Selection of interviewers, supervisors and personnel
Emphasis in the selection process is placed on criteria that are considered to be important for the research process and that were presented earlier. For instance, if subjects from a certain race are included in the study, it is beneficial and advisable to consider interviewers from this race; if mostly women are included in the study and when sensitive issues are investigated it is usual to employ female interviewers. The criteria that are taken to be important and that were discussed in the previous chapter should be taken into account in the selection process.

During selection the researcher discusses with the applicants the work conditions, payment and duration of the study. Normally, an attempt is made to select interviewers who will be acceptable to the respondents, and who will not cause any unnecessary problems during the research, such as refusing to cooperate, being antagonistic or causing conflict or distortions of some kind.

Training of interviewers
This involves the interviewers in studying the interview schedule, practising interviewing and developing skills associated with the research topic, as discussed in Chapter 11.

Arranging work conditions, payment and duration of employment
This is more significant when a large number of interviewers are employed and when they are employed under different conditions. In any case, determining these issues at this step of the research helps to organise the study more effectively and also to estimate the duration and costs of the study.

When computer-aided collection is employed, computers and relevant programs need to be made available, appropriate rooms arranged for housing the computers and of course suitable personnel employed. If interviews are to be made in the house of the respondent, provision of portable computers must be considered.

Approaching the respondent
This might be accomplished either by telephone, mail or personal visit. As a rule, the person who approaches the respondent introduces himself or herself, explains the purpose of the visit, the aim of the study and how the subjects were selected, offers details about the agency conducting the study and the

sponsor(s), as well as the method of recording (tapes, taking notes, etc.), assures the subject that confidentiality and anonymity will be respected and asks for cooperation.

Dealing with refusals
Although respondents in most cases agree to be interviewed, in some cases they do not. The interviewer should, therefore, be prepared to discuss such refusals and attempt to motivate the respondents to take part in the study. It is up to the interviewer to help respondents to overcome their initial hesitation and to make them see the research as interesting and worthwhile and to decide to participate in it. For this reason, it is often recognised that personal visits result in a higher response rate than if contacts are made by telephone or mail.

Choosing the time and place
If the respondent agrees to be interviewed, arrangements will be made for the time and place of the interview, which will be determined on the basis of factors related to the research objective, resources available and the respondents. In ideal terms the time is arranged to suit these needs and also the interests of the respondents.

Conducting the interview
The actual interview involves asking questions and recording the answers as instructed by the researcher. Depending on the type of interview, the interviewer might ask questions as stated in the interview schedule, or as required by the situation. In all cases, attention will be given to non-responses. All questions should be answered and schedules checked for completion.

When standardised interviewing is performed the three minimum requirements are: *completeness, uniformity* and *objectivity*. These suggest that all questions be asked and the responses recorded in the given order and as instructed, in the same way throughout the study, and in an unbiased and unbiasing manner.

Field supervision
Supervision is related to whether and how interviews are performed. The researcher must make sure that the interviews are in fact conducted and also that they are carried out as instructed. Supervisors will monitor the process of interviewing, take the necessary steps to achieve the set goals and report to the project director when and if required.

Ensuring adherence to ethics and honesty
This is a task that interviewers must be made aware of during the training period, and an issue that the researcher must make sure to control as much as possible. Supervising as well as telephoning respondents randomly, and asking them relevant questions, might help to prevent violations of these principles in the remaining part of the study.

Returning the completed interviews to the researcher
How and when interview data are to be returned to the researcher is an issue that is negotiated between the interviewer and the researcher. Return of the

material after it has been collected is the best arrangement. Researchers should be in a position to monitor the study progress and to intervene when necessary. When computers are used this task is not relevant, since the data are usually transferred automatically to the data bank as soon as the interview is completed.

Checking interviews for completeness, and eventual faults and errors
Checking is done by the interviewer, but researchers also go through the interview records when they receive them. Some researchers refuse to pay interviewers for incomplete or illegible interviews, while others make other arrangements for incomplete interviews (e.g. paying a fraction of the arranged remuneration or a small fee covering the interviewer's travel costs only).

b   Telephone interviewing

The process of data collection in telephone interviewing follows the same steps as those employed in general interviewing. The only difference between the two lies in the selection of interviewers, who are expected to have the qualities required for the particular form of interviewing, for approaching the respondents and asking the questions. Obviously, telephone interviewers are required to have different qualities, background and experience from ordinary interviewers. Nevertheless, on the whole, the procedure employed here is similar to that explained in the previous section.

As stated earlier, computers might be employed in interviewing in general as well as in telephone interviewing. In such cases, a part of data collection can be performed by the computer.

4   Questionnaires

The steps followed when using questionnaires as methods of data collection are similar to those employed in interviewing. Here there are no interviewers but other assistants are required. Preparing the questionnaires, checking for errors, problems, accuracy, etc. and printing the required copies as well as the envelopes with return addresses would have already been accomplished during the designing of the study and corrected by means of pre-tests and pilot studies. The tasks to be accomplished now are: (1) mailing or delivering the questionnaire to the respondents of the study; and (2) coping with non-responses.

5   Non-response in survey research

Dealing with respondents who fail to return questionnaires is one of the most serious survey problems. Whether a non-response rate is acceptable or is considered a problem is an issue addressed by researchers in different ways. Some researchers are content with a response rate of 10 per cent, while for others a 75 per cent response rate is taken to be a very good rate. (To compute the response rate divide the number of returned questionnaires by the number of delivered questionnaires and multiply the quotient by 100. This gives the percentage response rate.)

In practice, non-response means a loss of valuable sources of information and affects the degree of representativeness of the study. For this reason, researchers make an effort to increase the response rate by employing social, psychological or economic techniques. Offering economic incentives, for instance, and/or appealing to moral or other principles are not unusual in social research. Nevertheless, avoiding non-response in the first place is the best measure, and knowing the reasons for it helps to design the survey in such a way that a high response rate can be achieved.

The reasons for respondents not participating in surveys are many and varied. With respect to interviewing, respondents usually do not take part in the study because: (1) they are unwilling to do so (for example, they disapprove of the research study, don't like the sponsor, do not have time or the spouse disapproves of it); (2) they cannot be interviewed due to communication problems that make interviewing impossible, that is, physical, mental or linguistic problems (e.g. handicapped persons or migrants); (3) the respondent is inaccessible (e.g. moved away, died or was not at home when visited) (see Becker, 1989; Puris, 1995).

In the case of questionnaires, the reasons for not returning the questionnaires are similar to those reported for interviews. There are, however, some additional reasons, for example the questionnaire may have been lost or was too complicated, or the respondent did not have time to complete it. Long and complicated questionnaires are quite often not only difficult to understand but also constitute a time-consuming task for certain groups of people.

a Non-response to questionnaires — the researcher's tasks

If after the closing date for returning the questionnaires a number of questionnaires are outstanding, the researcher should introduce some measures to increase the response rate. Here are some ways of handling this issue.

Reminders

In the first place, sending reminders to those who did not return the questionnaire or to all respondents, depending on the research design, is the right step towards improving the response rate.

Particular attention should be paid to the principle of *anonymity*. If anonymity is not an issue, sending out reminders is of course very easy. In most cases, however, researchers guarantee anonymity and often responses are returned to the researcher anonymously; as a result, the names of the respondents who have not returned the questionnaires are unknown.

The correct way of handling this problem is to send reminders to all respondents, noting that if they have already responded they should ignore the note. This is a legitimate approach but an expensive one. A number of researchers tend to employ a less honest method. They mark the question-naires in one of many ways so that they can identify the questionnaire sent to each respondent. This allows the researchers to know the identity of those who have not responded to the study and to send them a reminder, just as if a letter was sent to all subjects. Although often used, this method is unethical.

Second reminders

Sending second reminders to all respondents, or only to those who have not returned the questionnaire after the return date for the first reminder has elapsed, is a step to take if the first attempt has not been successful. The same procedure as that introduced above is employed.

Direct telephone contact

When both reminders have proved unsuccessful, the researcher may approach the remaining respondents by telephone, urging them to return their question-naires. This procedure is associated with the same problems referred to above and is approached in the same way.

What follows?

Employing the above techniques helps to increase the response rate very significantly. As regards the questionnaires that remain unanswered, the researcher will most likely concentrate on the available numbers and, depending on the response rate, make relevant decisions about continuing the study (and if so under what conditions) or abandoning the project. The latter option is rather unusual, unless the response rate is extremely low and there are no ways of remedying the problem.

b   Reducing or avoiding non-response

Achieving a 100 per cent response rate is very rare, but there are ways that can help to attain a high response rate. Some of these are initiated before the survey starts and they help to prevent a low response rate, while others are introduced after the survey and these help to increase the response rate by motivating the respondents to return the questionnaire.

In the case of interviews, approaching the respondents persistently until they relent is reported to be a successful method of combating non-response. Offering rewards to 'difficult' respondents is another. Finding substitute respondents and getting information about the respondent through a third person (where possible) are further techniques.

To prevent non-response is even more difficult. Screening the sampling frame to eliminate drop-outs (dead persons and movers), using a not-too-large sample, approaching the respondents as gently and politely as possible and presenting the survey in an attractive way are quite often very helpful. If the interviews are long, demanding, intruding and sensitive, offering rewards might not be a bad way to make the survey more attractive. Some research institutes, for instance, offer financial rewards or presents for every completed questionnaire or interview.

When questionnaires are employed non-response becomes a more serious problem since there is no opportunity for the researcher to try to persuade the respondent to complete the questionnaire. The only way of motivating the respondent to do so is, as stated above, to send reminders to all subjects urging them to complete the questionnaire. Two to three reminders might be sufficient. After the third reminder it is very unlikely that any further attempt will be successful.

As discussed above, sending reminders can produce confusion and mistrust, particularly due to the fact that surveys are anonymous and thus the researcher is not supposed to know the names of non-respondents. Many writers are of the opinion that this problem can be prevented if approached as follows (see Berger *et al.*, 1989; Flick *et al.*, 1991; Roth, 1987):

- For the cover letter, content, timing, length and appearance are very important and must be considered very seriously.
- The cover letter should be closed and addressed as required by the nature of the study and the respondent (Dear Sir, Dear Householder, Yours sincerely, With regards, etc.).
- Confidentiality but not anonymity should be promised.
- Reminders to all respondents, not only to non-respondents, should be sent.
- Reminders to non-respondents only, but using initials or number, or just Sir, Madam, etc. should be used.
- Reminders only to non-respondents, but using the name on the letter only (not on the card or questionnaire), can be sent. The subject should be assured that when the questionnaire is returned the identity of the respondent cannot be defined.

c Some considerations

The above precautions can help to combat non-response, but only to a certain extent. Besides, some of the measures seem to be ways of remedying low response rates rather than positively promoting a high response rate. Such an increase can be achieved in a number of ways. The following statements might, according to a number of writers (see Lamnek, 1988; Mahr, 1995; Puris, 1995; Selltiz *et al.*, 1976), give some pointers in the right direction:

- *Approach*   The more serious, trustworthy and friendly the cover letter, the more likely it is that the questionnaire will be accepted and completed.
- *Explanation*   The more clearly the purpose, nature, usefulness and sponsorship of the study is explained, the more likely it is that the questionnaire will be completed.
- *Honesty*   The more honest, direct and concise the cover letter, the more likely it is that the questionnaire will be answered.
- *Length of cover letter*   The shorter the cover letter the better.
- *Principles*   The more convinced the respondent is of the anonymity and confidentiality of the study, the more likely he or she is to answer the questionnaire.

- *Reminders*   The more convinced the respondent is about the use of re-minders and their relationship with anonymity, the more trust is generated and the more likely it is that the questionnaire will be answered.
- *Rationale*   The more convinced the respondent is of the rationale of the study and the reasons for taking part in it, the more likely it is that the questionnaire will be completed.
- *Time required*   The more specific the indication of the time required for the completion of the questionnaire, the more likely it is that the respondent will complete it.
- *Size*   The smaller the size of the questionnaire, the more likely it is to be completed.
- *Degree of difficulty*   The easier it is for the questionnaire to be completed (e.g. enclosing a self-addressed, pre-stamped envelope), the more likely it is for the respondent to complete it.
- *Sensitivity*   The less sensitive the question content, the more likely it is that the questionnaire will be completed and returned.
- *Method of return*   The easier it is for the questionnaire to be returned, the more likely it is that it will be returned.
- *Time of completion*   A questionnaire is more likely to be completed and returned if administered at a time convenient to the respondent and at which the respondent is likely to be at home.
- *Administration*   Questionnaires are more likely to be completed if delivered personally and if arranged to be picked up by the researcher at a set date.
- *Rewards*   Promising rewards for completed questionnaires in general, or for completing them by a certain date in particular, is found to produce high response rates.
- *Return dates*   Setting too long or too short periods for questionnaire completion is reported to cause high non-response rates.
- *Appeal*   The more appealing and attractive the cover letter, the more likely it is that the questionnaire will be completed and returned.
- *Layout and format*   The more appealing and attractive the layout and format of the questionnaire, the more pleasant it is to answer the questions, and the more likely it is that it will be completed and returned.
- *Appearance*   The more impressive the colour of paper, type of print and type of mailing, the more likely it is that the questionnaire will be completed.
- *Trust*   The more trustworthy the questionnaire, for example by ensuring confidentiality and anonymity, the more likely it is that the questionnaire will be completed and returned.

d   Interview response rate

Many of the points made above with regard to questionnaires are also appli-cable in the context of interviews. In addition, when interviews are employed it is suggested by many researchers and writers (e.g. Puris, 1995; Becker, 1989; Berger *et al.*, 1989) that consideration of issues such as the following might prove helpful:

- *Approach*   The more personal, honest, brief and pleasant the approach when visiting the respondent for the first time, the more likely it is that the respondent will participate in the study.
- *Explanation*   The clearer and fuller the explanation of the survey, including the sponsor, purpose, time required, anonymity and confidentiality, the more likely it is that the respondent will agree to take part in the study.
- *Appeal*   The more appealing and attractive the presentation of the study and the more useful it is presented to be, the more likely it is that the respondent will agree to be interviewed.
- *Honesty*   The more honest, 'polite, frank, reassuring and modest' the researcher, the more likely it is that the respondent will take part in the study.
- *Respect*   The more respected the respondent feels in his or her role as an 'expert' to be consulted rather than as a person to provide information, the more likely it is for the interview to take place.
- *Trust*   The more successful the researcher in eliminating mistrust, insecurity, fears, confusion, doubts and ambiguity, the more likely it is for the respondent to agree to take part in the study.
- *Impression*   The more impressed the respondent is with the overall sincerity and appearance of the study, the more likely it is for the interview to take place.
- *Arrangements*   The more favourable and convenient the interview arrangements are for the respondent, and the more considerate the approach (e.g. phoning before visiting), the more likely it is for the interview to be completed.
- *Friendliness*   The more friendly and discreet the researcher, the more likely it is for the respondent to agree to be interviewed.
- *Sponsors*   Interviews conducted for the government, universities or other institutions are more likely to attract the cooperation of the respondent than interviews conducted for other sponsors or for the personal interest of the interviewer.
- *Purpose*   The more worthwhile the purpose of the interview, the more likely it is for the respondent to agree to be interviewed.

In summary, the most successful way of reducing the non-response rate is prevention. Knowing the ways respondents react to elements of the questionnaire or the survey helps in its planning so that non-response can be avoided or its rate greatly reduced.

6   Documentary methods

The single task to be accomplished in data collection where documentary methods are employed is reading the documents and recording the occurrence, prominence, evaluation and intensity of the recording units. If computers are employed, for example in the context of content analysis, this step will include feeding the computer with the necessary material (if this has not been done already) and instructing the computer to perform the required tasks. Recording of data will be done by the computer. Details about how information is to be extracted from the documents have been given earlier.

7   Observational research

a   General overview

Data collection varies with the type of observation employed in the research, especially with respect to participant and non-participant observation. Nevertheless, some common steps in both models of observation can be identified. The steps that must be undertaken when observation is employed are given below.

Step 1: Establishing contact with the subjects
If the observation is to take place in a laboratory, arrangements will be made for the subjects to be gathered in this place. If the observation is to be performed in a natural setting, the observer approaches the setting and establishes the necessary 'contact' with the subjects in their natural environment.

Step 2: Observing the observation unit(s)
This will be done according to the arranged methods. Structured observation will concentrate on the categories established during research design. But even in unstructured observation some points will soon be developed to direct the performance of the observer.

Step 3: Recording the data
Taking notes is the standard method of recording. Using mechanical assistance, for example with recording machines and so on, is useful but can only be employed when structured observation is used. Electronic recording (film, video, etc.) is equally useful.

Step 4: Observing the rules of ethics
This relates to the extent to which observation takes place, the way the information gathered is used, and to whether the respondents are aware of being observed or their rights being violated.

b   Tasks to be performed in participant observation

Gaining entry into the setting
This involves making arrangements for the observer to become a member of the group under study. In most cases this is arranged by the chief researcher, usually during the designing of the study. In some cases gaining entry into the setting is a time-consuming exercise and is therefore initiated long before the exercise begins.

Becoming familiar with the setting, and performing the observation

This is a difficult task, especially when it involves a radical change in the lifestyle of the observer. Entering a factory, a religious sect or a gang is often difficult; but 'getting familiar' with the members' lifestyles and beginning to function as 'one of them' is much more demanding and difficult.

The critical issue in participant observation is how to be a member of the group under investigation and to observe without affecting the setting. A wise suggestion is to be honest, vague and/or impressive. It is suggested that it is better to tell the truth (but not in detail), to explain that the observer is interested in a social environment but not in the particular environment she or he is observing, and that the observer is interested in learning from the others who are the experts.

Observers should be neutral, not take sides, develop trust in the group they observe, not challenge the position of the subjects, not disrupt the functioning of the group, participate in all activities of the subjects, and avoid establishing strong relationships with a few members of the group. When their identity as observers is known, they should not act as experts, give advice or direct the behaviour of the subjects; they should not be directed by subjects regarding what, when and how to observe. The presence of the observer and the use of questions should not alter the environment or the routines of the group life.

Recording the observation data

The recording of information should include every detail of the setting, the people and other elements of observation. In ideal terms conversations should be recorded verbatim and in the actual language of the subjects, and should not be summarised in general laws or patterns of behaviour before they are adequately studied and evaluated. Every experience is considered to be important and interesting and should be recorded, irrespective of the impression it makes on the researcher at the time of data collection.

Although observing the subjects is easy since the observer lives in the group and with the members of the group, recording observations is not. Recording information that most of the time is new, complex and specific when the observer has to avoid disclosing his or her real identity is not only difficult but in certain cases almost impossible. The chief researcher will have developed techniques of coping with this problem, and such techniques vary from case to case.

Observation records are delivered to the researcher, who in turn will process them. When the researcher is also the observer, and this is the most common occurrence, records will be treated according to the method of analysis and presentation employed by the researcher. In any case, information will be collected right through the duration of the study and processed by means of the method chosen during the design stage.

Closure

When the information required is collected, the process of observation is terminated. How this takes place depends on many factors, but primarily on the nature of the study and the degree of the observer's involvement in the life of the group. Normally, the observer is expected to depart in a natural, friendly and objective manner, which does not disturb in any way the observation setting or the relationship with the observed.

8   Experiments

Experiments are more strictly designed and executed than many other methods of data collection. This is especially so for laboratory experiments, which follow a systematic and rather strict procedure. The steps to be followed during the stage of data collection are given below.

Step 1
Approach the research situation and arrange for the experiment to take place. Ensuring access to a laboratory to suit the requirements of the study is one of the most important tasks to be accomplished at the beginning of data collection. In certain cases a special laboratory may be used for the purpose of data collection; in other cases, an ordinary room might serve as a laboratory. This is the case when attitudes of students are studied and tests of the attitudes are measured in the classroom, while projecting a video can be organised in any school room.

Step 2
Select the respondents in the context of groups as required (experimental and control groups). The procedure of choosing the members of the two types of groups was explained earlier. Here, the experimenter approaches the population and determines the membership of the groups.

Step 3
Control for variables as required. Steps 1 and 2 above can be completed before data collection begins. In this case, data collection will start with the establishment of the experimental conditions and the measures that help to control certain variables. What this involves varies from case to case. It must be specified, however, by the researcher in the design of the experiment, and expressed in the instructions. Controlling for variables is a very significant part of experimental research.

Step 4
Plan the time, place and conditions of the experiment and arrange for these to take place. Although these are practical aspects of the experimental procedure, they are as significant as any other aspect of the study. These procedures help to bring subjects to the experiment and also to conditions that guarantee valid and successful data collection.

Step 5
Arrange for the pre-testing of both groups to be executed, thereby identifying the strength and qualities of the dependent variable (pre-test). Administering the test offers the basis for the argument that is to be developed in the study. This test varies from one experiment to another, and its structure and content is to be determined by the researcher.

Step 6
Introduce the experimental group to the stimulus as planned. This again will contain some procedure: a film, a visit to a slum, an excursion to the outback,

dancing in a bar with a group of teenagers, etc. This is at the heart of the experiment and must be conducted with care.

Step 7
Measure the dependent variable (post-test). The test to be conducted here may be similar to that employed in the pre-test. In any case, the experimenter is expected to administer the test and collect the results as specified in the instructions.

Step 8
Compute the difference between the pre-test and post-test scores. This is a mechanical task which is quite often performed by the computer. The figures gathered in this way offer the basis for analysis and interpretation of the experimental data.

Field experiments
Data collection through field experiments follows a similar procedure, adjusted to the nature of this method. Field experiments are conducted in natural settings. For this reason they do not require laboratories and measures to control variables of the kind needed when laboratory experiments are employed. Nevertheless, the actual logic of experimentation employed in standard experiments is employed here too. Whether a pre-test is administered depends on a number of factors. The design will specify the exact steps to be undertaken in every form of field research. In general terms, the field experimenter will have to accomplish the following tasks.

Step 1
Identify the field in which the experiment takes place. The nature of the field varies according to the study object.

Step 2
Arrange the experimental conditions. These conditions will vary from case to case, and while in some cases it might involve just minor manipulation of the environment, in other cases interference may be more obvious.

Step 3
Induce the stimulus according to the instructions.

Step 4
Record eventual changes. This recording will provide the data for further analysis.

9   Case-study research

Data collection in case-study research concentrates on the cases that have been selected to be studied. Data collection is accomplished by means of the methods defined in the case-study protocol. Such methods include the use of documents, archival records, interviews, observation and physical artifacts.

The preparations needed at this stage of research relate mainly to the methods of data collection, and the preparations are not significantly different from those discussed above in the context of other methods. When interviews are used, interviewers must be employed and relevant material produced to make interviewing possible. If observation is used, observers must be appointed and the relevant arrangements made to allow observation to take place and so on.

What is different from our previous discussion is that the collection of data must be undertaken in the context of each case and analysed/evaluated in this context before entering another case. Cases are often approached separately without cross-case analysis. Each case study consists of a whole study and is not related to other cases. Results will not be gathered together. When, for instance, the study includes three cases, data will be collected from the first case, then from the second and finally from the third case, each of them constituting separate sources for individual analysis and evaluation.

The principles of data collection are those discussed earlier in this volume. Nevertheless, some writers suggest that case-study research might involve additional principles, directly related to data collection. An example of such suggestions is given below. Here researchers are advised (see, for example, Yin, 1991) to consider the following points:

- *Use multiple sources of evidence* Individual sources are thought to have limitations, which can be overcome by considering information from other sources; in addition, multiple sources offer a broader spectrum of analysis and a higher construct validity.
- *Create a case-study data book*, which allows easy analysis and evaluation of the information, and also provides a store of data others can read and further analyse and evaluate. The book may include notes, documents, tabular material and narratives.
- *Maintain a chain of evidence*, which will help to establish high reliability of the data since it allows the reader to follow the line of thought through all steps of the argument. Citation of evidence and presentation of vital information in a structured and systematic way makes this task easy and the evidence convincing.

Additional general principles, which are used also in other types of data collections, include the following:

- Maintain high standards of objectivity.
- Obey the code of ethics.
- Be accurate and systematic.
- Consider data collection as an element of the research, not an end in itself.
- Follow the instructions of the researcher.
- Avoid action that could generate distortions and errors.
- Report any unusual and unexpected occurrence to the researcher.
- Be fair and honest (no cheating in any way).

10   Summary

Data collection by means of other methods is not very different from those presented in this chapter. The general rule is that data collection is just an execution of the plans developed during the stage of research design. This design specifies exactly what is to be done, where, how, when and under what conditions. With a design well formulated and systematically set, data collection becomes just a routine. What follows then is *data analysis,* a complex and demanding process which will allow the researcher to formulate answers to the research questions. Data analysis is the focus of the remaining part of this book. The next chapter initiates the basic elements of data analysis as it is practised in qualitative and quantitative research.

Key concepts

Pre-tests	Closure
Non-response	Data collection
Pilot studies	Qualitative analysis

PART III Data analysis

14

Analysis and interpretation

As we saw in the previous chapter, the preparatory work for the initial stages of the research is put into practice during the stage of data collection, which itself produces useful and relevant information. In general terms, such data will be expressed in the form of ticks, circles or other notations on response sheets, or in piles of pages full of text and other information. It is the task of the researcher to study these data and search for trends, patterns and relationships that are relevant to the research question.

The aim of this task is to make sense out of the information gathered through the previous stages of the research, and to identify the meaning the data contain. The ticks, circles and other notations are converted into statements, propositions or conclusions, which ultimately will answer the research question. And the pages of text will need to be converted to a form that will convey the central message hidden behind the lines and paragraphs of the pages. This process of data processing and of converting raw data into meaningful statements is called analysis and interpretation of data.

To explain this process is the purpose of this chapter. More particularly, in the following discussion we shall introduce the methods of data analysis most common among social scientists. We shall consider the ways in which quantitative researchers work with raw data, but we shall also explore the techniques that qualitative investigators have developed to deal with raw data, and the underlying philosophy of their approach.

A Qualitative analysis

1 Introduction

Qualitative research is based on the theoretical and methodological principles of interpretive science. As a result, qualitative analysis contains a minimum of quantitative measurement, standardisation and mathematical techniques. In most cases, its process brings together collection and analysis of data in such a way that identifying data leads automatically to their analysis, which in turn directs the researcher to the area in which new data should be sought and identified, in order to be analysed again (Carspecken and Apple, 1992). This process leads to the development of new concepts and theories by relating evidence to abstract concepts and to theory generation.

In this standard form, analysis is part of data collection and evaluation. While further data are collected analysis continues and evaluation and interpretation follow, and the circular process is repeated until all units have been studied and the research issue is saturated (Patton, 1990). For this type of traditional qualitative research, data collection, analysis and evaluation are one and the same process. Nevertheless, qualitative analysis never finishes in the field; in most cases qualitative analysis is completed after data collection, as it is done in quantitative research. In such cases, the result of this collection/analysis process is a large amount of data, that is, qualitative data, which is different from quanti- tative data in at least the following ways (see Miles and Huberman, 1994): (1) they appear in words and extended text and in numbers; (2) they have been collected in a variety of ways, including observation, interviewing, studying documents, etc.; and (3) they need to be processed before they are ready for use.

In general, qualitative analysis is not as abstract as quantitative analysis, and is not guided by a large body of formal knowledge either. During data analysis, the investigator searches for patterns of data, for example in the form of recurrent behaviours, events, etc., and when such patterns are identified, interprets them, moving from description of empirical data to interpretation of meanings. Nevertheless, during the past 25 years qualitative analysis has undergone a reorganisation in structure and process, which has resulted in a relative reorientation of the underlying method on the one hand and in the establishment of a diverse structure on the other. While traditional practice is still applied by many researchers, additional approaches have been introduced which make qualitative analysis a pluralist procedure. The reason for this is not the shift in theory and ideology alone; it is also the development of new methods and acceptance of old ones in the context of qualitative methodology, which has enriched its structure and its methods of analysis.

An example of such change is the development of the symbolic interactionist methodology of the Iowa School, which is quite different from that of the Chicago School, the 'mother' school of interactionism. The analysis that is performed under symbolic interactionism, Iowa style, is so extensive that it resembles more a mild form of quantitative analysis than a qualitative one. Methods of data collection are similar to quantitative methods and quantification is not at all excluded from the analysis.

The majority of qualitative researchers, however, work in a qualitative context. Glaser and Strauss (1967), for instance, introduced an approach that is geared towards developing what they termed *grounded theory*. But while the majority of qualitative researchers see analysis as a description of events and of development of concepts, categories and hypotheses, others suggest more complex forms of operation and assign qualitative research a more ambitious purpose.

Buehler-Niederberger (1985) sees in qualitative analysis a process of working around a hypothesis, trying to establish whether and to what degree such a hypothesis corresponds to the facts identified in each case studied. If it does not correspond to facts, the hypothesis is reformulated; this process continues until a universal relationship is established. Barton and Lazarsfeld (1979), on the other hand, see in qualitative analysis a rather different process. In their view, analysis involves the study of single cases, which are expected to lead to the establishment of classes of similar phenomena (classification, establishing typologies) and to systematic comparisons; these are in turn expected to lead to identification of factors that influence relationships or behaviour processes, leading in that way to more integrated answers to the research question. Critical researchers, finally, see in qualitative research a critical appraisal of reality, with the purpose of emancipating and liberating respondents. Qualitative research is a complex issue, and making sense of qualitative data is not an easy task (Coffey, 1996).

2 Varieties of data analysis

Introduction

The first steps of qualitative analysis are made during the process of data collection. During that time, data are collected, coded, conceptually organised, interrelated, evaluated and used as a spring-board for further data collection. Collection is thus merged with analysis. Field researchers may regularly meet with colleagues to discuss their findings, compare notes, check consistency and draw conclusions which will help to establish guidelines for further work. Here analysis is conducted while the researcher is still working in the field and before data collection has been finalised. This process follows a cyclical path that goes from data reduction to data organisation and to interpretation of the data, and then to further data collection, reduction, organisation and so on which involve data processing and analysis.

The cyclical process of analysis

More specifically, the steps of the process of concurrent or preliminary analysis are conducted as shown below. Obviously, this process does not include elements of analysis in the traditional sense; however, it involves data transformation from the raw state to a form that allows them to be used constructively, and this is a form of analysis.

Stage 1: Data reduction

This refers to the process of manipulating, integrating, transforming and highlighting the data while they are being presented. Summarising, coding and categorising are some ways of doing this. Data reduction helps to identify important aspects of the issue in question, to focus data collection, sampling and methods, and arrive at conclusions.

In qualitative research, reduction involves careful reading of the recorded material, identification of the main themes of the studied process, behaviour and so on, and categorisation of the material for the purpose of analysis or presentation as stated above. The rules of data reduction in this case vary from case to case, and seem to be directly governed by the study objective and the theoretical assumptions of the framework employed. In most cases quantitative considerations are excluded. In other cases some measurement is taken for granted.

When participant observation or in-depth interviewing is employed, data reduction occurs during observation or interviewing. Information is collected, processed, analysed and so on, and this process continues until the research is completed. In these cases it is difficult to separate the elements of collection, reduction and analysis from each other.

Stage 2: Data organisation
This is the process of assembling information around certain themes and points, categorising information in more specific terms and presenting the results in some form. The most common form of presentation is text, but matrices, charts, graphs and so on are also used (Miles and Huberman, 1994).

Stage 3: Interpretation
This involves making decisions and drawing conclusions related to the research question. Identifying patterns and regularities, discovering trends and explanations are aspects of this process, which will allow the development of some firm views to guide the research further, namely more data collection and reduction, organisation and interpretation and then further data collection and reduction and so on. The research that follows will help to refine, confirm and test the validity of the conclusions drawn so far. This process will continue until saturation has been achieved.

3   During- and after-collection analysis

Qualitative research is by no means uniform. Wolcott (1992) lists more than 20 research strategies or methods of qualitative research, while Tesch (1990) brings that number to 27. In a more recent publication, Wolcott (1994) summarises research operations into three groups, namely description, analysis and interpretation, which in rough terms does not differ from the research model introduced earlier in this book. This diversity relates not only to qualitative research *per se* but also to types of qualitative analysis. The methods presented below are only a few of those applied by qualitative methodologists in the area of data analysis. They are all ways of handling data in qualitative research and provide guides regarding not only data analysis but also developing methods to be used for the same purpose. They are not uniform or integrated into a few guiding models; after all, qualitative research is based on the notion of subjectivity, which allows personal expression and individuality, not only in approaching subjects but also in generating and analysing data.

What really happens when data are collected, reduced, organised and interpreted varies from case to case. For this reason, the methods employed by researchers when analysing data vary significantly. Strauss (1987, 1991), for instance, suggests a model of qualitative analysis involving a process that goes from *coding* to the development of *concepts* and then, with the assistance of *memos*, to new *categories*. This process leads, finally, to the development of *hypotheses* and to *grounded theories*.

Whatever happens during the process of data collection, and regardless of the extent to which analysis goes, there is always some work left for analysis after completion of data collection. In most cases the bulk of analysis does take place later. Researchers have developed special techniques to assist with this task of analysing data during and after data collection. Miles and Huberman (1994) propose a set of methods that can be summarised as follows: (1) use of summary contact sheets; (2) using codes and coding; (3) pattern coding; (4) memoing; (5) case analysis meeting; (6) interim case summary; (7) vignettes; (8) prestructured case; and (9) sequential analysis. In a different fashion, Neuman (1991: 419–28) refers to the following methods: (1) successive approximation; (2) illustrative method; (3) analytic comparisons; (4) method of agreement; (5) method of difference; (6) domain analysis; (7) ideal types; and (8) cultural analysis.

The difference between these methods is obvious, and while some writers might concentrate on some aspects of the process, others relate to different aspects. Similarly, while some methods relate to certain aspects of the process of analysis others relate more closely to the whole research process. In the following we shall look at all these methods in turn as presented by Neuman and by Miles and Huberman in their works, beginning with Neuman's typology.

a   Neuman's typology

Successive approximation
The method of successive approximation begins with some basic observations and the resulting assumptions about the existence of concepts. Following this, the researcher checks these concepts against evidence from the data, trying to see whether the concepts fit the evidence. As a result of this, concepts are modified and new concepts emerge. Then new evidence is collected and contrasted with the concepts. This process of iteration or recycling through the steps is continued until the end of analysis.

In this process, concepts are contrasted with empirical data, and theories with empirical evidence. As a result of this, concepts approximate the level of completeness and accuracy of the empirical evidence, are modified through the repeated iterations and in this way reach successively a high level of accuracy.

The illustrative method
The aim of this method is, as the title indicates, to illustrate the degree of validity of a theory. The process of analysis begins with a set of theory models, which help to establish *empty boxes*, which are ultimately filled through the research process. Questions are answered and assumptions tested. The evidence collected through the study will offer the arguments that confirm or reject the theory.

Analytic comparison
This method is similar to the illustrative method, the difference being that there are no empty boxes to fill. Instead, the researcher develops, on the basis of already established theories or through induction, ideas or assumptions about the data. On the basis of these ideas and assumptions, the researcher

then attempts to identify regularities in the data, compares such regularities with different ideas and assumptions, and then attempts to establish the regularities, first in a restricted area and then at a more general and abstract level. Regularities in specific settings become gradually more general and obtain validity outside that specific setting.

The method of agreement

In this method the researcher is directed towards commonalities in data. In the first place analysis concentrates on cases that have a common outcome, and identifies causes and effects of elements of interaction. In this context an attempt is then made to ascertain cases that have a common cause. In this way features are eliminated as causes if they are not common across cases that have a common outcome.

The method of difference

In the method of difference the researcher compares sets of cases that are similar in some ways but different in others. Comparisons between them allow the researcher to draw some important conclusions.

Domain analysis

A domain is a fundamental element and a crucial unit in a culture. There are three types of domain, the *folk domain*, the *mixed domain* and the *analytic domain*. Domains have three major elements or parts: the cover term, that is, the name of the domain; the included terms, which are subtypes or parts of the domain; and the semantic relationship, which shows how included terms relate to the domain.

The researcher who employs domain analysis concentrates on identifying and analysing *domains*. In a more concrete way, researchers scrutinise notes looking for cover terms and organise information into included terms, identify semantic relationships, look for examples of domains in the notes, compare them for similarities and differences, and search for more domains until all have been identified. Expanding this research towards classifying and organising domains into larger sets and more dominant themes that explain and interpret the culture setting is the next step of analysis.

Ideal types

Stemming from Max Weber, ideal types have been used extensively in the social sciences in the area of theory as well as of research. Here, ideal types are used as models for the purpose of comparison. Actual events and issues identified in the notes are compared with ideal types of these events, issues, etc. and their specific and unique elements emerge. In a different way, when analogies are made, ideal types are used to demonstrate the extent to which real cases are close to these types.

Cultural analysis

In this method, which — as the title indicates — was originally employed in cultural studies, the researcher reviews the data, looking for a number of points, such as: the intention people had when they developed certain cultural elements; the way these elements were received by others; the internal structures, patterns or symbols displayed in these elements of culture; and finally the connection that exists between the cultural element in question and the social world.

b   The methods of Miles and Huberman

Miles and Huberman (1994) distinguish between early analysis and drawing and verifying conclusions, both of which follow a set of steps. With regard to early analysis, these writers propose the methods described below.

The contact summary sheet

During their study, researchers construct contact summary sheets, which are used as a basis for analysis. The sheets contain a set of questions that are relevant to the central issue of the study. As soon as sufficient information is gathered researchers review their notes and material and answer these questions, in that way producing an information summary of the progress so far. This sheet is then used as a guide for further research, such as refining codes or categories and adjusting the research design, and as a form of communication between the researchers when more than one fieldworker is involved in the study.

Codes and coding

Codes and categories are applied as tools of analysis by many researchers; they are keywords which are used to categorise or classify text. We have already seen how these tools are being employed in the context of grounded theory. They are considered an integral part of qualitative research (Bodgan and Bilkin, 1992). When coding text, the researcher assigns a symbol or keyword to a section of text, giving a particular meaning to or labelling a section of the material. Such codes are generated in many ways, before, during and some-times after data collection.

Miles and Huberman (1994) identify many types of codes, such as descriptive, interpretative and explanatory codes, but pattern coding seems to be very significant.

Pattern coding

Pattern codes are developed to identify emergent themes, configurations or explanations, integrating material into a coherent and meaningful unit. This form of coding is a type of data reduction in the sense that it groups already summarised information into 'a smaller number of sets, themes or constructs'. The four functions of pattern coding are (1) reduction of data into a smaller number of analytic units; (2) analysis of data during collection, and focusing on further work; (3) elaboration of a cognitive map, that is, a schema that helps to educidate the research field; and (4) facilitating cross-case analysis and comparisons (Miles and Huberman, 1994: 69).

Memoing

Memos are summaries of ideas about codes and their relationships and vary in content, direction and length. Strauss referred to this analytical device as analytic memos, and described them as ideas or thoughts about coding. There are many types of memos and there are also many memos in each study, often one memo for each theme or concept. They help integrate data and demonstrate connectedness with each other and with a general concept or category. Such memos are central to the process of data collection and analysis in qualitative research, and are used to link empirical data to abstract concepts. They offer the basis for data analysis and for generating hypotheses and later for grounded theory.

Case analysis meeting

This device is used when there are many sites and many fieldworkers involved in the study, and it brings together all participants to brief them about the progress of the study as well as eventual problems. This, as well as being part of the analysis itself, helps to direct collection and analysis of further data as well as revise and update codes, categories and sampling procedures.

Interim case summary

This is a progress summary, which covers what has been achieved so far and also what is still left to investigate, and states the agenda for the next wave of collection, reduction and analysis of data (Miles and Huberman, 1994).

Vignettes

A vignette is a focused description of typical and representative events (e.g. brief time, actor(s) or space) that occur in the study. It is written in a narrative, story-like style, is brief and follows the sequence in which it appears in real life.

Prestructured case

This entails an outline, an empty shell, in which the researcher will place the data to be collected in the study. Obviously, this outline is constructed before data collection has begun (hence prestructured). It is developed on the basis of exploratory research, that is, after the researcher has visited the field site, and is adjusted and amended several times before data collection begins.

Sequential analysis

Qualitative analysis takes place in waves, each wave following the previous one and providing additional information. A single analysis is never full, complete, valid or sufficient. A sequential analysis follows the initial analysis and includes a deeper re-evaluation of the steps conducted earlier (coding, memoing, etc.) arriving at richer and more powerful explanations. Sequential analysis may also include the involvement of other researchers in order to provide a different input into the analysis and another view on the meaning of the findings.

4   Qualitative analysis in specific contexts

Qualitative analysis may employ one or more of the methods discussed above, or may use other techniques developed in the context of the qualitative framework underlying the particular study and which are required by the individual method of data collection. In a number of cases analysis will be conducted during data collection; but in many cases analysis will be completed after all data are collected. When the method of data collection is interviewing or participant observation, the during-collection analysis is rather limited. Information can only make sense when interviews are transcribed and listened to later. This is more obvious when more than one interviewer/observer is employed. Below, we shall see how analysis is performed when data collection has been facilitated through interviewing, observation or case study.

Qualitative interviews
With regard to qualitative interviews, the analysis follows a number of patterns which deserve special consideration. In one form, this type of analysis takes place *after data collection*; here, the interviews have been completed and the answers recorded on video or audio cassettes. In addition to the analysis which took place during the interview, the four steps presented will assist in completing the work associated with the research question and arrive at some valid answers. A model of analysis made up of five steps can be described as follows.

Step 1: Transcription
The first step of analysis is to transcribe the data from the original form (video, tape, etc.) onto paper. Following this, the researcher 'cleans' and edits the manuscript by eliminating typographical errors and contradictions in the text.

Step 2: Checking and editing
Next comes checking and editing of transcripts, relating parts of data and preparing data for (further) analysis.

Step 3: Analysis and interpretation
This step entails data reduction, and analysis. Here categories will be developed, coding and data reduction will be completed and using one or more of the methods listed above an attempt will be made to identify trends in the data.

Step 4: Generalisation
The findings of the individual interviews are then generalised and differences and similarities identified, allowing the development of typologies.

Step 5: Verification
This involves a process of checking validity of interpretations by going through the transcripts again alone or with the assistance of other researchers. This will allow the researcher to verify or modify hypotheses already arrived at previously.

Qualitative observation
Analysis of data in observational research follows the principles of the methodology that underlies the study, and most aspects of this process have already been discussed in the appropriate place. When triangulation is employed, the data of each method will be analysed separately and then evaluated — in comparative or other terms —as a set.

When observation is developed in a qualitative context (e.g. in participant observation) the analysis is based on an open and flexible approach, using an unstructured and unstandardised design and a close relationship between the observer and the observed, a perception of reality as constructed in interaction and interpreted by the participants, free of structural constraints (e.g. set concepts, hypotheses, operational definitions, strictly defined research units) and a high degree of closeness to the everyday life of the participants and the nature of the situation.

Analysis in an observational study of the qualitative model is directed towards establishing concepts, testing and modifying them permanently, classifying them into categories, comparing them constantly, perhaps (following the suggestion by Glaser and Strauss) developing substantive theories and from there finally establishing a formal theory, namely a *grounded theory*.

Case study

In case-study research, analysis contains a number of methods that in essence attempt to address the initial propositions of the study. There are several techniques employed in case-study analysis; the following are the most common (Pelz, 1981; Yin, 1991).

Pattern-matching

This technique compares the empirically verified pattern with a pattern predicted at the outset of the study. It is argued that if predicted and observed patterns coincide there is strong internal validity of the findings.

Explanation-building technique

In this technique explanation is based on a series of iterations, which proceed as follows: initially a statement or proposition is made about the study object; then the findings of the study are compared with this proposition; if there is a discrepancy between proposition and findings, the proposition is revised according to the findings; the revised proposition is then compared with new findings and evidence; if discrepancies are recorded, the proposition is revised again; then the new revision is again compared with the findings for the third, fourth, fifth time, the proposition being revised each time as required. This process is repeated as many times as is needed.

Time-series analysis

A number of researchers employing case-study research analyse their findings by means of time-series analysis. In simple terms, in this technique trends over a certain period of time are compared with one theoretical proposition specified before the onset of the study and with a rival proposition. This comparison indicates which proposition is correct.

For example, it may be argued that the introduction of the *De Facto Relationships Act* has resulted in higher proportions of people entering *de facto* relationships (time-series pattern I); another proposition is that the introduction of the Act has not had any effect on the proportion of people living in *de facto* relationships (time-series pattern II — rival trend). Case-study research in this area employs time-series analysis to see whether the data support one model or the other, that is, whether the Act encouraged an increase in the proportion of people living in cohabitation or not. A comparison between the empirical data and each of the two propositions will show which time-series pattern matches the empirical data.

Making repeated observations

This technique directs the analysis towards repeating observations at various levels, that is, over time, across sites and across embedded units. Examples of this technique are observing subjects in spring and autumn, observing units embedded in case A, case B and case C and observing units in various locations (e.g. NSW, Vic. and the NT). Comparisons between these observations are considered in the context of analysis of the subject matter.

Case-study survey

Here the survey is directed towards data already available and operates at a secondary level. This secondary analysis follows a strict procedure, such as development of a code book used for coding the material under consideration and studying the data on the basis of the codes and categories included in the code book. The data resulting from this process are then analysed according to the preferences of the researcher or the requirements of the study object and the theoretical proposition that underlies the study.

5   Interpreting the findings of qualitative analysis

Interpreting data and drawing relevant conclusions that will answer satisfactorily the research question is one of the most significant steps of the research process, but also the step about which very little has been written. There are no existing rules to guide the researcher about how to interpret the data. And while guides, in the form of numbers or meanings, might be offered, the type and direction of the actual interpretation is left exclusively to the researcher.

If this is the case for quantitative researchers, one can imagine how difficult it is in qualitative research where rules and standards are rejected in favour of hints, guides, feelings and subjective interpretations of meanings. It is therefore surprising that a structured discussion on drawing conclusions (resembling that used by quantitative researchers) is found in Miles and Huberman's book, *Qualitative Data Analysis* (1994). The way of thinking, the type of approach and the actual propositions offered are very interesting and warrant a brief description, which hopefully will stimulate students to discuss this issue further.

Miles and Huberman (1994) ask whether meanings identified in a given study are valid, repeatable and right, and discuss how to confirm meanings, avoid bias and assure quality of conclusions. They propose four groups of tactics which are to be employed when drawing and verifying conclusions. These are (1) tactics for generating meaning; (2) tactics for testing or confirming findings; (3) standards for the quality of conclusions; and (4) documentation. The first group of tactics will be described briefly below; the other groups have already been referred to in earlier parts of the text.

It is worth noting that there may be qualitative researchers who will not agree with the idea of setting up a set of tactics to guide interpretation of data or with the necessity or validity of certain tactics. The authors' 13 tactics are described below.

Noting patterns, themes
Interpretations are strengthened by trends and patterns shown in the data. Thus, a way of drawing valid conclusions is searching for and identifying patterns and trends in the material collected through the study.

Seeing plausibility
A second way of helping to draw conclusions is to ensure plausibility. Trends and patterns, but most of all conclusions, must make sense, fit into the logic and the research principles and be plausible. Many tactics are expected to be used to check the plausibility of the data.

Clustering
Here, Miles and Huberman (1994) propose that events, sites, actors and processes that have similar patterns or characteristics must be sorted into categories and grouped together. This allows the researcher to discuss what happens in the research unit with more confidence, and to 'move to higher levels of abstraction'.

Making metaphors
The authors suggest that researchers should not only write but also think metaphorically, because metaphors are richer, more complete, data-reducing, pattern-making, excellent de-centring devices and ways of connecting facts with theory. Obviously, this is a way of reaching higher levels of abstraction and of facilitating the making of conclusions.

Counting
Although quantitative considerations are not at the heart of qualitative research, identifying the presence and frequency of occurrence of significant and recurrent events is a part of qualitative analysis. This is particularly so when the purpose of the study is to compare sets of events and explain their relationship or identify trends in data, to verify assumptions and to protect against bias. As Miles and Huberman put it, doing qualitative analysis with the aid of numbers is a good way of seeing how robust our insights are.

Making contrasts/comparisons
This entails establishing similarities and differences between sets of data, that is, aspects of elements of the research object, persons, roles, activities or cases. This is presented by the authors as the 'classic way to test a conclusion'.

Partitioning variables
Splitting a variable is thought to assist in making the issue more diverse and in finding coherent, integrated descriptions and explanations. This is advisable when the variable does not relate to another variable as anticipated; the procedure is expected to bring elements of the findings closer to each other and to help in making valid conclusions.

Subsuming the particular into the general

Analysis encourages the development of conclusions when the researcher relates empirical data to general concepts and categories and continues thus until categories are saturated. This is a theoretical and conceptual activity that allows the investigator to reach higher levels of abstraction, which legitimate valid conclusions.

Factoring

This concept, whatever its content and purpose, does not seem to fit squarely into a qualitative framework, which by nature is against quantification and statistical analysis. Yet, Miles and Huberman explain that it comes from factor analysis and aims at reducing data and identifying patterns of action, for example what units *do* or *have* in common. With this tactic, researchers attempt to discover factors that underlie the process under investigation, and generate factors through the analysis. Identifying factors in a situation displays trends and patterns and allows further interpretation of the findings.

Noting relationships between variables

The relationship between variables can be ascertained by using matrix displays or other ways of studying interrelationships between parts of the data. This relationship is, in terms of substance, not very different from that studied by quantitative researchers as we shall see soon. Establishing valid relationships between variables provides a sound basis for drawing conclusions about the research findings.

Finding intervening variables

In a similar fashion, establishing the presence and effects of intervening variables on other variables results in a complex set of relationships, and clarifies trends in the data, which allow more general and valid statements about the issue under investigation.

Building a logical chain of evidence

After relationships between variables have been established, evidence supporting certain trends or assumptions begins to appear. Ascertaining a logical chain of evidence can obviously support trends and patterns in the research unit and allows interpretations.

Making conceptual and theoretical coherence

By means of analysing and categorising data and interrelating variables, one moves from data to constructs and from there to theories. Miles and Huberman suggest that in this way one can tie the findings to 'over-arching, across-more-than-one-study propositions that can account for the now and why of the phenomena under study'.

This discussion is not only more detailed than those presented earlier. It is also closer to a quantitative analysis than any other method presented so far, and more than many qualitative researchers would be prepared to accept. The suggestion to use counting, variables and factoring is not a part of the standard tools of qualitative research and one many qualitative researchers find incompatible with the basic assumptions of the research methodology they employ.

6 Statistical procedures and computer-aided analysis

Statistical methods have always been available for use in qualitative analysis: measures for nominally scaled data are suitable. As far as choice of specific procedures, relevant methods and evaluation of results are concerned, the methods employed by quantitative researchers can be employed. These procedures will be introduced in the next chapter. However, there are theoretical, ideological and methodological limitations to this.

Computers can be, and are being, used in qualitative research in the context of both pure qualitative research, where analysis is done the traditional way, and the so-called 'enriched' qualitative research (Weitzman and Miles, 1994; Richards and Richards, 1994; Contrad and Reinharz, 1984; Drass, 1980). Computers are used as word-processing aids to manipulate the text as well as to categorise and to classify information. Computers also help with logical analysis of data; they compare and classify categories, for example by using Boolean algebra (Ragin, 1987). Computer programs employ techniques that allow the qualitative researcher to manipulate data in a way similar to that in quantitative research. However, as we shall see later, computers can perform more and more complex functions.

There are now many programs that have been developed for specific use in qualitative research. Apart from the basic word-processing programs, which are used in low-level analysis of qualitative data, AQUAD, ATLAS/ti, HyperQual, HyperRESEARCH, MAX, MECA, Metamorph, NUDIST, Knosis, 'Qualpro', 'The Ethnograph', The TextCollector, The WordCruncher and ZyINDEX are popular (see Flick *et al.*, 1991; Richards and Richards, 1987, 1994; Weitzman and Miles, 1993, 1994).

The extent to which computers and computer programs are used by qualitative researchers depends on the nature of the study, type of analysis and ideology of the researcher. The range of functions provided by such programs is wide and allows researchers to employ the type of program they consider most appropriate. Briefly the types of functions offered by computer programs are shown below:

1 *Recording/storing*   Computers assist researchers with the recording and storing of data. This not only provides clean and clear text, but also allows easy corrections, adjustments and further manipulation, which under normal circumstances are not available in manual recording. Word-processing programs and specific programs for data analysis are employed for that purpose.
2 *Coding*   Computers allow researchers to isolate segments of text and code it accordingly for future retrieval and linking with other segments of the text. In addition, such programs allow researchers to make side notations on the margins.
3 *Retrieving/linking*   Coded segments of text can be retrieved and set in separate files and/or linked with other parts of the text, facilitating within- and between-part searches and linkages. Programs can also do content analysis, count frequencies of codes and produce quantitative results.

4 *Displaying*   Results of search and retrieval can be displayed by the computer in a variety of ways. Highlighting relevant sections one at a time is one way; gathering related segments of text together in a file is another. Finally, computer programs can display results graphically.

5 *Integrating*   More advanced computer programs have the capacity to develop classifications, categories, propositions and semantic networks and establish links between them, to the extent that they can build and/or test theories.

Although most computer programs employed for qualitative analysis contain modules for recording, coding and retrieving data, higher-level functions such as linking, displaying and integrating are available in a few programs only. ATLAS/ti, HyperRESEARCH, MECA, MetaDesign, NUDIST and QCA are a few examples of programs with advanced capabilities.

The use of computers offers many advantages to researchers (Tesch, 1989; Ragin and Becker, 1989). Apart from saving time, reducing work and the need for resources, they allow higher accuracy and flexibility in the analysis, more systematic organisation of data, easier access to text and codes, easier and more successful text manipulation and easier text reproduction and sharing. This has made the use of computers in qualitative research very popular. Although many qualitative researchers still avoid the use of computers in the analysis of data, others use computers as a functional ingredient of the everyday research routine.

B Quantitative analysis

1 Introduction

Types of quantitative analysis
There are three major types of quantitative analysis: primary analysis, secondary analysis and meta-analysis (Glass, 1976). *Primary analysis* refers to an original analysis conducted by the researcher that produces findings on a specific topic. The analysis of data produced by a study of the effects divorce has on children, which considered original (first-hand) information, is a primary analysis. The analysis of existing findings by another researcher, perhaps using different or more refined methods, is a *secondary analysis*. Such an analysis focuses on already gathered and analysed data and conducts an analysis for the second or third time. *Meta-analysis* is the analysis of information already gathered and analysed from several studies. In this and the following chapters we predominantly refer to primary analysis; but before we continue with this, a few words on meta-analysis are in order.

Meta-analysis
Meta-analysis was initially developed in the 1970s by Glass (1976), and has become relatively popular among social researchers (Mann, 1990; Cook *et al.*,

1992; Hunter, 1990). It is a form of standardisation of findings of diverse individual studies and prepares them for collective analysis (Kulik and Kulik, 1992). An example of meta-analysis is a review of several typical studies of the effects of divorce on children, which aims to draw conclusions about the common message conveyed by these findings.

Why do we use meta-analysis? The answer to this question is simple. Consider the following example: If there were several studies reporting on the effects of divorce on children and all have produced findings using different measures, for example one using a chi-square, the other an ANOVA and the third a *t*-test, integration of the findings in a way that would allow integration of the data would have been difficult. A meta-analysis transforms the different metrics to a common denominator 'such as Z's and one-tailed probability levels for significance and product-moment correlations, Fisher's Z's, and Cohen's *ds* for effect size' (Mullen and Miller, 1991: 429), allows comparisons to be made and facilitates an integration of these diverse findings.

Despite its popularity as a method of social research, meta-analysis has its critics (Wachter, 1988, 1990). The concern of these critics is related to the way conclusions are drawn from diverse and often incompatible methods, samples and environments. First of all, meta-analysis is sensitive to the type of studies included in the sample and the way they are chosen. But apart from this, it is argued that the individuality of the sample studies is ignored and so are the conditions under which they were conducted (quality of samples, quality of research, quality of design, etc.). Often studies are not comparable. As a result of this, the units included in the individual studies can be different, and therefore a meta-analysis may relate to an artificially constructed sample of incompatible and different units which cannot be drawn together in a logical context, thus not allowing valid conclusions.

Doing quantitative analysis

In quantitative studies the process of analysis has the general purpose of summarising and relating data. More specifically, the process of data analysis involves six major activities, namely (1) data preparation, (2) counting, (3) grouping, (4) relating, (5) predicting and (6) statistical testing. This can be done manually and/or mechanically. Manual analysis is generally restricted to small studies and simple research questions. Nevertheless, even when the data are analysed manually, the use of calculators is inevitable and taken for granted. Mechanical analysis is usually taken to mean the use of computers. With the development of electronic devices and sophisticated models, analysis has become electronic rather than mechanical, but also more simple, more accurate, more reliable and less time consuming than in the past.

Analysis of data provides researchers with facts and figures that allow them to interpret results in the context of the community and to make statements about the significance of the findings for the individual and society. Examples of some major activities will be discussed in later sections of the book, but before we explain the steps in data analysis a brief description of each of the six major activities in quantitative analysis listed above is given, followed by a short discussion on the use of computers in data analysis.

Data preparation

This mainly involves all those forms of manipulation that are necessary for preparing the data for further processing, whether manual or electronic, such as coding, categorising answers to open-ended questions, editing and checking, as well as preparation of tables. When computers are used entering data in the computer is the first step of data analysis.

Counting

This includes the mechanical task of registering the occurrence and frequency of occurrence of certain answers or research items. This is performed manually and/or electronically.

Grouping and presentation

This procedure involves ordering of similar (or the same) items into groups. This results in distribution of the data, presented in the form of tables and graphs, which can be performed manually or electronically.

Relating

This involves cross-tabulations and statistical tests to explain the occurrence and strength of relationships. This can be done manually or electronically.

Predicting

This is a process of extrapolating trends identified in the study into the future. Statistical methods help researchers to complete this task, which can be accomplished manually or mechanically.

Significance testing

Tests of significance are, finally, employed during the process of analysis. As in previous cases, testing can be done manually or electronically.

---

2   Electronic data processing

The use of computers in the analysis of data has become a common procedure and a taken-for-granted task of the modern researcher, especially when a quantitative large-scale study has been conducted and/or sophisticated forms of analysis are anticipated. Nevertheless, the use of computers in data analysis does not restrict itself to the area of quantitative studies and survey research. As stated earlier, even qualitative researchers have become interested in computers and have started to use their assistance to a significant degree. This is done when, for instance, qualitative data are being 'quantified' and so made accessible to computer analysis. Apart from this, computer developments have reached the stage where they can process qualitative data *per se* and assist the qualitative researcher, if not as much as the quantitative investigator, at least to a significant degree.

However, the main thrust of computer-aided analysis seems to concentrate on quantitative research and on statistical analysis. This is the area where computers were used for the first time in social research, and where the level of development has, in the past five years, been highest. The programs currently employed in social research in general and in statistical analysis in particular are numerous, and the models employed very sophisticated and diverse.

As mentioned above, the first computer programs developed to aid the quantitative researcher with the analysis of data were geared mainly towards statistical analysis. Since then, the trend has been directed towards better, more powerful and more user-friendly programs, and then towards less statistical and more 'processual' tasks. Programs have been developed, for instance, to assist with the collection of data when personal interviews, telephone interviews, self-administered interviews or questionnaires are employed. The achievements in this area have been tremendous and the options almost unlimited.

The researcher has now been relieved of the burden of tedious and time-consuming mathematical/statistical operations; complex analyses have become just a routine, advanced statistical analysis is no longer the privilege of a few experts and the degree of accuracy has increased enormously. To a certain extent, computers have displaced many of the tasks that statisticians performed in the past, and courses in statistics have, to a certain extent, been replaced (or augmented) by computer courses.

The use of statistical packages has already changed the nature of social research in general and of data analysis in particular. For many social investigators, doing social research without computers is almost unthinkable. Electronic data processing and computer-aided research are believed to have many advantages for the individual researcher, as well as for social science in general and for the community. The following are considered to be the most important advantages:

- Fast data processing and analysis of huge amounts of data.
- Fast completion of complex mathematical/statistical models.
- Relatively cheap data processing and analysis.
- Easy handling of enormous amounts of data.
- A high level of accuracy.
- Making sophisticated statistical models accessible to non-statisticians.

Nevertheless, there are researchers, and particularly statisticians, who see many disadvantages in the use of computers in social research. In the 1970s the American Statistical Association criticised many computer programs for having a low quality, no standards of control and no standards of evaluation, and decided in 1973 to form the Committee of Evaluation of Program Packages in order to evaluate the efficacy of available programs and to oversee the development of new ones. This critique went beyond deficiencies of individual programs; it also addressed the issue of using such programs in lieu of statistics. The main points against computer-aided statistical packages for social research presented by the association were the following:

- Packages limit the options of users of statistics: many statistical functions were not included in the packages and thus were not available to these users.

- Since the use of packages was easy, they could be misused, particularly due to the fact that they did not require a good understanding of statistical prerequisites.

The outcome of this criticism was not as successful as statisticians had originally expected. The number of statistical packages has increased rapidly ever since, and has become more integrated into social research than ever before. Apart from this, there seems to be a shift of interest from statistics courses to computer courses dealing with statistics.

3   Data preparation in quantitative analysis

As stated above, quantitative analysis often begins with preparation of the data so that they can be used in manual or electronic analysis.

The type of information collected during the stage of data collection varies in nature and quantity from study to study. Basically, it depends on the method of collection used. In certain cases, for example, when participant observation is employed, the gathered information offers, when the data have been collected, a clear description of the answers sought in the study. For this reason, data preparation is not required in such studies. In other cases, however, for example when surveys are employed, the information gathered is hidden behind interview schedules, comments and symbols, and an indication regarding the direction of the answers of the study is practically impossible without further work.

In these cases, the first step towards clarifying the collected data and allowing analysis and interpretation is data preparation and reduction, for example a translation of the collected information into a form that can be further manipulated by the analyst and/or the computer. Data preparation first involves coding, editing and checking. After this is accomplished, a decision is made about whether the data will be analysed manually or by means of computers. When electronic data processing is employed, the data will first be entered in the computer.

a   Coding data

Coding is a process in which statements and answers are translated into numbers. This facilitates easy reduction of the data, analysis, storage and dissemination of the data. In a question about the gender of the respondent, for instance, the answer categories 'Male' and 'Female' will be substituted by 1 and 2 respectively, and counting of frequencies will refer not to 'Males' and 'Females' but to 1s and 2s. This is preferable for many reasons but mainly because it is easier to handle numbers than words, particularly when computers are used. This method also helps to minimise errors.

Coding must include categories that are accurate, unidimensional, mutually exclusive and exhaustive and it can be performed either before the study is completed, that is, before the data are collected (pre-coding) or after data collection (post-coding).

Pre-coding

In pre-coding, *numerical codes* are assigned to response categories during the construction of the questionnaire or the interview schedule; an example of a pre-coded statement is shown below.

Example A: 'Examinations should be abolished from all university courses.'

Strongly agree	1
Agree	2
Disagree	3
Strongly disagree	4

The digits 1, 2, 3 and 4 are called the *values,* and the response categories strongly agree, agree, disagree and strongly disagree are referred to as *value labels.* Analysis of the data normally refers to the values, and these are the figures which will be entered in the computer.

Post-coding

Post-coding is used mainly when open-ended questions are used. Here after the answers have been read and evaluated, values and value labels are developed and recorded. These values will be used later for analysis.

Using a code book

When pre-coding is not complete, when open-ended questions are used, when more than one coder is employed and when large and complicated question-naires are used, a code book is necessary in order to facilitate accuracy and uniformity in coding. The code book includes information about how to assign numerical codes for response categories, including value labels and values. If the questionnaires have been fully pre-coded, a code book will not be required.

Missing cases

It is imperative that all questions are answered. It is possible, however, that some questions have no response (i.e. an answer was not required for a particular respondent or questions were not answered at all or adequately). Coding in these cases has to be adjusted accordingly. The general practice is that when pre-coding or post-coding, 'missing values' are considered a separate category and are coded separately. Certain numerals (e.g. 9 or 99) are used for this purpose.

A similar approach is employed when 'Don't know' or 'Not applicable' appears on the questionnaire. How these and similar responses are coded is a question that will be answered in the code book.

b   Editing and checking data

It is important that information appearing on a questionnaire is clear, legible, relevant and appropriate. It is therefore essential that the researcher takes every precaution to ensure that these standards are upheld. In addition, interview schedules and questionnaires must be edited before they are passed on to the assistants for further processing.

Further, investigators are expected to monitor coding in order to prevent errors or bias. Coder reliability is significant and is usually checked in two contexts, the reliability of the coder (i.e. that the coder maintains a stable and uniform pattern of coding, and that variability in coding is avoided) and intercoder reliability (checked by testing how uniform the pattern of coding is when performed by several coders). Coders will, of course, use a code book that explains how to code the responses and how to avoid distortions. However, it is possible that instructions are misinterpreted and unconscious bias might occur in the work of coders. Such problems can be prevented by monitoring the coders systematically.

c   Feeding the computer

Coded data are fed to the computer for further processing and analysis. In most cases, this is done by means of computer cards, computer paper or magnetic tape, or through the computer terminal. The latter has now become the rule for the majority of researchers employing electronic data analysis.

d   Manual preparation of data

Manual processing is usually employed when qualitative methods are used, when a small sample is used, when the questionnaires or interviews employed are not very long and when the instruments employ many open-ended questions.

Manual reduction of the data is also employed in small quantitative studies and when accessibility to computers is impossible or inappropriate. As in electronic data reduction, coding is also considered here. Data reduction in this case starts with the construction of mock tables (or dummy tables) in which the title, heading and the variables are given, without any numerical values. The researcher reads the answers to the questions and records the values of each response category separately. The scores of each response category are placed in the already constructed dummy table.

4   Processing open-ended questions

Unlike closed questions, open-ended questions need some special processing before they are transferred onto the computer card or before they are processed manually by the researcher.

In general, the content of the answers is carefully studied and then fitted into a pattern of categories, which is developed after the responses have been studied. These categories are accurate, unidimensional, mutually exclusive and exhaustive and allow some degree of quantification if a quantitative framework is employed. If the question was, for instance, about the discipline employed by teachers in a certain school, the responses might be interpreted in terms of whether the teachers were authoritarian or democratic (if this was the aim of the question). This might not be obvious by the wording of the answers, but can be identified when analysing the meaning of the respondents' statements. The categories 'authoritarian' and 'democratic' should be marked onto the questionnaire or interview schedule, in order to indicate the direction of the respondent's answer. The long and general answer is this way 'reduced' into one concept (value label), and further to a number (value).

Processing open-ended questions is more time consuming than the processing of closed questions, and can cause distortions and problems, especially when several assistants are involved in this task. Knowledge of the subject and extreme care are two attributes the researcher has to possess in order to guarantee that the processing of these questions is free from bias and distortions.

5   Counting

When electronic analysis is employed, counting is the task of the computer. In most cases this process will also include — depending on the instructions given to the computer — other activities, such as grouping, relating and testing. Nevertheless, counting is the first step of analysis, which will provide the raw material needed for further analysis. What goes on inside the computer while it is counting is not of importance to the beginner and is also beyond the limits of this treatise. What is important is that all answers given by the respondents will be considered and adequately registered.

When the data are analysed manually, counting is undertaken by the research assistant or the researcher, and involves the hard, long, sometimes tedious, and tiring job of computing the individual responses of the subjects to each question. Some form of grouping the answers together will also be undertaken during counting. Since this process is entirely left up to the researcher, and since it is exposed to possible problems and distortions, further discussion of this issue is necessary.

Counting of the answers has in the past been accomplished in two ways. Some researchers take their unit of counting as the instrument (questionnaire, interview schedule or response sheet); others use questions or items as their unit of counting.

When the instrument used is taken as the unit of counting, the researcher studies the response sheet(s) corresponding to each subject, identifies the answer given to each question, and registers it in the dummy tables (or other structures) developed during the previous step of the research. When all answers of the first interview (if interview was used in the study) have been recorded, the researcher proceeds with the second interview, then with the third and so on until all interviews have been processed and the data recorded. The characteristic of this approach is that instruments (e.g. interviews) are processed separately, so that the researcher can observe the total response of the subject and can make a judgement about the position of the subject in the context of the research issue.

When the question or item is taken as the basis for counting, the researcher studies questions or items rather than each instrument at a time. In this case, the researcher reads the answer given to the first question of the first interview (if interview was the instrument of data collection), records the answer, reads the first question in the second interview and records the answer and so on until all the first questions in all interviews have been recorded. When this is completed, the researcher will study the second question, then the third question in all interviews and so on until all questions have been studied.

Both methods are equally effective and are employed by social scientists who decide to analyse their data manually. The first method obviously has the advantage of offering a complete picture of the respondent, as against the second method, which presents segments of the response of the subjects at a time. The second method, on the other hand, enables the researcher to get a clear idea about the total response of subjects to a certain issue, and even to set out some anomalies that might have taken place during data collection.

Although both methods have advantages and disadvantages, in practical terms they seem to be rather a matter of preference. Researchers find one method more convenient than the other, without considering one being inferior to the other. This view is well justified by the fact that at this stage the researcher's interest is counting rather than evaluating or interpreting, and both methods seem to be useful and effective.

C Data analysis using computers

1 Using SPSS

When computers are used, the whole process of analysis acquires a new dimension. Let us see how this works by using an example. Assume you have conducted a survey of 16 students by using a questionnaire containing five questions. These questions were about the students' *sex* (male, female), *class* (upper, middle, lower), *religion* (Christian, Buddhist, Jewish, Agnostic — there were no other religious denominations in that university), *living arrangements* (living alone, living with friends, living with relatives, living at home) and *scholastic achievement* (excellent, very good, good, poor). After the questionnaires have been completed the results are placed in table form, as shown in Table 14.1.

How can we enter these data in the computer? Computers communicate and operate with numbers. For this reason, before we enter the results in the computer, we convert words to numbers. For 'male' we put 1; for 'female' 2. Similarly, we use 1 for 'lower class', 2 for 'middle class' and 3 for 'upper class'. We use, further, 1 for 'Christians', 2 for 'Buddhists', 3 for 'Jewish' and 4 for 'Agnostic'. We also use 1 for 'living alone', 2 for 'living with friends', 3 for 'living with

Table 14.1 Raw data

Student	Question 1 Sex	Question 2 Class	Question 3 Religion	Question 4 Living arrangements	Question 5 Scholastic achievement
1	Male	Lower	Christian	With family	Good
2	Male	Middle	Buddhist	With family	Very good
3	Female	Middle	Christian	Alone	Good
4	Female	Lower	Buddhist	Alone	Good
5	Male	Middle	Jewish	With family	Excellent
6	Female	Upper	Jewish	With family	Very good
7	Female	Middle	Buddhist	Alone	Good
8	Male	Upper	Jewish	With relatives	Excellent
9	Male	Lower	Agnostic	With friends	Poor
10	Female	Middle	Christian	With friends	Good
11	Female	Lower	Agnostic	Alone	Good
12	Male	Upper	Buddhist	With family	Very good
13	Male	Middle	Christian	With friends	Good
14	Male	Lower	Agnostic	With friends	Poor
15	Female	Upper	Jewish	With family	Excellent
16	Female	Lower	Agnostic	Alone	Poor

relatives' and 4 for 'living at home'. Finally, 1 is used for 'poor' school performance, 2 for 'good' performance, 3 for 'very good' and 4 for 'excellent' school performance. In addition, we abbreviate the names of the two last questions; consequently, 'living arrangements' becomes 'living' and 'scholastic achievement' becomes 'achieve'. Remember, the numbers are what we call the *values,* and the corresponding statements describing the answers are the *value labels.* If we replace the words with the numbers and amend the variable names as suggested, the set-up looks as in Table 14.2. We call this a *data matrix.*

In this form the results contained in the data matrix can be transferred onto the computer. The student numbers are not required and are therefore omitted. Numbers as well as the names of the columns will be transferred. Numbers will be entered in columns. How this is accomplished varies according to the program we use.

2   Entering data in SPSS

To demonstrate how computers are used in data analysis we will use SPSS (Statistical Program for Social Sciences, Version 6.2.1 for Windows 3.1).

Table 14.2 Numerical data

Student number	Question 1 Sex (Variable 1)	Question 2 Class (Variable 2)	Question 3 Religion (Variable 3)	Question 4 Living (Variable 4)	Question 5 Achieve (Variable 5)
1	1	1	1	3	2
2	1	2	2	3	3
3	2	2	1	1	2
4	2	1	2	1	2
5	1	2	3	4	4
6	2	3	3	4	3
7	2	2	2	1	2
8	1	3	3	3	4
9	1	1	4	2	1
10	2	2	1	2	2
11	2	1	4	1	1
12	1	3	2	4	3
13	1	2	1	2	2
14	1	1	4	2	1
15	2	3	3	4	4
16	2	1	4	1	1

Other versions and computer programs employ similar procedures. The first step towards using computers in data analysis is to enter the data in the computer. But before we do this there is a need for some preliminary instructions.

To simplify our instructions we shall use abbreviations, which you must become familiar with before you begin the actual entry. The most important abbreviations are:

- *A string of commands connected by* > This sign means 'click on'. For example, the string Statistics > Summarise > Crosstabs means: click on 'Statistics', then click on 'Summarise', and finally click on 'Crosstabs'. We shall use this string frequently, so make sure that you know how to use it.
- *Transfer* This instruction comes in the following form: *Transfer age to the 'Variables' box.* This means that you should highlight the variable age and click on the arrow (➤) that stands in front of the box where the variable is to be transferred.
- *Activate* When you are asked to *activate* an option in a window, you simply click on the little circle ○ or □ that stands in front of that option. For instance, if the instruction is *Activate 'Correlations'*, you must click on the box in front of the word 'Correlations'.

Other short cuts will be introduced later. Now let us look at how we define variables, and then how we enter data in the SPSS data matrix. But before we do that we must familiarise ourselves with the SPSS display window. When we switch the PC on and get into the SPSS, the *data editor* window appears labelled **Newdata**. This contains empty boxes (the cells) arranged in columns and rows. This is where we enter the data. At the top of the columns (shaded row) the cells contain a faint **var.** This is where the name of the variable will be entered. The left-hand side column contains the identification number for each respondent.

Apart from the data editor window, there is the *output* window, which is hidden behind the data editor window and has the title **!Output.** This window is activated when the computer (following our command) produces results (output). In Windows 3.1, to switch back to the data editor window, click on the - sign at the top-left side of the active window and then on **next.** (Find out how to do this in Windows 95 or newer versions.)

The process of entering data in the computer entails two steps: (1) the naming of variables and (2) the entering of data. Naming variables is a simple process which has the purpose of giving variables a name, defining the values and value labels and giving instructions to the computer about how to register missing values. This process will prepare the computer to receive and place the data in the right context. In the example shown above, each question contains a variable. Hence, the name of the variable will replace the **var** at the top of the column, and the corresponding numbers will be placed below the variable name. Entering the data will commence after the naming of variables is completed. We first begin with the process of naming a variable.

a   Naming variables

To name the variables/columns we must be at the data editor window and in the column in which we intend to set a variable. As mentioned above, naming the variables entails four elements:

1 *Giving a name to the variable*   Such names are sex, class, marital status, etc. Remember only 8 characters fit in the name box.
2 *Specifying the variable label*   The variable label is the full name of the variable, which normally is larger than the variable name. For instance, the variable name may be 'Livarr', and the variable label 'Living arrangements'.
3 *Specifying values and value labels* for each variable. The value labels of sex are male and female and the corresponding values 1 and 2 respectively.
4 *Specifying values for missing data* for each variable. Given that our values in each variable are below 9, the value for missing values will be 9; otherwise it would have been 99.

To define variables, their labels, values and value labels we proceed as follows.

➤ Click on any cell of the first column	This will specify the variable you wish to define.
➤ Choose **Data** > **Define variable**	This will bring you to the 'define variable' window.
➤ At the highlighted square type **SEX**	This defines the variable; the name is SEX.
➤ Click on **labels . . .**	This will bring you to the 'define labels' window.
➤ In the box next to **Variable Label** type the full variable name (if required)	The variable name may be abbreviated; the variable label may be in full.
➤ In the box next to **Value** type **1** and in the box next to **Value label** type **Male**	This tells the computer that 1 means Males.
➤ Click **Add**	This will attach this value to the variable SEX.
➤ Go back to **Value** and type **2** in the box and in the box next to **Value label**, type **Female**	This indicates that 2 means Females.
➤ Click on **Add**	This will attach this value to the variable SEX.
➤ Click on **Continue**	This will bring you back to the 'define variable' window.
➤ Activate **Discrete missing values** and type **9** where the cursor stands	This will set missing values to 9.
➤ Click on **OK**	At the top of the first column, the description **var** has been replaced by the variable name SEX.

This is how a variable is named (here the variable SEX). This process will be repeated for each variable separately. The steps are the same, except for the variable name, values and value labels, which depend on the nature of the variable. Some variables have two and others more than two labels.

b   Data entry

It is technically possible to enter data in the computer before the variables have been named. However, this is not correct procedure, particularly if you are dealing with many variables. It is advisable to name variables before data are entered in the computer.

Method 1: Entering listed data
The entry of data in the data file is very simple. The data listed in Table 14.2 can be typed in the SPSS data page column by column, in the same way that tables are typed in any word-processing program. For example, to type the column **sex** in the computer, we click on the first cell under the variable **sex**. This cell will be activated. Then we simply type in the first number, which is 1, and hit **enter** (this will activate the next cell), then the second number,

which is 1, and hit **enter** then type the third number, which is 2, and hit **enter** again. Continue this until all the numbers of this column are entered. To enter the figures for the second variable we follow exactly the same steps. We click on the first cell under the second variable name, enter the first number, then the second, the third and so on until all numbers have been entered.

Method 2: Entering grouped data
When data refer to individual responses of subjects ('listed data'), they are entered in the computer as shown above. However, there are cases in which researchers are dealing with grouped data, either resulting from their studies or obtained through other means, for example through figures from the Australian Bureau of Statistics or from studies of other researchers. In these cases, individual data are not available. Hence, data must be entered in the computer in a grouped form.

Let us look at an example. A sample of 100 males and 100 females were asked to state whether they were in favour of the monarchy. The responses were as shown in Table 14.3.

Table 14.3   Attitudes to the monarchy by gender

Attitudes	Males	Females	Total
In favour	25	58	83
Against	62	33	95
Undecided	13	9	22
Total	100	100	200

We simply enter each number separately by specifying first the number's row position, second the number's column position and third the number value. Hence, the number 25 will be entered in the computer as 1 1 25, because 25 is in row 1 and column 1. Similarly, the number 33 will be entered as 2   2 33 because 33 is in row 2 and column 2; and the number 9 as 3   2   9 for similar reasons. The order in which these numbers are entered in the computer is shown in Table 14.4.

Table 14.4   New data

1	1	25
1	2	58
2	1	62
2	2	33
3	1	13
3	2	9

This is now the new table, containing three variables and the corresponding data. We enter these data as described above. We name the three variables and define their values and value labels. The first column is named **Attitude** (positive = 1; negative = 2), the second becomes **Gender** (male = 1; female = 2) and the third is named **Count** (we enter no values). There are three value labels for attitudes, two for sex and none for count. To complete the process of entering data in the computer in tabular form we proceed as follows.

1 Name variables, values and value labels as shown above
2 Enter the three columns in the computer as shown above
3 Choose **Statistics** > **Summarise** > **Crosstabs**
4 Transfer **Attitudes** to the **Rows** box
5 Transfer **Sex** to the **Column** box
6 Choose **Data** > **Weight cases**
7 Activate **Weight cases by**
8 Transfer **Count** to the **Frequency variable** box
9 Click on **OK**

Your figures have now been adjusted to correspond to their respective variables, and can be used in this format for statistical analysis. Before we leave this section you should remember that there are at least two ways of entering data in the computer: method 1 and method 2. Remember, method 1 refers to listed (single) data, and method 2 refers to table (tabular) data. When we begin doing analysis of data later, reference will be made to method 1 and method 2. Now you know what they refer to.

D Summary

The analysis of the data allows the researcher to manipulate the information collected during the study in order to assess and evaluate the findings and arrive at some valid, reasonable and relevant conclusions. While in quantitative research this process is relatively clear and unambiguous, in qualitative investigations it is 'cloudy' and confusing.

The issue here concerns mainly the procedures employed in qualitative analysis, as well as the extent to which counting and quantification can go. The opinions of the experts vary on this point. Equally fluid is the issue about the stage at which analysis can take place. While the majority of qualitative researchers place analysis during the time of data collection, for others analysis can also take place after data collection. (Some writers even speak of anticipatory data analysis, which in fact takes place before data collection.) For instance, when in-depth interviews, observation or narrative interviews are employed for data collection, the responses and activities of the respondents are often recorded on paper or tape and subsequently studied and 'analysed'. As stated above, what follows is transcription, individual analysis of records, generalisation and control.

Be that as it may, data analysis follows a systematic pattern which enables the researcher to organise data in a constructive way and to facilitate further and more meaningful operations. Such operations include graphic presentation of the findings, identification of trends and dispersion in the data, associations between variables considered in the study, and tests of significance. These operations will be considered in the remaining chapters of the text. Next we shall consider in detail the forms in which data can be presented, in both quantitative and qualitative studies.

Key concepts

Coding	Code book
Selective coding	Paper tapes
Successive approximation	Counting
Domain analysis	Axial coding
Explanation-building technique	Pattern-matching
Analytic comparison	Ideal types
Method of difference	Cultural analysis
Post-coding	Time-series analysis
Checking	'The Ethnograph'
Storing	Pre-coding
Tallying the frequencies	Editing
Open coding	Paper cards
Illustrative method	Manual preparation
Method of agreement	

15

Data presentation

The process of grouping the data, that is, integrating the responses in terms of their origin and degree of similarity, was introduced in the previous chapter when we were discussing the process of counting. In the discussion that follows, grouping will be dealt with in more detail. In addition, we shall introduce other aspects of grouping and some aspects of arithmetical operations employed by social researchers to gain an overview of the data as a whole system of information *per se*, as well as the relationship between its parts.

In quantitative research, the most common forms of grouping and presentation of data are distributions, tables and graphs. Here data are integrated in a form that provides, at a glance, summarised information about the research topic or aspects of it. In a similar fashion, qualitative data are presented and grouped in many diverse ways; matrices, figures and context charts are three examples. In the discussion that follows we shall look briefly at a few typical ways of presenting data in quantitative and qualitative research.

A Presentation of data in quantitative research

1 Distributions

Distributions are one of the most common ways of presenting data. A distribution is a form of organisation or classification of scores obtained for the various categories of a particular variable. There are several types of distributions, for example frequency distributions, proportional or percentage distributions and cumulative distributions. In social research frequency distributions are the most common.

Frequency distributions

Frequency distributions display the frequency of occurrence of certain categories in a range of scale values. This indicates that distributions normally contain two important elements: a scale with a number of values and corresponding observations. Consequently, a frequency distribution is constructed in two steps.

Step 1

A scale that displays the scores ranging from the highest to the lowest is constructed. This process is called rank order distribution or an *array of scores*.

Step 2

The raw scores are tallied and then the tallies are converted into frequencies.

Constructing a frequency distribution results in a frequency table, which is very common in social research and which will be discussed later in this section.

Frequency distributions appear in at least two forms, the ungrouped and the grouped distributions. (1) In an *ungrouped distribution* the scores have not been collapsed into categories; each score value represents a separate class of values. For instance, if the distribution presents the ages of the members of a club, each age value (e.g. 18, 19, 20 and so on) will be presented separately in the distribution, together with the corresponding frequencies. (2) In a *grouped distribution* the scores are collapsed into categories, so that two or three scores are presented together as a group. In our example, the distribution will contain groups such as 18–20, 21–23, 24–26, etc. These groups are usually referred to as *class intervals*.

When class intervals are to be included in the construction of distributions, their number and a definition of their width must be considered. The answer to this question cannot be given in absolute terms, since it depends on several factors, such as the purpose of the study and personal preferences of the investigator. In practical terms, the number of intervals must be kept to a manageable and meaningful proportion.

The question regarding the width of the intervals has been addressed in a similar manner. In some cases it is guided by the purpose of the investigation: if specific and detailed information is required narrow intervals are used, otherwise wide intervals are employed. In other cases the width is determined by using quantitative procedures as shown below.

Step 1

Calculate the range of the data by subtracting the smallest score from the largest score of the distribution, then add 1.

Step 2

Divide the result obtained above by the desired number of intervals. This is the width of each interval.

If the lowest score was 18 and the highest 41, and if the desired number of intervals was 8, the interval width would be $(41 - 18 + 1)/8 = 3$.

Percentage distributions

This type of distribution contains percentages rather than absolute frequencies. This has the advantage that comparisons between distributions with
unequal numbers of cases can be made. Percentage distributions can be
ungrouped or grouped, and their use is very common among social researchers.

Cumulative distributions

A cumulative distribution does not contain in each item the observations that
fall in the relevant category (as in the other types of distributions) but consists
of the number of cases up to and including a specified scale value. They
appear in an ungrouped or grouped form.

More information about these distributions is presented below, when the
tables resulting from such distributions are discussed.

2 Tables

Tables are the most common way of presenting data and usually contain a
vast amount of information. They enable the researcher to gain an overall view
of the findings, to identify trends and to display relationships between parts of
the findings. Below we explore the structure and types of tables in detail.

a Table structure

Tables contain five elements:

1 *A title*, which contains a clear and specific description of the table.
2 *A heading*, that is, a label of the columns or rows.
3 *The body of the table*, containing the information offered in the table,
   which can be in the form of either absolute numbers and/or proportions.
   The intersections of rows and columns are the *cells* of the table.
4 *Marginals*, which are sums of the columns and rows.
5 *Footnotes*, containing additional information explaining the origin of the
   information provided in the table, commenting on the data, and describing
   the strength of the relationships between the variables, such as level of
   significance, chi-square value, details about cell information and source of
   information.

b Types of tables

Tables vary in a number of ways. While some are small and simple, others
are large and complex. Tables also vary in terms of their content. Whereas
some contain one variable, others contain many variables. With regard to the
number of variables, tables can take the forms described below.

Univariate tables
This type of table describes one variable and presents its values in the form of a frequency.

Bivariate tables
These describe two variables and are referred to as contingency tables. One variable — the dependent variable — is presented in the rows and the other — the independent variable — in the columns.

Multivariate tables
These tables describe many variables. They are quite often very difficult to read, and writers seem to prefer to split them into smaller tables, usually bivariate or trivariate ones.

c   Working with tables

Immediately after counting, the resulting tables and distributions are quite often long, asymmetrical and non-functional. This might be due to unexpected answers, methodological problems, unforeseeable events and other causes. As a result, some of the items in the table might be extremely underrepresented and they may not need to be included in the table as a separate category. In other cases the list of values might be extremely long and need some reduction.

In a table of the age of respondents, for instance, the ages might be given in single years starting with 1 and ending with 99 or above. Restructuring the table or distribution into one containing intervals might be one way of reducing the size of the table. Grouping the ages of the respondents into 'under 25', '26–50', '51–75', '76–100' and '101 or more' is an arbitrary sub-division which might be functional and effective.

If intervals are preferred when presenting variables, there are some issues that the investigator should seriously consider. Such issues are, for instance, the size and number of class intervals, the range, the upper and lower limits of the distribution, and the arithmetical interpretation of the limits of the class intervals (score limits, exact limits, etc.). Some researchers may make arbitrary decisions about these issues. Others may follow rules such as 'one should prefer not fewer than 10 or more than 20 class intervals' or that 'a class interval of 3 is ideal' and so on. Although such rules may be drawn from extensive experience with research, the best decision is the one made with reference to the purpose of analysis and the nature of the study. What is considered as ideal and preferable for one study might be dysfunctional and ineffective for another. The size of the sample, the range of the distribution, the type of analysis and the objective of the study are some of the factors that may affect the decisions regarding the construction of a particular distri-bution. (A method of determining the interval width was presented above.)

Although the construction of intervals varies from study to study, there are some issues on which researchers seem to agree. Intervals are taken by most researchers to be equal and uniform. If 3 is the interval thought to be the most relevant for the study, it is employed right through the distribution. Also, it is common practice to start with the highest score first and to proceed to the lowest.

The following definitions of relevant concepts might be useful:

* *The class interval* is that part of the range ordered into a group; for example, in the age distribution 1–5, 6–10, 11–15 and 16–20, the four subdivisions (1–5, 6–10, etc.) are the class intervals.
* The *class width* is the difference between the lowest and the highest number in a class interval.
* *Class limits* are the numbers that define the boundaries of a class interval. For example, in the class interval 1–5, 1 and 5 are the class limits; 1 is called the lower limit and 5 the upper limit.
* *The range* is the difference between the lowest and the highest values in a distribution.
* *The midpoint* is the value that lies between the upper and the lower limits of a class interval. For instance the midpoint in the class interval 1–5 is 3.
* *Frequency* is the number of observations in each item, category or class interval.
* An *open-ended class* is a class that has only one limit. The classes 'under 5 years', 'under $2.00', '65 years and over' are open-ended classes.

d Rules of presentation

Presentation of the data is based on a set of rules that researchers are expected to follow. The rules most frequently listed by a number of writers (see Becker, 1989; and Mahr, 1995) are the following:

* *Clarity* Information should be presented clearly, and without ambiguity and confusion.
* *Simplicity* Information should be easily readable.
* *Economy of space* Neither excessive spacing nor undue crowding should occur when data are presented.
* *Order of variables* Independent and dependent variables should be presented in their correct places.
* *Appearance* Tables and graphs should have a pleasant appearance.
* *Accuracy* Marginals should accurately correspond with cell values, and footnotes with relevant references.
* *Objectivity* Figures contained in tables or graphs should not be misleading and should not encourage erroneous conclusions.

e Tables using SPSS

The easiest way of constructing tables is to use the computer. SPSS has a number of ways of presenting tables, for example frequency tables for one variable or crosstabs for two or more variables. The steps followed to construct a table are shown below.

Univariate tables
1 Choose **Statistics > Summarise > Frequencies**
2 Transfer the variable you wish to put in the table to the **Variable(s)** box
3 Click on **OK**

This gives you tables containing the following: value, frequency, percentage, valid percentage and cumulative percentage. An example from a study of the frequency of conflicts among Australian couples is given below.

```
CONFLICT       Conflicts and Violence


                                        Valid    Cum.
Value label  Value  Frequency  Percent  Percent  Percent

Very often   1.00      10        4.0      4.0      4.0

Often        2.00      45       18.1     18.1     22.2

Sometimes    3.00      64       25.8     25.8     48.0

Never        4.00     129       52.0     52.0     52.0

                      ----     -----    -----    -----
             Total    248      100.0    100.0    100.0
```

Another way of setting up univariate tables is shown below:

1 Choose **Statistics > Custom tables > Tables of frequencies**
2 Shift the variable you wish to put in the table to the **Frequencies for** box
3 Click **OK**

The output contains less information than the one displayed above. Try this in your computer to see the difference.

Crosstabs
There are at least two ways of obtaining crosstabs with SPSS. They are shown below.

Method 1
1 Choose **Statistics > Custom tables > General tables**
2 Transfer one variable to rows and one to columns
3 Click on **OK**

Method 2

1 Choose **Statistics > Summarise > Crosstabs**
2 Set variables in boxes for rows and columns
3 Click on **OK**

Employing method 2 to demonstrate the crosstabulation between place of residence (farm or city) and overall happiness of 124 farm families and 124 city families, we obtain the table shown below:

```
15 Jul 97 SPSS for MS WINDOWS Release 6.1


HAPPINES   Overall happiness   by   PLACE   Place of residence

                            PLACE              Page 1 of 1
                 Count
                 Col Pct | Farm      City
                                                Row
                           1.00|     2.00| Total
    HAPPINES     ─────────
                 1.00         6         7        13
      Very low              4.8       5.6       5.2

                 2.00         4         5         9
      Low                   3.2       4.0       3.6

                 3.00        38        43        81
      Moderate             30.6      34.7      32.7

                 4.00        41        39        80
      High                 33.1      31.5      32.3

                 5.00        35        30        65
      Very high            28.2      24.2      26.2

                 Column    124       124       248
                 Total     50.0      50.0     100.0

Number of Missing Observations:   0
```

3 Graphs

Graphs are figures that offer a visual presentation of the results. Most consist of a skeleton and a body. While the skeleton in such graphs is the same, the shape of their body usually varies from one type to the other. Other graphs use circles, bars, columns, maps, pictures or other figures to display relevant information.

In most cases, the format of the graphs consists of two lines placed at right angles to each other intersecting at the lower left-hand part of the figure and are called *coordinate axes*. The point of intersection is called the *origin*. The horizontal line is called the *X*-axis or *abscissa*, and the vertical line the *Y*-axis or *ordinate*. The values of the independent variable are scaled along the abscissa. In ordinal scales the lowest values are placed on the left-hand end and the highest values on the right-hand end of the line; if the scale is nominal, values can be placed in any order. If a zero is present (ratio scale), it is placed close to the right of the intersection of the axes.

The values of the dependent variable are marked off along the vertical axis, that is, along the ordinate. The origin serves as the zero point; values above the origin are positive and increase when moving away from the zero point. Values beneath the origin are negative.

The body of a graph consists of the figure constructed between the axes, and can be a curve, a number of adjacent blocks or a number of separate bars. Each type of graph has a characteristic shape and body.

4   Types of graphs

There are many types of graphs employed by researchers to display visual information about their findings. This section will introduce some of the most common graphs and explain their structure and purpose.

Line graphs
Line graphs (or line charts) consist of a number of dots (corresponding to values of the dependent and independent variables) joined with straight lines, and are very frequently used in social research. Line charts can be *single,* containing one line only, or *multiple,* containing more than one line. An example of a multiple line chart is shown in Figure 15.1.

The principle of plotting a line graph on the coordinates is *the rule of the right angles*, and involves the following steps:

Step 1: Ascertain the value of the independent variable on the *X*-axis and starting from this point draw a line parallel to the *Y*-axis.
Step 2: Ascertain the value of the dependent variable and, starting from this point, draw a line parallel to the *X*-axis.
Step 3: Ascertain the point of intersection of these lines.
Step 4: Repeat Steps 1–3 for all values.
Step 5: Connect the points of intersection of the lines with straight lines.

SPSS and other computer programs provide an array of options for line graph presentation, and make the construction of line graphs easier, more accurate and certainly more presentable! We shall see later how to construct a line graph using SPSS.

The histogram
A histogram is plotted on the coordinates by using the values of the dependent and independent variables. The process is basically similar to that of constructing a line graph explained above. The difference between these two types of graphs is that instead of points being plotted, in the histogram

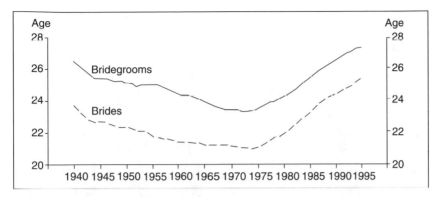

Figure 15.1 Multiple line chart: marriage age of bridegrooms and brides at first marriage
Source: ABS (1997), *Australian Social Trends, 1997*, Canberra: AGPS, p. 27.

vertical bars are drawn adjacent to each other. Histograms display continuous scale values, shown by there being space between the bars (see Figure 15.2).

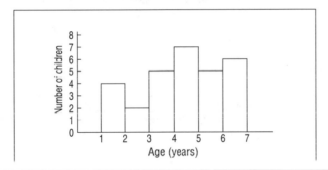

Figure 15.2 Histogram: number of children by age

A histogram can be transformed into a line graph by joining the midpoints of the tops of the blocks with straight lines.

The bar graph

A bar graph is similar to a histogram in that it consists of bars that indicate the strength of the values of the variable. However, bar graphs are different from histograms in that the bars are not joined together but are set apart from each other; this indicates that there is no quantitative relationship between them. They are employed when the independent variable is nominally scaled and display values with discrete intervals. They can be vertical (Figure 15.3) or horizontal (Figure 15.4).

Bars are continuous, of the same thickness and distance from each other, and they do not touch each other. They are usually arranged in the graph arbitrarily (although researchers often tend to place them in decreasing order).

Bars appear in a number of shapes and forms. There are *simple bar graphs* (which present single values at a time), *clustered bar graphs* (presenting sets

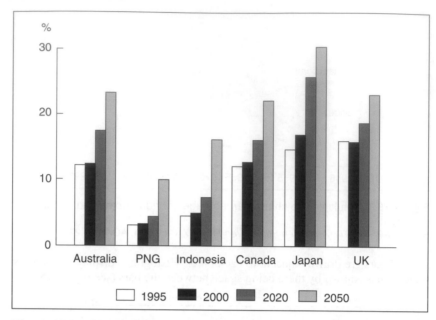

Figure 15.3   Clustered vertical bar graph: projected proportion of population aged 65 years and over, selected countries
Source: ABS (1996), *Projections of the Populations of Australia, States and Territories*, Canberra: AGPS, p. 37.

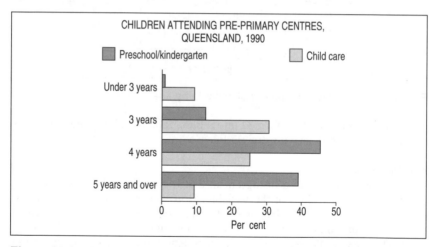

Figure 15.4   A clustered horizontal bar graph: children attending pre-primary centres, Queensland, 1990
Source: ABS (1992), *Queensland Pocket Year Book 1991*, Canberra: AGPS, p. 29.

of bars at a time), and *stacked bar charts* (which present bars containing more than one value). Figures 15.3 and 15.4 are examples of clustered bar charts; Figure 15.5 contains a stacked bar chart.

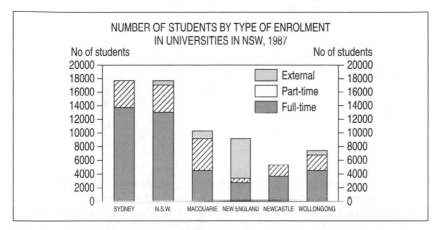

Figure 15.5 Stacked bar chart: number of students by type of enrolment in universities in NSW, 1987
Source: ABS, NSW Pocket Year Book 1988, Canberra: AGPS, p. 13.

The ogive

Ogives are graphs that visually describe the values of cumulative distributions as in line graphs. Cumulative distributions show how many scores fall into or below one point or interval. Thus, ogives are line graphs which present cumulative distributions.

Profiles

Profiles are line graphs or data curves in which the independent variable is marked off on the ordinate (*Y*-axis) and not on the abscissa (*X*-axis). Profiles are relatively common and can accommodate more than one curve, thus allowing comparisons between responses of various groups. In a special form profiles are used to display the findings obtained by means of the technique of semantic differentials, allowing the responses to be entered in a form that allows comparisons.

The scattergram

A scattergram is employed to demonstrate the relationship between two variables. It employs the same structure as a line graph or a histogram but does not use curves or bars but rather dots congregated in a certain way and making up a certain shape. This shape denotes the type of relationship between the variables. The process of plotting scattergrams is similar to that discussed in the context of histograms.

Interest in the scattergram is primarily centred not on the individual scores but rather on the general direction of the dots. As we shall see later, the direction of the grouped dots will indicate whether the variables are correlated or not, and if they are, whether there is a strong, weak, positive or a negative correlation between them (see Figure 15.6).

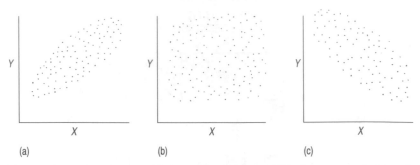

(a)   (b)   (c)

Figure 15.6   Scattergram. Scattergrams demonstrate the type and strength of the relationship between two variables, for example a strong and positive relationship (a), a strong and negative relationship (c), or no relationship at all (b).

The pie chart

In pie charts, data are presented in the form of a circle, with each entry occupying a segment that is proportional to its size. Pie charts (also called pie graphs) are an easy way of displaying relationships between the whole and its parts as well as comparisons between the parts (Figure 15.7).

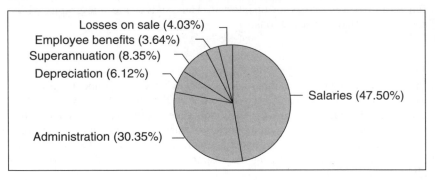

Figure 15.7   Pie chart: composition of operating expenses
Source: Department on Finance, *Annual Report, 1993–94*, Canberra: AGPS, p. 182.

The population pyramid

Consisting of many levels and presenting one or two variables, population pyramids are very common and very useful. They consist of one or more sets of horizontal bars indicating the strength of the variables presented in the graph, thus allowing comparisons to be made between various population groups. Comparing the state and/or growth of various age groups of the same or different gender, time or geographic location are a few examples (see Figure 15.8).

The cartograph

This type of graph presents the values of variables in map form, which is marked with relevant symbols to indicate their presence, frequency or strength.

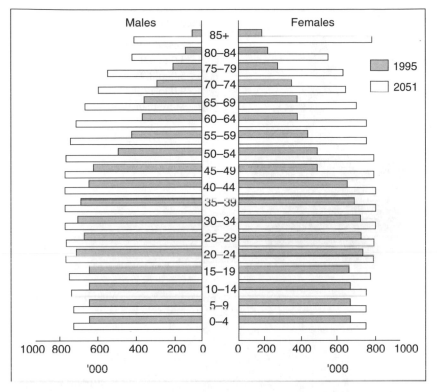

Figure 15.8 Population pyramid: projected population of Australia, 1995 and 2051
Source: ABS (1996), *Projections of the Populations of Australia, States and Territories, 1995 and 2051*, Canberra: AGPS, p. 31.

These criteria are indicated in various forms: for example by shading (Figure 15.9) (e.g. with dark shading meaning high frequency and light shading low frequency); with pie graphs incorporated in the maps; with bars or columns; using dots or other shapes, such as coins, barrels, cars or houses, indicating the presence or absence, or strength or frequency of appearance of these items in the various geographic areas.

A stem and leaf display

This method of presentation was developed by John Tuckey (1977) and includes both a tabular and a graphical display, allowing a visual presentation of trends of relatively small sets of data in detail. As the name indicates, it contains two elements, a *stem* and a *leaf*, which are separated by a vertical line. Stem entries are placed on the left of the line and can be simple integers or intervals, representing a part of a number, for example the tens, hundreds, etc.; leaf entries are on the right and display the remaining part of the number. In the example 3 | 6 7 8, the stem contains the entry 3 and the leaf the entries 6, 7 and 8. This indicates that the numbers presented here are 36, 37 and 38.

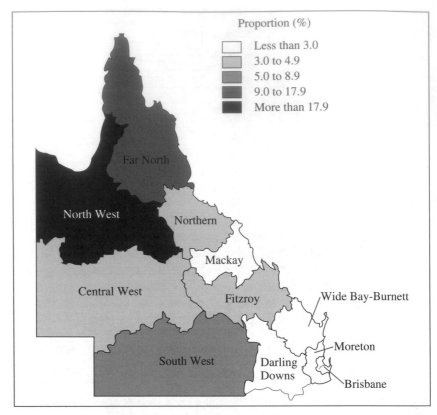

Figure 15.9   Cartograph: Aboriginal and Torres Strait Islander people as a proportion of total population, Queensland, 1991
Source: ABS (1997), *Queensland Families. Facts and Figures*, Brisbane: Qld Govt Printer, p. 21.

Stem and leaf entries may include one or more integers, but leaf entries containing more than one integer must be separated by a comma; in addition, placeholders should be entered next to the stem indicating the number of integers per entry. If, for instance, each leaf entry contains two integers, two placeholders (e.g. ** or ..) must be placed to the right of the stem entry. If for instance the entry '246' is to be placed, this can be done either as 24│6 or as 2** │46.

If a large number of leaf entries are made for each stem, and if more detailed information is to be presented in the display, the range of each stem can be divided into two or more sections, each of which must be indicated by the use of relevant placeholders. An * for instance, placed next to the stem may mean that next to it entries from 0 to 4 must be placed; similarly, a . placed to the right of the stem may be defined to mean that next to it entries ranging from 5 to 9 must be placed, as we shall see next.

Double-stem display
Using two different placeholders allows a double-stem display, that is, a division of a range into two parts, each of which is being defined by the placeholder as shown above. For example, if the set 10, 11, 12, 13, 14, 15, 16, 17, 18, 19 is to be displayed, and if a double-stem display is to be used, * may stand for entries ranging from 0 to 4, and . for entries ranging from 5 to 9. The above set could then be displayed as follows:

$$1* \mid 0\ 1\ 2\ 3\ 4$$
$$1.\ \mid 5\ 6\ 7\ 8\ 9$$

Five-stem display
The stem range can be divided into five parts, allowing more detailed information about trends in the data set. In this case, five placeholders are set, each covering one-fifth of the total range of the stem. The most common placeholders and their ranges are, for instance, * for 0 to 1, t for 2 and 3, f for 4 and 5, s for 6 and 7, and . for 8 and 9. Using the above example, a five-stem display would be as follows:

$$1* \mid 0\ 1$$
$$1t \mid 2\ 3$$
$$1f \mid 4\ 5$$
$$1s \mid 6\ 7$$
$$1.\ \mid 8\ 9$$

In summary, this form of presentation of data allows single or multiple displays. The form employed in each case depends on the purpose of the display and the degree of accuracy and detail required.

The pictograph
This form of presentation is common when the amount of certain products or populations or occurrence of incidents are displayed. When car accidents are depicted in a pictograph the picture of one car may stand for 1000 car accidents, two cars for 2000, three cars for 3000 and so on. Fractions of cars (e.g. one-half, one-third or one-quarter) represent fractions of 1000. A similar ratio may be used when presenting the density of population in various parts of a city or district, or the number of crimes committed by various ethnic groups. The figure of one man may represent 1000 crimes committed by men, two men 2000 crimes and so on.

Products and animals can be presented in a similar fashion. The proportion of wool exports per year, for instance, may be presented in pictures (whole or fractions) of bales; the amount of wool may be shown in a picture showing a number of bales per country, with each bale corresponding to 1000 bales; and the daily consumption of milk by male and female students in milk cartons or fractions of a milk carton.

Such forms of presentation provide a vivid and realistic impression of the state of affairs in certain contexts as well as trends and developments in these areas (Figure 15.10).

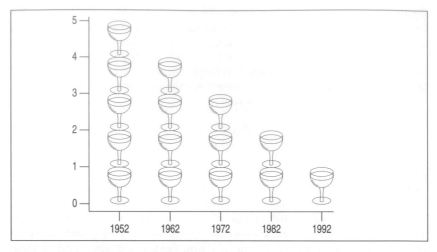

Figure 15.10 Pictograph. Such graphs display a variety of variables and relationships in pictures. This example displays the answer to the question 'How many glasses of wine does a woman have to drink before she believes all men are bastards?' The answer is obvious.
Source: *The Bookseller*, 10 July 1992, p. 51.

5 Chart display using SPSS

Bar chart/ Histogram

1 Choose **Statistics > Summarise > Frequencies**
2 Transfer the variable you wish to graph to the **Variable(s)** box
3 Click on **Charts**
4 Activate bar chart and/or histogram and then click on **Continue**
5 Click **OK**

Pie graph

1 Choose **Graph > Pie** (this will bring you to the Pie Graphs window)
2 Click on the **O** in front of your presentation choice
3 Click on **Define**
4 Transfer the variable you wish to display to **Define Slices by:** box
5 Click on **Titles**
6 Type title 1 (and title 2 and footnotes if required) in the appropriate box
7 Click on **Continue** and then on **OK**

Similar steps are employed to obtain bar graphs, line graphs, area graphs and histograms.

B Presentation of data in qualitative research

1 Introduction

Qualitative researchers employ various methods to present their data visually. While some employ methods of presentation used by quantitative researchers in their original or in a modified form, in other cases different forms of presentation are used. Certainly, tables and graphs are useful tools of presentation in qualitative research, but the structure of presentation does not seem to adhere to any strict rules and procedures, given that graphs and tables in qualitative research are always tailored to serve the needs of the particular study.

Such methods seem to be developed by researchers for a particular study to meet their personal styles, but those proven useful are accepted by other researchers and after some time they become an element of qualitative research. Miles and Huberman, for instance, presented some of the methods used in their studies in a well-read publication (1994), many of which are very interesting and used widely among other qualitative researchers. In the following discussion we shall report on some of the techniques presented and justified theoretically and methodologically by these writers. The following are a few examples of the types of displays reported by these writers.

2 Matrices

A matrix is a type of data presentation that, to a large extent, resembles and is equivalent to a table. It contains a title, a heading, cells and other forms of information similar to those of the tables typical of quantitative research, but it differs in its purpose and nature.

Matrices are a form of summary table. They contain verbal information, quotes, summarised text, extracts from notes, memos, standardised responses and, in general, data integrated around a point or research theme that makes sense. In the main, matrices contain information about and explain aspects of research, and allow the researcher to get a quick overview of data related to a certain point. In this sense they serve a similar purpose to that of tables employed in quantitative research.

Matrices can become very complex and also serve many diverse goals. In one form (*checklist matrix*) they present integrated data on a summative index or scale, thus organising several components of a single, coherent variable (Miles and Huberman, 1994). In another form matrices contain information ordered according to time (*time-ordered matrix*) or according to roles (*role-ordered matrix*). The former can be thought of as a table with its columns arranged according to a time sequence, demonstrating what happened and when as the research was progressing from one point of time to the next. In the latter, the table rows contain verbal information about the views of role occupants on a specific issue of the project. A combination of the elements of matrices is also possible (e.g. role by time or role by group matrix).

Matrices can be ordered according to a central theme (*conceptually clustered matrix*), or according to outcomes and dependent variables (*effects matrix*) or present forces that are at work in particular contexts showing processes and outcomes (*site dynamics matrix*); they can present a series of events displayed in any possible order (*event listing*) or in the form of a *causal network*. In this case, the matrix presents a field of interrelationships between dependent and independent variables, describing causal connections between them.

It must be noted that models such as those described above, although of qualitative nature, have some strong quantitative overtones which might not be accepted by traditionally orientated qualitative researchers. Terms such as variables, for instance, defined as dependent and independent, especially when a notion of causation is attached to them, are elements that many researchers may find incompatible with qualitative analysis. This illustrates how diverse the field of qualitative research is.

Building matrices

How a matrix is to be constructed is a process that relates more to the personal ingenuity, competence and creativity of the researcher than to rules and principles. Miles and Huberman admit that there are no fixed canons for constructing a matrix, and that there are no *correct* matrices, only *functional* matrices (Miles and Huberman, 1994: 240–1). They nevertheless recommend that researchers follow some 'rules of thumb' when working with matrices. Such 'rules' suggest that matrices should be kept to one page display; should include between 15 and 20 variables in rows and columns; be constructed by keeping in mind that they can and will be changed, regrouped and modified by adding new rows and columns; that rows and columns be kept fine-grained so that adequate differentiation is possible; and that new matrices may evolve out of other matrices as the research unfolds.

3   Figures

Figures are as useful in qualitative research as matrices. They combine lines and curves with verbal comments and indicators. However, there is no set format of organisation and construction; how a figure will be constructed and what format it will take depend on the complexity of data and on the ability and imagination of the fieldworker (Miles and Huberman, 1994).

4 Charts

Miles and Huberman describe a form of charts they call *context charts*. This chart presents in graphic form the interrelationship that exists between elements of the environment, for example roles and groups that make up the context in which behaviour develops (Miles and Huberman, 1994). Context is a significant factor in the understanding of behaviour. This chart offers a visual presentation of behaviour in context.

5 Displays in qualitative research

Displays are employed in qualitative research for many and diverse purposes. To a certain extent, displays substitute for the work accomplished by means of statistics. In this sense, charts, matrices and figures are to provide the information which mathematical figures and coefficients provide in quantitative research. They present visual information which allows the researcher to make sense of the collected information and this way to draw relevant conclusions. There are several types of displays, each of which vary in type and complexity and serve a different purpose. Miles and Huberman (1994) offer a very detailed discussion of these types of displays; a brief discussion of such displays follow.

Within-case displays
The first group of displays is the within-case displays, which have the purpose of exploring and describing conclusions related to a single case study. The types of displays used in this context are (1) partially ordered displays (including context charts, checklist matrix and the transcript as poem display); (2) time-ordered displays (such as event listing, critical incident chart, event-state network, activity record, etc.); (3) role-ordered displays (e.g. role-ordered matrix, and role-by-time matrix); and (4) conceptually ordered displays (such as conceptually clustered matrix, thematic conceptual matrix, fork taxonomy, cognitive maps and effects matrix).

Types of displays which not only intend to describe but also to provide explanations and predictions also belong in this group. Such displays are the case dynamic matrix, which displays 'a set of forces for change and traces the conceptual processes and outcomes' (Miles and Huberman, 1994: 148) and the causal network which displays the various variables and their interconnections.

Cross-case displays
The second group of displays involves more than one case. Some of these displays aim to explore and describe conclusions; others aim to order and explain findings. Some are partially ordered displays, others are case-ordered displays

and time-ordered displays. Many of these displays are matrices, graphs and tables. But other types of displays are also used; the scatterplot is an example. Here a relative affinity to quantitative research is evident. This is more so when we explore the second part of this group, which relates to ordering and explaining. Here a strong emphasis is placed on predicting and variable analysis as well as on causal analysis (causal chains and causal networks), which for many qualitative researchers do not belong to the qualitative methodology.

6 Summary

The examples given by Miles and Huberman (1994) are interesting, important and paradigmatic in at least two ways. On the one hand they show how types of data presentation established by researchers are gradually introduced in qualitative practice; a number of these techniques will probably not be taken up by other researchers, but others will certainly be. As a result, a technique developed for a specific purpose and for a specific project becomes a technique in qualitative research. In addition, their examples provide a guide as to how data can be presented in qualitative research, which is very useful for researchers and students of social research.

Key Concepts

Distributions	Matrices
Bivariate tables	Cumulative distributions
Midpoint	Class width
Tables	Marginals
Multivariate tables	Class limits
Open-ended class	Graphs
Frequency distributions	Univariate tables
Class interval	Class range
Cells	Histogram
Bar graphs	Scattergrams
Population pyramids	Area diagrams
Stem and leaf display	Ogives
Normal curve	Cartographs
Body diagrams	Profiles
Pie graphs	Picture diagrams

16

Central tendency and dispersion

Statistical methods assist significantly in the analysis of data. For many researchers, analysis of data means statistical analysis and that any analysis cannot be successful without statistical operations. This point is contested by qualitative researchers; however, as we have already seen, even qualitative research lends itself to statistical analysis.

In this chapter examples of some elementary techniques will be introduced. These techniques relate to three groups of measures, namely to relational measures, measures of central tendency and measures of dispersion. Relational measures show how to relate parts of data to each other or to the whole; measures of central tendency show what the main trend is in the data; and measures of dispersion describe the spread of data. We begin with the relational measures.

1   Relational measures

Relational measures relate parts of a group of scores to each other or to the whole, for instance the relationship of males to females or the relationship of males to the whole group or to 100.

The measures we shall consider here are rate, ratio and percentage.

Rate
This is a measure used to compare values that are not a part of the same variable. It can measure the frequency with which a value occurs compared to the possible frequency with which this value could occur (Reid, 1987: 54). Rate is then expressed in the following relationship:

$$\text{Rate} = \frac{\text{number of actual occurrences}}{\text{number of possible occurrences}}$$

For instance, the graduation rate at Monash University is the number of graduations at this university divided by the number of graduations at all universities in Victoria. Likewise, if the number of people killed in car accidents in NSW is 1200 and the number of deaths in that state for the same period of time is 4800, the rate of deaths caused by car accidents is 0.25. Rates are useful when comparing variables in different populations over time.

Ratio

'Ratio' describes the relationship of parts of a group to each other, and is computed by the following formula:

$$\text{Ratio} = \frac{\text{number of members of group A}}{\text{number of members of group B}}$$

If for instance there are 37 female students and 26 male students at the introductory sociology lecture, the ratio of male students (group A) to female students (group B) will be:

$$\text{Ratio} = \frac{26}{27} = 0.7$$

This suggests that the ratio of males to females is 7:10 (7 to 10); multiplied by 100 this figure becomes 70, which means that there are 70 male students for every 100 female students. The ratio of female students to male students will similarly be:

$$\text{Ratio} = \frac{37}{26} \times 100 = 1.42 \times 100 = 142$$

This means that the ratio of females to males is 1.4:1, or 1.42 females for each male, or that there are 142 female students for every 100 male students.

Percentage

While ratio relates two subgroups to each other, percentage compares a subgroup (n) to the total group (N). This is computed using the following formula:

$$\text{Percentage of } n = \frac{n}{N} \times 100$$

Using the above example where the number of male students was 26, the number of female students was 37 and the total number of students 63, the percentage (%) of the male students is:

$$\text{Percentage of male students} = \frac{26}{63} \times 100 = 41.27\%$$

The percentage of female students is:

$$\text{Percentage of female students} = \frac{37}{63} \times 100 = 58.73\%$$

A way of checking the accuracy of the results is to add up the percentages of the subgroups. If they add up to (about) 100 the computations are correct.

2 Measures of central tendency

Measures of central tendency are very popular and are the most commonly used statistical measures, not only by social scientists but also by people in everyday life. These measures represent the average or typical value in a distribution; in this sense, they summarise the entire distribution, by providing information about the main trend of the units of the population in question.

There are many ways of determining central tendency, and there are also many relevant techniques that help to compute these measures. In this chapter we shall introduce the most common measures: the mean, the mode and the median. We begin with the mean.

a   The mean

The mean is by far the most important measure of central tendency, and also the most popular one among social scientists. It describes the central trend of the results or the average of all observations. Such measures are very common in everyday life. Everyone uses means when saying, for instance, that the average Australian believes in justice, that the average woman rejects patriarchy, and that the average wage of the Australians born overseas is lower than the average wage of those born in Australia.

The computation of the mean varies according to the nature of the data. The mean of listed data (those corresponding to individual scores, for example those presented in Example A) is computed in a manner that is different from that of grouped data (those set in frequencies, for example those shown in Example B).

Listed data
The computation of the mean in *listed data* is quite simple; it can be accomplished by adding up all scores and dividing the sum so obtained by the number of scores. For instance, if we were to compute the mean of the number of books read by five students during the holidays, and the number of books for each student was 2, 2, 3, 4 and 4, the mean would have been 2 + 2 + 3 + 4 + 4 = 15, divided by the number of scores, 5, which equals 3. Consequently, the mean is 3. This means that the average number of books read by these five students is 3. We use the symbol $\bar{x}$ (read: ex bar) to indicate the mean.

The mean for ungrouped data is computed by means of the following formula:

$$\bar{x} = \frac{\Sigma x}{n} \qquad\qquad \textbf{(16.1)}$$

This formula displays exactly what we stated above, namely that the mean is the sum of the values of observations (Σx), divided by the number of observations (n). Σ (sigma) is a Greek letter that means 'the sum of'. Let us discuss an example.

Example A: In a sociology test the following scores have been recorded:

27, 17, 47, 52, 42, 37, 32, 27, 22, 17, 27, 37, 17, 32, 37, 27, 17,

22, 42, 57, 47, 27, 37, 32, 27, 22, 17, 12, 32, 27, 22, 17, 12, 27

Since the data are ungrouped, we add up all the scores (Σx) and divide by the number of observations (n). Since $\Sigma x = 993$ and $n = 34$:

$$\bar{x} = \frac{\Sigma x}{n} = \frac{993}{34} = 29.2$$

This shows that the average score in the sociology test was 29.2.

Grouped data I (frequencies)

Quite often the data are available in a grouped form, where observations or scores appear in frequencies. In such cases the computation of the mean proceeds in a different manner. To demonstrate this let us consider the distribution given in Example B, which is a grouped presentation of the scores introduced in Example A.

Example B: Frequency of scores of sociology students

Score x	Frequency f	Product of x,f fx
12	2	24
17	6	102
22	4	88
27	8	216
32	4	128
37	4	148
42	2	84
47	2	94
52	1	52
57	1	57
	$n = 34$	$\Sigma(fx) = 993$

In order to compute the mean in this distribution, a slightly different formula is employed. This is as follows:

$$\bar{x} = \frac{\Sigma fx}{n} \tag{16.2}$$

According to Formula (16.2), in order to compute the mean we need n as well as the product of x and f (fx), which is required in order to calculate *the sum of products*. For this reason a new column is required in the frequency table describing the factor. The value of n will be computed from the second column, namely the f column. The frequency table (shown in Example B) is complete, and provides the information needed to compute the mean.

Employing Formula (16.2), we find:

$$\bar{x} = \frac{\Sigma fx}{n} = \frac{993}{34} = 29.2$$

Grouped data II (class intervals)

It is quite common for distributions to include class intervals instead of single numbers, as shown in Example C. In order for the mean to be computed the same procedure as above is employed. However, this might cause some confusion to the beginner since there are two values of x to consider, the lower and the upper limits. In such cases, in order to compute the mean we take the midpoint instead. This way the intervals are transformed into single numbers. When this is accomplished, the computation follows the procedure employed for grouped data, as shown in Example C.

Example C: Age groups of unmarried mothers

Age group x	Midpoint x	Frequency f	Product xf
16–18	17	5	85
19–21	20	9	180
22–24	23	16	368
25–27	26	11	286
28–30	29	14	406
		$n = 55$	$\Sigma(xf) = 1325$

The mean age of the unmarried mothers of this particular group is:

$$\bar{x} = \frac{\Sigma fx}{n} = \frac{1325}{55} = 24.09$$

b   The mode

The mode is the category with the largest number of observations. If, for instance, in a sociology test 6 students received an A, 9 a B, 16 a C, 7 a P and 4 an F, C is the mode because it is the most frequent category. As shown here, the mode is not computed mathematically but is identified logically on the basis of its relationship with other values. It is a measure you can *see*, rather than one you need to calculate.

While there can only be one mean in a distribution, with regard to the mode the situation is different. Distributions can have one mode (unimodal distributions), two modes (bimodal distributions), more than two modes (multimodal distributions) or even no mode at all (non-modal distributions), when, for instance, all observations in the distribution are the same.

The mode is a useful measure but it is not used very widely in the social sciences, except for nominal data and when a quick description of the trend in the data is needed.

c   The median

The median is the point on a distribution that divides the observations (not their values) into two equal parts, so that half of the observations are above and half below this point. For example, in the distribution 36, 33, 30, 28, 26, 23, 18, 12, 11, 8, 4, showing the reading hours per week reported by the 10 students of a history class, the median is 23 because it divides the distribution into two parts with equal numbers of scores; there are five scores each side of 23. Similarly, in the distribution 150, 125, 110, 75, 68, 40, 23, 20, 18, 15, 12, the median is 40. Note that when computing the median, it is the number of observations rather than the actual values of the observations that counts.

The way of computing the median depends on the nature of the distribution. In listed distributions, such as those presented above, the computation is very simple. It only involves rank ordering of the scores and identifying the score that divides the distribution into halves. This process becomes more involved when there is an even number of scores and the median falls between two scores, when there is a large number of scores and frequencies are required, or when there are tied scores.

When there is an even number of scores, the median is the mean of the two adjacent middle scores. For example, in the distribution 18, 16, 15, 13, 11, 9, 7, 5, the point that divides it into two equal parts lies between 13 and 11. Consequently, the median is the mean of these two scores, namely 12.

In the following we shall explain how the median is computed in ungrouped and grouped distributions.

Grouped data (frequencies)
Let us first look at a distribution without intervals. Consider the following example: in a small study of 102 same-sex couples in Sydney's Western Suburbs it was found that the number of children per unit was as shown in Example D.

Example D: Number of children per unit	
Number of children *x*	Frequency *f*
1	12
2	46
3	23
4	11
5	8
6	2

What is the median age of the children? To compute the median we follow the steps shown below:

1 The observations are set in a rank ordered form. This is already done in Example D.
2 The *midpoint observation* is defined. This is half of the sum of the frequencies (the sum of 12, 46, 23, 11, 8 and 2, which is 102, divided by 2). The midpoint observation is then half of 102, which is 51.
3 The frequency at which the midpoint observation occurs is located by adding up the frequencies from one end of the distribution. The frequency that contains the midpoint observation, that is, the frequency that is added last and gives a sum that exceeds the midpoint observation, in Example D is 46 (12 + 46 = 58; and 2 + 8 + 11 + 23 + 46 = 88) because 51 is reached only after 46 is added to 23 (if one counts from below) or to 12 (if one adds from above).
4 The category to which the observation containing the midpoint observation corresponds is located. In our example this category is 2 (i.e. 2 children).
5 Consequently the median number of children is 2.

It is quite possible that, when counting from above and from below, two different midpoints are identified and for this reason two medians are computed. In such cases the average score of the two medians is the true median.

Grouped data (with intervals)

Let us now consider an example with intervals. The obvious problem with computing the median in such a case is that after the midpoint observation is identified, it will point to a category that includes several figures. If, for instance, the category that corresponds to the observation containing the midpoint is 25–34, a specific median cannot be determined because it points to all numbers between 25 and 34. In order to compute the median in such cases, the following formula is employed.

$$\text{Median} = l + \frac{\left(\frac{N}{2}\right) - cn}{n} \times w \qquad (16.3)$$

where the letter l stands for the lower limit of the category that contains the midpoint observation (if the interval is 20–25, l is 20); N represents the number of observations included in the study, which is the sum of the frequencies; and cn stands for the cumulative number of observations of the category that immediately precedes the category containing the midpoint (this means that first the cumulative frequency is computed, the category containing the midpoint defined, and then the category above it is taken); n stands for the number of observations contained in the midpoint category (here we refer to the frequency column); and w stands for the width of the category.

This formula offers one way of computing the median; there is another way of computation which is, however, beyond the limits of this book.

Let us now compute the median in a distribution with intervals, by using the example of the age of single fathers (see Example E).

Example E: Age groups of single fathers		
Age group	Frequency *f*	Cumulative frequency *cn*
16–18	5	5
19–21	9	14
22–24	16	30
25–27	11	41
28–30	14	55

To compute the median in this distribution we operate as follows:

1 The cumulative frequency (*cn*) is calculated by adding each frequency to frequencies above it; for example, the first frequency is 5, the second frequency is 14 (i.e. 5 + 9), the third frequency is 30 (i.e. 16 + 9 + 5), the fourth frequency is 41 (11 + 16 + 9 + 5), and the last frequency is 55 (i.e. 14 + 11 + 16 + 9 + 5).

2 The midpoint observation and the category that contains it are computed. In Example E it is 55 divided by 2, which is 27.5. The midpoint is in 30 and the corresponding interval is 22–24 (in exact terms it is 21.5–24.5).

3 Formula (16.3) is used. Following the definition of the symbols discussed above, $l = 22$, $N = 55$, $cn = 14$, $n = 16$ and $w = 2$ (if w represents the *exact interval* it will be computed by subtracting the lower limit, namely 21.5, from the upper limit, 24.5, and will be 3).

Employing Formula (16.3):

$$\text{Median} = l + \frac{\left(\frac{N}{2}\right) - cn}{n} \times w = 22 + \frac{\left(\frac{55}{2}\right) - 14}{16} \times 2$$

$$= 22 + \frac{27}{16} = 22 + 1.68 = 23.68$$

d   Mean, mode and median

Each of the measures discussed above, mean, mode and median, provides specific information about the trend demonstrated in the data and is used when this specific information is required and when conditions allow it. Nevertheless, which measure should be chosen in each case? In order to answer this question we should carefully study the distribution and examine two major factors, namely the type of measurement and the shape of the distribution. Table 16.1 summarises the suitability of these measures for the various levels of measurement.

Table 16.1   Levels of measurement and central tendency

Level of measurement	Measure
Nominal	Mode
Ordinal	Mode, median
Interval	Mode, median, mean
Ratio	Mode, median, mean

Overall, there is agreement among researchers (e.g. Foddy, 1988; Sofos, 1990) that the following points may serve as a guide when deciding which measure is the most suitable:

- The mode is chosen if the variable is nominally scaled, although it can be used for all types of data.
- The mean is chosen if the variable is ordinal, interval or ratio.
- If the distribution shows a central tendency, the mean or median is a better measure; if there is no central tendency the mode is preferable.
- If the distribution is skewed, the median is a better measure. This is particularly so for distributions of interval data. When the skewness is extreme and if the distribution contains ordinal data the mode may be a better choice (Foddy, 1988: 74).
- If further measures are to be considered (e.g. standard deviation) the mean should be preferred.
- If a quick but rough measure is acceptable, the mode can be helpful.
- If information about the central trend is wanted, the mean is the best choice.
- If information is needed about the location of cases in the two halves of the distribution, the median is a better measure.

Despite the advantages and disadvantages of these measures, or perhaps because of them, social scientists seem primarily to employ the arithmetic mean as the measure of central tendency. The other methods are only marginally used. The mean has many mathematical properties that are very important, not only for providing a guide for central tendency but also for being necessary for computing other measures. It is also a stable measure, not being easily affected by shifts in a few data, and it is a clear and direct method obtained from raw data, irrespective of their order.

3   Measures of dispersion

a   Introduction

The measures we presented above are employed to demonstrate central tendency, that is, the general trend that is evident in the findings of the study. These are useful measures, which help to define the direction demonstrated by the data, and present a summary impression of some major traits of the population. Knowing, for instance, that the average IQ in a group of secondary school students is 120 gives us a very good indication of the level of intelligence of the members of that group and provides useful information to those teaching these students.

Measures of dispersion are equally useful and informative; they inform, however, of a different quality of the data, namely the degree to which the data are spread around the mean. Measures of dispersion show how close to or far away from the main stream of the data the observations are. If, for example, the average IQ is 120, how low is the lowest and how high is the highest score? How many low or high scores are in the distribution? And what is the average of the individual deviation of the scores from the mean? Such information is provided by means of the *measures of dispersion*. In this section we shall introduce the most common methods of computing such measures.

b   Variance and standard deviation

Variance and *standard deviation* are the two most popular measures of dispersion in the social sciences. The standard deviation is the square root of the variance; and hence the variance equals the square of the standard deviation.

In simple terms, *the variance is the average of the distances of the individual scores from the mean.* The procedure for computing the variance is the same as that of the mean, namely adding the distances of the individual observations from the mean and dividing them by their number. Due to the fact that half of the scores lie above and the other half below the mean, half of the differences from the mean are positive and half are negative; the calculation of the mean of the differences from the mean is thus impossible, for the sum of the distances is inevitably zero. For this reason, the variance is calculated by using the squared deviations from the mean. Thus, *variance is the mean of the squared deviations of the observations from the mean.* Let us explain this in an example (see Example F). Assume that we are interested in the spending habits of a group of 10 primary school students. We asked them to state the amount of money they spend weekly at school; the results are presented in Example F.

Example F: Distribution of amount of money spent by primary school students at school

Students	Amount ($)
A	5
B	7
C	3
D	9
E	16
F	12
G	8
H	4
I	2
J	14

By adding up the observations and dividing by 10 (the number of students) we can calculate the average amount of money spent at school, which is $8. If we plot the observations on the coordinates, we obtain a figure which, as well as showing the place of the observations in relation to each other, also shows the distances of each score from the mean (see Figure 16.1).

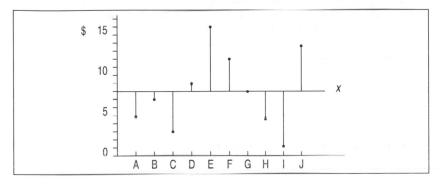

Figure 16.1   Amount of money spent at school

This figure shows that the distances of the scores from the mean vary from one case to another, some of them being below the mean and some above it. The variance demonstrates the average distance of these scores from the mean.

c Computation of variance and standard deviation

There are four basic formulae of variance employed by statisticians, two for ungrouped and two for grouped data.

Example G: Variance of the amounts of spending money from the mean

Students x	Amount $x - \bar{x}$		$(x - \bar{x})^2$
A	5	-3	9
B	7	-1	1
C	3	-5	25
D	9	1	1
E	16	8	64
F	12	4	16
G	8	0	0
H	4	-4	16
I	2	-6	36
J	14	6	36
$\bar{x} = 8$		$\Sigma(x - \bar{x}) = 0$	$\Sigma(x - \bar{x})^2 = 204$

Listed data I
The first formula of variance is a translation of the definition of variance into mathematical symbols. This formula is:

$$s^2 = \frac{\Sigma(x - \bar{x})^2}{N - 1} \qquad\qquad (16.4)$$

This formula defines variance in mathematical terms and symbols. It tells us to subtract the mean from each score, square what we get, add up the results and then divide by the number of scores. In practice this can be a longwinded method of calculation. Formula (16.5) gives a more practical computational procedure, as we shall see soon.[1]

As you will recall, to calculate a mean we add up all the scores and divide the sum by the number of scores. Similarly, the variance is the sum of the squared deviations from the mean, divided by the number of scores. It is a measure of the average spread from the mean. To compute the variance we need x, $x - \bar{x}$ and $(x - \bar{x})^2$. Their value can be calculated as shown in Example G. Note that each column corresponds to each of the factors of the formula.

Returning to Formula (16.4) we find that:

$$s^2 = \frac{\Sigma(x - \bar{x})^2}{N - 1} = \frac{204}{9} = 22.67$$

Thus the variance is 22.6 ($s^2 = 22.6$). Given that, by definition, the standard deviation (s) is the square root of the variance (s^2), s is the square root of s^2 and therefore the square root of 22.6 (which is 4.76). Consequently, the standard deviation is 4.76 ($s = 4.76$).

The results suggest that the standard deviation of the amounts spent weekly by students at school is \$4.76; in simple terms this means that the average deviation from the mean amount of money (i.e. from \$8) spent by students is \$4.76.

Listed data II
This method is called the *raw-score method* and is widely used in the social sciences. The advantage of this method is that it requires neither computation of the mean nor calculations of the deviation from the mean and thus the computations are markedly easier than in the previous method.

The formula employed in the raw-score method looks more complicated than Formula (16.4); it is, however, much easier and less time consuming to compute. The formula is:

$$s^2 = \frac{\Sigma x^2 - \dfrac{(\Sigma x)^2}{N}}{N - 1} \qquad\qquad (16.5)$$

---

[1]Social researchers distinguish between the standard deviation for a population (σ) and for a sample (s). In effect, the only difference between the computation employed in each case is that their formulae have different denominators: the denominator of the formula for s is $N - 1$, whereas the denominator for σ is N. In terms of value, the difference between the two formulae is significant for small samples only; the closer the sample is to 100, the smaller the difference and for samples larger than 100, there is no difference. Given that in quantitative studies (where it is more likely that statistical procedures are used) samples are usually large, in social research use of one or other formula makes no difference.

To compute s^2 it is necessary to calculate (1) the sum of the squared scores, Σx^2, and (2) the squared sum of the scores, $(\Sigma x)^2$. In other words it is necessary to square all the scores and add up all the products to get Σx^2, and to add up all the scores, thus obtaining Σx, and then square the sum to get $(\Sigma x)^2$. Let us compute the standard deviation in Example H.

Example H: Standard deviation of scores from the mean

x	x^2
5	25
7	49
3	9
9	81
16	256
12	144
8	64
4	16
2	4
14	196
$\Sigma x = 80$	$\Sigma x^2 = 844$

Using Formula (16.5) we find:

$$s^2 = \frac{844 - \dfrac{80^2}{10}}{10 - 1} = \frac{844 - 640}{9} = \frac{204}{9} = 22.67$$

$$s = \sqrt{22.67} = 4.76$$

Thus, the standard deviation score computed using the raw-score formula is the same as the score obtained using Formula (16.4).

Grouped data I

The formula employed when we deal with grouped data is similar to Formula (16.4) with the exception that the formula for the grouped data takes into account the frequency (f) of appearance of the individual scores. For this reason, the construction of the table and computation of the standard deviation are similar to those in Formula (16.4). The formula for grouped data is:

$$s^2 = \frac{\Sigma f(x - \overline{x})^2}{N - 1} \tag{16.6}$$

According to this formula, in order to compute the standard deviation the following factors are required: x, $x - \overline{x}$, $(x - \overline{x})^2$, $f(x - \overline{x})^2$ and $\Sigma f(x - \overline{x})^2$. These factors indicate the type and number of columns we need to set up in the table to compute the standard deviation. Let us look at an example.

In a recent sociology test the scores of 30 students were distributed between 1 (high distinction) and 5 (failed) as shown in Example I.

Example I: Distribution of test scores

x	f	$x - \bar{x}$	$(x - \bar{x})^2$	$f(x - \bar{x})^2$
1	1	−2	4	4
2	5	−1	1	5
3	18	0	0	0
4	5	1	1	5
5	1	2	4	4
$\bar{x} = 3$	$n = 30$			$\Sigma f(x - \bar{x})^2 = 18$

Employing Formula (16.6) we find:

$$s^2 = \frac{\Sigma f(x - \bar{x})^2}{N - 1} = \frac{18}{29} = 0.62; \quad \text{and } s = \sqrt{0.62} = 0.79$$

The standard deviation of the test scores is 0.79. This means that the average deviation of the scores from the mean (3) is 0.79.

Grouped data II

This method has the same qualities as the raw-score method discussed above under 'Listed data II'. The standard deviation is computed without calculating the mean or the difference of the scores from the mean. The relevant formula is:

$$s^2 = \frac{\Sigma fx^2 - \dfrac{(\Sigma fx)^2}{N}}{N - 1} \tag{16.7}$$

As in the previous cases, in order to compute the standard deviation it is necessary to calculate x^2, fx^2 and fx. From these values Σfx^2 and $(\Sigma fx)^2$ will be computed. Let us look at the figures in Example I again, here shown in Example J.

Example J: Distribution of test scores

x	f	x^2	fx^2	fx
1	1	1	1	1
2	5	4	20	10
3	18	9	162	54
4	5	16	80	20
5	1	25	25	5
			$\Sigma fx^2 = 288$	$\Sigma fx = 90$

Employing Formula (16.7) we find:

$$s^2 = \frac{288 - \frac{90^2}{30}}{30 - 1} = \frac{288 - 270}{29} = \frac{18}{29} = 0.62; \quad \text{and } s = \sqrt{0.62} = 0.79$$

Thus, the variance is 0.62, and the standard deviation is 0.79, which is the value obtained using Formula (16.6).

d The range

The range is another measure of variability. As the title indicates, this measure demonstrates the range that the distribution covers, from the lowest to the highest score. For this reason, its computation is quite simple; it describes the distance between the highest and the lowest score of a distribution, and is thus computed by subtracting the lowest score from the highest score.

Obviously, the range is quite different from the standard deviation. While the latter considers the spread of the data on the basis of their distance from the mean, the range does not refer to or depend on the value of the mean. Rather it refers to the continuum of the scores contained in the distribution, and shows how far apart its two extreme scores are. Let us study two examples.

Example K: The 10 students of class A in a Sydney primary school were found to spend the following weekly amounts of money on sweets (in dollars):

10, 9, 9, 8, 8, 8, 7, 7, 7, 7

In a grouped form the data show that one student spent $10, two spent $9, three $8 and four $7. The range here is 10 – 7 = 3 ($3); this means that the students have similar spending patterns, since the difference between the person who spent the highest amount and the one who spent the lowest amount is just $3.

Let us look at another example.

Example L: In another class of the same grade and school the 10 students interviewed each spent the following amounts of money on sweets (in dollars):

5, 7, 3, 9, 16, 12, 8, 4, 2, 14

Following the same procedure, we find that the range is 16 – 2 = 14, i.e. $14. The range demonstrates here that there is a large difference in the spending patterns of the members of the second group of students. This group is rather diverse.

A study of the central tendency of both distributions shows that *on average* both groups spent the same amount of money; the mean in both groups is $8. The range, however, indicates that a conclusion stating that both groups are therefore similar in their spending habits is misleading. The range shows that these groups are diverse in their spending patterns and not uniform as the mean suggests. The information offered by the range is not as specific as that offered by standard deviation; it is, however, very useful indeed.

e   Interquartile range

This measure is a version of the range except that it excludes from the computation the two ends of the distribution. More precisely, it leaves out the lower and upper quarter of the distribution. In this way extreme cases (outliers) which can skew the range value are excluded. To compute the interquartile range we proceed as follows:

1 Rank order the scores from the highest to the lowest.
2 Devide the distribution into four equal parts (first, second, third and fourth quarters or, better, *quartiles*).
3 Subtract the lowest score of the second quartile from the highest score of the third quartile. The difference is the *interquartile range*.

For instance, if the income of 20 students ranged from $20 to $250 per week and we wished to compute the interquartile range, we would rank the students according to their income from the highest to the lowest, divide them into four groups (quartiles) and subtract the income of the student at the bottom of quartile 2 (e.g. $31.00) from that of the student at the top of quartile 3 (e.g. $69.00). The difference between these two amounts ($38.00) is the inter-quartile range. This measure is more realistic than the range (in our case $230.00) because it excludes outliers, such as $250.00 in our example.

4   Computing $\bar{x}$, the median, the mode and s^2 using SPSS

Although the computation of the measures of central tendency and dispersion is easy, it also is tedious and time consuming. In any case it is not as easy as when computers are used. As a result there is no researcher who will compute these measures manually. The ease and speed of computation by computer and the high degree of accuracy have made manual computation obsolete. To work out these measures using SPSS you first enter the data in the computer; then while at the data editor window you proceed as follows:

1 Click on **Statistics > Summarise > Frequencies**
2 Transfer the variable for which you need information to the **Variable(s)** box
3 Click on **Statistics** (at the bottom of the window)
4 Activate the desired statistic (mean, median, mode, standard deviation, variance and range)
5 Click on **Continue**
6 Click on **OK**

The computer will display all activated measures on the same screen. For Example D the computer output will be as follows:

```
CHILDREN
                                      Valid    Cum
Value Label  Value  Frequency  Percent  Percent  Percent

             1.00      12        11.8     11.8     11.8
             2.00      46        45.1     45.1     56.9
             3.00      13        22.5     22.5     79.4
             4.00      11        10.8     10.8     90.2
             5.00       8         7.8      7.8     98.0
             6.00       2         2.0      2.0    100.0

             Total    102       100.0    100.0

Mean       2.637   Median    2.000      Mode    2.000
Std dev    1.184   Variance  1.402      Range   5.000

Valid cases    102       Missing cases    0
```

The results are self-explanatory; the mode is 2 because it is the category with the largest number of observations; and the value of the median is the same as that computed above manually.

5   Comparing scores and standard deviations

Scores and standard deviations offer useful information if interpreted inside but not outside their distribution. For instance a test score of 80 is larger than a score of 75, but if the mean of the distribution of the former is 78 and the mean of the distribution of the latter is 55, a score of 75 may have a higher value than a score of 80. In a similar fashion, a standard deviation of 6 is larger than a standard deviation of 3, but this is not necessarily so if the former refers to a distribution of 10 respondents and the latter to one of 100.

To have a realistic value and to allow comparisons these measures need to be brought down to a common denominator or, better, to be standardised. This is done for scores by means of the *standard scores* and for standard deviations by means of the *coefficient of variation*.

a   Standard scores (z-scores)

As stated above, although raw scores offer specific information about the position of a respondent on a scale, they are of little use if comparisons are to be made between different distributions. Standard scores offer a handy and effective method for expressing relationships and allowing comparisons between raw scores. Let us study this in an example (Example M).

> *Example M*: Two male students have applied for a scholarship which is granted on the basis of academic standards and achievement in the end-of-the-year examinations. The first student studies psychology and his score is 65; the second student studies history and his score is 70. On face value, the scores indicate that the history student should receive the scholarship, for his score is higher than the score of the other student. The question here is: Does the score 70 indicate that the history student has a higher achievement than the psychology student?

The logic behind this question is whether scores taken from two different scales can be compared. If both scores had come from the same distribution it would have been very simple to evaluate the actual value of the scores and to decide about who deserves the scholarship. But this is not so in our example.

To allow a valid comparison between these two scores and to make the decision about the scholarship easier, the *z*-score is employed.

Standard scores (or *z*-scores) transform raw scores from different distributions into a common distribution, which has the same mean (a mean of zero) and the same standard deviation (a standard deviation of 1). Standard scores convert raw scores into standard units of standard deviation. A *z* of 2 means that the raw score is two standard deviations above the mean. A negative *z*-score indicates that the score is below the mean. A *z*-score of –1.5 means that the score in question is one and a half standard deviations below the mean.

Raw scores are converted into standard scores (*z*-scores) by means of the following formula:

$$z = \frac{x - \overline{x}}{s}$$ (16.8)

The transformation is fairly simple. How raw scores are converted into standard scores is shown in Example N, which uses the scores for the two students in Example M.

Example N: Raw scores converted to standard scores.
Student 1: Assume that this student's raw score of 70 came from a group of students in which the mean was 71 and the standard deviation 6. The conversion into a standard score proceeds as follows:

$$z = \frac{x - \bar{x}}{s} = \frac{70 - 71}{6} = -\frac{1}{6} = -0.17$$

This shows that the score 70 is slightly below the mean; more accurately, it is 0.17 standard deviations below the mean. In simple terms this shows that the student in question performed slightly below average in the examination.

Student 2: Assume that the score 65 came from a distribution of scores in which the mean was 58 and the standard deviation 3. The conversion of this score into a standard score follows the same procedure:

$$z = \frac{x - \bar{x}}{s} = \frac{65 - 58}{3} = \frac{7}{3} = +2.3$$

This shows that the score 65 is an excellent score, being 2.3 deviations above the mean. In simple terms student 2's performance in the examination was far above the average.

The information provided by the two standard scores offers a valid basis for comparison, because it employs the same framework: both standard scores have a common mean and standard deviation and they are evaluated on the basis of the same standards. Therefore, their difference is more meaningful than the difference between the raw scores.

b   Computing z-scores using SPSS

1   Enter raw scores in the computer
2   Choose **Statistics > Summarise > Descriptives**
3   Transfer the variable you wish to standardise to the **Variable(s)** box
4   Click on the square in front of **Save Standardised values as variables** box
5   Click on **Continue**
6   Click on **OK**

To convert raw scores to *z*-scores using SPSS you proceed as follows:

The computer will display in the output window information which tells you that a new variable has been added to your data, showing also the name under which this variable has been saved. If you switch over to the Newdata screen, you will see that *z*-scores have been added alongside the original raw scores. These scores can be statistically treated as any other set of data.

c   The coefficient of variation

The coefficient of variation (also known as coefficient of relative variation) serves a purpose that is similar to that of z-scores: it allows researchers to compare standard deviations and decide whether one is larger than another. This is done by relating standard deviation to the mean and converting it to a percentage. Consequently, to compute the coefficient of variation *we divide the standard deviation by the mean and multiply the result by 100*. The formula for the coefficient of variation (CV) is as follows:

$$CV = \frac{s}{x} \times 100 \qquad (16.9)$$

Let us look at an example.

> *Example O*: A researcher investigated the amount of money spent on Fridays after work by members of a large union, and recorded their educational status. The data collected produced a standard deviation of $25.00 for spending and of 6 for education (in years of education). Obviously, income seems to have a larger standard deviation than education, but does this mean that the variability of the former is larger than the variability of the latter? The mean for spending is $50.00 and the mean number of years of education is 10 years.

To answer the research question we substitute the values in the formula and obtain the following figures:

$$CV_{spend} = \frac{25}{50} \times 100 = 50\% \quad \text{and} \quad CV_{educ} = \frac{6}{10} \times 100 = 60\%$$

Given that the coefficient of variation for education is larger than the coefficient for money spent on drinking, one can conclude that, despite the fact that the standard deviation for spending is larger than the standard deviation for education, variability in years of education is larger than in spending on drinking.

Key concepts

Ratio	Median
Mean	Range
Mode	Percentage
Variance	Group data
z-score	Standard deviation
Rate	Standard scores
Listed data	

17

Associations

A Correlation

1 Introduction

It is exceptional for social research to produce descriptions or measurements of single variables. Most social researchers are interested in the relationship between events, and try to ascertain the existence of such relationships, their strength and their direction. For this reason, the analysis of data, or at least a large part of it, tends to concentrate on the relationships between variables.

There are many ways of evaluating the type, direction and strength of such relationships. Some measures include two variables, others contain more than two. Whereas some relate to nominal data, others refer to ordinal or interval/ratio data. For instance, such measures provide a useful tool for examining the relationship between a high education level of women and liberal social attitudes; between socioeconomic status of parents and scholastic achievement of their children; between poverty and criminality; and between high technology and rates of divorce.

Measures of correlation are employed to explore three points, namely:

1 *presence or absence of correlation*, that is, whether or not there is a correlation between the variables in question;
2 *direction of correlation*, that is, if there is a correlation, whether it is positive or negative; and
3 *strength of correlation*, that is, whether an existing correlation is strong or weak.

Existence, direction and strength of correlation are demonstrated in the coefficient of correlation. A zero correlation indicates that there is no correlation between the variables. The sign in front of the coefficient indicates whether the variables change in the same direction (*positive correlation*) or in opposite directions (*negative correlation*), except for nominal measures, where the sign has no meaning, in which case coefficients describe only the strength of the relationship (a high or a low association) between the variables of the study. The value of the coefficient shows the strength of the association, with values close to zero meaning a weak correlation and those close to 1 a strong correlation, as we shall see later. A correlation of +1 is just as strong as one of –1; it is the direction that is different.

2   Overview of relevant options

The selection of the appropriate measure of association is based on a number of factors. Of these, the type of distribution (being continuous or discrete), the structure and characteristics of the distribution and the level of measurement of the data are the most significant. In addition, the availability of computers and relevant computer programs have a relative effect on the choice of measures.

The options are many; Table 17.1 displays the popular measures, at least in the area of social sciences, grouped according to level of measurement. In this section only one measure for each level of measurement will be discussed. These are Yule's Q, ϕ, Spearman's rho and Pearson's r.

Table 17.1   Association tests based on level of measurement

Level	Association tests
Nominal	Yule's Q, Lambda test, Contingency coefficient (C), Tschurprow's T, Cramer's V and ϕ coefficient
Ordinal	Spearman's rank-order correlation, Tau-α, Gamma coefficient, Sommer's d and Tau-β
Interval/ratio	Pearson's product-moment correlation

The degree of difficulty as well as the relevance of such measures to social scientists in general and to sociologists in particular vary to some extent. In this section we shall present an overview of how correlational measures are used, computed and interpreted. More procedures and more specialised and complicated tests can be found in relevant readings. Although the list covers only the minimum of measures related to association it does present a test for each possible level of measurement, offering a good start for an analysis of association between variables.

3   Nominal measures of association

In nominal measurement, data are classified in categories by means of numbers or other symbols. For this reason, nominal data cannot be analysed with statistical techniques that employ higher levels of measurement. The methods used are based on the differences that occur between certain values (e.g. expected and observed values) or on predictions made about one variable, derived from available knowledge about the other.

The computation and interpretation of these measures are fairly straight-forward. What is important to remember is that their coefficients range from 0 to 1, with 0 being the lowest level of their value. Negative values have no meaning. The closer the values are to 1, the stronger is the relationship between the variables, and the closer they are to 0, the weaker is the relationship. Three nominal measures of association will be considered in this section: Yule's Q, the ϕ coefficient and Cramer's V.

a Yule's Q

Yule's Q is a popular measure of association for nominal data and a method which is very easy to compute. Named after a famous nineteenth century statistician (Quetelet), this measure rests on the principle that *if values are set in a four-cell table, the cross-products of the internal diagonal cells will be equal when no relationship exists between the two variables* (Eckhardt and Ermann, 1977: 134). This principle is reflected in the formula given below:

$$Q = \frac{AD - BC}{AD + BC} \tag{17.1}$$

A, B, C and *D* refer to the cells of the relevant table. The computation of Yule's Q is very simple and involves the following steps:

Step 1: First we set up a four-cell table with its cells clearly marked using letters from *A* to *D* as shown in Table 12 in Example A.

Step 2: Substitute the values in the formula and compute Q.

Example A: A study of attitudes to feminism including 60 males and 60 females carried out in a country town of NSW produced the data presented in Table 12. How can the relationship between attitudes and gender be described?

Table 12 Attitudes to feminism by gender

Attitudes	Females		Males		Total
Positive	45	A	10	B	55
Negative	15	C	50	D	65
Total	60		60		120

Employing the relevant formula we find:

$$Q = \frac{AD - BC}{AD + BC} = \frac{(45 \times 50) - (10 \times 15)}{(45 \times 50) + (10 \times 15)} = \frac{2100}{2400} = 0.875$$

What does 0.875 mean? The value of Q is compared with H_o, which proposes that there is no difference, that is, no expected association between the variables. If Q is low, H_o is accepted; if Q is high, H_o is rejected. In our example, given that the value of Q is high, H_o is rejected, which means that there is a strong association between the variables.

b   Phi (ϕ) coefficient

Yule's Q, although simple in logic and computation, has not been included in any of the major computer-assisted statistical packages and is therefore not used as much as other nominal measures. Researchers tend to use other measures instead. Of these measures, two that are relatively powerful and also popular are ϕ and Cramer's V. They are also available in most popular computer programs. Both will be discussed in the next chapter because they are employed also in conjunction with chi-square tests. We shall introduce them briefly next. We begin with the ϕ coefficient.

The characteristics of ϕ are that, like Yule's Q, it is suitable for 2×2 tables, it is computed by means of a simple formula (Formula 17.2), it relies on the chi-square (to be introduced in the next chapter), and is interpreted the same way as Yule's Q. Its value ranges from 0 to 1; in general, if the ϕ value is close to 0, the strength of the relationship is fairly weak; if it is about 0.4 to 0.7 it is moderate; and if it is above 0.8 it is strong or very strong.

$$\phi = \sqrt{\frac{\chi^2}{N}} \qquad\qquad (17.2)$$

For example, with $\chi^2 = 9.36$ and $N = 85$, ϕ will be as follows:

$$\phi = \sqrt{\frac{9.36}{85}} = \sqrt{0.1101176} = 0.33$$

This suggests that the strength of the relationship between the variables in question is fairly weak.

c   Cramer's V

This is another measure of association between nominal variables. Its advantage over the ϕ coefficient is that it can be employed when tables are larger than 2×2. This measure (also known as Cramer's ϕ) possesses all the characteristics listed above for the ϕ coefficient, is interpreted the same way and is calculated using Formula (17.3):

$$\text{Cramer's } v = \sqrt{\frac{\chi^2}{N(k-1)}} \qquad\qquad (17.3)$$

where k is the smaller value of the number of rows and columns, and N the sample size. For instance, if in a table there were 3 rows and 4 columns, k would be 3 (since it is smaller than 4); if there were 6 rows and 4 columns, k would be 4. This measure is interpreted similarly to the ϕ coefficient.

Let us now employ V in an example. If a study in which $N = 65$ and $k = 3$ produced a chi-square of 23.45, Cramer's V would be as follows:

$$\text{Cramer's } V = \sqrt{\frac{23.45}{65(3-1)}} = \sqrt{\frac{23.45}{130}} = \sqrt{0.1803846} = 0.424717$$

This indicates that there is a moderate association between the variables in question.

d   Computing ϕ and V using SPSS

In SPSS, the computation of ϕ and Cramer's V is simple, and is a part of the computation of chi-square tests. Both measures are computed simultaneously, and their values are shown together with the chi-square value. Relevant instructions for computing these measures will be given in the next chapter.

4   Ordinal measures of association

Ordinal measures are characterised by their emphasis on ranking and on pairs. They derive their coefficient from ranking pairs, expecting that knowledge of the rank order of the pairs of one variable will allow some degree of prediction about the rank order of the other variable. Of the various measures employed in ordinal data, Spearman's rho is the most common.

a   Spearman's rank-order correlation coefficient

This is a fairly simple, useful and very popular *ordinal* measure of association mainly of two ordinal variables. It relates two ordered sets of ranks (not magnitudes), and allows a prediction about one set from the other. This is facilitated by means of the formula:

$$r_s = 1 - \frac{6\sum D^2}{N(N^2 - 1)} \tag{17.4}$$

The only factor that needs to be calculated in this formula is the sum of the squared difference of the ranks, namely $\sum D^2$; N is already known. To calculate this factor we proceed as follows:

Step 1
A table with the two sets of categories and rank orders is constructed.

Step 2
The ranks are subtracted and the difference is entered in a new column under *D* (differences).

Step 3
The differences are squared and the products entered in another column under D^2 (squared differences).

Step 4
The squared differences are summed, giving the sought value.

Step 5
The known values are placed in the formula and the coefficient is computed. Let us apply these steps in an example.

Example B: A group of psychology students ($N = 14$) is ranked from 1 to 14 according to test scores and also according to their popularity; the ranks are as follows: Student **A** 3, 4; **B** 14, 12; **C** 12, 13; **D** 2, 1; **E** 13, 14; **F** 1, 2; **G** 8, 6; **H** 10, 11; **I** 4, 3; **J** 7, 8; **K** 5, 7; **L** 11, 10; **M** 6, 5; and **N** 9, 9. Is there an association between popularity and test results? To answer these questions rho is computed as shown above. The results are given below.

Ranking of test results

Students	Test ranking	Popularity ranking	D	D^2
A	3	4	−1	1
B	14	12	2	4
C	12	13	−1	1
D	2	1	1	1
E	13	14	−1	1
F	1	2	−1	1
G	8	6	2	4
H	10	11	−1	1
I	4	3	1	1
J	7	8	−1	1
K	5	7	−2	4
L	11	10	1	1
M	6	5	1	1
N	9	9	0	0
				$\Sigma D^2 = 22$

Employing Formula (17.4) we find:

$$r_s = 1 - \frac{6 \times 22}{14(14^2 - 1)} = 1 - \frac{132}{2730} = 1 - 0.048 = 0.952$$

The result shows (1) that there is an association between popularity and test results (the coefficient is not 0); (2) that this association is very strong; and (3) that the association is positive.

Tied ranks

The procedure described in Example B contains a straightforward process of elementary calculations without major complications. One difficulty may arise when tied ranks occur, that is, when two or more subjects are given the same rank. The rule here is that these subjects receive the average rank score, and the ranks of the remaining subjects are adjusted accordingly. For instance, if five subjects were ranked and one was ranked first, three second and the other last, the actual ranks of these five respondents would be 1, 3, 3, 3 and 5. The second, third and fourth position are all allocated rank 3.

Significance of rho

Is the correlation coefficient significant? This is tested by means of a special table containing the critical values of rho. A version of that table containing the significance level for 0.05 and 0.01 (the most popular options) is given in Table 17.2. Note that this table can be used for positive and negative observations but only up to 30 observations. When N is more than 30 a different measure (*t*-statistic) is employed. The degree of significance is tested in the following way:

- In column 1 of Table 17.2 the value of N that corresponds to the number of cases (sample size) of the test is located. (If the table has no odd numbers, the value of N directly below the sample size is taken (for example, if N is 13, take 12). In our case N is 14.
- The appropriate column is chosen by defining the type of test (one-tailed or two-tailed test) and the significance level; then, the critical value that corresponds to N is located in the appropriate column. This is the *critical value* of rho. In our example, the critical values are 0.456 and 0.645 (for one-tailed tests) and 0.544 and 0.715 (for two-tailed tests) respectively.
- Rho is compared with the critical value: If r is equal to or greater than the critical value, rho is significant. In our example, the coefficient is 0.952. Since the absolute value of our coefficient is larger than each of the critical values, the value of r is significant.

For larger samples (over 30) and when the table of the critical values of r is not adequate, the value of t is employed to test the significance of r. t is evaluated in the context of the *t*-table. If the corresponding value in the table is equal to or smaller than the *t*-value, rho is significant at the specified level.

Evaluation

Spearman's rho is a very useful and effective measure of association. Nevertheless, it should be approached with caution when it includes (1) a large number of 'ties'; and (2) when scores are skewed.

Table 17.2   Critical values of Spearman's rho

N	Significance level (one-tailed tests)		Significance level (two-tailed tests)	
	0.05	0.01	0.05	0.01
5	0.900	1.000	1.000	- - - - -
6	0.829	0.943	0.886	1.000
7	0.714	0.893	0.786	0.929
8	0.643	0.833	0.738	0.881
9	0.600	0.783	0.683	0.883
10	0.564	0.746	0.648	0.794
12	0.506	0.712	0.591	0.777
14	0.456	0.645	0.544	0.715
16	0.425	0.601	0.506	0.665
18	0.399	0.564	0.475	0.625
20	0.377	0.534	0.450	0.591
22	0.359	0.508	0.428	0.562
24	0.343	0.485	0.409	0.537
26	0.329	0.465	0.392	0.515
28	0.317	0.448	0.377	0.496
30	0.306	0.432	0.364	0.478

Source: E.G. Olds (1940), 'The 5% significance levels for sums of squares of rank differences and a correction', *Annals of Mathematical Statistics*, 20, pp. 117–18.

b   Computing rho using SPSS

There are two methods of computing Spearman's rho. In both cases data must have been entered in the PC (method 1) before the methods can be used. They are shown below.

Method A

1 Choose **Statistics > Correlate > Bivariate**
2 Shift the variables to be correlated to the **Variable(s)** box
3 Click on the squares in front of **Spearman**
4 Click on **OK**

This procedure, employed using the data in Example B, will produce the results shown below. Note that the coefficient is the same as that computed manually and the rho is significant at the 0.000 level!

```
- - - SPEARMAN     CORRELATION     COEFFICIENTS - - -

TEST           .9516

               N(    14)

               Sig .000

               POPULARITY

(Coefficient / (Cases) / 2-tailed Significance)

"  .  " is printed if a coefficient cannot be computed
```

Method B

```
1  Choose Statistics > Summarise > Crosstabs
2  Shift one variable to the Rows box and the other to the Columns box
3  Click on Statistics at the bottom of the window
4  Click on the square box in front of Correlations
5  Click on Continue and then on OK
```

This will give you the values of Spearman's rho, together with ASE1, Val/ASE0 and approximate significance. Entering the data in Example B in the computer and following the steps introduced above produces the results shown below. The figures are self-explanatory. Note that information for Pearson's coefficient is also included in the output!

				Approximate
Statistic	Value	ASE1	Val/ASE0	Significance
---------	-----	-----	--------	----------
Pearson's R	.95165	.01593	10.73151	.00000*4
Spearman Correlation	.95165	.02272	10.73151	.00000*4

```
*4 VAL/ASE0 is a t-value based on a normal
approximation, as is the significance

Number of Missing Observations: 0
```

5   Interval/ratio measures of association

a   Pearson's product-moment correlation coefficient, *r*

This is the most common measure of association of variables scaled on an interval level. This measure considers not ranks of pairs but rather magnitudes of observations, and can be computed in three ways: (1) by means of computers, the easiest and most reliable method; (2) through the plotting method, by plotting and examining the least-squares line; and (3) by means of the following formula:

$$r = \frac{N\Sigma XY - (\Sigma X)(\Sigma Y)}{\sqrt{\{N\Sigma X^2 - (\Sigma X)^2\}\{N\Sigma Y^2 - (\Sigma Y)^2\}}} \tag{17.5}$$

In the following discussion we shall attempt all three methods, beginning with the plotting method.

The plotting method

Computing the correlation using this method implies the construction of a scattergram, with the two variables being placed on the two axes of the graph. Each pair of scores is then plotted on the scattergram. The resulting shape and direction of the dots indicate the type, strength and direction of correlation. Widely spread dots indicating no direction, as in (b) in Figure 17.1, suggest that there is no correlation; dots congregating around a line beginning from the origin of the graph and making a 45° angle with the abscissa, as in (a) in Figure 17.1, indicate a positive correlation; dots displaying a form similar to that of (c) in the figure indicate a negative correlation. The more linear and the closer together the dots the stronger the relationship, and vice versa.

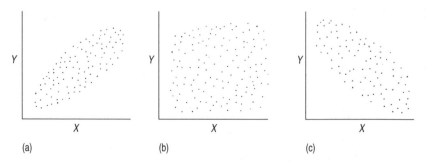

(a)   (b)   (c)

Figure 17.1   Scattergrams. (a) Strong positive relationship; (b) no relationship; (c) strong negative relationship

Plotting a scattergram using SPSS

Example C: A researcher wishes to examine the relationship between education of women and their degree of liberation. The hypothesis is that the degree of liberation is associated with their degree of education (educational status). To test this hypothesis 10 women are studied in terms of the variables in question. Education and liberation have been rated on a 15-point scale and each woman has been given a score for each of the variables according to her responses. The pair-scores obtained for education and liberation are: 2, 3; 4, 5; 5, 3; 6, 5; 7, 6; 8, 9; 9, 7; 11, 13; 13, 10; and 14, 11 respectively.

The steps to follow to obtain a scattergram are as follows.

1 Choose **Charts > Scatter**
2 Click on **Simple**
3 Click on **Define**
4 Transfer 'education' to the **Y Axis** box and 'liberation' to **X Axis** box
5 Click **OK**

These instructions will generate the output shown in Figure 17.2. The shape of the scores indicates a positive correlation. The fact that they do not form a line but are more or less spread around it suggests that the correlation is not perfect but still strong.

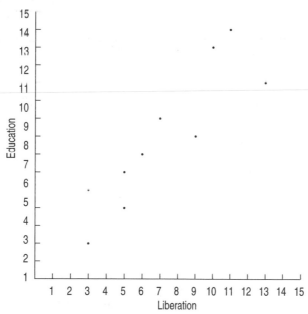

Figure 17.2 Scattergram showing a strong and positive correlation between education and liberation

Employing the formula

Computing the relationship between two variables by means of Formula (17.5) is more complicated than the plotting method; it offers, however, more information and is more accurate. To obtain the values of the elements of the formula, we first place the scores in a table, and construct columns for their squares and products. Employing the data in Example C, we obtain the results given in Table 17.3. The scores of the women have been placed in the first two columns. The squares and the products of the scores are shown in the remaining three columns.

Table 17.3 Correlation between liberalism and education of women

Education scores X	Liberation scores Y	X^2	Y^2	XY
2	3	4	9	6
4	5	16	25	20
5	3	25	9	15
6	5	36	25	30
7	6	49	36	42
8	9	64	81	72
9	7	81	49	63
11	13	121	169	143
13	10	169	100	130
14	11	196	121	154
$\Sigma X = 79$	$\Sigma Y = 72$	$\Sigma X^2 = 761$	$\Sigma Y^2 = 624$	$\Sigma XY = 675$

Substituting the values obtained through the table in Formula (17.5), the correlation coefficient for this example is:

$$r = \frac{10 \times 675 - 79 \times 72}{\sqrt{(10 \times 761 - 79^2)(10 \times 624 - 72^2)}} = \frac{1062}{\sqrt{1369 \times 1056}}$$

$$= \frac{1062}{\sqrt{1445664}} = \frac{1062}{1202.36} = 0.883$$

This coefficient is positive and high, indicating a strong and positive association between the variables. This verifies the trend depicted in the scattergram.

Interpretation of **r**

As stated at the beginning of this chapter, a correlation coefficient indicates both the type of correlation and the strength of the relationship. A *positive correlation*, indicated by a coefficient having a positive sign, suggests that the two variables are associated in such a way that an increase/decrease in one variable is associated with an increase/decrease in the other. The common statement made by researchers in this case is 'the higher X the higher Y' or 'the lower X the lower Y'. In a more concrete example, if a positive correlation is identified the statement might be that 'the higher the degree of dependence, the greater the chance for a person to hold a lower status in a system'; or 'the lower the class status, the lower the chance of a person attending tertiary institutions'.

A *negative correlation*, signified by a coefficient with a negative sign, suggests that there is an inverse relationship between the variables. In this case an increase in one variable is associated with a decrease in the other. The relevant statement in a study of feminism and traditionalism may be: 'the higher the degree of commitment to feminism, the lower the observance of traditional sex-differentiated household tasks'.

A *zero correlation* suggests that there is no systematic relationship between the two variables, and changes in one variable are not associated with changes in the other.

The *strength* of the relationship in a correlation is indicated by the position of the coefficient in its continuum.

The *range* of the coefficient is between −1 and +1. The correlation is generally considered to be:

- *very low* if the coefficient has a value under 0.20;
- *low* if the coefficient has a value between 0.21 and 0.40;
- *moderate* if the coefficient has a value between 0.41 and 0.70;
- *high* if the coefficient has a value between 0.71 and 0.91;
- *very high* if the coefficient is over 0.91.

This list offers a guide only to interpreting a coefficient value; it is not a rule to be followed. Nevertheless, most of the social scientists who employ *r* seem to interpret it as stated above.

The significance of *r*

Does the identified relationship between the variables described by the correlation coefficient, *r*, correspond with the relationship that actually exists in the population, or is it a reflection of sampling or other methodological problems or procedures? In other words are the variables in the population related in the same way and to the same degree as they are found to be in the study and as they are described by the coefficient?

There are several ways of testing the significance of *r*; the simplest of all employs the critical values of *r* as summarised in relevant tables. The procedure is the same as that introduced above when we were discussing the significance of Spearman's rho. To test the significance of Pearson's *r* we compare its value with the critical value of *r* given in the table especially constructed for Pearson's *r*, as indicated by the relevant degrees of freedom and level of significance. An *r* is significant if it is equal to or greater than the relevant critical value of *r*.

b   Computing Pearson's r using SPSS

There are two methods of computing Pearson's *r*. After entering the data in the computer we follow the following steps:

Method 1

1   Choose **Statistics > Correlate > Bivariate**
2   Transfer the variables to be correlated to the **Variable(s)** box
3   Click on the square in front of **Pearson**
4   Click on **OK**

Using the figures obtained in Example C, this procedure will produce the output shown below. It is clearly shown that the correlation coefficient for education and liberation is 0.8833, which is the same as the one obtained manually above. (The correlation coefficient between education and education, as well as liberation and liberation is obviously 1.) The correlation coefficient of 0.8833 is significant at the 0.001 level (P = 0.001).

```
 - - - CORRELATION COEFFICIENTS - - -
            Education          Liberation

Education   1.0000             .8833
            (    10)           (    10)
            P = .              P = .001

Liberation  .8833              1.0000
            (    10)           (    10)
            P = .001           P = .

(Coefficient / (Cases) / 2-tailed Significance)

 " . " is printed if a coefficient cannot be computed
```

Method 2

1   Choose **Statistics > Summarise > Crosstabs**
2   Transfer variable 1 to the **Rows** box
3   Transfer variable 2 to the **Columns** box
4   Click on **Statistics** at the bottom of the window
5   Click on the square box in front of **Correlations**
6   Click on **Continue** and then on **OK**

If we use the figures presented in Example C, the computer will display the following information. Note that the Spearman correlation is included also in the output!

```
- - Correlation coefficients - - -

                                    Approximate
Statistic      Value    ASE1     Val/ASE0  Significance


- - - - - - - - - -    - - - - -   - - - - -   - - - - - - - -   - - - - - - - - - -


Pearson's R    .88326   .03525   5.32818    .00070
Spearman       .92075   .04401   6.67495    .00016
Correlation

Number of Missing Observations: 0
```

The output given here is somewhat different from the one produced through Method 1. Going through crosstabs produces the same figures, offers information for Pearson's *r and* Spearman's rho, gives details for ASE1 and Val/ASE0 and is relatively easier to read. The important findings are, however, (a) the value of the coefficient (0.88326), which is very high (indicating a very strong, positive correlation), and (b) its significance, which is equally high.

c   Coefficient of determination

It must be stressed that the coefficient of correlation measures the type and strength of linear correlations, but it does not necessarily imply a cause–effect relationship. Nevertheless, this measure can offer very useful information. If squared, for instance, the coefficient of correlation gives the coefficient of determination. This measure describes the common variance, that is, the degree of variability shared by the two variables. The symbol of this coefficient is r^2. This measure is very useful, primarily because it offers an index of predictability: it allows the researcher to make predictions about one variable if the degree of determination is known.

The coefficient of determination displays the proportion of variance in one variable that is explained by the other variable. If the coefficient is 0.81 (which is the equivalent of a coefficient of correlation of 0.9), 81 per cent of the variation is accounted for by the linear relationship with the other variable. The remaining variance cannot be explained by the other variable.

This remaining amount of variance not explained by the other variable is expressed in the *coefficient of non-determination*, and is the difference between 1 and the coefficient of determination. Obviously, the two co-efficients must add up to 1.

For example, if the correlation coefficient is 0.88, the coefficient of determination is 0.77 and the coefficient of non-determination 0.23. Consequently a variable can explain 77 per cent of the variation in the values of the other. The remaining 23 per cent of variation is unique to both distributions and cannot be explained by the correlated variables.

B Regression and prediction

Regression is a method that allows social scientists to make predictions about the value of one variable (Y) if another variable (X) is known. This is an asymmetrical measure, since it allows one-direction predictions only. Predictions are made by means of the regression line, the definition of which is given by a formula containing the intercept and the slope of the line. The regression formula is as follows:

$$Y = a + bX \tag{17.6}$$

where Y and X are variables, a and b constants. The constant a stands for the value of Y when X is zero and represents the Y-intercept. The constant b together with X (bX) represents the slope of the line.

The regression line is a straight line plotted on a scattergram. It is constructed by means of the method of least squares, which places the line in such a position that the squares of the vertical distances of the plots from the line are the smallest possible. The regression line is one of many but is the line of best fit. The line reduces the variance of all the distances and also passes through the mean of each variable. The position of the line on the scattergram depends on the values of a and b (which can be computed independently) and on the value of X, which can be arbitrarily defined by the researcher. Thus, to determine the value of Y, the following steps are taken:

1 b is computed by means of Formula (17.7).
2 a is computed by means of Formula (17.8).
3 These values are substituted in Formula (17.6).
4 Any two of the given values of X are substituted in Formula (17.6) where a and b are known, and the two corresponding Y-values are computed.
5 Two selected X-values and the corresponding Y-values are plotted on a scattergram.
6 The two plots are joined, which gives the regression line, thus allowing an estimation of the remaining values of Y by drawing vertical lines on the independent variable towards the regression line and horizontal lines across to the dependent variable. The point of crossing of this line is the value of the dependent variable that corresponds to the value of the independent variable that is on the foot of the line crossing the abscissa.

Computation of b is done by means of Formula (17.7)

$$b = \frac{N(\Sigma\,XY) - (\Sigma X)\,(\Sigma Y)}{N(\Sigma X^2) - (\Sigma X)^2} \qquad\qquad (17.7)$$

From the computations in Table 17.3 we have $\Sigma X = 79$, $\Sigma Y = 72$, $\Sigma XY = 675$, $\Sigma X^2 = 761$, $N = 10$, $(\Sigma X)^2 = 6241$. Therefore:

$$b = \frac{10(675) - (79)(72)}{10 \times 761 - 6241} = \frac{6750 - 5688}{7610 - 6241} = \frac{1062}{1369} = 0.775$$

This means that for each unit change in X, Y changes by 0.775 units. The value of a is obtained by means of Formula (17.8):

$$a = \frac{\Sigma Y - b(\Sigma Y)}{N} \qquad\qquad (17.8)$$

Substituting our values in Formula (17.8):

$$a = \frac{72 - 0.775 \times 72}{10} = \frac{72 - 55.8}{10} = \frac{16.2}{10} = 1.62$$

This suggests that the regression line crosses the Y-line at 1.62. The formula of the regression line now is:

$$Y = 1.62 + 0.775X$$

Taking $X_1 = 6$ and $X_2 = 11$, Y_1 and Y_2 become:

$$Y_1 = 1.62 + 0.775 \times 6 = 10.495; \; Y_2 = 1.62 + 0.775 \times 11 = 18.595$$

Knowing these values, we can now plot the values on the scattergram and after joining the two plots we can secure the regression line.

C Summary

The measures of association introduced in this chapter are very popular, very useful and effective, and also very easy to compute and interpret. They are used to measure the relationship between two variables, the strength of the relationship and the direction of the relationship. These measures are used also for nominal data and therefore in qualitative investigations.

Of these methods Pearson's r is the most popular. With regard to nominal data researchers seem to have their own personal preferences. While some do not use statistics at all, others seem to prefer ϕ and Cramer's V. The latter seems to be more popular now than before, especially with the expansion of the use of computers.

Overall, measures of association are a key tool of statistical analysis. In some areas they are used as the only statistical measure, but in most cases they are used in conjunction with measures of central tendency and dispersion, and more so with regression. In all cases, they offer useful information that assists researchers to identify correlations between variables and make relevant predictions. Unfortunately the scope of this text does not allow a more detailed discussion on regression. Information on this must be sought elsewhere.

Key concepts

Correlation	Negative correlation
Spearman's rho	Regression
Pearson's r	Sommer's d
Zero correlation	Positive correlation
Prediction	Coefficient of determination
Yule's Q	
Gamma	

18

Tests of significance

1 Introduction

In the previous chapter it was shown how associations between variables could be conceptualised and measured. We saw that there are statistical techniques which are employed to determine the degree of association between variables, regardless of their level of measurement. These methods are very commonly used and help the researcher to gain an insight into the way parts of the findings relate to each other.

In this chapter we shall address another relationship, this time between the study and the society; the findings and the people; the sample and the target population. We shall introduce the way in which researchers make inferences about the target population, by generalising the findings beyond the boundaries of the sample. In this sense, the relationship we intend to focus on in this chapter is between *statistics* (attributes of the sample) and *parameters* (attributes of the population).

Making generalisations is an important element of the research process, and one that is close to the purpose of almost every investigation. Most studies are conducted with the purpose of being able to produce findings that can be generalised in some way or another to the whole population. To assure this, researchers employ several techniques. Some of these techniques relate to sampling procedures, guiding the selection of the respondents so that they come from all possible groups, assuring representativeness of the sample. Others check the significance of differences identified in the study.

Checking the significance of differences is facilitated by means of *significance tests*. These tests follow a strict procedure, beginning with setting a *research hypothesis*, formulating the *null hypothesis* and the *alternative hypothesis*, computing test statistics and then checking whether the null hypothesis can be rejected.

There are several types of tests of significance. Whether a researcher chooses one or the other depends on three factors, namely on:

1 whether the distributions are scaled on a nominal, ordinal or interval/ratio level;
2 whether there are one or more samples (one-sample tests, two-sample tests, *k*-sample tests); and

3 whether the samples are related or independent, that is, whether the samples are matched or chosen independently.

One-tail and two-tail tests

There are two types of tests: one-tail tests and two-tail tests. *One-tail tests* begin with the premise (stated in the alternative hypothesis) that population parameters are different from those hypothesised and also show the direction of that difference. For instance, they may test the hypothesis that men are less religious than women; or that older students achieve higher grades than younger students. In more technical terms, when two means are tested, one is considered to be either *greater than* or *less than* the other. One-tail tests are *directional*: they specify the direction of the difference.

The *two-tail tests* are based on the assumption that the population parameters are different from those hypothesised. They do not suggest any direction of the difference. For instance, two-tail tests may test the hypothesis that men and women have different views on religion; or that older and younger students achieve different grades. In more technical terms, when two means are tested, it is stated that the means are different from each other. Two-tail tests are often used in exploratory studies, when knowledge of the research topic is limited. These tests are *non-directional* (Kraemer and Thieman, 1987: 26).

Parametric and non-parametric tests

Tests are also divided into parametric and non-parametric tests. The *parametric tests* are based on the assumption that the variable being investigated is normally distributed in the population, and they employ the concept of the normal curve. *Non-parametric* tests do not adhere to the principle of normality.

2   Tests of significance: an overview

Tests of significance are many and diverse and are an integral part of every quantitative study. In the discussion presented in this section we shall pay attention to only a few tests, introducing their purpose and relevance, showing briefly how their values are derived and interpreted.

The main points that will be covered when discussing these tests are:

• when and under what conditions specific tests are employed;
• how they are computed (by hand and using SPSS); and
• how their values are interpreted.

A summary of the most common tests of significance grouped according to level of measurement and number of samples is given in Table 18.1. This table is by no means exhaustive.

In the following discussion we shall present only a sample of the most common tests of significance according to level of measurement, beginning with nominal-level tests.

Table 18.1   Overview of tests of significance

| Number and | Non-parametric tests | Parametric tests | |
| | | | |
type of samples	Nominal level	Ordinal level	Interval/ratio level
One	χ^2–test (Goodness-of-fit test)	Kolmogorov–Smirnov test	*t*-test
Two independent	χ^2–test of independence Fisher's exact test *z*-test for proportions	Mann–Whitney *U*-test Wald–Wolfowitz runs test	*t*-test
Two dependent	McNemar test	Sign test Wilcoxon test	*t*-test
More than two independent	χ^2–test	Kruskal–Wallis *H*-test	ANOVA
More than two dependent	Cochran *Q*-test	Friedman test	ANOVA

Sources: S. Siegel (1956), *Non-parametric Statistics for Behavioral Sciences*, London: McGraw-Hill; R.G. Knapp (1985), *Basic Statistics for Nurses*, New York: Wiley and Sons.

3   Nominal-level tests

There are several nominal-level tests of significance employed by researchers. The choice of the particular test depends on a number of factors, such as type of samples and degree of dependence between them. The tests presented or referred to in this section are listed in Table 18.2.

Table 18.2   Some significance tests used at the nominal level

Number of samples	Type of samples	Significance test
One sample	N/A	χ^2 goodness of fit *z*-test for proportions
Two samples	Independent	χ^2 test of independence Fisher's exact test
	Dependent	McNemar test
k–samples	Independent	χ^2 test
	Dependent	Cochran *Q*-test

a   The chi-square test (χ^2)

Chi-square (χ^2) (pronounced kye square) tests are the most popular and most frequently used tests of significance in the social sciences in general and in sociology in particular. Basically, they provide information about whether the collected data are close to the value considered to be typical and generally expected, and whether two variables are related to each other.

There are two types of chi-square tests, namely the *goodness-of-fit test* and the *test of independence*. Both are based on the same principles: the data obtained in a study (observed frequencies) are compared with the expected data (expected frequencies); their actual difference determines the level of significance.

The general procedure employed to calculate chi-square in both cases is also similar; it contains the following steps:

1 A simple table or a contingency table is constructed.
2 The observed frequencies are identified.
3 The expected frequencies are ascertained.
4 The expected frequencies are subtracted from the observed frequencies.
5 The differences are squared and then divided by the number of expected frequencies.

In both types of chi-square tests the results are interpreted in the same way. This is done as follows:

1 H_o (null hypothesis) is formulated.
2 The degrees of freedom and the critical value of χ^2 are ascertained.
3 The critical value of chi-square is compared with the chi-square score.
4 If the χ^2 value is greater than or equal to the critical value, the null hypothesis is rejected and the difference is considered to be significant. If chi-square is less than the critical value, the null hypothesis is accepted; the difference is not significant.

We begin our discussion by introducing the goodness-of-fit test.

The goodness-of-fit test: one variable

Introduction
In simple terms, this test is employed to ascertain whether the findings of a study reflect the real values of the population. In statistical terms the test will show whether the observed frequencies *fit into the theoretical* (expected) frequencies of the population in question. The basic formula is:

$$\chi^2 = \sum \frac{(f_o - f_e)^2}{f_e} \tag{18.1}$$

where f_o stands for the observed frequencies and f_e stands for the expected frequencies. According to the formula, in order to ascertain the chi-square value the expected frequency is subtracted from the observed frequency, the difference is squared and then divided by the number of expected frequencies. To illustrate the computation of chi-square, consider Example A.

Example A: Three hundred (300) women were asked to state whether they were in favour of women's liberation, women's emancipation or traditionalism. After the responses were recorded it was found that 100 women were in favour of the first, 150 in favour of the second and 50 in favour of the third option. Is the difference between the numbers of women opting for a certain category significant? Do the differences indicate that there is a similar diversity in the population? Can one assume that the differences are caused by factors related to methodology or sampling? To answer these questions we employ the chi-square test.

Preferences of women for the three options

Liberation	Emancipation	Traditionalism	Total
100	150	50	300

Computation

To compute the chi-square, Formula (18.1) is used. For this, the observed frequencies f_o and the expected frequencies f_e are required; f_o have already been identified as 100, 150 and 50. The expected frequencies (f_e) are the average of the observed frequencies, that is, 100. This estimation is based on the logical assumption that women will respond in equal numbers to these options, but this assumption need not be correct. The null hypothesis (H_o), which in very simple terms is the 'devil's advocate', suggests that there is no significant difference between the three groups, and that in reality their views are equally distributed among these options.

The chi-square test will show whether H_o is true or false. If chi-square is equal to or larger than its critical value, H_o is rejected. This means that the differences in our data are significant. Let us now compute chi-square:

$$\chi^2 = \frac{(100-100)^2 + (150-100)^2 + (50-100)^2}{100} = \frac{0^2 + 50^2 + (-50)^2}{100} = 50$$

The computation of chi-square can also be presented in a table, as shown in Example B.

Example B: Computation of χ^2

Ideology	f_o	f_e	$f_o - f_e$	$(f_o - f_e)^2$	$(f_o - f_e)^2/f_e$
Liberation	100	100	000	0000	00
Emancipation	150	100	+50	2500	25
Traditionalism	50	100	−50	2500	25

$$\sum \frac{(f_o - f_e)^2}{f_e} = 50$$

Thus, chi square is 50.

We have now determined the value of chi-square; the step that follows is to test whether our chi-square value is significant. To test the significance of chi-square we have to compare the chi-square value with its critical value as presented in the relevant statistical table. Chi-square is significant only if it is equal to or greater than that critical value. In order to accomplish this we need to know two additional values, namely the degrees of freedom (contained in the first left-hand column of the table), and the significance level indicated in the heading of the table. Let us introduce these two new concepts.

Degrees of freedom

The degrees of freedom are computed by the following formula:

$$df = k - 1 \qquad\qquad (18.2)$$

where k indicates the number of categories, which in our case is 3. The degrees of freedom are thus: $df = k - 1 = 3 - 1 = 2$. This suggests that we shall search for the critical value in the second row of the table of critical values.

Significance level

The significance level indicates the risk of rejecting H_0 when it should have been accepted, which we are prepared to take. This is referred to as alpha (α). The α value most commonly used by social researchers is 0.05. In such cases, we accept that there is a 5 per cent probability of rejecting a true H_0. (Another way of saying this is that, if we were to randomly take a number of samples from the same population, a difference as great as that at the 0.05 level would occur by chance only once in 20 samples — only once in 100 for the 0.01 level). The study is more precise if the differences are significant at the 0.01 level; here we reduce this probability to 1 per cent. In our example we might choose a significance level of 0.05.

Interpretation

Now that we have the chi-square value, the degrees of freedom and the level of significance, we are able to determine whether the chi-square is significant.

Remember the following:

- An interpretation can, in the first place, only say whether H_0 is rejected or accepted (or better not rejected).
- Our H_0 suggests that, despite the observed differences, there is no significant difference between the numbers of women opting for certain ideologies, and that the frequencies in the population are equal.
- If H_0 is rejected, the differences are significant.
- H_0 is rejected only if the value of chi-square is equal to or greater than the critical value; otherwise H_0 is accepted.

Looking now at the critical-value table, we find that the critical value of our chi-square for 2 degrees of freedom and at the significance level of 0.05 is 5.99. Since the value of our chi-square, that is, 50, is greater than its critical value, 5.99, our chi-square is significant and H_o *is rejected.* This means that there is no sufficient reason to accept H_o, and thus the observed differences are significant: the observed differences represent differences in the population. If we persist in our testing and select higher levels of significance it will be shown that our chi-square is significant at all levels.

Goodness-of-fit test: computation using SPSS
To compute the goodness-of-fit chi-square test we first have to enter the data in the computer. For the first example, this involves (a) naming the variable (e.g. ideology), (b) setting the values (1 for liberalism, 2 for emancipationism and 3 for traditionalism) and (c) entering one by one the scores. The column containing the ideology values will ultimately contain 100 times the value 1, 150 times the value 2 and 50 times the value 3. Having entered the data, we proceed as follows:

1 Choose **Statistics > Non-parametric tests > Chi-square**
2 Transfer Ideology to the **Test Variable** box
3 Activate **All categories equal** (click on the circle in front of it)
4 Click on **OK**

Upon completion of this procedure the computer produces the figures shown below:

```
– – – – – – – – – – Chi-Square Test

IDEOLOGY
                              Cases
               Category   Observed   Expected    Residual

Liberation     1.00         100      100.00          .00
Emancipat      2.00         150      100.00        50.00
Tradition      3.00          50      100.00       -50.00
                            ––––
               Total        300

     Chi-Square         D.F.            Significance
     50.0000             2                 .0000
```

This display shows that the chi-square value is 50 (the same as that computed by hand) and that with 2 degrees of freedom p = 0.0000. This means that the observed differences are significant.

The chi-square test of independence: two variables
This test is principally the same as the goodness-of-fit test and is employed when two nominal-level variables are being studied. The basic differences between these two chi-square tests are related to the method of obtaining the

expected frequencies and the area of employment of the tests. The test of independence does not employ theoretical assumptions about the distribution of frequencies in the population.

The main question regarding the test of independence is not about the 'fit' of the observed values of one variable in the theoretical model; rather it is about whether the two variables are independent from or related to each other. H_o always states that the variables studied are independent. The chi-square test of independence will help us decide whether to accept or reject this hypothesis.

Computation

There are two basic methods of computing the chi-square test of independence. The first method is simple and employs basic arithmetic procedures. The second method is similar to that presented in the context of the goodness-of-fit test with the exception of the way of defining f_e, which is a rather long and time-consuming procedure. For this reason the first method is more frequently used than the other. Both methods will be presented in this section; but before we discuss these methods, let us introduce an example.

Example C: A researcher wishes to measure the relationship between gender and social orientation (here: liberal, conservative). A study of 100 males and 100 females was carried out for this purpose ($N = 200$), which demonstrated that 66 males were liberal, 34 males were conservative, 43 females were liberal and 57 females were conservative (see below).

Social orientation of males and females

Social orientation	Males		Females		Row total
Liberal	66	A	43	B	109
Conservative	34	C	57	D	91
Total	100		100		200

The question here is about whether, on the basis of the obtained results, there is a relationship between gender and social orientation, that is, whether, say, females are more liberated than males. Are these variables related to each other? In the language of the chi-square test, are the variables dependent or independent? As we know already, H_o *suggests that the variables gender and social orientation are independent*. Let us see how the chi-square test of independence can be of assistance.

Computation: Method I

This method follows the steps discussed in the introductory part of this section, and consists of the following steps:

Step 1:
A contingency table with distinct cells and marginals is established. Gender is placed in the columns, social orientation in the rows. The actual values are shown in the contingency table (see Example C). The four central cells of the table are marked with the capital letters *A, B, C, D*.

Step 2:
Now the following formula is employed:

$$\chi^2 = \frac{N(AD - BC)^2}{(A + B)(C + D)(A + C)(B + D)} \qquad (18.3)$$

Step 3:
The values corresponding to the capital letters are substituted into the formula:

$$\chi^2 = \frac{200\,(66 \times 57 - 43 \times 34)^2}{(66 + 43)\,(34 + 57)\,(66 + 34)\,(43 + 57)} = \frac{200 \times 5\,290\,000}{99\,190\,000} = 10.666$$

The value of chi-square is 10.66.

Computation: Method II
The values of f_o, f_e, $f_o - f_e$, $(f_o - f_e)^2$ and $(f_o - f_e)^2/f_e$ are set in a table. The expected values are computed by using the following formula:

$$f_e = \frac{RT \times CT}{N} \qquad (18.4)$$

where *RT* stands for row total and *CT* for column total. *N* is the grand total (200).

Example D: Computation of χ^2

f_o	f_e	$f_o - f_e$	$(f_o - f_e)^2$	$(f_o - f_e)^2/f_e$
66	54.5	11.5	132.25	2.43
43	54.1	−11.5	132.25	2.43
34	45.5	−11.5	132.25	2.90
57	45.5	11.5	132.25	2.90
			$\sum \dfrac{(f_o - f_e)^2}{f_e}$	= 10.66

Substituting into Formula (18.4), f_e is computed:

for 66
$$f_e = \frac{109 \times 100}{200} = 54.5$$

for 43
$$f_e = \frac{109 \times 100}{200} = 54.5$$

for 34 $$f_e = \frac{91 \times 100}{200} = 45.5$$

for 57 $$f_e = \frac{91 \times 100}{200} = 45.5$$

Note that both observed values have the same values of RT and CT.

When all values are computed the results obtained are as shown in Example D, where the chi-square value is 10.66.

It should be stressed that chi-square tests can also be employed where contingency tables are larger than 2×2. The formula employed in each case is the same, and the computation of f_e is the same, irrespective of the number of row values or column values. The test in such cases is usually referred to as the chi-square test for k independent variables.

Interpreting chi-square
The chi-square test of independence is interpreted in the same way as the goodness-of-fit test. The only difference is with the calculation of df, which in the chi-square test of independence is computed by means of Formula (18.5):

$$df = (r-1)(c-1) \tag{18.5}$$

where r stands for the number of rows and c for the number of columns. Since in our example there are two rows and only two columns, the degrees of freedom are:

$$df = (2-1)(2-1) = 1 \times 1 = 1$$

From the table of critical values for chi-square, at the 0.05 significance level the corresponding value is 3.84. Remember that H_o asserts that the two variables are independent, and that it will only be accepted if chi-square is smaller than the critical value. In our example chi-square is 10.66, which is larger than the critical value. This means that H_o is rejected and with it the assumption that the variables are independent. Thus it is not reasonable to assert that social orientation is not related to gender.

Computation of the chi-square test of independence using SPSS
To compute the test of independence we first have to enter the data in the computer. The way in which this will be done depends on whether we have listed data, that is, individual responses, or tabular data, data set in a table. It is therefore important that we consider these two methods separately.

SPSS for tabular data
Given that in Example C we have tabular data, we use Method II above to enter the data in the PC. The first column is named Ideology with two values (1 for liberal and 2 for conservative); the second column is named Gender and has been assigned two values (1 for males and 2 for females). The third column contains the figures we call Count. After having entered the data into the computer, we proceed as follows:

1   Choose **Statistics > Summarise > Crosstabs**
2   Transfer Ideology to the **Rows** box
3   Transfer Gender to the **Columns** box
4   Choose **Data > Weight cases**
5   Activate **Weight cases by** box
6   Transfer Count to **Frequency variable** box
7   Click on **OK**
8   Click on **Statistics**
9   Click on the square in front of **Chi-square**
10 Click on **OK** to move to the next window and then click on **OK** again

These instructions generate information which is beyond what you may need at this stage. Apart from reproducing the table we started with (above), the computer shows the chi-square value, degrees of freedom and the significance level. The important information is in the last part of the display, which is reproduced below.

	Chi-Square Value	DF	Significance
Pearson	10.66640	1	.00109
Continuity Correction	9.75905	1	.00178
Likelihood Ratio	10.76660	1	.00103
Mantel Haenszel test for linear association	10.61307	1	.00112

Minimum Expected Frequency - 45.500

The information we are interested in at this stage is in the first line of the output, namely Pearson's chi-square value and its significance. The chi-square value is 10.66640 (the same as that computed by hand) and the level of significance is 0.00109. If we were to use only one piece of information from the display, this would have been the significance. If the chi-square is significant (less than 0.05) we reject the hypothesis. The actual chi-square value is of little importance. For our example, these data suggest that we can reject the null hypothesis of no differences, and argue that the differences in the observed data are significant.

SPSS for listed (ungrouped) data
In most cases, data come in a raw form from surveys or other methods of data collection, as a part of the matrix, and are already in the computer. They are set in columns and can be picked up by the researcher in any form of analysis, for significance tests, correlational analysis or other tests. What we need to know is that in such cases, data will consist of 'values', such as 1 and 2 (for males and females), 1, 2 and 3 (for positive, neutral and negative), and so on. The computer will then process the data and produce the desired values.

If we have to enter the data into the computer first we do so by naming the variables and setting their values and value labels; these are ideology and gender, and the values are 1 (liberal) and 2 (conservative) for the former, and 1 (male) and 2 (female) for the latter. Then we enter the respective values in columns, as shown earlier in this volume. To compute the chi-square, we proceed as follows:

1 Choose **Statistics > Summarise > Crosstabs**
2 Transfer Ideology to the **Rows** box
3 Transfer Gender to the **Columns** box
4 Click on **Statistics**
5 Click on the square in front of **Chi-square**
6 Click on **OK** to move to the next window and then click on **OK** again

This is a less cumbersome way than the one employed for tabular data. Still, the results are the same. The figures shown in the computer display are identical to those reproduced above. Obviously, the computer operates the same way in both cases; only the entry of data and their preparation for processing vary.

The φ coefficient and Cramer's V

The chi-square tests we examined above offer information about whether the obtained data and their differences are significant, or whether the variables in question are related to each other. However, chi-square values depend very much on the size of the sample, making it difficult for the researcher to determine whether differences in the results are due to the nature of the relationship between the variables or due to sample size. To demonstrate the strength of the relationship as well as to show whether differences are due to sample size, two measures are commonly employed: the φ (read phi) coefficient and Cramer's *V*.

The range of the values of these measures is between 0 (no association) and 1 (perfect association). This is more true for Cramer's *V* than for the φ coefficient, which, when it relates to tables larger than 2×2, can achieve values greater than 1. For this reason, φ is restricted to 2×2 tables only.

These two measures are almost identical, with Cramer's *V* being an extension of φ. For 2×2 tables they produce identical results. For this reason, and also given that φ can effectively be used with 2×2 tables only, Cramer's *V* is commonly used. However, since both measures are used together in SPSS, in the following discussion we shall briefly consider both of them.

The φ coefficient

This is computed by means of Formula (18.6) below and is interpreted according to the value of its coefficient, which for 2×2 tables ranges from 0 to 1. If the value of the coefficient is close to 0, the strength of the relationship is fairly weak; if it is about 0.4 to 0.7 it is moderate; and if it is above 0.8 it is strong or very strong.

$$\phi = \sqrt{\frac{\chi^2}{N}}$$

(18.6)

Substituting the value of chi-square obtained above (Example C) in Formula (18.6) we obtain:

$$\phi = \sqrt{\frac{10.66}{200}} = \sqrt{0.0533} = 0.23$$

This suggests that the strength of the relationship between gender and social orientation is fairly weak.

Cramer's V
This is another measure of the strength of relationship between variables employed with tables having two rows but several columns. This measure (also known as Cramer's ϕ) is computed by means of Formula (18.7):

$$\text{Cramer's } V = \sqrt{\frac{\chi^2}{N(k-1)}} \qquad (18.7)$$

where k is the number of rows or columns, whichever is the smaller. For instance, if in a table there were 3 rows and 4 columns, k would be 3 (since it is smaller than 4); if there were 6 rows and 4 columns, k would be 4.

Let us now employ V in an example. In a study of 120 subjects chi-square was found to be 21.36; if the table had 2 columns and 3 rows, Cramer's V would be as follows:

$$\text{Cramer's } V = \sqrt{\frac{10.66}{200(2-1)}} = \sqrt{\frac{10.66}{200}} = 0.0533 = 0.23$$

Here as well as in ϕ the coefficient is interpreted rather liberally, without strict adherence to the guidelines applied in other measures of association. Statisticians (e.g. Argyrous, 1996: 321) advise that there is no direct interpretation of values between 0 and 1, suggesting that the only indication we can obtain from these coefficients is that if they are below 0.1 they are very weak.

SPSS for the ϕ coefficient and Cramer's V
The computation of the ϕ coefficient and Cramer's V is the same as the computation of chi-square. While calculating chi-square we instruct the computer to compute the value of ϕ coefficients as well. The computation entails the following steps:

1 Choose **Statistics > Summarise > Crosstabs**
2 Transfer Ideology to the **Rows** box
3 Transfer Gender to the **Columns** box
4 Click on **Statistics**
5 Click on the square in front of **Chi-square**
6 Click on **Phi and Cramer's V**
7 Click on **OK** to move to the next window and then click on **OK** again

Using data from Example C, we obtain the following values:

	Chi-Square Value	DF	Significance
Pearson	10.66640	1	.00109
Continuity Correction	9.75905	1	.00178
Likelihood Ratio	10.76660	1	.00103
Mantel-Haenszel test for linear association	10.61307	1	.00112

Minimum Expected Frequency - 45.500

Statistics	Value	ASE1	Val/ASE0	Approximate significance
Phi	.23094			.00109 *1
Cramer's V	.23094			.00109 *1

*1 Pearson chi-square probability
Number of missing values 0

The figures given in the above display are self-explanatory. In addition to the information obtained previously when computing the chi-square, this display offers information for the ϕ coefficient and for Cramer's *V*. Both values are the same, and so is their significance, which is high indeed.

The z-test for a single proportion

The *z*-test for proportions is similar to the chi-square test, with one basic difference, namely that it is used for data expressed in proportions. It mainly deals with the question of whether the differences between proportions are significant. H_o states that there is no difference between the proportions and the differences shown in the data are not significant.

The value of *z* (when $N < 30$) is computed by means of Formula (18.8) and its value is interpreted as in the chi-square test, with the difference that here reference is made to the normal curve table. If *z* is equal to or larger than the critical value, H_o is rejected.

$$z = \frac{(P_{sa} -/+ 0.005) - P_{po}}{\sqrt{\dfrac{P_{po}(1 - P_{po})}{N}}} \qquad \textbf{(18.8)}$$

P_{sa} indicates the proportion of the sample;
P_{po} indicates the proportion of the population;
−/+ means that we can use either sign, depending on the relationship between the proportions:

- If the proportion of the sample is larger than the proportion of the population we use the minus sign $(P_{sa} > P_{po} = -)$.

• If the proportion of the sample is smaller than the proportion of the population we use the plus sign ($P_{sa} < P_{po} = +$).

Let us see how this works in an example.

Example E: A university lecturer is of the opinion that the proportion of students using SPSS in his university is much smaller than that of other Australian universities (this is reported to be 15 per cent). To determine the proportion of students using SPSS, the lecturer interviewed all 86 students of the research class and found that 19 students (i.e. 22 per cent) were using SPSS. Does this mean that the proportion of students using SPSS in his university is larger than that of other universities? *z* can help us to answer this question.

H_o states that there is no difference between the proportions of social research students using SPSS at this and other universities. To determine the value of z, we employ Formula (18.8); since the sample proportion (22 per cent) is larger than the population proportion (15 per cent) we employ the formula with the minus (−) sign in front of 0.005. Substituting for the proportions and the sample size in the formula we find:

$$z = \frac{(0.22 - 0.005) - 0.15}{\sqrt{\dfrac{0.15(1 - 0.15)}{86}}} = \frac{0.065}{\sqrt{\dfrac{0.1275}{86}}} = \frac{0.065}{0.0385032} = 1.688$$

Having established the value of z, we proceed as in chi-square tests. The critical value for the 0.05 significance level ($\alpha = 0.05$) is +1.64. Since the value of z is greater than its critical value, we can reject H_o. This means that the difference between the proportions is significant and that the proportion of students at the new university using SPSS is larger than that of other universities.

Computing the z-test for a single proportion using SPSS

Computing the z-test value using computers is quicker and easier. The steps to follow are shown below. Remember to set the data in the computer in one column. The name of the variable can be SPSSUSER; the values can be 1 for SPSS users and 2 for non-users. The computer will count those marked with 1, will compute the proportion and compare it to that of the population. Let us now look at the steps:

1 Choose **Statistics > Non-parametric tests > Binomial**
2 Transfer SPSSUSER to the **Test Variable List** box
3 Type 0.15 in the **Test Proportion** box over the existing number
4 Click on **OK**

The computer responds with the following display:

```
- — — — - Binomial Test

  SPSSUSER Students Using SPSS

  Cases
                                      Test Prop. =.1500
         19 = 1.00                    Obs. Prop. =.2209
         67 = 2.00
         —                            Z Approximation
         86    Total                  1-Tailed P =.0454
```

The information that is important for us is at the bottom of the display, which shows that p is equal to 0.0454. Since p is less than the alpha 0.05, we can reject H_o.

4 Ordinal-level tests

The number of ordinal tests of significance are as many and diverse as the significance tests for the nominal level. They vary mainly according to the number of samples they relate to as well as the type of samples, that is, whether they are dependent or independent. Examples of these tests are presented in Table 18.3.

Table 18.3 Ordinal-level tests of significance

Number of samples	Type of samples	Significance tests
One sample	N/A	Kolmogorov–Smirnov test
Two samples	Independent	Wald–Wolfowitz runs test
		Mann–Whitney *U*-test
	Dependent	Sign test
		Wilcoxon test
k samples	Independent	Kruskal–Wallis *H*-test
	Dependent	Friedman test

Ordinal-level tests are not used as frequently as nominal and interval/ratio tests in the social sciences. For this reason, in this section only a brief description of these tests will be given. In this description an attempt will be made to demonstrate the main characteristics of the tests, where and how they are employed and how to interpret their findings.

a   The Kolmogorov–Smirnov test

This is an ordinal-level, one-sample test employed when the researcher is interested to know about the relationship between the data and the expected values, and more generally about whether the observed values reflect the values of a specific distribution of the population. In this sense this is a goodness-of-fit test similar to the chi-square test.

The test is computed and interpreted in a similar way to the chi-square goodness-of-fit test; it is basically computed from the observed and expected values. However, from these values this test calculates the cumulative values of both observed and expected values, subtracts the latter from the former, selects the largest absolute difference between the two, and compares the value of the difference with the critical value from a special table developed for this test. If the difference is equal to or larger than that value, the difference is significant and H_0 is rejected. Selection of the level of significance takes place as in other tests.

Simply, D (the test value) is significant if H_0 is rejected, and H_0 is rejected if D is equal to or greater than the critical value.

b   The Mann–Whitney U-test

This test is suitable for answering the question about whether two samples have the same distribution, that is, whether they come from the same population. It has the following characteristics:

- It is a non-parametric test (perhaps the most powerful).
- It requires two independent samples (drawn independently).
- It tests the null hypothesis about the identity of population distributions.
- It is an ordinal-level test.

The test produces two values (U_1 and U_2). The interpretation of these values follows the already known steps of testing significance, namely the comparison of the test values with the critical values of this measure. Since the U-test produces two values we shall also have to undertake two comparisons. The critical values are obtained by locating N_1 and N_2 in the table; their intersection is the critical value.

c   The sign test

This is a popular test and is appropriate:

- for ordinally scaled data;
- for data that were collected by means of two samples;
- when the samples are related (randomly selected and matched); and
- when the difference between the central tendency of the two samples is tested.

H_0 asserts that there is no difference between the two sets of data. The sign test will, on the basis of the computed values, indicate whether H_0 will be accepted or rejected.

d The Wilcoxon test

This test is similar to the sign test employed when the significance of the difference between two samples is tested. In addition to considering the sign of the difference, it also takes into account the strength or magnitude of the difference. In this sense the Wilcoxon test is more powerful than the sign test.

Because this test deals with matched pairs and because it uses the sign to determine the significance of the difference, it is usually referred to as the Wilcoxon matched-pairs-sign-ranks test.

This test has the following characteristics:

- It is an ordinal-level test of significance.
- It relates to data of two related (matched) samples.
- It tests the direction and degree of difference between samples.
- It relates to differences of central tendencies.

H_o states that there is no difference between the scores obtained before and after exposure to the stimulus. The alternative hypothesis can be either that there is a difference between the scores (two-tail test), or that the scores after exposure to the stimulus will be higher than the scores prior to exposure (one-tail test). This test is employed if N is less than 25. If N is larger than 25 a version of the z-test is employed.

e The Kruskal–Wallis H-test

This test demonstrates the following characteristics:

- It is an ordinal-level test.
- It presents a one-way analysis of variance.
- It links together k (i.e. more than two) samples.
- It deals with independent samples.

The null hypotheses states that there are no differences between the samples, namely that all samples come from the same population. To determine whether H_o is true, we employ the procedure discussed in the chi-square test. To reject H_o, Kruskal–Wallis H must be *equal to or larger than* the critical value.

f The Friedman test

This test is also known as the Friedman two-way analysis of variance test, or the Friedman test for k samples. It is characterised by the fact that:

- it is an ordinal-level test;
- it is employed when samples are matched; and
- it can be used when k (more than two) samples are considered.

This test answers the question about whether matched subjects respond differently to different types of treatment. The test value is χ_r^2. The interpretation of this value follows the steps already discussed in the previous section. The test value is compared with the critical values in the chi-square table and if it is *equal to or larger than* the critical value, H_o is rejected.

5   Computing ordinal-level tests using SPSS

Although the computation of ordinal-level tests is simple and straightforward, it is also menial and time consuming. For this reason, researchers use electronic means to compute them. Most computer statistical packages — including SPSS — have facilities for dealing with ordinal-level variables, and the computation is simple, accurate and quick.

The instructions presented below will guide you to the specific measures in your SPSS. Given that the number of measures is large and the procedures employed to compute their values are similar if not identical, in this section we shall not show how each measure is computed individually but rather where to look for the relevant measures. It is assumed that by now you will have developed the skills required to follow the computer's instructions, which in all cases are self-explanatory.

The SPSS groups the measures introduced in this section under the general name of *non-parametric tests*. Consequently the path you need to follow to find these measures is **Statistics > Nonparametric tests**. When you click on Nonparametric tests a list of measures is displayed containing the following: chi-square, binomial, runs, one-sample K–S, 2 independent variables, *k* independent variables, 2 related samples and *k* related samples. Each of these items contains one or more of the tests introduced in this section. A list of these tests per list item is given below:

List items	Non-parametric tests
Chi-square . . .	Chi-square test
Binomial . . .	Binomial test
Runs . . .	Runs test
One sample K–S . . .	One sample Kolmogorov–Smirnov test
2 independent variables . . .	Mann–Whitney *U*; Wald–Wolfowitz, Kolmogorov–Smirnov *Z*, etc.
k independent samples . . .	Kruskal–Wallis *H*; Median
2 related samples . . .	Wilcoxon; Sign; McNemar
k related samples . . .	Friedman; Kendall's *W*; Cochran's *Q*

This list shows where to find each test and how to address it. For instance, McNemar test is in the 2-related-samples group; consequently the path to this test is **Statistics > Nonparametric tests > 2 related samples > McNemar**. In a similar fashion, the path you will use to get to Friedman's test is **Statistics > Nonparametric tests > k related samples > Friedman**. From there, you only need to follow the program instructions.

6   Interval/ratio-level tests

Having introduced the nominal-level and ordinal-level tests of significance, we now direct our attention to the interval/ratio-level tests. In these sections we shall discuss the most common interval/ratio-level tests. They are also called *parametric tests of significance* and they are based on the assumption that populations are normally distributed, employing the notion of the normal curve. Table 18.4 displays the interval/ratio significance tests that will be presented or referred to below, arranged according to the number of types of samples tested.

Table 18.4   Interval/ratio-level significance tests

Number of samples	Type of samples	Significance tests
One sample	N/A	*t*-test
Two samples	Independent	*t*-test
	Dependent	*t*-test
k samples	Independent	Simple ANOVA
	Dependent	Multiple ANOVA

Obviously, the only two (and most common) tests to be considered are the *t*-test and the analysis of variance (ANOVA). We will discuss these in the following sections, beginning with the *t*-test.

7   The *t*-test

The *t*-test is a very popular and useful test. In the past, a *t*-test was used primarily for small samples; for large samples the *z*-test was used. At the present time statisticians use the *t*-test for both small and large samples indiscriminately (Argyrous, 1996: 223). Its main characteristics are shown below:

- It is an interval/ratio test.
- It is a parametric test.
- It is employed when one or two samples are considered.
- It is employed when parameters are unknown.

T-tests can be employed for single samples and for two samples. In the former, test statistics are compared to population parameters. In the latter, the *t*-test tests the significance of differences between statistics of two samples: *independent* or *dependent* samples. More specifically, in one-sample tests, the *t*-test compares the sample mean with the population mean. In two-sample tests, the means of the two samples are compared. In the following we will consider single-sample and two-sample *t*-tests in turn.

a   The one-sample *t*-test

As the name indicates, when this test is employed we only have one sample to work with. In such cases, a single-sample *t*-test compares the sample mean and the population mean and tests whether there is a significance difference between them. Let us see a few examples.

Example E: The equal opportunity officer of a university wanted to check whether women are employed in high-level positions as much as in other institutions. She examined the university records using salary as a measure. Do women in this institution earn on average as much as women in other institutions? From existing information she knows that women in tertiary institutions earn on average $55 000 per year. An examination of the university records shows that at the university in question women earn $52 000 annually. Is the difference significant? A *t*-test will help answer this question.

Example F: Similarly, a local real estate agent argues that houses in his town are on average lower in value than houses in NSW. He knows that the average price of a three bedroom house in NSW is $135 000, and that the average price of a house in his town is $131 000. Are houses in that community cheaper than in other parts of NSW? Is the numerical difference between the two prices (means) significant?

Let us take another example, and also apply a *t*-test to show how the significance of the difference in such cases is tested.

Example G: A sociology lecturer suspects that female sociology students at a country university are more conservative than their counterparts at other Australian universities. To test this hypothesis she surveys the 26 female students in the third-year sociology class by employing the conservatism scale and obtains the following scores: 3.8, 3.9, 3.9, 4, 4, 4, 4.4, 4.5, 4.8, 5, 5.4, 5.6, 5.8, 5.9, 5.9, 6, 6.3, 6.6, 6.9, 6.9, 6.9, 7.1, 7.4, 7.8, 7.9, 7.9. The mean score is 5.715 and the standard deviation (*s*) is 1.384. Given that the average conservatism score for sociology students at other universities is 4.4, can the lecturer conclude that female sociology students at the country university are more conservative than other female sociology students?

The *t* will help us to answer this question. To calculate the *t*-value we employ Formula (18.9):

$$t = \frac{\bar{x} - \mu}{\dfrac{s}{\sqrt{N-1}}}$$
    (18.9)

With $\bar{x} = 5.715$, $\mu = 4.4$, $s = 1.384$, and $N = 26$ the value of t will be:

$$t = \frac{\bar{x} - \mu}{\frac{s}{\sqrt{N-1}}} = \frac{5.715 - 4.4}{\frac{1.384}{\sqrt{26-1}}} = \frac{1.315}{\frac{1.384}{5}} = \frac{1.315}{0.2768} = 4.75$$

The value of μ is generally hypothesised or derived theoretically.

Interpretation of t

The t-value is tested in the context of the table of t distribution. The relevant table value is located by means of alpha and the degrees of freedom. The latter is computed using the formula $N - 1$. If alpha is 0.05 and the degrees of freedom 25 ($26 - 1 = 25$), for a one-tail test the table value is 1.708. The null hypothesis states that there is no significant difference between the sample mean and the population mean (here 4.4). If the value of t is equal to or larger than the table value, H_o is rejected. Since 4.75 is greater than 1.708, H_o is rejected. This means that there is a significant difference between the two means, and that country female sociology students are more conservative than female sociology students at other universities.

b   Computing one-sample *t*-test using SPSS

To compute the one-sample t-test we proceed as follows:

> **1** Enter the data in the PC in one column and name it (e.g. 'Conserv'
>   — the variable label is Conservatism)
> **2** Choose **Statistics > Compare means > One-sample T Test**
> **3** Transfer Conserv to the **Test variable(s)** box
> **4** Type 4.4 in the box next to **Test Value** (this is the population mean
>   we use as the basis for comparison)
> **5** Click on **OK**

The computer responds with the following display:

```
One Sample t-tests


                           Number
Variable                   of Cases  Mean     SD      SE of Mean

CONSERV Conservatism 26              5.7154   1.384   .271


Test Value = 4.40

Mean            95%      CI      |
Difference      Lower    Upper   |    t-value   df    2-Tail Sig

1.32            .756     1.874   |    4.85      25    .000
```

This display contains more than we asked for. The figures that are most important for us are the *t*-value (4.85) and the two-tail significance (0.000). They are almost identical to those computed manually above. These figures indicate the following: (1) that the p value (0.000) is less than the alpha value (0.05) and therefore we can reject the null hypothesis; and (2) that the differences between the means are significant. Hence, the conservatism score of female rural sociology students is different from that of their other Australian counterparts.

Equally useful is the information provided by the 95% confidence intervals; in our example the interval limits are: lower = 0.756 and upper = 1.874. Since this interval does not contain 0, we can reject the null hypothesis that there is no difference between the means of the groups in question. Hence it is reasonable to assume that female country students are more conservative than female students at other universities. (An interval that includes 0 is one that has one negative and one positive limit.)

c   The two-sample *t*-test

Equally common are *t*-tests for two samples; in these tests the researcher checks the differences between the means of two samples. Two such types of tests are: one referring to independent samples and one to dependent samples. *Dependent samples* are also referred to as paired samples or matched samples; their characteristic is that they include pairs of data referring to the same person or to twins or matched subjects, for instance when a subject was tested before and after a stimulus or early in the morning and late in the afternoon. The *t*-test is expected to test the differences between each pair of data. *Independent samples* are those which include individual subjects (not pairs) chosen randomly, for instance when mean scores of males and females, students of morning classes and evening classes or religious and non-religious students are compared. We begin with the *t*-test for independent samples.

The t-*test for independent (unrelated) samples*
The following are the main characteristics of this test:

- It is a parametric test.
- It is an interval/ratio test.
- It refers to two independent samples.
- It tests the differences between means.
- Knowledge of population parameters is not required.

This test employs Formula (18.10):

$$t = \frac{\bar{x}_1 - \bar{x}_2}{\sqrt{\dfrac{S_1^2}{N_1} + \dfrac{S_2^2}{N_2}}} \qquad\qquad (18.10)$$

Example H: A researcher was interested in the study habits of first-year students, and particularly the hours male and female students studied on Sundays. A survey of 22 male and 22 female students was conducted in which the respondents were asked to state how many hours they studied on Sundays. The results are given below. The descriptive statistics which were computed for both groups show that the mean and standard deviation are 6.455 and 2.405 for female students and 3.045 and 1.43 for male students respectively. Can we argue that on average females studied longer during the specified times than males? Is the difference between the two means significant? The *t*-test will help us answer this question.

| | Scores | |
Males	Females	Descriptive statistics
8	3	
9	4	
9	3	
7	2	$\bar{x}_1 = 6.2727$ *(for males)*
6	4	
7	5	$\bar{x}_2 = 3.2727$ *(for females)*
7	1	
5	3	$s_1 = 2.5853$ *(for males)*
10	2	
8	2	$s_2 = 1.6383$ *(for females)*
9	7	
10	4	$N_1 = 22$ *(for males)*
8	3	
5	2	$N_2 = 22$ *(for females)*
5	7	
5	2	
3	3	
4	5	
3	2	
2	1	
1	4	
7	3	

Computing t

Substituting our values in Formula (18.10) we obtain:

$$t = \frac{6.2727 - 3.2727}{\sqrt{\dfrac{2.5853^2}{22} + \dfrac{1.6383^2}{22}}} = \frac{3}{\sqrt{0.4258092}}$$

$$= \frac{3}{0.6525405} = 4.5974157; \text{ or } 4.60$$

Interpretation of t

What does $t = 4.60$ mean? To answer this question we compare the t-value with the critical values of t, which can be found in the t sampling distribution table. For this, we need the alpha and degrees of freedom. Alpha is set at the 0.05 level; df can be computed by means of Formula (18.11):

$$df = (N_1 - 1) + (N_2 - 1) \qquad\qquad \textbf{(18.11)}$$

Substituting the values for N_1 and N_2 in Formula (18.11):

$$df = (22 - 1) + (22 - 1) = 21 + 21 = 42$$

Given that there is no critical value for 42 degrees of freedom, we take the one below it (40 df). The corresponding critical value for 40 df and for an alpha of 0.01 is 2.424. Since the t-value is larger than the critical value (4.60 > 2.424), we can reject H_o and state that there is a statistically significant difference between the length of study of male and female students on Sundays. Liberally interpreted this means that it is reasonable to assume that on average males study longer than females on Sundays.

Computing t for Independent samples using SPSS

The data will be entered in the computer as shown in the table below. To save space we set the data in several columns. You must set them in two columns only, one for gender and one for hours of study. Gender has two values and value labels (1 for male and 2 for female); the other variable requires no values and value labels.

Hours of Sunday study by gender of respondents

Gender	Hours	Gender	Hours	Gender	Hours	Gender	Hours
1	8	1	10	1	3	1	7
1	9	1	8	2	1	2	3
2	3	1	9	1	4	2	2
1	9	1	10	2	3	2	7
1	7	1	8	2	2	2	2
1	6	2	2	1	3	2	3
1	7	1	5	2	2	2	5
1	7	1	5	2	7	2	2
2	4	2	4	1	2	2	1
1	5	1	5	1	1	2	4
2	3	2	5	2	4	2	3

After entering the data in the computer (two column and 44 rows), we are ready to begin with the computation. To compute the t-value using SPSS we proceed as follows:

1 Choose **Statistics > Compare means > Independent samples *t*-test**
2 Transfer Hours to the **Test variable** box, and Gender to the **Grouping variable** box
3 Click on the **Define** group box
4 Type 1 in the Group 1 box, and 2 in the Group 2 box (since the grouping variable has two values, 1 and 2)
5 Click on **Continue**
6 Click on **OK**

After clicking on OK (step 6 above), the computer displays the following data:

```
t-tests for independent samples of GENDER Gender of
students

                            Number
Variable                    of Cases Mean    SD     SE of Mean

HOURS Sunday study hours
male                          22        6.2727 2.585 .551
female                        22        3.2727 1.638 .349

Mean Difference = 3.0000
Levene's Test for Equality of Variances: F= 6.285 P= .016
t-test for Equality of Means                        95%

Variances  t-value df    2-Tail Sig SE of Diff CI for Diff

Equal      4.60    42     .000       .653       (1.683,4.317)
Unequal    4.60    35.52 .000        .653       (1.676,4.324)
```

There is a lot of information in these lines, but the points you must consider first are those related to the following questions: What is the *t*-value? Is there a difference between the means? Is this difference significant? The answers to these questions are contained in the data displayed on the screen:

1 The *t*-value is 4.60 (last two lines, second column). Note that it is the same as that computed manually and shown above.
2 The mean difference is 3.0000 and this is relatively large.
3 The level of significance of this difference is given in the last two lines of the display. One line is for equal variables and the other for unequal variances. In our case, the level of significance is the same for equal and unequal variances but in many instances they are not. Which one should we take for our study?

The answer to this question depends on the results of Levene's test for Equality of Variances given above in the display. If the p value is below 0.05 we reject the hypothesis that the variances are equal, and therefore consider our samples to have unequal variances. If the p value of Levene's test is over 0.05, we cannot reject the hypothesis of equality of variances and assume that the variances of our samples are equal. Given that our p is less than 0.05, we reject H_o and assume that our samples have unequal variances.

In practical terms, what really counts is not the numerical value of the *t* but rather its level of significance. Consequently, if we need to obtain a quick answer to the question about the significance of the difference between the means, we only need to consider the 'Two-tail sig' column in the last two lines: the values of significance contained in this column are interpreted as in any other hypothesis-testing procedure discussed in the context of other tests of significance.

In the past, when most computations were made by hand different tests were employed for samples with equal and unequal distributions. As you see from the computer display above, computer programs make computations not only quick and reliable but also give values for both types of tests.

The t-test for two dependent (related) samples

The *t*-test discussed above is employed when data have been obtained through studies employing independent samples. When the samples are dependent, paired or matched, other tests are employed to test the differences between the means. The *t*-test for dependent samples demonstrates the following characteristics:

- It is an interval/ratio test.
- It is a parametric test.
- It studies two samples.
- It tests the data of two matched samples.
- It tests the difference between raw scores.

The computational formula of this form of *t* is as follows:

$$t = \frac{\Sigma D / N}{\sqrt{\dfrac{\Sigma D^2 - ((\Sigma D)^2 / N)}{N(N - 1)}}} \tag{18.12}$$

where ΣD stands for the sum of the differences between the paired scores, $(\Sigma D)^2$ the square of the sum of the differences and ΣD^2 the sum of the squared differences. Let us demonstrate this test in one example.

Example 1: A social scientist argues that personal experience can change the attitudes of people towards minority groups such as homosexuals. To test this assumption 10 students are selected randomly; their attitude towards homosexuality is measured and the pre-test scores recorded. Subsequently, the subjects are introduced to a group of homosexual activists, who in the context of a national campaign were lobbying in favour of relevant law reforms. During this meeting, which lasted for 4 hours, the 10 subjects had an opportunity to talk to homosexuals and to discuss with them some issues they considered to be crucial. A day after the confrontation, a test was conducted and the results recorded (post-test). The question here is whether there is a difference between the two sets of scores, that is, whether the attitudes of the students have changed or not. The null hypothesis suggests that there is no difference between the scores. To test this a table is set up as described below.

Computation of *t*-test for related samples

Students	Pre-test scores	Post-test scores	D	D²
1	15	13	2	4
2	12	10	2	4
3	22	21	1	1
4	11	8	3	9
5	25	24	1	1
6	18	17	1	1
7	26	25	1	1
8	10	9	1	1
9	11	7	4	16
10	13	11	2	4
			$\Sigma D = 18$	$\Sigma D^2 = 42$

To compute *t* the procedure is as follows:

1 The table containing the pre-test scores and the post-test scores is set up (see Example I above).
2 The differences between the individual scores of each subject (D) are computed, the differences are squared (D^2) and the differences and squares of the differences ($\Sigma D)^2$ are summed up.
3 The numerator and the denominator of Formula (18.12) are computed separately and the relevant values obtained as shown below. The value of the numerator is:

$$\frac{\Sigma D}{N} = \frac{18}{10} = 1.8$$

Substituting our values for D, D^2 and N in the denominator of Formula (18.12), we obtain:

$$\sqrt{\frac{42 - \frac{18^2}{10}}{10(10-1)}} = \sqrt{\frac{42 - \frac{324}{10}}{10(10-1)}} = \sqrt{\frac{42 - 32.4}{90}} = \sqrt{\frac{9.6}{90}} = \sqrt{0.107} = 0.3271$$

Substituting these values into Formula (18.12):

$$t = \frac{1.8}{0.3271} = 5.5029; \text{ or } 5.51$$

Interpretation of t

The *t*-value is assessed in the context of the *t*-table. In order to ascertain the critical value of *t*, alpha and the degrees of freedom are needed; they are computed using the formula $N - 1$. Hence $df = 10 - 1 = 9$. Thus the critical value of *t* for 9 *df* and at a 0.05 level is 2.262 (two-tail test). As a rule, if the value of *t* is equal to or larger than the critical value, *t* is significant and H_o is rejected. Since $5.45 > 2.262$, the null hypothesis is rejected; this means that there is a significant difference between the scores obtained before and after the contact with the external stimulus.

Computing the t-*value for paired samples using SPSS*

The steps employed for independent samples applies also for paired samples, with some differences. One point you must keep in mind is that data are entered in two columns in pairs. While in the previous example we put all scores in one column and all respondents in the other, here we put scores in each column, one for 'before' and one for 'after'. The main steps are as follows:

1 Choose **Statistics > Compare means > Paired samples t-test**
2 Click on both variables, one after the other and then transfer them to the **Paired variables** box
3 Click on **Options**
4 Set Confidence interval to 95%
5 Click on **Continue**
6 Click on **OK**

This will generate the following screen display:

```
- - - t-tests for paired samples - - -
```

Variable	Number of pairs	Corr	2-tail Sig	Mean	SD	SE of Mean
AFTER				16.3000	6.075	1.921
	10	.993	.000			
BEFORE				14.5000	6.770	2.141

Paired Differences						
Mean	SD	SE of Mean		t-value	df	2-tail Sig
1.8000	1.033	.327		5.51	9	.000
95% CI (1.061, 2.539)						

The interpretation here is similar to that of independent samples. The vital information is given in the last two lines and especially the figures on the right-hand side of the display: the *t*-value is 5.51 and with 9 degrees of freedom it is significant at the 0.000 level. Hence, H_o that the means are equal is rejected. Consequently, the differences between the means are significant. The scores obtained after they were subjected to the stimulus were significantly higher than those obtained before the stimulus.

8   Analysis of variance (ANOVA)

This is one of the most powerful and most common tests employed in the social sciences and is suitable for interval/ratio-level distributions. It is known either as analysis of variance or as the *F*-test and is used as a simple factorial, general factorial or multivariate factorial test; these tests are also known as single or one-way (when one criterion is used), as two-way (when two criteria are used), or as *N*-way (factorial) analysis (when more criteria are used). It is called the *F*-test after its creator, Sir R. D. Fisher.

ANOVA is similar to the *t*-test. The main characteristic and the advantage of the *F*-test over other tests is that it is employed when more than two variables are studied. It is a parsimonious test, that is, a single test that produces results which would otherwise have required several tests. For instance, if we were to compare eight ethnic groups to identify eventual differences in their attitudes to monarchy, and used *t*-tests, we would have needed 28 tests (number of tests = $N(N-1)/2 = 8(8-1)/2 = 56/2 = 28$). These comparisons could be facilitated by means of one *F*-test only.

a   Conditions of ANOVA

ANOVA is employed if certain conditions are met. Three such conditions are independence, normality and homogeneity of variance, as shown below:

1 *Independence*: that scores are independent from each other.
2 *Normality*: that scores are normally distributed.
3 *Homogeneity*: that variances are equal.

As stated above there are several types of ANOVA. The two most common are *one-way* and *two-way* ANOVA. The nature and use of these two types of ANOVA will be explained below. But before we begin the discussion, it is important that their concepts are clarified.

One-way analysis of variance is employed when there is one independent variable (factor) and one dependent. The independent variable is a qualitative variable (males, females; ethnic groups, marital status, etc.); the dependent variable is a quantitative variable. There are two variables, but we are looking at whether the sample groups vary systematically in one way, or with regard to one aspect only. Examples of such variable arrangements in one-way analysis of variance are:

Qualitative independent variable	Quantitative dependent variable
Factor: Does **marital status** .... *Levels:* single, married, divorced, etc.	affect **overall happiness** very happy, happy, unhappy, very unhappy
Factor: Does **gender** .... *Levels:* Male, female	affect level of **scholastic achievement?** very high, high, moderate, low, very low
Factor: Does **level of performance** .. *Levels:* HD, DI, CR, PS, FL	affect **educational aspirations?** very high, high, moderate, low, very low
Factor: Does **level of education** .... *Levels:* Primary, secondary, tertiary	affect level of **familism?** very high, high, moderate, low, very low

Again, the comparison relates to *two* variables but to *one* specific element (e.g. effects of marital status on overall happiness; effects of gender on scholastic achievement; effects of test performance on educational aspirations, and of education on familism).

A two-way analysis of variance includes two criteria of classification as well as two independent variables and one dependent variable. For instance, if we ask about the effects of education on familism this requires a one-way analysis of variance, but if we add gender as another independent variable and ask whether gender and education together (i.e. males with high and low education and females with high and low education) have an effect on familism, this requires a two-way analysis of variance. In a similar fashion, if we ask about the effects of social class on overall happiness we employ one-way analysis of variance; but if we relate social class and marital status to overall happiness we employ a two-way analysis of variance. In two-way analysis of variance we have two factors: in the first example these were gender and education; in the second example they were social class and marital status. Two-way analysis of variance is complex and requires more attention and therefore is beyond the scope of this text. We shall concentrate here only on the nature and computation of one-way analysis of variance.

b   Computing ANOVA

As stated above, a one-way analysis of variance is employed when there are two variables but one factor and a one-way classification. In technical terms, ANOVA works on the following *assumptions*:

- The *total variation* (*TV*) can be split into components, each of which has a certain source of variation; such components are the *within-sample variation* (*WV*) and the *between-samples variation* (*BV*), both of which make up the *total variation*. In statistical terms, $TV = WV + BV$.
- The samples are randomly selected.

- The population is normally distributed.
- The samples are independent.
- The samples have a common variance.

In its simple form, the *F*-test is computed using Formula (18.13):

$$F = \frac{\dfrac{BV}{k-1}}{\dfrac{WV}{k(n-1)}} \qquad (18.13)$$

where *BV* is the between-sample variation, *WV* the within-sample variation, *k* the number of categories, groups or samples, and *n* the number of respondents in the group (not the total sample). The computation of *F* proceeds as follows:

1 A table is set up with scores and squared scores for each group (see Example J below).
2 The sums for all columns (for scores and squared scores) are computed.
3 The total variation (*TV*) is computed, using Formula (18.14):

$$TV = \Sigma x^2 - \frac{(\Sigma x)^2}{N} \qquad (18.14)$$

The value of Σx^2 is obtained by adding up the squared scores of each group. The value of $(\Sigma x)^2$ is computed by squaring the sum of the scores of each group. *N* is the number of respondents in all the groups, that is, the sum of the respondents of all samples.
4 The within-sample variation (*WV*) is computed by employing the above formula for each group separately and adding up the scores for each group. Note that *N* here refers to the number of respondents in the group for which *WV* is computed. There will be as many *WV*s as there are groups in the study.

$$MV = \Sigma x^2 - \frac{(\Sigma x)^2}{n} \qquad (18.15)$$

5 The between-samples variation (*BV*) is computed using the following formula:

$$BV = TV - WV$$

6 *k* – 1, which is the *df* for *BV*, and *k*(*n* – 1), the *df* for *WV*, are computed. *k* stands for the number of groups or categories; *n* refers to the group size (not the total sample).
7 The values obtained above are substituted in Formula (18.13) to obtain the *F*-score.

Example J: A researcher is interested in the effectiveness of texts as learning instruments in tertiary institutions. To test this, five texts are chosen, each of which is assigned to a group of five students who were instructed to use the texts for the duration of the term. After the term, the members of these groups were tested and the results recorded; the results are as shown in the table below. Are the differences recorded in the tests significant?

The null hypothesis suggests that there are no differences. As in other tests, the aim of the *F*-test is to test the null hypothesis. To do this the *F*-statistic has first to be computed.

Test scores of five groups of students

Group A		Group B		Group C		Group D		Group E	
X_1	X_1^2	X_2	X_2^2	X_3	X_3^2	X_4	X_4^2	X_5	X_5^2
7	49	4	16	6	36	7	49	8	64
4	16	9	81	5	25	9	81	6	36
5	25	3	9	4	16	8	64	7	49
4	16	5	25	6	36	7	49	9	81
6	36	5	25	6	36	7	49	9	81

$\Sigma x_1 = 26$; $\Sigma x_1^2 = 142$; $\Sigma x_2 = 26$; $\Sigma x_2^2 = 156$; $\Sigma x_3 = 27$; $\Sigma x_3^2 = 149$; $\Sigma x_4 = 38$; $\Sigma x_4^2 = 292$; $\Sigma x_5 = 39$ $\Sigma x_5^2 = 311$

Application of the F-test to Example J

Let us employ this procedure in our example. The relevant steps are as follows:

1 A table is established with scores and squares of scores (see Example J).
2 The means of scores and squared scores are computed.
3 *TV* is computed:

$$TV = 1050 - \frac{24\,336}{25} = 1050 - 973.44 = 76.56$$

4 The values of *WV* are computed for the five groups:
   For *A*:

$$WV = 142 - \frac{26^2}{5} - 142 - \frac{676}{5} = 142 - 135.2 = 6.8$$

   For *B*:

$$WV = 156 - \frac{26^2}{5} = 156 - \frac{676}{5} = 156 - 135.2 = 20.8$$

   For *C*:

$$WV = 149 - \frac{27^2}{5} = 149 - \frac{729}{5} = 149 - 145.8 = 3.2$$

For D:

$$WV = 292 - \frac{38^2}{5} = 292 - \frac{1444}{5} = 292 - 288.8 = 3.2$$

For E:

$$WV = 311 - \frac{39^2}{5} = 311 - \frac{1521}{5} = 311 - 304.2 = 6.8$$

Thus:

$$WV = 6.8 + 20.8 + 3.2 + 3.2 + 6.8 = 40.8$$

5 BV is computed:

$$BV = TV - WV = 76.56 - 40.8 = 35.76$$

6 $k-1$ and $k(n-1)$ are computed:

$$k - 1 = 5 - 1 = 4; \quad k(n - 1) = 5(5 - 1) = 20$$

7 F is computed by substituting the above values in Formula (18.13):

$$F = \frac{\dfrac{BV}{k-1}}{\dfrac{WV}{k(n-1)}} = \frac{\dfrac{35.76}{4}}{\dfrac{40.8}{20}} = \frac{8.94}{2.04} = 4.3824$$

The values obtained from the above computations are usually presented in a summary table, known as 'Analysis of variance summary table'. The results for Example J are shown in Table 18.5.

Table 18.5   The ANOVA summary table for Example J

Source of variation	Sum of squares	df	Mean square	F
Between groups (BV)	35.76	4	8.94	4.3824
Within group (WV)	40.80	20	2.04	
Total	76.56	24		

Interpretation of F

What does $F = 4.38$ mean? First the table that contains the critical values of F (*CVF*), which is found in most major texts on statistics, is examined. *CVF* is located by using as a guide the *df* for *BV*, which are across the top of the table, and the *df* for *WV*, which are down the left-hand column of the table. The intersection of the two gives the critical value of F. If the F-value is equal to or greater than *CVF*, the null hypothesis is rejected; if it is less than *CVF*, the null hypothesis is not rejected.

In our example, the *df* for *BV* and *WV* are 4 and 20 respectively. Thus the relevant *CVF* at a 0.05 significance level is 2.87. Since the F-value (4.3824) is greater than *CVF*, the null hypothesis is rejected. Thus, the difference between the scores is significant and consequently there is a difference between the texts as a source of learning.

c Computing ANOVA using SPSS

Performing an ANOVA as small as the one above indicates that doing statistical analysis manually is not only tedious and time consuming but also dangerous in the sense that there is no guarantee that the results are accurate. For this reason there is no researcher who will perform an ANOVA manually. The ease with which computers perform such operations and the access to computer programs make manual computation of ANOVA an issue of the past.

To compute the one-way ANOVA we proceed as shown below. It is important, however, to place the data in the computer so that it is clear where each score belongs. Each group should be numbered from 1 to 5, and each score must be identified according to the group to which it belongs. For instance, the scores of the various groups will be set in the columns as follows:

Column 1	Column 2
7	1
4	1
5	1
4	1
6	1
4	2
9	2
3	2
5	2
5	2
6	3
5	3
4	3
6	3
6	3
7	4
9	4
8	4
7	4
7	4
8	5
6	5
7	5
9	5
9	5

From here the steps are simple and straightforward:

1 Enter data in two columns; test scores in one column named **scores** (dependent variable) and groups in another column named **groups**, with values ranging from 1 to 5 for group 1 to group 5 (this is the independent variable or factor)
2 Choose **Statistics > Compare means > One-way ANOVA...**
3 Transfer variable scores to the **Dependent list** box
4 Transfer groups to the **Factor** box
5 Click on **Define range**
6 Type 1 in the **Minimum** box and 5 in the **Maximum** box (this refers to the values of the 5 groups)
7 Click on **Continue**
8 Click on **OK**

Upon completion of these steps, the computer will generate the following table:

```
                    * * * ONEWAY * * *

            Variable SCORES      Test scores
           by variable GROUPS    Student groups

                  Analysis of variance

                           Sum of   Mean     F       F
    Source of Variation D.F. Squares Squares Ratio   Prob.

    Between groups        4    35.7600 8.940   4.3824  .0105
    Within groups        20    40.8000 2.0400
    Total                24    76.5600
```

In essence, this table contains information which is the same as the one constructed manually above; the *F*-ratio shown in the table (4.3824) is identical to that computed above. Similarly, the interpretation of *F* is also the same. This shows that *F* is significant at the 0.05 level; this means that it is unlikely that the population means in our example are the same. There are further interesting points contained in the *F*-table; for instance:

1 Although the size of *F* in itself can say very little about its significance, a large *F*-value is more likely to indicate differences between the means than a small *F*-value.
2 Given that the *F*-value is the ratio of the between-groups variation (*BV*) mean square to the within-groups variation (*WV*) mean square (e.g. $8.940/2.040 = 4.3824$):
   (a) the closer this ratio is to 1, the smaller is the *F*-ratio, and the more likely it is that the null hypothesis is true; and
   (b) the futher away this ratio is from 1, the larger the *F*-ratio, and the more likely it is that the null hypothesis is not true.

3 The *F* probability tells us that the likelihood of obtaining a ratio of 4.3824 or larger while the null hypothesis is true is 0.0105, about one in a hundred, which is an acceptable risk.

4 Of the figures given in the computer display, the one that offers the most information is the *F* Prob. If this value is less than 0.05, we can reject the hypothesis.

Another example

To establish whether power structure in marriage affects the quality of life of spouses a survey was conducted. Unlike previous studies which had looked at authoritarian and democratic families and the degree of satisfaction, this study, when investigating satisfaction, differentiated between authoritarian and democratic couples who accepted the power structure of their family and those who disputed it. This resulted in four groups of respondents, namely: authoritarian accepting, authoritarian disputing, democratic accepting and democratic disputing. In this example only ten respondents from each group will be considered. The results are as shown below:

Group	Score	Group	Score	Group	Score	Group	Score
1	8	2	4	3	9	4	6
1	9	2	5	3	8	4	5
1	7	2	6	3	8	4	4
1	8	2	5	3	7	4	4
1	9	2	4	3	9	4	5
1	7	2	4	3	8	4	6
1	9	2	5	3	9	4	5
1	8	2	6	3	7	4	4
1	9	2	5	3	8	4	4
1	8	2	4	3	9	4	5

On the basis of the data shown above, can we argue that the model of power structure in marriage affects in any way the degree of satisfaction of the spouses? We shall employ one-way analysis of variance to show whether this is the case.

Before we begin our analysis, we enter the data in the computer by setting the score and the corresponding group number. The column containing the group numbers (1, 2, 3 or 4) can be labelled *groups*, and the column containing the satisfaction scores can be named *scores*. The values and value labels for the variable 'groups' may be set as 1 for authoritarian accepting, 2 for authoritarian disputing, 3 for democratic accepting, and 4 for democratic disputing. After the data have been entered, the steps to follow are shown below:

1 Choose **Statistics > Compare means > One-way ANOVA**
2 Transfer variable scores to the **Dependent list** box
3 Transfer groups to the **Factor** box
4 Click on **Define range**
5 Type 1 in the **Minimum** box and 4 in the **Maximum** box (this refers to the factor values, which are from 1 to 4)
6 Click on **Continue**
7 Click on **OK**

Upon completion of these steps the computer displays the following information:

```
- - - - - - - - - - O N E W A Y - - - - - - - - - -

                Variable SCORES      Test scores
              by variable GROUPS     Spouse groups

                    Analysis of Variance

                          Sum of   Mean     F      F
      Source of Variation D.F.  Squares Squares  Ratio  Prob.

      Between Groups        3    115.6000 38.5333 61.9286 .0000
      Within Groups        36     22.4000   .6222
      Total                39    138.0000
```

The results indicate that the *F*-ratio is high and also significant at the 0.0000 level. Hence, we can reject the H_o that the means of the samples are equal. In a liberal interpretation, we can argue that the four groups of spouses have different levels of satisfaction.

9   Summary

In this chapter we discussed the most popular tests of significance. Briefly, chi-square tests, *t*-tests and ANOVA are the most common tools of testing the significance of the findings, and constitute the minimum level of quantification the quantitative researcher is expected to be familiar with. Obviously, those employing qualitative methods may not need to worry about statistics, and certainly not about *t*-tests and ANOVA. However, understanding the basics of statistical operations is a necessary precondition for anyone who is involved in serious social research.

The measures presented in this chapter are basic and relatively limited in depth and breadth. Full statistical analysis involves more than these measures. Although most statistical analyses begin with these operations, they advance further and include more complex and more demanding statistical measures. Two-way analysis of variance and multiple regression have now become basic requirements for any seriously thinking quantitative researcher, and are often the key to the door of international journals.

Although this might sound daunting to the beginner, these statistical measures are not as difficult as they appear to be. The use of computers has eliminated the mathematical and computational elements of statistics and has made statistical computations accessible also to less mathematically minded readers. Statistical analysis rests now on logic rather than on arithmetic. We already saw in this chapter how easy it is to compute ANOVA by using SPSS.

This development is more than welcome, not only because it helps expand the use of statistics to a wider spectrum of researchers but also for another reason: given that many international journals only publish papers entailing high levels of statistical operation (some journals do not consider papers for publication unless they use at least multiple regression analysis), access to statistical analysis widens the range of outlets of the results. Obviously, knowledge of the statistical measures introduced in this and previous chapters is more than useful.

Now that you have become familiar with the basics of significance testing, the way is open to more challenging statistical operations, to be sought in other sources.

Key Concepts

Tests of significance	Wald–Wolfowitz runs test
Interval/ratio-level tests	Friedman test
χ^2 test of independence	*t*-test
McNemar test	Ordinal-level tests
Kolmogorov–Smirnov test	χ^2 goodness-of-fit test
Wilcoxon test	*z*-test for proportions
z-test	Sign test
Nominal-level tests	Mann–Whitney *U*-test
χ^2 test	Kruskal–Wallis *H*-test
Fisher's exact test	Analysis of variance
One-way analysis of variance	Two-way analysis of variance
Cochran's *Q*-test	Parametric tests
Non-parametric tests	Nominal-level tests
One-tail tests	Two-tail tests

PART IV Publication

19

Reporting

1 Introduction

The last step of the research process is publication of the data, that is, the dissemination of information which was collected during the investigation. This is an important step because it is the only way for research findings to reach the community and become public knowledge and to encourage the community, interest groups and the government to take notice of it. For the community and even the experts, research reports *are* the research; and research is what is contained in these reports. Hence, bad research reports often mean bad research. Researchers are to be aware of this.

In this chapter we shall discuss a number of issues related to what report writing entails, and how to approach this part of the research process so that reports become a crucial, beneficial and constructive way of communicating clearly and accurately the findings to the readers. We will introduce some of the ways in which reports can be conveyed to the community, the factors which must be taken into account when research reports are prepared, and the items they should contain to be complete, useful and effective. We begin with the factors which influence the process of reporting.

2 Factors of reporting

Given that the research report is the face of the investigation, it is important that the report reflects the research process and the research outcomes accurately, adequately and effectively. It should reflect technical as well as political and ethical issues, for research reports depend very much on at least three important factors, namely ethical considerations, the nature of the reader for whom the report is prepared and the purpose of the report. The person who prepares the report must be aware of these important factors.

Ethics
As stated in the first chapter of this volume, research must adhere to ethical standards; and this pertains also to the manner in which reports are written. For instance, (1) research reports are required to present an accurate, honest and realistic account of the findings, without the intent to misrepresent the findings or mislead the reader; (2) plagiarism should be avoided: use of another writer's work or ideas without quotation or in an edited form is not acceptable; (3) limitations of the research caused by any reason must be disclosed in the report; (4) persons who contributed to the completion of the study and/or of the report must be duly acknowledged; and (5) a report will be prepared only if allowed by the sponsors and within the parameters specified in the agreement.

The reader
The report must also be written in a manner which will make it accessible to the intended reader. Readers have different linguistic competencies and their knowledge of scientific terminology varies significantly. Consequently, it is expected that the language in which the report is prepared is that of the consumer. In a similar fashion, the length of the report, the amount of details contained in it, the extent to which technical aspects are included and the depth of analysis and discussion will vary according to the nature of the reader. Obviously talks given to concerned community groups will be different from reports submitted to the sponsor, papers presented in conferences or articles published in professional journals. In all cases, the report is expected to be clear, honest, thorough and informative; however, diversity of content, presentation and structure cannot be avoided.

Purpose
The nature and content of the reports vary according to the purpose of the research undertaken and of the report. Descriptive studies result in publications presenting descriptive findings, and exploratory studies generate reports containing exploratory data. In a similar fashion studies based on action research will entail plans of action which will show interest groups and the government what is to be done to achieve the goals supported by the research. Finally, the purpose of the report, that is, whether it is just to inform the reader, to report to the sponsor or the government or to generate public debate or public action, has a strong impact on the manner in which it is presented as well as on the content and structure of the report.

Nevertheless, regardless of the nature of the audience, the question of ethics and the purpose of the report, every report is expected to be prepared in a certain form and adhere to certain standards. There is a common understanding among researchers that findings are presented in a certain manner and according to certain standards (Wolcott, 1990). These standards refer to a number of elements that the writer must be fully aware of and consider. They usually refer to three major areas, namely content, structure and presentation of the report. Whether the findings are published in one way or another depends on several factors, some of which will be discussed later.

3   Reporting outlets

Research findings are reported through a number of channels. Some may be published in newspapers only, others in journals, monographs, books or conferences. Publishing using a number of channels is very common as this promotes a wider and more varied readership. In summary, the findings can be published in the following:

- *Newspapers*   Here the general public is informed of the central trends of the findings, but there is little control over the content, since this is decided by the journalists. Often, findings are overdramatised and sensationalised and give only a partial description of the findings. Nonetheless, newspapers do help publicise the findings and bring them to the attention of the public.
- *Newsletters*   Findings published in newsletters address readers with a special interest and some political orientation. Here members of interest groups are addressed as general readers and given detailed information in a simple manner.
- *Conferences*   More specific and more complex are the findings presented in conferences, where experts in specific areas are addressed. Researchers present preliminary or complete findings, allowing for direct response on the part of colleagues to major points of the findings.
- *Monographs*   This outlet allows for larger reports which are more detailed and less formal than those presented in journals and books. Unless monographs are prepared in the form of books, perhaps as part of a series, the author has no editor or publisher to restrict the form, type, style and content of the report. This gives more freedom to the author but also more risk, since there is no opportunity for feedback on the quality of presentation and marketability of the product.
- *Journals*   Journals provide an outlet for summarised, concise, detailed and critical publication of findings. This is the most common method of disseminating knowledge and also the one that many writers aspire to use in their work. In most cases, journal articles will present only a part of the findings, with a social investigation leading to a series of journal articles.
- *Books*   This is perhaps the best and most respected method of publication of research findings. The wider boundaries and focus allow for almost unlimited length and complete coverage of the data collected. The only limitation for reporting findings in a book is an economic one, and is controlled by the publishers who only publish such findings if there is a prospect for profit. Given that research often is specialised and the findings are of interest to only a small group of readers, the prospect of publishing data in book form is rather slim.

There are many more outlets for publishing findings. Workshops for interested people and/or the sponsors and seminars are two of them. Media interviews, particularly for radio or television stations, are other forms of dissemination of knowledge obtained through research. However, most researchers would rank books as the best form of publishing data, followed by refereed journal articles and monographs. Nevertheless, as far as the suitability of these outlets is concerned, the only difference between them is the groups of people they address. Related to this is also the fact that authors have little say about whether their work will be published in one way or another. The proportion of research book proposals accepted is reported to be very low, and the acceptance rate of articles submitted for publication is — in certain journals at least — equally low. For some journals the acceptance rate is as low as 10 per cent!

4   Structure and content

Deciding where to publish research findings is an important issue, and the nature of the research and the research findings as well as the social significance of the findings are important contributing factors. However, other factors, such as content, structure and presentation of the report, are equally important, not only for making publication of the reports easier but also for disseminating research findings in a clear, accurate, unbiased and useful manner. Briefly, researchers preparing research reports must be fully aware of (1) what is to be included in the report, (2) how the information contained in the report should be structured, and (3) how the text is to be presented. All three elements of the report are equally important, should be well integrated and given adequate consideration. They will be discussed briefly below. Since structure and content are closely related to each other, they will be discussed together.

Generally, the content of the report is expected to adhere to certain rules; the following are some of the most important:

- The content of the report should communicate and discuss the findings of the project, as well as problems and frustrations experienced during the study.
- The content should be presented in a simple and orderly way, with every aspect of the project being properly introduced and explained, and with the presentation directed towards pre-set aims and the whole structure organised according to accepted standards and practices.
- Although no single report structure is fully accepted by writers and publishers, it is a practice in the social sciences that the structure of the publication covers a number of points.

In the following we will address briefly the main elements of the main part of the report.

a   The main body of the report

There are usually five main parts in a report: the introduction, methodology, findings, discussion and conclusion. The five parts must be presented symmetrically and proportionally. In addition, it should be kept in mind that although all parts of the report are important, the sections 'Findings' and

'Discussion' are the most important. For this reason, the other sections of the report are relatively smaller. As a general guide, the introduction and method usually do not exceed 10 per cent of the report, except for when relevant literature or methodology are controversial and require special attention (in which case they may be presented in a separate section entitled 'Literature review') or when a complicated methodology is used. Similarly, conclusions and recommendations make up only a small proportion of the report

Introduction

Here, the author describes, explains and introduces the topic of the report; the purpose and significance of the research; the findings of the exploratory study (if any); a review of the literature; problems encountered; and finally adjust-ments undertaken to arrive at the topic ultimately studied and presented in the report. Briefly the main questions considered in this section of the report are:

- What is the research topic?
- Why is there a need to research this topic, and who will benefit from this?
- What has been found/said by other researchers/writers in this area?
- Is everything said/done in the past on this topic correct?
- Are there gaps, deficiencies, etc. that justify the research introduced in this report?
- What is the view of the researcher on past research and policy on the research topic?
- What is hypothesised by the researcher?
- What are the expected outcomes of this study?

These questions are expected to set the research topic in the context of current research, debates and policies and show why the reader should be interested in the report, why the report is important and what the reader will gain from studying this report.

Method

This section will inform the reader in simple terms about how the research was done. Many professional journals have already established set patterns regarding how this section should be referred to and what to include. Some call this section 'method', others 'methodology'. In a similar fashion some are strict about the elements that are to be included in the section as well as the names of the sections used, while others are less strict on names and aspects contained in this section. Overall, this section includes issues regarding meth-odological framework, sampling procedures, instrumentation, data collection, data analysis and interpretation, and problems encountered by the researcher during the study. Briefly, this entails all the steps introduced when discussing the steps of the research process. In a summary form, the methodology section will include the following.

Research design

- How has the research question been addressed?
- What type of methodology has been employed in the study?
- What is the overall framework that contains the research process?

Sampling
- Who are the respondents who took part in the study?
- What was the size and composition of the sample?
- What were the sampling procedures used to select the sample?
- What are the measures employed to avoid errors?
- What is the degree of generalisability expected?
- What are the characteristics of the population?

Methods of data collection
- What are the methods of data collection employed in the study and why?
- What were the actual procedures of data collection, including ways of preventing or correcting non-response?
- How were validity and reliability assured in the study?
- What types of pre-tests and pilot studies were employed in the investigation, and what were their findings?

Instrumentation
- What precisely is it that you have studied, and what are the relevant variables?
- How were the variables operationalised?
- What types of instruments were used to measure the variables?
- What type of scales and response categories were used in the research?
- What are the working hypotheses, null hypothesis and alternative hypotheses?

Data analysis
- How were data analysed?
- Were statistical measures and computing employed?

Ethics
- How were ethical issues addressed in the study?

Results

In this section the results are presented. This is usually the largest part of a report, and its specific content depends on the nature of the topic and the methodology employed and the extent to which presentation can go. It includes largely a direct description of variables and relationships between variables in the form of statements, tables, figures, graphs and/or other types of presentation. Point by point, and step by step, the findings are presented here, following the structure of the instrument used or the order of the topics as categorised by the researcher.

Findings are presented in a summary form so that a general impression of trends is created. Presentation in the forms of central tendency and dispersion, aided by frequency tables and graphs integrated in the text, is a common way of presenting the findings. Following this, cross-tabulations and estimations regarding associations between the variables are undertaken. This will show whether factors of the issue in question are interrelated or interdependent. If regression analysis was used in the study, the findings will be presented in this section. Finally, the results of significance tests, if employed, will be presented here to strengthen the significance of relationships or differences reported in this section. In a question form, the issues considered in this section are:

- What are the answers to the questions raised in the previous sections of the study?
- How can the findings be presented in a summary form?
- What graphs can be used to present visually the trends identified in the study?
- Are there any associations evident in the study which can explain inter-dependence between relevant factors?
- Can the findings allow predictions to be made on the basis of figures ascertained on one variable?
- How significant are differences reported in this study?
- Why should we trust the findings?
- Are there any problems which can reduce the validity of the findings presented in this section?
- Does the presentation of the findings conform with ethical standards?

The presentation of the findings and the associated quantitative and ideological/ethical considerations will provide a platform for further critical elaboration. This is presented in the next section.

Discussion

The presentation of the findings is followed by a discussion of the most important points. The findings are summarised, explained and interpreted, establishing more general trends and departing from individual observations and individual data. Without repeating the findings or departing fully from the facts identified in the study, this section will facilitate a more general debate of the significance of the findings. Such a discussion takes place in a logical, theoretical and political context and attempts to integrate the findings into theories, into the purpose of the study, and into its main hypotheses. Ultimately the discussion of the findings offers some more general answers to the research questions and explains many issues included in the research problem. In addition, eventual weaknesses of the methods employed in the study will be explained adequately, and possible effects on the results and the resulting limitations of the study will be disclosed. In point form, the main issues which are usually addressed in this section are:

- What is the general meaning of the findings?
- How do the findings relate to the main assumptions/questions introduced earlier on in this report?
- How do findings fit with trends reported in the relevant literature?
- What theories, views or opinions do these findings support or reject?
- Do the findings support plans and programs related to the issue in question?

It is quite possible that findings are discussed in the same section as they are presented. In such cases the sections 'Findings' and 'Discussion' are merged into one, usually labelled 'Presentation and discussion of the findings'. In either case, the discussion section should not introduce new data or new elements of analysis. Discussion means just that, discussion of the results presented in the previous section of the report.

Conclusions and recommendations
Most reports contain a section headed 'Conclusions', 'Summary and conclusions' or 'Conclusions and recommendations'. Here the author puts the results of the study in a normative context and makes some general or specific recommendations, the implementation of which is expected to solve the problems studied in the project. In this section the findings are set along side the research question and an attempt is made to show what implications these findings have for the research topic and the community in general. In addition, attention is given to gaps in our knowledge identified in the study which deserve further attention.

Following the formulation of conclusions, researchers usually make recommendations regarding action that is required to respond to the situation identified in the study. Obviously action theorists will put more emphasis on this point than positivists, but the general trend is for the researcher to take a stance on the issue in question, to consider the conclusions made and to state, directly or indirectly, what action is recommended in this area. In summary, the following are some issues which are addressed in this section of the study:

• What are the implications of the findings for the issue in question and the community in general?
• Are there any gaps in our knowledge of the issue in question and relevant theory?
• What can be done to improve the state of affairs in this sector of our community?
• Who should take action in this context, the individual, interest groups, the community or the government?

This section is one which busy readers will read only, or which they will place more emphasis on. It is therefore wise to construct this section in such a way that it will offer an accurate, legitimate and fair reflection of the study and of the research report.

b   Other sections of the report

References
Every report is expected to contain a list of references: literature referred to in the report should be adequately documented and listed in alphabetical order at the end of the report. Referencing can be done in many ways. Which way will be used depends on the guidelines adopted by the publisher, or on the author's preference if the report is published privately. Hence the question here is not about whether such references should be made or not but rather in what way. Journals and publishers as well as other academic bodies (universities or professional bodies) have already established ways of referencing which are widely used in Australia and other countries. The Harvard system, for instance, is one such way. But other systems are equally popular. Using one or the other seems to be a matter of preference rather than a reflection of the quality of the system. Writers of reports are supposed to be aware of the different referencing systems because the choice of such a system depends on the type of publication rather than on the preference of the author.

Abstract

An abstract is an accurate, comprehensive, concise and informative summary of the report. It provides a useful summary of the report (between 150 and 200 words), allowing the reader to gain an insight into the findings of the study. An abstract is a mini-report where the reader will find sufficient information about the purpose and outcome of the study, and ultimately decide whether to read the report or not. For this reason, careful preparation of the abstracts is advised.

A good abstract is a true reflection of the study and its findings, and has the purpose of telling the reader *what* the study was all about, what the report intends to do, *how* the study was conducted, with what *results* and with what *success*. In point form, it answers the following questions:

- What was the purpose of the study?
- How was the study conducted (including sample type/size, methods of data collection and data analysis)?
- What were the main findings of the study?
- What were the main conclusions?

Submission of abstracts with reports is a compulsory requirement for articles published in professional journals and is gradually becoming more common than before. The types of publications in which abstracts are not required are books, monographs and newsletters.

Optional elements

Finally, the report may include acknowledgements, a list of contents and an appendix. All three parts are optional and are included in the report only if required or relevant.

Acknowledgements are given either in a separate section or as a footnote attached to the title of the paper or to some part of the introduction. A *list of contents* is generally required when large reports are produced. It usually provides detailed information or the main points or chapters of the report only. *Appendixes*, finally, provide an opportunity for the researcher to place in the report elements of the study which although important do not fit into the body of the report. Such elements are the full questionnaire, pictures, maps, lengthy tables and other peripheral material that can help the reader understand the findings better and place the whole research in a more constructive context.

5   Presentation

a   Conveying the message

If content denotes *what* is included in the report, presentation refers to *how* the content should be displayed. The main points pertinent to this issue are language and style. Beyond this, however, there are several other points that are important. The following standards are considered (e.g. Becker, 1989; Martin, 1988; Puris, 1995) to be significant.

- *Clarity* Reports should be written clearly; confusing and ambiguous statements should be avoided.
- *Precision* The author should avoid generalities and vague statements.
- *Legibility* The report should be legible not only for academics and specialists but for all intended readers.
- *Completeness* No parts of the study should be left out of the report. All issues should be given adequate emphasis.
- *Objectivity* Subjectivity and emotionality should be avoided. Reports are expected to convey information about the findings of the research; opinions and subjective views should be presented so that they are clearly identifiable as such, especially in the conclusion. Facts and value judgements should be separated.
- *Fairness* Findings should be presented in a fair and unbiased manner.
- *Verifiability* Information presented in the report must be readily verifiable.
- *Impersonality* Most writers believe that reports should be written in the third person. Statements such as I believe that . . . or I found that . . . are considered inappropriate.
- *Ethics* As stated above, the report should comply with the code of ethics.

While these points are generally accepted among many researchers, there is a controversy about the validity of some of these guidelines. Critical theorists and feminists will consider them inappropriate, particularly in regard to objectivity, detachment and impersonality.

b   Writing style

The quality of the style employed in a report is an important element of report writing and varies from case to case. The style used in a conference presentation is different from that used when writing for a professional journal or for a book prepared for the general reader. These styles are different and yet legitimate and acceptable in their context. As stated above, the criterion here that makes the difference is the reader but also the standards of the context in which it is published. Conference organisers often specify the style of presentation and so do editors of professional journals. In this sense style is not an expression of the quality of the research but rather a matter of preference. There is therefore very little one can say about which style one should use when preparing a report. The answer is to use the style prescribed by the publisher of the report.

Nevertheless, there are some common stylistic standards agreed upon by many writers. Although agreement on such standards is becoming weaker with time, and standards seem to be accepted more by some groups of writers than others, they seem to be preferred by writers and deserve to be mentioned.

Again, it is advisable that report writers consult with their publisher to establish the nature of the preferred style.

First or third person?
Many writers, editors and publishers insist that the third person is used. It is preferable to say 'It has been found in the present study . . .' rather than 'I found in my study . . .'. In both cases the message is the same but conventions support the former rather than the latter.

Active or passive voice?
In a similar manner, conventions prescribe that the passive voice is preferred to the active voice. Many writers would say 'Women were found to suffer more than men . . .' rather than 'The researcher found that women suffer more than . . .'. As in the previous example, the message is the same, but the expression varies. However, there is a gradual shift from passive to active expression. Increasingly more journals accept 'active' expressions more than before, while others do not seem to pay attention to this point. It is accepted as long as the usage is consistent throughout the report.

Past or present tense?
Whether the writer uses the past or present tense depends on the issues referred to in the text. Nevertheless, the rule is that reports of research findings are made in the past tense. This is logical given that the research being reported in the report happened in the past. It is logical to say that 'there were more women than men in favour of censorship' than '. . . there are more women than men in favour of censorship'; apart from the fact that the latter is incorrect (women were in favour of equality at the time of the study — five years ago — but are they now?), it seems to imply a generalisation of the finding, which may not be correct

Sexist language?
The general agreement among writers is that sexist language should not be used. This requirement has already been institutionalised among researchers, at least with regard to the use of certain expressions. Adherence to non-sexist expressions is a must. For instance, researchers are male and female; there is therefore no justification for referring to the researcher uniformly and consistently as he or she. Using both pronouns (he or she, he/she or (s)he) is one solution to the ideological issue, but also one that is often awkward in construction and difficult to read. It is preferable to use pronouns in plural instead. The sentence '*The respondent* has the right to be asked for *his/her* consent' can be better written as '*Respondents* have the right to be asked for *their* consent'. There is ample literature on the topic of sexist writing which the writer must consult if in doubt.

Writing style is not an integral part of the social research process, that is, of the creation of knowledge. Nevertheless it is a part of the research process, and an important one indeed. It is the part which will help disseminate findings to the interested parties in a clear, accurate and acceptable manner, and in this sense it deserves as much attention as any other part of the research process.

6   Size

The size of the report depends, among other things, on the nature of the research, the type of publication and on the readers to whom it is addressed. Nevertheless, overly long reports must be well justified. The rule here is that the report should be as small as possible and as large as necessary. Small studies are usually reported in journals, where their size does not exceed, on average, 4000 words. Large studies are reported in books or monographs.

7   Self-assessment

It is wise before the report leaves the hands of the author for reasonable assurance to be given that it presents a true reflection of the findings and that it meets the standards of report writing. The author should check the report point by point, so that if there are any errors or omissions they will be detected before it is printed. Writers of a diverse interest and origin (e.g. Becker, 1988; Judd *et al.*, 1991; Selltiz *et al.*, 1976; Puris, 1995) have referred to a number of points they think must be considered when assessing a report. These points make up the following detailed and useful list.

a   The abstract

- Is the abstract relevant, adequate, complete and concise?
- Is it overstating/understating the findings?
- Is it objective and informative?
- Does it include the problems, methods, summary of the results and conclusions?

b   The main body of the report

- Is the structure symmetrical and proportionately divided?
- Is it complete, readable, clear, precise, objective, fair, verifiable and impersonal?
- Does it comply with ethical standards?
- Does each part of the report fulfil its purpose?

The introduction
- Does it introduce the topic and variables adequately?
- Is the literature review pertinent, exhaustive and accurately reported and evaluated?
- Are the hypotheses clearly stated, pertinent to the main issues of the study and verifiable?
- Are the variables adequately and accurately measured and operationalised?

The method
- Are populations and research units clearly defined?
- Are the variables operationalised and the indicators explicitly stated?
- Are methods and instruments adequately chosen, explained, employed and justified?
- Are methods and instruments sufficiently guarded against bias, violation of the code of ethics and errors to ensure validity and reliability?
- Have extraneous variables been controlled adequately?

The findings
- Are the findings complete, readable and adequately organised and presented?
- Do they correspond to the research hypotheses and the basic points of the research question?
- Are visual displays of the data well integrated in the text and easy to read?

The discussion
- Are the findings adequately interpreted and generalised?
- Are interpretations legitimate in terms of the nature of the study?
- Are all issues presented in the previous sections equally considered?
- Is the discussion free of bias and violations of the code of ethics?
- Were limitations of the study considered when generalising the findings?

The conclusions
- Are the conclusions related to the main elements of the research question?
- Are the conclusions justified by the research and its limitations?
- Do they cover all important aspects of the study?

c The references/bibliography

- Are the references and bibliography presented according to the standards and guidelines set by the publisher?
- Does this section cover all sources used in the report?

d General

- Does the presentation of the report and the information provided allow replication?
- Does it show flow and continuity?
- Is the title relevant and adequate?
- In objective terms, is the report worth publishing?

The report is often given to colleagues for comments and criticism. A neutral and objective opinion of the procedures, methods, analysis and interpretation helps the writer to present a more objective and valid study. In certain cases writers have been reported to show parts of their report to respondents or key informants for comments; such comments have been found to be very helpful indeed.

8 The book

Most of the aspects referred to above are also valid for putting together a book. Nevertheless, writing a report to meet the requirements of as serious a publication as a book entails many elements that require more serious thought and much more work.

In general, a book will contain most of the elements presented above but here the publisher plays a very important role in the shape and final presentation of the book. Marketing involving the 'readership' and the level at which the publisher thinks it should be pitched are factors that have a profound influence on the structure and content of the book. In general, according to a number of writers (see Yin, 1991) a book reporting the findings of, for example a qualitative study, may take one of the following styles.

Analytic structure
In principle, the content of the book and its structure resemble that discussed above in relation to publishing reports. The outline of a book usually includes an introduction, explaining the purpose and significance of the research, the research methods employed, the findings presented at length in a number of chapters, including analysis and discussion as the information is presented, and an epilogue presenting critical issues and some recommendations.

Theory-building structure
Here the presentation of the material centres on the theory that is supported by the study. Elements of the theory constitute the main points of the book, presented in separate chapters together with the relevant data that support the theory.

Nevertheless, there is no definite way of presenting a report in a book. Provided that the theoretical and methodological parts of the study and the findings are presented, and that the argument can be followed, the structure is acceptable. Structure in most cases is a negotiable issue. The points made above in the section 'Presentation' must be followed.

Comparative structure
When the report relates to field studies or case studies, not only the methodology but also the underlying theory and theme of the discussion are unique and therefore affect the way a book will be prepared and presented. In such cases most of the points made above are still valid. Others may not be. The analytic structure and the theory-building structure are pertinent here, too. But other structures, such as comparative structure, chronological structure, suspense structure and unsequented structure (Yin, 1991) are equally valid.

The fact that case studies, for instance, are based on the analysis of cases that are often dealt with separately makes it possible for writers to present their findings in a comparative way. Here the findings are described repeatedly from various points of view and with different descriptive models.

Chronological structure
Here the material collected through a case study is presented in chronological order, following the development of the case history.

Suspense structure

This report structure is the inverse of that presented in the analytic model. The central finding that dominates the theme of the report is presented first and the details, plus the methodological explanations, follow later.

Unsequented structure

In this model the chapters are presented as separate entities without a particular relationship to the others. Their order can change without a loss of quality.

Case studies

With regard to case-study reports, the publication could employ any of the above structures and take the form that best corresponds with its nature. It may come out as a single case narrative with descriptions, tables, graphs, pictures and so on. It may appear as a multiple case report with multiple narratives, as a question–answer report or as a cross-case report presenting a separate theme per chapter rather than a case per chapter.

9   From research findings to policy and practice

Research never reaches the public, the stakeholders and the policy makers unless brought to their attention. Even bringing the finding to the attention of the authorities does not guarantee that action will be taken to rectify eventual problems. Findings can be shelved away before action is taken. To encourage action in the area covered by the research, investigators employ tactics like those mentioned when talking about action research. Action here is not guaranteed but it is the closest one can get to putting findings, decisions and conclusions into practice.

Action research proceeds in steps, using increasingly more involvement of the public in putting pressure upon the authorities to give the findings the credit they deserve and implement relevant policies. Here the researcher, after the findings have been analysed and discussed and after conclusions are drawn, brings them to the attention of the public. More specifically, pressure groups or advisory groups are formed and are given access to the findings, and are asked to make suggestions as to how to address the problems, what action to take, who to talk to to begin action and when.

Action or pressure groups are very useful not only because they provide ideas and suggestions about how to proceed further but also because of their numbers. When many people become aware of the presence and significance of a problem, they can communicate the findings to more people and finally develop a network of like-thinking individuals who can exert pressure upon the government to take action. And the government is more sensitive to public pressure than to reports which can be hidden away and become invisible.

For those who see social research as a way of achieving emancipation, and who consider action as an element of the research process, planning action after the findings have been secured is as important as planning research before it has begun. Setting the parameters of the research straight, working continuously towards disseminating the findings to as many people as possible and planning the way to put pressure upon the government to implement the findings are part of the everyday research practice.

10   The politics of publishing

The majority of social researchers see no incentive in getting involved in action research. In many cases this is not possible and in other cases they see no possibility of getting the government interested in doing what research findings suggest. Also, there are studies which provide no clear directives for social action, and more strength and support is needed before one goes further. In the first instance, research findings need to be communicated to more people before action is prepared. In these and other cases, the step that follows the completion of the report is publication.

In these cases, authors are interested in publishing their reports in a way that will guarantee a wide distribution of the findings so that the research is communicated to the largest range of readers. However, publishing is more than putting words in print. It entails excessive political and ideological manoeuvring, negotiation and convincing (Brown, 1992). Whether manuscripts will be accepted for publication by book publishers or not depends on many factors, of which quality of the report, social relevance, economic considerations and ideological imperatives are a few. Publication in journals is easier, in the sense that market factors and (to a lesser extent) social relevance are less significant. Similarly, publication in newspapers depends more on social relevance than on quality of the study, while newsletters and monographs published by the author or sponsor of the study find no difficulties with publication.

Quality of the report is an important factor: high-quality manuscripts are more likely to reach the shelves of a bookseller or to be accepted by journals for publication than poor-quality reports. However, this is not always the case. Publication is a function of more than one of the above listed factors. With regard to journal articles, the decisive factor is reviewers' reports; and this constitutes a possible problem for many reports. When biased reviewers infiltrate editorial boards of journals and publishing houses, this issue becomes critical. Personal interests, economic considerations and ideological convictions are a few reasons why some valid and relevant research findings remain unpublished. Groups or persons who consider the findings critical of personal interests or ideological principles usually do not support the publication and where possible do not 'allow' the report to be published. Academic quality here is not of primary importance.

In a similar fashion, companies or political parties who have contracted the research may not publish the research report unless it supports their views and practices. For instance, a company that receives a report proving that the toxic waste it produces causes severe damage to the flora of the surrounding area in a radius of 50 km will do its best to keep such a report unpublished.

Similarly, interest groups may make a strong effort to keep reports from being published if such reports do not correspond with their ideals. This may be done either in a direct or an indirect way; it may also be done on the basis of ideological standards or economic principles. Individuals who review manuscripts can decide the fate of a report on the basis of personal and ideological convictions rather than on academic grounds.

As far as books are concerned, publishers are interested in manuscripts which are of high quality and promise high returns for their investment. And while a combination of academic quality and business interests is the ideal, some publishers take the former while others consider the latter to be more important. Publication proposals are often rejected on the grounds of a weak market. To overcome this problem and to allow the publication of less marketable (i.e. specialist literature) but academically sound and vigorous studies, special publishers have been established. Some universities have organised their own publishing operations (referred to as university presses) for this purpose.

It must be kept in mind that the success of a research project is not always reflected in the amount or type of publication. The success of projects is measured in terms of their soundness and the type of findings they produce. It is not unusual to see excellent research findings in self-published reports or in sponsor-supported publications. Success is also measured in terms of the extent to which publications have initiated structural and/or political changes. Action research may not reach the shelves of booksellers but may reach the social order in a more decisive manner than books and articles together.

Key concepts

Analytic structure	Suspense structure
Chronological structure	Theory-building structure
Comparative structure	Unsequented structures

Glossary

Abnormality   Any situation that is generally not considered to be normal.

Abstat   A computer program for statistical analysis of research data, mainly for IBM PCs and CP/M operating computers.

Action research   Research orientated towards bringing about change, often involving respondents in the process of investigation, with the researchers being aware of their influence on the research process by being a part of the environment they study.

Age pyramid   A line graph showing the age structure of a population.

Analysis of variance   A test of significance of data related to many samples.

Analytical interviews   Interviews based on a theoretical foundation aimed at *analysing* research objects.

Association   The relationship between two or more variables.

Authenticity   The state of being original, natural, not influenced (qualitative research).

Bias   A systematic error in data collection.

BMDP ('Biochemical programs')   A statistical program for computer-assisted analysis of research data, mainly for the medical profession.

Bogardus scale   A scale developed by Bogardus to study social distance between people or between people and groups.

Boomerang effect   The situation where a measure achieves the opposite of what it was intended to achieve.

Canonical correlation   A form of correlation between two groups of variables employing factor analysis.

Case study   A qualitative method of data collection (or a research design) concentrating on studying single cases.

Category   A group of people demonstrating the same or similar traits without having face-to-face relationships.

Causal relationship   A relationship where one variable effects changes in another.

Causal research   A form of research aimed at establishing or testing causal relationships between variables.

Causality   The quality characterising two variables between which there is a causal relationship.

Central tendency   An attribute of distributions showing the general trend of the data and measured by means of the mean, median and mode.

Chart   A statistical package for computer analysis of research data.

Chicago School A school of thought founded by Mead, Park and Thomas which established a theoretical and methodological direction known as symbolic interactionism.

Chi-square test A test of significance for the comparison of empirical frequencies for nominal values.

Clinical interviews Interviews employed to provide information of specific causes of problems or types of illness, employed predominantly by psychologists but also social workers, welfare officers and sociologists.

Cluster analysis A form of analysis developed by Tyron, Holzinger and Harman used to study variables by integrating similar objects and grouping them together into clusters.

Cluster sampling A form of sampling procedure in which the primary selection unit is a 'cluster' (a school, a hospital, a soccer team, etc.).

Code A symbol or set of symbols used in measurement and analysis in place of responses collected through social research. In grounded theory: the result of coding; can be a category or a relationship of categories.

Code book Book containing a set of rules and guidelines regarding coding.

Coding The process of assigning symbols to elements of research instruments for the purpose of entering the data into computers. In the context of grounded theory: the process of conceptualising data.

Cohort analysis A study of cohorts to ascertain trends and developments over time.

Cohorts Groups of respondents with the same traits (date of birth, date of marriage, etc.) constituting a part of the population.

Communality A common factor variance; a measure of the degree to which variables vary together.

Community studies Empirical studies employing a variety of methods and techniques that attempt to study communities as whole units.

Compunication A new concept developed to describe communication involving computers.

Computer interviews Computer-aided interviews in which the interviewer is replaced partly or fully by a computer.

Concept A word that labels or classifies an object, event or experience.

Conduit A statistical program for computer-assisted analysis of research data.

Constant A factor that remains unchanged.

Content analysis A method of studying the content of documents in order to establish their meaning.

Content validity The type of validity that refers to the extent to which it covers all possible aspects of the research topic.

Context analysis The view that objects should be studied and interpreted within their context.

Contingency A form of correlation related to nominal data.

Contingency analysis A method developed by Osgood in the area of content analysis employed to study relationships between parts of text.

Control A procedure employed in experimental research with the purpose of hindering factors or variables from affecting in any way a certain variable.

Control group The group selected in experimental studies that is not exposed to the experimental stimulus.

Control question   A question employed to test the validity of the response given to another question.

Convergent interview   A type of unstructured interview involving respondents with divergent views and interviewers who plan together the process of interviewing and discuss the results of each interview before they proceed with the next interview.

Correlation   A statistical measure of relationships between variables describing the presence, direction and degree of association between them.

Correlation matrix   A matrix containing the values of the coefficient of correlation between the variables in question.

Co-variance   A measure of the degree of common variance between variables.

Cross-sectional study   A study containing units belonging to the same period of time. (Opposite to panel or trend studies.)

Cross-validation   A method of ascertaining validity by checking groups of data against other groups of data from the same study.

CSS ('Complete statistical system')   A statistical computer program for a selective number of computers.

Cumulative data   Frequencies established by adding low-value scores to the score with next highest value.

'Daisy professional'   A computer program for statistical analysis of research data, suitable for Apple II computers.

DATA-X   A statistical package for statistical analysis of research data for PET computers.

Deduction   The process of establishing logical conclusions from general and abstract to specific and concrete phenomena.

Delphi method   A method of data collection that relies on the opinion of experts.

Demography   A method of study introduced for the first time by Guillard in 1855 to describe or analyse structure and change of populations.

Demoscopy   A method of study employed to study opinions and attitudes, using mainly survey research. Formally developed in 1920 in the USA by Gallup.

Dependent variable   A variable that is explained or affected by another variable.

Depth interview   Unstandardised, roughly structured interview; also known as a clinical interview.

Design   A plan; as a research design it contains all steps of the research process (examples: survey design, experimental design).

Diagnostic interviews   Interviews employed to *diagnose* aspects of reality.

Dispersion   The degree to which elements of distribution are spread away from the mean.

Disproportional sampling   A form of stratified sampling in which the units included in the sample are disproportional to those of the stratum of the population.

Dogmatic hermeneutics   A branch of hermeneutics that adheres to certain dogmatic principles, such as in religion or ideology.

Dummy variable   An artificial variable.

Elite interviews   Interviews with *elites*, that is, well-known personalities, prominent and influential people.

Empiricism   A school of thought stressing the significance of experience as the source of all knowledge.

Equivalence reliability   Reliability across indicators.

Ethnocentrism   The trend to see one's own culture as the centre of life and its elements as the standards of evaluation of other cultures.

Ethnography   A discipline with the task of describing life customs, etc. of people living in various (predominantly primitive) cultures. A branch of ethnology.

Ethnology   A discipline with the task of studying social structure and culture of primitive societies (in Europe) but also of modern societies (USA and England — there known as social anthropology or cultural anthropology).

Ethnomethodology   A sociological discipline developed by Garfinkel (1967) that places emphasis on the methods and procedures employed by people when they define and interpret everyday life. It is the study of commonsense knowledge, its creation and use in natural settings.

Experiment   A research method that studies under systematic and controlled conditions predominantly causal relationships.

Experimental group   The group selected in an experimental study that is exposed to the experimental stimulus.

Exploration   A method of data collection and a research model employed in quantitative and qualitative studies.

Extrapolation   Estimation of missing external values by means of knowledge of internal values.

Factor analysis   A method of multivariate statistical analysis of variables.

Falsification   The process of disproving the validity of a hypothesis.

Fine analysis   A method employed in the context of objective hermeneutics.

Focused interviews   Semi-structured interviews set to explore deeply a specific object or a certain point of the research topic.

Formal theory   The last step of theory development employed in the context of grounded theory.

Free interviews   Another name for unstructured, unstandardised and open interviews.

'General inquirer'   A computer program employed in content analysis to compute various indices.

GENSTAT ('A general statistical program')   A statistical program for computer analysis of research data.

'Graph/stats II'   A statistical package for computer-assisted analysis of research data for BBC microcomputers.

Grounded theory   A type of theory thought to emerge out of the direct study of social reality; introduced by Glaser and Strauss. Offers one of the bases of qualitative or interpretative research.

Group discussion   A method of data collection in which information is collected in the context of a group by means of some form of discussion.

Guided interview   A form of semi-structured interview.

Gutman scale   An ordinal scale for attitude measurement.

Hallo effect   The influence that the response to a question has on the way other questions of the same context will be answered.

Hard interviews   Interviews in which structure and presentation are authoritarian and resemble formal interrogation.

Hawthorne effect   An expectation effect; related to the respondents' knowledge of being observed.

Hermeneutics   A school of thought aimed at studying and interpreting texts and other manifestations of cultures.

Histogram   Graphic presentation of a distribution consisting of blocks equal to the values of the units of the distribution.

Historicism   The school of thought that states that the course of society is governed by historical laws; the discovery of these laws can help to predict the future of a society.

Homogeneity   The quality of coming from the same origin, being the same or having identical attributes.

Hypothesis   An assumption, an educated guess, which can be tested.

Idiographic   Approaching reality through description (opposite to nomological).

Independent variable   A variable that does not need to be explained by, or is not affected by, another variable.

Index   A summary of indices of theoretical and arithmetic nature.

Indicator   A directly observable trait used to empirically define a variable.

Individual interviews   Interviews with one person at a time.

Induction   The process of making conclusions from the specific and concrete to the general and abstract.

Inductive statistics   Inferential statistics.

Inferential statistics   The type of statistics that makes conclusions from data derived through sampling and projects them onto the population.

Informative interviews   A term used to designate interviews that are set to provide information of a *descriptive* nature.

Inquiring interviews   A concept used to designate interviews in which the respondent is an *informant* with a lot of freedom and opportunities in offering data.

Instruments   Tools of research employed in the context of a methodology.

Intensive interview   A form of interviewing employing an unstructured and unstandardised approach, emphasising informal questioning, looking for deep and accurate information and considering the needs and preferences of the interviewee.

Interaction analysis   A model of studying patterns of interaction in small groups, developed in the 1950s by Bales.

Interaction effect   Changes in a variable caused by changes in another variable to which it is related.

Inter-cohort analysis   Analysis of two or more cohorts in two or more periods of time.

Interpolation   Estimation of missing internal values on the basis of knowledge of external values.

INTER-STAT   A computer program for statistical analysis of research data, mainly for Apple II computers.

Interview   A method of data collection that gathers information through oral questioning.

Interviewer bias   Data distortion stemming from the presence and/or certain traits of the interviewer.

Interviewer guide   A set of questions and instructions used by the interviewer during interviewing.

Interviewer training A process of training aimed at preparing research assistants to perform interviews.

Intra-cohort analysis Analysis of the same cohorts in two or more periods of time.

Items Elements of a whole, for example of a scale or questionnaire. It can be a question, a statement or stimulus, for which the opinion of the subjects is sought.

Laboratory experiments Experiments conducted in a laboratory under strictly controlled conditions.

Lambda coefficient A measure of association between nominally scaled variables.

Likert scale A scale introduced by Likert employing a set of response categories ranging from very positive to very negative, one of which the respondent has to choose.

Linear regression A method of estimating the value of a dependent variable when the values of two intervally scaled and normally distributed variables are known.

Logical positivism A branch of positivism known as empiricism according to which reality can be experienced only through the senses.

Longitudinal studies Studies using the same sample and the same techniques carried out more than once (panel studies).

Matching A method of choosing subjects in experimental research.

Mean The average value.

Median The value that divides an ordinally ranked distribution into two equal parts.

Metatheory The theory that explores the ways in which other theories must be formed in order for them to become successful.

Methodic Sum of research methods employed in a particular project.

Methodology The science of methods; the theory of methods.

Mode The value, in a distribution, with the highest number of observations; the most frequent value.

'Modistat' A statistical package for statistical analysis of research data for MSDOS, PCDOS and Compaq computers.

Multiple-choice question A question with a set of given responses.

Multiple-choice test A test containing multiple-choice questions.

Multiple correlation A form of correlation between a dependent variable and a group of independent variables.

Multivariate statistics Statistical methods dealing with more than one variable.

Narrative interviews Interviews that encourage the respondent to describe in detail or reconstruct a part of his or her life. The influence of the interviewer in this form of interview is minimal.

Neutral interviews Interviews that lie between hard and soft interviews and in which the interviewer takes a factual, distanced, friendly and impersonal position.

Nominal scales Scales in which items can only be defined as equal or unequal/same or different.

Nomological Being based on, related to or accepting law-like, generally valid standards; endeavouring to establish law-like statements.

Non-parametric statistics   Part of inferential statistics that assumes no metric, but topological data or normal distribution.

Null hypothesis (H$_0$)   A hypothesis that defines traits of a sample and on which hypothesis testing is based; H$_0$ states that differences in the samples are caused by chance or methodological procedures and that they have the same traits as the population.

'Number cruncher stat system'   A computer program for statistical analysis of research data, for Macintosh computers.

Objectivity   The notion that the social scientist should exclude subjective influences on the research process.

Observation   A method of data collection employing vision as the main medium of collection.

Open-ended questions   Questions without given response options.

Open interviews   Unstructured and unstandardised interviews.

Openness   The notion held by qualitative researchers according to which research should be open to changes according to the needs of the research process.

Operationalisation   The process of translating abstract concepts into workable (operational) indicators.

Ordinal scales   Scales in which elements are arranged according to their relationship to each other (greater, smaller, older, etc.).

OSIRIS   A statistical package for computer-assisted analysis of research data.

Outlier   Extreme value in a distribution that lies outside the rest of the distribution.

Panel studies   Studies using the same sample and the same techniques carried out more than once (longitudinal studies).

Paradigm   From the Greek *paradigma*. The underlying presuppositions and world view scientists have of their discipline (Kuhn). The image a disciple has of its subject matter (Friedrichs). *Examples*: the social facts paradigm; the social definitions paradigm; and the social behaviour paradigm.

Parameter   A numerical value of the population, displayed using Greek letters.

Partial correlation   A form of correlation computed under the assumption that all other variables are held constant.

Participant observation   A form of observation in which the observer becomes a member of the group or a part of the situation he or she observes.

Participatory action research (PAR)   A form of research characterised by participation of members of the community in the research process.

Path analysis   A statistical method employing multiple regression to study causal relationships in recursive models.

Percentile   A measure of dispersion.

Personal interviews   Interviews during data collection in which the interviewer and interviewee communicate with each other in a face-to-face situation.

Pictograms   A form of presenting data through pictures, for example pictures of coins, persons, animals, cars.

Pie graph   Graphic presentation of data in the form of a pie divided into sections, each of which corresponds to the measured value of the variable.

Pilot study   A complete replica of the main study employed in a fraction of the sample.

Placebo effect The effect thought to be caused by a stimulus that has no power to produce such effects.

Positivism A school of thought developed by Comte seeing reality as the sum of sense impressions, equating social sciences with natural sciences, employing a deductive logic and quantitative research methods, and assuming that life is regulated through natural laws, which social sciences have to uncover and document.

Pre-test A small-scale test administered before the introduction of a study aiming at measuring the efficacy of one or more elements of the main study.

Priestly sociology A sociology working in and for the status quo of an established order.

Product-moment correlation A form of correlation measuring the relationship between intervally scaled variables.

Prophetic sociology A sociology critical of the status quo, interested in discovering system deficiencies and inconsistencies and aiming at informing the community and achieving a more humane society.

Proportional stratification The choice of units in stratified sampling where the number of units are proportional to those of the population.

Propositions A set of logically interrelated concepts establishing some degree of regularity.

P-STAT ('Princeton statistical package') A computer program for statistical analysis of research data.

Pygmalion effect The effect caused by the trend of respondents to adjust to structures and conditions previously defined by the researcher.

Qualitative methods Methods of social research that employ no quantitative standards and techniques; based on theoretical and methodological principles of symbolic interactionism, hermeneutics and ethnomethodology.

Quantitative methods Methods employing quantitative theoretical and methodological principles and techniques and statistics.

Quota sampling A sampling procedure that allows interviewers to choose the respondents in the context of given quotas.

Random sampling A type of sampling employing the theory of probability as the basis of choice of respondents.

Randomisation The process of choosing and ordering units at random.

Range A measure of dispersion describing the distance from the lowest to the highest value of the distribution.

Rank-order correlation A form of correlation that measures the relationship between two ordinally ranked variables.

Rating scale An ordinal scale in which respondents assign values to a research object according to a set of response categories.

Reactivity Any form of change caused by the process of measurement.

Regression analysis A method employed to study the relationship between variables, especially the extent to which a dependent variable is a function of one or more independent variables.

Regression curve The graphic presentation of the regression equation.

Reliability Consistency; the quality of an instrument to produce the same results when employed under the same conditions.

Reliability tests Tests designed to measure reliability (retests, split-half tests, parallel-tests, etc.).

Representative reliability   Reliability across groups.

Representativeness   The attribute of a sample to reflect all relevant elements of the population, and so to represent the population in the research study.

Residual category   The response category in a set of responses that is intended to cover all unspecified answers (e.g. 'other'); the set of influences that cannot be specified or controlled further.

Retest   A reliability test based on testing identical respondents and with identical methods as those of the original study.

Rho   The name of Spearman's coefficient of correlation.

Rotation   A technique of rotating factors in factor analysis in order to determine the optimal matrix of factor loading.

Sample   A group of units chosen to be included in a study.

Sampling   A method of choosing samples.

SAS ('Statistical analysis system')   A statistical computer package for social scientists.

Saturation study   A study that includes all members of the population.

Scaling   The process of construction of the scales commonly used to study attitudes and opinions.

Secondary analysis   Analysis of data already collected in the context of another study.

Self-destroying prophesy   A prediction that fails to become true because it became known.

Self-fulfilling prophesy   A prediction that became true because it became known.

Semantic differential   A scaling method employing standardised pairs of concepts placed at the end of a seven-point continuum on which the respondents are expected to place their responses.

Semi-standardised interviews   Interviews in which the questions are only partly standardised.

Semi-structured interviews   Interviews with a given structure but with relative freedom to formulate the questions and to determine their order and presentation.

Sensualism   The notion held by positivists that the only valid sources of knowledge are the senses.

Significance   A criterion related to the validity of data.

Simple random sampling   A method of sampling employing probability in the selection of the units.

Snowball sampling   A sampling technique in which the respondents are chosen according to information supplied by already studied subjects.

Social distance scale   The Bogardus scale.

Sociogram   Graphic presentation of sociometric data.

Sociomatrix   Tabular presentation of sociometric data.

Sociometry   A method of studying social preferences between members of a group, developed by Moreno.

Soft interviews   A form of interview in which the interviewer exercises no power over the interviewee but offers a guide and assistance only in the task of answering the questions.

Spearman's rho   The coefficient of Spearman's correlation.

'Spida'   A computer program for statistical analysis of research data.

Split-half method   Method of testing reliability by halving the data and comparing the correlation coefficients of the halves.

SPSS ('Statistical programs for social scientists')   A popular method of statistical analysis by means of computers.

Spurious correlation   A correlation that does not hold when conditions change or another variable is introduced.

Stability reliability   Reliability across time.

Standard deviation   The square root of the variance.

Standardised interview   A form of interview using strict content and procedures, ensuring uniformity in approaching the respondents and in collecting the data.

'Statease'   A statistical program for computer analysis of research data, devised for Apple computers.

'Statfast'   A statistical package for analysis of research data mainly for Macintosh computers.

'Statflow'   A statistical program for computer-assisted analysis of research data.

Statistics   Numerical values of a sample displayed using English letters (the opposite of parameters).

'Statpak'   A computer package for statistical analysis of research data.

'Statpro'   A computer program employed for statistical analysis of research data.

'Statworks'   A computer statistical package for analysing research data.

Stratified sampling   A sampling technique in which the population is divided into strata and samplings are taken from each stratum.

Substantive theory   A type of initial theory developed as a prelude to formal theory employed in grounded theory.

Survey   A method of data collection employing a systematic and structured verbal or written questioning.

System of coordinates   A two-dimensional graph employed to display research data.

Taxonomy   A systematic classification of units into groups or categories.

Teleology   The theoretical presupposition that social behaviour, structures and phenomena are explained by their purpose or ends.

Telephone interviews   Interviews conducted by telephone.

Tests of significance   A test aiming to ascertain whether a difference is significant; or to measure the probability error between H_0 and the alternative hypothesis; or to test the degree to which differences in data are random or caused by the methodology, or that they are real.

Theory   A set of logically and systematically interrelated propositions describing and explaining social phenomena.

Thurstone scale   A scale employed to measure attitudes and opinions, developed by Thurstone.

Trend studies   Longitudinal studies using different samples at each stage of investigation.

Triangulation   A research approach employing more than one method of data collection and analysis.

Validity   The ability to produce findings that are in agreement with theoretical or conceptual values. The capacity to measure what a method is intended to measure.

Variance   A measure of dispersion; the average distance of the elements of a distribution from the mean.

Verification   The process of empirical validation, mainly of hypotheses.

Bibliography

Abercrombie, N., Hill, S. and Turner, B. (1988), *The Penguin Dictionary of Sociology*, Harmondsworth, UK: Penguin.

Agnew, N.M. and Pyke, S. W. (1991), *The Science Game: An Introduction to Research in the Social Sciences* (5th edn), Englewood Cliffs, NJ: Prentice-Hall.

Alcoff, L. (1988), 'Cultural feminism vs post-structuralism: the identity crisis in feminism', *Signs*, **13**, 3, pp. 405–36.

Anderson, G. (1989), 'Critical ethnography in education: current status, and the new directions', *Review of Educational Research*, **59**, 3, pp. 249–70.

Arbeitsgruppe Bielefelder Soziologen (eds) (1973), *Alltagswissen, Interaktion und gesellschaftliche Wirklichkeit*, vol.1, *Symbolischer Interaktionismus und Ethnomethodologie*; vol 2 (1976), *Ethnotheorie und Ethnographie des Sprechens*, Reinbeck (bei Hamburg): Rowohlt.

Arbeitsgruppe Bielefelder Soziologen (1976), *Kommunikative Sozialforschung*, Munich: Fink.

Argyrous, G. (1996), *Statistics for Social Research*, Melbourne: Macmillan.

Atkinson, J.M. and Heritage, J. (1984), *Structure of Social Action. Studies in Conversational Analysis*, Cambridge: Cambridge University Press.

Aufenanger, S. and Lenssen, M. (eds) (1986), *Handlung und Sinnstruktur. Bedeutung und Anwendung der objektiven Hermeneutik*, Munich: Kindt.

Australian Vice Chancellors Committee (1990), *Guidelines for Responsible Practices in Research and Dealing with Problems of Research Misconduct*.

Babbie, E.R. (1990), *Survey Research Methods* (2nd edn), Belmont CA: Wadsworth.

Bailey, K.D. (1982), *Methods of Social Research*, New York: The Free Press.

Bailey, K.D. (1988), 'Ethical dilemmas in social research. A theoretical framework', *American Sociologist*, **19**, pp. 121–37.

Baker, T.L. (1988), *Doing Social Research*, New York: McGraw-Hill.

Barton, A.H. and Lazarsfeld, P.F. (1979), 'Einige Funktionen von qualitativer Analyze in der Sozialforschung', in C. Hopf and E. Weingarten (eds), *Qualitative Sozialforschung*, Stuttgart: Clett-Cotta, pp. 41–89.

Bauer, W. (1994), *Qualitative Forschung mit Gastarbeitern*, Weimar: Ganz Verlag.

Becker, B. (1989), *Grundlagen soziologischer Methodologie*, Frankfurt: Selbstverlag.

Becker, H.S. (1963), *Outsiders: Studies in the Sociology of Deviance*, New York: The Free Press.

Beed, T.W. and Stinton, R.T. (eds) (1985), *Survey Interviewing: Theory and Techniques*, London: Allen & Unwin.

Berelson, B. (1952), *Content Analysis in Community Research*, Glencoe, Ill.: The Free Press.

Berg, B.L. (1989), *Qualitative Research Methods for the Social Sciences*, London: Allyn and Bacon.

Berger, H., Wolf H.F. and Ullmann, E. (eds) (1989), *Handbuch der Sozialistischen Forschung. Methodologie, Methoden, Technicken*, Berlin: Akademie Verlag.

Bergmann, B. (1991), *Sozialtheorie und Soziologie*, Stuttgart: Selbstverlag.

Bergmann, J.R. (1991), 'Konversationsanalyse', in U. Flick *et al.* (eds), *Handbuch Qualitative Sozialforschung*, Munich: Psychologie Verlags Union, pp. 213–18.

Blaikie, N. (1988), 'Triangulation in social research. Origins, use and problems', Paper presented at the Conference of the Sociological Association of Australia and New Zealand, Canberra.

Blumer, H. (1969), *Symbolic Interactionism: Perspectives and Method*, Englewood Cliffs, NJ: Prentice-Hall.

Blumer, H. (1973), 'Der methodologische Standort des Symbolischen Interaktionismus', in Arbeitsgruppe Bielefelder Soziologen (eds), *Alltagswissen, Interaktion und gesellschaftliche Wirklichkeit*, Reinbek (bei Hamburg): Rowohlt, pp. 80–146.

Blumer, H. (1979a), *Critiques of Research in the Social Sciences*, New Brunswick, NJ: Transaction Books.

Blumer, H. (1979b), 'Methodologische Prinzipien empirischer Wissenschaft', in K. Gerdes (ed.), *Explorative Sozialforschung*, Stuttgart: Enke, pp. 41–62.

Bogdan, R.C. and Biklin, S.K. (1992), *Qualitative Research for Education. An Introduction to Theory and Methods,* Boston, MA: Allyn and Bacon.

Bogumil, J. and Immerfall, S. (1985), *Wahrnehmungsweisen empirischer Sozialforschung. Zum Selbstverstaendnis des sozialwissenschaftlichen Forschungsprozesses*, Frankfurt am Main: Campus Verlag.

Bradburn, N.M. and Sudman, S. (1988), *Polls and Surveys. Understanding What They Tell Us*, San Francisco: Jossey-Bass.

Brieschke, P.A. (1992), 'Reparative praxis: rethinking the catastrophe that is social science', *Theory into Practice*, **XXXI**, 2, pp. 173–80.

Bromley, D.B. (1986), *The Case-Study Method in Psychology and Related Disciplines*, New York: Wiley.

Brown, R.H. (1992), *Writing the Social Text. Poetics and Politics in Social Science Discourse,* New York: Allyn and Bacon.

Bryman, A. (1984), 'The debate about quantitative and qualitative research: a question of method or epistemology?', *British Journal of Sociology*, **35**, pp. 75–92.

Bryman, A. (1988), *Quantity and Quality in Social Research*, London: Unwin Hyman.

Bude, H. (1984), 'Rekonstruktion von Lebenskonstruktionen — eine Antwort auf die Frage, was die Biographieforschung bringt', in M. Kohli and G. Robert (eds), *Biographie und soziale Wirklichkeit. Neue Beitraege und Forschungsperspektiven*, Stuttgart: Metzler, pp. 7–28.

Buehler-Niederberger, D. (1985), 'Analytische Induction als Verfahren der qualitativen Methodologie', *Zeitschrift fuer Soziologie*, **6**, pp. 475–85.

Bulmer, M. (1979), 'Concepts of the analysis of qualitative data: a symposium', *Sociological Review*, **27**, pp. 651–77.

Burgard, W. and Lueck, H.E. (1991), 'Nichtreactive Verfahren', in U. Flick *et al.* (eds), *Handbuch Qualitative Sozialforschung*, Munich: Psychologie Verlags Union, pp. 198–202.

Burgess, R.G. (1982), *Field Research: A Sourcebook and Field Manual*, London: Allen & Unwin.

Burgess, R.G. (1984), *In the Field. An Introduction to Field Research*, London: Allen & Unwin.

Burns, R.B. (1990), *Introduction to Social Research in Education*, Melbourne: Longman Cheshire.

Callan, V.J. (1991), 'Methods for studying Australian families', in K. Funder (ed.), *Images of Australian Families*, Melbourne: Longman Cheshire, pp. 136–46.

Carspecken, P.F. and Apple, M. (1992), 'Critical qualitative research: theory, methodology and practice', in M.D. LeCompte, W.L. Millroy and J. Preissle (eds), *The Handbook of Qualitative Research in Education,* San Diego: Academic Press, pp. 507–54.

Chadwick, B.A., Bahr, H.M. and Albrecht, S.L. (1984), *Social Science Research Methods,* Englewood Cliffs, NJ: Prentice-Hall.

Cicourel, A. (1970, 1974), *Methode und Messung in der Soziologie,* Frankfurt am Main: Shurkamp.

Coffey, A. (1996). *Making Sense of Qualitative Data: Complementary Research Strategies,* Thousand Oaks, CA: Sage.

Collins, E.C. (1992), 'Qualitative research as art: toward a holistic process', *Theory into Practice,* **XXXI**, 2, pp. 181–6.

Committee on the Status of Women in Society (1986), *The Treatment of Gender in Research,* Washington DC: American Sociological Association.

Contrad, P. and Reinharz, S. (1984), 'Computers and qualitative data', *Qualitative Sociology,* **7**, pp. 4–15.

Converse, J.M. and Presser, S. (1986), *Survey Questions. Handcrafting the Standardised Questionnaire,* Beverly Hills, CA: Sage.

Cook, J.A. and Fonow, M.M. (1990), 'Knowledge and women's interests: issues of epistemology and methodology in feminist sociological research', in J.M. Nielsen (ed.), *Feminist Research Methods. Exemplary Readings in the Social Sciences,* London: Westview Press, pp. 69–93.

Cook, T.D., Cooper, H., Cordray, D.S., Hartman, H., Hedges, L.V., Light, R.J., Louis, T.A. and Mosteller, F. (1992) *Meta-analysis for Explanation. A Casebook,* New York: Russell Sage Foundation.

Cook, T. and Reinhardt, C.S. (eds) (1979), *Qualitative and Quantitative Methods in Evaluation Research,* Beverley Hills, CA: Sage.

Crabtree, B.F. and Miller, W.L. (1992), *Doing Qualitative Research,* Newbury Park, CA: Sage.

Crawford, H.J. and Christensen, I.B. (1995), *Developing Research Skills: A Laboratory Manual,* Boston: Allyn and Bacon.

Danner, H. (1979), *Methoden Geisteswissenschaftlicher Paedagogik,* Munich: E. Reinhardt.

Denzin, N.K. (1970, 1978, 1989), *The Research Act: A Theoretical Introduction to Sociological Methods* (3rd edn), Englewood Cliffs, NJ: Prentice-Hall.

Department of Health, Education and Welfare (1975), 'Protection of human subjects — technical amendments', *Federal Register,* **40**, pp. 11854–8.

De Vaus, D.A. (1985), *Surveys in Social Research,* Sydney: Allen & Unwin.

Dick, B. (1987), *Convergent Interviewing,* St Lucia, Qld: Interchange.

Drass, K. (1980), 'The analysis of qualitative data: a computer program', *Urban Life,* **9**, pp. 332–3.

Dreher, M. and Dreher, E. (1991), 'Gruppendiscussionverfahren', in U. Flick *et al.* (eds), *Handbuch Qualitative Sozialforschung,* Munich: Psychologie Verlags Union, pp. 186–8.

Drew, C.J., Hardman, M.L. and Hart, A.W. (1996), *Designing and Conducting Research. Inquiry in Education and Social Science,* London: Allyn and Bacon.

Eckhardt, K.W. and Ermann, M.D. (1977), *Social Research Methods. Perspective, Theory and Analysis,* Toronto: Random House.

Edwards, A.L. (1957), *Techniques of Attitude Scale Construction,* New York: Appleton-Crofts.

Eichler, M. (1988), *Non-Sexist Research Methods: A Practical Guide,* Boston: Allen & Unwin.

Eichler, M., Lenton, S., Bridribb, S., Haddad, J. and Ross, B. (1985), *A Selected Annotated Bibliography on Sexism in Research,* Ottawa: Social Sciences and Humanities Research Council of Canada.

Ellgring, H. (1991), 'Audiovisuell unterstuetzte Beobachtung', in U. Flick *et al.* (eds), *Handbuch Qualitative Sozialforschung*, Munich: Psychologie Verlags Union, pp. 203–8.

Ellis, L. (1993), 'Operationally defining social stratification in human and nonhuman animals', in L. Ellis (ed.), *Social Stratification and Socioeconomic Inequality: A Comparative Biosocial Analysis*, New York: Praeger, pp. 15–35.

Ellis, L. (1994), *Research Methods in the Social Sciences,* Oxford: Brown and Benchmark.

Engel, U. and Weggenig, U. (1991), 'Statistische Auswertungsverfahren nominalskalierter Daten', in U. Flick *et al.* (eds), *Handbuch Qualitative Sozialforschung*, Munich: Psychologie Verlags Union, pp. 237–42.

Fay, B. (1980), *Social Theory and Political Praxis*, London: Allen & Unwin.

Fay, B. (1987), *Critical Social Science: Liberation and its Limits*, Ithaca, New York: Cornell UP.

Fee, E. (1986), 'Critiques of modern science', in R. Bleier (ed.), *Feminist Approaches to Science*, New York: Pergamon Press, pp. 42–56.

Fine, G.A. (1988), 'The Ten Commandments of writing', *The American Sociologist*, **19**, pp. 152–60.

Firestone, W.A. (1993), 'Alternative arguments for generalizing from data as applied to qualitative research', *Educational Researcher,* **22**, 4, pp. 16–23.

Fischer, W. and Kohl, M. (1987), 'Biographieforschung', in W. Voges (ed.), *Methoden der Biographie- und Lebenslaufforschung*, Opladen: Leske und Buderich, pp. 23–50.

Flick, U., Kardorff, E. von, Keup, L., Rosenstiel, V. and Wolf, S. (eds) (1991), *Handbuch Qualitative Sozialforschung*, Munich: Psychologie Verlags Union.

Foddy, W. H. (1988), *Elementary Applied Statistics for Social Sciences*, Sydney: Harper and Row:

Foddy, W.H. (1993), *Constructing Questions for Interviews and Questionnaires. Theory and Practice in Social Research,* Melbourne: Cambridge University Press.

Freeman, C.R. (1980), Phenomenological sociology and ethnomethodology', in J.D. Douglas *et al.* (eds), *Introduction to the Sociologies of Everyday Life*, Boston: Allyn and Bacon, pp. 113–54.

Frey, James H. (1989), *Survey Research by Telephone*, Newbury Park, CA: Sage.

Friedrichs, J. (1987), *23. Soziologentag 1986. Sektions- und Ad-hoc Gruppen*, Opladen: Westdeutscher Verlag.

Fuchs, W. (1984), *Biographische Forschung. Eine Einfuehrung in Praxis und Methoden*, Opladen: Westdeutscher Verlag.

Gadamer, H.-G. (1960, 1975), *Warheit und Methode, Grundzuege einer philosophischen Hermeneutik*, Tuebingen: Mohr.

Gardner, G. (1976), *Social Surveys for Social Planners*, Sydney: Holt, Rinehart and Winston.

Garfinkel, H. (1967), *Studies in Ethnomethodology*, Englewood Cliffs, NJ: Prentice-Hall.

Geer, J.G. (1988), 'What do open-ended questions measure?', *Public Opinion Quarterly*, **52**, pp. 365–71.

Geldsthorpe, L. (1992), 'Response to Martyn Hammersley's paper "On Feminist Methodology"', *Sociology, The Journal of the British Sociological Association*, **26**, 2, pp. 213–18.

Gerdes, K. (ed.) (1979), *Explorative Sozialforschung*, Stuttgart: Enke.

Girtler, R. (1984), *Methoden der qualitativen Sozialforschung. Anleitung zur Feldarbeit*, Wien: Boehlau.

Glaser, B.G. (1992), *Emergence vs. Forcing: Basics of Grounded Theory Analysis,* Mill Valey, CA: Sociology Press.

Glaser, B.G. and Strauss, A.L. (1967), *The Discovery of Grounded Theory. Strategies for Qualitative Research*, Chicago: Aldine.

Glaser, B.G. and Strauss, A.L. (1979), 'Die Entdeckung genenwartsbezogener Theorie: Eine Grundstrategie qualitativer Sozialforschung', in C. Hopf and E. Weingarten (eds), *Qualitative Sozialforschung*, Stuttgart: Enke.

Glass, G.W. (1976), 'Primary, secondary and meta-analysis of research', *Educational Researcher,* **5**, pp. 3–8.

Guba, E.G. (1990), *The Paradigm Dialog*, Newbury Park, CA: Sage.

Guba, E.G. and Lincoln, Y.S. (1989), *Fourth Generation Evaluation,* Newbury Park, CA: Sage.

Guilford, J.P. (1965), *Fundamental Statistics in Psychology and Education*, New York: McGraw-Hill.

Habermas, J. (1988), *On the Logic of Social Sciences*, Oxford: Polity Press.

Hakim, C. (1987), *Research Design: Strategies and Choices in the Design of Social Research*, London: Allen & Unwin.

Hammersley, M. (1991), *Reading Ethnographic Research: A Critical Guide*, London: Longman.

Hammersley, M. (1992a), 'On feminist methodology', *Sociology, The Journal of the British Sociological Association*, **26**, 2, pp. 187–206.

Hammersley, M. (1992b), *What is Wrong with Ethnography?*, London: Routledge.

Hammersley, M. and Atkinson, P. (1983), *Ethnography: Principles in Practice*, New York: Vintage Books.

Harding, S. (1986), *The Science Question in Feminism,* Ithaca, NY: Cornell UP.

Harding, S. (ed.) (1987), *Feminism and Methodology*, Bloomington: Indiana UP.

Harding, S. (1990), 'Feminism, science, and the anti-enlightenment critiques', in L. Nicholson (ed.), *Feminism/Postmodernism*, New York: Routledge, pp. 83–106.

Hartfield, G. (1972, 1982), *Woerterbuch der Soziologie*, Stuttgart: Kroener.

Harvey, L. (1990), *Critical Social Research*, London: Unwin Hyman.

Heinze, T. (1987), *Qualitative Sozialforschung. Erfahrungen, Probleme, Perspektiven* (2nd edn 1992), Opladen: Westdeutscher Verlag.

Hermanns, N. (1991), 'Narratives interview', in U. Flick *et al.* (eds), *Handbuch Qualitative Sozialforschung*, Munich: Psychologie Verlags Union, pp. 182–5.

Hermans, H., Tkocz, C. and Winkler, H. (eds) (1984), *Berufsverlauf von Ingenieuren: biographieanalytische Auswertung narrativer Interviews*, Frankfurt am Main: Campus Verlag.

Hess, Juergen P. (1982), *Empirische Sozialforschung und automatisierte Datenverarbeitung*, Berlin: Max-Plank Institute fuer Bildungsforschung.

Hildebrand, B., Mueller, H., Beyer, B. and Klein, D. (1984), 'Biographiestudien in Rahmen von Milieustudien', in M. Kohli and G. Robert (eds), *Biographie und soziale Wirklichkeit. Neue Beitraege und Forschungsperspektiven*, Stuttgart: Metzler, pp. 29–52.

Hopf, C. (1991), 'Qualitative Interviews in der Sozialforschung. Ein Ueberblick', in U. Flick *et al.* (eds), *Handbuch Qualitative Sozialforschung*, Munich: Psychologie Verlags Union, pp. 177–81.

Hopf, C. and Weingarten, E. (eds) (1979), *Qualitative Sozialforschung*, Stuttgart: Clett Cotta.

Huber, G.L. (1991), 'Computerunterstuetzte Auswertung qualitativer Daten', in U. Flick *et al.* (eds), *Handbuch Qualitative Sozialforschung*, Munich: Psychologie Verlags Union, pp. 242–8.

Hughes, J.A. (1990), *The Philosophy of Social Research* (2nd edn), London: Longman.

Hunter, J.E. (1990), *Methods of Meta-analysis: Correcting Error and Bias in Research,* Newbury Park, CA: Sage.

Hurrelman, K. and Ulich, D. (eds) (1980), *Handbuch der Sozialisationsforschung*, Opladen: Beltz.

Husserl, E. (1950), *Gesammelte Werke*, The Hague: M. Nijhoff.

Jacob, E. (1987), 'Traditions of qualitative research: a review', *Review of Educational Research*, **51**, pp. 1–50.

Jacob, E. (1988), 'Classifying qualitative research', *Educational Researcher*, **17**, pp. 16–24.

Johnson, D.P. (1989), *Sociological Theory*, New York: Wiley and Sons.

Judd, C.K., Smith, E.L. and Kidder, L.H. (1991), *Research Methods in Social Relations*, New York: Harcourt, Brace, Jovanovich.

Juettemann, G. (ed.) (1985), *Qualitative Forschung in der Psychologie. Grundfragen, Verfahrensweisen, Anwendungsfelder*, Weinheim: Beltz.

Kahn, R.L. and Cannell, C.F. (1957), *The Dynamics of Interviewing: Theory, Technique, and Cases*, New York: Wiley and Sons.

Kellehear, A. (1993), *The Unobtrusive Researcher. A Guide to Methods,* Sydney: Allen & Unwin.

Keller, E.F. (1980), 'Feminist critiques research: a forward or backward move?', *Fundamenta Scientiae*, **1**, pp. 341–9.

Keller, E.F. (1985), *Reflections on Gender and Science*, New Haven, CT: Yale University Press.

Kidder, L.H. (1981), *Research Methods in Social Relationships*, New York: Holt, Rinehart and Winston.

Kimmel, A.J. (1988), *Ethics and Values in Applied Social Research*, Newbury Park, CA: Sage.

Kimmon, S. (1990), *Theoretical Statistics*, Acron (Mimeograph).

Kirk, J. and Miller, M.L. (1986), *Reliability and Validity in Qualitative Research*, Beverley Hills, CA: Sage.

Kleining, G. (1988), *Das rezeptive Interview*, Bielefeld: University of Bielefeld.

Kleining, G. (1991), 'Das qualitative Experiment', in U. Flick *et al.* (eds), *Handbuch Qualitative Sozialforschung*, Munich: Psychologie Verlags Union, pp. 263–5.

Koeckeis-Stangl, I. (1980), 'Methoden der Sozialisationsforschung', in D. Ulrich and K. Hurrelmann (eds), *Handbuch der Sozialisationsforschung*, Opladen: Beltz, pp. 312–70.

Koenig, R. (ed.) (1978), *Das Interview. Formen, Technik Auswertung*, Cologne: Kiepenheuer and Witsch.

Kohli, M. (1987), 'Normalbiographie und Individualitaet. Zur institutionellen Dynamik des gegenwaertigen Lebenslaufregimes', in J. Friedrichs (ed.), *23. Soziologentag 1986. Sektions- und Ad-hoc Gruppen*, Opladen: Westdeutscher Verlag, pp. 432–5.

Kohli, M. and Robert, G. (eds) (1984), *Biographie und soziale Wirklichkeit. Neue Beitraege und Forschungsperspektiven*, Stuttgart: Metzler.

Konegen, N. and Sondergeld, K. (1985), *Wissenschaftstheorie fuer Sozialwissenschaftler*, Opladen: Leske und Budrich.

Kraemer, H.C. and Thieman, S. (1987), *How Many Subjects? Statistical Power Analysis in Research*, London: Sage.

Krejcie, R.V. and Morgan, D.W. (1970), 'Determining sample size for research activities', *Educational and Psychological Measurement*, **30**, pp. 607–10.

Kromrey, H. (1986), *Empirische Sozialforschung*, Opladen: Fernuniversitaet Gesamthochschulen.

Krueger, B. (1983), *Theoretische Methodologie*, Leipzig: Selbstverlag.

Krueger, H. (1983), 'Gruppendiskussion. Ueberlegungen zur Rekonstruktion sozialer Wirklichkeit aus der Sicht der Betroffenen', *Soziale Welt*, **34**, pp. 90–109.

Kuechler, M., Wilson, T.P. and Zimmerman, D.H. (eds) (1981), *Integration von qualitativen und quantitativen Forschungsansaetzen*, Manheim: ZUMA-Arbeitsbericht 81/19.

Kuhn, T. (1970), *The Structure of Scientific Revolutions*, Chicago: University of Chicago Press.

Kulik, J.A. and Kulik, C.C. (1992), 'Meta-analysis: historical origins and contemporary practice', *Advances in Social Science Methodology,* **2**, pp. 53–79.

Kuzel, A.J. (1992), 'Sampling in qualitative inquiry', in B.F. Crabtree and W.L. Miller (eds), *Doing Qualitative Research*, Newbury Park, CA: Sage, pp. 31–44.

Lamnek, S. (1988), *Qualitative Sozialforschung*. Band 1: *Methodologie*; Band 2: *Methoden und Techniken*, Munich: Psychologie Verlags Union.

Lancy. D.E. (1993), *Qualitative Research in Education: An Introduction to the major Traditions*, New York: Longman.

Lather, P. (1991), *'Getting Smart: Feminist Research and Pedagogy with/in the Postmodern*, New York: Routledge.

Lather, P. (1992), 'Critical frames in educational research: feminist and post-structural perspectives', *Theory into Practice*, **XXXI**, 2, pp. 87–99.

LeCompte, M.D. and Goetz, J.P. (1982), 'Problems of reliability and validity in ethnographic research', in *Review of Educational Research*, **52**, pp. 31–60.

Legewie, H. (1991), 'Feldforschung und teilnehmende Beobachtung', in U. Flick *et al.* (eds), *Handbuch Qualitative Sozialforschung*, Munich: Psychologie Verlags Union, pp. 189–92.

Lenssen, M. and Aufenanger, S. (1986), 'Zur Rekonstruktion von Interaktionsstrukturen. Neue Wege zur Fernsehanalyze', in S. Aufenanger and M. Lenssen (eds), *Handlung und Sinnstruktur. Bedeutung und Anwendung der objektiven Hermeneutik*, Munich: Kindt, pp. 123–204.

Likert, R.A. (1932), 'A technique of measurement of attitudes', *Archives of Psychology*, **140**, pp. 44–53.

Lin, N. (1976), *Foundations of Social Research*, London: McGraw-Hill.

Lincoln, Y. and Guba, E. (1985), *Naturalistic Inquiry*, Beverley Hills, CA: Sage.

McCall, G.J. (1979), 'Qualitaetskontrolle der Daten bei teilnehmender Beobachtung', in K. Gerdes (ed.), *Explorative Sozialforschung*, Stuttgart: Enke, pp. 141–57.

McNiff, J. (1992), *Action Research: Principles and Practice*, London: Routledge.

McQuarrie, E.F. (1996), *The Market Research Toolbox: A Concise Guide for Beginners*, Thousand Oaks, CA: Sage.

Maanen van, J. (ed.) (1983a), *Qualitative Methodology*, Beverley Hills, CA: Sage.

Maanen van, J. (1983b), 'Reclaiming qualitative methods for organisational research. A preface', in J. van Maanen (ed.), *Qualitative Methodology*, Beverley Hills, CA: Sage, pp. 9–18.

Madron, T.W., Tate, C.N. and Brookshire, R.G. (1987), *Using Microcomputers in Research*, Beverley Hills, CA: Sage.

Mahr, W. (1995), *Politische Struktur der Sozialforschung*, Leipzig: Selbstverlag.

Mann, C. (1990), 'Meta-analysis in the breech', *Science*, **249**, pp. 476–80.

Mariner, J. (1986), *Anwendung von Gruppendiscussion in Soziologie*, Munich: Blasaditch.

Marshall, C. and Rossman, G.B. (1989), *Designing Qualitative Research*, Beverley Hills, CA: Sage.

Martin, K. (1988), *Methodologisches Denken*, Hamburg: Selbstverlag.

Maxwell, J.A. (1992), 'Understanding and validity in qualitative research', *Harvard Educational Review*, **62**, 3, pp. 279–300.

Mayntz, R., Holm, K. and Hoebner, P. (1978), *Introduction to Empirical Sociology*, Harmondsworth: Penguin.

Mayring, P. (1983), *Grundlagen und Techniken qualitativer Inhaltsanalyze*, Dissertation, Univ. of Munich.

Mayring, P. (1985), 'Qualitative Inhaltsanalyze', in H. Juettemann (ed.), *Qualitative Forschung in der Psychologie. Grundfragen, Verfahrensweisen, Anwendungsfelder*, Weinheim: Beltz, pp. 187–211.

Mayring, P. (1988), *Qualitative Inhaltsanalyse. Grundlagen und Techniken*, Munich: Dt Studien Verlag.

Mayring, P. (1991), 'Qualitative Inhaltsanalyse', in U. Flick *et al.* (eds), *Handbuch Qualitative Sozialforschung*, Munich: Psychologie Verlags Union, pp. 209–12.

Menzel, A. (1936), *Griechische Soziologie*, Viena and Laipzig: Hoelder–Piechlor–Tempsky.

Merten, K. (1983), *Inhaltsanalyse. Einfuehrung in Theorie, Methode und Praxis*, Opladen: Westdeutscher Verlag.

Miles, M.B. and Huberman, A.M. (1984a), *Qualitative Data Analysis: A Sourcebook of New Methods*, Beverley Hills, CA: Sage.

Miles, M.B. and Huberman, A.M. (1984b), *Qualitative Data Analysis: An Expanded Sourcebook* (2nd edn), Thousand Oaks, CA: Sage.

Miles, M.B. and Huberman, A.M. (1994), *Qualitative Data Analysis: An Expanded Sourcebook*, Beverley Hills, CA: Sage.

Miller, C. and Treitel, C. (1991), *Feminist Research Methods. An Annotated Bibliography*, New York: Greenwood Press.

Mills, C.W. (1959), *The Sociological Imagination*, London: Oxford University Press.

Minichiello, V., Aroni, R., Timewell, E. and Alexander, L. (1990), *In-Depth Interviewing. Researching People*, Melbourne: Longman Cheshire.

Morgan, D.L. (1996), 'Focus groups', in J. Hagan and K.S. Cook (eds), *Annual Review of Sociology*, vol. 22, Palo Alto, CA: Annual Reviews, pp. 129–152.

Morgan, D.L. (1997), *Focus Groups as Qualitative Research*, Newbury Park, CA: Sage.

Moser, C.A. and Kalton, G. (1971), *Survey Methods in Social Investigation*, London: Heinemann.

Mucchielli, R. (1973), *Das Gruppeninterview. Theoretische Einfuehrung*, Salzburg: Mueller.

Mueller, U. (1979), *Reflexive Soziologie und empirische Sozialforschung*, Frankfurt am Main: Campus Verlag.

Mullen, B. and Miller, N. (1991), 'Meta-analysis', in C.K. Judd, E.L. Smith and L.H. Kidder (eds), *Research Methods in Social Relations*, New York: Harcourt, Brace, Jovanovich, pp. 425–49.

Murray, M.J. and Hay-Roe, H. (1986), *Engineered Writing. A Manual for Scientific, Technical and Business Writers*, Tulsa, Oklahoma: PennWell Books.

Nagler, K. and Reichhertz, J. (1986), 'Kontaktanzeigen. Auf der Suche nach dem anderen den man nicht kennen will', in S. Aufenanger and M. Lenssen (eds), *Handlung und Sinnstruktur. Bedeutung und Anwendung der objektiven Hermeneutik*, Munich: Kindt, pp. 84–122.

Nebraska Sociological Feminist Collective (1988), *A Feminist Ethic for Social Science Research*, Lewiston: Edwin Mellen Press.

Neuman, W.L. (1991, 1994), *Social Research Methods*, London: Allyn and Bacon.

Nicholson, L. (ed.) (1990), *Feminism/Postmodernism*, New York: Routledge.

Nielsen, J.M. (ed.) (1990), *Feminist Research Methods. Exemplary Readings in the Social Sciences*, London: Westview Press.

Oakley, A. (1981), 'Interviewing women: a contradiction in terms', in H. Roberts (ed.), *Doing Feminist Research*, London: Routledge, pp. 30–61.

Oevermann, V., Allert, T., Konav, E. and Krambeck, J. (1983), 'Die Methodologie einer "objectiven Hermeneutik"', in P. Zedler and H. Moser (eds), *Aspekte qualitativer Sozialforschung. Studien zu Aktionsforschung empirischer Hermeneutik und reflexiver Sozialtechnologie*, Opladen: Leske und Budrich, pp. 95–123.

Oja, S. and Smulyan, L. (1989), *Collaborative Action Research: A Developmental Approach*, London: Falmer.

Olds, E.G. (1940), 'The 5% significance levels for sums of squares of rank differences and a correction', *Annals of Mathematical Statistics*, **20**, pp. 117–18.

Oppenheim, A.N. (1992), *Questionnaire Design, Interviewing and Attitude Measurement*, London: Pinter.

Osgood, C.E., Suci, G.J. and Tannenbaum, P.H. (eds) (1957), *The Measurement of Meaning*, Urbana, Ill.: University of Illinois Press.

Pannas, N. (1996), Πολιτικη και Κοινη Γνωμη (Politics and Public Opinion), Leipzig: Selbstverlag.

Parten, M. (1950), *Survey Polls and Samples*, New York: Harper and Row.

Patton, M. (1990), *Qualitative Evaluation and Research Methods*, Newbury Park, CA: Sage.

Pelz, D.C. (1981), *Use of Innovation in Innovating Processes by Local Govermnents*, Ann Arbor: CRUSK, Institute for Social Research, University of Michigan.

Peoples, J. and Bailey, G. (1988), *Humanity: An Introduction to Cultural Anthropology*, St Paul, MN: West Publishing.

Pilcher, J. and Coffey, A. (eds) (1996), *Gender and Qualitative Research,* Aldershot: Avebury.

Poloma, M.M. (1974), *Contemporary Sociological Theory*, New York: Macmillan.

Puris, X. (1995), *The Complexity of Research Measures* (in Greek), Paris: Ajax.

Ragin, C.C. (1987), *The Comparative Method*, Berkley: University of California Press.

Ragin, C.C. and Becker, H.S. (1989), 'How the microcomputer is changing our analytic habits', in G. Blank *et al.* (eds), *New Technology in Sociology: Practical Applications in Research and Work,* New Brunswick, NJ: Transaction Books.

Ramazanoglu, C. (1992), 'On feminist methodology: male reason versus female empowerment', *Sociology, The Journal of the British Sociological Association*, **26**, 2, pp. 207–12.

Rassenberger, J. (1989), *Computerintegrierte Informationsverarbeitung in der empirischen Sozialforschung*, Nuernberg: Institut fuer Freie Berufe.

Ravagniani, M. (1991), *The Circumstantial Relationship. A Study of the Meaning of Care to Staff Working in a Group Home for People with Intellectual Disabilities*, MA Thesis, Deakin University.

Reichertz, J. (1991), 'Objective Hermeneutik', in U. Flick *et al.* (eds), *Handbuch Qualitative Sozialforschung*, Munich: Psychologie Verlags Union, pp. 223–7.

Reid, S. (1987), *Working with Statistics*, Cambridge: Polity Press.

Reinecker, H. (1987), 'Einzelfallstudie', in E. Roth (ed.), *Handbuch Qualitative Sozialforschung*, Munich: Psychologie Verlags Union, pp. 277–91.

Reinharz, S. (1983), 'Experiential analysis: a contribution to feminist research', in G. Bowles and R. Duelli-Klein (eds), *Theories of Women's Studies*, Boston: Routledge and Kegan Paul, pp. 162–91.

Reinharz, S. (1992), *Feminist Methods in Social Research*, New York: Oxford University Press.

Richards, T. (1986), NUDIST: *User's Manual*, Melbourne: Replee.

Richards, L. and Richards, T. (1987), 'Qualitative data analysis: can computers do it?', *The Australian and New Zealand Journal of Sociology*, **23**, 1, pp. 23–35.

Richards, T. and Richards, L. (1994), 'Using computers in qualitative analysis', in N. Denzin and Y. Lincoln (eds), *Handbook of Qualitative Research,* Thousand Oaks, CA: Sage.

Ritzer, G. (1983), *Sociological Theory*, New York: Knopf.

Roberts, H. (1981), *Doing Feminist Research*, London: Routledge and Kegan Paul.

Rorty, R. (1985), 'Solidarity or objectivity?', in J. Rajchman and C. West (eds), *Post-analytic Philosophy*, New York: Columbia University Press, pp. 3–19.

Rorty, R. (1989), *Contingency, Irony, and Solidarity*, Cambridge: Cambridge University Press.

Roth, E. (ed.) (1987), *Sozialwissenschaftliche Methoden. Lehr- und Handbuch fuer Forschung und Praxis*, Munich: Oldenburg.

Sayers, J., Evans, M. and Redclift, N. (eds) (1987), *Engels Revisited: New Feminist Essays*, London: Tavistock.

Scheele, B. (1991), 'Dialogische Hermeneutic', in U. Flick *et al.* (eds), *Handbuch Qualitative Sozialforschung*, Munich: Psychologie Verlags Union, pp. 274–8.

Schensul, J.J. and Schensul, S.L. (1992), 'Collaborative research: methods of inquiry for social change', in M.D. LeCompte, W.L Millroy and J. Preissle (eds), *The Handbook of Qualitative Research in Education*, New York: Academic Press, pp. 161–200.

Schrag, F. (1992), 'In defence of positivistic research paradigms', *Educational Researcher*, **21**, 5, pp. 5–8.

Schuetz, A. (1969), *Der sinnhafte Aufbau der sozialen Welt*, Wien: Shurkamp.

Schuetze, F. (1979), *Die Technik des narrativen Interviews in Interaktionsstudien. Dargestellt an einem Projekt von kommunalen Machtstrukturen*, No. 1, Bielefeld: University of Bielefeld, Arbeitsberichte und Forschungsmaterialien.

Schwartz, R. and Jacobs, J. (1979), *Qualitative Sociology: A Method to the Madness*, New York: The Free Press.

Selltiz, C., Jahoda, M., Deutsch, M. and Cook, S.W. (1960), *Research Methods in Social Relations*, New York: Holt, Rinehart and Winston.

Selltiz, C., Wrightsman, L.J. and Cook, S. W. (1976), *Research Methods in Social Relations*, New York: Holt, Rinehart and Winston.

Shaw, C.R. (1930, 1966), *The Jack Roller. A Delinquent Boy's Own Story*, Chicago: University of Chicago Press.

Silverman, D. (1985), *Qualitative Methodology and Sociology*, Aldershot: Gower Pub. Co.

Simons, H. (ed.) (1989), *Rhetoric in the Human Sciences*, Beverley Hills, CA: Sage.

Singleton, R. Jr., Straits, B., Straits, M. and McAllister, R. (1988), *Approaches to Social Research*, New York: Oxford University Press.

'Small-Sample Techniques', *The NEA Research Bulletin*, **38** (Dec. 1960), p. 99.

Smith, J. (1990), 'Alternative research paradigms and the problem of criteria', in E. Guba (ed.), *The Paradigm Dialog*, Newbury Park, CA: Sage, pp. 167–87.

Smith, J.K. (1992), 'Interpretive inquiry: a practical and moral activity', *Theory into Practice*, **XXXI**, 2, pp. 100–6.

Sofos, N. (1990), *Quantitative Analyse*, Berlin: Selbstverlag.

Spitznagel, A. (1991), 'Projective Verfahren', in U. Flick *et al.* (eds), *Handbuch Qualitative Sozialforschung*, Munich: Psychologie Verlags Union, pp. 272–4.

Sprague, J. and Zimmerman, M.K. (1989), 'Quality and quantity: reconstructing feminist methodology', *American Sociologist*, **20**, pp. 71–86.

Sproull, N.L. (1988), *Handbook of Research Methods: A Guide for Practitioners and Students in the Social Sciences*, London: The Scarecrow Press.

Stanley, L. (ed.) (1990), *Feminist Praxis: Research, Theory and Epistemology in Feminist Sociology*, London: Routledge.

Stanley, L. and Wise, S. (1983), *Feminist Consciousness and Feminist Research*, London: Routledge and Kegan Paul.

Stergios, L. (1991), *Theory Construction and Social Research*, Athens: Selbstverlag.

Stewart, D.W. and Shamdasani, P.N. (1990), *Focus Groups: Theory and Practice*, Newbury Park, CA: Sage.

Strauss, A.L. (1987, 1990), *Qualitative Analysis for Social Scientists*, New York: Cambridge University Press.

Strauss, A.L. (1991), *Grundlagen qualitativer Sozialforschung. Datenanalyse und Theoriebildung in der empirischen Sozialforschung*, Munich: Wilhelm Fink Verlag.

Suls, J.M. and Rosnow, R.L. (1988), 'Concerns about artifacts in psychological experiments', in J.G. Morawski (ed.), *The Rise of Experimentation in American Psychology*, New York: Yale University Press, pp. 153–87.

Terhardt, E. (1981), 'Intuition — Interpretation — Argumentation. Zum Problem der Geltungsbegruendung von Interpretationen', *Zeitschrift der Paedagogik*, **27**, 5, pp. 769–93.

Tesch, R. (1990), *Qualitative Research: Analysis, Types and Software Tools*, New York: Falmer.

Tesch, R. (1989), 'Computer software and qualitative analysis: a reassessment', in Blank *et al.* (eds), *New Technology in Sociology: Practical Applications in Research and Work*, New Brunswick, NJ: Transaction Books.

Thomas, J. (1993), *Doing Critical Ethnography* (Qualitative Research Methods Series, No. 26), Newbury Park, CA: Sage.

Thomas, W.J. and Znaniecki, F. (1958), *The Polish Peasant in Europe and America*, New York: Octagon Books.

Timasheff, N.S. and Theodorson, G.A. (1976), *Sociological Theory. Its nature amd Growth*, New York: Random House.

Tuckey, J. (1977), *Exploratory Data Analysis*, Reading, MA: Addison-Wesley.

Turner, J.H. (1982), *The Structure of Social Theory*, Homewood, Ill.: The Dorsey Press.

Vlahos, N. (1984), *Sociological Methodology* (in Greek), Athens: Phantom.

Voges, W. (ed.) (1987), *Methoden der Biographie- und Lebenslaufforschung*, Opladen: Leske und Budrich.

Volmerg, U. (1983), 'Validitaet im interpretativen Paradigma. Dargestellt an der Konstruktion qualitativer Erlebensverfahren', in P. Zedler and H. Moser (eds), *Aspekte qualitativer Sozialforschung. Studien zu Aktionsforschung empirischer Hermeneutik und reflexiver Sozialtechnologie*, Opladen: Leske und Budrich, pp. 124–43.

Wachter, K.W. (1988), 'Disturbed by meta-analysis?, *Science,* **241**, pp. 1407–8.

Wadsworth, Y. (1984), *Do It Yourself Social Research*, Melbourne: Victorian Council of Social Service.

Wadsworth, Y. (1991), *Everyday Evaluation of the Run,* Melbourne: Action Research Issues Association.

Wahl, K., Honig, M.S. and Gravenhorst, L. (1982), *Wissenschaftlichkeit und Interessen. Zur Herstellung einer subjectivitaetsorientierter Sozialforschung*, Frankfurt am Main: Shurkamp.

Walker, R. (ed.) (1985), *Applied Qualitative Research*, Aldershot: Gower Pub. Co.

Wallace, R.A. and Wolf, A. (1986), *Contemporary Sociological Theory*, Englewood Cliffs, NJ: Prentice-Hall.

Wang, M. and Mahoney, B. (1991), 'Scales and measurement revisited', *Health Values,* **15**, pp. 52–6.

Weitzman, E. and Miles, M.B. (1993), *Computer-aided Qualitative Data Analysis: A Review of Selected Software,* New York: Center for Policy Research.

Weitzman, E. and Miles, M.B. (1994), *Computer Programs for Qualitative Data Analysis,* Thousand Oaks, CA: Sage.

Wells, A. (1978), *Contemporary Sociological Theory*, Santa Monica, CA: Goodycar.

Wells, L.E. and Rankin, J.H. (1991), 'Families and delinquency: a meta-analysis of the impact of broken homes', *Social Problems,* **38**, pp. 71–93.

Werner, O. (1982), 'Microcomputers in cultural anthropology: ALP programs for qualitative analysis', *BYTE*, pp. 250–80.

Westkott, M. (1990), 'Feminist criticism of social sciences', in J.M. Nielsen (ed.), *Feminist Research Methods. Exemplary Readings in the Social Sciences*, London: Westview Press, pp. 58–68.

Whyte, W.S. (1943), *Street Corner Society*, Chicago: University of Chicago Press.

Whyte, W.F. (ed.) (1991), *Participatory Action Research*, Newbury Park, CA: Sage.

Wilke, H. (1986), *Eine Analyse der Nutzung statistischer Programmpakete in der Sozialforschung*, Berlin: Quorum.

Williamson, J.B., Karp, D.A. and Dalphin, V.H. (1977), *The Research Craft: An Introduction to Social Science Methods*, Boston: Little, Brown and Co.

Wilson, T.P. (1981),'Qualitative vs quantitative methods in social research', in M. Kuechler *et al.* (eds), *Integration von qualitativen und quantitativen Forschungsansaetzen*, Manheim: ZUMA-Arbeitsbericht 81/19, pp. 487–508

Winter, R. (1987), *Action Research and the Nature of Social Inquiry: Professional Innovation and Educational Work*, Avebury: Gower Pub. Co.

Witzel, A. (1982), *Verfahren der qualitativen Sozialforschung. Ueberblick und Alternativen*, Frankfurt am Main: Campus Verlag.

Wolcott, H.F. (1990), *Writing up Qualitative research*, Newbury Park, CA: Sage.

Wolcott, H.F. (1992), 'Posturing in qualitative research', in M.D. LeCompte, W.L. Millroy and J. Preissle (eds), *The Handbook of Qualitative Research in Education*, San Diego: Academic Press, pp. 3–52.

Wolcott, H.F. (1994), *Transforming Qualitative Data: Description, Analysis, Interpretation*, Thousand Oaks, CA: Sage.

Woldman, P. (1992), *Action Learning and Community Economic Development*, Nundah, Qld: Prosperity Press.

Yin, Robert K. (1991), *Case Study Research. Design and Methods*, Newbury Park, CA: Sage.

Zaharlik, A. (1992), 'Ethnography in anthropology and its value for education', *Theory into Practice*, **XXXI**, 2, pp. 116–25.

Zaharlik, A. and Green, J.L. (1991), 'Ethnographic research', in J. Flood, J. Jensen, D. Lapp. and J. Squire (eds), *Handbook of Research on Teaching the English Language Arts*, New York: Macmillan, pp. 205–25.

Zedler, P. and Moser, H. (eds) (1983), *Aspekte qualitativer Sozialforschung. Studien zu Aktionsforschung empirischer Hermeneutik und reflexiver Sozialtechnologie*, Opladen: Leske und Budrich.

Index